ONCE
IT'S OPEN SEAS

THE CAMBRIDGE UNIVERSITY HANDBOOK

1984-85

The right of the University of Cambridge to print and sell all manner of books was granted by Henry VIII in 1534. The University has printed and published continuously since 1584.

CAMBRIDGE UNIVERSITY PRESS

CAMBRIDGE

LONDON NEW YORK NEW ROCHELLE

MELBOURNE SYDNEY

1984

Published by the Press Syndicate of the University of Cambridge
The Pitt Building, Trumpington Street, Cambridge CB2 1RP
32 East 57th Street, New York, NY 10022, USA
10 Stamford Road, Oakleigh, Melbourne 3166, Australia

ISBN 0 521 31810 6

Printed in Great Britain by the University Press, Cambridge

73rd Edition
Revised to 25 July 1984

CONTENTS

1	THE UNIVERSITY	*page* 1
	Officers	2
	Matriculation	9
	Affiliation	13
	Incorporation	17
	Degrees in virtue of office	18
	M.A. status	18
	B.A. status	19
	The University Library	19
	The Fitzwilliam Museum	20
	Madingley Hall	22
2	THE COLLEGES	23
	Admission	24
	Overseas Candidates	24
3	UNIVERSITY EXAMINATIONS AND DEGREES	27
4	COURSES OF STUDY FOR DEGREES, DIPLOMAS, AND CERTIFICATES	42
	Anglo-Saxon, Norse, and Celtic	42
	Archaeology and Anthropology	49
	Architecture	69
	Chemical Engineering	79
	Classics	86
	Computer Science	105
	Development Studies	109
	Economics and Politics	110
	Education	134
	Engineering	152
	Electrical Sciences Tripos	1[illegible]
	Production Engineering Tripos	

4 Courses of Study for Degrees, Diplomas, and Certificates (*continued*)

English	*page* 172
Geography	188
History	194
History of Art	214
Land Economy	221
Latin-American Studies	231
Law	235
Mathematics	248
Medical Sciences	255
Medicine and Surgery	267
Modern and Medieval Languages	273
Music	323
Natural Sciences	332
Oriental Studies	370
Philosophy	391
Polar Studies	401
Social and Political Sciences	403
Theology and Religious Studies	416
Veterinary Medicine	451

5 Research and Courses of Advanced or Further Study	458
6 University Scholarships and Other Awards	465
University scholarships	466
Awards offered by other bodies	492
University Careers Service	498
aining for the Ministry	501
	503

PREFACE

The Cambridge University Handbook is designed to include most of the information, particularly about courses, which a prospective candidate for admission to Cambridge will need, and which an undergraduate will usually wish to have readily available.

The *Handbook* is not a substitute for the University Ordinances. Much of it is based on the Ordinances, and it contains an abridged account of some of them, but it must not be regarded as having the authority of the actual regulations. These are to be found in the latest edition of the *Statutes and Ordinances of the University of Cambridge* (published every three years*) and the *Amending Statutes and Supplementary Ordinances* (published in each year in which the Statutes and Ordinances are not published) as they are amended from time to time by Grace or by notice published in the *Cambridge University Reporter.*

A complete list of University administrative and teaching officers, members of University bodies, and representatives of the University on other bodies may be found in a special issue of the *Cambridge University Reporter* and also in the *Commonwealth Universities Yearbook.* A booklet entitled *University of Cambridge: Information and Regulations*, a copy of which is issued to every freshman, gives a full account of the regulations relating to residence and discipline and also information about medical and dental arrangements, libraries, and museums. The *Cambridge Admissions Prospectus* is published each year by the Cambridge Tutorial Representatives for the guidance of candidates applying between March and September for entry in October the following year. It contains details of individual Colleges, their Tutors, teaching Fellows, and Directors of Studies and may be obtained on application to any College or to the Cambridge Inter-Collegiate Applications Office, Kellett Lodge, Tennis Court Road, Cambridge CB2 1QA.

The Editor is grateful for help received from many quarters, and he will be glad to have his attention drawn to any mistakes that he may have made.

* Latest edition, 1982.

UNIVERSITY REGISTRY

1 August 1984

1
THE UNIVERSITY

The University is a self-governing body; the legislative authority is the Regent House, which consists mainly of the teaching and administrative staff of the University and Colleges. The Senate, which consists of all holders of the M.A. or higher degrees, has now only certain formal duties, other than meeting for the discussion of Reports made by the Council of the Senate and other bodies. The chief administrative body of the University is the Council of the Senate, which is elected by the Regent House. The General Board of the Faculties co-ordinates the educational policy of the University and the Financial Board supervises its financial affairs.

The nominal and ceremonial head of the University is the Chancellor, who is elected for life. The Vice-Chancellor is a head of a College who is nominated for election by the Council of the Senate and normally holds office for two years. He presides over Congregations of the Regent House, at which degrees are conferred, and is Chairman of the Council of the Senate and the more important of the many Boards and Syndicates which manage the affairs of the University.

Changes in the Ordinances, or regulations, of the University are proposed by the Board or Syndicate concerned in the form of reports which, after being approved for publication by the Council of the Senate, are published in the *Cambridge University Reporter*. Such reports can be commented on by members of the Senate at Discussions which are held once a fortnight in Full Term. A report may be amended after remarks made in a Discussion. Subsequently a Grace, which is a motion for the approval of recommendations made in a report, is submitted to a vote of the Regent House. Minor amendments of Ordinances are proposed in Graces which the Council of the Senate submit for the approval of the Regent House without the formality of Report and discussion. Ordinances may not infringe the University Statutes. The procedure for making amendments of the Statutes is the same as for the Ordinances, but such amendments require the approval of the Queen in Council, after the approval of the Regent House has been obtained.

The educational and research activities of the University are organized in Faculties, some of which are subdivided into Departments. All are answerable to the General Board of the Faculties

Through the Faculties, the University is responsible for lectures and laboratory work. The University also conducts all examinations and awards degrees; but it is the Colleges which select students for admission, arrange the tuition of undergraduates either individually or in small groups, and see to the welfare, both academic and personal, of undergraduates. All undergraduates admitted by the Colleges must, however, satisfy the University's matriculation requirements.

Cambridge University Reporter

The *Cambridge University Reporter* is the official newspaper of the University and is published every Wednesday in Full Term; extra numbers are published as occasion requires. The *Reporter* can be ordered from the Cambridge University Press Publishing Division, Edinburgh Building, Shaftesbury Road, Cambridge CB2 2RU. The annual subscription is £22.50, post free, and the terminal subscription £7.50, post free. Single copies cost 35p each (60p postage paid).

All University announcements and reports to the Regent House are published in the *Reporter* and there are the following special issues: the Lecture-list, which is published at the beginning of the Michaelmas Term (and costs 80p, £1.60 postage paid), with lists of additions and corrections published at the beginning of the Lent and Easter Terms; the List of University Administrative and Teaching Officers, etc., which is published at the beginning of each term; the Awards number which is published in November; the list of examination timetables which is published in April; the Class-list issues, which are published in June (students going out of residence before the results of their examinations are announced are able to arrange with some newsagents for the relevant issue to be posted to them); and the College Accounts (costing £1.10, £1.70 postage paid).

Administrative officers

Chancellor: His Royal Highness The Prince Philip, Duke of Edinburgh, K.G., P.C., K.T., O.M., G.B.E.

Vice-Chancellor (1984–85): Professor Sir John Butterfield, O.B.E., M.D., F.R.C.P., Master of Downing College. (The Vice-Chancellor is elected, a ... at a time, for two years, from among the Heads of Colleges.)

... (1984–85): K. J. Pascoe, M.A., of St John's College, and R. B. ... SC.D., of Emmanuel College. (The Proctors are disciplinary ...ninated by the Colleges in rotation.)

... Fleet, M.A., PH.D.

... *of the Faculties:* K. J. R. Edwards, M.A.

...ne, M.A.

Professors

(as from 1 October 1984)

Aeronautical Engineering (Francis Mond)	Vacant
Agriculture (Drapers)	Sir James Beament, SC.D.
American History (Paul Mellon)	Mrs C. Erickson, M.A.
American History and Institutions (Pitt)	R. H. Wiebe (for the year 1984–85)
Anatomy	Vacant
Ancient History	M. K. Hopkins, M.A. (from 1 October 1985)
Ancient Philosophy (Laurence)	M. F. Burnyeat, M.A.
Ancient Philosophy and Science	G. E. R. Lloyd, MA., PH.D.
Anglo-Saxon (Elrington and Bosworth)	R. I. Page, LITT.D.
Animal Embryology (Charles Darwin)	R. A. Laskey
Animal Pathology	E. J. L. Soulsby, M.A.
Applied Economics	Hon. W. A. H. Godley, M.A.
Applied Mathematics	Vacant
Applied Numerical Analysis (John Humphrey Plummer)	M. J. D. Powell, SC.D.
Applied Thermodynamics (Hopkinson and Imperial Chemical Industries)	Vacant
Arabic (Sir Thomas Adams's)	Vacant
Archaeology (Disney)	A. C. Renfrew, SC.D.
Architecture	C. A. St J. Wilson, M.A.
Astronomy and Experimental Philosophy (Plumian)	M. J. Rees, M.A., PH.D.
Astronomy and Geometry (Lowndean)	J. F. Adams, M.A., PH.D.
Astrophysics	D. Lynden-Bell, M.A., PH.D.
Biochemistry (Sir William Dunn)	Sir Hans Kornberg, SC.D.
Biology (Quick)	R. R. A. Coombs, SC.D.
Botany	R. G. West, SC.D.
Cell Biology (John Humphrey Plummer)	J. B. Gurdon
Cell Physiology	Lord Adrian, M.A., M.D.
Chemical Engineering (Shell)	J. F. Davidson, SC.D.
Chemistry	A. D. Buckingham, PH.D.
Chemistry	Sir Jack Lewis, SC.D.
Chemistry (Alexander Todd Visiting)	J-M. P. Lehn (for the year 1984–85)

Chinese	G. Dudbridge, M.A., PH.D. (from 1 October 1985)
Civil Law (Regius)	P. G. Stein, M.A., LL.B.
Classical Archaeology (Laurence)	A. M. Snodgrass, M.A., PH.D.
Clinical Biochemistry	C. N. Hales, M.D., PH.D.
Clinical Oncology (Cancer Research Campaign)	N. M. Bleehen, M.A.
Community Medicine	R. M. Acheson, M.D., SC.D.
Comparative Law	J. A. Jolowicz, M.A.
Comparative Philology	Vacant
Computer Science	D. J. Wheeler, B.A., PH.D.
Computer Systems	R. M. Needham, M.A., PH.D.
Criminology (Wolfson)	A. E. Bottoms, M.A.
Divinity (Lady Margaret's)	Miss M. D. Hooker, M.A.
Divinity (Norris-Hulse)	N. L. A. Lash, M.A., PH.D., D.D.
Divinity (Regius)	S. W. Sykes, M.A. (from 1 October 1985)
Ecclesiastical History (Dixie)	C. N. L. Brooke, LITT.D.
Economic History (1971)	B. E. Supple, PH.D.
Economics (1965)	P. Dasgupta, PH.D. (from 1 January 1985)
Economics (1970)	F. H. Hahn, M.A.
Education	P. H. Hirst, M.A.
Electrical Engineering	A. N. Broers, PH.D.
Energy Studies	R. J. Eden, M.A., PH.D.
Engineering (1875)	D. E. Newland, M.A.
Engineering (1966)	J. E. Carroll, M.A., PH.D.
Engineering (1966)	M. F. Ashby, M.A., PH.D.
Engineering (1966)	A. N. Schofield, M.A., PH.D.
Engineering (1971)	J. Heyman, M.A., PH.D.
Engineering (1974)	A. G. J. MacFarlane, SC.D.
Engineering (1977)	K. L. Johnson, M.A.
Engineering (Rank)	J. E. Ffowcs Williams, M.A.
English (1966, Grace 1 of 1 Dec. 1965)	I. R. J. Jack, LITT.D.
English (1966, Grace 2 of 1 Dec. 1965)	Mrs A. Barton, PH.D.
English (1983)	D. S. Brewer, LITT.D.
English Law (Rouse Ball)	D. G. T. Williams, M.A., LL.B.
English Literature (King Edward VII)	C. B. Ricks, M.A.
Ethology	P. P. G. B. Bateson, SC.D.

European Prehistory	J. M. Coles, SC.D.
Experimental Psychology	N. J. Mackintosh, PH.D.
Fine Art (Slade)	J. Bialostocki (for the year 1984–85)
French (Drapers)	T. C. Cave, M.A., PH.D. (from 1 October 1985)
Genetics (Arthur Balfour)	J. R. S. Fincham, SC.D.
Geography (1931)	M. D. I. Chisholm, M.A.
Geography (1974)	R. J. Chorley, SC.D.
Geology (Woodwardian)	Vacant
Geophysics	C. H. Chapman, M.A., PH.D.
German (Schröder)	D. H. Green, M.A.
Greek (Regius)	E. W. Handley, M.A.
Haematological Medicine (Leukaemia Research Fund)	F. G. J. Hayhoe, M.D.
Hebrew (Regius)	J. A. Emerton, D.D.
Histology	Vacant
History of the British Commonwealth (Smuts)	D. A. Low
History of Western Art	A. M. Jaffé, LITT.D.
Human Physiology	P. A. Merton, M.D.
Imperial and Naval History (Vere Harmsworth)	D. K. Fieldhouse, LITT.D.
Industrial Relations (Montague Burton)	Vacant
Information Engineering	F. Fallside, M.A.
International Law (Whewell)	D. W. Bowett, LL.D.
Italian (Serena)	P. Boyde, M.A., PH.D.
Land Economy	G. C. Cameron, M.A.
Latin (Kennedy)	M. D. Reeve
Latin-American Studies (Simón Bolívar)	Vacant
Law	S. F. C. Milsom, M.A.
Laws of England (Downing)	G. H. Jones, LL.D.
Legal Science (Arthur Goodhart)	R. C. J. Van Caenegem (for the year 1984–85)
Linguistics	P. H. Mathews, M.A.
Mathematical Physics (1967)	J. C. Taylor, M.A., PH.D.
Mathematical Physics (1978)	H. K. Moffatt, PH.D.
Mathematical Statistics	D. G. Kendall, M.A.
Mathematics	Sir Peter Swinnerton-Dyer, Bt., M.A.

Mathematics	J. H. Conway, M.A., PH.D.
Mathematics (Lucasian)	S. W. Hawking, PH.D.
Mathematics (Rouse Ball)	J. G. Thompson, M.A.
Mathematics for Operational Research (Churchill)	P. Whittle, M.A.
Mechanics	Vacant
Medicinal Chemistry (Herchel Smith)	L. D. Hall
Medicine	I. H. Mills, M.D.
Medieval and Renaissance English	J. E. Stevens, M.A., PH.D.
Medieval History	J. C. Holt, M.A.
Membrane Biophysics	D. A. Haydon, M.A.
Membrane Physiology	I. M. Glynn, M.D.
Metallurgy (Goldsmiths')	D. Hull
Mineralogy and Petrology	E. R. Oxburgh, M.A.
Modern History	D. E. D. Beales, M.A., PH.D.
Modern History (Regius)	G. R. Elton, LITT.D.
Modern Languages	H. B. Nisbet
Morbid Anatomy and Histology	G. A. Gresham, M.D., SC.D.
Music	A. Goehr, M.A.
Natural Philosophy (Jacksonian)	A. H. Cook, SC.D.
Neurosensory Physiology	F. W. Campbell, M.A.
Obstetrics and Gynaecology	C. P. Douglas, M.A.
Organic Chemistry (1702)	R. A. Raphael, M.A.
Organic Chemistry (1969)	A. R. Battersby, SC.D.
Paediatrics	J. A. Davis, M.A.
Pathology	P. Wildy, M.A., M.B., B.CHIR.
Pharmacology (Sheild)	A. W. Cuthbert, M.A.
Philosophy	Miss G. E. M. Anscombe, M.A.
Philosophy (Knightbridge)	T. J. Smiley, M.A. PH.D.
Philosophy of Science	Miss M. B. Hesse, M.A.
Physic (Regius)	Sir John Butterfield, M.D.
Physical Chemistry (1920)	J. M. Thomas, M.A.
Physical Chemistry (1978)	B. A. Thrush, SC.D.
Physics (1966)	V. Heine, PH.D.
Physics (1974)	B. D. Josephson, M.A., PH.D.
Physics (Cavendish)	Sir Samuel Edwards, M.A., PH.D.
Physics (1982)	Vacant
Physics (John Humphrey Plummer)	Vacant
Physiology	R. D. Keynes, SC.D.
Physiology of Reproduction (Mary Marshall and Arthur Walton)	P. A. Jewell, M.A., PH.D.
Plant Biochemistry	D. H. Northcote, SC.D.
Political Economy	R. C. O. Matthews, M.A.

Political Science	Q. R. D. Skinner, M.A.
Psychiatry	Sir Martin Roth, M.A.
Pure Mathematics	A. Baker, M.A., PH.D.
Pure Mathematics (Sadleirian)	Vacant
Radio Astronomy (1971)	A. Hewish, M.A., PH.D
Radiology	T. Sherwood, M.A.
Sanskrit	Vacant
Slavonic Studies	Vacant
Social Anthropology (William Wyse)	E. A. Gellner
Spanish	C. C. Smith, M.A., PH.D.
Surgery	R. Y. Calne, M.A.
Tumour Immunology (Sheila Joan Smith)	P. J. Lachmann, SC.D.
Veterinary Clinical Studies	A. Steele-Bodger, M.A.
Zoology	G. Horn, SC.D.

Readers

(*as from 1 October 1984*)

African History	J. Iliffe, M.A., PH.D.
Algebra	J. E. Roseblade, M.A., PH.D.
American Literature	P. A. Tanner, M.A., PH.D.
Architecture and Urban Studies	M. Echenique, M.A.
Astrophysics	N. O. Weiss, M.A., PH.D.
Biochemistry (Sir William Dunn)	J. C. Metcalfe, M.A., PH.D.
Biochemistry of Macromolecular Studies	R. N. Perham, SC.D.
Chemical Engineering	C. N. Kenney, SC.D.
Comparative Anaesthesia	L. W. Hall, M.A.
Developmental Genetics	M. Ashburner, SC.D.
Early Christian and Jewish Studies	E. Bammel, M.A.
Econometrics	N. E. Savin, M.A.
Economics	R. E. Rowthorn, M.A.
Egyptology (Herbert Thompson)	J. D. Ray, M.A.
Elastodynamics	J. A. Hudson, M.A., PH.D.
Electrical Engineering	K. C. A. Smith, M.A., PH.D.
Engineering	D. S. Whitehead, M.A., PH.D.
Engineering	L. C. Squire, M.A.
English Legal History	D. E. C. Yale, M.A., LL.B.
English Legal History	J. H. Baker, M.A., PH.D.
English Literature	J. B. Beer, M.A., PH.D.
English Literature	G. Storey, M.A.
Experimental Embryology	M. H. Johnson, PH.D.
Fluid Mechanics	J. C. R. Hunt, M.A., PH.D.
French Literature	Mrs D. Coleman, M.A.
Functional Analysis	G. R. Allan, M.A., PH.D.

High Energy Physics	J. G. Rushbrooke, M.A., PH.D.
Historical Anthropology	A. D. J. Macfarlane, M.A., PH.D.
History of Mathematics	D. T. Whiteside, PH.D.
History of Modern Political Thought	D. Forbes, M.A.
Immunology	A. J. Munro, M.A., PH.D.
Indian Studies	F. R. Allchin, M.A.
Indian Studies	K. R. Norman, M.A.
Inorganic Chemistry	B. F. G. Johnson, M.A.
Inorganic Chemistry	M. Gerloch, SC.D.
International Law	E. Lauterpacht, M.A., LL.B.
Invertebrate Physiology	J. E. Treherne, SC.D.
Law	J. A. Weir, M.A.
Literary History	H. H. Erskine-Hill, PH.D.
Mathematical Analysis	D. J. H. Garling, M.A., SC.D.
Mathematical Biology	A. W. F. Edwards, SC.D.
Mathematical Physics	P. V. Landshoff, M.A., PH.D.
Mechanical Metallurgy	J. F. Knott, PH.D.
Medieval Art	G. D. S. Henderson, M.A., PH.D.
Medieval Islamic Studies	M. C. Lyons, PH.D.
Medieval Latin Literature	E. P. M. Dronke, M.A.
Metabolic Disease	J. M. Walshe, SC.D.
Metaphysics	D. H. Mellor, M.A., PH.D.
Microelectronics	H. Ahmed, PH.D.
Modern English History	M. J. Cowling, M.A.
Neurobiology (Zoology)	M. Burrows, M.A., PH.D.
Neurobiology (Physiology)	J. G. Robson, M.A., PH.D.
Organic Chemistry	D. H. Williams, SC.D.
Pharmacology	E. K. Matthews, M.A.
Physics	A. Yoffe, SC.D.
Physics	A. Howie, M.A., PH.D.
Physics of Geochemical Measurement	J. V. P. Long, M.A., PH.D.
Physiology	R. G. Edwards, M.A.
Physiology	J. T. Fitzsimons, M.D.
Plant Biophysics	Miss E. A. C. MacRobbie, M.A.
Politics	J. M. Dunn, M.A.
Process Metallurgy	J. A. Charles, SC.D.
Radio Astronomy	J. E. Baldwin, M.A., PH.D.
Roman Historical Epigraphy	Miss J. M. Reynolds, M.A.

Smuts Reader	C. A. Bayly, PH.D.
Sociology	A. Giddens, PH.D.
Structural Mechanics	C. R. Calladine, M.A.
Structure and Properties of Materials	L. M. Brown, M.A., PH.D.
Tectonic Geology	W. B. Harland, M.A.
Tectonics	D. P. McKenzie, M.A., PH.D.
Veterinary Physiology	R. S. Comline, SC.D.
Zoology	M. J. Wells, SC.D.

Matriculation

Matriculation marks the formal admission of a student to membership of the University, and a College may not allow an unmatriculated student *in statu pupillari* to remain in residence after the division of his first term. Every candidate for matriculation must subscribe to the following declaration by signing the Matriculation Registration Form:

> 'I promise to observe the Statutes and Ordinances of the University as far as they concern me, and to pay due respect and obedience to the Chancellor and other officers of the University.'

A student is deemed to be matriculated from the beginning of the term in which a completed Matriculation Registration Form and satisfactory evidence of his qualification to matriculate are received by the Registrary.

To qualify for matriculation, a student must have been admitted to a College and, unless he is a Graduate Student or an Affiliated Student, or belongs to some other class of person approved by the Council of the Senate as qualified to matriculate, he must have satisfied the examination requirements for matriculation or be deemed by the Matriculation Board to have satisfied the examination requirements. In special circumstances (e.g. if a candidate's education has been seriously hampered by illness) the Matriculation Board have power to allow individual candidates to matriculate without fully satisfying the examination requirements.

A candidate will satisfy the examination requirements for matriculation if:

(*a*) he has obtained a pass in an examination in the Use of English or in an approved alternative,[1] or a Grade A, B, or C in a G.C.E. examination at Ordinary level in English Language,

(*b*) he has a pass in a G.C.E. examination (or a Grade A, B, or C at Ordinary level in 1975 and after) in:

one language other than English,
one approved mathematical or scientific subject,
two other approved subjects,

and (*c*) he has passed at Advanced level in any two approved subjects; provided that a pass in the three Parts of the First M.B. Examination is deemed to be the equivalent of passes in two approved scientific subjects at Advanced level, and a pass in two Parts of the First M.B. Examination is deemed to be the equivalent of a pass in one approved scientific subject at Advanced level.

A list of approved subjects in G.C.E. is published in the Cambridge Admissions Prospectus.

Examinations approved as alternatives to G.C.E. examinations

A candidate will satisfy the examination requirements for matriculation, at Ordinary level, if he has in one or more of the following examinations passed at the prescribed standard in the subjects specified above for the G.C.E.:

(*a*) A School Certificate or Malaysia Certificate of Education in the medium of English, awarded by the Cambridge Local Examinations Syndicate; or a certificate of having passed in certain subjects in the examination for one of these certificates. Standard: a pass with credit or with the note 'very good' in a School Certificate.

(*b*) A Cambridge Higher School Certificate, or a certificate of

[1] The following papers are approved: *Use of English* set by the Cambridge Local Examinations Syndicate, the Oxford and Cambridge Schools Examination Board, the Southern Universities' Joint Board for School Examinations, the Welsh Joint Education Committee, the Northern Ireland G.C.E. Committee, and the Associated Examining Board; *Test in English* set by the Joint Matriculation Board; *Certificate of Proficiency in Use of English* set by the Oxford Delegacy of Local Examinations; *English* (*Ordinary*, in which attainment of band A, B, or C constitutes a pass, or *Higher*) in the Scottish Certificate of Education; and *Certificate of Proficiency in English* set by the Cambridge Local Examinations Syndicate.

having passed in certain subjects. Standard: a pass in a subject as a subsidiary subject or a principal subject (a pass in a principal subject is deemed to be a pass at Advanced level).

(*c*) A Scottish Certificate of Education or a certificate of having passed in certain subjects. Standard: attainment of band A, B, or C in the Ordinary Grade (a pass in the Higher Grade is deemed to be a pass at Advanced level).

Special provisions

Graduates of approved Universities. Graduates of an approved university may be deemed to have satisfied the examination requirements for matriculation.

Mature Students. A mature student who is recommended by a College as fit to undertake a course leading to an Honours Degree may be deemed by the Matriculation Board to have satisfied the examination requirements for matriculation.

Candidates from the Commonwealth or from the Republic of Ireland or from countries using a European language, other than English, as the medium of instruction.[1] A candidate who produces a certificate showing that he is qualified for admission without further examination to an approved university, in a country in the Commonwealth other than in India or Pakistan,[2] or in the Republic of Ireland or in a country using a European language, other than English, as the medium of instruction,[3] may be deemed by the Matriculation Board to have satisfied, or partly to have satisfied, the examination requirements for matriculation if his qualification for such admission includes either the passing of an examination, or the satisfactory

[1] It is advisable that applications on behalf of such candidates should be submitted to the Matriculation Board before the student comes into residence. Unless the certificate shows on its face that it would admit the holder to a university, it should be accompanied by a sufficiently authenticated declaration by a government official or officer of a university, embassy, legation, or consulate of a specified country, testifying that the certificate would entitle the holder to enter, without further examination, on a regular course of study in a university. When certificates are in any other language than English, Latin, French, German, Italian, Portuguese, or Spanish, they should be accompanied by an English translation, attested by a public, diplomatic, or consular officer, or by a notary or public translator.

[2] Save for special cause, the Matriculation Board will exercise this power only when the candidate is ordinarily resident in the country in question.

[3] Save for special cause, the Matriculation Board will exercise this power only when the candidate is a national of the country in question or when his education has been conducted in the language of that country.

completion of a course of study, in the subjects specified for General Certificates of Education.

Candidates from India or Pakistan. A candidate who has attained the first class in an examination leading to the degree of Bachelor of Arts or Bachelor of Science, or the first or second class in the Examination for the degree of Bachelor of Arts or Bachelor of Science, in any university of India or Pakistan approved for the purpose, may be deemed to have satisfied the examination requirements for matriculation provided that, in some examination leading up to the degree of Bachelor of Arts or Bachelor of Science in that university, he has passed in an Oriental language, in Mathematics or Science, and in English.

Candidates from the United States of America. A candidate educated in the United States of America who has taken the tests of the College Entrance Examination Board may be deemed to have satisfied the examination requirements for matriculation if he has taken the following tests and has attained therein a standard approved by the Matriculation Board:

(*a*) The Scholastic Aptitude Test (Verbal and Mathematical Sections).

(*b*) Achievement Tests in:

(i) English Composition,
(ii) one language,
(iii) one of the following: Biology, Chemistry, Mathematics, Physics,
(iv) American History and Social Studies, *or* European History and World Cultures, *or* Literature, *or* a second language, *or* a second subject from (iii).

Candidates from Homerton College for the Qualifying Examination in Education. Members of Homerton College who at the end of their second year of study in the College have passed an intermediate examination conducted by the College for such candidates are deemed to have satisfied the examination requirements for matriculation.

Affiliation

Any person who before matriculation in the University of Cambridge has received or become qualified to receive a degree from another Institution for the education of adult students is entitled, on or after matriculation, to be approved as an affiliated student, provided that (*a*) when he became qualified for the degree he had been a member of one or more such Institutions for not less than three academical years; (*b*) the degree has been approved for the purpose by the Council of the Senate. In particular cases the Council of the Senate may approve as an affiliated student a member or former member of an Institution for the education of adult students who does not fulfil these requirements. Candidates for admission as affiliated students should make initial enquiry to one of the Colleges.

A Tutor must apply for approval of a pupil as an affiliated student not later than the division of the term next following that in which he first resides in the University, and approval has effect from the beginning of his first term of residence. An affiliated student is deemed to have satisfied the examination requirements for matriculation, and the first term of residence is reckoned as his fourth for the purposes of the regulations for Triposes, degree examinations in Music, and degrees other than the Ordinary B.A. Degree or the M.Phil., M.Sc., M.Litt., and Ph.D. Degrees, and for studentships, scholarships, prizes, and other awards.

The effect of these provisions is that an affiliated student may proceed to the B.A. Degree with honours in two years, but that if he is a candidate for the Ordinary B.A. Degree three years will be necessary.

An affiliated student has the following additional privileges, but he may not take Part II of any Tripos as his first Tripos examination later than the sixth term after his first term of residence, unless the regulations for a particular Tripos specifically allow it:

Anglo-Saxon, Norse, and Celtic

An affiliated student may take the Anglo-Saxon, Norse, and Celtic Tripos in his second year and, if he obtains honours, proceed to the B.A. Degree under the same conditions as if he had obtained honours in another Honours examination also.

Archaeology and Anthropology

An affiliated student may take Part II of the Archaeological and Anthropological Tripos in his second year under the same conditions as if he had obtained honours in Part I.

Architecture

An affiliated student may, if the Faculty Board permit, take Part I B of the Architecture Tripos in his first year.

Chemical Engineering

An affiliated student may, if the Chemical Engineering Syndicate permit, be a candidate either for Part I of the Chemical Engineering Tripos in his first year or for Part II in his first or second year under the same conditions as if he had obtained honours in Part I.

Classics

An affiliated student may take Part II of the Classical Tripos in his second year under the same conditions as if he had obtained honours in Part I or, if the Faculty Board of Classics permit, take Part II of the Tripos in his first year under the same conditions as if he had obtained honours in another Honours examination in the year next preceding.

Computer Science

An affiliated student may, if the Computer Syndicate permit, take the two-year examination option for the Computer Science Tripos in his second year, and, if he obtains honours, he may proceed to the B.A. Degree under the same conditions as if he had obtained honours in another Honours Examination also.

Economics

An affiliated student may, if he passes or gains exemption from the Economics Qualifying Examination in Elementary Mathematics, take Part II of the Economics Tripos in his second year under the same conditions as if he had obtained honours in Part I.

Education

An affiliated student may take the Qualifying Examination for the Education Tripos in his first year and, if he passes that examination, the Tripos in his second year, and if he obtains honours in the Tripos, he may proceed to the B.A. degree on the same conditions as if he had obtained honours in another Honours Examination also.

Engineering, Electrical Sciences

An affiliated student may, if the Faculty Board permit, take Part II of the Engineering Tripos, or the Electrical Sciences Tripos in his first or second year under the same conditions as if he had obtained honours in another Honours examination.

English

If the Faculty Board of English allow it in his case, an affiliated student may take in his second year *either* Part I of the English Tripos, *or* Part II of the English Tripos subject to the regulation for that Part which applies to candidates who have not previously obtained honours in Part I of the English Tripos; and if he obtains honours, he may proceed to the B.A. Degree as if he had obtained honours in another Honours examination also.

Geography

An affiliated student may, if the Faculty Board permit, take Part II of the Geographical Tripos in his first or second year under the same conditions as if he had obtained honours in another Honours examination.

History

An affiliated student may, if the Faculty Board allow it in his case, (*a*) be a candidate for Part II in his first or second year or a candidate for Part I in his second year and (*b*) may proceed to the B.A. Degree after obtaining honours in either Part of the Tripos under the same conditions as if he had obtained honours in another Honours Examination also, provided that a candidate offering either Part of the Tripos may be required by the Faculty Board to take an additional paper or papers.

History of Art

An affiliated student may take the History of Art Tripos in his second year and, if he obtains honours, proceed to the B.A. Degree under the same conditions as if he had obtained honours in another Honours examination also.

Land Economy

An affiliated student may take the Land Economy Tripos in his second year and, if he obtains honours, proceed to the B.A. Degree as if he had obtained honours in another Honours examination also.

Law

An affiliated student may, if the Faculty Board of Law permit, take Part II of the Law Tripos in his first or second year without having obtained honours in Part IB; and he may claim certain privileges as a candidate for the LL.M. Degree.

Mathematics

An affiliated student may take Part II of the Mathematical Tripos in his first or second year under the same conditions as if he had obtained honours in Part IB of the Tripos.

Medical Sciences

An affiliated student may proceed to the B.A. Degree after obtaining honours in Part IA and Part IB of the Medical Sciences Tripos under the same conditions as if he had obtained honours in another Honours examination also.

Modern and Medieval Languages

An affiliated student may take Part II of the Modern and Medieval Languages Tripos in his second year under the same conditions as if he had obtained honours in Part I or, if the Faculty Board of Modern and Medieval Languages permit, in his first year under the same conditions as if he had obtained honours in another honours examination in the year next preceding or in his third year after spending an authorized year abroad under the same conditions as if he had obtained honours in another honours examination in the year next but two preceding.

Music

An affiliated student may take Part IB of the Music Tripos in his first year and, if he obtains honours therein, Part II of the Music Tripos in his second year.

Natural Sciences

An affiliated student may: (*a*) take Part IB of the Natural Sciences Tripos in his first year; (*b*) if the Faculty Board concerned permit, take Part II of the Natural Sciences Tripos or, if the History and Philosophy of Science Syndicate permit, take Section II of Part II (General) of the Natural Sciences Tripos, in his first or second year as if he had obtained honours in Part IB.

Oriental Studies

An affiliated student may take Part II of the Oriental Studies Tripos in his second year under the same conditions as if he had obtained honours in Part I of the Tripos or, if the Faculty Board of Oriental Studies permit, in his first year under the same conditions as if he had obtained honours in another honours examination in the year next preceding.

Philosophy

An affiliated student may take Part IB of the Philosophy Tripos in his first year or his second year. If he takes it in his second year and obtains honours, he may proceed to the B.A. Degree under the same conditions as if he had obtained honours in another Honours examination also. He may also take Part II in his first or second year without having obtained honours in any Honours examination; provided that, if he takes Part II under Regulation 7 for the Philosophy Tripos in his first year or in the year after being a candidate for another Honours examination, he must offer Papers B1 and B2 of Part II of the Classical Tripos, and that if he takes Part II under Regulation 7 in his second year and has not been a candidate for another Honours examination he must offer Papers B1, B2, and B3 of Part II of the Classical Tripos.

Social and Political Sciences

An affiliated student may proceed to the B.A. Degree after offering six papers and obtaining honours in Part II of the Social and Political Sciences Tripos in his second year under the same conditions as if he had obtained honours in another Honours examination also. He is thus precluded from offering at the end of the second year of actual residence only four papers for Part II.

Theology and Religious Studies

An affiliated student may take in his second year Part II of the Theological and Religious Studies Tripos under the same conditions as if he had obtained honours in another Honours Examination in the year next but one preceding, and, if he obtains honours, proceed to the B.A. Degree.

No affiliated student may take Part II of a Tripos as his first Tripos Examination later than the sixth term after his first term of actual residence, unless the regulations for a particular Tripos specifically allow it.

Incorporation

A graduate of the University of Oxford or of Trinity College, Dublin may be admitted by incorporation to a degree which in the opinion of the Council of the Senate is equivalent to the highest degree which either of those Universities has conferred upon him provided that:

(i) he has been matriculated as a member of the University;

(ii) he has attained the age of twenty-four years or the Council of the Senate see fit to exempt him from this provision;

(iii) he has satisfied the Council of the Senate that he qualified for his degree by residence as well as by passing the examinations and performing the exercises required;

(iv) he has been admitted to a University office or a Headship or a Fellowship (other than an Honorary Fellowship) of a College or holds a post in the University Press specially designated under Statute J, and

(v) if he holds a University office or a post in the University Press or a Fellowship of a College to which initially he was not appointed or elected to the retiring age, he has already held a University office or offices or such a post or posts in the University Press or a Fellowship or Fellowships (other than an Honorary Fellowship) of a College or of different Colleges, or any combination of these, for a total period, which need not be continuous, of at least three years.

Applications together with the necessary evidence must be sent direct to the Registrary.

M.A. Degree under Statute B, III, 6

The degree of Master of Arts may be conferred on a person qualified under Statute B, III, 6 provided that he satisfies conditions (i), (ii), (iv), and (v) specified above for incorporation. Applications together with the necessary evidence must be sent to the Registrary.

M.A. status

Certain persons may be granted the status of Master of Arts provided they have attained the age of twenty-four years and have been matriculated. These persons include Graduate Students or other persons to whom the Council have previously granted the status of Bachelor of Arts, for so long as they are not of standing to proceed to the degree of Master of Arts. Enquiries may be made at the University Registry.

A person holding M.A. status may not be a candidate for any examination leading to a B.A. or Mus.B. Degree nor may he compete for any emolument for which undergraduates only are eligible.

B.A. status

Graduate Students who are not graduates of the University and have not the status of Master of Arts have the status of Bachelor of Arts, as have certain Oxford graduates while in Cambridge. This status may also be conferred by the Council on other persons who have attained the age of twenty-one years and have been accepted for admission to a College and who are not reading for a B.A. or equivalent degree.

A person holding B.A. status may not be a candidate for any examination leading to B.A. or Mus.B. Degree nor may he compete for any emolument for which undergraduates only are eligible.

The University Library

In the early fifteenth century, the first known catalogue of the University Library listed 122 books. There are now well over three million books housed in the present Library, which comprises a building designed by Sir Giles Scott and opened in 1934 and an extension, to the designs of Gollins, Melvin, Ward and Partners, added to it in 1971. Under the provisions of the Copyright Act, the Library may claim a copy of every work published in the British Isles. Among the collections for which it is famous are Bishop Moore's library (30,000 volumes), the Bradshaw Collection of Irish books, the Wade collection of Chinese books, the Acton Historical Library (60,000 volumes), the Taylor-Schechter collection of Hebrew fragments from the Cairo Genizah, the Sir Geoffrey Keynes collection, the Bible Society Library, and important collections of incunabula – books printed before 1501 – and manuscripts.

Throughout its history the Library has provided open access to a large proportion of its books. Virtually all the stacks in the 1934 building are open-access, the closed-access stacks being concentrated in the 1971 extension, which also houses reading rooms for Manuscripts, for Rare Books, for Periodicals and Reserved Books, and for Official Publications. The 1934 building houses the main Reading Room (containing the principal collection of reference works: bibliographies, encyclopedias, dictionaries, etc.), the Map Room (with a collection of some 920,000 maps and 10,000 atlases) and the Music Department. Details of these rooms and their times of opening are available at the Library.

The Library is open on Saturdays from 9 a.m. to 1 p.m. and on other weekdays from 9 a.m. to 7.15 p.m. (10 p.m. during the

Easter Full Term). There is no entry to the Library during the last quarter of an hour before the time of closing.

The Library is closed on all Sundays, on Christmas Eve and the following days up to and including the New Year public holiday, on Good Friday and the three following days, on the August Bank Holiday, and from 16 to 23 September both days inclusive.

The day for the annual return of books is 15 September.

Resident members of the University *in statu pupillari* and Bachelors of Arts, Law, Medicine, Surgery, Music, Veterinary Medicine or Education and holders of a Diploma or Certificate of the University must apply at the Library in person for tickets of admission.

Tutors of Colleges may borrow from the Library not more than five volumes for each resident pupil who has kept or been allowed at least six terms and has obtained honours or intends to be a candidate for honours, in a Tripos Examination, or who is an Affiliated Student. Special forms, which must be dated and signed by the Tutor, are available for books borrowed in this way.

Graduate students, other than Affiliated Students, following a course of study leading to a Tripos Examination or to a degree, diploma, or certificate of the University may borrow from the Library not more than five volumes.

Books so obtained must be returned in a fortnight or by the day for the annual return of books, whichever is earlier; and they may not be borrowed again for the same person before the second day after their return.

The fine for not returning a book by the specified day is 30p for the first day, 60p for the first week or part of a week (including the 30p for the first day), and 60p for every subsequent week or part of a week, or twice those amounts in the case of 'Special Order' books.

A leaflet, *Introduction for New Readers*, is given to all readers when they first use the Library. The *Readers' Handbook* is available on request in the Entrance Hall.

The Fitzwilliam Museum

The Fitzwilliam Museum collections range over a wide field. The fine arts and the applied arts are both extensively represented, and there is in addition a department of antiquities and a library.

The principal feature of the Museum is the series of picture galleries occupying the whole of the upper floor. The collection covers a period from the late Middle Ages to the present day, and includes paintings from all the main European schools. Among other paintings of outstanding quality is a group of Venetian pictures by Titian, Tintoretto, and Veronese. Drawings, water-colours, and prints, with Italian maiolica and some sculpture and furniture, are also shown in these galleries.

The main collections of applied arts, portrait miniatures, and illuminated manuscripts are displayed in the galleries on the lower floor, together with the antiquities, which comprise an Egyptian and Western Asiatic Department, and a Greek and Roman Department. Of chief importance is the collection of ceramics, which is among the foremost in Great Britain; it is particularly strong in English pottery, but includes also many fine examples of English and Continental porcelain, and of Far Eastern and Islamic wares. Another exceptional collection is that of English glass. Other applied arts which are represented include silver (both English and Continental), metalwork, carvings, jewellery, textiles (including a very good collection of English samplers), and arms and armour. A group of Renaissance bronze statuettes, mostly Italian, and a series of medals from the work of Pisanello onwards, are displayed in association with the paintings.

The collection in the Coin Room is one of the most important in this country. It consists of a fully representative collection of coins, medals, and seals, including in particular very fine Greek coins and an unrivalled collection of medieval coins. Admission is for students only.

The Print Room contains another particularly good collection. Its chief riches are prints by Dürer and other early German masters, and by Lucas van Leyden, etchings by Rembrandt, and extensive series of English and French portrait prints, and of political caricatures.

The Library, open to members of the University and scholars, contains over 55,000 volumes. In addition there are 800 medieval manuscripts, many of them illuminated, and of the finest quality, and a collection of early printed books. The music collection of over 900 volumes is one of the best in Great Britain. Among other collections are autographs and literary manuscripts.

Special Exhibitions are held in the Adeane Gallery, the most considerable gallery for this purpose in East Anglia.

The Museum is open free to the public as follows:

Tuesdays to Saturdays	Lower Galleries	10 a.m.–2 p.m.
	Upper Galleries	2 p.m.–5 p.m.
Sundays	2.15 p.m.–5 p.m.	

The Museum is closed from 24 to 31 December, on New Year's Day, and on Good Friday; and on Mondays, except on Easter Monday and on the Spring and August Bank Holidays. On these Mondays the Museum will be open as on Tuesday to Saturdays.

Madingley Hall

Madingley Hall, a country house four miles west of Cambridge, was acquired by the University in 1948 and is now administered by the Board of Extra-mural Studies. The Hall is used as a residential centre for adults who attend the 200 short courses (usually of one to five days' duration) which the Board organizes each year for the general public; and a similar number of conferences and courses is held there in conjunction with other public and educational institutions and with some commercial and industrial organizations. Up to sixty residents can be accommodated, mainly in single rooms. It is sometimes possible for University teachers or those engaged in research to stay at Madingley for periods between a few days and several months.

All enquiries about the programme of public courses, arrangements for specially commissioned courses and conferences or residence at the Hall should be addressed in the first instance to the Director of Extra-mural Studies, Madingley Hall, Madingley, Cambridge, CB3 8AQ. Telephone: Madingley (0954) 210636.

2

THE COLLEGES

NOTE

Details of the individual Colleges, their Tutors, teaching Fellows, and Directors of Studies are included in the *Admissions Prospectus* which is published by the Cambridge Tutorial Representatives each year in March for the guidance of candidates applying between March and September for entry in the following year. The prospectus may be obtained on application to any College or to the Cambridge Intercollegiate Applications Office, Kellett Lodge, Tennis Court Road, Cambridge, CB2 1AQ. Because of the cost of postage, a leaflet printed on airmail paper and containing all essential information is usually sent to applicants from overseas.

General

Each College is a self-governing body; the control of its affairs rests with its Head and Fellows or, in some Colleges, with a smaller executive body elected by them from among themselves. There are twenty-four Colleges which admit both undergraduate and graduate students in any subject. Two Colleges (Newnham and New Hall) admit women only: two Colleges admit men only (Magdalene and Peterhouse*); and the remainder admit both men and women (Christ's, Churchill, Clare, Corpus Christi, Downing, Emmanuel, Fitzwilliam, Girton, Gonville and Caius, Jesus, King's, Pembroke, Queens', Robinson, St Catharine's, St John's, Selwyn, Sidney Sussex, Trinity, Trinity Hall). Darwin College and Wolfson College primarily admit only graduate students of either sex. Clare Hall (an Approved Foundation) and St Edmund's House (an Approved Foundation) admit graduates of either sex. Lucy Cavendish Collegiate Society (an Approved Society) for women only admits mature and affiliated undergraduates as well as graduates. Hughes Hall (an Approved Society) admits students for a one-year postgraduate course of study and training for the teaching profession, and also a small number of affiliated students. Wolfson College and St Edmund's House also admit a small number of mature student undergraduates and of affiliated students. Homerton College (an Approved Society) admits men and women only for the B.Ed. Degree course.

* Peterhouse is proposing to admit women in October 1985.

Under the authority of the governing body of each College certain officers are responsible for College teaching and for the detailed work of its administration. They include Lecturers and Directors of Studies, one or more Bursars, one or more Deans, who are responsible for services in the College Chapel and sometimes for College discipline, the Praelector, traditionally known as the Father of the College, who presents its members for degrees, and, most important of all from the point of view of the undergraduate, one or more Tutors, who advise their pupils not only about their studies but also on every kind of problem arising out of College and University life on which they may need advice, and who represent them in all their dealings with the University. A Tutor controls the educational and business arrangements arising out of his pupils' relations with the College.

Admission

Full details of the procedure for admission to Cambridge and of awards offered by the Colleges are published annually in the *Cambridge Admissions Prospectus*, a copy of which is sent to all schools which prepare candidates for admission to universities. The prospectus may be obtained on application to any College or to the Cambridge Inter-Collegiate Applications Office, Kellett Lodge, Tennis Court Road, Cambridge, CB2 1QA. In general, candidates seeking admission as undergraduates should apply in the spring or summer of the year before that in which they wish to be admitted.

Homerton College uses a different application procedure from other Colleges. A full description of the B.Ed. course can be found in the Homerton prospectus, obtainable on request from Homerton College, Cambridge CB2 2PH.

Enquiries about admission for research or for any of the courses for graduates other than the course for the Certificate in Education should be made to the Secretary, Board of Graduate Studies, University of Cambridge, 4 Mill Lane, Cambridge, CB2 1RZ. Enquiries about the course for the Certificate in Education should be made to the Department of Education, 17 Trumpington Street, Cambridge, CB2 1PT.

Overseas Candidates

About 10 per cent. of the students in the University, or roughly 1,000, are from overseas. Most of them are graduates with a good degree when they come to Cambridge. The Colleges do not normally admit undergraduates who do not intend to work for one of the qualifications offered by the University and there are normally no facilities for overseas students who wish to spend 'a junior year' abroad or 'transfer year' at Cambridge. Eight Colleges are, however, ready to accept a small number of such students. These Colleges are: Churchill, Clare, Fitzwilliam, Girton, Magdalene, Peterhouse, Queens' and Lucy Cavendish (for mature and affiliated women students only).

A student proposing to spend three years in Cambridge working for a B.A. Degree should apply to the Tutor for Admissions of one (and one only) of the Colleges stating his or her age, present qualifications, other qualifications which he or she may hope to obtain by the time of his or her admission, and his or her proposed subject of study. The applicant should do this preferably by 30 June but in any case not later than 30 September in the year before that in which he or she wishes to be admitted.

An applicant holding an approved degree of an overseas university may be granted the privileges of affiliation and can then be admitted to the B.A. Degree in two years instead of the usual three, after passing one Part only of a Tripos, generally Part II (see p. 13). Applications to Colleges should be submitted as early as possible, preferably by 30 September (for admission in October of the following year), and otherwise by the closing date, which is 31 October – although some Colleges may consider applications received after the closing date. Early application will increase a candidate's chance of a place.

A prospective graduate student should apply, in the first instance, to the Secretary of the Board of Graduate Studies, 4 Mill Lane, Cambridge, CB2 1RZ. In addition to being asked to complete an application form, he will be required to give particulars of his qualifications and the names of Professors or others under whom he has worked, and to whom reference can be made. He will also have to state his subject of research or give an outline of his proposed thesis. Information concerning fellowships, scholarships, grants, etc., for which prospective graduate students from Commonwealth countries are eligible, is contained in *Scholarships Guide for Commonwealth Postgraduate Students* published by the Association of Commonwealth Universities (36 Gordon Square, London, W.C.1H 0PF) and which can be obtained from that address, or from booksellers.

If overseas students require further information about the University before applying to a College, they should write to the Registrary, The University Registry, The Old Schools, Cambridge,

CB2 1TN, or, in the case of Graduate Students, to the Secretary of the Board of Graduate Studies.

Overseas students seeking admission as undergraduates (but not those seeking admission as affiliated students) must also submit an application form to the Universities Central Council on Admissions (U.C.C.A.). The U.C.C.A. handbook and application form can be obtained from the U.C.C.A. office, GPO Box 28, Cheltenham, Glos., GL50 1HY or, usually, from the students' High Commission or Government Agency in London. U.C.C.A. will inform an applicant what costs are involved and these must be prepaid. The application form must be returned by 15 October of the year previous to that in which admission is required. Even if a student has a preference for Cambridge, he will be well advised to mention on his U.C.C.A. form other universities by which he would wish to be considered if he fails to secure a place at the university of his first choice.

The Government introduced charges for overseas visitors for treatment under the National Health Service from 1 October 1982. These charges do not apply to students on a course at a university lasting over six months. Nevertheless, students are advised before arrival to consult their College Tutor regarding taking out a health insurance policy especially if dependants are involved. Overseas visitors from the E.E.C. countries and from those countries where there is a reciprocal agreement* are exempt from being charged under the N.H.S.

*Countries with reciprocal agreements are: Austria, Bulgaria, Czechoslovakia, German Democratic Republic, Gibraltar, Guernsey, Hong Kong, Hungary, Isle of Man, Jersey, Malta, New Zealand, Norway, Poland, Portugal, Romania, Sweden, Union of Soviet Socialist Republics, Yugoslavia.

3

UNIVERSITY EXAMINATIONS AND DEGREES

UNIVERSITY EXAMINATIONS

Most University examinations are held once in every academical year, towards the end of the Easter Term. The dates of most examinations are prescribed by Ordinance and may be found in the *Cambridge Pocket Diary*.

Examination entry

The College is responsible for entering candidates *in statu pupillari* for examinations, but if a candidate fails to keep his Tutor fully informed of his intentions he may incur a fine for late entry.

A first list of candidates, then a corrected list, and lastly a final list with a programme giving the time and places of examinations, are published successively from December onwards and are posted in each College. Every candidate is expected to make certain that he has been correctly entered for his examination and to inform his Tutor at once if there is an error in his entry in any of the lists.

Conduct in examinations

No candidate may enter an examination room later or leave earlier than thirty minutes after the beginning of a session except with the consent of the Supervisor or Senior Invigilator. A candidate may not take into an examination room or have in his possession during an examination any unauthorized book or paper, nor may he remove from the room any paper except the question paper and any books or papers which he may have been authorized to take in. During an examination a candidate may not communicate with any other candidate, nor may he leave his place except with the consent of the Supervisor or an Invigilator. Should a candidate act in such a way as to disturb or inconvenience other candidates, he shall be warned and may, at the discretion of the Supervisor, Invigilator, or Examiner, be dismissed from the session. Candidates attending a practical examination must comply with the safety requirements of the laboratory in which the examination is held.

Candidates may apply to the Examiners if they think that there is a misprint or other error in the paper, and also may inquire whether they may take some particular point for granted in answering a question. For these purposes an Examiner will be present for the first twenty minutes of each session.

Candidates affected by illness or other serious hindrance

If a candidate for any University examination, except one for which candidates are required to be Graduate Students or one leading to the M.B., B.Chir. Degrees or the Vet.M.B. Degree, is absent from the whole examination because of illness or other grave cause, the Council of the Senate may, after receiving proof of that cause and evidence of his attainments:

(i) give him leave to degrade, including leave, where required, to present himself as a candidate for the same examination;
(ii) allow him the examination;
(iii) allow him one, or, where that is consistent with the regulations for the Ordinary B.A. Degree, two Ordinary Examinations;
(iv) declare him to have attained the honours standard. This allowance is given only when the candidate would, if successful in the examination, have been declared by the Examiners to have attained the honours standard.

If a candidate is prevented by illness or other grave cause from attending part of the examination, the Examiners may be authorized by the Council of the Senate to declare him to have deserved honours or to have deserved to have passed the examination, whichever is appropriate. The Examiners may not make such a declaration unless they judge the candidate to have acquitted himself with credit in a substantial part of the examination and unless they either are unable to include him in the list of successful candidates or would otherwise have to award him a class that would in their opinion misrepresent his abilities. If the Examiners are unable to do so, the Council may take one of the four courses set out above.

If a candidate has been hindered by illness or other grave cause in preparing for an examination which he takes and fails, the Council may also take one of the four courses set out above.

It is very important that any examination candidate who

(1) *finds that his preparation for the examination is seriously hindered;*
(2) *withdraws from the examination;*
or (3) *completes it under a disability,*

should inform his Tutor of the fact and of the full circumstances, whatever the cause, at the earliest possible moment.

Examinations leading to the B.A. Degree

Examinations for honours leading to the B.A. Degree are known as Tripos Examinations. Most Tripos Examinations are divided into Parts but a few are undivided. It is possible to offer various combinations of subjects by taking Part I of a Tripos in one subject at the end of the first or second year and Part I or Part II of another Tripos, or one of the undivided Triposes, at the end of the third. An account of the regulations and subjects for each Tripos Examination and of the regulations governing the standing of candidates is given in the next chapter, and is summarized in the Table below.

A candidate obtains honours by the inclusion of his name in one of the classes or under the heading 'Declared to have deserved honours' in the class-list or by his being allowed the examination by the Council.

No one who is, or is qualified to be, a member of the Senate, or is, or has been, registered as a Graduate Student, shall be a candidate for honours in an honours examination.

Qualifying Examinations or Preliminary Examinations for Triposes are not honours examinations but 'examinations proper to an honours course'. In any year in which he does not take a Tripos Examination (or in certain subjects a Qualifying Examination) a candidate for honours is likely to be advised by his College to sit for a Preliminary Examination. Failure to take or pass a Preliminary Examination does not in itself debar a student from proceeding to a Tripos Examination.

Tables of standing required for Honours Examinations

In the following tables standing is shown by reference to years and not to terms as in the Ordinances. The tables do not show any differing requirements in the numbers of papers to be offered by candidates according to their standing. No account is taken of the privileges of Affiliated Students. The tables are therefore only an approximate guide, and for complete accuracy the relevant Ordinances should be consulted.

I. Examinations taken as the first Honours Examination

Examination	Year of standing required
Anglo-Saxon, Norse, and Celtic	2
Archaeology and Anthropology, Part I	1
Architecture, Part I A	1
Classical, Part I	1 or 2
Economics, Part I	1
Engineering, Part I A	1
Engineering, Part I B	2
English, Part I	1 or 2
Geographical, Part I A	1
Historical, Part I	2
Law, Part I A	1
Law, Part I B	2
Mathematical, Part I A	1
Mathematical, Part I B	1 or 2
Medical Sciences, Part I A	1
Modern and Medieval Languages, Part I	1 or 2
Music, Part I A	1
Natural Sciences, Part I A	1
Oriental Studies, Part I	1 or 2
Philosophy, Part I A	1
Philosophy, Part I B	2, 3, or 4
Theological and Religious Studies, Part I A	1
Theological and Religious Studies, Part I B	2

II. Examinations taken after one or more Honours Examinations

Examination	Year of standing required		Remarks
Anglo-Saxon, Norse, and Celtic	3 or 4	‡	
Archaeological and Anthropological, Part I	3	*	
Archaeological and Anthropological, Part II	3 or 4	‡	
Architecture Tripos, Part IA	2 or 3	*	
Architecture Tripos, Part IB	2, 3, or 4	*	Part IA of same Tripos must precede
Architecture Tripos, Part II	3 or 4	‡	Part IB of same Tripos must precede
Chemical Engineering, Part I	3 or 4	*	Specific requirements for preceding exam
Chemical Engineering, Part II	4 or 5	*	Part I of same Tripos must precede
Classical, Part I	2, 3, or 4	‡	Not after MML I with Latin or Greek
Classical, Part II	3 or 4	‡	
Computer Science			
(i)	3 or 4	*	
(ii)	3 or 4	†	
[1]Economics, Part II			
(i)	3		After Part I of same Tripos
(ii)	3 or 4	‡	After any other Tripos
Education			
(i)	3, 4, or 5		Ed.Q.E. must immediately precede
(ii)	2		B.Ed. candidates (Homerton)
Electrical Sciences	3 or 4	‡	Part IA may not be the sole preceding exam
Engineering, Part IA	2 or 3	*	
Engineering, Part IB	2, 3, or 4	‡	
Engineering, Part II	3 or 4	‡	Part IA may not be the sole preceding exam
English, Part I	2, 3, or 4	‡	

[1] Candidates must be exempt, or obtain exemption, from E.Q.E.M.
* To be taken in the year after another Honours Examination.
† To be taken in the year next but one after another Honours Examination.
‡ To be taken in the year after or next but one after another Honours Examination.
§ The previous Honours Examination must have been taken not earlier than the candidate's second year.

Examination	Year of standing required		Remarks
English, Part II	2, 3, or 4	‡	
Geographical, Part IA	2 or 3	*	
Geographical, Part IB	2, 3, or 4	*	
Geographical, Part II			
(i)	3 or 4	‡	Part IA may not be the sole preceding exam
(ii)	3 or 4	*	After Part IB
Historical, Part I	3 or 4	‡	
Historical, Part II	3 or 4	‡	
History of Art	3 or 4	‡	
Land Economy			
(i)	3, 4, or 5	†	
(ii)	3, 4, or 5	*	
Law, Part IB	2, 3 or 4	*	Faculty Board may grant special permission
Law, Part II	3 or 4	‡	Part IB of same Tripos must precede. Faculty Board may grant special permission
Mathematical, Part IA	2 or 3	*	
Mathematical, Part IB	2, 3, or 4	‡	
Mathematical, Part II	2, 3, or 4	‡	Part IA may not be the sole preceding exam
Mathematical, Part III	3 or 4	§	
Medical Sciences, Part IA	2 or 3	*	Not after NST IA including Physiology
Medical Sciences, Part IB	2, 3, or 4	*	Part IA must precede
Medical Sciences, Part II (General)	3 or 4	‡	Section I or II only after Parts IA and IB. Section III only after NST IA and IB
Modern and Medieval Languages, Part I	2, 3, or 4	‡	
Modern and Medieval Languages, Part II			
(i)	3 or 4	‡	If Honours obtained after first year
(ii)	3 or 4	†	If Honours obtained in first year. Or next but two if year spent abroad with approval of Faculty Board

* To be taken in the year after another Honours Examination.
† To be taken in the year next but one after another Honours Examination.
‡ To be taken in the year after or next but one after another Honours Examination.
§ The previous Honours Examination must have been taken not earlier than the candidate's second year.

Examination	Year of standing required		Remarks
Music, Part IB	2 or 3	*	
Music, Part II	3 or 4	*	Part IB of the same Tripos must precede
Natural Sciences, Part IA	3	*	
Natural Sciences, Part IB	2	*	
Natural Sciences, Part II (General)	3 or 4	§	
Natural Sciences, Part II	3 or 4	§	
Oriental Studies, Part I	2, 3, 4, or 5	‡	
Oriental Studies, Part II			
(i)	2, 3, or 4	‡	After Part I of the same Tripos
(ii)	2, 3, 4, or 5	‡	After any other Tripos
Philosophy, Part IB	2, 3, or 4		
Philosophy, Part II	3, 4, or 5	‡	Part IA may not be sole preceding exam
Production Engineering, Part I	3 or 4	*	After Part IB or Part II Engineering
Production Engineering, Part II	4 or 5	*	Part I of same Tripos must precede
Social and Political Sciences, Part II	3 or 4	‡	
Theological, and Religious Studies, Part IA	2, 3, or 4	*	Not after another Part of same Tripos
Theological and Religious Studies, Part II			
(i)	3, 4, or 5	*	After Part IB or Honours exam other than Part IA
(ii)	3, 4, or 5	†	After Part IA or Honours exam other than Part IB

* To be taken in the year after another Honours Examination.
† To be taken in the year next but one after another Honours Examination.
‡ To be taken in the year after or next but one after another Honours Examination.
§ The previous Honours Examination must have been taken not earlier than the candidate's second year.

DEGREES

Degrees are conferred at Congregations in the Senate-House. These ceremonies are held three times in each term and once in the Long Vacation, usually on Saturdays at 2 p.m.* Although the degree of B.A. may be conferred at most Congregations, candidates for that degree are more likely, unless their circumstances are unusual, to be admitted to it on one of the two days in June set apart as days of General Admission to Degrees. Candidates may be admitted to degrees by proxy.

Entry of candidates

Any qualified person who wishes to take a degree should communicate with the Tutor or Praelector of his College. Anyone who wishes to proceed to the B.A. Degree on some date other than a day of General Admission, or to some other degree at any Congregation, should give early notice to his College. Except with the approval of the Vice-Chancellor, no degree other than those of B.A., LL.M., Mus.B., Vet.M.B., and B.Ed. may be conferred on a day of General Admission.

Academical dress

In general, all men being admitted to degrees must wear at the ceremony in the Senate-House dark clothes, black shoes, white ties, and bands with their academical dress. Women wear a plain black or dark coat and skirt with a plain white blouse, or a plain black or dark dress, and black shoes; their stockings need not be black, but must not be of a bright colour.

A person being admitted to a degree by incorporation or to the degree of M.A. under Statute B, III, 6 wears the gown and hood of the degree that he is to receive. A graduate of the University being admitted to a degree wears the gown and hood of the highest degree that he has hitherto received from the University. A possessor of the status of B.A. or M.A. who is not a graduate of the University and is being admitted to a degree other than the degree of M.A. under Statute B, III, 6 or to a degree by incorporation shall wear the gown appropriate to his status and the hood of the degree, or of the higher of the two degrees, that he is to receive. An undergraduate being admitted to a degree wears his undergraduate gown, and the hood of the degree, or of the higher of the two degrees, that he is to receive.

The order of seniority of degrees is prescribed by Ordinance.

* The Congregation in March usually now starts at 1.30 p.m.

Presentation

At each Congregation, after supplicats (motions for the approval of the conferment of degrees) have been read by the Senior Proctor, degrees are conferred. When his turn comes, each candidate is led forward by the officer presenting him (generally, except for higher degrees, the Praelector of his College) who takes him, right hand by right hand, to the Vice-Chancellor and pronounces the formula of presentation, stating that the candidate is qualified for the degree by his character and his academic attainments. The candidate then kneels and places his hands together between those of the Vice-Chancellor, who pronounces the formula of admission to the degree. The graduate rises, bows to the Vice-Chancellor and withdraws. He may then leave the Senate-House at the next permissible opportunity.

Certificates of Degrees

A certificate of every degree is issued without charge on graduation. A fee of £1 is charged for a certificate issued from the University Registry attesting matriculation or the passing of any examination, or the class obtained by a candidate in a Tripos Examination or for the repetition of a degree certificate. For more detailed certificates a fee of £2.50 is charged.

Bachelor of Arts by honours

A candidate for this degree must have kept or been allowed nine terms and have obtained honours

(*a*) in Part II of any Tripos (except Section I of Part II (General) of the Natural Sciences Tripos), or in the Anglo-Saxon, Norse, and Celtic Tripos, the Computer Science Tripos, the Education Tripos, the Electrical Sciences Tripos, the History of Art Tripos, or the Land Economy Tripos;

or (*b*) in any two Honours Examinations, except that he may not count for this purpose (i) both Part IA and Part IB of the same Tripos, (ii) any two Parts IA, or (iii) both Part IB of the Natural Sciences Tripos and another Honours Examination (other than Part II of a Tripos);

(*c*) in any three Honours Examinations.

If, however, he completed the examination requirement in any term earlier than his eighth he must *either* produce a 'Certificate of Diligent Study' (i.e. a certificate from his College that since completing this requirement he has been engaged upon academic studies suited to his attainments and has been regular and diligent therein), *or*, not earlier than in the last but one of the terms that he needs for a degree, pass an examination leading to the Ordinary B.A. Degree, the examination for the Diploma in Mathematical Statistics, or in Computer Science, or the LL.M. Examination (provided that if he elects to proceed to the LL.M. Degree he is not also entitled to proceed to the B.A. Degree). It is not possible for a candidate to qualify for the B.A. degree and a one-year M.Phil. degree simultaneously.

For details of other courses leading to the B.A. Degree with honours that are open to Affiliated Students, see p. 17.

The Ordinary degree of Bachelor of Arts

No candidates are admitted to the University as candidates at the outset for the Ordinary B.A. Degree and the degree is mainly intended for those who fail to pass a Tripos Examination or a Tripos Qualifying Examination and so become ineligible to proceed to the B.A. Degree by honours.

In order to qualify for the Ordinary degree a candidate must

(*a*) keep nine terms;

(*b*) accumulate three Ordinary Examinations.

A candidate cannot accumulate more than one Ordinary Examination by the end of his first year nor more than two by the end of his second year, nor, except with the permission of the Council of the Senate, may he take more than one examination leading to the Ordinary B.A. Degree in the same term, and then only after his second year.

Ordinary Examinations are accumulated as follows:

(i) A pass in a Preliminary Examination or a Tripos Qualifying Examination always counts as the equivalent of one Ordinary Examination, as does being classed in one language in Part I of the Modern and Medieval Languages Tripos or in a Part of a Tripos taken in a candidate's first year.

(ii) Being classed in a Part of a Tripos taken in a candidate's second year counts as the equivalent of one Ordinary Examination if he already has one to his credit and otherwise as the equivalent of two Ordinary Examinations.

(iii) An allowance of one Ordinary Examination may be made by the Council of the Senate to a candidate who has not passed a Preliminary Examination or a Tripos Qualifying Examination, and of one or two Ordinary Examinations to a candidate who has not passed a Tripos examination, but has performed sufficiently well to justify that allowance.

(iv) The Examiners may make an allowance towards the Ordinary B.A. Degree to a candidate for an Honours Examination who has not been classed but who has performed sufficiently well to justify it, which gives him one Ordinary Examination if he is in his first year or has one Ordinary Examination to his credit and otherwise two Ordinary Examinations.

(v) A pass in an actual Ordinary Examination counts as one Ordinary Examination. A performance of at least the standard for an allowance towards the Ordinary B.A. Degree in an Honours Examination which the Council of the Senate have allowed a candidate to take as though it were an Ordinary Examination counts either as one Ordinary Examination or as two, as the Council may decide.

The Ordinary Examinations in Greek, Latin, English, History, Law, certain Modern and Oriental Languages, Geography, Medical Sciences, Philosophy, Theology, and certain of the Natural Sciences are described where their subjects are dealt with in the following chapter.

Bachelor of Divinity

A candidate for the B.D. Degree must be a graduate of the University of at least five years' standing from admission to his first degree in the University (or in another University if he has also been admitted to the M.A. degree under Statute B, III, 6 or a degree by incorporation) and must submit a dissertation or published work; he must also establish his competent knowledge of Christian Theology.

Bachelor of Education

A candidate for the B.Ed. Degree must have kept five terms, passed the Ed.Q.E., obtained honours in the Education Tripos, and satisfied the Examiners for the Tripos in practical teaching ability.

Bachelor of Law

A candidate for the LL.B. Degree must ordinarily have kept three terms and have passed the LL.B. Examination. It is not available to anyone who has not passed that examination before October 1982.

Bachelor of Medicine

A candidate for the M.B. Degree must have kept three terms and have passed the prescribed examinations.

Bachelor of Music

A candidate for the Mus.B. Degree must have kept nine terms and have passed the two Sections of the prescribed examination.

Bachelor of Surgery

A candidate for the B.Chir. Degree must have kept three terms and have passed the prescribed examinations.

Bachelor of Veterinary Medicine

A candidate for the Vet.M.B. Degree must have kept nine terms and have passed the prescribed examinations, the last of which cannot be completed until the end of his sixth year.

Master of Arts

A candidate for the M.A. Degree must be a Bachelor of Arts of the University of at least two years' standing, and six or more years must have passed after his first term of residence. The College will usually notify its members when they are of standing to proceed to the M.A. Degree. Each candidate is required to give notice to the College of the day on which he proposes to take the degree.

Master of Law

A candidate for the LL.M. Degree must *either*

(i) be a Bachelor of Law of the University who has passed the LL.B. Examination before October 1982 and be of at least six years' standing from the end of his first term of residence and at least two years' since his admission to the B.A. or LL.B. Degree. He must submit a dissertation; *or*

(ii) must ordinarily have kept three terms and passed the LL.M. Examination.

Master of Letters

A candidate for the M.Litt. Degree must be a registered Graduate Student who shall pursue a course of research under supervision, ordinarily for not less than six terms, and submit a dissertation embodying the results of his course (see Chapter 5).

Master of Music

A candidate for the Mus.M. Degree must be a Bachelor of Music of the University of at least two years' standing, and must pass the prescribed examination, which is in two Parts. Part I, which is held in March, is a written and oral examination. Part II is an exercise in the form of a musical composition, written for the occasion, and conforming to the detailed provisions of the regulations. A Bachelor of Music who has been approved for the degree of Mus.M. may be admitted to that degree three years after he has been admitted to the Mus.B.

Master of Philosophy

A candidate for the M.Phil. Degree must normally be a graduate of a university. To qualify for the degree he must pursue a course of study of either one year or two years under supervision and pass the prescribed examination. The examination after the two-year course consists of written papers, a thesis, and may include an oral examination. The examination after the one-year course consists of written papers or a thesis or both, and may include an oral examination on the thesis. No one may qualify simultaneously for the B.A. degree and the one-year M.Phil. degree.

Master of Science

A candidate for the M.Sc. Degree must be a registered Graduate Student who shall pursue a course of research under supervision, ordinarily for not less than six terms, and submit a dissertation embodying the results of his course (see Chapter 5).

Master of Surgery

A candidate for the M.Chir. Degree must be a holder, of at least five years' standing, of an approved medical degree and also a holder of a primary degree of the University or of the M.A. degree under Statute B, III, 6 or a degree by incorporation (in the latter two cases of at least two years' standing), must pass a clinical examination, and must submit a thesis or published work. Further details may be obtained from the Secretary of the M.Chir. Committee, at the Medical School.

Doctor of Divinity

A candidate for the D.D. Degree must be a Bachelor of Divinity of the University of at least three years' standing or a holder, of at least twelve years' standing, of another degree of the University or a degree of another university (in the latter case holding also the M.A. degree under Statute B, III, 6 or a degree by incorporation), and must submit a dissertation or published work.

Doctor of Law

A candidate for the LL.D. Degree must be of at least eight years' standing from admission to his first degree of this University or of another University (in the latter case holding also the M.A. degree under Statute B, III, 6 or a degree by incorporation), and must submit proof of distinction by some original contribution to the advancement of the science or study of Law.

Doctor of Letters

A candidate for the Litt.D. Degree must be of at least eight years' standing from his first degree of this University or of another University (in the latter case holding also the M.A. degree under Statute B, III, 6 or a degree by incorporation), and must give proof of distinction by some original contribution to the advancement of science or of learning.

Doctor of Medicine

A candidate for the M.D. Degree must be a holder, of at least four years' standing, of an approved medical degree and also a holder of a primary degree of the University or of the M.A. degree under Statute B, III, 6 or a degree by incorporation (in the latter two cases of at least two years' standing). He must submit a dissertation specially composed for the purpose and may also submit published work in support of his dissertation. In certain circumstances he may be allowed to submit published work only. He will undergo a *viva voce* examination on work submitted, as well as on other medical subjects, and may be required to take a clinical examination.

Doctor of Music

A candidate for the Mus.D. Degree must be of at least eight years' standing from his first degree of this University or of another university (in the latter case holding also the M.A. degree under Statute B, III, 6 or a degree by incorporation), and must give proof of distinction in musical composition. He must submit not more than three works (printed or otherwise) including either an oratorio, an opera, a cantata, a symphony for orchestra, a concerto, or an extended piece of chamber music.

Doctor of Philosophy

A candidate for the Ph.D. Degree must be a registered Graduate Student who shall pursue a course of research under supervision ordinarily for not less than nine terms, and submit a dissertation embodying the results of his course (see Chapter 5). Under special regulations, a candidate may proceed to the Ph.D. Degree if he can give proof of a significant contribution to scholarship by the submission of published work and an oral examination. Candidature for the Ph.D. Degree under the special regulations is confined to graduates of the University who must be of at least six years' standing from admission to their first degree of this University or of another university (in the latter case holding also the M.A. degree under Statute B, III, 6 or a degree by incorporation).

Doctor of Science

A candidate for the Sc.D. Degree must be of at least eight years' standing from his first degree of this University or of another university (in the latter case holding also the M.A. degree under Statute B, III, 6 or a degree by incorporation), and must give proof of distinction by some original contribution to the advancement of science or of learning.

4

COURSES OF STUDY FOR DEGREES, DIPLOMAS, AND CERTIFICATES

ANGLO-SAXON, NORSE, AND CELTIC

The course of study leading to the Anglo-Saxon, Norse, and Celtic Tripos is primarily concerned with the culture and history of the British Isles between the departure of the Romans and the coming of the Normans. It provides a diverse education of general value or, if desired, a stage in the training of future scholars in this field. All the main forms of evidence can be studied, a student being free to place the emphasis where he chooses. For instance, he can pursue a principal interest in history or literature or in one region or period. If he is an historian, he can learn to correlate the various kinds of evidence and to read the documents in their original languages; if his interest is predominantly literary, he can study a literature of his choice against its cultural background and in comparison with other literatures. If he wishes, he can also extend his interest by studying, for example, Middle English as well as Old English, or the history of the Vikings in their homelands, or Celtic literatures until the end of the Middle Ages. He has an option of preparing a short dissertation to give some experience of research. No previous knowledge of the subjects studied is required, although some knowledge of Latin is useful.

This Tripos is not divided into Parts. A student can qualify for an Honours Degree by taking it, either first or second, in combination with a Part of some other Tripos, although an Affiliated Student can qualify for an Honours Degree on this Tripos alone. According to a student's interests it combines well with English, or History, or Modern and Medieval Languages, or Classics, or Archaeology and Anthropology, or History of Art, or Theological and Religious Studies. A student who is preparing for this Tripos after obtaining Honours in a Part of another Tripos may spend either one year or two, but the Department expresses a strong preference for two;* any other student spends two years. A student who is spending two years may take a Preliminary Examination at the end of his first year.

* If he wishes to spend two years, after spending two years obtaining honours in another Tripos, and is receiving an L.E.A. grant, he is strongly advised to apply through his Tutor for his grant for his fourth year not later than the beginning of his fourth term at the University.

The Anglo-Saxon, Norse, and Celtic Tripos

The examination consists of the following papers:

1. England before the Norman Conquest

An introduction to the history and civilization of England from the age of the Anglo-Saxon settlements to the Norman Conquest. A candidate will be required to use primary sources in the original languages or in translation.

2. The Vikings

An introduction to the political, social, and religious history of the Vikings in their homelands and during their expansion to east and west. Their history in the British Isles is excluded in so far as it is included in Papers 1 and 3. Particular attention is paid to primary sources, notably those in Old Norse, with discussion of the historical value of the Sagas of Icelanders. A knowledge of Old Norse, although useful, is not essential. There will be recommended texts, including groups of Old Norse works to be read in translation.

3. The Celtic-speaking peoples from the fourth century to the twelfth

An introduction to the history and civilization of the Celtic-speaking peoples of the British Isles and Brittany from the collapse of the Roman Empire to the Norman invasions. A candidate will be required to use primary sources in the original languages or in translation.

4. Latin literature of the British Isles, 400–1100 (also serves as Paper 10 of Part I and Paper 16 of Part II of the English Tripos)

An introduction to the Latin prose and poetry of England, Wales, and Ireland during the period specified. An advanced knowledge of Latin is not expected when preparation is begun, although some knowledge of the language is desirable. There will be set texts in the original language and recommended texts in translation. A candidate will be required to show detailed knowledge of set texts and to write essays on recommended texts as well as on set texts.

5. English literature before the Norman Conquest (also serves as Paper 9 of Part I and Paper 15 of Part II of the English Tripos)

An introduction to the language and literary characteristics of Old English prose and poetry. There will be set texts in the original language, including a substantial part of *Beowulf*. A candidate will be required to translate passages from the set texts and to write essays on selected topics.

6. Old Norse literature (also serves as Paper 11 of Part I and Paper 17 of Part II of the English Tripos)

An introduction to the language and literary characteristics of Old Norse prose and poetry. There will be set texts in the original language and recommended texts in translation. A candidate will be required to translate passages from the set texts and to write essays on selected topics.

7A. Medieval Welsh language and literature I (also serves as Paper 12 of Part I and Paper 18A of Part II of the English Tripos)

An introduction to the language and literature of Wales from the beginnings to the end of the Middle Ages. There will be set texts in the original language, including selections from the 'Mabinogion', from the early poets, and from Dafydd ap Gwilym and other later poets, and there will also be recommended texts in the original language. A candidate will be required to translate an unseen passage of Middle Welsh and extracts from the set texts. He will be required also to write essays on selected topics and/or to comment on the linguistic or literary characteristics of passages from the recommended texts.

7B. Medieval Welsh language and literature II (also serves as Paper 18B of Part II of the English Tripos)

This paper is intended for those who have taken Paper 7A or have reached an equivalent standard when preparation is begun. There will be set and recommended texts in Old and Middle Welsh. A candidate will be required to translate extracts from these set texts, and to translate other passages, of which some will be drawn from the recommended texts and some will be unseen. There will be two further groups of set texts, one of them in Medieval Cornish and Breton and the other in Middle Welsh. A candidate will be required to translate extracts from either or both of these further groups of texts. He will be required also to write essays on selected topics in medieval Welsh, Cornish or Breton language and literature, or in comparative Celtic philology.

8A. Medieval Irish language and literature I (also serves as Paper 19A of Part II of the English Tripos)

An introduction to the language and literature of early medieval Ireland, in particular until the end of the tenth century. There will be set texts in the original language, including selections from the early lyric poetry and from the prose sagas and religious prose, and there will also be recommended texts in the original language. A candidate will be required to translate an unseen passage of Old Irish and extracts from the set texts. He will be required also to write essays on selected topics and/or to comment on the linguistic or literary characteristics of passages from the recommended texts.

8 B. Medieval Irish language and literature II (also serves as Paper 19 B of Part II of the English Tripos)

This paper is intended for those who have taken Paper 8 A or have reached an equivalent standard when preparation is begun. Irish language and literature from the beginnings to the end of the Middle Ages are studied. There will be set and recommended texts in the original language. A candidate will be required to translate extracts from the set texts, and to translate other passages, of which some will be drawn from the recommended texts and some will be unseen. He will be required also to write essays on selected topics in medieval Irish language and literature or in comparative Celtic philology.

9. Palaeography, diplomatic, and the editorial process

An introduction to the processes by which extant sources written in the languages studied for Papers 1–8 have been transmitted and of the scholarly methods by which these sources are converted into a usable form. The history of script, the manuscript as a physical object, the history of the forms of legal instruments, and the various editorial approaches and techniques are studied. A candidate will be required to answer a compulsory practical question and to write essays on selected topics.

10. Special subject I, specified by the Faculty Board of English from time to time

In a year for which a subject is specified, the paper will consist of a detailed consideration of a predominantly historical topic related to more than one field of study in the Tripos. A candidate will be required to use primary sources in the original languages or in translation. He will be expected to show a knowledge of relevant literary and linguistic evidence, and he will have to show familiarity with both Germanic and Celtic societies.

No subject has been specified for 1985.

11. Special subject II, specified by the Faculty Board of English from time to time (also serves as Paper 20 of Part II of the English Tripos)

In a year for which a subject is specified, the paper shall consist of a detailed consideration of a predominantly literary topic related to more than one field of study in the Tripos. There will be recommended texts in each of the relevant Germanic and Celtic languages. A candidate will be required to show a knowledge of at least two of these languages and to write essays on selected topics. In his essays he will have to show familiarity with both Germanic and Celtic literatures, although not necessarily in the original languages.

No subject has been specified for 1985.

12. Anglo-Saxon England in the pagan period (also serves as option (*c*) in Paper 5 in Archaeology of Part II of the Archaeological and Anthropological Tripos and Paper O8 of Part II of the Classical Tripos)

An introduction to the archaeology and history of the Anglo-Saxon peoples from the age of the settlements to *c*. 650. A candidate will be expected to show familiarity with archaeological, historical, and linguistic evidence.

13. Early medieval literature and its background (Paper 8 of Part I of the English Tripos)

14. Chaucer (Paper 3 of Part II of the English Tripos)

15. Medieval English literature, 1066–1500 (Paper 4 of Part II of the English Tripos)

16. History of the English language (Paper 13 of Part II of the English Tripos)

A candidate will be required to answer three questions from Section A only.

17. Medieval Latin literature, from 400 to 1300 (Paper 12 of Part II of the Modern and Medieval Languages Tripos)

18. The Teutonic languages, with special reference to Gothic, Anglo-Saxon, Early Norse, Old Saxon, and Old High German (Paper 121 of Part II of the Modern and Medieval Languages Tripos)

19. A period of European history: A.D. 284–962 (option (*a*) of Paper 14 of Part II of the Historical Tripos)

20. Special subject in the history of art (a pair of papers on a special subject announced for the History of Art Tripos which in any year has been approved for the purpose of this regulation by the Faculty Board of English)

In **1985** and **1986**: Irish, Pictish, and Anglo-Saxon Art, *c*. 600–*c*. 800 (Papers 12 and 13 of the History of Art Tripos)

A candidate who has spent two years preparing for the Tripos must offer six papers; a candidate who has spent one year in preparation is required to offer only five papers. No candidate can offer a paper he has already taken in another Tripos Examination. A candidate cannot offer both Papers 7A and 7B or both 8A and 8B; nor can he offer more than two of Papers 13–20.

A candidate may apply to the Faculty Board of English not later than the division of the Lent Term for permission to submit a dissertation on any subject within the scope of the Tripos. The application must specify the proposed subject of the dissertation and the whole scheme of papers that the candidate intends to offer. A candidate whose application is granted shall offer one paper less than the number of papers that he would otherwise be required to choose. The Faculty Board may require that such a candidate shall not offer more than one paper from among Papers 13–20. The dissertation must show evidence of reading, of judgement and criticism, and of power of exposition, but not necessarily of original research, and shall be of not less than 5,000 and not more than 10,000 words in length (inclusive of notes and appendices). A candidate will be required to declare that the dissertation submitted is his own work and does not contain material which he has already used for a comparable purpose, and to give full references to sources used. The dissertation must be typewritten, and submitted to the Secretary of the Faculty Board of English so as to reach him not later than the first day of Full Easter Term. The Examiners have power at their discretion to examine a candidate *viva voce* on the dissertation and on the general field of knowledge within which it falls.

The Preliminary Examination for the Anglo-Saxon, Norse, and Celtic Tripos

The examination consists of the following papers:

1. England before the Norman Conquest
2. The Vikings
3. The Celtic-speaking peoples from the fourth century to the twelfth
4. Latin literature of the British Isles, 400–1100
5. English literature before the Norman Conquest
6. Old Norse literature
7. Medieval Welsh language and literature

8. Medieval Irish language and literature

9. Palaeography

A candidate must offer three papers.

A student who is not a candidate for the examination may offer Paper 4 or 5 or 6 or 7 in accordance with the regulations for the Preliminary Examination for Part I of the English Tripos, and his marks will be communicated to his Tutor.

A list of set texts and recommended reading may be obtained from the Professor of Anglo-Saxon and other members of the Department, and from the office of the Faculty of English.

ARCHAEOLOGY AND ANTHROPOLOGY

There are in these subjects courses of study followed by candidates for:

The *Archaeological and Anthropological Tripos*, which is divided into two Parts.

The *Preliminary Examinations* for each subject of Part II of the Tripos.

The *M.Phil. Degree* (one-year course) *in Archaeology, Biological Anthropology*, and *Social Anthropology*.

Papers from this Tripos can be taken in the *Anglo-Saxon, Norse, and Celtic Tripos* (p. 42); in Part II of the *Classical Tripos* (p. 86) and in the Diploma in *Classical Archaeology* (p. 102); in Part II (General) of the *Medical Sciences Tripos* (special subject, Physical Anthropology, (p. 263); in the *Oriental Studies Tripos* (p. 370); and in Part II of the *Social and Political Sciences Tripos* (p. 403).

The Archaeological and Anthropological Tripos

Part I

The first part of the Tripos provides an introduction to four interlocked but relatively discrete subjects: (*a*) Archaeology, (*b*) Physical Anthropology, (*c*) Social Anthropology, (*d*) Sociology.

The central field of study is variation in the cultural, social, and biological conditions of man. This is viewed through the perspective of time since the appearance of early precursors of man (which is dealt with by physical anthropology), over the millennia during which man developed his culture (the subject matter of archaeology), and in contemporary mankind, ranging from the hunters and gatherers of aboriginal Australia to the developing new nations of Africa and Asia, and to our own society. Physical anthropology deals with man's relationships with other primates and the fossil evidence for hominid evolution, and with biological aspects of man's interaction with his environment, and the extent and origin of biological variation within and between human populations. Archaeology is concerned with the development of man through time and the elaboration of his culture. The social anthropological study of contemporary and historical societies includes the analysis of the bodies of knowledge and beliefs, technological skills and social norms of conduct that make up their ways of life. Sociology is the study of social institutions and processes, of the social context of ideas, and of the individual as a member of society, with its main emphasis on industrial societies.

The course of study for Part I of the Tripos lasts one year. It is anticipated that most candidates will confine their studies to three of the four subjects. There are two lecture courses in each subject. Candidates for Part I may be first-year undergraduates intending to go on to Part II of the Tripos or intending to transfer to another Tripos (e.g. Social and Political Sciences). The course is also open to third-year undergraduates from other Triposes (e.g. Medical Sciences).

Part II

Social Anthropology. The Part II in Social Anthropology is designed as a two-year course for those who have read some anthropology or sociology in the previous year. Undergraduates who change to this subject from some different field will not be at any great disadvantage providing they can attend the lectures for Paper 5 of the Part I. The first year of the two-year syllabus includes the study of subsidiary subjects, linguistics, social psychology, or statistics and computing. In the same year, students undertake work on a special region of the world, e.g. South Asia, Latin America, Europe, New Guinea, West Africa, or East Africa. Each year three of those areas are offered as options. All students take a paper on the Third World. For students wishing to study Social Anthropology as part of their general education, rather than to acquire skills and background for post-graduate research, the regulations allow undergraduates to complete the Tripos in one year, after taking a two-year Part I in another subject. Such students omit the Preliminary examination, but should make arrangements with their Director of Studies for supervision in the previous Long Vacation term.

The concerns of social anthropology are closely related to those of sociology, but include the full range, historical and geographical, of human societies and cultures. Attention is paid both to pre-industrial societies and to the non-industrial sectors of more complex ones, and to contemporary urban communities. With regard to methods, emphasis is placed upon techniques of intensive field research, use of comparative study, formal analysis, and sociological enquiry. The courses offered attempt to introduce students to the comparative study of politics, kinship, religion, and non-industrial economics. Optional papers may be taken in theories of social dynamics, the study of social change, urban and ethnic studies, comparative medicine, population studies and development. Other topics include the study of myth and ritual, the role of women, systems of exchange, modes of production and reproduction, micro-politics, the ethnography of disputes, and the use of force.

Students wishing to take some papers in Social Anthropology with papers from other fields in the social sciences may do so in the framework of Part II of the *Social and Political Sciences Tripos* (see p. 405).

Physical Anthropology. Physical Anthropology can be taken as a two-year Part II course by students from Part I of the Tripos. The subjects examined at the end of the Preliminary year (which includes a long vacation course as an integral component) are shown below (p. 62). Human biology is studied at a much greater depth than in Part I, and students with no science background will find it very challenging. First-year students intending to take Part II Physical Anthropology are advised to discuss their choice of Part I courses with a staff member.

Transfer to a two-year Part II in Physical Anthropology is also possible from other Triposes, especially Part IA of the Natural Sciences or Medical Sciences Triposes. A one-year course is available for students who have completed Part IB of the Medical Sciences Tripos or who have taken biological subjects in Part IB of the Natural Sciences Tripos. Students taking the one-year course are advised to attend during the preceding Long Vacation term.

The course for the Tripos Examination covers three main branches:

(*a*) The comparative anatomy, ecology, behaviour, and evolution of the primates; the fossil evidence for hominid evolution in relation to the palaeoecological and archaeological records. (*b*) Biological variation in human populations and its genetic basis. The course stresses polymorphic systems, but also deals with continuous variation, including psychometric traits. (*c*) Human adaptability in different environments; ecological aspects of nutrition and disease; growth; biological aspects of demography. Students are also required to select one of several options for more detailed study, or to complete a project and submit a dissertation. Practical work includes biometric and laboratory studies, and the statistical analysis of data.

Archaeology. Archaeological research has made possible the study of human societies through long periods of time; the evidence is steadily improving in quality and variety.

The Part II Archaeology course, designed as a self-contained two-year study (which can be taken by undergraduates transferring from other disciplines without serious disadvantage), considers the theoretical premises upon which a study of the past can be based and the way in which that study has developed. Students also discuss and receive practical training in the field-methods used and in the retrieval and analysis of archaeological evidence in the laboratory. Teaching in comparative technology, both ancient and modern, is given from the University's museum collections.

Undergraduates also choose, from a range of area and period options, a series of problems to study in detail. These currently include European (prehistoric or historic), Asian and African (including Egyptian) Archaeology.

Practical experience is offered through participation in a number of departmental and other research projects.

Part I

Part I is taken at the end of the first year. It may also be taken at the end of his third year by a student who has obtained honours in another Tripos Examination in his second year. A candidate takes five papers; he shall be permitted but not required to select his papers from more than three groups.

Subjects of examination

The subjects of examination are as follows:

Group A. Archaeology

1. (*a*) The development of early societies

The paper will deal with the principles and history of Archaeology and with aspects of world prehistory, from the origins of human culture to the development of agriculture, social ranking, and state formation, with particular reference to the Near East (including Egypt), the Far East, and Mesoamerica.

2. The archaeology of Europe and neighbouring areas

The paper will examine the archaeological evidence for the origins of agriculture, metallurgy, urbanism, and civilization in Europe and neighbouring areas.

Group B. Physical Anthropology

3. Human biology, ecology, and population structure

Human biology and ecosystems. Climatic and nutritional adaptations in evolutionary and comparative perspective. The ecology of disease and growth. Genetic differences and their social implications. Biosocial influences on the structure of populations.

4. Prehistory and human evolution

Chronological and environmental frameworks for human evolution. Man as a primate: behaviour and adaptation. The evolution of hominids and their artefacts; technology and ecology.

Group C. Social Anthropology

5. Human society: organization, evolution, and development

The topics covered are the study of human society in its comparative and developmental perspective. The technology and productive systems in hunting, pastoral, and agricultural economies and their contact with industrial systems; systems of exchange and markets. Political and legal systems, simple and complex; feud and war; the organization and development of state structures; from traditional authority to bureaucracies, incorporation within nation states. Family, marriage, and kinship in simple and complex societies; changing kinship in modern societies. Religion and society, from community to world religions; ritual systems, diviners, and prophets; ancestor worship and cargo cults; conversion to old faiths and the emergence of new religions.

6. Culture, society, and communication

The nature and uses of language and writing. Communication in time and space. Learning and interaction. Symbolic and non-verbal communication.

Group D. Sociology

7. Theoretical foundations of sociology

The scope of sociology. The development of sociological thought. Distinct concepts, modes of analysis, and methods of enquiry. An introduction to theoretical issues and debates in modern sociology.

8. Industrial societies

The historical development of specialized political and economic institutions. Social and psychological effects of industrial conditions. Social stratification and occupational differentiation. Urbanism. Demographic factors and domestic organization in industrial society. Crime and delinquency.

Part II

Part II may be taken in the third or fourth year by a candidate who has obtained honours in a Tripos Examination one or two years before.

There is an examination for Part II in each of the following three subjects:

Social Anthropology, Physical Anthropology, Archaeology.

Every candidate for Part II must offer one of these subjects. The scheme of papers set in each subject is as follows:

Social Anthropology

A candidate must offer Papers 1–4, and

either (*a*) two papers from among Papers 5–7,

or (*b*) one paper from among Papers 5–7, and a dissertation on a topic approved by the Faculty Board which falls within the field of social anthropology, provided that a candidate may not submit a dissertation on a topic falling within the scope of any of the papers that he is offering in the examination.

A candidate who chooses to offer a dissertation must submit his proposed title, together with a brief outline of the contents of the proposed dissertation, and a statement of the papers that he intends to offer in the examination, through his Tutor to the Secretary of the Faculty Board so as to reach him not later than the second Monday of the Full Michaelmas Term next preceding the examination. Each candidate must obtain the approval of the title of his dissertation by the Faculty Board not later than the end of the Full Michaelmas Term next preceding the examination. After the Faculty Board have approved a candidate's proposed title no change may be made in it without the approval of the Faculty Board, but a candidate may submit a revised title to the Secretary of the Faculty Board by the division of the following Lent Term for the approval of the Faculty Board. Titles received by the Faculty Board after that date will be considered only in the most exceptional circumstances. Each dissertation must be typewritten unless a candidate has obtained previous permission from the Faculty Board through his Tutor to present his dissertation in manuscript, may be of not more than 6,000 words in length (exclusive of footnotes, appendices, and bibliography), must show knowledge of relevant anthropological material, and must be submitted through the candidate's Tutor so as to reach the Secretary of the Faculty Board not later than the division of the Easter Term in which the examination is held. Each dissertation must be accompanied by (*a*) a brief synopsis on a separate sheet of paper of the contents of the dissertation, and (*b*) a certificate signed by the candidate that it is his own original work, and that it does not contain material that has already been used to any substantial extent for any comparable purpose. The Examiners have power, at their discretion, to examine a candidate *viva voce* on his dissertation and on the general field of knowledge within which it falls.

The details of the papers are:

1. Non-industrial economics (also serves as Paper 5 of Part II of the Social and Political Sciences Tripos)

The organization of production, consumption, and exchange. Wealth, capital, and labour. Land tenure and property. Technology and social organization. Social inequality. Systems of exchange.

2. Religion, ritual, and ideology (also serves as Paper 6 of Part II of the Social and Political Sciences Tripos)

Religion and magic, witchcraft, totemism, prophetic cults, mythology, and cosmology. Morality in relation to ritual practices and beliefs. Comparative religion. Symbolism and thought.

3. Kinship, marriage, and the family (also serves as Paper 7 of Part II of the Social and Political Sciences Tripos)

The comparative study of the family, kinship, and kin groups; marriage, affinity, and divorce; bride-wealth and dowry; inheritance, succession, and descent; the organization of domestic groups; sex and procreation; changing family structures.

This paper attempts to cover the kinship and family of non-European, peasant, and industrial societies, but there is a sufficient choice of questions to enable students to concentrate upon two of these fields.

4. Political anthropology (also serves as Paper 8 of Part II of the Social and Political Sciences Tripos)

Caste and class. Local, occupational, and other forms of groupings. Stateless societies and the evolution of the state. Kingship, chiefship, and achieved leadership. Stratification. Councils and courts. Micropolitics. Ritual aspects of government. Feud and warfare. Law and custom; sanctions. Judicial institutions.

5. Special topic in social anthropology

Candidates are required to offer one of a number of special subjects.

The topics prescribed will be:

In **1985**: *Either* Comparative medicine;
or Anthropology and development.

In **1986**: *Either* Population studies;
or Anthropology and development.

6. Change, development, and decline (also serves as Paper 9 of Part II B of the Social and Political Sciences Tripos)

Major theories of social dynamics, change, and evolution. History and social anthropology: theory and practice. Changes in modes of livelihood and technology. Ancient society, feudalism, capitalism, colonialism, and postcolonial societies. Religion and social change. Frameworks for comparison.

7. Urban and ethnic studies (also serves as Paper 10 of Part II of the Social and Political Sciences Tripos)

Urban studies, based on intensive field research in Britain and elsewhere. Urbanized and urbanizing societies. The comparative study of city life, the urban workplace, the inner city; poverty and marginality. Country and town, and movement between them. Ethnicity, colour, and migration. Anthropology and the community.

Physical Anthropology

A candidate must offer all the papers and a practical examination, except that he may, with the permission of the Faculty Board obtained before the division of the Lent Term next preceding the examination, submit in place of Paper 4

either (*a*) a dissertation, of not more than 10,000 words on some subject in physical anthropology approved by the Board, which must be submitted to the Secretary of the Faculty Board so as to reach him not later than the division of the Easter Term;

or (*b*) one paper from Social Anthropology or Archaeology.

The practical examination may include or consist wholly of a *viva voce* examination. The Examiners will also take into account such practical work done by candidates during the courses leading to the examination as shall from time to time be determined by the Faculty Board of Archaeology and Anthropology.

The details of the papers are:

1. Human genetics and variation

This paper requires a knowledge of human genetics and variation, with particular emphasis on polymorphism in living populations.

2. Primate biology and evolution

This paper requires a knowledge of the biology of living Primates and of human and primate evolution.

3. Human ecology and adaptability

This paper covers various aspects of human ecology and adaptability, in particular climatic adaptation, epidemiology, growth, and population aspects of nutrition.

4. Special subject in physical anthropology

One of the following subjects:

For **1985** and **1986**: *Either* Primate behaviour *or* Topics in mammalian and primate evolution *or* The human biology of a geographical region.

ARCHAEOLOGY

A candidate must offer Papers 1, 2, 5, and 6, and one of the options (*a*), (*b*), (*c*), (*d*), (*e*), (*f*), or (*g*) for Papers 3 and 4, provided that

(*a*) a candidate who offers one of options (*a*), (*b*), (*c*), (*d*), (*f*) or (*g*) for Papers 3 and 4 may offer in Paper 5 a special subject set for any one of those six options; if he offers option (*c*) he must offer Paper 3 in that option and *either* Paper 4 in the same option *or* any one of Papers 2, 3, or 4 of the Anglo-Saxon, Norse, and Celtic Tripos;

(*b*) a candidate who offers option (*e*) for Papers 3 and 4 must offer for Paper 5 a special subject set for option (*e*);

(*c*) a candidate, with the permission of the Faculty Board obtained Tripos for Paper 5 if already offering it as either Paper 3 or Paper 4, or *vice versa*;

(*d*) a candidate, with the permission of the Faculty Board obtained before the division of the Lent Term next preceding the examination, may submit in place of Paper 5 a dissertation of not more than 8,000 words, excluding bibliography and references, on a subject approved by the Board which concerns a special subject prescribed for one of options (*a*), (*b*), (*c*), or (*d*) for Papers 3 and 4 or a thesis for option (*f*) for Papers 3 and 4 in accordance with the regulations for the Classical Tripos. He shall submit his dissertation to the Secretary of the Faculty Board so as to reach him not later than the division of the Easter Term, and he shall be required to attend an oral examination, at a time to be determined by the Examiners, on the subject of his dissertation and on other aspects of the special subject with which his dissertation is concerned.

The details of the papers are:

1. History and scope of archaeology

The history of archaeological research. Its relations with the humanities and the natural sciences. Quaternary research. Prehistory and proto-history. Application of archaeological method to historical times.

2. Methods and techniques of archaeology

Field archaeology, including air photography. Excavation. Classification and dating. Identification and interpretation of finds. Limitations of archaeological data.

3, 4. The archaeology of a special area. A pair of papers on one of the following options must be taken:

(*a*) The Old Stone Age

The prehistory of man from the earliest times up to the origins and spread of food-production; archaeology, geological sequence, and physical types.

(*b*) Europe, including the British Isles, from the Neolithic to the end of the Early Iron Age

The Archaeology of Crete, Greece, the Cyclades, Italy, and Sicily, from the Neolithic Age to the beginning of the historic period; and of Malta and the West Mediterranean Islands, Southern France, and Iberia, from the Neolithic Age to the Roman Conquest. The Archaeology of the Neolithic, Bronze, and Early Iron Ages in the British Isles, North-western, Northern, and Central Europe.

(*c*) Europe and the British Isles from the beginning of the Roman to the end of the medieval period

These papers will have particular reference to the north-western provinces of the Roman Empire, including Britain, to northern Europe during the migration and Viking periods, and to medieval Britain.

(*d*) India and the Far East from the earliest settlements to the end of the third century B.C.

Paper In. 21 of the Oriental Studies Tripos, and one paper set on the Far East.

(*e*) Egypt and Western Asia[1]

[2]*Either* Papers As. 3 and E. 19 *or* Papers As. 3 and As. 16 of the Oriental Studies Tripos.

(*f*) Classical archaeology

Any two of Papers D1, D3, D4, and D5 of Part II of the Classical Tripos.

(*g*) India and Mesopotamia

5. Special subjects in an option specified for Papers 3 and 4

In **1985** and **1986** the options will be:

(*a*) African archaeology *or* Pleistocene chronology and palaeology.

[3](*b*) *Either* Prehistoric agriculture in Europe;[4]
or Ethnoarchaeology.

(*c*) *Either* Anglo-Saxon England in the pagan period (Paper 12 of the Anglo-Saxon, Norse, and Celtic Tripos);
or Agriculture, industry, and trade of the North-Western Roman Provinces.

(*d*) *Either* Indian art and archaeology, 500 B.C.–A.D. 400 (Paper In. 22 of the Oriental Studies Tripos);
or State formation in East Asia.

(*e*) *Either* Akkadian specified texts (Paper As. 1 of the Oriental Studies Tripos);
or Civilization in Mesopotamia (Paper As. 14 of the Oriental Studies Tripos);

[1] A candidate offering option (*e*) for Papers 3 and 4 must offer for Paper 5 either of the special subjects set for option (*e*), but a candidate offering one of the other options for Papers 3 and 4 may offer for Paper 5 a special subject set for *any* one of options (*a*), (*b*), (*c*), (*d*), (*f*), or (*g*).

[2] In **1986** the papers will be:
Either As. 13 and E. 19 *or* As. 13 and As. 16 of the Oriental Studies Tripos.

[3] Add '*or* Archaeology of the Americas' for **1986**.

[4] Delete the words 'in Europe' for **1986**.

or Special subject in Assyriology (Paper As. 15 of the Oriental Studies Tripos);

or Special subject in Egyptology (Paper E. 18 of the Oriental Studies Tripos).

[1](*f*) *Either* (i) Prehellenic archaeology (Paper D 3 of Part II of the Classical Tripos);

or (ii) Greek and Roman sculpture (Paper D4 of Part II of the Classical Tripos);

or (iii) Archaeology of the Western Provinces of the Roman Empire (Paper D5 of Part II of the Classical Tripos).

cr (iv) Early Hellenic archaeology (Paper D1 of Part II of the Classical Tripos).

(*g*) *Either* Indian art and archaeology, 500 B.C.–A.D.400 (Paper In. 22 of the Oriental Studies Tripos);

or [2]History of the Ancient Near East (Paper As. 3 of the Oriental Studies Tripos).

Note (*i*): a candidate offering option (*e*) for Papers 3 and 4 must offer for Paper 5 either of the special subjects set for option (*e*), but a candidate offering one of the other options for Papers 3 and 4 may offer for Paper 5 a special subject set for *any* one of options (*a*), (*b*), (*c*), (*d*), (*f*), or (*g*).

Note (*ii*): a candidate may not offer Paper D5 of Part II of the Classical Tripos for Paper 5 if already offering it as either Paper 3 or Paper 4, or *vice versa*.

Note (*iii*): a candidate may not offer Paper D4 of Part II of the Classical Tripos for Paper 5 if offering option (*c*) for Paper 3.

6. Oral and practical

A test of the candidate's power of recognizing and describing archaeological material from the areas and period specifically studied. The examiners may take into account practical work done by the candidate during the courses leading to the examination.

A candidate who offers Part II in Archaeology must take a practical

[1] In **1986** (*f*) will become:

(*f*) *Either* (1) Prehellenic archaeology (Paper D1 of the Classical Tripos);

or (2) A prescribed subject connected with early Hellenic archaeology or early Greek art (Paper D2 of the Classical Tripos);

or (3) A prescribed subject connected with Classical (Greco-Roman) art or the archaeology of the Greek and Hellenistic world (Paper D3 of the Classical Tripos);

or (4) Archaeology of the western provinces of the Roman Empire (Paper D4 of the Classical Tripos).

[2] In **1986** it will be History of Mesopotamia (Paper As. 13).

examination and Papers 1, 2, 5, and 6, and Papers 3 and 4 in one of the options (*a*)–(*f*). A candidate who in Papers 3 and 4 offers one of options (*a*), (*b*), (*c*), (*d*), (*f*), or (*g*) may offer in Paper 5 the special subject set for any one of those six options; if he offers option (*c*) he must offer Paper 3 in that option and either Paper 4 in the same option or any one of Papers 1, 2, or 3 of the Anglo-Saxon, Norse, and Celtic Tripos. A candidate who in Papers 3 and 4 offers option (*e*) must offer in Paper 5 either of the special subjects for option (*e*).

A candidate, with the permission of the Faculty Board obtained before the division of the Lent Term next preceding the examination, may submit in place of Paper 5 a dissertation of not more than 8,000 words, excluding bibliography and references, on a subject approved by the Board which concerns a special subject prescribed for one of options (*a*), (*b*), (*c*), or (*d*) for Papers 3 and 4, or a thesis for option (*f*) in accordance with the rules for theses in the Classical Tripos. He must submit his dissertation to the Secretary of the Faculty Board so as to reach him not later than the division of the Easter Term, and he will be required to attend an oral examination on the subject of his dissertation and on other aspects of the special subject with which his dissertation is concerned.

The Preliminary Examination for Part II, Social Anthropology

The examination consists of four papers as follows:

1. Theory, problems, and enquiry
2. Special areas

Candidates are required to offer one of the special areas specified by the Faculty Board for **1985**:

(*a*) Africa, with special reference to East Africa.
(*b*) Asia.
(*c*) The Pacific, with special reference to New Guinea.

3. A paper on one of the following subjects:

(*a*) General linguistics (Paper 111 of Part II of the Modern and Medieval Languages Tripos).
(*b*) Anthropology and social psychology.
(*c*) Statistics and computing for the social sciences.

4. The Third World

Candidates must offer all four papers.

The Preliminary Examination for Part II, Physical Anthropology

The examination consists of three papers as follows:

1. Human biology

The paper is divided into Sections A and B, and candidates are required to answer at least one question from each section.

Section A covers the physical basis of heredity; gene action and the control of protein synthesis; and other biochemical topics. Section B will cover topics in physiology and immunology.

2. Comparative anatomy and evolutionary biology

The paper is divided into Sections A and B, and candidates are required to answer at least one question from each section.

Section A covers histology; comparative functional anatomy, including primate studies; and growth and development. Section B will cover topics related to the **1985** options for Part II Physical Anthropology, including animal behaviour, and may include questions on methods of analysis in physical anthropology; evolutionary principles and mechanisms, palaeo-environments, and dating techniques; and population genetics.

3. Practical

The practical examination covers the subjects examined in Papers 1 and 2 and may require statistical calculations. A candidate must also present for the inspection of the Examiners, not later than the division of the Easter Term, a record of practical work done by him.

Candidates must offer all three papers.

The Preliminary Examination for Part II, Archaeology

The examination consists of two papers as follows:

1. Aims and methods of archaeology.
2. Special areas.

Candidates are required to offer one of the special areas specified by the Faculty Board for **1985**: (*a*) Old Stone Age; (*b*) Europe, including the British Isles from the Neolithic to the end of the Early Iron Age; (*c*) Europe and the British Isles from the beginning of the Roman to the end of the medieval period; (*d*) Egypt; (*e*) Western Asia; (*f*) Classical archaeology; (*g*) India and Mesopotamia; (*h*) India and the Far East.

Candidates must offer both papers and a practical examination, which will include the submission of practical work done during the course.

Examinations for the M.Phil. Degree

(See p. 458)

The Faculty offers the following one-year postgraduate courses which lead to the M.Phil. Degree:

Archaeology.
Social Anthropology.
Biological Anthropology.

Archaeology

The scheme of examination, at the choice of the candidate, consists of Option A or Option B.

Option A. Archaeology

(*a*) a thesis, of not more than 15,000 words in length, including footnotes, appendices, but excluding bibliography, on a topic approved by the Degree Committee for the Faculty of Archaeology and Anthropology;

and

(*b*) three written papers, each of three hours' duration, as follows:

1. The principles of archaeology.
2. The practice of archaeology.
3. Aspects of world archaeology.

This paper includes the following sections, from which every candidate, subject to the approval of the Degree Committee, must select one, on which he will be required to answer three questions:

(i) Palaeolithic archaeology.
(ii) Bio-archaeology
(iii) Mesopotamian archaeology.
(iv) South Asian archaeology.
(v) African archaeology.
(vi) Later European prehistory.
(vii) The archaeology of early historic Europe.
(viii) The archaeology of ancient Egypt.
(ix) Quantitative analysis.
(x) Ethnoarchaeology.
(xi) East Asian archaeology.
(xii) Archaeology of the Americas.

The Degree Committee may announce, not later than the end of the Easter Term of the preceding academical year, that a particular section or sections are not available;

(*c*) a practical examination designed to test the candidate's powers of understanding evidence from survey and fieldwork, and of recognizing and describing archaeological material related to the section of Paper 3 selected by him.

The examination includes, at the discretion of the examiners, an oral examination upon the thesis and written papers.

Option B. Museum Practice and Archaeology

(*a*) a thesis, of not more than 15,000 words in length, including footnotes and appendices, but excluding bibliography, on a topic approved by the Degree Committee for the Faculty of Archaeology and Anthropology, which must fall within the field of study covered by either Paper 2 or Paper 3 in (*b*) below;

and

(*b*) three written papers, each of three hours' duration, as follows:

Paper 1. Archaeological theory and practice.

Paper 2. Museum practice.

Paper 2 will contain two sections and candidates must answer questions from both sections:

(i) The history, functions, and organization of museums.

(ii) Archaeological work in the museum.

Paper 3. Aspects of world archaeology (Paper 3 of Option A).

Any section, to be chosen by the candidate, subject to the approval of the Degree Committee, from those available for Paper 3 in Option A above.

A candidate who chooses Option B must undertake practical work during a period of experience spent in a museum having archaeological collections, the nature of the practical work and the length of the period being determined by the Degree Committee for the Faculty of Archaeology and Anthropology. He must present for the inspection of the examiners a record of this practical work bearing, as an indication of the good faith of the record, the signature of the museum curator under whose supervision it was performed. A statement concerning the candidate's period of experience, certified by the Head of the Department of Archaeology, must be submitted to the examiners.

The examination may include, at the discretion of the examiners, an oral examination upon the thesis and upon the general field of knowledge within which it falls.

Biological Anthropology

The course of study consists of lectures and seminars, plus appropriate practical work. The following areas of study form the syllabus for the course: Human variation, population structure, ecology and adaptation, primatology, palaeoanthropology, and research methods.

A knowledge of the topics covered in the courses for Part II Physical Anthropology is required.

The scheme of examination consists of:

(*a*) a thesis of not more than 20,000 words, including tables, footnotes, appendices, and bibliography, on a subject in biological anthropology approved by the Degree Committee for the Faculty of Archaeology and Anthropology;

and (*b*) six essays, each of about 2,000 words, and each on a subject which is related to one or more of the six areas of study set out in the syllabus and has been approved by the Degree Committee for the Faculty of Archaeology and Anthropology. At least one essay must incorporate the results of an experimental or a biometrical project.

The examination includes an oral examination on the subject of the thesis and, at the discretion of the Examiners, on the subjects of the essays.

Social Anthropology

The scheme of examination consists of *either* Option A *or* Option B *or* Option C as follows:

Option A. Social Anthropology

(*a*) a thesis, of not less than 7,500 and not more than 10,000 words in length, including footnotes, tables, appendices, and bibliography, on a subject approved by the Degree Committee for the Faculty of Archaeology and Anthropology, which has special reference to community organization, but which must not fall within the field of any paper or essay offered by the candidate under (*b*) below, *or* the alternative below;

and (*b*) three written papers, to be chosen by the candidate, subject to the approval of the Degree Committee, from the following list of papers:

1. Social anthropology, with special reference to the economics of non-industrial societies.
2. Social anthropology, with special reference to politics.
3. Social anthropology, with special reference to kinship and the family.
4. Social anthropology, with special reference to ritual and religion.

Option B. Social anthropology with special reference to the work of a museum

(i) a thesis, of not less than 7,500 and not more than 10,000 words in length, including footnotes, tables, appendices, and bibliography, on a subject approved by the Degree Committee for the Faculty of Archaeology and Anthropology, which has special reference to material culture, but which does not fall within the field of any paper or essay offered by the candidate under (ii) below, or under the alternative below;

and (ii) two written papers, to be chosen by the candidate, subject to the approval of the Degree Committee, from papers 1–4 under Option A above;

and (iii) one written paper as follows:

5. Social anthropology, with special reference to the work of a museum.

(i) *Option C. Social anthropology and the community*

(i) a thesis, of not less than 7,500 and not more than 10,000 words in length, including footnotes, tables, appendices, and bibliography, on a subject approved by the Degree Committee for the Faculty of Archaeology and Anthropology, which has special reference to community organization, but which does not fall within the field of any paper or essay offered by the candidate under (ii)–(iii) below, or under the alternative below;

and (ii) Paper 3 and one other paper, to be chosen by the candidate, from Papers 1, 2, and 4 under Option A;

and

(iii) *either* one written paper, as follows:

Paper 6. Anthropology and the community;

or an essay on *either* anthropology in relation to medicine, *or* anthropology in relation to population studies, whichever of those subjects is announced by the Degree Committee for the examination in a particular year. Such an essay must be of not more than 6,000 words in length, exclusive of footnotes, appendices, and bibliography.

In place of any one or more of the written papers in Options A, B, or C, a candidate may, by special permission of the Degree Committee, only granted after considering his experience and special qualifications, offer the same number of essays, each of not more than 6,000 words in length, exclusive of footnotes, appendices, and bibliography, and each on a topic to be chosen by the candidate, subject to the approval of the Degree Committee falling within the field of one out of a list of subjects specified from time to time by the Degree Committee.*

* The Degree Committee have specified the following list of subjects within the field of one of which a candidate may, until further notice, propose a topic in which instruction is offered, other than in the M.Phil. courses themselves, for approval by the Degree Committee. The candidate after discussion with his supervisor should propose to the Degree Committee by the first meeting of the Michaelmas Term what course of instruction he proposes to follow. This field of study will be examined by an essay and by oral examination, the title of the essay to be sent to the Degree Committee for approval by the Division of the Lent Term.

Comparative studies in anthropology. Connected to a current research project, and using material from the Human Relations Area files and other data.

The use of historical methods and sources. Materials would include the records of the village of Elmdon, and the historical records of selected English villages from the fourteenth to the nineteenth centuries.

The use of computing in the social sciences. Experimental data-input systems and retrieval systems, with emphasis on data-processing and/or numerical techniques, statistics in relation to the collection and analysis of social science data.

Psychology and anthropology. Using lectures provided by SPS and other bodies, and organized to fit the needs of particular candidates.

Anthropology in relation to medicine. Making use of an existing course, and an existing project in medical anthropology.

Anthropology in relation to population studies. Making use of an existing course, and concerned with practical contributions to current world problems.

Linguistics and anthropology. Making use of the teaching for anthropological linguistics by the Department of Linguistics.

Anthropology and development studies. An enquiry into sociological and anthropological aspects of development, making use of teaching and research available in the University.

Myth, folklore, and oral literature. Using lecture courses and research programmes available in the University.

The examination may also, at the discretion of the Examiners, include an oral examination upon the thesis, and upon the essays if any are offered, and upon the general field of knowledge in which they fall.

Further details of the courses of study may be obtained from the Department of Social Anthropology, Downing Street, Cambridge.

ARCHITECTURE

A student reading architecture will attend courses in the School of Architecture and will take the appropriate examinations for the Tripos. These examinations are held in three stages: Part IA at the end of the first year, Part IB at the end of the second year, and Part II at the end of the third year. This three-year course leads to an Honours Degree and provides a basic education and training in architecture: it also qualifies for exemption from the Part I Examination of the Royal Institute of British Architects. The course concentrates on the study of known problems of building and of the built environment. Studies may be either individual or collective. They all involve the presentation of studio-work in which specialized studies are brought into relationship in the finished design and this studio-work forms the major educational process throughout the course. After taking the three-year course, a student may apply to take a further two-year course, leading to the Diploma in Architecture, which qualifies for exemption from the Part II Examination of the Royal Institute of British Architects. The course includes both the study of certain special subjects in the field of urban studies and studio-work.

The qualification for membership of the Royal Institute of British Architects can be obtained by the satisfactory completion of the School courses and the compulsory two years of practical training required by the Royal Institute of British Architects, one year of which should be taken before the Diploma course.

The Department of Architecture has also a centre of research work in the Martin Centre for Architectural and Urban Studies.

Students have the use of the Faculty Library, housed in the Department of Architecture, and in addition have available the library of the Fitzwilliam Museum and the University Library. Most College libraries also possess useful collections of reference works.

Apart from College Entrance Scholarships, there is the following award made within the Department:

Anderson and Webb Scholarship. This Scholarship, which at present amounts to £70 a year, is offered by the Royal Institute of British Architects to be held by a student in the Department of Architecture. It is now tenable for one year and is awarded at the end of the First Year to the most promising candidate.

School subjects

The minimum requirements which lead to exemption from the examinations of the Royal Institute of British Architects are passes in five G.C.E. subjects of which two must be at A-level. The following subjects are compulsory, either at A or O level: English Language and either Mathematics or a science subject. (If, however, the science subject is Botany, Zoology, Biology or Geology, Mathematics is also compulsory.)

Recommended reading

The following books are recommended for reading by students coming to Cambridge to read Architecture:

S. Giedion, *Space, Time and Architecture*, Harvard University Press, 1973; E. H. Gombrich, *The Story of Art*, Phaidon, 1966; Kidson, Murray and Thompson, *A History of English Architecture*, Penguin Books, 1965; Le Corbusier, *Towards a New Architecture*, Architectural Press, 1946; N. Pevsner, *An Outline of European Architecture*, Penguin Books, 1943; S. E. Rasmussen, *Experiencing Architecture*, Chapman and Hall, 1959; V. Scully, *Modern Architecture*, Prentice-Hall International, 1961; J. Summerson, *The Classical Language of Architecture*, B.B.C. Publications, 1963, Methuen and Co., 1964; N. Pevsner, *Pioneers of Modern Design from William Morris to Walter Gropius*, Penguin Books, 1953; Reyner Banham, *The Architecture of the Well-tempered Environment*, Mainstone; C. Norberg-Schulz, *Meaning in Western Architecture*, Studio Vista, 1975.

Recommended for further reading

J. Summerson, *Heavenly Mansions and Other Essays on Architecture*, Cresset, London, 1949; J. Summerson, *Architecture in Britain 1630–1830*, Penguin Books, 1953; G. Webb, *Gothic Architecture in England*, Longmans, Green and Co., 1951; Henry Russell Hitchcock, *19th and 20th Century Architecture*, Penguin Books, 1968; Kevin Lynch, *Image of the City*; March and Steadman, *Geometry of the Environment*, RIBA Publications, 1971; Victor Olgyay, *Design with Climate*, Princeton University Press, 1963; R. Wittkower, *Architectural Principles in the Age of Humanism*, Academic Editions, London, 1973.

The Architecture Tripos

The Architecture Tripos consists of three Parts: Part I A, Part I B, and Part II. The normal programme for an undergraduate who intends to spend three years reading architecture will be as follows:

Part I A of the Tripos at the end of the first year;
Part I B of the Tripos at the end of the second year;
Part II of the Tripos at the end of the third year.

All candidates taking Part II should have taken Part I A and Part I B but provision is made for candidates who change to architecture after having spent one year in another subject.

Part I A

The examination for Part I A consists of three sections:

Section A. Six written papers as follows:

1. Introduction to the history of architecture

The paper deals with a selective introduction to the architectural history of Western Europe and North America from classical antiquity to the early twentieth century.

2. Approaches to architectural thought and practice

The paper deals with an introduction to theoretical writings on architecture from the mid-eighteenth century to the mid-twentieth century, related to the architectural practices of the time.

3. Introduction to design theory

The paper may include questions on the fundamental nature of architectural theory and some of the ways in which specific theories have been brought to bear in the design of particular buildings.

4. Fundamental principles of construction

The paper may include questions on the development of construction methods, the elementary principles of construction of small buildings, and the basic properties of construction materials.

5. Fundamental principles of structural dssign

The paper may include questions on the elementary principles of structural design of buildings, on simple statics, stress analysis, and strength of structural materials.

6. Fundamental principles of environmental design

The paper may include questions on the elementary principles of environmental control in buildings and servicing of buildings.

Section B. Studio-work.

Section C. Course-work.

A candidate for Part IA must offer all six papers in Section A; and for Section B, must satisfy the Examiners in studio-work carried out during the year, and attested by satisfactory evidence and presented for the inspection of the Examiners on the first day of the written examination; and for Section C, must satisfy the Examiners in course-work presented in an appropriate form recording work done by him, and bearing, as an indication of the good faith of the record, the signature of teachers under whose direction the work was performed, and presented for the inspection of the Examiners on the same day.

Part IB

The examination for Part IB consists of three sections:

Section A. Five papers as follows:

1. Introduction to Architectural History

Periods from the architectural history of Europe and North America are specified from time to time. The periods in **1985** and **1986** will be:

(*a*) Housing in Britain, 1890–1950.

(*b*) Modern Movement in Europe between the Wars.

(*c*) Aspects of Russian Architecture.

(*d*) The Classical Tradition in 18th Century Architecture in France and England.

(*e*) Aspects of the History of the garden and its meaning.

(*f*) Origins and developments of 'Art Nouveau'.

(*g*) Aspects of American Architecture, 1893–1973.

2. Theories of architecture, urbanism, and design

This paper may include questions on

(*a*) the nature of architectural elements and systems, their mathematical description and analysis, and approaches to synthesis;

(*b*) concepts and ideals which, since the mid-eighteenth century, have contributed to the development of modern architectural theory;

(*c*) the development of modern urban theory, the mathematical description and analysis of urban systems, and approaches to urban design and policy.

3. Principles of construction

This paper may include questions on the principles governing the use of constructional elements in complex building types, properties of materials, dimensional co-ordination, analysis of simple methods of enveloping space.

4. Principles of structural design

This paper may include questions on the structural aspects of architectural design, the behaviour of structural elements under load, the use of load-bearing brickwork, steel, and reinforced concrete, systems of roof spanning and their calculation, the mathematical and graphical determination of simple structural systems.

5. Principles of environmental design

This paper may include questions on the principles of environmental control and functional design, the practical applications of the principles of thermal response, of acoustics, and of lighting in buildings, micro-climate, planning and designing for user needs.

Section B Studio-work.

Section C Course-work.

A candidate is required:

(*a*) to offer all five papers in Section A;

(*b*) for Section B, to present for the inspection of the Examiners, on the first day of the written examination, a portfolio of studio-work attested by satisfactory evidence and carried out during the academical year in which he presents himself for examination;

(*c*) for Section C, to present for their inspection, on the same day, records in an appropriate form of course-work done by him, and bearing, as an indication of the good faith of the record, the signatures of the teachers under whose direction the work was performed.

The Examiners are provided by the Head of the Department with assessments of all the course-work performed by the candidates of which records have been presented under (*c*).

Part II

The scheme of the examination for Part II consists of three sections and is as follows:

Section A (i) One paper on the historical aspects of architecture and urbanism (Paper 1); one paper on the theoretical aspects of architecture and urbanism (Paper 2); a thesis on an approved subject.

(ii) Three papers (Papers 3–5) on the technical aspects of the theory and practice of construction and of structural and environmental design.

Section B Studio-work.

Section C Course-work.

A candidate for Part II is required:

(*a*) for Section A, to offer Papers 3–5 and

either Paper 1 and a thesis on an approved subject falling within the field of Paper 2,

or Paper 2 and a thesis on an approved subject falling within the field of Paper 1;

(*b*) for Section B, to present for the inspection of the Examiners, on the first day of the written examination, a portfolio of studio-work attested by satisfactory evidence and carried out during the academical year in which he presents himself for examination;

(*c*) for Section C, to present for the inspection of the Examiners, on the first day of the written examination, records in an appropriate form of the course-work done by him, and bearing, as an indication of the good faith of the record, the signatures of the teachers under whose direction the work was performed.

The Examiners are provided by the Head of the Department with assessments of all the course-work performed by the candidates of which records have been presented under (*c*).

Each candidate must submit the proposed subject of his thesis through his Tutor to the Secretary of the Faculty Board not later than the end of the third quarter of the Michaelmas Term next preceding the examination and must obtain the approval of the Faculty Board for his subject not later than the end of that term.

The proposed subject must fall within a topic or period selected from a list of prescribed subjects in *either* the history of architecture and urban development *or* the theory of architecture, urbanism, and design; the list will be published by the Faculty Board not later than **1** June in the year next preceding the examination. The subjects prescribed for **1985** and **1986** will be:

1. Theories of design and urban development in the twentieth century.
2. The City and its meanings: origins.
3. The contemporary City.
4. Aspects of the history of the Garden and its meaning.
5. Aspects of American Architecture 1893–1973.
6. Aspects of Russian Architecture.
7. Advanced technical studies: construction methods, environmental analysis and a design related to special functional requirements.

Each thesis must be between 7,000 and 9,000 words (inclusive of notes). Theses must be typewritten (unless previous permission has been obtained to present it in manuscript) and must be submitted through the Tutor to the Secretary of the Faculty Board so as to reach him not later than the first day of Full Easter Term in which the examination is to be held.

In both Parts I and II the Examiners may impose such oral and practical tests as they think fit, and in drawing up the class-list they will take into account the candidate's performance in all such tests, and in the studio-work and course-work, as well as in the written papers and theses, together with the assessment of his course-work presented by the Head of the Department. A candidate may be required to attend a *viva voce* examination in the subject of any thesis he has submitted.

The Diploma in Architecture[1]

The Diploma is awarded to members of the University who have diligently attended a two-year course prescribed by the Faculty Board and have passed the First and Second Examinations for the Diploma.

The First and Second Examinations are held once a year during the last half of the Easter Term.

First Examination

The First Examination will consist of studio-work, course-work, and a dissertation.

(*a*) The *studio-work* must be carried out during the academical year in which a candidate presents himself for examination, and

[1] A candidate may not make use of material that he has already submitted in the examination for the M.Phil. Degree.

must be submitted to the Examiners not later than the last Wednesday of Full Easter Term.

(*b*) The *course-work* must consist of three essays, each on a topic proposed by the candidate through his Tutor to the Secretary of the Diploma Committee so as to reach him not later than the end of the first quarter of the Michaelmas Term; the candidate must obtain the approval of the Diploma Committee for his topics not later than the division of the Michaelmas Term. A candidate must propose one topic in the history, theory, and practice of each of the following subject-areas: (i) architecture, (ii) urban and regional development, (iii) building technology. Each essay must be of not less that 2,500 words and not more than 3,000 words and must be submitted to the Examiners not later than the first day of Full Lent Term.

(*c*) The *dissertation*, which must be of not less than 5,000 words and not more than 7,500 words, must be on a topic which is related to one of the candidate's approved topics for an essay and may make use of material submitted as part of his essay; the topic for the dissertation must be proposed through the candidate's Tutor to the Secretary of the Diploma Committee not later than the first day of Full Lent Term, and the approval of the Diploma Committee for the topic obtained not later than the end of the first quarter of the Lent Term. The dissertation must be submitted to the Examiners not later than the first day of Full Easter Term.

The essays and dissertation must be in English and must be typewritten unless previous permission has been obtained from the Diploma Committee to present the written work in manuscript. A candidate may be called for a *viva voce* examination in connexion with his studio-work, or dissertation, or essays, or any combination of these.

Second Examination

A candidate for the Second Examination must work in Cambridge under the supervision of the Diploma Committee during three Full Terms of an academical year; provided that the requirement to work in Cambridge may for special reasons approved by the Diploma Committee be waived by the Committee for the whole or part of that period in respect of a particular candidate.

The Second Examination consists of studio-work and a dissertation. The studio-work must be carried out during the academical year in which the candidate presents himself for examination, and must be submitted to the Examiners not later than the last Wednesday of Full Easter Term. Each dissertation must relate to a topic approved by the Diploma Committee in the field of planning, architecture, or building technology. Each candidate must submit the proposed topics of his studio-work and of his dissertation through his Tutor to the Secretary of the Diploma Committee so as to reach him not later than the end of the third quarter of the Michaelmas Term, and must submit his dissertation to the Examiners by a date to be announced annually by the Diploma Committee; this will be not later than the division of the Easter Term. Dissertations must be typewritten in English, and must be of not less than 10,000 words and not more than 20,000 words. A candidate may be called for a *viva voce* examination in connexion with his studio-work or his dissertation, or his studio-work and his dissertation.

Examination in Architecture for the M.Phil. Degree (one-year course)

The scheme of examination for the one-year course of study in Architecture for the degree of Master of Philosophy consists of:

(*a*) a thesis, of not more than 20,000 words in length, excluding appendices and bibliography, on a topic approved by the Degree Committee for the Faculty of Architecture and History of Art, which must fall within the field of history and theories of architecture;

and

(*b*) an exercise consisting, subject to the approval of the Degree Committee, of *either*

(i) three essays not exceeding 5,000 words each on topics to be chosen by candidates from the list of subjects published by the Degree Committee (all of which are to be taken from the same field of study as that of the thesis in (*a*)); provided that at the discretion of the Degree Committee a candidate may substitute a drawn exercise for not more than one of the essays; *or*

(ii) a drawn project on a topic approved by the Degree Committee from the same field of study as that of the thesis in (*a*);

provided that, if a candidate for the M.Phil. Degree has previously been a candidate either for the First Examination or for the Second Examination for the Diploma in Architecture, he may not offer in the examination for the degree a thesis or an essay on a subject that overlaps significantly with the dissertation or with any of the essays that he offered for either of the Examinations for the Diploma.

The examination may, at the discretion of the Examiners, include an oral examination upon the thesis and upon the general field of knowledge within which it falls; such an oral examination may include questions relating to one or more of the other pieces of work submitted by the candidate under (*b*) above.

CHEMICAL ENGINEERING

In this subject there are courses of study followed by candidates for:

The *Chemical Engineering Tripos*, which is divided into two Parts.
Certificates of Advanced Study in Chemical Engineering.
Certificates of Post-graduate Study in Chemical Engineering.

A chemical engineer is concerned with industrial processes, products, and methods of operation, in which there are changes in the composition and properties of matter. These operations may involve chemical reactions, changes of temperature or state, mixing or separation, and size reduction, or other chemical or physical operations. The qualified chemical engineer can contribute during the pre-operational and operational phases of an industrial project, and a wide range of activities is open. He, or she, may become a design engineer, a plant construction engineer, or a plant manager. On the other hand many chemical engineers work in research and development, where the tasks may not seem very different from those carried out by pure scientists. Such research is, however, directed towards improving processes or products, and is constrained by economic feasibility. In all these jobs the chemical engineer is concerned with the application of science to industry, and for this reason needs a basic training in chemistry, physics, mathematics, and computing, with a good grasp of related branches of engineering and technology.

The education of a chemical engineer is based on a sound understanding of the principles of thermodynamics and chemical kinetics, and of fluid mechanics. The course at Cambridge includes many examples taken from industrial applications, and an important feature – as of any engineering course – is a training in application of scientific methods to practical situations. The course is not confined to the operations of the chemical industry; indeed it is widely recognized that many of the concepts of chemical engineering can be applied to a very wide range of industries, and as a consequence chemical engineers are being employed in increasing numbers in many other branches of industry.

The accepted need to lay the main emphasis on the scientific background naturally raises the question as to why it should be an advantage to study engineering as a separate discipline rather than the pure sciences on which it is based. The answer is that engineers have tended to develop the basic sciences on different lines from the current studies of pure scientists, and indeed some branches of science have been originated by engineers in response to their needs; for example the science of thermodynamics evolved partly from engineers' requirements for better heat-engines. Thus in engineering departments in general, and chemical engineering departments in particular, the training is in those branches of sciences most likely to be of value in industry. There is also a different attitude of mind as between an engineer and a pure scientist. The engineer is primarily concerned with getting things done and making things work, and only uses theory as a means to these ends. The engineer must therefore be prepared to obtain and use partial solutions to otherwise insoluble problems; he, or she, must develop an almost instinctive feeling for what are reasonable and what are unreasonable approximations, and a readiness to combine scientific method with empiricism to obtain the best answer possible in the existing state of knowledge. As a consequence engineering courses concentrate more on the development of an ability to formulate and solve specific problems than do most of their scientific counterparts. This stress on getting things done, together with the development of scientific and technical initiative, means that chemical engineering offers much as an education, irrespective of its attraction as a profession.

The first necessity for any engineer is a wide and sound scientific training. Potential chemical engineers while at school should concentrate on their normal scientific activities. A sound knowledge of chemistry is essential, and candidates for the Chemical Engineering Tripos should have taken 'A' level chemistry in the G.C.E., whether they approach Chemical Engineering via the Natural Sciences or the Engineering Tripos. However, a liking for and ability in the more mathematical and physical fields is a prerequisite for success in chemical engineering.

Students of other universities who have graduated in either pure science or engineering may attend the course as Affiliated Students, and obtain the B.A. Degree in two years by taking Parts I and II of the Chemical Engineering Tripos. Graduates in chemistry should note that the courses are somewhat mathematical in outlook and they should have shown considerable ability in the more physical parts of their studies. Graduates in engineering should note that the course presumes that they have taken chemistry at least to G.C.E. 'A' level.

The courses leading to both parts of the Chemical Engineering Tripos are as follows:

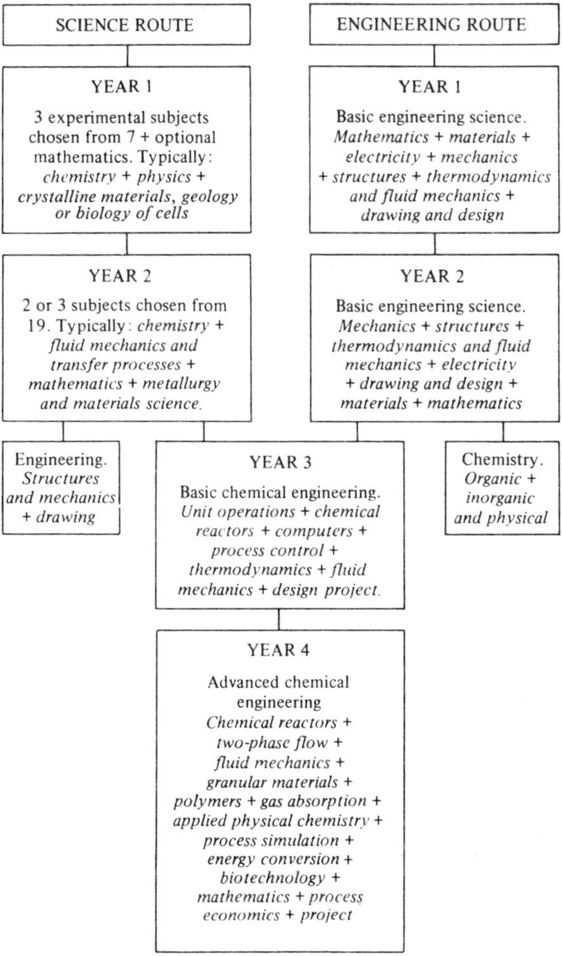
SCIENCE ROUTE
ENGINEERING ROUTE
YEAR 1
3 experimental subjects chosen from 7 + optional mathematics. Typically: *chemistry + physics + crystalline materials, geology or biology of cells*
YEAR 1
Basic engineering science. *Mathematics + materials + electricity + mechanics + structures + thermodynamics and fluid mechanics + drawing and design*
YEAR 2
2 or 3 subjects chosen from 19. Typically: *chemistry + fluid mechanics and transfer processes + mathematics + metallurgy and materials science.*
YEAR 2
Basic engineering science. *Mechanics + structures + thermodynamics and fluid mechanics + electricity + drawing and design + materials + mathematics*
Engineering. *Structures and mechanics + drawing*
YEAR 3
Basic chemical engineering. *Unit operations + chemical reactors + computers + process control + thermodynamics + fluid mechanics + design project.*
Chemistry. *Organic + inorganic and physical*
YEAR 4
Advanced chemical engineering *Chemical reactors + two-phase flow + fluid mechanics + granular materials + polymers + gas absorption + applied physical chemistry + process simulation + energy conversion + biotechnology + mathematics + process economics + project*

The Chemical Engineering Tripos

The Chemical Engineering Tripos is divided into two Parts. Part I is normally taken at the end of the third year in the University and Part II at the end of the fourth year. Whilst Part I satisfies the academic requirements of the Institution of Chemical Engineers, Part II gives an opportunity to study the subject in greater depth, to consider recent advances, and to undertake some original work instead of the more usual laboratory classes. Candidates who satisfy the examiners for Part II, having already obtained the B.A. degree, are awarded a Certificate of Advanced Study.

The first two years at the University are spent reading for either the Natural Sciences Tripos, Part I B, or the Engineering Tripos, Part I B. Natural scientists who are going on to Chemical Engineering take the subjects Chemistry and Fluid Mechanics in their second year.

The choice between taking the Natural Sciences Tripos or Engineering Tripos first is largely personal. There is a natural tendency for students who are mainly interested in the construction and design of equipment to proceed via the Engineering Tripos and those who are mainly interested in the chemistry and physics of processes to proceed via the Natural Sciences Tripos. However, these subdivisions need not be permanent and a competent person with due practical training can move from one branch of the profession to the other without difficulty.

Part I

The course for Part I of the Chemical Engineering Tripos (which normally occupies the third undergraduate year) begins in the second week in July with a 'Long Vacation term' lasting about four weeks. The Tripos Examinations are held towards the end of May.

The examination consists of four written papers, each of which is of three hours' duration.

Papers 1, 2, and 3 will each be on Chemical Engineering Principles and will contain questions on applied chemistry, thermodynamics, fluid and particle mechanics, transfer processes, applied mathematics, control theory, and chemical engineering operations. They may also contain questions on technical and economic aspects of the chemical industry, industrial management, and other topics at the discretion of the Examiners.

Paper 4 will consist of two sections for which the examinations may be held on separate days:

Section 1. General Engineering, will be taken by candidates who have previously obtained honours in the Natural Sciences Tripos, and will contain questions on selected aspects of engineering, for example, structures, mechanics, electricity.

Section 2. Chemistry, will be taken by candidates who have previously obtained honours in the Engineering Tripos, Part IB.

An Affiliated Student or a student admitted to the examination for Part I by leave of the Chemical Engineering Syndicate will take the section prescribed for him by the Chemical Engineering Syndicate.

Every candidate for Part I must satisfy the Examiners that he can make simple laboratory tests and experiments appropriate to the subjects of examination, that he can make and interpret drawings, and that he can apply his knowledge to the design of chemical engineering processes. To satisfy themselves on these points the Examiners may impose such oral or practical tests as they may think fit and may require each candidate to submit a report on selected experimental or other work carried out by him under the direction of a member of the Chemical Engineering Department.

Part II

The Part II examination consists of four written papers each of which is of three hours' duration.

Papers 1, 2, 3, and 4 will each be on Chemical Engineering Principles and will contain questions on applied chemistry, thermodynamics, fluid and particle mechanics, transfer processes, applied mathematics, control theory, and chemical engineering operations. The Examiners may also include questions on technical and economic aspects of the chemical industry, industrial management, and any chemical engineering topics of current interest.

Every candidate for Part II must satisfy the Examiners of his ability to perform original work, in the form either of a theoretical or experimental investigation or of a design project. In this connexion the Examiners may impose such oral or practical tests as they think fit, and may require each candidate to submit a written report on work carried out by him under the direction of a member of the Chemical Engineering Department.

Certificates of Advanced Study in Chemical Engineering

A Certificate of Advanced Study in Chemical Engineering is awarded to a member of the University who obtains honours in Part II of the Chemical Engineering Tripos having previously completed the examination requirements for the B.A. Degree.

Certificates of Post-graduate Study in Chemical Engineering

Certificates are awarded for advanced study and training in research in Chemical Engineering. A candidate must have been admitted as a Graduate Student, on the recommendation of the Degree Committee of the Faculty concerned, by the Board of Graduate Studies, who will fix the date of commencement of his candidature. He must also *either* (*a*) have graduated, or have completed the examination and residence requirements for graduation, in the University, and have been classed in Part II of the Mathematical, Natural Sciences, or Engineering Tripos, or in the Chemical Engineering Tripos, *or* (*b*) if not a member of the University, satisfy the Degree Committee of his fitness to study for the Certificate.

The course of instruction extends over three consecutive terms, but a candidate may be permitted in exceptional circumstances to spend up to two years in study for the Certificate.

The study and training include (*a*) courses of lectures, and (*b*) practical work carried out in one or more of the following ways: (i) experimental or theoretical exercises of an advanced type, (ii) training in research by means of assistance with a piece of research, (iii) training in research by means of an original research investigation, (iv) training in some technique.

Each candidate is required to submit a dissertation and to take an oral examination, which may include practical tests, on the subject of the dissertation and on the general field of knowledge within which it falls, and which may be supplemented by a written examination. In addition he may be required to take one or more written papers. By the end of the second term of his candidature a candidate must send to the Secretary of the Board of Graduate Studies the proposed title of his dissertation for approval by the Board. He must submit two copies of his dissertation to the Secretary of the Board of Graduate Studies during the third term of his candidature, unless he has been granted an extension; a statement of the sources from which his information is derived must be included.

A candidate for a Certificate may be allowed to count the whole or some part of the period for which he has been a candidate towards a course of research for the degree of Ph.D., M.Sc., or M.Litt., but if such an allowance is made he will not be entitled to receive a Certificate so long as he remains on the register of Research Students, nor subsequently if he should submit a dissertation for the degree of Ph.D., M.Sc., or M.Litt. A candidate is not entitled to receive a Certificate until he has kept at least three terms.

A candidate who is not awarded a Certificate may not be a candidate again nor may he be a candidate for any other Certificate of Post-graduate Study.

CLASSICS

In this subject there are courses of study followed by candidates for:

The *Classical Tripos*, which is divided into two Parts.

The *Preliminary Examinations* for Part I and Part II of the Classical Tripos.

Examinations for the Ordinary B.A. Degree in Greek *and in* Latin.

The *Diploma in Classical Archaeology*.

The Classical Tripos

The civilization of ancient Greece and Rome is of fundamental importance for the comparative study of societies and cultures and, more especially, for the understanding of the origins of modern Europe. The Classical Tripos approaches the study of classical antiquity through the original sources; and candidates for admission must possess a competent command at least of Latin. Most will also have a good knowledge of Greek, and this of course is a great advantage. However, the course is also suitable for those with little or no experience of Greek before acceptance. For such students intensive and systematic instruction in the language will be provided. The Tripos is usually completed in three years but may occupy four (see below under Part II). After reading Classics some students go on to further academic work and to teaching in schools and universities, but these do not represent a majority. Classical graduates follow a wide variety of careers and find that the Classical Tripos offers a valuable educational preparation for life in business, industry or administration.

The Tripos is divided into two Parts:

The course for Part I covers the main aspects of classical civilization: literature, history, philosophy, art and architecture. All students take papers in Greek and Latin literature, together with two papers chosen from the other three fields of study. The course is intended to develop students' knowledge of the Greek and Latin languages; to give them the opportunity of learning about their chosen fields through the study of particular texts and other primary sources; and to introduce them to the techniques of classical scholarship. As well as serving as a preparation for more specialized classical studies, Part I is designed to provide a course of wide scope that is balanced and satisfying in itself. Thus it is suitable for candidates who intend to read another Tripos in their third year, particularly one of those to which a first-hand knowledge of the classical background is relevant, such as Archaeology and Anthropology, English, History, Law, Philosophy, or Theology.

It is usual to take Part I at the end of the second year of residence. The regulations in fact allow a student to take it at the end of the first year, but few will have read widely enough in the ancient authors before coming to Cambridge to do this with profit. Part I may also be taken after a Part I in another subject by candidates who attained a good standard in Greek and Latin at school, unless they have already offered classical Greek or Latin in Part I of the Modern and Medieval Languages Tripos.

Part II offers an opportunity for the student to explore in depth some particular aspect or aspects of the classical world and also, for those who wish, to investigate related aspects of other cultures and disciplines. The subject is divided into five groups of papers concerned with (A) Literature, (B) Philosophy, (C) History, (D) Archaeology, (E) Language, representing five fields of study, and a sixth group, X, representing a combination of two or more of these fields of study. For their main field of study candidates (including those who spend two years reading for Part II) choose one of these groups A, B, C, D, E; they must offer at least two papers from the group and may offer three. These must be supplemented by additional papers, as detailed below. The options for additional papers include certain specially designated papers in other Triposes. These latter are at present chosen from the following Triposes: Anglo-Saxon, Norse, and Celtic, English, History, History of Art, Modern and Medieval Languages, Natural Sciences, Philosophy, and Theology.

Part II is usually taken at the end of the third year, but may be taken at the end of the fourth, i.e. after two years' study. The option of taking Part II after two years is commonly chosen by Affiliated Students who already hold a first degree from another University; it is also recommended for those candidates who attained a good knowledge of Greek and Latin at school but preferred to read Part I of another Tripos on coming into residence.

All candidates for Part II are expected to show themselves capable of broader thinking about their subject as well as detailed work in one or two branches of it, and their capacity to do so is tested in the examination by an English Essay on a classical topic.

Details of the examinations are as follows:

Part I[1]

Candidates are required to offer seven papers, each of three hours, as under:

Paper 1 or 2; Papers 3, 4, 5, and 6; and two papers chosen from among Papers 7–9.

In addition, a candidate may offer Paper 10 or 11 or both these papers.

The papers are:

1. Passages for translation from Greek authors

2. Less difficult passages for translation from Greek authors

The passages set will be selected from Homer and from Attic writers in prose and verse. The paper is intended for candidates who had little or no Greek at entrance.

3. Passages for translation from Latin authors

4. Passages for translation from Greek and Latin authors

These may include some passages taken from authors less generally familiar than those set in Papers 1, 2, and 3. Candidates are required to translate two passages from Greek and two passages from Latin. Less difficult Greek passages are set for candidates offering Paper 2.

5. Greek literature

The paper consists of three sections. Section (*a*) contains questions on Greek books prescribed from time to time by the Faculty Board. Section (*b*) contains passages for appreciation and analysis chosen from a schedule of Greek books which are prescribed from time to time by the Faculty Board. Section (*c*) contains questions on Greek literature which will also be based on this schedule, but credit will be given for knowledge of Greek books not included in the schedule. Candidates offering Paper 1 are required to answer four questions, one from section (*a*) and at least one from each of sections (*b*) and (*c*). Candidates offering Paper 2 are required

[1] The following papers, or the parts dealing with Greek, may be offered by candidates offering Classical Greek for Part I of the Modern and Medieval Languages Tripos: Papers 1, 2, 4, 5, 7, 8, 9, 10.

to answer four questions, including at least one and not more than two from section (*a*). If two are answered from section (*a*), they must be on different books. Candidates offering classical Greek for Part I of the Modern and Medieval Languages Tripos are required to attempt questions on Greek literature as follows:

option A: four questions, including at least one and not more than two from section (*a*).

option B or C: four questions, one from section (*a*) and at least one from each of sections (*b*) and (*c*).

Set texts in Section (*a*):

In **1985**: Sophocles, *Oedipus Tyrannus*, Theocritus, *Idylls* 1, 2, 3, 6, 7, 11, 13, 14, 15, 18, 24, 28.

In **1986**: Theocritus, *Idylls* 1, 2, 3, 6, 7, 11, 13, 14, 15, 18, 24, 28. Aristophanes, *Thesmophoriazusae*.

Schedule of Greek books prescribed for Sections (*b*) and (*c*) in **1985**:

Homer: *Iliad* I–XII; *Odyssey* XIII–XXIV; Hesiod: *Works and Days*; Lyric and elegiac poetry as in D. A. Campbell, *Greek Lyric Poetry* (2nd ed., 1972); Pindar: *Pythians*; Aeschylus: *Oresteia*; Sophocles; *Antigone*, *Oedipus Tyrannus*, *Philoctetes*; Euripides: *Hippolytus*, *Troades*, *Bacchae*; Aristophanes: *Acharnians*, *Clouds*, *Frogs*; Menander; *Dyscolus*, *Epitrepontes*; Theocritus: *Idylls* I–VII, X–XI, XIII–XVI, XVIII, XXII, XXIV, XXVI, XXVIII; *Epigrams* 4, 17–19, 21, 22; Callimachus: *Hymns* I, II, V; Epigrams by Asclepiades, Callimachus, a selection of Meleager (2, 4, 5, 6, 7, 11–20, 23, 25, 29, 31, 34, 37, 38, 43, 46, 52, 53, 54, 56, 69, 70, 72, 79, 85, 88, 107, 109, 110, 115, 123, 129, 132) (as in Gow–Page, *Hellenistic Epigrams*); Apollonius: *Argonautica* III; Herodotus I; Thucydides, I, II; Plato: *Apology*, *Crito*, *Symposium*; Lysias I, XII, XXIV; Demosthenes: *Olynthiacs*; Aristotle: *Poetics*, *Rhetoric* III; Lucian: *Verae Historiae*; Longus: *Daphnis and Chloe*.

In **1986**:

Homer: *Iliad* I–XII; *Odyssey* I–XII; Homeric *Hymn to Demeter*; Hesiod: *Works and Days*; Lyric and elegiac poetry as in D. A. Campbell, *Greek Lyric Poetry* (2nd ed., 1972); Pindar: *Olympians*; Aeschylus: *Oresteia*; Sophocles: *Oedipus Tyrannus*, *Philoctetes*, *Trachiniae*; Euripides: *Bacchae*, *Electra*, *Helen*; Aristophanes: *Birds*, *Frogs*, *Thesmophoriazusae*; Menander: *Dyscolus*, *Epitrepontes*; Theocritus: *Idylls* I–III, VI–VII, XI, XIII–XV, XVII–XVIII, XXIV, XXVIII; Moschus: *Europa*; Callimachus: *Hymns* II, V, VI; Epigrams by Asclepiades, Callimachus, a selection of Meleager (2, 4, 5, 6, 7, 11–20, 23, 25, 29, 31, 34, 37, 38, 43, 46, 52–4, 56, 69, 70, 72, 79, 85, 88, 107, 109, 110, 115, 123, 129, 132 as in Gow–Page, *Hellenistic Epigrams*);

Herodas: I, III; Apollonius: *Argonautica* III; Herodotus: I; Thucydides: I, II; Plato: *Apology*, *Ion*, *Symposium*; Lysias: I, XII; Demosthenes: *Olynthiacs*; Aristotle: *Poetics*; Lucian: *De Historia Conscribenda*; Longus: *Daphnis and Chloe*.

6. Latin literature

The paper consists of three sections. Section (*a*) contains questions on Latin books prescribed from time to time by the Faculty Board. Section (*b*) contains passages for appreciation and analysis chosen from a schedule of Latin books which are prescribed from time to time by the Faculty Board. Section (*c*) contains questions on Latin literature which will also be based on this schedule, but credit will be given for knowledge of Latin books not included in the schedule. Candidates are required to answer four questions, one from section (*a*) and at least one from each of sections (*b*) and (*c*).

Set texts in Section (*a*):

In **1985**: Virgil, *Georgics* III, IV, Petronius, 26.7–90.6.

In **1986**: Petronius 26.7–90.6; Propertius III.

Schedule of Latin books prescribed for sections (*b*) and (*c*) in **1985**:

Plautus: *Amphitryo*, *Rudens*; Terence: *Adelphoe*; Lucretius III, IV; Catullus; Virgil: *Eclogues*, *Georgics* III, IV, *Aeneid* I–VI; Horace: *Satires* I, *Odes* II, III, *Epistles* I; Tibullus I; Propertius I, IV; Ovid: *Amores* I, *Ars Amatoria* I, *Metamorphoses* VIII; Lucan V, VI; Juvenal 1, 3, 4, 5, 7, 8, 10; Cicero: *In Catilinam* I, *Pro Caelio*, *Pro Archia Poeta*, *De Amicitia*; Livy I; Seneca: *Agamemnon*; selection of letters (5, 7, 11, 12, 15, 28, 33, 47, 51, 53, 56, 63, 77, 79, 82, 84, 87, 90, 114); Petronius: *Cena Trimalchionis*; Pliny: selection of letters (as in *Fifty Letters*, ed. A. N. Sherwin-White, 1969); Suetonius: *Nero*; Tacitus: *Annals* XIII, XIV, *Dialogus*; Quintilian XII; Apuleius: *Cupid and Psyche*

In **1986**:

Plautus: *Amphitryo*, *Casina*; Terence: *Adelphoe*; Lucretius: I, III; Catullus; Virgil: *Eclogues*, *Georgics* I, IV, *Aeneid* I–VI; Horace: *Satires* I, *Odes* II, III, *Epistles* I, *Ars Poetica*; Tibullus: I; Propertius: I, IV; Ovid: *Amores* I, *Ars Amatoria* I, *Metamorphoses* III; Lucan: I; Persius: I; Statius: *Thebaid* X; Juvenal: I, III, IV, V, VII, X; Cicero: *In Catilinam* I, *Pro Archia Poeta*, *Pro Caelio*, *Somnium Scipionis*, *Orator* 1–32, 75–120, 168–238; Livy: I; Seneca: *Medea*, selection of letters (5, 11, 12, 18, 21, 28, 47, 53, 90, 122); Petronius: *Satyricon* 26.7–90.6; Suetonius: *Nero*; Tacitus: *Annals* XIII–XIV, *Dialogus*; Apuleius: *Metamorphoses* I, II 1–17, III 19–25, XI 1–15.

7. Greek and Roman history with reference to prescribed authors

This paper is divided into three sections. Section (*a*) consists of a single question containing a number of passages, from works of ancient authors prescribed from time to time by the Faculty Board, each of which requires an answer to the question appended to it. Section (*b*) contains questions on Greek history, and section (*c*) contains questions on Roman history. In sections (*b*) and (*c*) credit is given for knowledge of ancient sources, on which specific questions may also be asked. Candidates are required to answer the question in section (*a*) and not fewer than three other questions, of which at least one must be chosen from section (*b*) and at least one from section (*c*).

In Section (*a*) the authors prescribed are:

In **1985** and **1986**:

(For *c.* 750–399 B.C.) Herodotus V–VI 60; Thucydides I–II 65; Xenophon, *Hellenica* I–II iii; Aristotle, *Constitution of Athens*, 5–41.

(For 445–323 B.C.) Thucydides I 22–88; I 115–II 65; Xenophon, *Hellenica* I–II iii; Aristotle, *Constitution of Athens*, 29–41; Demosthenes I, V, IX, XIV, XV; Arrian, *Anabasis* I and VII 1–19.

(For 218–44 B.C.) Polybius VI 3–26; Livy XXVI; Appian, *Civil War* I 1–26; Sallust, *Catiline*; Cicero, *Ad Q.F.* I i and *Pro Marcello.*

(For 81 B.C.–A.D. 68) Sallust, *Catiline*; Cicero, *Ad Q.F.* I i and *Pro Marcello*; *Res gestae divi Augusti*; Tacitus, *Annals* I and XIV.

8. Greek and Roman philosophy and religion with particular reference to Plato

This paper is divided into two sections. Section (*a*) contains questions on a prescribed dialogue or prescribed dialogues of Plato. Section (*b*) contains questions on ancient philosophers and philosophical systems and on religion. Candidates are required to answer four questions of which at least one and not more than two must be chosen from section (*a*).

Section (*a*): In **1985** and **1986**: prescribed dialogues, Plato, *Republic*, 475–535.

9. Greek and Roman art and architecture

The paper will be divided into three sections. Section (*a*) will consist of a single question involving comments on photographs. Section (*b*) will cover the Greek art and architecture in the fifth century B.C. Section (*c*) will cover Roman Italy, *c.* 80 B.C.–A.D. 68. Candidates for the Classical

Tripos will be required to attempt section (*a*) and three other questions, including at least one from each of sections (*b*) and (*c*).

10. Translation from English into Greek prose and verse[1]

This paper is divided into two sections. Section (*a*) contains two passages for translation into Greek prose, one passage for translation into Greek verse (iambics), and one passage for translation into Greek verse (elegiacs). Section (*b*) contains one passage for translation into Greek verse (iambics), longer than that set in section (*a*). Candidates are required to attempt *either* any two passages chosen from section (*a*) *or* the single passage from section (*b*).

11. Translation from English into Latin prose and verse

This paper is divided into two sections. Section (*a*) contains two passages for translation into Latin prose, one passage for translation into Latin verse (hexameters), and one passage for translation into Latin verse (elegiacs). Section (*b*) contains one passage for translation into Latin verse (hexameters), and one passage for translation into Latin verse (elegiacs), each longer than the corresponding passage set in section (*a*). Candidates are required to attempt *either* any two passages chosen from section (*a*) *or* one passage chosen from section (*b*).

Part II[2]

Part II may be taken at the end either of the third or of the fourth year of residence, but no one, except an Affiliated Student, may be a candidate for honours in Part II unless he has already obtained honours in Part I or in another Honours Examination not more than two years before.

No student may present himself as a candidate for Part II on more than one occasion.

Subjects of examination[3]

The examination consists of an Essay paper, papers assigned to five groups A, B, C, D, E, representing five fields of study, and to a sixth

[1] Candidates are expected to show a knowledge of the general principles of Greek accentuation.

[2] The detail below describes the examination to be held in **1986**. For the examination to be held in 1985, see the *Handbook* for 1983–84.

[3] Advisers to students who wish to begin to read for Part II of the Classical Tripos are appointed annually; a list of the Advisers, together with the times at which they are available for interview, is published in the *Cambridge University Reporter* during the Easter Term.

group, X, representing a combination of two or more of these fields of study, and certain papers from other Triposes (Group O). The essay paper, or an extended essay, carries half the weight assigned to other papers.

A candidate who takes Part II in one year must offer

(*a*) the Essay paper;

and (*b*) two papers belonging to a single group, chosen from among the five Groups A, B, C, D, E;

and *either* (*c*) two additional papers chosen from Groups A, B, C, D, E, X, and from the Schedule of Optional Papers;

or (*d*) one additional paper chosen from Groups A, B, C, D, E, X, and from the Schedule of Optional Papers, together with a thesis on a topic proposed by himself and approved by the Faculty Board;

provided that no candidate may offer more than three papers from Group D or more than one paper from the Schedule of Optional Papers.

A candidate who takes Part II in two years must offer

(*a*) the Essay paper;

and (*b*) two papers belonging to a single group, chosen from among the five Groups A, B, C, D, E;

and *either* (*c*) three additional papers chosen from Groups A, B, C, D, E, X, and from the Schedule of Optional Papers;

or (*d*) two additional papers chosen from Groups A, B, C, D, E, X, and from the Schedule of Optional Papers, together with a thesis, as prescribed in Regulation 25, on a topic proposed by himself and approved by the Faculty Board;

provided that no candidate may offer more than three papers from Group D or more than two papers from Group X or more than one paper from the Schedule of Optional Papers.

A candidate may be examined *viva voce* on the field of study of a group from which he offers two or more papers, provided that the scope of such an examination will be restricted to the subjects of the papers which the candidate has offered.

In place of the Essay paper a candidate may submit an extended essay of not less than 3,000 and not more than 5,000 words (inclusive of notes), on a topic proposed by himself and approved by the

Faculty Board. The topic proposed for the essay must fall within the field of Classics and must not coincide substantially with the subject of any of the papers that the candidate is offering in the examination. Each candidate must submit the proposed title of his essay, together with a statement of the scheme of papers that he intends to offer in the examination, and the title of any thesis that he intends to offer, through his Tutor to the Secretary of the Faculty Board, so as to reach him not later than the division of the Lent Term next preceding the examination. Each candidate must obtain the approval of the title of his essay by the Faculty Board not later than the end of Full Lent Term. When the Faculty Board have approved a candidate's title, no change may be made to it, or to his scheme of papers, or to the title of any thesis that he intends to offer, without the further approval of the Faculty Board. A candidate is required to declare that the essay is his own work and that it does not contain material which he has already used to any substantial extent for a comparable purpose. Except for Greek quotations, which may be written by hand, essays must be typewritten, unless a candidate has obtained previous permission from the Faculty Board to present his essay in manuscript, and must be submitted to the Secretary not later than the first day of the Full Easter Term in which the examination is to be held.

Details of the papers are:

ESSAY PAPER

The paper will contain a number of topics, for an essay in English, connected with the history, language, literature, thought, archaeology, and art of the Greeks and Romans. Candidates may be asked to treat any of the subjects in relation to later developments.

GROUP A (LITERATURE)

Paper A1. A prescribed Greek author or authors, and a prescribed Latin author or authors

This paper contains questions on a Greek author or authors and on a Latin author or authors. The works prescribed are taken from among the major works of Greek and Latin literature.

In **1986**: Homer and Virgil.

Paper A2. A prescribed Greek author

In **1986**: Aeschylus, with special reference to *Agamemnon*.

Paper A3. A prescribed Latin author

Papers A2 and A3 include questions on a prescribed portion or portions of the works of the author prescribed. In each paper candidates are required to answer at least one question on the textual criticism of the prescribed portion or portions.

In **1986**: Ovid's amatory works, with special reference to *Amores* II and III.

Group B (Philosophy)

Paper B1. Plato

This paper includes questions on a prescribed portion or portions of the works of Plato.

In **1986**: Plato, *Theaetetus*.

Paper B2. Aristotle

This paper includes questions on a prescribed portion or portions of the works of Aristotle.

In **1986**: Aristotle, *Metaphysics* Z.

Paper B3. Ancient philosophers other than Plato and Aristotle from Thales to Marcus Aurelius

Candidates who also offer both Paper B1 and Paper B2 are required to attempt at least one question on the Presocratic philosophers and at least one question on Hellenistic philosophy. For other candidates there will be no restriction on choice of questions.

Group C (History)[1]

Paper C1. A prescribed period or subject of Greek history

In **1986**: Demosthenes and Athens.

Paper C2. A prescribed period or subject of Roman history

In **1986**: Rome and the Western Empire, A.D. 41–161.

A candidate who offers this paper may not also offer Paper D4.

Paper C3. A prescribed subject taken from ancient history

In **1986**: Famine and Food Supply in Classical Antiquity.

[1] In each of Papers C1, C2, C3 candidates will be required to attempt one question on the literary, epigraphical, and archaeological sources for the period or subject prescribed. These papers may contain questions that involve a knowledge of geography and topology and of the political, legal, and social antiquities of the period or subject prescribed but they will not require a technical knowledge of archaeology.

Group D (Archaeology)

Paper D1. Prehellenic archaeology

Paper D2. A prescribed subject connected with early Hellenic archaeology or early Greek art

In **1986**: Early Hellenic archaeology.

Paper D3. A prescribed subject connected with Classical (Greco-Roman) art or the archaeology of the Greek and Hellenistic world

In **1986**: Classical (Greco-Roman) art.

Paper D4. Archaeology of the Western Provinces of the Roman Empire

Group E (Language)

Paper E1. Elements of comparative linguistics

This paper will cover the principles of the comparative method and of historical reconstruction and their applications to Indo-European phonology, morphology, syntax, and lexicon. A knowledge of the relevant phenomena in Vedic will be required.

[1]*Paper E2. The Greek language*

This paper will cover the history of the Greek language and its dialects to the late Hellenistic period.

In **1986**: the prescribed texts are: F. Solmsen, E. Fraenkel, *Inscriptiones Graecae ad inlustrandas dialectos selectae* nos. 1, 6, 8, 12, lines 1–23; 20, lines 121–69; 22, 24, 35; 40, col. II line 45–col. III line 39; 44, lines 1–20; 51, 60, 63; Homer, *Iliad* x, 1–41.

[1]*Paper E3. The Latin language*

This paper will cover the history of the Latin language to the end of the Roman Empire.

In **1986**: the prescribed texts are: *Inscriptiones Latinae Liberae Rei Publicae*, ed. Degrassi (1957 and 1963), nos. 2, 3, 23, 24, 76, 123, 132, 170, 286, 310, 311, 489, 504, 1197. *Recueil de Textes Latins Archaïques*, ed. Ernout (1973), nos. 126, 137, 149 tabb. 4–12. *Fragmenta Poetarum Latinorum*, ed. Morel (1927); Naevius, nos. 4, 12, 19, 29, 30, 32, 33, 36, 45.

[1] Each of Papers E2 and E3 are divided into two sections, (*a*) prescribed texts, which will include portions for translation and comment; (*b*) the historical phonology, morphology, syntax, and lexicon of the language. In each paper candidates are required to answer questions from both sections.

Vulgärlateinisches Uebungsbuch, ed. Slotty (1960), part I, nos. 2, 12, 69, 104, 139, 153; part II: Petronius capp. 40–2.

Group X

There will be not more than three papers in this group, X1, X2, X3, whose subjects will be prescribed from time to time by the Faculty Board of Classics. The subjects will be of an inter-disciplinary nature, requiring knowledge related to more than one of the fields of study represented by Groups A, B, C, D, and E.

In **1986**: Women in Antiquity: Perspectives from literatu re, science and art.

Group O[1]

O1. General linguistics (Paper 111 of Part II of the Modern and Medieval Languages Tripos).

O2. Greek literature, thought, and history, since 1888 (Paper 104 of Part II of the Modern and Medieval Languages Tripos).

O3. Tragedy (Paper 2 of Part II of the English Tripos).

O4. History and Theory of literary criticism (Paper 9 of Part II of the English Tripos).

O5. Metaphysics (Paper 1 of Part IB of the Philosophy Tripos).

O6. History of political thought to *c.* 1750 (Paper 19 of Part I of the Historical Tripos).

O7. Medieval Latin literature from 400 to 1300 (Paper 12 of Part II of the Modern and Medieval Languages Tripos).

O8. Christian life and thought to A.D. 461 (Paper 22 of the Theological and Religious Studies Tripos).

O9. Anglo-Saxon England in the pagan period (Paper 12 of the Anglo-Saxon, Norse, and Celtic Tripos).

O10. The transformation of the Roman world (Paper 15 of Part II of the Historical Tripos).

O11. The transformation of the Roman World (Paper 14 of Part II of the Historical Tripos).

O12. Scientific ideas and practice from antiquity to the Renaissance (Paper 1 of Section II of Part II (General) of the Natural Sciences Tripos).

O13. The triumph of Classicism: Architecture in England, France and Germany, 1750–1830 (the pair of Papers 10–11 of the History of Art Tripos).

[1] These are the papers for **1986**. For the papers in **1985** see the *Handbook* for 1983–84.

Thesis

A candidate who chooses to offer a thesis must submit the proposed title of his thesis, together with a statement of the scheme of papers that he intends to offer through his Tutor to the Secretary of the Faculty Board so as to reach him not later than the fifth day of the Full Michaelmas Term next preceding the examination if he is taking the examination in one year, and not later than the last day of the Lent Term next but one preceding the examination if he is taking the examination in two years. In the case of a candidate taking the examination in one year, the topic of his thesis must be closely connected with the subject of a paper belonging to one of the six Groups A, B, C, D, E, X, provided that a candidate may not submit a thesis on a topic that falls within the general area of any of the papers that he is offering in the examination, and that a candidate who chooses to offer three papers from Group D may not submit a thesis on a topic that falls within the general area of that group. In the case of a candidate taking the examination in two years, the topic of his thesis must fall within the field of Classics and must not coincide substantially with the subject of any of the papers that he is offering in the examination. Each candidate must obtain the approval of the title of his thesis by the Faculty Board not later than the end of the third quarter of the Michaelmas Term next preceding the examination if he is taking the examination in one year, and not later than the end of the third quarter of the Easter Term next preceding the examination if he is taking the examination in two years. When the Faculty Board have approved a candidate's title, no change may be made to it, or to his scheme of papers, without the further approval of the Faculty Board. The length of the thesis must not exceed 10,000 words (inclusive of notes). A candidate will be required to give full references to sources used and to declare that the thesis is his own work and that it does notc ontain material which he has already used to any substantial extent for a comparable purpose (including an extended essay). The Board will expect the thesis to show detailed knowledge of the relevant primary sources and to provide evidence of ability to select a topic of interest, to handle it in an enterprising manner and with sound and independent judgement, and to present it with clarity and precision. Except for Greek quotations, which may be written by hand, theses must be typewritten, unless a candidate has obtained previous permission from the Faculty Board to present his thesis in manuscript, and must be submitted to the Secretary so as to reach him not later than the first day of the Full Easter Term in which the examination is to be held. The candidate will also be examined *viva voce.*

The Preliminary Examination for Part I

(*each paper* 3 *hours*)

The examination consists of six papers as follows:

1. Greek translation
2. Alternative Greek translation

The paper contains passages for translation from the following Greek books prescribed by the Faculty Board of Classics, together with two passages for unseen translation, one verse, one prose, from the authors of the prescribed Greek books:

Homer, *Odyssey* XVIII; Euripides, *Troades*, 1–121, 292–325, 353–423, 608–781, 680–781, 860–1059, 1156–1208, and 1260–1286; Lysias, XII, 1–17 and 41–80; Plato, *Symposium* 198–end; Thucydides, I, 13–19, 89–121.

3. Latin translation
4. Classical questions

The paper contains questions on:

(*a*) Greek and Latin literature;
(*b*) Greek history from *c.* 750 to 323 B.C., and Roman history from 218 B.C. to A.D. 69;
(*c*) Greek and Roman philosophy and religion;
(*d*) Greek and Roman art and architecture.

Candidates are required to answer four questions taken from any one or more of the above-named sections.

5. Greek prose and verse composition
6. Latin prose and verse composition

Every candidate must offer *either* Paper 1 *or* Paper 2, and Papers 3 and 4. Papers 5 and 6 are optional, but the Examiners will give credit for proficiency in these papers; candidates are not required to attempt both prose and verse.

The Preliminary Examination for Part II

The papers for this examination are taken from among the papers for Part II of the Classical Tripos. It is usual for Affiliated Students to take the Preliminary Examination at the end of their first year. Every candidate must offer the Essay paper, one paper chosen from Papers 1–3 of one of Groups A–F, and one other paper which may be *either* another paper from Papers 1–3 of the same or of a different group,

or a paper which may be offered as a subsidiary paper,

or a paper from Group O;

provided that a candidate choosing one or two papers from Group A may substitute Paper A4 for *either* Paper A2 *or* Paper A3, and provided that a candidate choosing one or two papers from Group C may substitute Paper C4 for *either* Paper C1 *or* Paper C2.

The Examinations for the Ordinary B.A. Degree

Greek

The examination consists of *either* (*a*) the five following papers, all of which must be taken:

1, 2, and 3. Passages for translation into English from specified books: Homer, *Iliad* XVIII–XXI, *Odyssey* VI–VII, Sophocles, *Philoctetes*, Euripides, *Hecuba*; Plato, *Phaedrus.*

4. Passages from unspecified books for translation into English, such passages being chosen from books comparable in style and difficulty to those specified for Papers 1, 2, and 3.

5. History and civilization, with special attention to the period 600–323 B.C.

or (*b*) the following papers from Part I of the Tripos:

either (i) Papers 1, 5, and 10,

or (ii) Papers 1, 4 (two Greek passages specified for candidates taking Paper 1), and 5, and two questions from any one of Papers 7, 8, and 9,

or (iii) Papers 1 and 5 and two questions from each of two of Papers 7, 8, and 9.

In the case of Paper 7 the question in section (*a*) must be attempted and one question chosen from section (*b*) of the paper; only passages in Greek must be selected for comment from section (*a*). In the case of Paper 8 one question must be chosen from section (*a*) and one from section (*b*) of the paper. In the case of Paper 9 two questions must be chosen from section (*b*).

For certain restrictions see the last paragraph under Latin, below.

Latin

The examination consists of *either* (*a*) the five following papers, all of which must be taken:

1, 2, and 3. Passages for translation into English from specified books: Lucretius III, Horace, *Odes*, III; Virgil, *Aeneid* X–XII; Livy V.

4. Passages from unspecified books for translation into English, such passages being chosen from books comparable in style and difficulty to those specified for Papers 1, 2, and 3.

5. History and civilization, with special attention to the period 78 B.C.–A.D. 117.

or (*b*) the following papers from Part I of the Classical Tripos:

either (i) Papers 3, 6, and 11,
or (ii) Papers 3, 4 (two Latin passages), and 6, and two questions from Paper 7 or Paper 9,
or (iii) Papers 3 and 6, and two questions from each of Papers 7 and 9.

In the case of Paper 7 the question in section (*a*) must be attempted and one question chosen from section (*b*) of the paper; only passages in Latin must be selected for comment from section (*a*). In the case of Paper 8 one question must be chosen from section (*a*) and one from section (*b*) of the paper. In the case of Paper 9 two questions must be chosen from section (*c*).

A student may not count towards the Ordinary B.A. Degree both the Special Examination in Latin or Greek and also anything that he may have to his credit as the result of the Preliminary Examination in Classics or Part I of the Classical Tripos; but in lieu of a Special Examination, a student who has passed the Preliminary Examination may take certain papers from Part I of the Tripos in one or the other language, and a student who has received an allowance on Part I of the Tripos or on the Preliminary Examination for his performance in one of the two languages may take certain papers from Part I of the Tripos in the other.

The Diploma in Classical Archaeology [1]

A candidate for the Diploma in Classical Archaeology must be approved by the Faculty Board of Classics and must *either* be a graduate of the University who has obtained honours in Part I or Part II of the Classical Tripos *or* be a graduate of another university who has passed with honours in that university an examination of a standard and scope comparable to that of Part I of the Classical Tripos *or* have produced other evidence to satisfy the Faculty Board of his fitness to study for the Diploma.

Before being admitted to the examination for the Diploma a candidate must obtain a certificate, signed by the Secretary of the Faculty Board of Classics, of having received instruction in Classical Archaeology under the direction of the Faculty Board for at least two terms. The certificate must be sent to the Registrary by 1 May in the year in which the candidate wishes to take the examination.

The Diploma is awarded to members of the University who have obtained certificates of instruction in Classical Archaeology, passed the examination, and kept at least three terms. No one may be a candidate for the Diploma on more than one occasion.

Subjects of examination

The examination for the Diploma is partly written and partly oral; all candidates will be examined *viva voce* on the subjects of the papers that they have offered. The following papers are set for three hours each:

1. Early Hellenic archaeology

2. Greek and Roman architecture

3. Prehellenic archaeology

4. Greek and Roman sculpture

Candidates will be required to attempt at least two questions on Greek sculpture.

[1] This entry applies to the examination to be held in 1985. The regulations have been changed for the examination in 1986. Details are available from the Faculty Board. The Part II examination referred to herein is the examination for 1985, details of which are to be found in the 1984–85 edition of the *Handbook*.

5. Archaeology of the Western Provinces of the Roman Empire

6. Section (*a*) Greek epigraphy;
   Section (*b*) Latin epigraphy

This paper includes facsimiles of inscriptions for transcription, translation and comment. Candidates will be required to answer at least one question from each section.

7. Ancient coinage

[1]A candidate who has not taken any paper of Group D in Part II must offer Papers 1, 2, and 4 and two other papers chosen from among Papers 3, 5, 6, and 7.

[1]A candidate who has taken Paper D3 only in Part II must offer Papers 1, 2, and 4 and two other papers chosen from among Papers 5, 6, and 7.

[1]A candidate who has taken Paper D4 only in Part II must offer Papers 1 and 2 and three other papers chosen from among Papers 3, 5, 6, and 7.

[1]A candidate who has taken Paper D5 only in Part II must offer Papers 1, 2, and 4 and two other papers chosen from among Papers 3, 6, and 7.

[1]A candidate who has taken three main papers from Group D in Part II must offer Papers 6 and 7 and

(*a*) if he took Paper D3 in the Tripos, Papers 4 and 5;
(*b*) if he took Paper D4 in the Tripos, Papers 3 and 5;
(*c*) if he took Paper D5 in the Tripos, Papers 3 and 4.

He must also offer an advanced essay on some subject or combination of subjects which he studied for Group D of Part II of the Tripos chosen by himself and approved by a committee appointed by the Faculty Board of Classics. A candidate must submit the subject for his essay through his Tutor to the Secretary of the

[1] In **1985**, a candidate must offer:

(i) if he has not taken any paper of Group D in Part II of the Classical Tripos, Papers 1 and 4 and three other papers chosen from among Papers 3, 5, 6, and 7;

(ii) if he has taken one paper from Group D in Part II of the Classical Tripos, all the Diploma papers other than that paper.

A candidate who has taken three papers from Group D in Part II of the Classical Tripos in the examination in 1984, or in 1985, will not be eligible to be a candidate for the Diploma.

Faculty Board so as to reach him not later than 15 November preceding the term in which he desires to present himself for examination, and must send his essay through his Tutor to the Secretary of the Board so as to reach him not later than the division of that Term.

COMPUTER SCIENCE

In this subject there are courses of study followed by candidates for:

The *Computer Science Tripos* (one-year or two-year course).
The *Preliminary Examination* for the two-year course.
The *Diploma in Computer Science.*

The Computer Science Tripos

There are two alternative courses for the Computer Science Tripos. One is the one-year course which is intended for students in their third year. These students will have spent their first two years reading for a part of another Tripos, which would normally be Mathematics, Natural Sciences, or Engineering. The other is a two-year course; students on this will similarly have spent their first year studying some other subject. The two-year course includes all the material in the one-year course together with additional material; in particular, students are required to complete a substantial project. Neither course for the Computer Science Tripos necessarily requires a high degree of mathematical preparation and the mathematics in Part IA of the Natural Sciences Tripos is quite sufficient; even this degree of formal mathematics need not be insisted on in the case of a student who is highly motivated towards the computer field. It is regarded as essential that all students who wish to take the one-year course should come up during their second Long Vacation in order to attend an introductory course.

Both courses provide a sound basis in programming languages, computer hardware, compilers, and operating systems. In addition there is a wide range of optional courses from which students may choose. Courses will be offered on computer graphics, computer design, memory protection, specialized computer languages, the theory of computation, mathematical software, data communication, numerical analysis, data base management, artificial intelligence, and algebraic manipulation by computer. Students who follow the two-year course will attend practical classes in a hardware laboratory and, in their final year, will spend much of their time working on a dissertation on an approved topic.

The examination consists of five written papers each of which is of three hours' duration. The details of the papers are:

Papers 1 and 2.

Papers 1 and 2 (only for candidates on the one-year course) are of such a nature as to test the candidate's knowledge of fundamentals of computer science. The subjects covered are programming languages, programming techniques, elements of the design of computers, computing circuits and computer systems, assembly language, elements of assembler and compiler design. Paper 2 includes an extended practical question relating to the design of a program for a specified purpose.

Papers 3 and 4.

Papers 3 and 4 are of such a nature as to enable candidates to show a specialized knowledge of some branches of computer science, or a deeper knowledge of topics also covered in Papers 1 or 2. The papers contain a choice of questions so that it is not necessary for a candidate to have a specialized or advanced knowledge of all branches of the subject.

Papers 5 and 6.

Papers 5 and 6 (only for candidates on the two-year course) cover more advanced aspects of programming languages, programming language theory, mathematical computation, computer hardware, real-time and distributed computing. Papers 5 and 6 will each include an extended practical question.

On the one-year course, Papers 1, 2, 3, and 4 must be offered. On the two-year course, Papers 3, 4, 5, and 6 must be offered, together with a dissertation. A candidate must submit the subject of his dissertation through his Tutor to the Head of the Computer Laboratory and must obtain approval for his subject by the division of the Michaelmas Term next preceding the examination. Two copies of the dissertation on the approved subject, which must be typewritten or computer printed and must not exceed 12,000 words in length, excluding appendices, footnotes, and bibliography, must be submitted by the candidate not later than the fifteenth day preceding the first day of the examination. The Examiners have power to require a candidate to present himself for a *viva voce* examination on the subject of his dissertation and on the general field of knowledge within which it falls.

Preliminary Examination for the two-year course

The examination consists of three papers as follows:

Papers 1 and 2 are of such a nature as to test the candidate's knowledge of fundamentals of computer science. The subjects covered are programming languages, programming techniques, elements of the design of computers, computing circuits and computer systems, assembly language, elements of assembler and compiler design. Paper 2 includes an extended practical question relating to the design of a program for a specified purpose.

Paper 3 is of such a nature as to enable candidates to show a specialized knowledge of some branches of computer science, or a deeper knowledge of topics covered in Papers 1 or 2.

Each paper is of three hours' duration and candidates are required to offer all three papers.

Diploma in Computer Science

Applicants for admission to the Diploma course should normally have at least a second-class Honours Degree in Mathematics, Science, or Engineering. The course covers the basic aspects of computer hardware and software, with additional material on topics such as data bases, data communication, computer graphics, numerical analysis and algebraic manipulation. Students have access to the computers in the Laboratory and have opportunities to follow up their own particular interests. The examination is in two Parts; Part A consists of four written papers taken near the end of the Easter Term, and Part B consists of a dissertation submitted during the following long vacation on an individually approved subject. Further information about the course may be obtained from the Head of the Computer Laboratory.

A candidate for the Diploma must be approved by the Computer Syndicate. He must satisfy the Syndicate that he has attained a standard in mathematics sufficiently high for him to profit by the course and must ordinarily be a graduate of a university. No one may be a candidate in the same year for the Diploma and for another Diploma or any Tripos.

An undergraduate who has completed the examination requirements for the B.A. Degree may attend the course of instruction for the Diploma and may take the examination. If he passes the examination, he will be entitled to receive a certificate to that effect but he will not be entitled to receive a Diploma.

An application for approval as a candidate should be sent, together with evidence of qualifications, to the Head of the Computer Laboratory so as to reach him well before the beginning of the Michaelmas Term in which the applicant wishes his candidature to begin. The course is approved by the Science and Engineering Research Council for tenure of advanced course studentships. Application for a studentship is made on behalf of an eligible student who has been provisionally admitted to the course. The quota of grants for allocation is generally small in comparison with the number of applicants.

The course of instruction extends over one academical year and requires regular attendance at the Computer Laboratory. To be awarded the Diploma candidates must have passed the examination and must have kept at least three terms.

A candidate who has taken the examination for the Diploma may not count any part of the period during which he has been a candidate for it towards a course of research for the degree of Ph.D., M.Sc., or M.Litt. A candidate who fails in the examination may not be a candidate again.

M.Phil. Degree in Computer Speech and Language Processing

For details of this one-year course, see p. 170.

DEVELOPMENT STUDIES

Candidates wishing to undertake Development Studies at Cambridge should refer to the following entries:

(i) P. 133. A course in the Economics and Politics of Development leading to the M.Phil. Degree is available in the Faculty of Economics and Politics.

(ii) P. 229. A course leading to a Diploma in Development Studies is available under the Board of Graduate Studies and the Degree Committee of the Department of Land Economy.

Other courses which may be of interest are:

The course leading to a Diploma in Economics (p. 131).

The course leading to an M.Phil. in Land Economy (p. 228).

The course leading to an M.Phil. in Social Anthropology (p. 65).

The course leading to an M.Phil. in Latin-American Studies (p. 231).

The course leading to an M.Phil. in International Relations (p. 212).

ECONOMICS AND POLITICS

In this field the courses of study offered to candidates are:

The *Economics Tripos.*
The *Preliminary Examination* for Part II of the Economics Tripos.
The *Diploma in Economics.*
The *M.Phil. Degree.*

The Economics Tripos

The Economics Tripos, as it has developed, allows candidates a broad range of options. Sociology is covered, there is broad provision for the study of politics, and training in the mathematical aspects of economics is on a firm basis. It will appeal to those interested in the study of society, whatever their speciality in school may have been: students trained in mathematics will find as much scope for their abilities as those who have specialized in history, geography, or languages.

The Tripos is based on a solid core of economics, pure and applied. It examines employment and unemployment, economic growth, price fluctuations, international trade, resource allocation, the distribution of income, and so on. Those who read for the Tripos can also study cognate subjects such as economic history, politics, sociology, and statistics. The Tripos is divided into two Parts:

Part I is taken at the end of the first year;
Part II is normally taken at the end of the third year.

Many candidates read Economics for three years, but the system allows considerable flexibility. A candidate may often combine Part I of the Economics Tripos and Part II of another Tripos, or Part I of another Tripos and Part II of the Economics Tripos.

For studying economic principles at the Part II level it is a great help if a candidate has a certain familiarity with elementary mathematical concepts. There is, therefore, an economics qualifying examination in elementary mathematics (E.Q.E.E.M.); this is normally taken in the candidate's Part I year, or just before starting the second year. The standard required is lower than for 'A' level in G.C.E., and anyone who has passed in mathematics at 'A' level (or has some equivalent qualification) is automatically exempt. Those who have to take E.Q.E.E.M. will be assisted to acquire the necessary understanding of elementary mathematics during their first year at Cambridge, and there are also provisions whereby certain people can be accepted for Part II without passing E.Q.E.E.M.

The examination for Part I, which is taken at the end of the undergraduate's first year, consists of four compulsory papers: three in selected aspects of political economy and one in British economic history. The scope of these papers is described in greater detail below. Even for those who do not intend to continue in economics this year of study will be valuable. It will give them more insight into many live issues on which sooner or later almost everyone has to form an opinion. Moreover, there are many careers in which a basic understanding of economic processes is a valuable professional qualification.

Part I of the Tripos provides an interesting consolidation and extension of studies for those who have taken economics at Advanced level, but it is in no way a requirement to have done so. The Tripos is also suitable for those with no previous study of the subject. It makes a particular appeal to students who have done some history at school, but whose main interests are in contemporary society; they will already know some of the background to the papers in economic history and politics, and will learn to analyse these subjects more rigorously. Part I will also be of interest to those who have done mathematics or natural sciences and are looking for a subject where they can apply their knowledge in a new field.

Part II provides the means to study several of the social sciences in some depth. At the end of the course everyone has to take three papers in economic principles and problems; in addition all candidates must take either three papers from a wide choice of optional subjects or one paper and a dissertation. It is possible to take special papers in industry, labour, economic theory, mathematical economics, international economics, banking and finance, the economic problems of underdeveloped countries, World Depression in the interwar years, Russian economic development since 1861, applied economic and social statistics, and the theory of statistics. In addition, the choice extends to papers from the Social and Political Sciences Tripos, on the sociology of economic life, the sociology of politics, and the sociology and politics of developing areas with special reference to South Asia or Latin America. Subjects can be combined in many ways so as to suit those of varied tastes, abilities, and previous training.

Part II of the Tripos offers many opportunities to the undergraduate who in his last years at school specialized in mathematics, and finds the mathematical method of thought congenial – he will be able to use mathematical methods in many parts of economic theory, and he will learn how the methods of mathematical statistics can be applied in quantitative studies and will get an idea of the computational problems involved. Such a training is essential to anyone who wants to become a mathematical economist or econometrician, and is also of great value to anyone contemplating a career in industry which calls for programming, operational research, or the use of computers. This field of work offers full scope to the mathematical qualities of clarity and rigour, and provides a challenging range of new problems in applied mathematics.

But a previous training in mathematics is by no means the only approach to economics. Much economic theory and useful quantitative work in applied economics and statistics can be handled without specialized mathematical training. Moreover, problems of economic policy also involve political and moral criteria which are essentially qualitative in nature. There is need for historical and institutional knowledge, and the ability to weigh the pros and cons of problems for which purely mathematical solutions are inadequate. People with a variety of gifts and tastes can gain from – and contribute to – the study of both economics and economic history.

Students may wish to consider the possibility of specializing in the study of Sociology. By acquiring a knowledge of sociological theory and methods of social investigation the student who is interested in such problems as social class, political authority, the family, work groups in industry, etc., will learn to study these subjects with some precision. By comparing the working of these social institutions in different societies, he will come to have a broader perspective on his own society.

Whatever discipline the student may have followed when he takes Economics Part II he will be enabled to study one social science in depth and see how it is related to allied social sciences. He will learn to combine rigorous and abstract reasoning with an understanding of the problems of public policy. His judgement will be strengthened and he will acquire the habit of applying scientific methods to the analysis of social issues.

As in all other subjects, only a minority of those who read for the Economics Tripos go on to a career of academic teaching and research. There is, however, a growing number of specialized occupations available to graduates in the social sciences. Both in industry and the civil service economists are to an increasing extent employed in a professional capacity, while statisticians are employed in the civil service and in industry and commerce, where they are engaged in sales forecasting, marketing problems, the control of industrial processes, and so on. With the coming of high-speed computers, programming methods, and operational research techniques, a new field of specialized jobs has opened up. The development of market research and the increasing professionalization of social administration and personnel management provide new scope for the trained sociologist.

But the Economics Tripos is not designed just to produce academics or specialists. A large proportion of graduates in economics go into business, public administration, and professions such as accounting, where they can make use of the habits of thought they have acquired at the University. Experience shows that employers recognize the practical utility of a training in the social sciences, and young men and women with a good degree have no difficulty in obtaining interesting and well-paid jobs.

Copies of booklists may be obtained from Directors of Studies or from the Secretary, Faculty of Economics and Politics, Sidgwick Avenue, Cambridge, CB3 9DD.

Part I

Part I is taken at the end of the first year. The subjects are:

1, 2, and 3. Selected aspects of political economy

The topics on which questions are set are as follows:

(*a*) *Employment, wages, and price-levels:* Keynes' general theory and developments stemming from it, such as the multiplier and accelerator; classical, Marxian, and neo-classical theories of employment and wage-level determination; links between the theories and national income accounts, introduction to social accounts and the national income ('Blue Book'); simple ideas on fiscal management; elementary models of inflation (including, where relevant, their microeconomic aspects); a discussion of the empirical findings on the causes of inflation;

(*b*) *Money and credit:* introductory discussion of concepts such as money, interest, and credit, and their relationship to the determination of interest rates; essential features of the financial institutions of modern economies in so far as they are relevant to the theory of money and credit; the quantity theory of money and credit and the Keynesian theory; alternative theories of the determination of interest rates; an outline of the empirical evidence relating to these theories; data sources, monetary policy, and its relationship with fiscal policy;

(*c*) *The balance of payments and international monetary problems:* components of the balance of payments and how balance of payments tables are set up; introduction to data sources; economic significance of various types of changes in the figures; recent trends in U.K. balance of payments; concepts of balance of payments equilibrium under various systems of international payments; exchange-rate variations and other adjustment mechanisms; interactions between internal and external factors; current problems, prospects, and policies in international trade and finance; problems of international liquidity; the development of international institutions;

(*d*) *Economic growth:* introduction to classical and modern ideas about economic growth and income distribution; concepts and conventions in measuring real GDP and productivity; the comparative growth experience of different countries;

(*e*) *Income distribution and poverty:* measurement, theoretical explanations, and social and economic implications of various aspects of the distribution of income and wealth among persons and groups; redistribution of income by taxation and public expenditure; poverty and the efficacy of various measures for alleviating poverty.

All three papers are based on a common core of economic analysis applied to the specified topics; however, the emphasis of each of the papers differs, as follows:

Paper 1 emphasizes theoretical issues (and some questions may be set which require knowledge of the history of economic thought).

Paper 2 emphasizes the application of quantitative methods to these topics; candidates are expected to have experience in using *National Income and Expenditure* (the 'Blue Book') and are expected to bring with them a copy of the latest September issue of the *Monthly Digest of Statistics, Economic Trends Annual Supplement*, or any other publication specified by the Faculty Board from time to time. Candidates are expected to display knowledge of concepts and elementary quantitative methods for analysing problems relating to these topics, and to display ability to use specific statistical methods as follows: the use of tables, graphs, and frequency distributions in summarizing and organizing statistical data; summary measures of central tendency and dispersion, especially mean, median, mode, standard deviation, interquartile range, interquartile ratio, and coefficient of variation; Lorenz curves and their simple applications; the construction and economic interpretation of index numbers in common use with particular reference to the Index of Retail Prices and the Index of Industrial Production; analysis of association between variables with the help of scatter diagrams using both economic and social data.

Paper 3 stresses the influence of political and some sociological considerations on these and related topics. It is concerned with the interrelationship between the exercise of economic and political power, account being taken of conflicts of interest between, and the relative power of, different classes and groups in society, as well as the constraints imposed by the relationship between, and organization of, political and economic structures. It will consider the processes by which policies come to be formulated and the way in which employers' organizations, trade unions, the City, the military, the political parties, the media, and the bureaucracy of the State influence the decision-making process. It will analyse the role of the State in relation to employment and wage policy, international economic policy, the rate of economic growth and poverty.

4. British economic history

This paper is concerned with four main themes in the industrial development of Britain between 1750 and 1955: the industrial revolution, problems of growth and trade in the mature economy up to 1914, the slump and recovery of the inter-war years, and new directions for the U.K. economy in the ten years after the end of World War II; it also covers some of the demographic and social changes associated with this industrial development. The specific topics which are covered in the course of the analysis of the main themes include the long-run growth of output, productivity, and the standard of living; the costs of growth; demographic changes; capital accumulation and technical progress; entrepreneurship; foreign trade, the export of capital, and the role of the Empire; changes in the industrial structure; the labour market; government economic policies. In addition, an attempt is made to demonstrate the relevance of simple theories of economic growth and development to the study of the historical development of the British economy.

Economics Qualifying Examination in Elementary Mathematics

The examination, which will consist of a single paper lasting three hours, will be held on the second day of Full Easter Term and the Friday before the first day of Full Michaelmas Term. The standard required is lower than that for 'A' level mathematics. The paper will be set in three sections, A, B, and C.

Candidates will be examined in the use of those concepts, notations, and methods in elementary mathematics which are commonly employed by lecturers and writers on elementary economic principles and quantitative economics. Section A will consist of questions on numerical techniques, Section B of questions involving graphical presentation and Section C of questions on the correct interpretation of the kind of mathematics students may meet in lectures or textbooks. Questions in Section C will be given substantially more weight than those in Sections A and B, which will be weighted equally. Candidates will be expected to answer at least one question from each section. As a general guide, correct answers to four questions from Sections A and B together and one from Section C will be sufficient to enable candidates to pass the examination.

Candidates who are taking Part I of the Economics Tripos, but are certain that they will not wish to take Part II are not required to pass the E.Q.E.E.M., though they are advised to follow the lecture course.

The Faculty Board will grant exemption from taking the E.Q.E.E.M. to the following candidates for Part II of the Tripos:

(*a*) Those who have passed a G.C.E. examination at Advanced level in an approved mathematical subject. The subjects listed below* and approved for Matriculation purposes would be acceptable.

(*b*) Those who have passed an examination in Mathematics approved by the Tutor as of a standard broadly equivalent to or higher than G.C.E. Advanced level.

(*c*) Those who have obtained honours in Part I of another Tripos and are regarded as suitable to be candidates for Honours in Part II of the Economics Tripos without having taken the E.Q.E.E.M. Candidates who have taken Part I in Mathematics, Engineering, or Natural Sciences would clearly be suitable for exemption in this category, and exemption would also be appropriate for candidates who have taken 'non-mathematical' Part Is if the Tutor considered that the Long Vacation before starting Economics should be devoted to preparation for the Economics course rather than the E.Q.E.E.M.

(*d*) Affiliated students regarded as suitable to be candidates for

* (*a*) Mathematics *or* Elementary Mathematics *or* Pure Mathematics *or* General Mathematics.

(*b*) Additional Mathematics *or* Further Mathematics *or* Higher Mathematics *or* Mathematics and Theoretical Mechanics *or* Mathematics for Science *or* Applied Mathematics *or* Mathematics with Statistics.

(*c*) Mathematics (Pure and Applied) *or* Statistics *or* Commercial Mathematics (*c* may not be counted with *a* or *b*).

(*d*) Physics *or* Applied Physics *or* Applied Electricity and Heat.

(*e*) Engineering Science.

(*f*) Physics-and-Mathematics.

Honours in Part II of the Economics Tripos without having taken the E.Q.E.E.M.

In order to gain exemption under any of these headings a candidate's Tutor must submit a certificate to the Secretary of the Faculty Board, from whom blank certificates may be obtained.

The Faculty Board have provided that they shall waive the requirement to pass the E.Q.E.E.M. for candidates who have obtained honours in Part I of the Economics Tripos, and have failed to pass the E.Q.E.E.M., but are recommended by their Tutors for exemption.

In order to gain exemption under this heading a candidate's Tutor must submit a recommendation to the Secretary of the Faculty Board, from whom blank certificates may be obtained.

Part II

Part II is taken at the end of the third year, except that a candidate who has obtained honours in another Tripos may take it at the end of his fourth year.* Every candidate, except as provided below, must take

(*a*) Papers 1, 2, and 3, *and*

(*b*) *either* (i) three or four papers chosen from among Papers 4–18;†

or (ii) one or two papers chosen from among Papers 4–18, together with a dissertation on an approved topic within the field of any one of Papers 4, 5, 7–10, and 13–18 or within a field from among other fields which the Faculty Board shall specify from time to time;

provided that

(1) each candidate must offer at least one paper from among Papers 4–12 and 16–18 or a dissertation on an approved topic within the field of any one of Papers 4, 5, 7–10, and 16–18 or within one of the other fields specified by the Faculty Board;

* A candidate who takes the examination in the year next after he has obtained honours in another Tripos shall be exempt from taking the E.Q.E.E.M. and offer Papers 1 and 2 and not less than two nor more than three papers chosen from among Papers 3–18. If he offers three such papers his performance in the one in which the Examiners judge his work to be least good shall only be taken into account if that would be to his advantage.

† Until further notice Paper 18 will not be set.

and (2) a candidate offering under (*b*)(ii) only one paper together with a dissertation will not be allowed to submit a dissertation on a topic within the field of that paper.

The Examiners in drawing up the class-list give a dissertation double the weight given to each of Papers 4–18, except that if under (*b*)(ii) above a candidate offers two papers and a dissertation they may give the dissertation equal weight if that would be to the candidate's advantage.

If under (*b*)(i) above a candidate offers four papers, the paper of these four on which the Examiners judge the candidate's performance to be least good will be taken into account only if that would be to the candidate's advantage, provided that at least one of Papers 4–12 and 16–18 will always be taken into account.

If under (*b*)(ii) above a candidate offers two papers and a dissertation, the paper of these two on which the Examiners judge the candidate's performance to be less good will be taken into account only if that would be to the candidate's advantage; provided that account will always be taken of a paper if

either (*a*) the candidate's dissertation topic falls within the field of the other paper

or (*b*) the other paper is one of Papers 13–15 and the candidate's dissertation also falls within the field of one of Papers 13–15.[1]

The Faculty Board of Economics and Politics provide not later than 1 June each year a list of topics on which a dissertation may be submitted for the Tripos to be taken in the following year. Candidates may alternatively submit their own suggested topics for approval. A list of approved topics for the dissertation and details of the timetable and procedure for the submission of topics and of the dissertation are available from the Secretary, Faculty of Economics and Politics, Sidgwick Avenue, Cambridge, CB3 9DD.

[1] In considering their choice from among the alternative papers candidates should bear in mind that the number of alternatives is such that clashes between the times of lectures cannot be entirely avoided and that there will be clashes in connexion with the following combinations of papers:

(*a*) Paper 5 and Paper 17;
(*b*) Paper 6 and Paper 9;
(*c*) Paper 6 and Paper 16;
(*d*) Paper 7 and Paper 14;
(*e*) Paper 12 and Paper 9;
(*f*) Paper 12 and Paper 14;
(*g*) Paper 12 and Paper 16;
(*h*) Paper 12 and Paper 17.

Papers 13, 14 and 15 will clash with other optional papers.

The papers are:

1, 2, and 3. Economic principles and problems

These papers deal with the scope and method of economics, with fundamental ideas, and with the application of the methods of economic analysis to economic problems. The papers are designed to afford scope for the exercise of analytical power in abstract reasoning and in interpreting economic data. A few questions of a more advanced analytical character may be set, but the papers as a whole are so framed as to be within the competence of those who have not made a study of advanced methods of analysis. A main object is to test the power of candidates to apply their theoretical reasoning to actual problems. Candidates are, therefore, expected to show a general knowledge and understanding of the role of the Government in economic affairs and of the workings and effects of the principal economic institutions in the fields of production and distribution, of money and banking, international economics, of employment, labour and wage determination. Knowledge of the British economy is a basic requirement. Candidates should be able to analyse British problems in their international setting. Some questions will be asked about international economic problems and institutions, and about the problems of different types of economy. The questions set will not require such detailed knowledge as may be appropriate in Papers 4–10, but an understanding of general principles. In Paper 3 candidates are required to answer one question only. Candidates are free to take to the examination their own copy of *Economic Trends Annual Supplement* for any year or any other publication specified by the Faculty Board from time to time, and will be told in advance what other statistical source material, if any, will be provided.

4. Labour

This paper has the following subject matter:

analysis of labour markets in relation to the determination of wages, conditions of work, and the distribution of employment; the market demand for labour by firms and other organizations, and the supply of labour by households; job selection and hiring procedures; discrimination, wage and salary differentials, and their relationship with the distribution of income and poverty; the concept of human capital; the influence of education on social mobility and occupational recruitment; labour turnover and lateral mobility;

power in trade unions, and its effects on union policy and labour markets; general features of British trade unionism, compared with other national movements; types of unions, and trends in union structure, growth, amalgamations and the TUC internal government; the relation between formal constitutions and the actual distribution of power; the shop steward system: its relation to formal constitutions, and to union leaders and members, and to the management of firms; union policies on collective bargaining, earnings distribution, employment and restrictive practices; strikes and other forms of industrial conflict; current issues in industrial relations, including legal controls on unions, strikes, and the collective bargaining system; other types of Government intervention in the labour market;

the causes of changes in the money wage-level, with special reference to the role of trade unions, wage and price interdependency; prices and incomes policies, with special reference to pay policies, possibilities and problems in the light of experience in the U.K. and other countries.

Candidates are expected to be familiar with the main empirical characteristics of the British labour market, including important recent studies, but they may also be asked questions relating to other countries.

Candidates are encouraged to consider the theoretical and factual issues involved in this paper in the light of both economic and sociological techniques of thought.

In this paper some questions may be set which permit candidates to show capacity to interpret and handle statistical evidence.

5. Economic theory and analysis

In this paper questions are set of a more advanced character than in Papers 1, 2, and 3, and the emphasis rests on the theoretical aspects of economics. The paper provides opportunity for the use of analytical methods of various types, but is so framed, taken as a whole, as to be within the competence of those who have no knowledge of advanced mathematics.

6. Mathematical economics

Candidates for this paper are examined in those parts of economic theory where mathematical methods of exposition offer particular advantages, e.g. of lucidity, conciseness, and rigour. They are expected to use such methods in the discussion of particular economic theories and economic models. In particular, it is a feature of this way of theorizing that assumptions are to be clearly stated and their relation to conclusions made precise.

Some questions in this paper will be marked with an asterisk. Extra credit will be given for answers to questions with asterisks, and a candidate will not obtain a first-class mark on the paper unless he completes at least one starred question. Relatively little credit will be given for answers to parts of questions.

7. Banking and credit

The paper has the following subject matter:

The nature of money and liquidity; demand for money by households and firms; the banking system; composition of the money stock and methods of control over money and credit; portfolio selection behaviour – especially that of banks and other financial intermediaries; the term structure of interest rates; capital markets and the finance of investment; developments in world capital markets – the origins, growth, and effects of the Euro-dollar system; the implications of international financial flows for domestic monetary management and the exchange rate; intervention in domestic economic policies by the World Bank and the International Monetary Fund.

The objectives and instruments of monetary policies, including: implications for the financial efficiency of banks, both commercial and central, and other financial institutions; interconnexions between fiscal and monetary policies, and their mutual interaction with balance of payments and exchange rate policies.

The paper will require knowledge of the relevant theories, institutions, and recent events in the U.K. and the international financial system. Questions may be set relating to the practices of other countries.

In this paper some questions may be set which permit candidates to show capacity to interpret and handle statistical evidence.

8. Public economics

The paper has the following subject matter:

The structure and accounts of the public sector; the pattern of public expenditure and taxation; reasons for and against particular categories of public expenditure: 'public goods'; the role of taxes, charges, and subsidies in dealing with externalities; applications of cost benefit analysis in the public sector; public sector pricing and investment policy; methods of monitoring public expenditure and its efficiency; incidence of expenditure and taxes; a detailed study of the main categories of taxes levied on households and companies, and their comparative advantages; economics of the public debt and its management; interconnexions between fiscal and monetary policies.

The paper requires knowledge of the relevant theories, institutions, and recent events in the U.K. Questions may be set relating to the practices of other countries.

In this paper some questions may be set which permit candidates to show capacity to interpret and handle statistical evidence.

9. The economics of underdeveloped countries

This paper deals with the origins of underdevelopment and its changing character, with the factors which have led to differences in economic growth and structure and in income distribution and living standards in less developed market and socialist economies, and with the effects of different national and international policies designed to promote development. Candidates are expected to show familiarity with the theoretical issues involved, with the actual economic conditions, problems, and policies in a number of less developed countries, and with the impact of the socio-political environment in which such policies operate.

In this paper, some questions are set which give candidates an opportunity to make use, in writing their answer, of a brief amount of empirical data provided on the examination paper. Such questions are designed to test candidates' knowledge of development economics and do not require elaborate arithmetical or statistical computations. They carry no more weight than any other question. Candidates may be required to answer one of these questions, but in this event at least three such questions will be set.

10. Industry

This paper has the following subject matter:

the modern business enterprise: the firm seen as a social organization and as an economic decision-making unit; the sociology of large-scale organizations: theories of bureaucracy; the composition and behaviour of main social groups within the enterprise; technology and market in relation to the structure of management; the professional in the organization; conflicts within management systems;

the industrial worker: theories of alienation and involvement; workers' productive behaviour, responses to economic incentives, etc.; the distribution of power in the enterprise, methods of management control, and their effectiveness; the distribution of, and relationship between economic and political power in western capitalist societies; sociological aspects of ownership and control; the rise of the managerial 'class' and its ideologies;

implications of the internal organization and functioning of the enterprise for its economic performance; alternative behaviour hypotheses including profit-maximizing, utility-maximizing, and satisficing hypotheses; problems of testing these hypotheses; some of their theoretical implications for theories of the firm, including theories of the growth of firms, and of business concentration; the economic analysis of the transnational enterprise;

changes in the structure of British industry: goods and services, the location of industry, small and large firms; the role of vertical integration, diversification, and of research and development expenditure in the growth of firms; market structure, business behaviour, and market performance; barriers to entry, oligopolistic groupings etc.; the relationship between structure, behaviour, and performance: theory and empirical evidence; the Government and industry: alternative policy approaches to the problems of monopoly and competition; policy on restrictive practices and monopoly in Britain, and some international comparisons.

Candidates are encouraged to consider the theoretical and factual issues involved in this paper in the light of both economic and sociological techniques of thought. Opportunity is given to refer to the historical experience of different societies.

In this paper some questions may be set which permit candidates to show capacity to interpret and handle statistical evidence.

11. Applied economic and social statistics

This paper is set in two Parts: Part 1 of three hours' duration and Part 2 of four hours' duration. It does not require the use of any advanced mathematical methods nor are proofs or commitment to memory of formulae to be expected; it deals with the simpler ways in which statistical data and methods can assist in the study of economic and social problems. Candidates are expected to be familiar with, and to use where appropriate, shortened or approximate methods of calculation. Mathematical tables (including tables of logarithms) and a list of the more complicated statistical formulae are provided.

In the first Part of the paper the candidate is required to answer a number of questions relating to statistical methods and sources and their applications and to show knowledge in each of these areas. In the second Part he is required to answer one question only from a selection designed to test ability to combine the use of source books and statistical methods in answering a problem in applied economics or in other social sciences.

Candidates are expected to show a knowledge of each of the following:

(*a*) *Statistical Methods:*

(i) the use of tables, graphs, and frequency distributions in summarizing and organizing statistical data; summary measures of central tendency, dispersion and skewness; the construction and interpretation of index numbers;

(ii) the use of sample statistics; sampling distributions (large samples): sample mean, sample variance, difference between sample means, difference between sample proportions; sampling distributions (small samples from parent normal populations): difference between sample means where population variances are the same, ratio of sample variances;

(iii) an elementary treatment of point and confidence interval estimation and hypothesis testing: in each case, the sample statistics used are those enumerated in (ii);

(iv) chi-square hypothesis testing: goodness of fit of observed data to hypothetical distribution; independence of two-way classification;

(v) regression: statistical estimation of the classical linear regression model where errors are independently and normally distributed with common variance, sampling distributions of regression coefficients and correlation coefficients; estimation and hypothesis testing; extension of the classical linear regression model, including heteroscedasticity, autoregressive errors and errors in variables;

(vi) non-parametric testing; use of Kendall rank correlation coefficient (tau);

(vii) simpler methods of seasonal correction;

(viii) conduct and use of economic and social surveys.

(*b*) *Statistical Sources:*

The topics covered include national income and expenditure; the incomes and expenditures of firms and households; production; prices; overseas trade and payments; population and vital statistics; labour; households and families; education; housing; and crime. The major general source books of United Kingdom statistics and their use, especially the *Monthly Digest of Statistics, Economic Trends* (including the *Annual Supplement*), the *Annual Abstract of Statistics, National Income and Expenditure* ('Blue Book'), and such international source books as the *O.E.C.D. Main Economic Indicators*; how to seek more detailed statistical information not included in these general source books (e.g. in the *U.K. Balance of Payments*, in the *Family Expenditure Survey, The Census of Production, The Census of Population*).

(*c*) *Econometric applications:*

The candidates will be expected to show familiarity with major econometric studies in areas to be specified by the Faculty Board from time to time. The Board will also specify the particular studies to be covered. The candidates will be expected to show knowledge of the statistical and economic problems involved in analysis of economic issues in these areas.

Candidates will be required to cover the following areas and books and articles until further notice:

(i) Econometric studies of consumer behaviour with particular reference to the following:

S. J. Prais and H. S. Houthakker, *The Analysis of Family Budgets*, Chaps. 5–8; M. Friedman, *A Theory of the Consumption*

Function, Chaps. 3 and 4; J. E. Davidson, D. F. Hendry, F. Srba, and S. Yeo, 'Econometric Modelling of the Aggregate Time-Series Relationship between Consumers' Expenditure and Income in the United Kingdom', *The Economic Journal*, Dec. 1978.

(ii) Econometric studies of the behaviour of firms with particular reference to the following:

A. Singh and G. Whittington, 'The Size and Growth of Firms', *The Review of Economic Studies*, Jan. 1975; R. L. Marris and A. J. B. Wood (Eds.), *The Corporate Economy*, Appendices A and B, pp. 389–427.

(iii) Econometric studies of U.K. imports with particular reference to:

H. S. Houthakker and S. P. Magee, 'Income and Price Elasticities in World Trade', *Review of Economics and Statistics*, May 1969; T. S. Barker, (Ed.), *Economic Structure and Policy*, Chap. 7; R. D. Rees and P. R. G. Layard, *The Determinants of U.K. Imports*, Government Economic Service, Occasional Paper, No. 3, 1972.

(iv) Econometric studies of U.K. exports with particular reference to:

M. Panič and T. Seward, 'The Problem of U.K. Exports', *Bulletin of the Oxford Institute of Economics and Statistics*, Feb. 1966; D. Stout, *International Price Competitiveness, Non-Price Factors and Export Performance*, N.E.D.O., 1977; T. S. Barker (Ed.), *Economic Structure and Policy*, Chap. 6.

(v) Econometric studies of pricing behaviour with particular reference to:

K. J. Coutts, W. A. H. Godley, and W. D. Nordhaus, *Industrial Pricing in the United Kingdom*, Chaps. 2–4.

(vi) Econometric studies of investment behaviour with particular reference to:

D. W. Jorgenson, 'Econometric Studies of Investment Behaviour: A Survey', *Journal of Economic Literature*, Dec. 1971; P. J. Lund, 'The Econometric Assessment of the Impact of Investment Incentives', in A. Whiting (Ed.), *The Economics of Industrial Subsidies*, H.M.S.O.; M. Desai, *Applied Econometrics*, Chap. 6.

(vii) Econometric studies of output, productivity and employment with particular reference to:

Z. Hornstein, J. Grice, and A. Webb (Eds.), *The Economics of the Labour Market*, a Chapter by S. G. B. Henry; *Cambridge Economic Policy Review*, 1978, Chap. 3; W. A. H. Godley and J. R. Shepherd, 'Long-Term Growth and Short-Term Policy', *National Institute Economic Review*, Aug. 1964.

(viii) Macroeconometric models of the U.K. economy with particular reference to:

M. V. Posner, *Demand Management*, Chaps. 1–4 and 7; M. Desai, *Applied Econometrics*, Chap. 8.

(*d*) *Interpretation and Use of Statistics:*

Interpretation of the meaning and validity of statistical data; the use of statistics to assist in forming judgements about the course of events and in testing economic or sociological hypotheses. Considerable importance is attached to a candidate's performance in this aspect of the subject in both Parts of the examination.

12. The theory of statistics

Candidates for this paper are expected to show both an understanding of the theory of statistics and an ability to apply statistical methods to economic problems and to perceive the limitations and difficulties inherent both in data and methods. The use of slide-rules, calculators, and statistical tables is permitted in the examination.

The paper poses questions involving estimation, hypothesis testing, and forecasting primarily in the context of statistical models of particular use in economic and social studies: the models include multiple regression, multivariate regression and simultaneous equations models; particular emphasis is placed on such problems as serial correlation, errors in variables, and identification. In addition questions on such topics as Bayesian estimation and inference, the design and analysis of sample surveys, sequential sampling, and non-parametric procedures may be asked.

Candidates are expected to attempt not more than four questions. Relatively little credit is given for answers to parts of questions.

13. The sociology of economic life (Paper 16 of Part II B of the Social and Political Sciences Tripos)

14. The sociology of politics (Paper 15 of Part II B of the Social and Political Sciences Tripos)

15. A subject in the field of sociology and politics

Until further notice the subjects specified for this paper, from which candidates are required to select one, will be:

The sociology and politics of South Asia.

The sociology and politics of Latin America.

The subjects are respectively the subject specified for Paper In. 28 of the Oriental Studies Tripos, and Paper 43 of Part IIB of the Social and Political Sciences Tripos.

16. A subject in economic history

This paper is entitled 'Economic development of Russia from 1860 to the present day'. Topics covered include the Emancipation of 1861, the Stolypin reforms, collectivization and other changes in land holding and the position of the peasantry; the condition of agriculture and its interaction with the industrial sector; the growth of industry and the industrial labour force; the contribution to economic growth of foreign capital and foreign trade; the role of the state in promoting economic development; the economic and political aspects of the policy debates of the 1920s; the system of planning and administration of the Soviet economy as it has developed since 1929.

The paper will be divided into two parts. Section A will include questions mainly on the pre-1917 period, Section B will include questions mainly on the post-1917 period. Questions requiring knowledge of both periods may be included in either section or in both sections. Candidates will be required to answer at least one question from each section.

Questions may be set on the current period, but candidates are not expected to have a detailed knowledge of the changes in the Soviet economy after 1965.

17. A subject in economic history

This paper is entitled 'World Depression in the interwar years'. Its main focus is on the causes and courses of the Great Depression of the 1930s, but the events of the 1920s including the inflation and deflation of 1919–21 also receive attention. Topics covered include the transfer problem and international monetary arrangements, the growth of protection and the development of trading blocs, monopolistic tendencies and changes in income distribution, technology and structural changes, the agrarian depression, and the comparative experience of different countries with regard to unemployment, especially following the trough of the cycle.

The main countries considered are Britain, France, Germany, U.S.A., and Japan, but the paper is not exclusively confined to these, and, in particular, the experience of some of the main primary producing countries is also studied.

18. A subject in economic history

This paper will not be set until further notice.

The Preliminary Examination for Part II

The examination is taken at the end of the second year and consists of the following papers:

Papers 1 and 2. Economic principles

These papers are concerned with the theoretical groundwork of the topics covered in Papers 1, 2, and 3 of Part II of the Economics Tripos, with emphasis on tools of analysis and their use. In Paper 2 some questions are included which deal with the history of economic thought.

Each of these papers contains one question which involves candidates in manipulating simple 'mathematical' models. The mathematical competence required is not higher than that required in passing E.Q.E.M. The required manipulative element accounts for approximately one third of the total weight to be accorded the question as a whole. The remaining two thirds is accounted for by a discursive element (which does not rule out but does not require further 'mathematical' manipulation). In both Paper 1 and Paper 2 the 'mathematical' question is set as one half of an either/or combination where the alternative question is in the same subject area as the 'mathematical' question but does not have a required 'mathematical' element.

Paper 3. Economic development

This paper provides an introduction to basic concepts and theories in development economics and to their application to the comparative industrialization and development experience of selected countries. It is designed to provide a useful foundation for candidates proposing to take Part II specialist options in development economics or in economic history as well as to constitute a self-contained one-year course for those interested in studying this field but not necessarily planning to continue with it further.

The concepts and theories to be covered are: explanations for the origins of 'underdevelopment'; theories concerning the transformation of pre-capitalist economies; the concept and measurement of 'development'; theories concerning the evolution of both capitalist and socialist modes of production and economic organization; the role of such factors as international economic relations, state policies, technological change, population growth and socio-political structure in the above-mentioned processes.

The examination is in two sections. Section (1) includes purely theoretical questions. Section (2) requires candidates to relate their analyses about topics to comparative historical evidence from Japan, Russia, China and India during the periods covered in the lectures for this course. Candidates will be required to answer *one* question from Section (1) and *two* questions from Section (2).

Paper 4. Sociology

The scope of sociology. Basic sociological concepts and principles as seen in the analysis of: social stratification and mobility; population, community and family; political mobilization and political parties; social control and deviance; education and social structure; urbanization; religion; relations between economic activity and social organization in industrial and pre-industrial societies.

Paper 5. Economic and social statistics

This paper deals with the manner in which statistics contribute to the study of economic and social problems and to the discussion of issues of public policy. Its main purpose is to test the candidate's ability to analyse problems in applied economics and similar problems of a sociological type, by bringing to bear on them relevant economic or sociological theory, knowledge of statistical sources, and relatively simple statistical derivations. It does not require mathematical analysis.

The examination will consist of a four-hour paper which will be set in such a way that candidates will be required to answer two questions which directly test their ability to use statistical techniques, and one question of an applied economic or sociological character. The latter question will carry as much weight as the first two. Candidates are expected to be familiar with and to use, where appropriate, shortened or approximate methods of calculation. Numerical tables will be provided.

Statistical techniques

The specific statistical techniques covered by the syllabus are given below:

(*a*) *The use of tables, graphs, and frequency distributions* in summarizing and organizing statistical data; summary measures of central tendency; dispersion and skewness; the construction and interpretation of index numbers.

(*b*) *The use of sample statistics:* sampling distributions (large samples): sample mean, sample variance, difference between sample means, difference between sample proportions; sampling distributions (small samples from parent normal populations): difference between sample means where population variances are the same, ratio of sample variances.

(c) *An elementary treatment of point and confidence interval estimation and hypothesis testing:* in each case, the sample statistics used are those enumerated in (b).

(d) *Regression:* statistical estimation of two-variable models where errors are independently and normally distributed with common variance; sampling distributions of regression coefficients and correlation coefficients; testing of hypotheses; estimation and interpretation of multiple regression coefficients (candidates will not be expected to estimate multiple regression equations with more than three variables).

(e) *Methods of Social Accounting*, including an introduction to the concept of an input–output table.

(f) *Economic time-series:* identification of the 'trend' and 'seasonal' components of economic time-series on the basis of simple assumptions.

Statistical sources

Candidates will be expected to have had experience in using the *Monthly Digest of Statistics*, the *Annual Abstract of Statistics, National Income and Expenditure* (the 'Blue Book'), *Economic Trends* including the Annual Supplement, and the *Handbook of International Economic Statistics for Use with the Cambridge Economics Tripos*; they should also have had more limited experience in seeking for more detailed information, not included in these general source books, in the *General Household Survey*, the *Family Expenditure Survey*, the *U.K. Balance of Payments* and the *Census of Population.*

Paper 6. Mathematics for economists and statisticians

This paper deals with those portions of linear algebra, differential and integral calculus, differential and difference equations, probability theory, and statistics which are the principal mathematical groundwork of the subjects covered in Papers 6 and 12 of Part II of the Economics Tripos. In each of the four sections of the examination there are three questions labelled (a), (b), and (c). In each section questions are in ascending order of difficulty from (a) to (c). Candidates can pass the examination by answering correctly only questions labelled (a). Candidates can obtain progressively higher marks by answering correctly questions from harder categories.

Papers 1–4 and 6 are set for three hours each.

A candidate may offer all or any of the six papers specified above, provided that

(a) in order to be included in the list of candidates who have passed the examination

(i) a candidate who has previously taken Part I of the Economics Tripos shall offer Papers 1, 2, and 5, and at least one other paper chosen from Papers 3, 4, and 6;

(ii) a candidate who has previously taken a Tripos Examination in Mathematics, Natural Sciences, or Engineering shall offer Papers 1 and 2 and at least one other paper chosen from Papers 3, 4, and 5;

(iii) any other candidate shall offer Papers 1 and 2 and at least one other paper chosen from Papers 3, 4, 5, and 6.

(*b*) if a candidate wishes to offer fewer papers than required under (*a*) above, his entry is made in accordance with Regulation 4 for entries and lists of candidates for examinations.

(*c*) if a candidate offers more papers than the minimum required under (*a*) above, his performance in the additional paper or papers will be taken into account by the Examiners only if that would be to his advantage.

(*d*) a candidate who offers Paper 6 may, in addition, submit such written work done by him during the course leading to the examination as shall from time to time be determined by the Faculty Board, bearing, as an indication of good faith, the signatures of the teachers under whose direction the work was performed. In drawing up the class-list the Examiners shall take account of this written work only if that would be to the candidate's advantage.

Candidates may use battery-powered electronic calculators.

The Diploma in Economics

Candidature for the Diploma in Economics is open to any member of the University who has not been classed in Part II of the Economics Tripos.

A candidate for the Diploma must be admitted as a Graduate Student. The Board of Graduate Studies will fix the date of commencement of his candidature.

At least three terms must have been kept by any candidate before he is qualified to receive the Diploma. He must pursue his studies for the Diploma in Cambridge under the direction of a Supervisor appointed by the Degree Committee and under any special conditions that the Committee may lay down in his case.

Not later than the fourth, nor earlier than the first, term after the term of the commencement of his candidature the candidate must satisfy the Examiners for Part II of the Economics Tripos in three papers, chosen from among the papers of Part II of the Economics Tripos and Paper 3 of the Preliminary Examination for Part II of the Economics Tripos, provided that one paper must be chosen from among Papers 1, 2, 3, 5, and 9 of Part II of the Economics Tripos, and that no candidate may offer both Paper 3 and Paper 11 of Part II. Subject to the approval of the Degree Committee, candidates for the Diploma who take Paper 11 of Part II may be permitted to make a different choice of questions from that available to candidates for the Tripos. The choice of papers must be approved by the Degree Committee, and in the three papers judged together the candidate must reach at least the standard of the first division of the second class. The Examiners will make a written report on each candidate's work to the Degree Committee.

Not earlier than the division of the second term, nor later than the end of the fourth term after the term of the commencement of his candidature, the candidate for the Diploma must send to the Secretary of the Board of Graduate Studies a thesis or essay not exceeding fifteen thousand words on a subject previously approved by the Degree Committee; the thesis or essay may, by special permission of the Board, be submitted later than the fourth term after the term of commencement of candidature. This thesis or essay will be referred to an Examiner appointed by the Degree Committee, who will report on it to the Degree Committee, who will consider the reports of the Examiners of the papers and of the thesis and will decide whether the candidate shall be entitled to receive the Diploma.

A Graduate Student who has been given leave by the Board of Graduate Studies to count the period or any part of it during which he has been a candidate for the Diploma towards a course of research for the degree of Ph.D., M.Sc., or M.Litt. will not be entitled to be awarded the Diploma so long as he remains on the register of Graduate Students, nor if he subsequently proceeds to the degree of Ph.D., M.Sc., or M.Litt.

M.Phil. Degree (one-year)

This is a qualification gained for advanced course work.

(*a*) *M.Phil. in Economics*

The examination takes the form of a three-hour written paper or an 8,000 word essay, or a combination of a three-hour written paper and a 4,000 word essay on each of four topics on which the Faculty offers M.Phil. courses; in place of one of these topics the candidate may submit an 8,000 word essay on a subject of his own choice which has been approved by the Degree Committee. In 1984–85, M.Phil. courses will be offered on Political Economy (four courses), Mathematical Economics (two courses), Applied Economics (two courses), Econometrics and Applied Econometrics (one course), Industrial Economics (two courses), Development Studies (two courses), and Economic History (one course).

(*b*) *M.Phil. in the Economics and Politics of Development*

The examination takes the form of three three-hour written papers in (1) Theories of Development, (2) Sociology and Politics of Development, (3) Applied Economics for Development and either an 8,000 word essay on a subject of the candidate's own choice which has been approved by the Degree Committee or one course chosen subject to the approval of the Degree Committee from the courses offered in (*a*) above.

In place of the examination described above, a candidate may, by special permission of the Degree Committee, granted after considering the candidate's experience, special qualifications, and proposed topic, offer

(*a*) a thesis of not more than 25,000 words in length, including footnotes, tables, appendices, and bibliography, on a subject approved by the Degree Committee;

and (*b*) three essays, each of not more than 4,000 words in length, including footnotes, tables, appendices, and bibliography, on subjects approved by the Degree Committee and falling respectively within the following fields:

1. Theories of development.
2. Sociology and politics of development.
3. Applied economics for development.

Further details of the courses may be obtained from the Secretary of the Degree Committee, Faculty of Economics and Politics, Sidgwick Avenue, Cambridge, CB3 9DD.

EDUCATION

Introduction

The University of Cambridge is concerned with the following courses of study in the field of Education: (1) a one-year postgraduate course leading to the award of the Postgraduate Certificate in Education; (2) a two-year course for undergraduates and affiliated students leading to an Honours B.A. Degree with a Certificate in Education; (3) a two-year course, for students who have already completed two years of study at Homerton College, leading to the B.Ed. Degree; and (4) a one-year course leading to the M.Phil. Degree. There are also facilities for research and an opportunity for those who have already completed the Certificate in Education course at the University to submit work towards a Diploma in Education.

ONE-YEAR COURSE FOR THE POSTGRADUATE CERTIFICATE IN EDUCATION

Regulations for the granting of Qualified Teacher status to graduates make it necessary for all those graduating after 31 December 1973 to complete successfully a year of professional teacher training for a Certificate of Education. This means that new graduates cannot obtain appointments to teach in maintained schools in England and Wales without taking a Certificate course.

At the present time, many changes are taking place in schools, both in the social context and in new developments in curricula and teaching methods. Intending teachers need to be aware of the opportunities provided by these changes, and to be equipped to respond to them in a professional way. The Postgraduate Certificate course therefore seeks to combine the learning of practical teaching techniques with the analysis of contemporary professional practice and an introduction to related theoretical studies. Students follow one of three programmes within the course, according to the type of teaching they wish to undertake, as follows:

S1 :the teaching of **one** main subject (with subsidiaries) in secondary schools;

S2: the teaching of **two** subjects in secondary schools;

P: the teaching of children aged 7–11 in primary schools.

General

Each year about 280 graduate students in the Faculty read for the Postgraduate Certificate in Education. All students must be members of a College (or an Approved Society). Cambridge graduates are usually allowed to continue membership of their own College for this extra year. Details of the application procedures are given on p. 136.

Pattern of study

There are three major elements of the course:

1. The study of teaching methods;
2. General principles of educational practice;
3. School experience and teaching practice.

The Secondary School Programmes are described below, and the Primary School Programme is described on p. 134.

The Secondary School Programmes S1 and S2

1. The Study of Teaching Methods

This part of the course differs according to which of the two secondary programmes, S1 or S2, the student is following.

The S1 programme

On admission to the S1 programme each student joins a main subject 'Methods' group and may also attend a number of 'Subsidiary' subject courses. Work in Methods groups deals with all aspects of the teaching of particular school subjects including, for example, classroom organization and management, the subject as part of a school curriculum, techniques and problems of teaching and learning, preparation of appropriate teaching materials, assessment procedures etc. Each week, experienced serving teachers, acting as teacher-tutors, take part in Methods sessions.

The main school subjects offered in the S1 programme are: Biology, Chemistry, Classics, English, Geography, History, Mathematics, Modern Languages, Physics, Religious Studies.

Applicants need to decide which of these main subject Methods groups they wish to enter. They are normally expected to have a degree qualification in their teaching subject which will enable them to cover the full range of secondary work up to University entrance standard. Applications from graduates in subjects related to the teaching subjects shown will be considered. It is not possible to change from one Methods group to another at any time after acceptance, without reapplication.

Modern Languages specialists should offer two languages, one of which must be French or German. Those who have not had a substantial period of residence abroad in the country of their major language (e.g. as an English Assistant or as a student at a foreign university) will not normally be considered. Russian and Spanish may be offered only as subsidiary subjects.

The *Classics* Methods course includes the teaching of Latin, Greek, Classical Studies and Ancient History. Classical Studies graduates may apply but should normally have Latin to at least A-level standard.

All *Science* specialists, whether they join the Biology, Chemistry or Physics Methods groups, also attend a Combined Science course. This caters for anyone who may teach combined or integrated science and is available as a subsidiary to non-scientists.

Subsidiary Courses. In addition to training for the teaching of their main subjects, students have the opportunity to attend subsidiary courses in the teaching of other subjects. The subsidiary courses most frequently offered include: Humanities, Combined Science, Mathematics, Computer Studies, French/German, Latin, Religious Studies, Games. Russian and Spanish are also available to students taking Modern Languages as their main subject.

The choice of subsidiary subjects should be discussed at the beginning of the year with both the main Methods and the subsidiary subject lecturers. Entry restrictions apply to certain subsidiary subjects; for example, some are only available to students taking particular main subjects, while others require relevant qualifications as a condition of entry.

Additional Courses and Activities open to all Students

Throughout the year all students are given the opportunity to acquire skills in educational technology (including, for example, TV and audio recording, graphics and display and the use of film, slide and overhead projectors) and some 'hands-on' experience with microcomputers. It is intended that all students will gain some appreciation of the use of microcomputers in education during the course. Other activities for interested students may include movement and drama, speech training, outdoor pursuits and special lectures.

The S2 programme

The work falls into two parts. Some of a teacher's skills are specific to particular subjects, and these skills are dealt with in **subject methods** courses. Other skills, such as those of classroom management and interaction, non-verbal communication and the use of questioning, are of more general application; these are dealt with in a course of **professional preparation.**

Students choose **two** subject methods courses. The first teaching subject receives slightly greater emphasis than the second. Subjects are chosen from the following groups (not more than **one** course may be chosen from the same group):

A: Mathematics, French, Biology.
B: Physics, Music, Drama.
C: Religious Studies, Chemistry.
D: English, Physical Education.

The following restrictions apply:

Drama and Physical Education are available only as second teaching subjects.

Students who take English as their first teaching subject must take the linked second subject of Drama.

Drama is only available to students who take English as their first teaching subject.

Science students must choose either a second science or Mathematics.

Students may normally only choose a subject as their second teaching subject if their degree contains some element of that subject, or if they have studied the subject at least to A-level. In the case of Drama, previous study is not required. Physical Education requires some expertise in at least one game. For Religious Studies, subjects such as Anthropology, History, Philosophy, or Sociology are acceptable as an alternative to Theology.

Further details of the entry qualifications for first and second teaching subjects in the S2 programme may be obtained from the Registrar, Homerton College.

2. General Principles of Educational Practice

The principles of educational practice, which form the general theoretical background to the practical side of the **S1** and **S2** programmes, are taught in various ways:

Situations. These sessions occur during the Michaelmas Term. Students take part in discussion, simulations or role-play exercises, in interdisciplinary groups with a member of staff attached to each. Each session presents a situation which might be encountered by a student or probationary teacher and considers possible courses of action. Readings are provided for each session. The topics covered include the motivation of pupils, classroom discipline, the assessment of pupils' work and ability, language in the classroom, curriculum issues, relationships between teachers and parents, values and bias in the classroom, the role of the teacher in school and community.

Themes. Each theme is a presentation of a major topic in education, such as discipline, and is linked with a particular 'Situation'.

Core Course. In the Easter Term all students spend one morning per week in intensive study of a topic of particular concern in education, e.g. the curriculum, selection and equality, education in a multi-cultural society. There is also a course on the teaching of slow learners and gifted children.

Special Topics. In the Easter Term, each student chooses two options from a list of Special Topics, which varies from year to year but which usually consists of over twenty titles. The time allocated to each Special Topic allows for study in some depth. Examples of the Topics which may be available are: the adolescent in school, moral education, education in a multi-racial society, simulation in the classroom, social class and education, educational technology, aspects of comparative education, developments in educational assessment, society and education in a particular historical period, schools and industry.

3. School Experience and Teaching Practice

There are three elements of school experience and teaching practice in the course.

Preliminary experience in a primary or secondary school

Students are expected to undertake a two-week period of school experience before the course begins. Students on the **S1** programme spend this time in a maintained primary school, students on the **S2** programme in a maintained comprehensive school. Students arrange their preliminary school experience through their own Local Education Authority, although pre-printed letters are provided for the purpose by the Faculty. Each student is provided with an observation guide which gives a clear indication of what to look for and find out about the school.

Work in schools in the Michaelmas Term

During the Michaelmas Term there are frequent opportunities to visit schools and to work with children. Wherever possible, students are encouraged to participate in lessons and discuss them with experienced teachers.

At least one visit is made to the school in which the student will undertake the main teaching practice.

Main teaching practice

The main practice, lasting a full school term, begins after Christmas, at the beginning of the school term. Each student is supervised by a member of the school staff who will help, advise and arrange a programme to include time for preparation and regular discussion of work. Lecturers from the Faculty visit all students during the term.

The Primary School (P) Programme

1. The Study of Teaching Methods

This course prepares students as generalist teachers of children in the 7–11 age-range.

The course covers generalizable teaching skills, such as classroom management, the use of individual, group and class methods and group interaction. Students consider the role of questioning and discussion techniques. In studying lesson planning, particular attention is paid to objectives, organization of material and methods of evaluation.

All students take a course in the development of reading skills and courses which introduce different ways in which children explore their world. These include the study of: English, Drama, Mathematics, Geography, History, Art, Music, Physical Education, Religious Education, Science.

Opportunities are provided for taking part in thematic work which integrates several of these areas and students are also given the opportunity to consider the place of the microcomputer in primary education.

2. General Principles of Educational Practice

During the Michaelmas Term and the first part of the Lent Term, major **themes** concerned with schools and teaching with particular reference to the junior age-range are presented. Topics include the task of the teacher, the nature of abilities, personality, language in the classroom, social relationships, children with special needs. Whenever possible, these are considered in a multi-cultural context. These topics are related to **situations** which are commonly encountered by students beginning teaching. Regular discussions take place and each session is supported by readings and by regular weekly work in school.

Special Topics during the Michaelmas and Lent Terms focus on sociological and philosophical ideas relevant to decision-making in the primary school.

3. School Experience and Teaching Practice

Preliminary school experience

Students are expected to undertake a two-week period of school experience in a maintained primary school before the course begins. Students arrange this through their own Local Education Authority, although pre-printed letters are provided for the purpose by the Faculty. Each student is provided with an observation guide which gives a clear indication of what to look for and find out about the school.

Work in schools during the Michaelmas Term

For most of the term students spend one morning each week working with children in a local school. They prepare programmes of work in English and Mathematics for small groups of children and, at the end of the series of visits, have an opportunity to engage in a collaborative project which may take the form of a play or some other presentation to the other children in the school.

Teaching practice

All primary students undertake two periods of teaching practice, each of approximately half a term, the first in the Lent Term, the second during the Easter Term. The period between these practices provides a time of reflection and further preparation in curriculum subject areas.

Each student works closely under the supervision of a member of the school staff and, in addition, is advised by a Faculty supervisor.

Postgraduate Certificate Examination

The assessment of the course is based on a combination of submitted work, a written examination paper and the assessment of performance in the teaching practice. The examination has the following three Sections:

Section I. Educational Theory

(*a*) a three-hour paper dealing with the principles of educational practice, based on the Situations and Themes course and other general courses given during the year. The paper for those who follow the primary programme is similarly based but set on a syllabus different from that taken by students who have followed the secondary programmes;

(*b*) two long essays (or equivalent pieces of work) on subjects from the two Special Topics in educational theory which have been chosen for study.

Section II. Course work on teaching methods

(*a*) one or two pieces of submitted work;

(*b*) an assessment of the student's contribution to the courses in teaching methods.

Section III. Practical teaching

Assessment by the Examiners on the basis of teaching practice reports from the schools concerned and from lecturers supervising the practice.

For those who fail in any Section of the examination, re-examination is possible on not more than two occasions subject to the permission of the Faculty Board and under conditions set in each case by the Faculty Board and the Examiners. Re-examination must normally take place within two years of the initial failure. A candidate failing in practical teaching is normally required to take a full school term of teaching practice in a subsequent academical year.

Award of the Certificate

The award of the Postgraduate Certificate in Education of the University of Cambridge is made to candidates who diligently attend and satisfactorily complete the course, and who satisfy the Examiners in Section III and in the examination as a whole. Such candidates may be recommended to the Department of Education and Science for the grant of Qualified Teacher Status. Students of exceptional merit may be awarded a pass with distinction.

Admission to the Course

The course is open to graduates of Cambridge and of other U.K. universities and to applicants with equivalent qualifications. In order to be admitted to the course, students must also hold G.C.E. O-Level passes in Mathematics and English Language, or equivalent qualifications. (For G.C.E. examinations taken in June 1975 or thereafter, a pass is regarded as Grade A, B or C.)

Full details of the application procedure are available in the Faculty of Education's P.G.C.E. prospectus, available on request from the Assistant Secretary of the Department of Education, 17 Trumpington Street or from the Registrar, Homerton College, from whom Faculty application forms are also available.

All applicants, whether from Cambridge or from other universities, are required to register their application with the Graduate Teacher Training Registry (G.T.T.R.). Full details are given in the P.G.C.E. prospectus, but applicants should note that applications will not be considered until the Faculty application forms, G.T.T.R. forms and references have all been received. As well as being accepted by the Faculty of Education, students must also be accepted by a College before being offered a place on the course. It is not, however, necessary to make a separate application for a College place. Students will not normally be accepted without interview.

Grants

Similar procedures apply in obtaining grants for the course as for undergraduate grants. Students will be told how to go about obtaining the grant once they are offered a place on the course. Arrangements can be made for students who are unable to obtain grants to enter as private students. Details of fees involved are supplied on request. The University fee is the normal undergraduate University Composition Fee. Colleges also charge fees, normally at their undergraduate rate.

Term dates and residence

The P.G.C.E. course has different official term dates from those of the University Full Terms, and the dates for the primary programme differ from those of the secondary programmes.

Secondary (S1 and S2). The Michaelmas (Autumn) and Easter (Summer) Terms are the same as the University Full Terms. The whole of the Lent (Spring) Term is spent on teaching practice in schools. The Lent Term is longer than Full Term, usually by a period of three or four weeks, the extension covering school term dates in most cases.

Primary (P). The Michaelmas Term is the same as the University Full Term. Students spend two periods, each of about half a term, on teaching practice. These periods fall in the latter part of the Lent and Easter Terms, and in each case the term extends beyond Full Term.

Term dates for 1984/85 are as follows: S1 and S2 programmes: 9 October–7 December (Michaelmas), 7 January–29 March (Lent), 16 April–7 June (Easter). **P** programme: 9 October–7 December (Michaelmas), 14 January–29 March (Lent), 16 April–21 June (Easter).

Students are expected to comply with Faculty and College requirements for residence.

TWO-YEAR EDUCATION TRIPOS COURSE (B.A. AND B.ED. DEGREES)

The course, which is at Part II stage, is open to two groups of students: firstly, undergraduates who have completed two years of study and have passed their Part I examinations, and affiliated students who already hold degrees from other universities. These students proceed to the B.A. Degree with a Certificate in Education. Secondly, students matriculated by Homerton College who have already undertaken two years' work in the College and who proceed to the B.Ed. Degree.

Both groups of students follow similar courses and are taught together, with the exception of certain courses specially arranged for B.A. students in the Michaelmas Term. Both groups take the same examinations – Qualifying Examination in Education at the end of the first year, and Education Tripos at the end of the second year. Students entering the course are required to have passed O-level English Language and Mathematics.

The aim of the course is to provide for those who intend to follow careers in Education, many as teachers but others in educational administration, counselling and guidance or educational research. The arrangements for the Tripos seek to make it possible for all students to follow a coherent, sustained course in which professional training and the study of educational theory are integrated and in which there is an opportunity to carry further the study of a subject other than education.

The course covers the main Sections of the examination and assessment in practical teaching. The examinations and their Sections as they will be for the academical year 1984–85 are set out below. However, changes in the structure of the course are under consideration which, if agreed, would affect those entering the first year of the two-year course in October 1985.

Qualifying Examination in Education (taken at the end of the first year)

This examination comprises three Sections:

Section I. Curriculum Study. Assessment is made of course work carried out on the teaching of a particular subject (or area of curriculum) or specific age-range of children. There are four assignments, which relate to courses taken during the year. In selecting their courses for this Section, candidates choose from one of three 'programmes' as follows:

A. for those intending to teach in junior schools (7–11). Special arrangements are necessary for B.A. candidates who may seek to take this. As much notice as possible should be given;
B. for those intending to teach more than one subject to pupils aged 9–13;
C. for those intending to teach their particular subject at secondary level.

Section II. Each candidate takes two two-hour papers chosen from the four courses whose details are as follows:

Paper 1. Psychology of Education

The paper is concerned with the following psychological aspects of the growth of understanding.

Growth and Structure of the Intellect. The nature and description of human cognitive abilities; patterns of cognitive growth and development; ways in which an understanding of cognitive growth might affect educational decisions.

Developmental Psycholinguistics. Language acquisition, understanding and use, language and cognition; models of interaction, assumptions and realities; learning, memory and language; language and the grasp of ideas.

Cognitive Styles. Individual and cultural differences; recent work on cognitive styles.

Paper 2. Philosophy of Education

Learning and Teaching. The major concepts associated with teaching and learning: e.g. learning, teaching, conditioning, training, instructing, learning by discovery, learning by discussion; logical and psychological aspects of learning and teaching; teacher–learner relationships.

Aims and Content of the Curriculum. The aims and objectives of the curriculum and their foundations in theory of knowledge and philosophy of mind; social and individual factors in curriculum design; choice and compulsion in the curriculum; curriculum integration and subject disciplines.

Paper 3. Sociology of Education

Culture and community. An introduction to concepts used in the study of culture and community: culture and sub-culture, culture and values, counter culture, youth culture.

Selected case studies. A consideration of British studies of local communities with particular reference to educational provision within them: Community Development Projects; Educational Priority Areas.

Relations between local and school cultures. Cultural and linguistic deprivation; culture of poverty; cultural difference and bi-culturalism; cultural imposition.

The economic bases of community and culture. The nature of the relationship between school and work; schools and urban development.

Paper 4. History of Education (specified periods)

The period specified for examination in **1985** is:

Education and Social Change in England from 1900–1965

English society and the context of educational change. Schooling in 1900: the divided pattern, elementary and secondary provision. Their growth and articulation, 1900–1940; selection and the educational process; the birth of the tripartite system. The Second World War and reconstruction; 1944 and conservative reform; the classical period of selectionism. The growth of the comprehensive idea; its acceptance, 1965. Independent and progressive schools. Higher education. The education of girls. Social change and educational opportunity, 1900–1965.

Section III. Each candidate normally offers two papers in one or two of the subjects in the schedule listed below. Details of the papers which may be offered are published a year before the examination. This notice will indicate where a dissertation may be substituted for a paper.

Schedule of subjects:

Archaeology and Anthropology (Archaeology)*
Classics
Economics
Engineering*
English
Geography
History
History of Art
Mathematics
Modern and Medieval Languages (French, German,† Italian,† Russian,† Spanish†)
Music
Natural Sciences (Biology,[1] Chemistry, Physics, History and Philosophy of Science)
Social and Political Sciences
Theology and Religious Studies

Education Tripos

The examination comprises three Sections:

Section I. Curriculum Study

Candidates will offer one paper (of three hours) or a dissertation on the teaching of a particular subject (or area of curriculum) or specific age-range of children, together with a piece of submitted work.

Section II. Educational Theory

Candidates will offer one advanced paper (of three hours) or a dissertation in the same subject as one of those offered in Educational Theory for the Qualifying Examination the previous year.

Paper 1. Psychology of Education

The development of personality. Theories and assessment of personality; temperament and the development of personality; personality and school attainment in childhood and adolescence.

Social psychology. Attitudes and values; group influences on the individual; social interaction and the school.

Language and cognition. Language acquisition, including the nature of first language skills, 'stages' in linguistic development, language environment factors, communicative competence; the involvement of language with intellectual development, including specific learning disabilities and the notion of operating a language.

* Candidates may not offer two papers in this subject.
† By special application.
[1] Biology includes animal biology, biology of cells, environmental biology, biology of organisms, and plant biology.

The shaping of intelligent behaviour with particular reference to: intelligence, creativity, cognitive styles, the growth and development of a particular concept or of thinking in a particular subject area.

Paper 2. Philosophy of Education

Education and values. The nature of values and their relationship with education: subjectivity, objectivity, interest, worthwhileness; education in values: moral education, political education, aesthetic education; problems in teaching values: neutrality, impartiality, commitment, indoctrination.

Participation and control in schools. Accountability between schools and the wider community; authority and responsibility in the classroom and the school; decision-making in schools; co-operation and competition; discipline, rules, and punishment.

The paper shall also contain questions on special topics of which notice will be given in the Michaelmas Term preceding the examination. One of these topics will normally have been studied.

Paper 3. Education, Society and the State

Education in industrial societies. Theoretical and conceptual alternatives for understanding the place of education in industrial societies. Reference to the 'founding fathers' of Sociology with discussion of more recent developments and later alternatives to their work in considering the relationship between educational and wider social systems. Post-Marxist, Weberian and Durkheimian methods of understanding the economic, political and cultural–ideological influences on schooling. Current understanding of schools as institutions of legitimation, domination and reproduction.

The paper will also contain questions on special topics of which notice will be given in the Michaelmas Term preceding the examination. One of these topics will normally have been studied.

Topics in 1985 are expected to be:

(*a*) the sociology of school deviance.
(*b*) educational policy and provision.
(*c*) community education.
(*d*) the sociology of the teaching profession.

Paper 4. Education and Society in Victorian Britain: issues and evidence

Popular, secondary, and higher education: assumptions and attitudes, resources, state intervention and private endeavour.

Section III

In this section there are three options. In each option the candidate may offer a paper or a dissertation. The three options are as follows:

(*a*) the Educational Theory subject offered in Section II of the Qualifying Examination which is not being offered in Section II of this examination (listed above);

(*b*) a subject in Educational Theory chosen from subjects specified by the Faculty Board which are in addition to those available in the first year of the course.

(*c*) one of the subjects offered by the candidate for Section III of the Qualifying Examination provided it is included in the list of subjects approved for this purpose.

The subjects specified in 1984–85 for Section III(*b*) are:

Paper 5. Comparative Education: Area Studies

Theory and practice of Communist education. The section will be mainly concerned with Marxist educational ideas and their practical applications as seen in the educational institutions of socialist countries, and will deal with the period from the Communist Manifesto to the present with references to influences from, and developments within, other pre-Marxist and Marxist 'schools' and periods. Among the topics on which questions may be set will be: the principle and practice of the polytechnical school in the U.S.S.R. and *one* other Communist country; the theory of the 'collective' and the formation of the Communist personality; the control and administration of education; the preparation of teachers; the curriculum in the U.S.S.R. and at least one other Communist country.

Wherever relevant, an awareness of the political, social, historical, and economic background, and of parallel problems of education in Britain, will be expected.

Paper 6. Quantitative Methods of Investigation in Education

Basic statistical techniques; test construction; research design and criticism; use of computer-assisted analysis.

Candidates for this paper will be required to submit course work.

School experience and teaching practice

Before the course starts, B.A. students undertake a two-week period of observation in a school. During their first year, they have opportunities for observation in schools. Before the beginning of the final year all students undertake a one-week period of school experience (a mixture of observation and teaching). This is carried out in the school in which the main teaching practice takes place. The main practice occupies most of the schools' autumn term (irrespective of University Term dates).

Award at the end of the course

A student who has obtained honours in the Tripos, and is qualified to proceed to the B.A. Degree, receives a Certificate in Education, if he has satisfied the Examiners in practical teaching ability. This is the recognised qualification for teaching. Students who have qualified for the B.A. Degree and the Certificate in Education are recommended to the Department of Education and Science for the award of Qualified Teacher Status, provided they satisfy the conditions in force at the time.

Candidates from Homerton who are classed in the Education Tripos and satisfy the Examiners in practical teaching proceed to the Honours B.Ed. Degree, a recognised qualification for teaching.

Enquiries and Admissions

For Cambridge undergraduates, enquiries and applications should be directed through College Tutors, but any interested students can obtain further preliminary information from the Secretary of the Department of Education at 17 Trumpington Street. Early application during an undergraduate's second year is advised.

The course leading to the B.A. Degree and Certificate in Education is open to affiliated students (see p. 137).

Applicants for the B.Ed. Degree should approach Homerton College.

Grants

Candidates for the B.Ed. Degree – the two-year Education Tripos course is the second half of a known four-year course and is, therefore, covered by initial grant.

Candidates for the B.A. Degree – in order to qualify for an award from a Local Education Authority for the course, undergraduates at Cambridge must obtain the written permission of their College Tutor to the transfer onto the Education Tripos course by 31 October of their second year of undergraduate study. They must also, by the same date, inform their Local Education Authority of their intention to transfer.

Affiliated Students – grants are awarded at the discretion of their Local Education Authority, but most Local Education Authorities are reluctant to support students who wish to work at undergraduate level for a second 'first' degree.

ONE-YEAR COURSE FOR THE M.PHIL. DEGREE

The Faculty of Education offers a one-year advanced course leading to the award of the M.Phil. Degree. The examination is by a combination of a thesis (not exceeding 15,000 words in length) on an approved topic and submitted essays.

In 1984–85, M.Phil. courses will be offered in Curriculum Design and Organisation, Mathematical Education, and The Psychological Investigation of Intellectual Development. Regulations have also been approved for a course in Moral and Religious Education, but this will not be available in 1984–85.

Further details of the courses and of entrance requirements may be obtained from the Secretary of the Department of Education, 17 Trumpington Street, Cambridge CB2 1PT.

RESEARCH IN EDUCATION

Applications are welcomed from those who wish to carry out research in Education for the M.Litt., M.Sc., or Ph.D. Degrees, which are degrees by dissertation.

The research interests of members of the teaching staff of the Faculty available to supervise research include developmental psycholinguistics; classroom interaction; curriculum development, planning and evaluation; education in certain overseas countries; analysis and evaluation of teaching; moral and social education; mathematical education; philosophy of education; social psychology in relation to education; sociology of education; history of education; urban education. Enquiries about other subjects should, however, be made as it may be possible to arrange the necessary supervision. Acceptance of a candidate for research will be dependent on the availability of suitable facilities and of specialist supervision in Cambridge.

Applicants are advised to write first of all to the Secretary of the Department of Education, 17 Trumpington Street, Cambridge,

CB2 1PT, who will provide further details of the application procedure and refer the enquiry to an appropriate member of staff. Formal application for admission is made through the Board of Graduate Studies and as part of the application for those intending research candidates are required to submit a statement of about 1,000 words outlining the nature of their research. Further details are given in the Graduate Studies Prospectus which may be obtained from the Secretary of the Board of Graduate Studies, 4 Mill Lane, Cambridge, CB2 1RZ.

UNIVERSITY DIPLOMA IN EDUCATION

Graduates who have completed a course of study in the Department of Education since 1952, and have received the Certificate in Education or the Postgraduate Certificate in Education, are eligible without further residence as candidates for the University Diploma in Education. They must write a thesis of 15,000–20,000 words on an approved topic in the field of Education. Those graduates who obtained a Certificate in Education from the University of Cambridge Education Syndicate in or before 1951 should consult the Secretary of the Degree Committee of the Faculty of Education as to their eligibility.

At least one year from the award of the Certificate in Education must have elapsed before a topic is proposed, and at least two years before a thesis is submitted.

The full regulations may be obtained on application to the Secretary of the Degree Committee, 17 Trumpington Street, Cambridge, CB2 1PT.

ENGINEERING

There are in this subject courses of study which may be followed by candidates for:

The *Engineering Tripos*, which is divided into three Parts, Part IA, Part IB, and Part II.
The *Electrical Sciences Tripos*, which is not divided into Parts.
The *Production Engineering Tripos*, which is divided into two Parts, Part I and Part II, with a Certificate in Manufacturing Technology.
The *degree of M. Phil. in Soil mechanics.*
The *degree of M.Phil. in Control engineering and operational research.*
Certificates of Post-graduate Study in Engineering.

Professional engineers may be employed in one of several fields (for example: aeronautical, chemical, civil, control, electrical, information, mechanical, nuclear, or production engineering) and their work may be in design, development, research, production, management, or sales. Before they can acquire the necessary specialist knowledge they must follow a course in the basic elements of engineering science. This begins at school, with mathematics and physics as the essentials, and may be continued in the Engineering Tripos at Cambridge.

In Parts IA and IB of the Engineering Tripos, covering the first two years of study, the student continues his study of applied mathematics. His knowledge of applied physics is developed, but emphasis is placed upon applications of direct importance to the engineer: electricity, magnetism and electronics with their application to the design of electrical machines, circuits, and control mechanisms; the strength and properties of materials and the analysis and design of structures in which they may be used; thermodynamics and its utilization in the design of engines for power production, as well as refrigeration; the application of mechanics to the design and manufacture of machinery; and fluid mechanics and its use in civil engineering as well as the design of aircraft, engines, and machines. This general course is taken by all Cambridge engineering undergraduates, but some specialization is provided within Part IB. It is important to note that the student entering the Department is not immediately required to make the choice of his specialist field of engineering (e.g. civil, mechanical, or electrical).

Following this wide-ranging course in engineering science given in Parts IA and IB, the student may take Part II of the Engineering Tripos or the Electrical Sciences Tripos, each of which is for one year. The student may also take the Production Engineering Tripos or the Chemical Engineering Tripos (details on p. 79) both of which last for a further two years. Advanced courses are offered in Part II of the Engineering Tripos, and in the Electrical Sciences Tripos. The student is required to concentrate on a few subjects and to study these in depth. He may specialize entirely in a major engineering field such as aeronautical, civil, electrical or mechanical engineering, or management studies, but alternatively he may opt to take papers in a variety of subject areas depending on his interests and abilities.

The Production Engineering Tripos provides the student with opportunity for extended study of manufacturing technology, design and production management. It is normally taken after reading Parts IA and IB of the Engineering Tripos and is itself in two parts covering two years of study. Much of the final year of this Tripos, that is the fourth year as an undergraduate, is spent carrying out projects in manufacturing industry.

Experimental laboratory work and computing are important parts of the undergraduate courses in engineering, as is training in engineering drawing, which is a vital means of communication for the professional engineer.

At the Post-Graduate level the Department offers advanced courses as well as opportunities for Research. A one-year Advanced Course in Production Methods and Management provides an introduction to the procedures and problems of production and management in industry. About three-quarters of this course takes place in industrial firms throughout the United Kingdom, and much of the time is spent in project work. One-year courses leading to the M.Phil. Degree are available in Soil Mechanics, in Control Engineering and Operational Research and from October 1985 in Computer Speech and Language Processing; in each of these lecture courses are examined in the Lent Term and a major research project is then undertaken.

Most areas of Engineering research are pursued in the Department. The majority of research students are registered for the Ph.D. Degree which provides an extensive training in research and is expected to take three years. Some students register for the M.Sc. which is expected to take two years or for the Certificate of Post-Graduate Study which is for one year. Many students also register for the Ph.D. Degree after completing the M.Phil. or Certificate of Post-Graduate Study, the time spent on these courses counting towards the three years required for the Ph.D.

Entrants to Post-Graduate courses and research degrees come from many British and Overseas Universities. Those who received their Undergraduate training in the Department often spend a period in industry before returning to academic work.

It should be emphasized that academic training is only part of the education of a professional engineer. Even with a research degree, a graduate cannot become a chartered engineer or a corporate member of a professional engineering institution without a period of practical experience in a responsible position.

The Engineering Tripos

The Engineering Tripos consists of three Parts, Part IA, Part IB, and Part II. During the first year all students follow similar courses, which lead to Part IA at the end of the year. At the end of the second year candidates for the Part IB Examination in 1985 will take a range of subject papers plus either a paper in Drawing and Design (General Option) or a special paper in Electricity (Electrical Option). From 1986 all candidates for PartB I will take five papers and two more chosen from a group of four.

A student who has obtained honours in Part IB or in another Tripos may take Part II in his third or fourth year.

The class-lists for each Part are arranged in three classes of which the second is divided into two divisions.

Full details of the examinations including those for the Electrical Sciences Tripos and Production Engineering Tripos are given below together with information about workshop qualifications and professional exemptions. Parts IA and IB of the Engineering Tripos have been modified and the changes will affect students admitted to read Part IA in 1984; Part II of the Engineering Tripos and the Electrical Sciences Tripos are at present being reviewed and are likely to be modified for the examinations to be held in 1987.

Part IA of the Engineering Tripos

The papers for Part IA consist of the following:

1. Mathematics.
2. Mechanical engineering.
3. Materials and structural mechanics.
4. Electrical and information engineering.

Each paper will be set for three hours and every candidate must offer all four papers.

The Examiners will take into account such course work done by the candidates as will from time to time be determined by the Faculty Board. For this purpose the Head of the Department of

Engineering will present to the Examiners detailed reports on the performance of each candidate in this course work. Details of the work required of candidates will be published by the Faculty Board by notice in the Department of Engineering not later than the beginning of the Full Michaelmas Term preceding the examination.

Details of these papers are as follows:

1. Mathematics

The paper consists mainly of questions on: vector methods, including vector calculus; ordinary differential equations; functions of several variables, including simple partial differential equations; series approximations, including Fourier series; linear algebra; numerical and computational methods for the above topics.

2. Mechanical engineering

The paper consists mainly of questions on: statics; kinematics and dynamics of a particle; the work equation applied to mechanisms; vibrations of mechanical systems with one degree of freedom; basic concepts of thermodynamics; the first and second laws; the application of these laws and of the conservation of mass and momentum to flow processes; the thermodynamic properties of pure substances; modelling of physical system behaviour, analogue and digital systems, differential and difference equations, transforms, and frequency response; basic control concepts, feedback and its use in control systems, stability theory for feedback systems.

3. Materials and structural mechanics

The paper consists mainly of questions on: the properties of engineering materials (including the moduli, strength, toughness, fatigue strength, creep strength, corrosion resistance, and wear resistance); the physical origins of the properties; the selection and use of materials in given engineering applications; equilibrium and displacements of bodies and assemblies; pin-jointed frameworks; states of stress and strain; constitutive equations; tubes and shafts; elastic and plastic theories of bending and torsion; buckling of struts; vibration of beams.

4. Electrical and information engineering

The paper consists mainly of questions on: simple electrical networks containing active and passive devices with elementary analogue and digital applications; the principles and uses of computers and microprocessors in information engineering; fundamental concepts of electromagnetic phenomena with elementary applications.

Part IB of the Engineering Tripos

The papers for Part IB in **1985** will be as given in the *Handbook* for 1983–84, p. 151.

The papers for Part IB in **1986** will be as follows:

1. Mechanics.
2. Thermodynamics and fluid mechanics I.
3. Information, systems, and control engineering.
4. Electrical engineering.
5. Materials.
6. Thermodynamics and fluid mechanics II.
7. Electrical and information engineering I.
8. Electrical and information engineering II.
9. Structural mechanics.

Each paper will be set for three hours.

Every candidate must offer Papers 1–5 and two papers chosen from Papers 6, 7, and *either* 8 *or* 9.

The Examiners will take into account such course work done by the candidates as will from time to time be determined by the Faculty Board. For this purpose the Head of the Department of Engineering will present to the Examiners detailed reports on the performance of each candidate in this course work. Details of the work required of candidates will be published by the Faculty Board by notice in the Department of Engineering not later than the beginning of the Full Michaelmas Term preceding the examination.

No candidate can obtain honours unless he has satisfied the Examiners

(*a*) that he has qualified in a practical course approved by the Faculty Board in one of the following subjects:

(i) surveying,
(ii) mechanical engineering,
(iii) electrical engineering;

(*b*) that he has such workshop or equivalent experience as may be determined from time to time by the Faculty Board of Engineering, see p. 167 below.

Details of the papers are as follows:

1. Mechanics

The paper consists mainly of questions on: rigid body statics applied to engineering problems; particle dynamics; rigid body dynamics in two dimensions; vibrations; kinematics and dynamics of simple machines; elementary treatment of gyroscopic action.

2. Thermodynamics and fluid mechanics I

The paper consists mainly of questions on: fossil fuels and the application of thermodynamic principles to combustion; other sources of energy including nuclear energy; heat transfer by conduction, radiation, and convection; heat exchangers; fluid statics; kinematics of fluid motion; dynamics of fluid motion including the effects of viscosity; model testing.

3. Information, systems, and control engineering

The paper consists mainly of questions on: basic principles of information and signal analysis, analogue and digital signals, power and energy spectra; basic principles of communication, encoding and decoding information, effects of noise, examples of communication systems; basic principles of systems and control, elementary control systems analysis, and design techniques; basic principles of acquisition, storage, and manipulation of digital information in computing systems, networking, use of computers in communication and control.

4. Electrical engineering

The paper consists mainly of questions on: methods of electrical instrumentation; electrical power, underlying principles of electrical machines; electronic circuit techniques.

5. Materials

The paper consists mainly of questions on: the properties of engineering materials (mechanical properties, chemical properties, electrical, magnetic, and optical properties); the origins of these properties and their control by processing; the selection and use of materials in given engineering applications.

6. Thermodynamics and fluid mechanics II

The paper consists mainly of questions on: multiphase transfer processes; thermodynamic power systems; turbomachines; fluid motion including free-surface flow and the effects of compressibility.

7. Electrical and information engineering I

The paper consists mainly of questions on: principles of digital systems and control; related digital electronics; elementary concepts in software engineering; fundamentals of optics applied to engineering; a further treatment of topics falling within the scope of Papers 3 and 4.

8. Electrical and information engineering II

The paper consists mainly of questions on: basic semiconductor physics; principles of operation and fabrication of semiconductor devices and integrated circuits; the fundamental laws of electromagnetism; transmission and reception of electromagnetic waves; a further treatment of topics falling within the scope of Papers 3, 4, and 5.

9. Structural mechanics

The paper consists mainly of questions on: the application of the bound theorems of plasticity to engineering problems; strength and deformation of soil bodies; elastic analysis of statically-indeterminate structures.

Part II of the Engineering Tripos†

The papers in Part II are as follows:

1. Structures I
2. Structures II
3. Soil Mechanics
4. Vibrations
5. Machine elements
6. Mechanics of prime movers
7. Dynamics
8. Civil engineering fluid mechanics
9. Electrical systems
10. Electronic devices
11. Control Engineering
12. Materials I
13. Materials II*
14. Economics
15. Statistics and operational research I
16. Industrial Sociology
17. Surveying
18. Mechanics of solids
19. Geotechnical engineering
20. Developments in power engineering
21. Thermodynamics
22. Internal combustion engines and power plant
23. Turbomachinery and power plant
24. Fluid mechanics I
25. Fluid mechanics II

† This entry applies for the years **1985** and **1986** but will be changed thereafter.

* This paper also serves as Paper I of Part I of the Production Engineering Tripos.

26. Acoustics
27. Aeronautics
28. (Temporarily in abeyance)
29. Statistics and operational research II
30. Statistics and operational research III

Papers 11, 14–16, 29, and 30 constitute a group of papers known as the Management Studies Group.

During the year leading to Part II, a student is required to submit reports on laboratory experiments or, if taking certain papers, course-work essays, and to undertake and to report on a substantial laboratory, design, or industrial project. Considerable weight is given by the Examiners to these reports and essays. In order to obtain honours a candidate must satisfy the Examiners that he has appropriate industrial or equivalent experience, see below.

Options in Part II of the Engineering Tripos

Every candidate must offer four papers from Papers 1–30 in accordance with *one* of the following options:

(A) he may choose from the Management Studies Group offering Papers 15 and 29 and any **two** of Papers 11, 14, 16, and 30;
(B) he may choose two pairs of papers from the sections (*a*)–(*y*) listed below;
(C) he may choose a pair of papers from the sections (*a*)–(*y*) listed below, and two other papers in Papers 1–30;

provided that for either of options (A) or (B):

(i) Paper 22 must not be offered with Paper 23,
(ii) Paper 22 must not be offered without Paper 21,
(iii) none of Papers 23, 25, and 27 may be offered without Paper 24,
(iv) neither Paper 29 nor Paper 30 may be offered without Paper 15;

and provided that for option (*c*):

(v) Paper 6 may not be offered with any of Papers 4, 11, or 18,
(vi) Paper 8 may not be offered with Paper 25.

The Faculty Board have power to restrict the choice of questions in Paper 15 which may be offered by a candidate who has previously obtained honours in or received an allowance on Part IB of the Mathematical Tripos.

The pairs of papers in Part II (see Options (*b*) and (*c*)) are:

(*a*) any two of:

1. Structures I, 2. Structures II, 3. Soil Mechanics, and 18. Mechanics of solids

(*b*) 3. Soil mechanics and 19. Geotechnical engineering

(*c*) any two of:

4. Vibrations, 5. Machine elements, and 11. Control engineering

(*d*)	4. Vibrations	and	7. Dynamics
(*e*)	4. Vibrations	and	26. Acoustics
(*f*)	5. Machine elements	and	6. Mechanics of prime movers
(*g*)	5. Machine elements	and	7. Dynamics
(*h*)	5. Machine elements	and	18. Mechanics of solids
(*i*)	7. Dynamics	and	11. Control engineering.
(*j*)	7. Dynamics	and	17. Surveying
(*k*)	7. Dynamics	and	18. Mechanics of solids
(*l*)	9. Electrical systems	and	10. Electronic devices
(*m*)	9. Electrical systems	and	11. Control engineering
(*n*)	11. Control engineering	and	15. Statistics and operational research I
(*o*)	12. Materials I	and	13. Materials II
(*p*)	12. Materials I	and	18. Mechanics of solids

(*q*) any two of:

14. Economics, 15. Statistics and operational research I, and 16. Industrial sociology

(*r*)	15. Statistics and operational research I	and	29. Statistics and operational research II
(*s*)	15. Statistics and operational research I	and	30. Statistics and operational research III
(*t*)	20. Developments in power engineering	and	21. Thermodynamics
(*u*)	21. Thermodynamics	and	22. Internal combustion engines and power plant
(*v*)	23. Turbomachinery and power plant	and	24. Fluid mechanics I
(*w*)	24. Fluid mechanics I	and	25. Fluid mechanics II

(*x*) 24. Fluid mechanics I and 26. Acoustics
(*y*) 24. Fluid mechanics I and 27. Aeronautics

The scope of the papers is as follows:

1. Structures I

The paper consists mainly of questions on the analysis and design of structures.

2. Structures II

The paper consists mainly of questions on reinforced and prestressed concrete, the theory of shells, instability and buckling, and structural connexions.

3. Soil mechanics

The paper consists mainly of questions on the general principles of soil mechanics and on the analysis of earthworks, foundations, and soil structures.

4. Vibrations

The paper consists mainly of questions on the theory of vibrations and the causes, measurement, isolation and suppression of vibrations in machinery and structures.

5. Machine elements

The paper consists mainly of questions on friction and wear, contact stresses, lubrication, bearings, cams, gears, and the topology, kinematics and synthesis of mechanisms.

6. Mechanics of prime movers

The paper consists mainly of questions on the theory of vibrations, including the whirling of shafts, and the causes and suppression of vibrations; the theory and design of automatic control systems; stress analysis, including applications to prime movers.

7. Dynamics

The paper consists mainly of questions on the principles of mechanical dynamics, including their application to wheeled vehicles, rotors and gyroscopic instruments, inertial navigation, and the motion and uses of artificial satellites.

8. Civil engineering fluid mechanics

The paper consists mainly of questions on wind loads on structures; pollution, flood control; loose-boundary hydraulics; coastal engineering.

9. Electrical systems

The paper consists mainly of questions on the systems applications of electrical engineering including instrumentation and control; telecommunications and radar; power transmission circuits and their protection.

10. Electronic devices

The paper consists mainly of questions on the characteristics and operation of electronic devices, and on the physical and electromagnetic theory applied to their design. These devices include microwave electron tubes; light-conversion devices used in TV; semiconductor devices operated at medium and high frequencies; and passive devices such as aerials and waveguides.

11. Control engineering

The paper consists mainly of questions on theory of linear systems, simple mechanical and electrical control systems, transfer functions and compensating networks, complex plane analysis, systems with random variables, sampled-data systems, relay control systems, simple non-linear systems, time-solution of matrix differential equations, and dynamic programming.

12. Materials I

The paper consists mainly of questions on the physical and chemical properties of engineering materials and the influence of those properties on the selection and use of materials.

13. Materials II

The paper consists mainly of questions on the properties of metals and non-metallic materials which are of significance in manufacturing processes and the effect of production processes upon the properties and functioning of materials.

14. Economics

The paper consists mainly of questions on the economics of the firm, factors affecting wages, profits and prices, financial control within firms, the forces affecting the level of activity and employment in the economy as a whole, current problems of economic policy.

15. Statistics and operational research I

The paper consists of three sections, A, B, and C. Section A contains questions mainly on statistics and mathematical programming; Section B contains questions mainly on advanced statistics and mathematical programming; and Section C questions mainly on methods of operational research. Candidates who have been classed in, or received an allowance on, Part IB of the Mathematical Tripos must take Sections B and C. All other candidates must take Sections A and C.

16. Industrial sociology

The paper consists mainly of questions on the social structure of industry and the relations between industry and society.

17. Surveying

The paper consists mainly of questions on geodetic astronomy, geodetic surveying, the adjustment of surveying networks, the design of surveying instruments, and photogrammetry and photo-interpretation.

18. Mechanics of solids

The paper consists mainly of questions on elasticity, plasticity, and their applications, including impact.

19. Geotechnical engineering

The paper consists mainly of questions on the properties and behaviour of soils and rocks, and on the analysis and design of earthworks, foundations and soil structures.

20. Developments in power engineering

The paper consists mainly of questions on nuclear engineering (fission and fusion), low-temperature engineering, and industrial thermal processes.

21. Thermodynamics

The paper consists mainly of questions on thermodynamic principles, chemical thermodynamics and combustion, radiation and two-phase phenomena.

22. Internal combustion engines and power plant

The paper consists mainly of questions on internal combustion engines, unsteady gas dynamics, turbo-charging, and a comparative review of power plant.

23. Turbomachinery and power plant

The paper consists mainly of questions on the aerodynamics of turbomachinery, jet engines, and a comparative review of power plant.

24. Fluid mechanics I

The paper consists mainly of questions on the fundamental principles of fluid flow; flow of inviscid fluid including the effects of compressibility; shock waves; boundary layers and convective heat transfer.

25. Fluid mechanics II

The paper consists mainly of questions on the development of the principles included in Fluid mechanics I and applications to practical flows; surface waves; turbulence.

26. Acoustics

The paper consists mainly of questions on the generation and propagation of sound; sound sources including flow-induced vibrations; simple properties of sound waves; techniques for the measurement and analysis of noise.

27. Aeronautics

The paper consists mainly of questions on the performance and stability of aircraft; the theory of wings and aerofoils, including effects of compressibility; more advanced topics in boundary layers.

28. (temporarily in abeyance)

29. Statistics and operational research II

The paper consists mainly of questions on mathematical model building, applied statistics, decision analysis, and production management.

30. Statistics and operational research III

The paper consists mainly of questions on optimization, stochastic processes, and time-series analysis.

The Electrical Sciences Tripos*

The Electrical Sciences Tripos is not divided into Parts. A student who has obtained honours in another Tripos (other than Part IA of the Engineering Tripos) may be a candidate in his third or fourth year. An Affiliated Student may, if he obtains permission from the Faculty Board of Engineering, be a candidate in his first or second year.

Subjects of examination

The examination consists of four written papers, each of three hours' duration.

The Examiners take into account laboratory work done by the candidates. For this purpose the Head of the Engineering Department presents to the Examiners a detailed report of the work done by each candidate in the laboratory. In order to obtain honours a candidate must satisfy the Examiners that he has had some industrial or equivalent experience, see below.

The scope of the papers is as follows:

Electricity (four papers)

The papers consist mainly of questions on electric and magnetic properties of matter, including solids, liquids, and gases, and theories of those properties; electron emission; production of high vacua; theory of electric circuits including those with both passive and active elements; electric measurements; equations of the electromagnetic field; electrical transmission of energy and of information; electric machinery.

The Production Engineering Tripos

The Production Engineering Tripos consists of two Parts, Part I and Part II. The course for the Tripos is one of those specially designated by the University Grants Committee as a high-quality first-degree course with a pronounced orientation towards manufacturing industry. A student who has obtained honours in Part IB of the Engineering Tripos may take Part I of the Production Engineering Tripos normally in his third year. If he obtains honours in Part I of that Tripos, he may then proceed to Part II in a fourth year.

* This Tripos is at present under review but the description here is appropriate for **1985** and **1986**.

For Part I of the Production Engineering Tripos the student follows a conventional course of lectures and practical work. The names of the candidates who obtain honours in Part I are arranged in three classes, the second class being divided into two divisions. For Part II a student spends a considerable portion of his time on case studies, project work, and work done in conjunction with industry. The names of candidates who obtain honours in Part II are not divided into classes, but for special excellence a mark of distinction may be awarded.

Part I of the Production Engineering Tripos

The examination consists of five written papers, each of three hours' duration. The Examiners take into account course work undertaken during the year. In order to obtain honours a candidate must satisfy the Examiners that he has appropriate industrial or equivalent experience, see below.

The scope of the written papers is as follows:

1. consists mainly of questions on production technology
2. consists mainly of questions on engineering design and manufacturing processes
3. consists mainly of questions on the organization and control of production systems
4. consists mainly of questions on human behaviour in industry, personnel management, and industrial relations
5. consists mainly of questions on financial aspects of industrial management.

Part II of the Production Engineering Tripos

The examination consists of two written papers, each of three hours' duration. The Examiners also take into account and attach considerable weight to course work undertaken during the year. In order to obtain honours a candidate must satisfy the Examiners that he has appropriate industrial or equivalent experience.

The scope of the written papers is as follows:

1. consists mainly of questions on technological aspects of production engineering
2. consists mainly of questions on managerial aspects of production engineering.

A **Certificate of Advanced Study in Manufacturing Technology** is awarded to a member of the University who obtains honours in Part II of the Production Engineering Tripos having previously completed the examination requirements for the B.A. Degree.

Workshop and Industrial experience Qualifications

The regulations for the Engineering Tripos, the Electrical Sciences Tripos, and the Production Engineering Tripos require candidates to furnish evidence of practical experience in industry.

Candidates for Part I B of the Engineering Tripos are required to spend a minimum of four weeks obtaining 'hands on' experience of manufacturing in mechanical, electrical, or civil engineering. If possible this experience is obtained with a company but the Department also sponsors suitable courses at Government Training Centres; applications should be made to the Workshops Superintendent in the Department.

Candidates for Part II of the Engineering Tripos, or for the Electrical Sciences Tripos, who have already obtained the Part I B Engineering Tripos workshop qualification, are required to spend four weeks in industry 'on the shop-floor' in close contact with the manual workforce. Some flexibility is permitted in satisfying this requirement, e.g. employment in workshops attached to research laboratories, or work on civil engineering sites may be acceptable. Work in a training workshop either in industry, a technical college, or in the Department will not be accepted for this qualification; nor will office work, e.g. designing, draughting, planning, computing, progressing, selling, costing, etc. The Department will allow candidates to reverse the order in which they obtain their practical experience.

Candidates for Part II or for the Electrical Sciences Tripos who have not taken Part I A or Part I B of the Tripos will be required to obtain four weeks of experience of either type in order to qualify for honours. Candidates for Part I or for Part II of the Production Engineering Tripos must obtain industrial experience under guidance from the Department.

Students and prospective students would be well advised, before entering an industrial establishment for the purposes of satisfying the Tripos regulations, to consult the Workshops Superintendent of the Department, who will inform them whether their intended period of training will in fact give them the required qualifications. It should be noted that these qualifications must be obtained *before* the relevant Tripos Examination is taken. Students are encouraged to complete their full requirements by the end of their second year.

Exemptions from the Examinations of Professional Institutions

A student may, by passing one or more of the University's examinations in Engineering, be exempted from certain examinations or sections of examinations held by the Engineering Institutions. The examinations which normally carry exemption are listed below; holders of qualifications which do not carry automatic exemption may be granted some measure of exemption if they apply individually to the Institution concerned. Exemptions carried by the examinations of the Production Engineering Tripos have not yet been determined.

Council of Engineering Institutions (*C.E.I.*)

Part I of the Engineering Tripos exempts from Parts I and II of the C.E.I. Examination provided that it is followed by the award of a degree.

Institution of Mechanical Engineers

Part II(F) of the Engineering Tripos exempts from Part III of the Institution Examination.

Institution of Electrical Engineers

A student who successfully completes *either* the Electrical Sciences Tripos *or* the Engineering Tripos, Part I, followed by a suitable combination of papers in Part II, *or* the Electrical Option of the Engineering Tripos, Part I, followed by Part II of the Engineering Tripos will be allowed complete exemption from the Institution Examination.

British Institute of Management

The Management Group of papers of Part II of the Engineering Tripos exempts from Part I of the Membership Examination.

Examinations for the M.Phil. Degree

Candidates for the M.Phil. Degree must have been admitted to the status of Graduate Student by the Board of Graduate Studies on the recommendation of the Degree Committee of the Faculty of Engineering.

The Department offers the following one-year postgraduate courses which lead to the M.Phil. Degree:

Control engineering and operational research.
Soil mechanics.

These courses are intended primarily for students who have a good first degree in engineering, but a degree in mathematics may be appropriate for the course in control engineering and operational research.

From 1985 the Department, in collaboration with the Computer Laboratory, will also offer the following one-year course leading to the M.Phil. Degree:

Computer speech and language processing.

This course is intended for students who have a good first degree in engineering, computer science, physics, mathematics, linguistics or experimental psychology.

Control Engineering and Operational Research

Students follow a main core of lecture courses in both control engineering and operational research. In addition they must choose to follow a number of advanced lecture courses from a selection available in either or both fields. A project forms an important part of the overall course and is the subject of a thesis submitted as part of the Examination.

The scheme of examination consists of:

(*a*) two written papers:
   1. Control and feedback in dynamical systems.
   2. Optimization and data analysis.

(*b*) not less than five and not more than eight essays or exercises, of a length and on topics approved by the Degree Committee:

and (*c*) a thesis, of not more than 15,000 words in length, including footnotes, appendices, and bibliography, on a subject approved by the Degree Committee.

The Examination includes an oral examination upon the thesis and the general field of knowledge in which it falls.

The scope of the written papers is defined as follows.

1. Systems

State-space dynamical theory, the general theory of feedback systems, and the theory and application of stochastic processes.

2. Models and their application

Optimization and mathematical programming theory, statistical theory the principles of modelling, and the analysis and use of industrial production and engineering models.

3. Advanced control and operational research techniques

Advanced topics in control engineering and operational research techniques in accordance with the notice to be published by the Faculty Board of Engineering during the Michaelmas Term preceding the examination.

Soil mechanics

Students follow lecture courses in the advanced theory of soil mechanics and lectures and practical courses in modern experimental techniques. A project forms a major part of the overall course and is the subject of a thesis submitted as part of the Examination.

The scheme of examination consists of:

(*a*) two written papers, each of which may include questions on theoretical soil mechanics and experimental soil mechanics;

and (*b*) a thesis, of not more than 15,000 words in length, including footnotes, appendices and bibliography.

The Examination includes an oral examination upon the thesis and the general field of knowledge in which it falls.

Computer Speech and Language Processing

Students will follow an introductory course of lectures aimed at bringing students of differing backgrounds nearer to a common basis. There will be integrated main lecture courses on speech and language processing together with shorter lecture courses on the adjacent subjects of phonetics, linguistics, psycholinguistics and experimental psychology. There will be experimental and computer-based coursework and a project forms an important part of the overall course and is the subject of a thesis submitted as part of the Examination.

The scheme of examinations consists of:

(*a*) two written papers, each of which may include questions on computer speech and language processing;

(*b*) not less than five and not more than eight essays or exercises of a length and on topics approved by the Degree Committee for the Faculty of Engineering;

and (*c*) a thesis, of not more than 15,000 words in length, including footnotes, appendices and bibliography, on a subject approved by the Degree Committee.

The Examination shall include an oral examination upon the thesis and the general field of knowledge in which it falls.

The scope of the written papers is defined as follows.

Papers 1 and 2

Knowledge of speech and language from the viewpoints of phonetics, linguistics, cognitive science and computer processing and the application of this knowledge in speech analysis, recognition and synthesis and in syntactic parsing, semantic interpretation and text and discourse planning.

Advanced Course in Production Methods and Management

The one-year Advanced Course in Production Methods and Management is run by the Department in co-operation with Lancaster University. It is designed to be an alternative to the first year of postgraduate training in industry and is approved for this purpose by the Institution of Mechanical Engineers and by the Institution of Production Engineers. The Course leads to no University qualification.

Students on the Course must (i) have been approved by the Selection Committee of the Department, (ii) either have become qualified for the B.A. Degree by obtaining honours in an Honours Examination of the University, or have obtained from another university a degree which the Selection Committee adjudge to be of a comparable standard, or have produced other evidence of fitness for the Course.

Application for admission to the Course should be sent to the Head of the Department of Engineering, Engineering Laboratory, Trumpington Street, Cambridge, CB2 1PZ, by 1 May of the year in which the student wishes to begin the Course.

ENGLISH

In this subject there are courses of study followed by candidates for:

The *English Tripos*, which is divided into two Parts.
The *Ordinary Examination* in English for the Ordinary B.A. Degree.

The English Tripos

The course of study for the English Tripos covers English literature from 1300 to the present day, with some reference to classical literature and related modern literature. A reading knowledge of one classical or modern European language is expected. Anglo-Saxon (Old English) is not compulsory; it is an optional subject in both Parts of the Tripos, and those intending to read it should make arrangements to do so as early as possible, preferably in their first year.

The Tripos is divided into two Parts. Part I is devoted principally to English literature; Part II includes various options involving classical and other literatures, and the history of ideas. This will be seen in the detailed syllabus that follows. A dissertation may be substituted in Part I for one specified paper in the Tripos. A dissertation is compulsory in Part II; a further dissertation may be offered in place of one optional paper in Part II.

Part I takes two years; Part II normally takes one year, though it is possible to spend two years on this Part. The ordinary assumption, however, is that the whole Tripos is a three-year course.

The school subjects most relevant to the Tripos, besides English itself, are Classics, Modern Languages and History. It is generally desirable that intending candidates should have taken an A level in French or some other modern European Language.

Either Part of the Tripos may be combined with a Part of another Tripos. The most suitable combinations are with Classics, Modern and Medieval Languages, or History. Students who have read Part I of any of these Triposes might well change to English for their second Part. Students who intend to change to English, either Part I or Part II, in their third year, after taking some other Tripos in their second year, should try to give some time to reading English literature during the first two years. They should also try to attend during that period some of the relevant courses of lectures provided by the Faculty of English. It is also possible to change to other Triposes after reading Part I English. The Anglo-Saxon, Norse, and Celtic Tripos makes a particularly suitable Part II for those who have by then become mainly interested in medieval English literature. Impulsive last-minute changes are not recommended; students are advised to form some comprehensive idea of the course they intend to pursue, whether both Parts of the English Tripos, or English combined with some other subject, as early as possible. On all these matters they should consult their Tutors and Directors of Studies.

Part I*

The papers in Part I* are as follows:

1. English literature and its background, 1300–1550.
2. English literature and its background, 1550–1700.
3. English literature and its background, 1700–1830.
4. English literature and its background, since 1830.
5. Shakespeare.
6. Literary criticism.
7. Foreign language and literature; passages for translation and comment.
8. Early medieval literature and its background (also serves as Paper 14 of Part II, and as Paper 13 of the Anglo-Saxon, Norse, and Celtic Tripos).
9. English literature before the Norman Conquest (Paper 5 of the Anglo-Saxon, Norse and Celtic Tripos).
10. Latin literature of the British Isles, 400–1100 (Paper 4 of the Anglo-Saxon, Norse, and Celtic Tripos).
11. Old Norse literature (Paper 6 of the Anglo-Saxon, Norse, and Celtic Tripos).
12. Medieval Welsh language and literature (Paper 7A of the Anglo-Saxon, Norse, and Celtic Tripos).

Each paper is set for three hours except Paper 6 which is set for three and a half hours.

Every candidate for Part I must offer:

either (*a*) Papers 1–7;

or (*b*) Papers 1 and 5; and four papers from among Papers 2, 3, 4, 6, 7; and one paper from among Papers 8–12;

or (*c*) Papers 1 and 5; three papers from among Papers 2, 3, 4, 7; and two papers from among Papers 8–12 which must include at least one of Papers 8–9.

* See p. 182 on the submission of an original composition in English for Part I.

provided that a candidate may, in substitution for one of Papers 2–5, submit a dissertation on a topic of literary interest falling within the scope of that paper, except that (i) no candidate may submit a dissertation of which the main emphasis is on literature written in a foreign language and (ii) if a candidate submits a dissertation in substitution for Paper 2 it must not be wholly or largely on Shakespeare.

If a candidate chooses to submit a dissertation, the topic must be approved by his Director of Studies and the approved topic notified through his Tutor to the Secretary of the Faculty Board not later than the division of the Lent Term next preceding the examination. A dissertation must not be more than 5,000 words in length (inclusive of notes and appendices, although appendices additional to this word limit may be allowed in special circumstances subject to the approval of the Faculty Board not later than the division of the Lent Term next preceding the examination) and must be accompanied by a list of the books and articles used in its preparation. A candidate is required to declare that the dissertation is his own work and does not contain material which he has already used to any substantial extent for a comparable purpose. A candidate may be called for *viva voce* examination in connexion with his dissertation. The dissertation must be typed, in English, with proper attention to style and presentation, marked with the candidate's name and College and the Part of the Tripos for which he is a candidate, and sent through his Tutor to the Secretary of the Faculty Board so as to reach him not later than the third day of the Full Easter Term in which the examination is to be held.

The scope of the papers in Part I is as follows:

1. English literature and its background, 1300–1550

Medieval texts are prescribed for special study; and passages are set from them for translation and explanation. Questions are set both on the literature and on the life and thought of the period. All candidates are expected to show such knowledge of the life and thought of the period as is necessary for understanding its literature.

For **1985**: Chaucer, *Troilus and Criseyde*, Book v; *Sir Gawain and the Green Knight*, lines 1–490; *Piers Plowman*, B Text, Passus 18, 'Harrowing of Hell' (ed. A. V. C. Schmidt, Everyman, 1978).

For **1986**: Chaucer, *Troilus and Criseyde*, Book III; *Sir Gawain and the Green Knight*, lines 1998–2530; *Piers Plowman*, B Text, Passus 18, 'Harrowing of Hell' (ed. A. V. C. Schmidt, Everyman, 1978).

2. English literature and its background, 1550–1700

Questions are set both on the literature and on the life and thought of the period, and on any books prescribed from time to time for special study. All candidates are expected to show such knowledge of the life and thought of the period as is necessary for understanding its literature.

In **1985** and **1986** a special element will be prescribed: Literature and death.

3. English literature and its background, 1700–1830

Questions are set both on the literature and on the life and thought of the period. All candidates are expected to show such knowledge of the life and thought of the period as is necessary for understanding its literature.

In **1985** and **1986** a special element will be prescribed: Literature and politics.

4. English literature and its background, since 1830

Questions are set both on the literature and on the life and thought of the period. All candidates are expected to show such knowledge of the life and thought of the period as is necessary for understanding its literature.

In **1985** and **1986** a special element will be prescribed: Literature and education.

5. Shakespeare

Questions are set requiring explanation and discussion of passages of a specific work or works. Questions are also set on other work of Shakespeare and matters of historical and critical interest relevant to his works.

For **1985**: *King Lear*, *Twelfth Night*.
For **1986**: *Othello*, *Twelfth Night*.

6. Literary criticism

Questions on literary criticism (critics or critical works may be specified or recommended for study); passages of English prose or verse for explanation, comment and appreciation.

Specified critics for **1985** and **1986**: Johnson and Coleridge.
The following works have been specified for special study:

Johnson: (i) from *Lives of the Poets*, the lives of Cowley, Milton, Waller, Dryden, Swift, Pope and Gray.

(ii) The Preface to his edition of Shakespear and the notes on the following plays: *Love's Labour's Lost*, *Henry IV, Parts 1 and 2*, *King Lear*, *Macbeth*, *Romeo and Juliet*, *Hamlet*, and *Othello*.

Coleridge: (i) *Biographia Literaria* (text as in the first edition, i.e. excluding the Aesthetic Essays sometimes reprinted alongside).

(ii) The following extracts from Coleridge's *Shakespearean Criticism* in two volumes, ed. T. M. Raysor (Everyman): vol. 1, section I, the Notes on *Romeo and Juliet*, *Hamlet*, *Othello*, *King Lear*, *Macbeth*, *Love's Labour's Lost*, *The Tempest*, and *Richard II*; Section II, 'Shakespeare's Poetry', 'Shakespeare's Judgment Equal to his Genius', and 'The Characteristics of Shakespeare'.

7. Foreign language and literature; passages for translation and comment

The paper includes one passage for unseen translation and one passage for comment from a prescribed text or texts in the following languages for which there is a candidate: classical Greek, French, German, Italian, classical Latin, medieval Latin, Russian, and Spanish. Candidates are not required to show knowledge of more than one of these languages.

The prescribed texts for each language in **1985** are:

French	M. Proust, *Du côté de chez Swann*, première partie: Combray.
German	G. Büchner, *Dantons Tod*, *Woyzeck*, in *Werke und Briefe*, ed. Werner Lehmann (D.T.V., no. 2065).
Greek	Aeschylus, *Prometheus Bound*, ed. D. Page, Classical Texts (Oxford, 1972).
Italian	Boccaccio, *Decameron*, 'Prologue' and 'First Day', ed. C. Segre (Milan: Mursia, 1977) or ed. C. Salinari (Rome: Laterza, 1979).
Latin (classical)	*Virgil*, *Eclogues*, ed. R. G. Coleman, C.U.P., 1977.
Latin (medieval)	*Carmina Cantabrigiensia*, ed. Walther Bulst, Heidelberg, 1950.
Russian	Mikhail Bulgakov, *Dni Turbiniykh*.
Spanish	J.-L. Borges, *Ficciones*, ed. G. Brotherston and P. Hulme (London: Harrap, 1976).

The prescribed texts in **1986** will be the same for German, Greek, Italian, Latin (both classical and medieval), Russian and Spanish. For French the text will be:

French J.-P. Sartre, *Les mots.*

8. Early medieval literature and its background

The period covered by this paper is 1066–*c.* 1350. English and French texts are prescribed for special study: and passages are set from them for translation and explanation. Questions are set on the English texts of the period; there are also questions on French texts, whether written in England or on the Continent, which stand in a significant relation to them. Candidates are expected to show such knowledge of the life and thought of the period as is necessary for the understanding of its literature.

In **1985** and **1986**: *La Chanson de Roland*, ed. Whitehead, lines 1671–1760, 2375–2475; *Le Mystère d'Adam*, ed. P. Aebischer or P. Noomen, lines 205–357; Chrétien de Troyes, *Yvain*, ed. Reid, lines 3341–3484; Marie de France, *Lais*, ed. Ewert: 'Laustic'; *The Owl and the Nightingale*, ed. Stanley, lines 1043–1290; *Ancrene Wisse*, ed. Shepherd: Section VII, 'On Love', pp. 19–27; *Early Middle English Verse and Prose*, ed. Bennett and Smithers, VIII (Lyrics).

9. English literature before the Norman Conquest

10. Latin literature of the British Isles, 400–1100 (Paper 4 of the Anglo-Saxon, Norse, and Celtic Tripos).

11. Old Norse literature (Paper 6 of the Anglo-Saxon, Norse, and Celtic Tripos).

12. Medieval Welsh language and literature I (Paper 7A of the Anglo-Saxon, Norse, and Celtic Tripos).

Part II

The papers for Part II are as follows:

GROUP A (Compulsory Papers)

1. Practical criticism.
2. Tragedy (also serves as Paper O 3 of Part II of the Classical Tripos).

Group B(i)

3. Chaucer (also serves as Paper 14 of the Anglo-Saxon, Norse, and Celtic Tripos).
4. Medieval English literature, 1066–1500 (also serves as Paper 15 of the Anglo-Saxon, Norse, and Celtic Tripos).
5. Special period of English literature (taken from the period after 1500 and before 1700).
6. Special period of English literature (taken from the period after 1700).
7. Special subject I.

Group B(ii)

8. English moralists.
9. History and theory of literary criticism.
10. The novel.
11. American literature.
12. Special subject II.

Group C(i)

13. History of the English language.
14. Early Medieval literature and its background (Paper 8 of Part I of the English Tripos).
15. English literature before the Norman Conquest (Paper 5 of the Anglo-Saxon, Norse, and Celtic Tripos).

Group C(ii)

16. Latin literature of the British Isles, 400–1100 (Paper 4 of the Anglo-Saxon, Norse, and Celtic Tripos).
17. Old Norse literature (Paper 6 of the Anglo-Saxon, Norse, and Celtic Tripos).

18A. Medieval Welsh language and literature I (Paper 7A of the Anglo-Saxon, Norse, and Celtic Tripos).

18B. Medieval Welsh language and literature II (Paper 7B of the Anglo-Saxon, Norse, and Celtic Tripos).

19A. Medieval Irish language and literature I (Paper 8A of the Anglo-Saxon, Norse, and Celtic Tripos).

19B. Medieval Irish language and literature II (Paper 8B of the Anglo-Saxon, Norse, and Celtic Tripos).

20. A special subject in early medieval comparative literature (in a year in which a subject is specified by the Faculty Board for Paper 11 of the Anglo-Saxon, Norse, and Celtic Tripos).

21. French literature, thought, and history, from 1594 to 1700 (Paper 5 of Part II of the Modern and Medieval Languages Tripos).
22. French literature, thought, and history, from 1690 to 1789 (Paper 6 of Part II of the Modern and Medieval Languages Tripos).
23. French literature, thought, and history, from 1789 to 1898 (Paper 7 of Part II of the Modern and Medieval Languages Tripos).
24. French literature, thought, and history, since 1890 (Paper 8 of Part II of the Modern and Medieval Languages Tripos).
25. Dante (Paper 14 of Part II of the Modern and Medieval Languages Tripos).
26. Medieval Latin literature from 400 to 1300 (Paper 12 of Part II of the Modern and Medieval Languages Tripos).
27. A special subject in Comparative Literature (i) and (ii) (Papers 123 and 124 of Part II of the Modern and Medieval Languages Tripos).
28. *A prescribed subject taken from or connected with Classical literature (Paper A4 of Part II of the Classical Tripos) in any year in which the subject Roman Renaissance and English Pastoral has been prescribed by the Faculty Board of Classics for that paper. (Not available in 1982 and 1983.)
29. General linguistics (Paper 111 of Part II of the Modern and Medieval Language Tripos).

Each paper is set for three hours except Paper 1 which is set for three and a half hours. The Faculty Board announce in every year one or more special subjects for Paper 7; they may in addition announce one or more special subjects for Paper 12.

Every candidate for Part II must offer:

(*a*) a dissertation on a subject in English literature since 1066;
(*b*) both papers from Group A;
(*c*) *either* two papers chosen from Groups B and C *or* one paper chosen from Groups B and C and a second dissertation;

provided that:

(i) a candidate may not offer any paper that he has previously offered for another Honours Examination;

* From 1 October 1985, Paper 28 will be deleted and Paper 29 will be renumbered 28.

(ii) a candidate may not offer both Papers 7 and 12 nor both Paper 9 and one of the Special Subjects for Paper 12 if the Faculty Board have specified that it may not be so combined when announcing that Special Subject; nor more than one of the papers from Group C(ii); nor both papers 18 A and 18 B or both 19 A and 19 B;

(iii) a candidate who has obtained honours in Part I of the English Tripos or any allowance on that examination towards a degree may not offer both Papers 5 and 6;

(iv) every candidate who has not previously obtained honours in Part I of the English Tripos must offer *either* at least one paper from Group B(i), *or*, in substitution and if he has obtained leave from the Faculty Board, one paper chosen from among Papers 1–5 of Part I of the English Tripos. An application for leave to offer one of these Part I papers must be sent through the candidate's Tutor to the Secretary of the Faculty Board so as to reach him not later than the division of the Michaelmas Term next preceding the examination and shall state the whole scheme of papers which the candidate proposes to offer, including the topic of his required dissertation and topic of his second dissertation (if offered). In determining whether to approve such an application the Faculty Board will take into consideration both the overall balance of the proposed scheme and the potential overlap between the papers to be offered under it. After the Faculty Board have approved a candidate's proposed scheme of papers, no change may be made in the scheme without the approval of the Faculty Board.

The dissertation under (*a*) above must be of not less than 5,000 and not more than 7,500 words in length (inclusive of notes and appendices, although appendices additional to this word limit may be allowed in special circumstances subject to the approval of the Faculty Board not later than the division of the Lent Term next preceding the examination), and must be on a topic in English literature since 1066 approved by the candidate's Director of Studies. The approved topic must be notified to the Secretary of the Faculty Board not later than the end of the Full Michaelmas Term next preceding the examination. A candidate may, if he wishes, choose a topic in the same field as that of any of the papers that he is offering. A candidate will be required to give full references to the sources used and to declare that the dissertation is his own work and does not contain material which he has already used to any substantial extent for a comparable purpose. A dissertation must show evidence of reading, of judgement and criticism, and of power of exposition. It must be typed, in English, with proper attention to style and presentation, marked with the candidate's name and College and the Part of the Tripos for which he is a candidate, and sent through the candidate's Tutor to the Secretary of the Faculty Board so as to reach him not later than the third day of the Full Easter Term in which the examination is to be held. A candidate may be called for *viva voce* examination in connexion with his dissertation.

Second Dissertation

A candidate for Part II who chooses under (*c*) above to offer only *one* paper from Groups B and C must submit a second dissertation in English of not less than 5,000 and not more than 7,500 words in length (inclusive of notes and appendices, although appendices additional to this word limit may be allowed in special circumstances subject to the approval of the Faculty Board not later than the division of the Lent Term next preceding the examination). This dissertation may be on any topic in the field of English and related studies, as indicated by the range of the English Tripos as a whole, excluding those papers not set by the Examiners for the English Tripos and the Anglo-Saxon, Norse, and Celtic Tripos which has been approved by the Faculty Board, provided that:

(i) if he is offering one of the papers from Group B(ii) the dissertation must be on a topic in English literature unless the Faculty Board (after considering the proposed topics of his dissertation and the whole scheme of the papers he intends to offer) allow him to submit a second dissertation on any topic in the field of English and related studies as indicated by the range of the English Tripos as a whole;
(ii) if he is offering one of the papers from Group C(ii), the dissertation must be on a topic in English literature.

Subject to the foregoing provisions, a candidate may choose a topic in the same field as that of any of the papers that he is offering, except that, if the topic of the dissertation which he is offering under (*a*) is in the field of one of his papers, the Faculty Board may at their discretion decline to allow for the second dissertation a topic in the field of the same paper. A candidate must give full references to the sources used and declare that the dissertation is his own work and does not contain material which he has already used to any substantial extent for a comparable purpose; a dissertation must show evidence of reading, of judgement and criticism, and of power of exposition. Each candidate must submit the proposed topic of his dissertation together with that of his dissertation required under (*a*), and the whole scheme of the papers he intends to offer, through his Tutor, to the Secretary of the Faculty Board so as to reach him not later than the division of the Michaelmas Term next preceding the examination. In determining whether to approve such an application the Faculty Board will take into consideration both the overall balance of the proposed scheme and the potential overlap between the subjects to be offered under it. After the Faculty Board have approved a candidate's proposed scheme of subjects, no change may be made in the scheme without the approval of the Faculty Board. The Secretary will communicate its approval or rejection to the candidate's Tutor. Whether the proposed topic is approved or not, a candidate may submit a revised topic so as to reach the Secretary of the Faculty Board by the division of the following Lent Term; topics received after that date will be considered by the Faculty Board only in the most exceptional circumstances. Dissertations must be typewritten, with proper attention to style and presentation, marked with the candidate's name and College and the Part of the Tripos for which he is a candidate, and must be sent through his Tutor to the Secretary of the Faculty Board so as to reach him not later than the third day of the Full Easter Term in which the examination is to be held. A candidate may be called for *viva voce* examination in connexion with his essay.

Original Compositions in Part I and Part II of the Tripos

A candidate may submit an original composition in English of not more than 5,000 words (exclusive of notes). This, if of sufficient merit, will be taken into account by the Examiners, who may examine him *viva voce* upon it. The submission of non-literary material is not allowed. Compositions must be typewritten, marked with the candidate's name and College and the Part of the Tripos for which he is a candidate, and must be sent through his Tutor to the Secretary of the Faculty Board so as to reach him not later than the third day of the Easter Full Term in which the examination is to be held.

The scope of the papers in **Part II** is as follows:

1. Practical criticism

Passages of English prose and verse for critical comment.

2. Tragedy

Tragedy ancient and modern in connexion and comparison with English Tragedy.

The paper will not be divided into sections. Candidates will be required to answer either *one* or *three* questions. They must, in the paper as a whole, show knowledge of both Greek and Shakespearean tragedy.

3. Chaucer

Candidates are expected to show a full and detailed knowledge of the works of Chaucer. Questions are set on those works and on Chaucer's relationship to his contemporaries and to the life and thought of his age.

4. Medieval English literature, 1066–1500

A specific literary subject is prescribed for special study. It is of a kind to require reading in early as well as in the late medieval English literature and may involve the study of related texts from other languages.

For **1985**: Allegory and Symbol, 1066–1500.

For **1986**: Medieval Romance.

The paper will be divided into two sections, A and B. Candidates will be required to answer three questions, at least one and not more than two questions being from Section A.

Section A will consist of (*i*) passages for comment taken from medieval texts written between 1066 and 1500 (including passages from the recommended works announced by the Faculty Board but not limited to those works); (*ii*) essay questions related to the list of recommended works.

Section B will consist of questions, some of a general or comparative nature, on allegory and symbol in medieval literature.

5. Special period of English literature (taken from the period after 1500 and before 1700)

Candidates are required to show a substantial knowledge of the literature of the period prescribed together with its life and thought.

For **1985** and **1986**: 1500–1557.

6. Special period of English literature (taken from the period after 1700)

Candidates are required to show a substantial knowledge of the literature of the period prescribed together with its life and thought.

For **1985** and **1986**: 1840–1880.

7. Special Subject I

The work of an author or of a group of authors, or a literary topic or genre, or a period not already prescribed for Papers 5 or 6, within the field of English literature, is prescribed for special study. Relevant texts may be recommended for study from time to time. The Faculty Board may from time to time prescribe a number of such special subjects of which one may be offered by candidates for this paper.

In **1985** and **1986**:

(*a*) Shakespeare and the development of English literature: Shakespeare and Jonson.
(*b*) Milton.
(*c*) Pope, Swift, and their circle.
(*d*) English drama and theatre.
(*e*) Modernism (but in **1986**: Twentieth century English poetry).

8. English moralists

Moral and philosophical aspects of English literature in relation to the history of philosophical thought. Candidates are expected to make full use of their existing interests in poetry, drama, and the novel. They are also given opportunities to show knowledge of English intellectual history including topics in moral, social, and political philosophy. Relevant foreign as well as English moral and philosophical authors may be specified or recommended for special study.

9. History and theory of literary criticism

The paper comprises historical, critical, and comparative questions on works and problems in the history of literary criticism and also of literary theory from the fourth century B.C. to the present day. A sufficient number of questions are set to enable candidates to choose questions on a limited chronological period (including the modern period).

10. The Novel

A critical and historical study of the novel, with special reference to the period from 1830 to 1930. Candidates are expected to have studied English novels in relation to selected foreign novels, American and European, and relevant foreign as well as English works may be recommended for study. Questions are also set on the history of the novel, including works and authors before 1830 and after 1930.

The paper will be divided into sections:

Section A will consist of general questions of an historical, comparative, theoretical, and critical kind which must be answered in relation to more than a single novel or a single novelist.

Section B will consist of questions which must be answered in relation to particular novels or novelists.

Candidates will be required to answer three questions, including at least one from each section.

11. American literature

The subject covered by the paper is American literature from 1820 to the present day. Questions will be set on the literature and on the life and thought of the period. A list of books may be prescribed for special study. All candidates will be expected to show such knowledge of the life and thought of the period as is necessary for understanding its literature.

The books prescribed for **1985** and **1986** are: James Fenimore Cooper, *The Deerslayer*; Ralph Waldo Emerson, 'The American Scholar', 'Self Reliance', 'Nature', 'The Over-Soul' (from *Essays, First Series*); 'The Poet', 'The Transcendentalist' (from Lectures on *The Times*); Henry David Thoreau, *Walden*; Nathaniel Hawthorne, *The Scarlet Letter*; Herman Melville, *Moby Dick*; Walt Whitman, *Song of Myself*; Mark Twain, *The Adventures of Huckleberry Finn*; Emily Dickinson, *Selected Poems* (ed. Ted Hughes); Henry James, *The Bostonians*; F. Scott Fitzgerald, *The Great Gatsby*; Wallace Stevens, *Selected Poems* (Faber); William Faulkner, *Absalom, Absalom!*; William Carlos Williams, *Selected Poems* (ed. Charles Tomlinson); Eugene O'Neill, *Long Day's Journey into Night*.

12. Special Subject II

For a year for which a subject is announced for this paper, the work of an author or of a group of authors, or a literary topic or genre, or a period not already prescribed for Paper 5, or 6, or 7, is prescribed for special study. Relevant foreign texts as well as English texts may be recommended for study from time to time. The Faculty Board may from time to time prescribe a number of such special subjects of which one may be offered by candidates for this paper.

For **1985** and **1986**: (*a*) Literature and the visual arts in England, 1725–1900.

(*b*) The literary representation of women.

13. History of the English language*

The paper will be set in two sections and candidates will be required to answer three questions, taken from either section or from both sections. Section A will comprise questions on the history of the English language, including historical grammar, up to *c.* 1600. Section B will comprise questions on the language of English literature since *c.* 1500, covering different forms of linguistic history and analysis. A list of set texts will be published for each section. Candidates offering this paper for the Anglo-Saxon, Norse, and Celtic Tripos and for Part II of the Modern and Medieval Languages Tripos will be required to answer three questions from Section A only.

For *Section A* in **1985**: D. Whitelock, *Sweet's Anglo-Saxon Reader* (15th or later edition), II, XXXI (C) (pp. 183, 283), XXXII (E and F), XXXIII (B); B. Dickins and R. M. Wilson, *Early Middle English Texts*, VI (lines 1–35 and 183–245), VIII (lines 1–165), XV, XVI, XVII (lines 60–135), XXII; K. Sisam, *Fourteenth Century Verse and Prose*, I, III, V (lines 1–91), X, XIII (B); C. C. Butterworth, *The Literary Lineage of the King James Bible*, pp. 313–336.

For *Section B* in **1985**: Spenser, *The Shepheardes Calendar*, 'June' and 'September'; Shakespeare, *Hamlet*, Act III, Sc. ii; Jonson, *Timber, or Discoveries made upon men and matter*, from *De vere Argutis* to *De piis et probis* (inclusive); Milton, *Paradise Lost*, Book 1, lines 1–437; *Guardian*, 40; Johnson, 'The Plan of a Dictionary of the English Language' and 'Preface to the English Dictionary'; Wordsworth's poems in the 1798 edition of *Lyrical Ballads* (ed. R. L. Brett and A. R. Jones, Methuen); Dickens, *Dombey and Son*, chapter XV (Penguin); D. H. Lawrence, 'Odour of Chrysanthemums' (*The Prussian Officer and Other Stories*, Penguin); T. S. Eliot, *The Waste Land* (*Collected Poems 1909–1962*, Faber).

The Preliminary Examination for Part I

There will be no Preliminary Examination for Part I in 1985, and until further notice.

The Examination in English for the Ordinary B.A. Degree

The examination consists of the five following papers, all of which must be taken: (1) Specified works of Chaucer, and one other

* An announcement concerning this paper in 1986 will be made in due course.

medieval text; (2) Shakespeare (three specified plays) and Milton (specified selections); (3) Representative English novelists (specified works); (4) Wordsworth and Keats (specified selections); (5) English Prose, including (*a*) précis, (*b*) questions on an introductory book on the history of the language, (*c*) passages from a book of selected prose for comments on the syntax, vocabulary, and idiom of various periods. Details of the books prescribed for the examination in **1985** can be obtained from the Faculty office.

A student may not count towards the Ordinary B.A. Degree both the Ordinary Examination in English and also anything he may have to his credit as the result of the Preliminary Examination for Part I of the English Tripos or Part I of the English Tripos.

GEOGRAPHY

In this subject there are courses of study followed by candidates for:

The *Geographical Tripos*, which is divided into three Parts.
The *Preliminary Examination* for Part II of the Tripos.
The *Ordinary Examination* in Geography for the Ordinary B.A. Degree.

The Geographical Tripos

Normally more than a hundred undergraduates are admitted each year to the Department of Geography. Almost all of these spend three years reading geography and take all Parts of the Geographical Tripos; no subsidiary subject is required. A few people, however, take a Part of the Geographical Tripos either before or after a Part of some other Tripos.

University geography differs from school geography in that it places greater stress upon analysis and provides opportunity for more intensive specialization in specific branches or areas. This is particularly true of Part II of the Tripos.

The normal programme for an undergraduate who intends to spend three years reading geography is as follows:

1. Part IA of the Tripos at the end of the first year.
2. Part IB of the Tripos at the end of the second year.
3. Part II of the Tripos at the end of the third year.

The course for Part IA aims at providing a general all-round training in the subject. It comprises teaching in Physical Geography, Contemporary Human Geography, Historical Geography, in the application of quantitative techniques and in the making and use of maps. In Part IB, a candidate must offer at least one paper in each of the three main branches of the subject and a compulsory paper in ideas and methods but otherwise may specialize. The course for Part II permits a candidate *either* to specialize *or* to draw his options widely within the discipline. A candidate has also to write a short dissertation on some area or topic, which will be taken into account by the Examiners.

The school subjects most relevant to the Tripos, besides geography itself, include mathematics, physical and biological sciences, geology, economics, and history. A modern language is also desirable, and a good general education is an important asset. A candidate who has not taken geography at school would not necessarily be at a disadvantage if his or her other subjects were cognate.

Undergraduates who transfer to the Geographical Tripos after taking a Part of some other Tripos may spend one year on Part IA or Part IB, or either one year or two years on Part II. Such undergraduates should consult their Directors of Studies well in advance on the question of preliminary reading, and this applies particularly to those who intend to read for Part II, owing to its more specialized nature. Some undergraduates who transfer, and some Affiliated Students, are not required to submit a dissertation for Part II. Triposes that combine most readily with a Part of the Geographical Tripos include Archaeology and Anthropology, History, Economics, Social and Political Sciences, Law, Natural Sciences (which includes Geology) and Land Economy.

General

The Geographical Tripos consists of three Parts, Part IA, Part IB and Part II. No student may present himself for more than one Part in the same term, and no student can be entered for the same Part more than once. Examiners may take account in each Part of laboratory and field work done by the candidates during their courses.

Part IA

Part IA is normally taken in the first year, or in the second year by a candidate who has obtained Honours in some other Tripos examination. The examination consists of five papers, all of which must be offered, as follows:

1. Physical geography

Aspects of geomorphology, climatology and related subjects in physical geography.

2. Environment and resources

Introduction to biogeography, population geography and natural resources.

3. Contemporary human geography

Aspects of economic, social and political geography, and related subjects in contemporary human geography.

4. Historical geography

Introduction to historical geography, with particular reference to the British Isles.

5. Geographical ideas and methods

Introduction to the history and philosophy of geography. Field and laboratory techniques, including cartography and statistics.

Part IB

Part IB is normally taken in the second year, either after a candidate has obtained honours in Part IA of the Geographical Tripos, or in another honours examination. The papers for Part IB are as under; a candidate must offer Paper 1 and in addition one paper from each of Groups A, B, and C, and any other two papers.

1. Geographical ideas and methods
Development of geographical ideas; techniques of analysis.

Group A

2. Human geography I
Geography of economic activities.

3. Human geography II
Economic and social aspects of urban geography.

4. Political geography
The geography of political problems and issues.

5. The geography of the Indian sub-continent

The social and political geography of the Indian sub-continent before and after Partition.

Group B

6. Historical geography I
The historical geography of North America.

7. Historical geography II
The historical geography of cities.

8. The cultural geography of prescribed areas

Two areas will be prescribed, of which candidates will be expected to show knowledge of one.

The areas prescribed in **1985** will be:
Melanesia.
Middle America.

Group C

9. Physical geography I
Processes and the landscape.

10. Physical geography II
Physical geography of the tropics. Aspects of the physical geography of the humid, semi-arid, and arid tropics, including biogeographical and human implications.

11. Physical geography III
Regional geomorphology.

Part II

Part II may be taken in the third or fourth year, either in the year next after a candidate has obtained honours in Part I B, or in the year or next year but one after he has obtained honours in another honours examination (other than Part I A). The papers in Part II are as follows; a candidate must offer any five papers:

1. Human geography I
The human geography of the United Kingdom.

2. Human geography II
The human geography of advanced countries.

3. Human geography III
The human geography of developing countries.

4. Human geography IV
Urban problems, planning, and policy.

5. Historical geography I
The geography of medieval Britain.

6. Historical geography II
The geography of the Industrial Revolution in Britain.

7. Historical geography III
The historical geography of France.

8. Historical geography IV

The methodology of historical geography.

9. Physical geography I

Fluvial geomorphology.

10. Physical geography II

Landscape evolution. The evolution of landforms in low latitudes during the Late Teritary and Quaternary.

11. Physical geography III

Coastal physiography.

12. Physical geography IV

Glacial studies. Physical glaciology, sea ice, and glacial geomorphology.

13. Biogeography

Geographical aspects of ecosystems. The biogeography of Eastern England; upland Britain and conservation; lowland heaths and coasts.

14. Resource management and conservation

The management and conservation of natural resources.

15. Methods of regional and spatial analysis

The structure and analysis of geographical systems, together with associated computer-based methods.

16. The geography of South Asia

17. The geography of the U.S.S.R.

18. The geography of Latin America

Dissertations for Part II

A candidate for Part II, except for

(*a*) an affiliated student; and

(*b*) a student who has not obtained honours in either Part IA or Part IB and takes Part II in the year after he has obtained honours in another Tripos

must submit a dissertation on some geographical subject. The subject of the dissertation must be approved by the Head of Department not later than the division of the Michaelmas Term preceding the examination. The text must not exceed 9,000 words and must be submitted in typescript (unless permission has been obtained to submit it in manuscript) not later than the division of the Lent Term preceding the examination. The examiners may examine a candidate *viva voce* upon it.

The Preliminary Examination for Part II

The papers in this examination are taken from amongst the papers for Part IB of the Tripos. Each candidate must offer four of those papers.

The Ordinary Examination in Geography for the Ordinary B.A. Degree

The examination consists of the five papers for Part IA of the Geographical Tripos.

A student may not count towards the Ordinary B.A. Degree both the Ordinary Examination in Geography and also anything he may have to his credit as the result of Part IA or Part IB of the Geographical Tripos.

HISTORY

In this subject there are courses of study followed by candidates for:

The *Historical Tripos*, which is divided into two Parts.
The *Preliminary Examination* for each Part of the Tripos.
The *Ordinary Examination* in History for the Ordinary B.A. Degree.
The *Diploma in Historical Studies*.
M.Phil. Degree in *International Relations*.

The Historical Tripos

The Historical Tripos is designed to allow the study of a wider range of historical subjects than is normally available at school, and to provide an opportunity for the investigation of these subjects at a deeper level, and from a greater variety of standpoints, than is possible in a school curriculum. Cambridge has for many years been strong in social and economic, as well as in political, religious and intellectual, history; candidates can choose from papers ranging chronologically from ancient Greece and Rome to the present day, and geographically from Britain and Europe to extra-European countries. There is increasing opportunity, as the course unfolds, to study the subject through primary source materials. The teaching system, based on a combination of lectures, seminars, and individual tuition, is intended to stimulate a spirit of historical enquiry, and to encourage undergraduates, by weighing and assessing the evidence, to reach their own conclusions.

The Tripos is divided into two Parts, the examination for Part I normally being taken at the end of the second year, and the examination for Part II normally at the end of the third year. The Preliminary Examination, held at the end of the third term of the first year, does not affect the degree classification.

The two principles governing the organization of the Tripos are:

(*a*) the provision of opportunities for increasing specialization over the course of the three-year period of study,

(*b*) the provision of an increasingly wide choice of subjects as the course proceeds.

All candidates for Part I take a General historical problems paper. A candidate is required to choose at least one of the five periods of English political and constitutional history and English economic and social history. He also makes three further choices from among papers covering other periods of English history, seven periods of European history, two periods in the History of political thought, Expansion of Europe, North American history since 1607, and The West and the 'Third World' from the First World War to the present day. In total a candidate takes six papers in Part I.

In Part II there is a wide range of subjects, and their time span is narrower. English and European history are divided into short periods which are studied at a greater level of intensity than in Part I; there are 'specified' subjects devoted to a particular theme or topic or to comparative studies; there are papers on extra-European history, on the History of political thought, and on Political Philosophy; and there are 'special' subjects which vary from time to time, and which allow close examination of short periods with particular attention to primary documents.

A candidate for Part II may choose to offer a dissertation of between 7,000 and 15,000 words on a topic in substitution for one of his Part II papers, but not in place of the General historical problems paper or a 'special' subject.

Compulsions governing the choice of subjects in Part II are as follows:

(*a*) All candidates (as in Part I) take a General historical problems paper.

(*b*) All candidates must take a 'special' subject.

(*c*) Candidates who in Part I of the Historical Tripos took no paper which fell mainly in a period before 1750 must take at least one such paper in Part II. It should also be noted that a period, or part of a period of English and European history studied in Part I cannot be studied again in Part II, although a candidate may take a 'special' or 'specified' subject in English or European history or write a dissertation on a topic which falls within a period he has studied in Part I.

(*d*) Candidates who in Part I of the Historical Tripos took no European paper must take at least one such paper in Part II.

Subject to his abiding by these provisos, a candidate in Part II can therefore, if he wishes, confine himself entirely to one general field, selecting his three subjects from either English, or European, or extra-European history; alternatively, he can range as widely as he likes, choosing something from each.

While the great majority of undergraduates reading history have specialized in history at school, this is not essential. Freshness of approach is often preferable to historical erudition, and a good working knowledge of French and German, for example, is likely to prove of considerably more value than close acquaintance while still at school with the more specialized products of modern historical scholarship. The best preparation for the Historical Tripos, before coming to Cambridge, consists of wide general reading and the cultivation of an interest in the present as well as in the past.

Although the full course in History at Cambridge is a three-year course, the division of the Tripos into two Parts makes it possible for an undergraduate to study History for only one or two of his three years and to take one Part of a Tripos in another subject for the remainder of his time at the University. It would be possible, therefore, to combine one Part of the Historical Tripos with one Part of another Tripos, such as Law, or Archaeology and Anthropology, or Fine Arts. While Part I of the Historical Tripos is a two-year course, and Part II is normally a one-year course, there is also an extended version of Part II, covering two years, for candidates who have taken Part I of another Tripos at the end of their first year, and wish to switch to Part II of the Historical Tripos.

Part I

Part I may be taken at the end of the second year of residence, or one or two years after obtaining honours in another Honours Examination, but not later than a candidate's fourth year. The scheme of examination is as follows:

Section A – *General Historical Problems*

1. General historical problems.

Section B – *English Political and Constitutional History*

2. English political and constitutional history, 500–1450.
3. English political and constitutional history, 1200–1600.
4. English political and economic history, 1450–1750.
5. English political and constitutional history, 1600–1870.
6. English political and constitutional history, since 1750.

Section C – *English Economic and Social History*

7. English economic and social history, 500–1450.
8. English economic and social history, 1200–1600.

9. English economic and social history, 1450–1750.

10. English economic and social history, 1600–1870.

11. English economic and social history, since 1750.

Section D – *European History*

12. European history, 776 B.C.–A.D. 284.

13. European history, 31 B.C.–A.D. 962.

14. European history, 284–1250.

15. European history, 962–1500.

16. European history, 1250–1715.

17. European history, 1500–1871.

18. European history, since 1715.

Section E – *Political Thought*

19. History of political thought to *c.* 1750 (also serves as Paper O 5 of Part II of the Classical Tripos).

20. History of political thought since *c.* 1750.

Section F – *Extra-European History*

21. Expansion of Europe since the fifteenth century to the First World War.

22. North American history since 1607.

Section G – *Additional Historical Subjects to be set from time to time*

23. The West and the 'Third World' from the First World War to the present day.

24. A subject in any aspect of History specified by the Faculty Board from time to time.

A candidate for Part I must offer papers as follows:

(*a*) if he takes the examination in the fourth, fifth, or sixth term after his first term of residence, or in the year next but one after he has obtained honours in another Honours Examination, or if he is an Affiliated Student who has been given leave by the Faculty Board to take Part I in the fourth, fifth, or sixth term after his first term kept, Paper 1 and five other papers;

(*b*) if he takes the examination in the year next after he has obtained honours in another Honours Examination, Paper 1 and four other papers;

provided that

(i) he offers at least one paper from Section B, at least one paper from Section C, and at least one paper from Sections D–G;

(ii) if he offers more than one paper either from Section B or from Section C or from Section D, he must not choose papers within that Section which overlap chronologically:

(iii) no candidate who has obtained honours in either Part of the Classical Tripos can offer Paper 12 or 13;

(iv) the Faculty Board may specify from among Papers 2–24 a paper or papers which an Affiliated Student who is a candidate under this regulation may or may not offer.

The details of these papers are as follows:

1. General historical problems

The purpose of this paper is to test candidates' ability to handle questions of historical method and broad historical themes. In particular, candidates are expected to show greater skill at sustained and wide-ranging historical analysis than is possible in the other Tripos papers, and to demonstrate their capacity to strike a balance between generalized argument and detailed examples.

Candidates are required to answer one question.

Some of the questions are designed to enable candidates to display a knowledge of historical theory and method, including the nature of historical explanation, the boundaries and connexions between different fields of historical study, relations with other disciplines, and critical analysis of the methods, concepts, and types of evidence used by historians.

Other questions are designed to test candidates' ability to deploy a connected argument supported by historical illustration about major themes of human development.

2–6. English political and constitutional history, from A.D. 500 to the present day

In these papers candidates are required to show knowledge of political and constitutional aspects of English history within the specified period.

Candidates may also be required to show knowledge of Irish, Scottish, and Welsh history and diplomatic history, where relevant to the period studied. Candidates are expected to show evidence of their ability to use and interpret contemporary documents. In each paper three questions must be answered, but no question will be specified as compulsory.

7–11. English economic and social history, from A.D. 500 to the present day

In these papers candidates are required to show knowledge of economic, social, and cultural aspects of English history within the specified period. Candidates may also be required to show knowledge of Irish, Scottish, and Welsh history, where relevant to the period studied. Candidates are expected to show evidence of their ability to use and interpret contemporary documents. In each paper three questions must be answered, but no question will be specified as compulsory.

12–18. European history, from 776 B.C. to the present day

These papers survey European history in the periods concerned, in its political, constitutional, cultural, economic, and social aspects. Each paper is set in two sections. In one section the major emphasis is on political and constitutional history; in the other section the major emphasis is on economic, social, intellectual, and cultural history. Candidates are also required to show knowledge of general aspects of European history. Candidates are required to answer three questions, at least one question from each section.

19. History of political thought to *c.* 1750

This paper deals with political ideas and theories in their relation to general history up to *c.* 1750. The paper will be divided into two sections. Section A contains questions on prescribed texts. Section B contains questions designed to test knowledge of trends and movements in the history of political thought derived from the study of the texts prescribed for Section A and of subsidiary texts announced by the Faculty Board. Candidates are required to answer three questions, but no question will be specified as compulsory.

20. History of political thought since *c.* 1750

This paper deals with political ideas and theories in their relation to general history since *c.* 1750. The paper is divided into two sections. Section A contains questions on prescribed texts. Section B contains questions designed to test knowledge of trends and movements in the history of political thought derived from the study of the texts prescribed for Section A and of subsidiary texts announced by the Faculty Board. Candidates are required to answer three questions, but no question will be specified as compulsory.

21. Expansion of Europe from the fifteenth century to the First World War

This paper deals comparatively with the growth of political, economic, and cultural relations between Europe and the rest of the world since 1400; and with their effects in world history. The subject consists of an historical introduction to the institutions and culture of the major societies of Africa and Asia; comparative analysis of the motives and forms of the expanding wealth and power of Europe; the effects of European expansion upon indigenous societies and the emergence of modern nationalisms; the politics and economics of European colonization and the development of colonial nationalism in the Americas (excluding the United States after 1776), Australasia, and North and South Africa; the general theory of imperialism and nationalism in the modern world.

22. North American history since 1607

This paper concentrates on the history of those parts of North America which now form the United States. Candidates are required to answer three questions.

23. Subject specified in **1985** and **1986**: The West and the 'Third World' from the First World War to the present day

This paper surveys the historical interaction between the West and the 'Third World' since 1918 in its political, economic, and strategic aspects. It deals with the effects of world economic fluctuations and of the two World Wars on Western societies and the development of modern nationalist movements; Western attempts at political and strategic adjustment including the process of decolonization; the emergence of the 'new states' and their evolution since independence; the nature and relevance of modern theories of imperialism, neo-colonialism, and under-development. Attention is given to those aspects of the social and economic structure of overseas societies that are pertinent to the explanation of major political trends.

Part II

Part II may be taken one or two years after obtaining honours in Part I, or in any other Honours Examination, but not later than a candidate's fourth year. The scheme of examination is as follows:

Section A – *General Historical Problems*

1. General historical problems

The detail of this paper is the same as for Part I (see p. 192).

Section B – *Special Subject*

2. Sources paper

3. Essay paper

Each candidate must choose one Special Subject from a list of Special Subjects published by the Faculty Board. With each of the subjects original authorities are specified some of which may be in a foreign language. A candidate is required to take two three-hour Special Subject examination papers. One of the papers deals exclusively with the original authorities; in the other paper three questions have to be answered.

In **1985**, the special subjects will be:

*A. Rome and the Western Empire, A.D. 41–161 (Paper C2, and possibly questions from Paper C3, of Part II of the Classical Tripos).
*B. England and the continent in the eighth century.
*C. The universities and society in England from the twelfth century to 1485.
*D. The Burgundian 'state' in fifteenth-century Netherlands.
*E. Social protest in Germany, 1520–26.
*F. Church, state, and society in late Stuart England, 1660–1714.
G. Slavery and servitude in the age of the American Revolution, 1763–1790.
H. The transformation of the British monarchy: political influence and public image during the reign of Queen Victoria.

* Candidates who have previously taken Part I and who did not offer in that Part a paper falling mainly in the period before 1750 will be able to meet the requirement to take a pre-1750 paper in Part II by offering one of the subjects marked with an asterisk.

I. Government, industry and the 'arms race': Britain, 1890–1914.
J. Gandhi, reform and agitation: Indian politics, 1916–1922.
K. The Fascist seizure of power in Italy: October 1918 to January 1925.
L. The political career of Charles de Gaulle, 1940–62.
M. Mau Mau: Origins, reactions and myths.
N. Title to be announced.

In **1986**, the special subjects will be:

*A. Rome and the Western Empire, A.D. 41–161 (Paper C2, and possibly questions from Paper C3 of Part II of the Classical Tripos).
*B. England and the Continent in the eighth century.
*C. The universities and society in medieval England from the twelfth century to 1485.
*D. The Burgundian 'State' in fifteenth century Netherlands.
*E. Social protest in Germany, 1520–26.
*F. Church, state and society in late Stuart England, 1660–1714.
G. The Philosophes and the Monarchs.
H. The drafting and ratification of the United States Constitution, 1787–88.
I. Clive and Warren Hastings.
J. Christian socialism in mid-Victorian England.
K. Rethinking the role of the State: Economic and social policy, 1922–35.
L. The political career of Charles de Gaulle, 1940–62.
M. Mau Mau: Origins, reactions and myths.
N. Nuclear strategy and Anglo-American relations, 1939–64

Section C – *Political Thought*

4. A period in the history of political thought

This paper deals with political ideas and theories in their relation to general history. Candidates are required to answer questions either (*a*) on the period up to *c*. 1750 or (*b*) on the period since *c*. 1750. Each period is divided into two sections. Section A contains questions on prescribed

* Candidates who have previously taken Part I and who did not offer in that Part a paper falling mainly in the period before 1750 will be able to meet the requirement to take a pre-1750 paper in Part II by oflering one of the subjects marked with an asterisk.

texts. Section B contains questions designed to test knowledge of trends and movements in the history of political thought, derived from the study of the texts prescribed for Section A and of subsidiary texts prescribed for Section A and of subsidiary texts announced by the Faculty Board. In each period three questions must be answered, but no question is specified as compulsory in either section of the paper.

5. Political philosophy (also serves as Paper 20 of Part II of the Social and Political Sciences Tripos).

This paper centres on the study of the nature and ends of the state, the grounds of political obligation, and the study of the main theories which have influenced the structure and functions of governments in the modern world. Candidates are expected to show some knowledge of modern intellectual movements and some ability to discuss political concepts and broad political issues in a critical and independent way. The main concepts and issues to be considered are as follows: the understanding of politics and of society generally; the question of the relations between political thought and action, and of the limitations on the possibility of political action; the concepts of authority, power and security; contract, rights, and representation; liberty, social justice, equality, welfare, and the public interest; the relations between law, moral attitudes, and political behaviour.

Section D – *Comparative and Thematic Studies*

6. A subject in economic history

For **1985** and **1986**: Business, literature and society, 1750–1950.

7. A subject in the history of international relations

For **1985** and **1986**: The development of the international system since the seventeenth century.

8. A subject in the history of ideas since *c.* 1500

In **1985** and **1986**: History and Historians from Guicciardini to Gibbon.

9. A subject in comparative and thematic studies

For **1985** and **1986**: Revolution (special subject, Paper 22, in Part II of the Social and Political Sciences Tripos).

10. A subject in comparative and thematic studies

For **1985**: The history of population and family structure.
For **1986**: Marriage in England, 1500–1800.

11. A subject in comparative economic and social history

The purpose of this paper is to introduce students to some of the approaches and techniques developed and applied by economic and social historians over the last fifty years. It requires not only the scrutiny of the assumptions which lay behind the work of particular historians or groups of historians, but also a working knowledge of the basic theoretical concepts and methods they have used.

The paper is set in two sections. Candidates are required to answer three questions and may answer all questions from one section, or from both. In both sections candidates are expected to understand the logic of explanation in the work of economic and social historians and to analyse the appropriateness and effectiveness of the application to historical study of the concepts and methods specified below.

Section A: Concepts and methods in economic history

This section is concerned with the ways economic historians have used aspects of economic theory in their historical work. Among the subjects to be studied are historical applications of national income accounting; trade cycle theory; counterfactual models of economic development; theories of the determinants of the level of and changes in income and employment, wages, and prices, with special reference to the work of Keynes; theories of surplus value; definitions of skill; and international trade and international payments.

Section B: Concepts and methods in social history

This section is concerned with the ways historians have applied quantitative methods and sociological concepts to the study of history. Special attention will be paid to demographic history. Candidates may be tested on the uses to which the following statistical techniques and sociological concepts have been put by historians: aggregative analysis; measurements of central tendency and dispersion; the analysis of time series; measurements of the relationship between variables; concepts of social stratification; kinship and family structure, measurements of literacy; approaches to the study of popular culture and mentality.

Candidates are not expected to master all these concepts and methods, but to concentrate on aspects of the study of economic and social history with which they are familiar or with which they wish to become familiar. Candidates may specialize in either quantitative or non-quantitative methods.

In **1985**: Concepts and methods in economic and social history.

In **1986**: European society and the First World War: Britain, France, Germany.

Section E – *Papers on English and European history*

12. A period in English history

Candidates must answer questions on one of the following periods:

(*a*) A.D. 500–A.D. 1200
(*b*) 1200–1450
(*c*) 1450–1600
(*d*) 1600–1750
(*e*) 1750–1870
(*f*) since 1870

13. A period in European history

Candidates must answer questions on one of the following periods:

(*a*) A.D. 284–962
(*b*) 962–1250
(*c*) 1250–1500
(*d*) 1500–1715
(*e*) 1715–1871
(*f*) since 1871

Section F – *Topics in English or European or English and European history*

14. A subject in ancient history

For **1985** and **1986**: The transformation of the Roman world (also serves as Paper O9 of Part II of the Classical Tripos).

15. A subject in medieval English history

For **1985** and **1986**: The Norman Conquest, 1042–1154.

16. A subject in medieval European history

For **1985** and **1986**: Byzantium and its neighbours (*c*. 900–1204).

17. A subject in modern English history

For **1985** and **1986**: Deviance, law, and social order in England, 1750–1914.

18. A subject in modern European history

For **1985** and **1986**: Continuity and change in France since the French Revolution.

19. A subject in English or European or English and European history

For **1985** and **1986**: Religious thought in England, 1485–1650.

20. A subject in English or European or English and European history

For **1985** and **1986**: The struggle for mastery in Germany, 1740–1880.

Section G – *Extra-European history*

21. A subject in African history

For **1985** and **1986**: The history of Africa from *c*. 1800 to the present day.

The paper deals with the history of the entire African continent. Candidates are expected to show a general grasp of the processes of African history including the principles of African social, economic, and political organization, the growth of African states and empires, the changes brought about by European influences, the emergence of modern nationalism, the terms of decolonization, and the problems of post-colonial government and economy. While candidates will be allowed to give special attention to one or more geographical regions, they will also be given the opportunity to draw comparisons between them. The paper is not divided into sections, but for purposes of both specialization and comparison, the continent will be considered to have the four following regions: North and North East Africa, including central and eastern Sudan, Ethiopia, and Somalia; South and South Central Africa, including Angola and Mozambique; East Africa, including Rwanda and Burundi; Western Africa, including the western Sudanic zone and Zaire (Congo).

22. A subject in Asian history

For **1985** and **1986**: The history of South Asia from the late eighteenth century to 1947.

In this paper the term South Asia is taken to mean the whole Indian subcontinent. The paper is broadly concerned with the development of South Asia during the specified period. Candidates are expected to show knowledge of the working of indigenous political and socio-religious systems; the rise of the British dominion; social and religious movements; economic, educational, and social developments (including land questions); the rise of national movements and Muslim separatism; India's place within the British Imperial system and its relations with the outer world.

23. A subject in North American history

In **1985**: U.S. foreign policy since the 1890s.

In **1986**: Economic and social history of the U.S.A., 1815–85.

24. A subject in extra-European history specified by the Faculty Board

This paper will not be available in **1985**.

In **1986**: Spain in America: Mexico and Peru, 1492–1821.

25. A subject in extra-European history

For **1985** and **1986**: The history of the Commonwealth from 1839 to the present day.

In this paper Commonwealth history is understood to mean a survey of Imperial and Commonwealth history from 1839 to the present day in its political, constitutional, economic, and strategic aspects. Candidates are expected to show knowledge of the more important contemporary documents bearing on the subject.

Knowledge of the internal history of individual Commonwealth countries is required only in so far as is necessary for an understanding of the emergence, development, and working of the Commonwealth as a whole.

A candidate for Part II must offer

(*a*) if he takes the examination in the year next after he has obtained honours in Part I of the Historical Tripos or in another Honours Examination, or if he is an Affiliated Student who has been given leave by the Faculty Board to take Part II in the first, second, or third term after his first term kept, Sections A and B (Papers 1–3) and

either two papers from Sections C–G

or one paper from Sections C–G and a dissertation on a topic approved by the Faculty Board within the range of the Historical Tripos as a whole, provided that a candidate must not submit a dissertation on a topic falling within the scope of Paper 1, or of the special subject that he is offering for Papers 2 and 3, or of any paper that he is offering from amongst Papers 4–11 and 14–25;

(*b*) if he takes the examination in the year next but one after he has obtained honours in Part I of the Historical Tripos or in another Honours Examination, or if he is an Affiliated Student who has been given leave by the Faculty Board to take Part II in the fourth, fifth, or sixth term after his first term kept, Sections A and B (Papers 1–3) and

either four papers from Sections C–G

or three papers from Sections C–G and a dissertation on a topic approved by the Faculty Board within the range of the Historical Tripos as a whole, provided that a candidate must not submit a dissertation on a topic falling within the scope of Paper 1, or of the special subject that he is offering for Papers 2 and 3, or of any Paper that he is offering from amongst Papers 4–11 and 14–25;

provided that

(i) no candidate may offer in Papers 2 and 3 a subject which he has already offered in Group C of Part II of the Classical Tripos;

(ii) no candidate who has obtained honours in Part II of the Classical Tripos may offer Paper 14;

(iii) no candidate may offer any paper that he has previously offered as a candidate for another Honours Examination;

(iv) (*a*) if he offers Paper 4, which will comprise not more than two periods, or Paper 12, which will comprise not more than six periods, or Paper 13, which will comprise not more than six periods, he will in each case offer not more than one of these periods and will declare in his entry for the examination which period he intends to offer;

(*b*) if he offers Paper 4 he must not choose a period which covers chronologically in whole or in part a paper that he has already offered from Section E in Part I;

(*c*) if he offers Paper 12 he must not choose a period which covers chronologically in whole or in part a paper that he has already offered from Sections B and C in Part I;

(*d*) if he offers Paper 13 he must not choose a period which covers chronologically in whole or in part a paper that he has already offered from Section D in Part I;

(v) the Faculty Board may specify from among Papers 4–25 a paper or papers which an Affiliated Student who is a candidate under this regulation may or may not offer;

(vi) a candidate who has previously obtained honours in Part I of the Historical Tripos but who did not offer in that Part a paper from among

either Papers 2–5, 7–10, 12–17 and 19

or Papers 25 and 26 (if available, and if the subject

specified for the paper fell mainly in a period before 1750)

must offer in Part II

either Papers 2 and 3, provided that the special subject selected by the candidate is one which has been announced by the Faculty Board as a subject falling mainly in the period before 1750

or one of the following papers, provided that the period selected by the candidate or the subject specified for the paper by the Faculty Board is a period or subject falling mainly in the period before 1750:

Papers 4, 8, and 12–16;

Papers 19–20, and 23–25 (if available);

(vii) a candidate who has previously obtained honours in Part I of the Historical Tripos but who did not offer in that Part a paper from among Papers 12–18 must offer in Part II a paper from among Papers 4, 7, 9, and any other papers on a subject in European history specified by the Faculty Board from time to time;

(viii) any restrictions imposed by provisos (vi) and (vii) on a candidate's choice of papers will apply also to the alternative of offering a dissertation under this regulation.

A candidate for Part II who chooses to offer a dissertation must submit the proposed title of his dissertation through his Tutor to the Secretary of the Faculty Board so as to reach him not later than the first Monday of the Full Michaelmas Term next preceding the examination; with his proposed title the candidate shall submit the number and the title of the paper with which it is associated and the number and title of each paper (other than Paper 1) that he intends to offer. Each candidate must obtain the approval of the title of his dissertation by the Faculty Board not later than the end of the Full Michaelmas Term next preceding the examination. After the Faculty Board have approved a candidate's proposed dissertation title no change may be made to it without the approval of the Faculty Board, but a candidate may submit a revised title to the Secretary of the Faculty Board by the division of the following Lent Term for the approval of the Faculty Board. Titles received by the Faculty Board after that date shall be considered only in the most exceptional circumstances. Each dissertation must be typewritten, unless permission has been given to present it in manuscript (and if this is considered insufficiently legible, it may have to be resubmitted in typescript), of not less than 7,000 and not more than 15,000 words in length (inclusive of footnotes and appendices, but exclusive of bibliography), must show knowledge of primary sources, and must be submitted through the candidate's Tutor so as to reach the Secretary of the Faculty Board not later than the end of the first week of Full Term in which the examination is held. Each dissertation must bear a motto but not the candidate's name and must be accompanied by (*a*) a sealed envelope bearing the same motto outside and containing the name of the candidate and his College, (*b*) a brief synopsis on a separate sheet of paper of the contents of his dissertation, and (*c*) a certificate signed by the candidate that it is his own original work and that it does not contain material that he has already used to any substantial extent for a comparable purpose. A candidate will be required to give full references to sources used. The Examiners will have power at their discretion to examine a candidate *viva voce* on his dissertation and on the general field of knowledge within which it falls.

The Preliminary Examination for Part I

The examination consists of five papers as follows:

1. General historical problems (Paper 1 of Part I).
2. English history: political and constitutional.
3. English history: social and economic.
4. European history from 776 B.C. to the present day.
5. Translation of foreign language passages.

Every candidate must offer Paper 5, unless he has obtained honours in another Tripos or is an Affiliated Student or is certified by his Tutor to have qualified for matriculation with the help of a non-European language, and three of Papers 1–4.

Paper 1 will be framed to enable candidates to display a knowledge of general aspects of history. Candidates will be required to answer one question.

The papers on English history run from the Anglo-Saxon period to the present day, and therefore encompass all five of the separate periods of English history set in Part I of the Historical Tripos. In Paper 2 candidates are required to show knowledge of political and constitutional aspects and also of general aspects of English history. Candidates may also be required to show knowledge of Irish, Scottish, and Welsh history and diplomatic history, where relevant to the period studied. Candidates are expected to show evidence of their ability to use and interpret contemporary documents. Four questions must be answered but no question will be specified as compulsory. In Paper 3 candidates are required to show knowledge of economic, social, and cultural aspects and also of general aspects of English history. Candidates may also be required to show knowledge of Irish, Scottish, and Welsh history, where relevant to the period studied. Candidates are expected to show evidence of their ability to use and interpret contemporary documents. Three questions must be answered, but no question will be specified as compulsory.

Paper 4 on European history covers the chronological span from 776 B.C. to the present day. The paper is set in two sections. In one section the major emphasis is on political and constitutional history; in the other section the major emphasis is on economic, social, intellectual, and cultural history. Candidates are also required to show knowledge of general aspects of European history. Candidates are required to answer three questions at least one of which must be chosen from each section.

In Paper 5 candidates are required to translate into English passages written in a foreign language. Two passages will be set in Latin, two in French, and two in German. One passage will be set in Greek, one in Spanish, one in Italian, and one in Russian. Candidates are expected to satisfy the Examiners in one passage in Latin or French or German, and in one additional passage which may be in Latin, in French, in German, or in one of the other languages set. Dictionaries may be used in the examination.

The Preliminary Examination for Part II

The papers for this examination are taken from among the papers for Part II of the Historical Tripos. A candidate who wishes to be classed must offer Paper 1, and any three other papers, except Paper 2, or Paper 3, or a paper which he would not be permitted to offer if he were a candidate for the Tripos examination.

The Examination in History for the Ordinary B.A. Degree

The examination consists of the following four papers, all of which must be taken:

1. General historical problems.
2. English history: political and constitutional.

3. English history: social and economic.
4. European History from 776 B.C. to the present day.

The papers in any year are the same as those for the papers in the Preliminary Examination for Part I.

The Diploma in Historical Studies

The Diploma is primarily but not exclusively intended to provide for those who intend to proceed to a research degree in Cambridge after taking a one-year postgraduate course in advanced historical studies. Candidature is open to students who, on the recommendation of the Degree Committee for the Faculty of History, have been admitted to the status of Graduate Student by the Board of Graduate Studies. Applications, together with evidence of qualifications, should be submitted to the Secretary of the Board of Graduate Studies not later than 31 July in the year preceding that in which the applicant wishes to present himself for examination. In exceptional circumstances, the Board may accept later applications.

Candidates must submit a thesis of not less than 15,000 or more than 30,000 words (including notes and appendices) on a subject approved by the Degree Committee. Candidates must submit to the Secretary of the Degree Committee, not later than the division of the Michaelmas Term, the proposed title of their dissertation.

Candidates are examined orally on the subject of their dissertation and on the general field in which it falls.

The M.Phil. course (one-year) in International Relations

(See p. 485)

The course of study includes lectures, seminars, and individual supervision. It is designed to give a general understanding of the nature and development of the modern international system, an appreciation of the nature and problems of the contemporary world, and an opportunity for the candidate to study at greater depth a subject suited to his needs and interests in those areas.

The syllabus of the course of study is as follows:

The rise of the nation-state and the modern system of relations between states; statecraft and diplomacy and their historical development; the concepts of national interest, balance of power, and international community; the roles of power and war; the relationship between the super-powers; the relationship between states at different stages of development; the theories of deterrence; modern international law and its development; the relationship of international law, policy, and economies; the legal and economic aspects of regional integration; international institutions and their development; the role of the U.N. and its agencies; the law of armed conflict and peaceful settlement of disputes; the economics of international trade and finance; the economics of growth and development; comparisons and contrasts between the economic development of different social systems.

The scheme of examination consists of (*a*) a thesis of not more than 25,000 words in length, including tables, footnotes, and appendices, but excluding bibliography, on a subject approved by the Degree Committee for the Faculty of History. The examination includes an oral examination upon the thesis and the general field of knowledge in which it falls; and (*b*) three essays, each not exceeding 2,000 words in length and on a set topic falling within one of the following fields, provided that not more than one topic is chosen from any particular field:

History and theory of international relations.
Strategic studies.
International economics.
International law.

HISTORY OF ART

The History of Art Tripos is intended for those who wish to study the history, criticism, and theory of the figurative arts as well as of architecture. The course does not provide studio-work in practical art.

To be entered as a candidate for the History of Art Tripos, it is necessary to have obtained honours in Part I of any other Tripos or to be accepted by the University as an Affiliated Student.

The courses and Tripos requirements are so arranged as to enable candidates to prepare to take Group (i) in one year, or Group (ii) in two* years. Candidates for Group (ii) are required to take a Preliminary Examination at the end of their first year of study.

The Head of the Department of the History of Art is responsible for arranging the teaching and for the issue of lists of recommended books. Teaching consists of lectures and classes in the Department (Scroope Terrace), and in the Fitzwilliam Museum. The Slade Professor of Fine Art is a member of the Faculty. His classes in the Department and his public lectures to the University are arranged in conjunction with the teaching of the Department.

Lectures and classes given by the staff of the Department are extensively augmented with teaching given by visitors appointed for their outstanding abilities in those fields of Art History related to the subjects of special study.

Prospective candidates, after consulting their College Tutors and present Directors of Studies, should arrange to call on the Director of Studies in the History of Art for their College as early in their Cambridge careers as possible, and *in any case not later than one week before the end of the Easter Full Term preceding the year in which they would begin to read specifically for the History of Art Tripos*, in order to discuss their likely suitability and plans for preliminary study and travel. Preparation for reading History of Art at Cambridge should include: as much looking at buildings and works of art in the original as may be feasible in this country and abroad; attendance at the Slade lectures, and at other 'open lectures' on the arts; an ability to read French at least, and, desirably, German or Italian or both. Really inadequate reading knowledge of these principal languages of Europe may debar candidates not only from satisfactory access to the documentary sources, but also from using secondary material

* If a candidate wishes to spend two years, after spending two years obtaining honours in another Tripos, and is receiving an L.E.A. grant, he is strongly advised to apply through his Tutor for his grant for his fourth year not later than the beginning of his fourth term at the University.

of critical importance. Total incapacity to cope with Latin sentences, even with a dictionary, is no less a handicap to those who wish to concentrate particularly on Medieval or Renaissance subjects.

Prospective candidates should make every effort to read the few books in the list below. These books have been selected as offering classic examples of the principal approaches to those fundamental problems of interpretation and method in art history with which undergraduates should become familiar before beginning their work for the History of Art Tripos. The number of books on this basic list has been kept to a minimum. Most are very easily obtainable; and all can be read in English. The styles of approach represented, and many of the problems and ideas involved, are applicable generally beyond the ostensible limits of each book's chosen field. Copies of other lists of books currently recommended for particular courses may be obtained by applying to the Secretary, University of Cambridge Department of the History of Art, 1 Scroope Terrace, Cambridge. Reference may be made to the Head of the Department of the History of Art at the same address for such other information about the courses and requirements as is not contained in the *Handbook*.

Some foreign travel during vacations is virtually essential. Grants towards the cost of this are generally obtainable either through special funds administered by Colleges, or, with the recommendation of the Department, from Local Education Authorities. But undergraduates must expect to have to provide a part of what is needed from their own resources. The Department as such can dispose of no finance for travel.

For books undergraduates have use of the Faculty Library housed at Scroope Terrace, from which they may borrow, and of the Fitzwilliam Museum Library nearby, where they may work but not borrow, besides the University Library, which is particularly rich in source books from the mid-sixteenth to the early nineteenth century. An increasing number of books of importance in modern criticism is becoming obtainable at more reasonable prices as paperbacks; and College Libraries are co-operating most helpfully in making available to their undergraduates additional copies of the most used books of general interest.

Recommended reading

The following books are recommended to all proposing to read for the History of Art Tripos:

C. Baudelaire, *The Painter of Modern Life and other essays*, ed. J. Mayne, London, 1964; M. Baxandall, *Painting and Experience in Fifteenth Century Italy*, Oxford, 1972; M. Baxandall, *The Limewood Sculptors of Renaissance Germany*, New Haven and London, 1980; O. Benesch, *The Art of the Renaissance in Northern Europe*, London, 1965; A. Braham, *The Architecture of the French Enlightenment*, London, 1980; B. Berenson, *The Italian Painters of the Renaissance*, London, 1952; J. Burckhardt, *The Civilisation of the Renaissance in Italy*, tr. S. G. C. Middlemore, London, 1945; D. Coffin, *The Villa d'Este at Tivoli*, Princeton, 1960; T. Comito, *The Idea of the Garden in the Renaissance*, Hassocks, 1979. J. Connors, *Borromini and the Roman Oratory*, Cambridge, Mass., 1980; R. Fry, *Cézanne: a study of his development*, London, 1927; J. Gage, *Colour in Turner*, London, 1969; M. Girouard, *The Victorian Country House*, New Haven and London, 1979. E. H. Gombrich, *Art and Illusion*, London, 1960; F. Haskell, *Patrons and Painters*, New Haven, 1980. F. Haskell and N. Penny, *Taste and the Antique*, New Haven, 1981. L. Heydenreich and W. Lotz, *Architecture in Italy 1400–1600*, Harmondsworth, 1974. M. Jaffé, *Rubens and Italy*, Oxford, 1977; H. W. Janson, ed., *Sources and Documents in the History of Art*, Prentice-Hall Inc., Englewood Cliffs, New Jersey; A. Katzenellenbogen, *The Sculptural Programs of Chartres Cathedral*, Baltimore, 1959; E. Mâle, *The Gothic Image*, London, 1913; J. M. Montias, *Artists and Artisans in Delft in the Seventeenth Century*, Princeton, 1982; G. Morelli, *Italian painters: Critical Studies of their works*, tr. C. J. Ffoulkes, London, 1892; O. Pächt, *The Rise of Pictorial Narrative in Twelfth-Century England*, Oxford, 1962; E. Panofsky, *Renaissance and Renascences in Western Art*, Stockholm, 1960; E. Panofsky, *Studies in Iconology*, New York, 1962; N. Pevsner, *An Outline of European Architecture*, London, 1960; M. Podro, *The Critical Historians of Art*, New Haven, 1983; J. Reynolds, *Discourses on Art*, ed. R. Wark, San Marino, 1959; F. Saxl, *Lectures*, London, 1957; M. Schapiro, *Word and Image*, Leyden, 1972; M. Schapiro, *Late Antique, Early Christian and Mediaeval Art*: Selected papers, London, 1980; G. Scott, *The Architecture of Humanism*, London, 1914; J. Summerson, *Architecture in Britain 1530–1830*, London, 1983; J. White, *The Birth and Rebirth of Pictorial Space*, London, 1957; H. Wölfflin, *Principles of Art History*. tr. M. D. Hottinger, London, 1932; H. Wölfflin, *Classic Art*, London, 1952.

The scheme of examination is as follows:

The Tripos consists of one Part. A student who has obtained honours in another Honours Examination may take the Tripos in his third or fourth year. A student may not be a candidate for the

Tripos on more than one occasion, or be a candidate for another University examination in the same term. The scheme of the examination is as follows:

Paper 1. Approaches to the History of Art, with reference to works of criticism

This paper deals with the influence of writers of classical antiquity upon the Renaissance approach to art and architecture; with changing attitudes towards both antiquity and the Middle Ages in the eighteenth century; with nineteenth-century and twentieth-century theoretical and critical approaches to art and architecture; and with recent developments in art historical methods, the growth of connoisseurship, formal and stylistic criticism, and sociological and iconographical interpretations of works of art and architecture.

and such number of **pairs of papers** on special subjects as the Faculty Board may announce from time to time. There will be no less than six pairs of such papers on special subjects. Each pair of papers will deal with a particular person, subject, or period in the History of Art. In each pair of papers, the second paper will consist of photographs of works of art requiring comment and interpretation.

A candidate for the Tripos must offer

(i) if he takes the examination in the year next after he has obtained honours in another Tripos, Paper 1; two pairs of papers on special subjects; and a thesis of between 7,000 and 9,000 words on a subject approved by the Faculty Board dealing with a particular person, work of art, subject, or period in the History of Art.

(ii) if he takes the examination in the year next but one after he has obtained honours in another Tripos, three pairs of papers on special subjects; and a thesis of between 7,000 and 9,000 words on a subject approved by the Faculty Board dealing with a particular person, work of art, subject, or period in the History of Art. Theses must be typewritten, unless previous permission has been obtained to present the thesis in manuscript.

The pairs of papers on special subjects in **1985** will be as follows:

2 and 3. Religious Art of the High Middle Ages in Northern Europe

The option investigates techniques of pictorial narrative in painting and sculpture, mainly of the twelfth and thirteenth centuries; the variety of interplay of pictorial imagery and the written word, in 'literal' illustrations, captions, inscribed verbal dialogue, etc.; the emergence in this period of new narrative and devotional subjects; the imagery of the saints; and the 'visionary' element in some representations of sacred scenes or persons. Special attention will be paid throughout to the evidence contained in illuminated books such as Psalters and Apocalypses in Cambridge collections.

4 and 5. The Figurative Arts in Tuscany, 1402–1482

The subject deals mainly with painting and sculpture of the Florentine and Sienese Schools. It begins with the submissions by Ghiberti and Brunelleschi of competition reliefs for the doors of the Bapistery in Florence. The major artists of the period will be studied individually, and an attempt will be made to assess their impact upon the pictorial conventions inherited from the previous century. Account will also be taken of the activity of artists like Gentile da Fabriano and Domenico Veneziano who came from other artistic centres to work in Tuscany. The period ends with the abandonment by Leonardo da Vinci of his unfinished painting of the Adoration of the Magi (Uffizi), and the departure for Rome of Ghirlandaio and Botticelli to work, among others, in the Sistine Chapel.

6 and 7. Rembrandt and Dutch art, 1600–1675

This option deals with the main currents of Dutch art between 1600 and 1675: historical and genre painting, portraiture, landscape, and still-life. The production of Rembrandt and his circle, as well as the work of his most important contemporaries (Frans Hals, Jan Vermeer, etc.) are studied. Special emphasis will be placed on relating these works to their social, religious, and cultural context.

8 and 9. Modern movements between the wars

This option deals with the art, architecture, and design of what has been loosely described as 'the Modern Movement', in their widest context within the period. A focus will be provided by the periodicals *De Stijl* and *L'Esprit Nouveau*, and the publications of the Bauhaus, which will be examined from the point of view of their effect on all the arts, including the theatre and film. Among the architects studied will be Oud, van Esteren, Gropius, Mayer, Breuer, and Le Corbusier; and among the artists Mondrian, van Doesburg, Klee, Kandinsky, Schlemmer, Moholy-Nagy, Ozenfant, and Leger.

Papers 10 and 11 will be: The triumph of classicism: architecture in England, France and Germany, 1750–1830

The paper concentrates on the architects who determined the form and style of the period: Adam, Chambers, Dance, Soane, Nash and Cockerell in England; Soufflot, Peyre and De Wailly, Gondoin, Boullée, Ledoux, and Percier and Fontaine in France; and Gilly, Schinkel and Klenze in Germany. Particular attention will be paid to interior design and furnishing, as well as to the relation of buildings to their settings, whether in town or country.

Papers 12 and 13 will be: Irish, Pictish, and Anglo-Saxon Art *c.* 600–*c.* 800

The subject deals with the growth of Early Christian insular art in illuminated manuscripts, stone and ivory carving and in metalwork, from the earliest recognizable examples of the Celto-Saxon style to its mature flowering in works such as the Gospel Book of Kells and the free-standing crosses on Iona. The variety of decorative motifs, the inventive combination of which characterises the style, will be studied, together with the wide range of religious imagery displayed, both narrative and symbolic. The influence of historical personalities such as Oswald, Wilfrid, and Egbert, on the scope and content of this art will be discussed, together with the controversial problem of where the most active centres of artistic creation were located.

There will be eight pairs of papers on special subjects in **1986**:

Papers 2 and 3 will be the same as papers 12 and 13 in 1985.

Papers 4 and 5 will be the same as papers 2 and 3 in 1985.

* Papers 6 and 7 will be new, Central Italian sculpture: Donatello to Michelangelo.

Papers 8 and 9 will be the same as papers 6 and 7 in 1985.

Papers 10 and 11 will be the same as papers 10 and 11 in 1985.

Papers 12 and 13 will be: Painting and sculpture in Britain in the romantic period

The paper deals with the growth of a self-consciously British art from the close of the eighteenth century until the accession of Queen Victoria,

* The detail of these papers will be published in *Reporter* in the Michaelmas Term 1984.

and includes an assessment of the response to the teaching of Reynolds and the practice of Hogarth, Wilson, and Gainsborough among younger artists. The rôle of institutions like the Royal Academy and the British Institution will be examined, as well as the expansion in the public patronage of painters and sculptors during and after the Napoleonic wars. The chief artists to be considered are Banks, Barry, Blake, Chantrey, Constable, Cotman, Crome, Danby, Flaxman, Fuseli, Girtin, Martin, Mulready, Nollekens, Palmer, Romney, Turner, Ward, West, and Wilkie, most of whom are well-represented in collections in and around Cambridge. It is intended to set them in the social, political, and cultural context of their times.

Papers 14 and 15 will be: Painting in France, 1770–1848

This option covers French painting during a period of extreme social and political change and deals with a number of major and minor artists of radically different types. It will begin with the early work of David, and will follow his development of an austere and authoritative style during the 1780s; work by his contemporaries such as Peyron, Regnault, and Vincent, and older but still functioning artists like Fragonard and Greuze, will also be considered. David archaism of the '90s, the rise of the Primitifs, and the early work of Ingres will be analysed, and attention will be paid to the artistic consequences of the Revolution.

*Papers 16 and 17 will be: Aspects of the history of colour in painting

The Preliminary Examination for the History of Art Tripos

The Examination in **1985** consists of a paper entitled 'Approaches to the History of Art, with reference to buildings and works of art in and around Cambridge', together with certain papers from among the History of Art Tripos, namely Paper 1 (Approaches to the History of Art, with reference to works of criticism) and one pair of papers on special subjects offered in the Tripos.

The paper entitled 'Approaches to the History of Art, with reference to buildings and works of art in and around Cambridge' offers an opportunity of investigating a wide range of art historical materials and methods through study of accessible works of art and architecture. Candidates are expected to have examined the nature of the artistic problems confronted in individual works, to have gained a knowledge of the practices, attitudes, and theories of the respective periods of those works, and to have noted the changes in attitude towards the works that are characteristic of subsequent periods.

* The detail of these papers will be published in *Reporter* in the Michaelmas Term 1984.

LAND ECONOMY

In this subject there are courses of study followed by candidates for:

The *Land Economy Tripos.*

The *Preliminary Examination* for the Land Economy Tripos.

The *M.Phil.* (*one-year*) in Land Economy.

The *Diploma* in Development Studies.

Land economy is the study of the use, management and development of land and other natural resources. It is set within a conceptual framework in which explanations are sought for the spatial distribution of population and of economic activity, the physical, economic and social characteristics of the settlement structure and the general pattern of man's use of the natural environment. Thus the student considers how, at various scales from individual land units through neighbourhoods, cities, regions and nations, and in a variety of philosophical and institutional contexts, competing claims for the use, management and development of land and the built environment are articulated and resolved. Such a study involves consideration both of factors which shape investment, employment, residential and other land use decisions in the private sector, as well as of the role of government in financing and shaping public investment in infrastructure, in guiding the operation of land markets and in otherwise influencing patterns of settlement and resource use. Conflicts between equity and efficiency in the use of land and of the built environment and the evaluation of alternative forms of development, taking account of the needs of efficiency, conservation and local interests, are examined predominantly, though not exclusively, within the setting of advanced mixed economics.

As an academic subject, land economy is a derivative one, drawing mainly upon theory and applied research in the social sciences and especially upon economics, law and politics. Ultimately, the student is concerned to integrate concepts from these disciplines in an understanding of interactions between individuals and societies and their environment, as expressed particularly in the spatial distribution of the population and the location of economic and other activity. Such issues as the future of the inner city; the consequences of changes in the regional balance of population and employment; the implications of a changing mix of public and private investment in housing; the desirability of reform of the nature and structure of land ownership, and the balance between conservation and development in both urban and rural contexts, all form a particularly stimulating challenge for students who wish to use theoretical analysis in framing answers to national and local policy concerns.

In the preliminary year of land economy, all students cover basic courses in the principles of economics, the economics of agriculture and of cities and regions, legal principles and land law, history and theories of land use and the built environment, statistics and quantitative methods. In the Tripos year students are given considerable scope either to select options which lead to a specialised understanding of particular aspects of land economy or alternatively to range widely across a variety of subjects.

Graduates in land economy are particularly suitable for employment in occupations dealing with land use in general and urban and rural development in particular. Many enter chartered surveying in both public and private sectors (successful completion of particular Tripos papers gives exemption from the professional examinations of the Royal Institution of Chartered Surveyors) and others take up careers in banking and other financial institutions, environmental planning, agriculture and urban and regional analysis, especially in central and local government.

School subjects

As a student will sit the Land Economy Tripos after taking Part I of another Tripos, the subjects he reads at school preparatory to entering the University should be selected, after due weight is given to his natural abilities, with an emphasis upon the subjects best suited as a preparation for the discipline in which he intends to take the Part I Tripos.

Economics, law and political science are the foundation disciplines of land economy so that students who have done social science subjects at school such as economics, government, economic history and geography may be particularly suited to the courses. Mathematics is also a useful general grounding.

Preparatory reading

Students intending to read Land Economy may obtain a preparatory reading list of books from the Department of Land Economy, 19 Silver Street, Cambridge, CB3 9EP.

The Land Economy Tripos

The Land Economy Tripos is in one Part and is read after Part I of another Tripos. As two years' reading is normally required, it is most conveniently taken after a one-year Part I, such as Archaeology and Anthropology, Economics, Geography, Modern Languages, Law, Mathematics, Natural Sciences, Philosophy, and Theology.

It is possible for undergraduates who have read a two-year Part I to take a form of the Land Economy Tripos after one further year's reading; but as the full range of papers is not taken, this is not wholly satisfactory on academic grounds and difficulties may arise, for example, over claiming exemption from subsequent professional examinations. It is possible, according to the Regulations for Triposes, to read Land Economy for the full two years after taking a two-year Part I (such as Architecture, Classics, English, History, Music, and Oriental Studies), but such a course would entail four years' residence. While many Colleges will allow this, problems may arise over continuing L.E.A. awards for a fourth year. Anyone contemplating such a course is strongly advised to consider its complications in consultation with the College to which he applies at the earliest possible opportunity.

The examination for the Tripos consists of the following papers:

1. Issues in land economy.
2. Urban and regional economic analysis.
3. Land law.
4. Investment appraisal and public policy analysis.
5. Planning theory and process.
6. Valuation theory and practice.
7. Comparative land policies.
8. Agriculture, forestry, and rural development.
9. Housing and housing policy.
10. Agricultural and natural resource development.

A candidate who takes the Tripos after completing a two-year course of study in Land Economy is required to offer Papers 1 and 2 and four chosen from Papers 3–10, of which at least one must be from Papers 3–5; such a candidate is allowed to submit, in place of any one paper, other than Papers 1 and 2, a dissertation on an approved topic substantially within the scope of the paper concerned, provided that he is also offering at least one paper from Papers 3–5. A candidate who takes the Tripos after completing a one-year course of study is required to offer Papers 1 and 2 and three chosen from

Papers 3–10, of which at least one must be from Papers 3–5; such a candidate is not allowed to offer a dissertation.

Any eligible candidate may apply through his Tutor for the permission of the Board of Land Economy, to be obtained before the division of the Lent Term next preceding the examination, to submit in place of any one paper other than Papers 1 and 2, and subject always to the requirement that he shall offer at least one paper chosen from Papers 3–5, a dissertation of not more than 6,000 words, exclusive of footnotes, on a topic approved by the Board which falls substantially within the scope of the paper concerned. The dissertation must contain full references to any sources used in its composition. Any candidate who avails himself of this provision must submit his dissertation through his Tutor to the Secretary of the Board by the end of the first week of the Full Term in which the examination is held. Each dissertation must be accompanied by a brief synopsis on a separate piece of paper of the contents of the dissertation, and a certificate signed by the candidate that it is his own original work. The Examiners have power to examine the candidate *viva voce* on the subject of his dissertation and on the general field of knowledge within which it falls, and to require him to resubmit his dissertation in typescript if, in their opinion, the original work submitted is not sufficiently legible.

The scope of the papers is more fully defined as follows:

1. Issues in land economy

This paper deals with contemporary issues in land economy. Examples include: the changing urban settlement pattern and the spatial distribution of industry and residences; regional and rural development; local government organization and finance; land ownership and decision-making; the structure and role of the development industries and related financial institutions; social objectives in the processes of land development and spatial economic change, and the role of public agencies in relation to social and economic objectives.

2. Urban and regional economic analysis

This paper deals with the economic analysis of urban and regional development (including the development of land in these contexts) and of policies designed to influence them. Topics include: theories of the location of economic activity (including industry and residences) at the regional and urban scale; theories of regional and urban economic development and change; regional and urban economic development policies; the organization of public finance and taxation in relation to urban and regional economic activity and the impact of fiscal policies; the theory of land prices and the structure of the property markets in urban areas; the economics of building development; the role of, and objectives and criteria for, public intervention in these fields.

3. Land law

This paper deals with the English law of leases and mortgages – their nature, creation, and extinguishment, and the rights and obligations of the parties thereto (but no question will be asked on priority of mortgages); the law of easements and profits (though no question will be asked on details of the Prescription Act 1832, local customary rights, or public rights) and of covenants affecting land, both leasehold and freehold; the law of licences; and a general survey of the statutory law of landlord and tenant relating to control of rent and security of tenure.

4. Investment appraisal and public policy analysis

This paper deals with the evaluation of decisions and policies relating to land use and the development of the built environment as well as to the wider issues of sub-national economic development by private entities and public agencies. The topics covered will include: the theory of capital and value; risk and uncertainty; rates of return, discounting, and investment appraisal; cost-benefit analysis; inflation accounting; and the design of, and problems associated with, the development of appropriate decision-taking criteria for private and public action.

5. Planning theory and process

This paper deals with principles and techniques for planning the use of the land to meet the needs of society. Topics will include: demographic, social, economic, and political pressures on land and natural resources; patterns of urbanization; the theory and philosophy of planning; the socio-economic and legal frameworks of planning; policies and practices in urban and rural development and conservation; planning methodology and techniques.

6. Valuation theory and practice

This paper deals with economic, proprietary, and statutory influences on value, and methods of appraisal and valuation of different forms of investment in real property. Topics will include: the structure of the land market and market analysis; the nature of value; principles and appraisal of investment and development; valuation methods in the United Kingdom and other countries, and statutory bases of value, including those prescribed for fiscal and compensatory purposes.

7. Comparative land policies

This paper deals with the evaluation of land policies and their contribution to economic and social development under different ideological and political conditions and in different countries and historical periods. Selective attention will be paid to the analysis of tenurial systems, to the reform of agrarian structures, to problems of urbanization and urban planning, to economic and socio-political parameters, to land policy instruments and to legal and historical origins.

8. Agriculture, forestry, and rural development

This paper deals with policy towards, and development of, agriculture, forestry, and the rural sector in industrialized market economies, with particular reference to the United Kingdom. The formulation of policy is studied in a context of economic, technical, political, and social pressure and change at the local, national, and supra-national levels.

9. Housing and housing policy

This paper deals with the operation of the housing system and the role of government housing policy in the United Kingdom. Topics will include: the present housing situation and policies and their evolution; the legal, economic, and institutional context; the housing system and housing markets; the identification and measurement of needs and effective demand; housing consumption and access to the housing system; production, investment, and housing supply, housing renewal; determination of housing costs and prices; the finance of housing (including subsidies and taxation); and the relationship of housing and housing policy to other sectors of the economy.

10. Agricultural and natural resource development

This paper deals with the contribution of economic theory to contemporary problems of resource scarcity and economic growth and development. The focus is on practical issues of resource management, energy, environment, employment, urban/rural economic relationships, and on associated international economic pressures which influence economic policy and private investment at national and regional levels.

The Preliminary Examination for the Land Economy Tripos

The examination consists of the following five papers of three hours each. Candidates must offer all five papers.

1. Economic principles and land economy

This paper deals with micro and macro economic principles of relevance to land economy.

2. Applied economics

This paper deals with economic principles and shows their relevance to the study of cities and regions and agricultural policy.

3. Land law

This paper deals with elements of English land law including concepts of property and tenure, the definition of land, the nature of land ownership and of interests in land, the machinery of equitable ownership, the buying and selling of land, and the law of torts affecting land. It also deals with the basic principles of English law and government, including (in outline) local government and the law of town and country planning.

4. Land use and the built environment

This paper deals with the development of the British land use and settlement pattern in the nineteenth and twentieth centuries, the evolution of land use planning ideas, principles of building economics, and the creation of the built environment.

5. Statistics and quantitative methods in land economy

This paper deals with statistical, econometric, and computing techniques of relevance to land economy.

Higher Degrees

Research students in the Department are currently investigating such problems as the role of local authorities in economic development; international changes in the structure of urban and regional labour demand; the integration of immigrants in English cities; the labour market implications of urban decline; the provision of urban housing in developed and developing countries; land tenure law and commodity price supports and their effect on the returns from land.

It is possible to read for research degrees over one, two, or three years, for the M.Phil., M.Litt., or M.Sc. and Ph.D. respectively. All are examined by dissertation only. For the M.Phil. there is a prescribed course of instruction in some aspects of research methodology. In all cases candidates are encouraged to attend University lectures and seminars relevant to their chosen topic.

Regular Departmental seminars are arranged to encourage research students to expound their latest discoveries and benefit from the exchange of ideas and constructive criticism of their colleagues and staff. In addition, discussion groups provide a forum for staff and research students to exchange views on important issues of land use and policy.

Awards for postgraduate study

The Board of Land Economy offer annually one or two Harold Samuel Studentships to finance studies leading to higher degrees. A successful applicant will be required to pursue research in economic, legal, or social matters relating to the use, tenure, or development of land. Candidature is open, but tenure of a studentship is conditional upon the student becoming a registered graduate student of the University. The electors will normally require a candidate to have obtained an honours degree in land economy, law, economics, geography, politics, sociology, history, agricultural economics, or town and country planning.

Graduates in these and other relevant subjects wishing to undertake research in the department are eligible for certain studentships and other awards offered by Colleges. Details of these can be obtained from Tutors' offices.

British students and others qualified by residence may be eligible for a studentship offered by the Economic and Social Research Council, the Natural Environment Research Council, the Ministry of Agriculture or other public body. These awards are highly competitive and in most years are in short supply, nominations in many instances being confined to the 'pool' stage of allocation.

Further information on graduate facilities, awards, and application procedures, and on Harold Samuel Studentships in particular, may be obtained from the Secretary for Research Studies at the Department.

Diploma in Development Studies

The Diploma in Development Studies is a one-year course-work postgraduate qualification of an inter-disciplinary nature. The course is designed to provide a programme of study for those concerned with problems of underdevelopment and the formulation, planning and execution of development policies. The course is the responsibility of the Board of Graduate Studies and the Degree Committee for the Department of Land Economy, advised by a Committee of Management with representation from the relevant Faculties and Departments concerned with the subject matter of the teaching, e.g. Economics and Politics, Social Anthropology, Social and Political Sciences, and Land Economy. Candidates are able to follow such other courses of lectures in other departments of the University which may be relevant to their particular needs and interests in the development context.

The examination consists of three written papers, each of three hours, as follows:

1. Theories of development

This paper offers the basic grounding required to understand development processes by introducing and explaining fundamental concepts and by showing how they have been applied to the analysis of development problems at the local, national, and international levels.

The aim is to survey ideas and ideologies of development in economic and social thought since the late eighteenth century; the contributions of the various social sciences to the subject, especially since the Second World War; theories of modernization and dependency; developing countries in the international system; global and national environmental issues.

2. Rural and urban development planning

This paper deals with development planning at the sectoral and local levels in the national context, and especially with the ways in which urban and rural communities can affect and are affected by it. Special attention will be paid to case studies, plans, and projects.

Rural development: land tenure, conversion and reform; individual, co-operative, and collective models and comparative post-reform performances; social and economic change at the village level; the penetration of capitalism in peasant economies; rural labour markets, household decision-making; cultural inhibitions with regard to development; popular religious and social dissent.

Urban development: urbanization theories in national and regional planning; migration determinants and dynamics; transformation of class structures and the emergence of an urban working class; urban management, finance, and housing policies; rural/urban inter-relationships.

3. The political economy of development

This paper deals with contemporary economic and political processes in developing countries. One aim is to develop students' competence in the numerical analysis of national income accounts and the application of social cost-benefit analysis, within the framework of an understanding of the political economy of development. The topics covered include macro- and micro-economics and their application to planning in poor and middle-income countries at the national, sectoral, and project levels. Another aim is to examine political processes both at the national level and at the local level: the role of the state, the bureaucracy, political parties, and the military, and relationships between the state and small-scale communities will be analysed. Emphasis will be placed on the effective contribution that economic theory and quantitative techniques can make to the practice of development planning, given the economic, political, and administrative constraints arising in these economies.

(See also M.Phil. Degree in the Economics and Politics of Development, p. 133.)

LATIN-AMERICAN STUDIES

M.Phil. (one-year course) in Latin-American Studies

The M.Phil. Degree in Latin-American Studies is intended to meet the needs and interests of graduates wishing either to gain knowledge of Latin America in preparation for a career associated with that part of the world, or to broaden their existing knowledge on an inter-disciplinary basis before proceeding to further study and research for a higher degree. Candidates need not have any previous training in specifically Latin-American areas of study, although such experience would of course be an advantage. They will be expected, however, to have obtained a reading knowledge of the Spanish or Portuguese languages before coming into residence, or to be prepared to do so within the first weeks of residence.

To qualify for the M.Phil. Degree, a candidate must pursue the prescribed course and pass the examination. He must also reside for three terms. To be admitted as a candidate, an applicant must normally be a graduate and must be admitted to the status of Graduate Student by the Board of Graduate Studies.

A candidate may not take the examination on more than one occasion nor may he be a candidate for any other University examination in the same term.

Applications should be sent to the Secretary of the Board of Graduate Studies by 15 July of the academical year next preceding that in which he wishes to take the examination, including evidence of proficiency in Spanish or Portuguese.

A candidate pursues his studies for the M.Phil. Degree in Cambridge under a Supervisor appointed by the Degree Committee of the Faculty of Geography and Geology.

The scheme of examination, which includes an oral examination on any thesis submitted and upon the general field of knowledge in which it falls, consists of:

(*a*) a thesis, not exceeding 15,000 words in length, including footnotes, tables, appendices, and bibliography, on a subject approved by the Degree Committee for the Faculty of Geography and Geology, which shall fall within the field of the group of papers in which the candidate offers two written papers:

and (*b*) three written papers, each of three hours, to be chosen by the candidate, subject to the approval of the Degree Committee, from the list of papers below. Each candidate must offer both papers from any one group together with any paper that is listed first in another group.

Group A

1. The agrarian sociology of the Andean zone

Institutions of land tenure from pre-Incaic period to the present day; ecological adaptations of the present economy; theories of peasant economy and capitalist agriculture; social movements and the impact of agrarian reform.

2. A topic in Andean agrarian sociology

Candidates must answer questions on one of the following topics: the historical development of peasant society and its economy; the impact of international trade on the establishment of capitalistic forms of agriculture; agrarian reform and peasant movements in Chile, Bolivia, and Peru; *la violencia* in Colombia; indigenismo and the indigenista novel.

Group B

3. The history of Mexico

The effects of Spanish conquest; demographic movements during the colonial period; the rise of the great estate; fluctuations in the mining economy; Creole patriotism; independence and the conflicts between Liberals and Conservatives; positivism and the export economy; the revolution and the P.R.I.; agrarian reform and modern industrialization.

4. A topic in the history of Mexico

Candidates must answer questions on one of the following topics: Conquest society in New Spain, 1519–70; Bourbon Mexico, 1763–1810; the Mexican Revolution, 1910–40.

Group C

5. Latin-American literature of the twentieth century[1]

Poetry, the essay, and the novel in Latin America from 1900 to the present day. Candidates may specialize in *either* Spanish-American literature, *or* in Brazilian literature, *or* in both.

[1] Candidates for this paper may offer themselves for examination in either Spanish-American or Portuguese-American literature, or in both.

6. Two authors in twentieth-century Latin-American literature

The following options are available:

(i) César Vallejo and Pablo Neruda.
(ii) Jorge Luis Borges and Julio Cortázar.
(iii) José María Arguedas and Mario Vargas Llosa.
(iv) Machado de Assis and Euclides da Cunha.
(v) Jorge de Lima and Carlos Drummond de Andrade.
(vi) Antônio Callado and Ariano Suassuna.

Group D

7. The ethnology of lowland South America[1]

The ethnography of the Amerindian population of lowland South America: culture history, language distribution, demography, ecology, modes of subsistence, kinship and social organization, politics and warfare, shamanism, mythology and ritual, with emphasis on comparison.

8. Kinship and social organization in lowland South America

Candidates are expected to undertake a comparative study of a particular culture area and to concentrate upon the relationship between kinship terminology, marriage practices, sex roles, and social structure.

Group E

9. Economic development in Latin America[2]

Post-war trends in the economic development of Latin America; industrialization and trade policies within a comparative framework; inflation and monetary developments; income distributional changes and their consequences; the role of the state; issues related to 'dependency' theory.

10. A topic in the economic development of Latin America

Candidates must answer questions on one of the following topics: the effect of economic growth on absolute and relative income changes among the urban and rural poor; aspects of planning; fiscal structures and public investment; problems of international finance and foreign investment.

[1] Candidates for this paper will be expected to have had previous training in anthropology.

[2] Candidates for this paper will be expected to have had previous training in economics.

A candidate may, by special permission of the Degree Committee, granted after considering the candidate's experience, special qualifications, and proposed topic, offer in place of (*a*) and (*b*) above a thesis of not less than 20,000 and not more than 30,000 words in length, including footnotes, tables, appendices, and bibliography, on a topic approved by the Degree Committee.

Every candidate must submit a proposed thesis topic to the Secretary of the Degree Committee for the Faculty of Geography and Geology not later than the division of the Michaelmas Term next preceding the examination. The Secretary will communicate to the candidate the Degree Committee's acceptance or rejection of his choice of topic not later than the end of Full Michaelmas Term.

Candidates must submit two copies of their thesis to the Secretary of the Board of Graduate Studies not later than the division of the Easter Term in which the examination is held, unless the Board grant an extension.

Further details of the course can be obtained from the Director of the Centre of Latin-American Studies, History Faculty Building, West Road, Cambridge.

LAW

In this subject there are courses of study followed by candidates for:

The *Law Tripos* and the Preliminary Examination for Part I B.
The *Ordinary Examinations* for the Ordinary B.A. Degree.
The examination for the degree of *Master of Law*.
The *Diplomas in Legal Studies* and *International Law*.
The *M.Phil. Degree in Criminology* (one-year course).

The University law course is intended to give a deeper appreciation of the working of legal rules and institutions than is obtainable from a merely vocational training. It seeks to do this by providing an opportunity to see law in its historical and social context and to examine its general principles and techniques. The problems studied involve questions of interpretation, of logical reasoning, of ethical judgement, of political liberty and social control.

Lawyers play many parts in society. They are employed not only in private practice but in the civil service, local government, the legal departments of industrial and commercial firms and banks, and international organizations. While a Law degree is not at the moment necessarily a sufficient qualification for practice in these fields, the intending lawyer will derive a benefit from reading Law at the University that he will not otherwise obtain from his later training; and it is therefore very desirable that the future practitioner should include at least some Law in his University courses.

Many undergraduates read Law who have no intention of becoming professional lawyers particularly those who intend to go into industrial management, commercial life or accountancy. The study of Law provides an intellectual discipline in a subject of wide human interest.

A student who intends to read Law at the University need not have taken any particular subject at school. Some knowledge of History is desirable, particularly in relation to the later study of Constitutional and International Law; but there is no reason why a student who has shown ability in any school subject should not read Law. Latin (to 'O' level) is helpful, especially for the study of Roman law, but it is not essential; many highly successful Law students come from purely scientific backgrounds.

Preliminary reading list

Students thinking of reading Law may be helped to make up their minds by reading the relevant section on Law in *University Choice*, ed. Klaus Boehm (Pelican Books), and should then study Glanville Williams: *Learning the Law* (Stevens paperback) and R. M. Jackson: *The Machinery of Justice in England.*

The following list is intended to provide, before a student comes into residence, a background to the subjects included in the first year's work, not to those in later years.

Roman law. B. Nicholas: *An Introduction to Roman Law* (Part I: History and Sources of the Law); Sir Henry Maine: *Ancient Law* (ed. Sir F. Pollock); R. H. Barrow: *The Romans* (Penguin Books); C. F. Kolbert: *The Digest of Justinian* (Penguin Books); J. A. Crook, *Law and Life of Rome.*

Criminal law. R. M. Jackson, *Enforcing the Law* (Penguin Books, but out of print) *or* R. M. Jackson, *The Machinery of Justice*, ch. IV; Barnard, *The Criminal Court in Action* (2nd ed.); Glanville Williams, *The Proof of Guilt* (1963); Barbara Wootton, *Crime and Penal Policy* (1978); H. L. A. Hart, *Punishment and Responsibility* (Oxford Paperbacks); Rupert Cross, *The English Sentencing System* (1975).

Constitutional law. H. Street, *Freedom, the Individual and the Law* (Penguin 1982); S. A. de Smith, *Constitutional and Administrative Law* (1981).

Law of Tort. R. W. M. Dias and B. S. Markesinis, *The Tort Law* (1984); J. A. Weir, *Casebook on Tort* (1983), Introduction; G. L. Williams and B. A. Hepple, *Foundations of the Law of Tort* (1976).

Visiting law courts

Any available opportunity should be taken of visiting law courts, and of working for a short time in a solicitor's office. Little will be learned about the substance of the law by listening, without preparation, to a case in court, but it will give greater insight into some of the problems that will be studied in the University.

The Law Tripos

The papers for the Law Tripos are divided into four groups and are as follows:

Group I

1. Roman law I.
2. Constitutional law.
3. Criminal law.
4. Law of tort.

Group II

10. Law of contract.
11. Land law I.
12. International law.
13. Roman law II.

Group III

20. Administrative law.
[1]21. Muslim law.
22. Family law.
23. Legal history.
24. Criminology.
25. Jurisprudence.
26. Criminal procedure and criminal evidence.
27. Equity.

Group IV

40. Commercial law.
41. Labour law.
42. Land law II.
43. Company law.
44. Contract and tort II.
45. Conflict of laws.
46. E.E.C. law.
47. Prescribed subjects (half-papers).

Each paper is of three hours' duration, except Paper 47 for each subject of which the examination consists of a half-paper of two hours' duration.

Part IA of the Tripos

This will be taken in the first year. A candidate must offer all the papers for Group I.

Part IB of the Tripos

This will be taken in the second year by a student who has obtained Honours in Part IA of the Law Tripos or in another Honours Examination, or who has not yet obtained honours in an Honours Examination. A candidate must offer five papers chosen from among Groups I, II, and III, provided that he may not offer any paper which he has previously offered.[2]

[1] This paper has been suspended until further notice.

[2] A candidate may offer Paper 3 in addition to the five papers chosen for Part IB, but the Examiners will disregard this fact and any marks awarded for it. In this way an undergraduate reading Law for one year after another Tripos will be able to be examined in the six subjects required if he is to gain exemption from Part I of the examinations for the entry to the barristers' and solicitors professions, although he is, as a candidate for honours in the Tripos, required to offer only five papers. A candidate reading Law for only one year may also take Paper 3 in the Preliminary Examination to Part IB of the Tripos in October.

Part II of the Law Tripos

This will normally be taken in the third year. A candidate must:

either offer five papers chosen from among Paper 3 (Criminal Law) and Groups III and IV,

or offer four papers chosen from among Paper 3 (Criminal Law) and Groups III and IV, and in addition participate in a seminar course and submit an essay in a subject prescribed by the Faculty Board or chosen by him from a number of subjects so prescribed,

provided that he may not offer any paper which he has previously offered.

Prescribed subjects (half-papers) (Paper 47)

The prescribed subjects (half-papers) are as follows:

In **1985**: Introduction to French law, landlord and tenant, discrimination, intellectual property, human rights, Muslim law, environmental and planning law, aspects of civil litigation.

Seminar subjects

A candidate may choose to substitute for one paper of Part II participation in a seminar course, together with the submission of an essay.

The procedure for prescribing the subjects and for notifying a candidate's intention of participating in a seminar course, are as follows:

(*a*) Subjects prescribed will be provisionally notified to Directors of Studies by the Faculty Board and will be published in the *Reporter* before the end of the Lent Term preceding the year in which seminars on the subjects are to be conducted. The subjects provisionally notified for seminar courses in **1985** are:

The family in society. The ethics of the criminal law. Explanation of criminal behaviour.

(*b*) A candidate wishing to take part in a seminar course must send his application to the Secretary of the Faculty Board before the end of the Full Easter Term preceding the year in which he wishes to take part. The Board has power to accept or reject applications, having regard to the number of candidates who offer to take part in each course, and the Secretary of the Faculty Board of Law will notify each candidate, before 31 July, of the acceptance or rejection of his application. Later applications, provided that they are submitted not later than the end of the first week of the Full Michaelmas Term in the academical year in which the seminar course is to be conducted, may be accepted at the discretion of the Board and, if an application is accepted, the candidate will be notified before the division of the Michaelmas Term.

(*c*) Subjects prescribed by the Faculty Board will be published in the *Reporter* before the end of the Long Vacation period of residence preceding the year in which seminar courses are to be conducted. Any subject prescribed by the Faculty Board may be withdrawn by the Faculty Board upon notice given in the *Reporter* within the first three weeks of the Full Michaelmas Term in the academical year in which the seminar course was to have been conducted. Each candidate who has applied to take part in that seminar course will be informed of its withdrawal by the Secretary of the Faculty Board.

(*d*) A lecturer conducting a seminar course will set each candidate an essay upon a given subject. Essays must not, without the consent of the lecturer, exceed 12,000 words including footnotes and appendices. Each essay must state the sources from which it is derived and must be prefaced with a declaration signed by the candidate that it represents his own work unaided except as may be specified by him in the declaration. The essay must be sent to the Secretary of the Faculty Board to reach him not later than the seventh day of the Full Easter Term in the year in which the examination is to be held. A candidate who submits his essay at a later time may be penalized. If the Examiners consider that an essay is not sufficiently legible, they may require that it be resubmitted in typescript.

Preliminary Examination for Part IB of the Tripos

This examination will be held at the beginning of each academical year for candidates who have turned too late to legal studies to become sufficiently prepared for Part IA in the previous Easter Term. Colleges may also require persons who have not been classed in Part IA to pass the Preliminary Examination as a condition of remaining in residence. It is not, however, strictly necessary to pass this examination to be eligible to sit Part IB of the Law Tripos. The examination will also enable an undergraduate reading Law for one year only to become a candidate for a single paper in the Tripos examination and thus gain full exemption from the first part of professional examinations.

The Preliminary Examination consists of all four papers in Group I. Candidates must offer all four papers; except that a student in his third year who has not been classed in Part IA of the Tripos and who intends to be a candidate for honours in Part IB may take Paper 3 only.

Exemption from professional examinations in England and Wales

As a result of the recommendations of the Ormrod Committee on Legal Education the professional bodies agreed to restrict entry into the legal profession (with some exceptions) to graduates. This change was to have occurred in 1978: it was then postponed to 1980 and is now being reconsidered altogether. Under the agreed scheme there was to have been a Common Professional Examination, common to both branches of the profession, but this never materialized. Both branches of the profession still have their independent qualifying examinations.

To gain exemption from those examinations a graduate will normally be required to have taken six 'core' subjects, as part of his degree course, before proceeding to his vocational training and the final (or Part II) examination. These six subjects, with the corresponding Cambridge papers (New Regulations), are:

1. Constitutional and administrative law (Paper 2).
2. Law of contract (Paper 10).
3. Criminal law (Paper 3).
4. Land law (Paper 11).
5. Law of tort (Paper 4).
6. Law of trusts (Paper 27).

A student who reads Law for one year at Cambridge will normally take Paper 3 (Criminal law) as a single paper, preferably in October, and offer the remaining five papers in the Law Tripos. Students reading Law for two or more years will have no difficulty including all six core subjects in their courses. It is understood that graduates who have not taken all the core subjects in their degree courses will be allowed to take the missing subjects in examinations held by the professional bodies.

At present there are no exemptions from the Part II professional examinations. Subjects taken at Cambridge may not, however, be repeated in Part II of the Bar Examinations.

Intending barristers

Applications for exemption must be made on forms which are obtainable from The Secretary, Council of Legal Education, Grays Inn Place London, WC1 5DX. The applicant should also request the Registrary of the University as soon as possible after publication of the University class-lists to inform the Council of Legal Education of the applicant's class or marks in the relevant examination or papers. A fee of £1 must accompany this request but no further fee is payable in respect of any subsequent request. The Council of Legal Education will inform the applicant whether exemption has been granted.

Intending solicitors

Applications for exemption must be made to the Secretary of The Law Society, on a form obtainable from him or from a Director of Studies.

Each year the University sends to the Law Society a list of those intending solicitors who have passed the six 'core' subjects, and an applicant whose Director of Studies, has given notification that he has passed in these subjects need not request a certificate from the Registrary, nor make individual application to the Law Society.

The Examinations in Law for the Ordinary B.A. Degree

Law Ordinary Examination I consists of three papers chosen from among groups I–III of the groups of papers for the Law Tripos.

Law Ordinary Examination II consists of three papers chosen from among Groups III–IV of the groups of papers for the Law Tripos.

A candidate for either of the Ordinary Examinations may not offer any paper which he has taken in a previous year in an examination which he has passed or on which he has received an allowance.

A student who has passed either of the examinations may not be a candidate again for the same examination.

The degree of Master of Law*

The LL.M. Degree can be obtained by Cambridge graduates and also by graduates of other universities and, in exceptional cases, by other students who have passed an examination in law.

A Cambridge graduate who takes the LL.M. Examination will normally do so in his fourth year. He may be allowed by his College to return into residence for that year, but he does not need to keep further terms and may therefore, if he wishes, take the examination while out of residence. To be a candidate for the LL.M. Examination he must *either* (i) have obtained honours in a Part of the Law Tripos (or reached honours standard if he was not a candidate for honours) *or* (ii) have become qualified to practise as a barrister or solicitor in England or Wales or Ireland or as an advocate or law agent in Scotland.

A graduate of another university who has been admitted as an Affiliated Student may, on application through his tutor, be a candidate for the LL.M. Examination in his second or later year if he has obtained honours in Part IB or Part II of the Law Tripos in a preceding year.

A student who is not qualified under either of the two preceding paragraphs may be allowed by the Degree Committee of the Faculty to take the LL.M. Examination after keeping at least two terms, if he has passed an approved examination in law with sufficient credit before coming into residence. On passing the LL.M. Examination he may then proceed to the LL.M. Degree when he has kept three terms. This leave may be granted to a graduate of another university who wishes to take the LL.M. Examination without first taking a Part of the Tripos; it may also be granted, in exceptional cases, to a person who is not a graduate but has shown special aptitude for legal study in professional or other examinations. In granting the leave the Degree Committee may require the student first to pass in one or more specified papers from the Law Tripos. Applications for this leave should, in the case of a student not yet in residence, be made to the Board of Graduate Studies *not later than 31 August preceding the examination*; in the case of a student in residence, to the Secretary of the Degree Committee not later than 1 November preceding the examination.

* This was previously known as the degree of Bachelor of Law. It has been changed so that it is immediately identifiable as a higher degree for a year of postgraduate study in law. Existing holders of the LL.B. retain the right to apply for the LL.M. Degree by dissertation. In addition, a change of statutes which would allow existing holders of the LL.B. to have their degrees re-designated as LL.M. degrees is awaiting Privy Council approval.

The following papers are prescribed for the LL.M. Examination to be held in **1985**:

Section A. English law: private law and conflict of laws

1. Taxation.
2. *Conflict of laws.
3. Restitution and remedies.
4. Credit and security.
5. International sales.
6. Advanced corporate and securities law.

Section B. Legal history: the history of English law

8. History of English civil and criminal law, 1485–1710.
9. Sources and literature of English law, 1200–1800.

Section C. Civil law: Roman law and the later Civil Law

12. History of European institutions.

Section D. International law: public international law

14. †Law of peace.
15. Law of international institutions.
16. Law of armed conflict and use of force (including settlement of disputes).
17. †Law of the sea.

Section E. Public law: British and comparative public law

18. Law and practice of civil liberties.
19. Judicial review of administrative action.

Section F. Comparative law and legal philosophy: historical and modern comparative law and jurisprudence

23. Jurisprudence.
24. Comparative aspects of private and procedural law.
25. *E.E.C. law.
26. International and comparative labour law.

A candidate must offer either four of the prescribed papers or three such papers and a thesis. His choice of papers is not restricted

* No candidate may offer both Paper 2 and Paper 25 without leave of the Faculty Board of Law.

† No candidate who offers Paper 14 together with Paper 17 may answer any questions specially designated by an asterisk in Paper 14; such questions refer to topics falling within the scope of Paper 17.

by their distribution among sections or otherwise, except in so far as the Faculty Board of Law shall provide. The Faculty Board announces such restrictions before the end of the Easter Term next before that in which the examination to which they apply is to be held. For 1983, no candidate may offer Paper 2 together with Paper 25 without the leave of the Faculty Board.

A thesis, which must be less than 5,000 and no more than 15,000 words in length, may be submitted on any topic approved for the purpose by the Faculty Board not later than the last day of Full Michaelmas Term in the academical year in which the candidate presents himself for the examination. The approval of the Faculty Board will not normally be given to a topic which does not fall within the scope of any of the prescribed papers nor will they normally approve a topic which falls within the scope of one of the other papers which the candidate is offering in the examination. In approving the topic the Faculty Board may direct that it shall qualify a candidate for the inclusion of his name in the class-list as having satisfied the Examiners in a particular section.

Each thesis must be prefaced by a declaration signed by the candidate that it represents his own work unaided except as may be specified by him in the declaration, and that the work has been done principally in the academical year in which he presents himself for the examination; and must contain a statement of, or notes on, the sources from which the thesis is derived, including any written work which the candidate has previously submitted or is concurrently submitting for any other degree, diploma, or similar qualification at any university or similar institution.

The thesis must be submitted to the Secretary of the Faculty Board of Law not later than 1 May preceding the examination.

The syllabuses and recommended reading lists for the prescribed papers may be obtained from the Secretary, Faculty Board of Law, Syndics Building, Mill Lane, Cambridge, CB2 1RP.

The Diplomas in Legal Studies and International Law

A candidate for the Diploma in Legal Studies or the Diploma in International Law must be admitted as a Graduate Student, on the recommendation of the Degree Committee of the Faculty of Law, by the Board of Graduate Studies, who will fix the date of commencement of his candidature. At least three terms must have been kept by a candidate before he is qualified to receive a

Diploma. He must study for it in the University for at least three terms under the direction of a Supervisor appointed by the Degree Committee and under any special conditions that the Committee may prescribe in his case, but a candidate who is a graduate of the University may, on the recommendation of the Degree Committee and with the approval of the Board of Graduate Studies, study at a university or institution outside England as a satisfaction in whole or in part of the requirement of study for a Diploma.

Not earlier than the end of the second, nor, except by special permission of the Degree Committee, later than the end of the fifth term after the term in which his candidature commenced, a candidate must send to the Secretary of the Board of Graduate Studies, with the prescribed fee, a thesis on a subject, previously approved by the Degree Committee, which falls within the field of Comparative Law or of International Law. The thesis must not exceed 20,000 words except with the special permission of the Degree Committee. It must afford evidence of serious study by the candidate, and of his ability to discuss a difficult problem critically. The Secretary of the Board of Graduate Studies will send the thesis to the Degree Committee, who after referring it to an Examiner, and considering his report, and the reports of the Supervisor will resolve that the Diploma be awarded or refused. The Degree Committee may allow a candidate to re-submit his thesis within a time limit fixed by them which will normally not extend beyond the end of the term following the notification of this decision.

A Graduate Student who has been given leave by the Board of Graduate Studies to count the period or any part of it during which he has been a candidate for the Diploma towards a course of research for the degree of Ph.D., M.Sc., or M.Litt., will not be entitled to be awarded the Diploma so long as he remains on the register of Research Students nor if he subsequently proceeds to the degree of Ph.D., M.Sc., or M.Litt.

The Examination in Criminology for the M.Phil. Degree (one-year course)*

This is a postgraduate degree obtainable in one academic year. It is open to graduates with a good degree in any subject, although in

* Applications for admission to the course should be submitted to the Board of Graduate Studies for consideration by the Institute of Criminology, which is part of the Faculty of Law and provides the relevant teaching.

practice the majority of students have degrees in law, psychology or social or political sciences. The scheme of examination consists of:

(*a*) an exercise in designing a proposal for, or in critically evaluating, a project of empirical research on a subject chosen from a list announced by the Examiners; a candidate's report on his research exercise must not exceed 3,000 words, including notes and appendices;

and

(*b*) a thesis of not more than 15,000 words, including notes and appendices, on a topic approved by the Degree Committee for the Faculty of Law, falling within one of the following areas of study:

The sociology of crime and deviance
Psychiatric and psychological aspects of crime and its treatment
The aims, effects, and problems of penal measures
The development of criminal law and the administration of criminal justice

and

(*c*) five essays, each of not more than 3,000 words in length, chosen by the candidate from lists of topics announced by the Examiners;

and

(*d*) one written paper containing questions from each of the areas of study defined in (*b*) above.

The examination may include, at the discretion of the Examiners, an oral examination upon the thesis and on the general field of knowledge within which it falls, and such an oral examination may include questions relating to one or more of the other pieces of work submitted by the candidate under (*a*) and (*b*) above.

In place of sections (*a*), (*b*), and (*c*) of the above scheme a candidate who has satisfactorily completed the written paper in (*d*) above may, by special permission of the Degree Committee for the Faculty of Law granted after considering his experience, special qualifications, and proposed topic, offer a thesis of not more than 30,000 words in length, including notes and appendices, on a criminological topic approved by them. The Examiners may, at their discretion, examine the student orally upon the thesis and on the general field of knowledge within which it falls.

The syllabus for the papers under (*b*) above is as follows:

(*a*) *The sociology of crime and deviance*

Definition of deviance. Social functions of deviance. Deviance and the media. Official statistics on crime and deviance, problems in interpretation. Some sociological perspectives: anomie, subcultural theories, control theory, labelling and interactionism, Marxist approaches, conflict theory, ethnomethodology. Sociology of juvenile justice.

(*b*) *Psychiatric and psychological aspects of crime and its treatment*

Defining the abnormal offender. Psychodynamic theories. Biological factors. Neurological disorder and psychopathy. Psychotic and neurotic offenders. Sexual crimes. Drugs, alcohol, and crime. Psychiatric provisions for abnormal offenders.

Psychological research on the courts, police, and penal institutions. Social learning theory. Developmental psychology research on dishonesty and moral judgement. Personality, attitudes, intelligence, and crime. The psychology of aggression. Experiments on deviance.

(*c*) *The aims, effects, and problems of penal measures*

Utilitarian and non-utilitarian justifications of penal measures. Problems in the measurement of intended and unintended effects of such measures. The ethical and administrative issues involved. The law and the mentally abnormal offender. Special sentences for dangerous, persistent, or young offenders.

(*d*) *The development of criminal law and the administration of criminal justice*

The scope, functions, and philosophy of the criminal law. Police organization. Criminal investigation. Discretion in prosecuting. The trial process: pretrial detention and bail, legal aid, plea negotiation, the jury, appellate review. The sentencing process, including proposals for non-judicial sentencing. Parole and other release procedures. Criminal legislation.

MATHEMATICS

In this subject, which is regarded as including mathematical physics, there are courses of study followed by candidates for:

The *Mathematical Tripos*, which is divided into four Parts.
The *Certificate of Advanced Study in Mathematics.*
The *Diploma in Mathematical Statistics.*

There are also courses of study in Computer Science (cf. p. 101) suitable to be taken after Part I A of the Mathematical Tripos, but there is no first-year course in computer science.

The Mathematical Tripos

The Tripos is divided into four Parts, I A, I B, II, and III. The normal course of study for a student in Mathematics is Part I A taken in the first year, followed by Part I B taken in the second year, and Part II in the third year leading to a B.A. Degree. Some students then stay on for a fourth year to take Part III. A small number of exceptionally able and well-prepared students take Part I B in their first year and Part II in their second year, so as to be able to take Part III or some other course in their third year.

Part I A

A candidate may take Part I A in his first year, or, if he has obtained honours in another Tripos, in the year after doing so but not later than his third year. In addition to serving as preparation for further Parts of the Tripos, Part I A provides a suitable course for students who wish to have only an introduction to mathematics and its applications before taking up their main subject (which might be physics, theoretical physics, chemistry, engineering, economics, etc.). Part I A consists of five papers, two of which are alternatives. Every candidate must offer Papers 3–5; in addition, a candidate offering Pure and Applied Mathematics must offer Paper 1, and a candidate offering Mathematics (with Physics†) must offer Paper 2.

Courses of lectures covering the examination syllabus for Part I A are given as follows; numbers of lectures are given in parentheses after course titles:

† The 'with Physics' option will not be available after 1 October 1985.

Analysis I (24).
Analysis II (24).
Algebra I (Groups) (24).
Algebra II (Vector Spaces) (24).
Probability and its Applications (24).
Vector Calculus (24).
Linear Systems (24).
Newtonian Dynamics and Special Relativity (24).
Electrodynamics (24).
Potential Theory (12).

As an alternative to the course described above, a student may take the option Part IA Mathematics (with Physics†) in which the courses Newtonian Dynamics and Special Relativity and Linear Systems are replaced by the following courses given for the subject Physics in Part IA of the Natural Sciences Tripos.

Concepts of Physics (24).
Thermal Physics (12).
Vibrations (12).

This option is designed to meet the needs of students who propose to transfer to the Natural Sciences Tripos to study Physics or Theoretical Physics.

Part IB

A candidate may take Part IB in his first or second year, or, if he has obtained honours in another Honours Examination, one or two years after doing so but not later than his fourth year. Four papers, each of three hours, will be set for examination and every candidate must offer all four papers. Courses given for Part IB are of three types: basic courses, which each candidate should attend most of; additional courses, which each candidate is advised to attend between one-half and two-thirds of; and a computing course. All courses (except for computing) will be examined on the same footing; the papers will be of a cross-section type. The course Introduction to Computational Mathematics, which comprises lectures and practical work, is assessed on the basis of notebooks handed in by the candidates, and no questions are set on it in the examination; the maximum credit available is about equivalent to that for a normal sixteen-hour lecture course, and the credit gained is added directly to the credit gained in the examination.

Courses of lectures are given for the Part IB year on the following topics:

† The 'with Physics' option will not be available after 1 October 1985.

Basic courses

Complex Variable (16).
Algebra III (16).
Introduction to Statistics (16).
Mathematical Methods (24).
Quantum Mechanics (16).

Additional courses

Rings and Modules (24).
Analysis III (24).
Markov Chains (12).
Introduction to Optimization (16).
Introduction to Topological Groups (12).
Fluid Dynamics I (24).
Principles of Dynamics (24).
Classical Theory of Fields (12).

Computing course

Introduction to Computational Mathematics.

Part IB of the Mathematical Tripos provides a firm foundation for a later more specialized study of pure mathematics or mathematical physics or other applications of mathematics. It is also possible to transfer at this stage to another Tripos; a student should first seek advice on whether he is adequately prepared for the proposed new course of study.

Part II

A candidate who has obtained honours in Part IB or in any other Honours Examination except Part IA may take Part II one or two years after doing so, but not later than his fourth year. Four papers, each of three hours, are set for examination and every candidate must offer all four papers. The first three of these contain concisely stated problems of medium length, commonly based on a piece of bookwork which may also be asked for. These papers are of cross-section type. The fourth paper contains one question on each course; the questions are designed to test the candidate's proficiency at sustained exposition of a topic, and not more than three may be attempted. Candidates are expected to be familiar with the content of about 136 lectures. No questions are set in the examination on the course Computational Projects in Applied Mathematics; credit is gained by the submission of notebooks by the candidate, and the maximum credit obtainable is approximately equivalent to that available for a twenty-four-lecture course. Students may be examined on any combination of the following courses of lectures, but the Secretary of the Faculty Board cannot always guarantee to arrange times of lectures so as to avoid clashes, especially over widely disparate subject-areas.

Groups (16).
Graph Theory (24).
Measure Theory (24).
Differential Analysis and Geometry (24).
Algebraic Geometry (24).
Algebraic Topology (24).
Linear Analysis (24).
Theory of Numbers (16).
Set Theory and Logic (16).
Stochastic Processes (16).
Principle of Statistics (24).
Convex Optimization (24).
Dynamic Stochastic Systems (16).
Probability Theory (24).
Statistical Theory of Communication (24).
Control Theory (24).
Nonlinear Differential Equations (24).
Methods of Mathematical Physics (24).
Representation Theory (16).
Galois Theory (24).
Riemann Surfaces (24).
Elementary Quantum Electronics (12).
Electrodynamics of Media (24).
Waves (24).
Seismic Waves (12).
Statistical Physics (24).
Foundations of Quantum Mechanics (24).
Partial Differential and Integral Equations (24).
Introduction to the Mechanics of Solids (16).
Fluid Dynamics II (24).
Applications of Quantum Mechanics (24).
Numerical Analysis (16).
General Relativity (16).
Approximation Methods (12).
Mathematical Economics (12).

Computing course

Computational Projects in Applied Mathematics.

Part III and the Certificate of Advanced Study in Mathematics

A candidate may take Part III in his third or fourth year if he has obtained honours in a Part of any Tripos Examination. In practice candidates from Cambridge have almost invariably taken either Part II of the Mathematical Tripos or Part II of the Natural Sciences Tripos in Physics or Theoretical Physics in the preceding year.

A graduate from another university or other applicant may take Part III in his first year provided he obtains the permission of the Degree Committee of the Faculty of Mathematics and is admitted by a College. The normal requirement is a first class degree in mathematics, physics, or engineering. Those interested in this possibility are invited to write to either the Head of the Department of Applied

Mathematics and Theoretical Physics (Silver Street) or the Head of the Department of Pure Mathematics and Mathematical Statistics (16 Mill Lane) for further information. Technically, candidates who take Part III on this basis are not candidates for honours since they do not obtain a degree, but their results are published and classified in the same manner as for the other candidates, although on a separate list.

Graduates of Cambridge or of another university who attain the honours standard in the examination for Part III are awarded the Certificate of Advanced Study in Mathematics.

The subjects of the examination are those which have been treated in lecture courses during the academical year. There are normally about sixty such courses, which range over the whole extent of pure mathematics, statistics and the mathematics of operational research, applied mathematics and theoretical physics. They are designed to cover those advanced parts of the subjects which are not normally given in first degree courses but which are an indispensable preliminary to independent study and research. Although many candidates are prospective Research Students, Part III also provides a valuable course in mathematics and in its applications for those who want further training before taking posts in industry, teaching, or research establishments.

Papers of two or three hours' duration are set on courses of sixteen or twenty-four lectures respectively. Candidates must either offer papers whose total duration is not more than nineteen hours, or they must offer papers whose total duration is not more than sixteen hours together with an essay on one of the assigned set of topics. Each essay must state the sources consulted and must be prefaced with a declaration signed by the candidate that it represents his own work unaided except as may be specified by him in his declaration. The Examiners may examine a candidate *viva voce* on the subject of his essay. Candidates have a free choice of the combination of courses which they offer, though naturally they tend to select groups of cognate courses. The final decision about which courses to offer and whether to submit an essay does not have to be made until the end of the first quarter of Easter Term.

Weekly supervision classes are provided for Part III students taking courses in the Department of Applied Mathematics and Theoretical Physics and there is a teaching officer of the Department who advises them on courses of study, future careers, and other similar matters. There is a work room and small library available for their exclusive use in the Department.

Students taking courses given by members of the staff of the Department of Pure Mathematics and Mathematical Statistics are encouraged to make personal contact with the Lecturers concerned and are invited to make use of the facilities provided by the Department in 16 Mill Lane.

The Diploma in Mathematical Statistics

The aim of the Diploma course is to equip graduates of predominantly mathematical preparation for the vocation of statistician. To this end it includes, not merely classes in mathematical and applied statistics as such, but also classes in probability, operational research, and other relevant options. The course normally extends for nine months from 1 October. Candidates have to be approved for admission to the course by the Degree Committee of the Faculty of Mathematics, which requires evidence of previous familiarity with probabilistic and statistical ideas as well as evidence of substantial mathematical competence.

Instruction for the course is given at the Statistical Laboratory in the Department of Pure Mathematics and Mathematical Statistics, 16 Mill Lane, Cambridge, under the general supervision of the Director of Studies for the Diploma in Mathematical Statistics, to whom completed application forms should be sent by 8 March if possible.

Classes, practicals, etc., are given at the Statistical Laboratory. Candidates are also required to undertake a practical project, usually in some other department of the University. Considerable importance is attached to this project; the project report is assessed and taken into account by the Examiners.

Each candidate is assigned two Supervisors; one is normally a University teaching officer in the Statistical Laboratory and the other is normally a member of the Department in which the candidate is to do his practical work.

A wide variety of fields of application is usually open to candidates within, for example, the sciences, medicine, agriculture, economics, engineering, operational research, criminology and linguistics.

Only a small number of candidates can work in any one applied field in a given year, and so intending candidates should suggest as wide as possible a range of practical topics in which they are or are prepared to become interested.

The examination consists of three theory papers (statistical theory and detailed methodology, probability and applications, stochastic processes and methods of operational research) and one practical paper. Hand machines are used in the practical examination, but all candidates receive instruction in the use of the University computer, and have access to this and various micro-computers throughout the course.

Candidates are encouraged to attend seminars and to be aware of research activity in the Laboratory. It is not uncommon for Diploma students to continue with a Ph.D., either in the U.K. or abroad.They also find careers in industry, computing, actuarial work, the Civil Service, consulting in statistics and operational research, and teaching.

MEDICAL SCIENCES

The Medical Sciences Tripos

The Medical Sciences Tripos can be read by candidates for Medical or Veterinary Degrees during their preclinical studies.

Parts I A and I B of the Tripos contain subjects which enable candidates to satisfy certain requirements for Medical and Veterinary Degrees and Section I of Part II (General) is taken by those who wish to spread the study of these subjects over three rather than two years. The subjects are treated as scientific disciplines without undue vocational bias.

All candidates read Anatomy, Biochemistry, and Physiology in their first year for Part I A. Courses in Medical Genetics and Medical Sociology are also given but are not examined in the Tripos; medical students have to pass a Second M.B. Examination in each; veterinary students have a Second Veterinary M.B. Examination in Medical Genetics. Undergraduates may then choose between the two-year and the three-year preclinical courses.

If they choose the former, they will read for Part I B more Anatomy and Physiology, but also Pathology and Pharmacology together with some Psychology if they are medical students or Veterinary Anatomy and Veterinary Physiology if they are veterinary students. In their third year they have a number of options. They may offer Section II of Part II (General) which comprises two of the Special Subjects Biological Resources, History of Medicine, Physical Anthropology, and Social Psychology. Alternatively, they may offer Part II or Part II (General) of the Natural Sciences Tripos. Those undergraduates who wish to proceed to a *two-year* course of clinical medicine (which is provided at Cambridge but not at London) must spend their third year reading a subject which is approved by the General Medical Council as constituting a 'year of medical study'. The Council's ruling is, however, liberal and such subjects as Physical Anthropology, Social and Political Sciences, and Zoology are likely to be acceptable. If a three-year clinical course is to be taken (as provided at London) then the third undergraduate year may be spent reading for any Tripos (e.g. History of Art or Law).

Undergraduates who choose to do the *three-year* preclinical course postpone Pathology and Pharmacology until their third year. For Part I B they take the same Anatomy and Physiology as in the two-year course; if medical students, they take also the same Psychology, and an Elective subject chosen from a list of about six;

if veterinary students, they take the Veterinary Anatomy and Veterinary Physiology of the two-year course but instead of Psychology and an Elective Subject, they have a course in Animal Behaviour.

Such undergraduates spend their third year reading for Section I of Part II (General), taking the same Pathology and Pharmacology courses as in the two-year course and also reading an Elective Subject from the list of about a dozen. Medical students do a further course in Psychology, whereas veterinary students take a further course in Animal Behaviour.

Transfers to the Medical Sciences Tripos are usually from the Natural Sciences Tripos. This may happen after Part I A provided, firstly, that the undergraduate's College is willing to make one of its limited quota places available and, secondly, that the candidate has *not* read Physiology in Part I A of the Natural Sciences Tripos. Such candidates take the two-year preclinical course, reading for Parts I A and I B of the Medical Sciences Tripos in their second and third years. Undergraduates who have read Physiology in Part I A and in Part I B of the Natural Sciences Tripos, and also two of the subjects Biochemistry, Pathology, and Pharmacology in Part I B of that Tripos, may transfer to Section III of Part II (General) of the Medical Sciences Tripos at the end of their second year, again provided that a quota place is available. Transfers from other Triposes require detailed advice. The provisions for Affiliated Students are similar to those in the Natural Sciences Tripos.

Part I A

Candidates are required to take the following papers for Part I A:

Anatomy
Biochemistry
Physiology

A suitable previous training for this Tripos is Chemistry, Physics, and *either* Biology (or Zoology) *or* Mathematics to Advanced Level in the General Certificate of Education. Candidates lacking Biology or Mathematics are advised to read these subjects if they are spending a third year in the sixth form.

The course is given by members of the Departments of Anatomy, Biochemistry, Community Medicine, Genetics, Pharmacology, and Physiology.

Teaching in anatomy includes lectures on the anatomy of tissues, on cytology and cytogenics, on early embryology, and on biometrics. Practical classes relate to these subjects. Medical students dissect the limbs and trunk and lectures are given on certain aspects of the anatomy of these parts. Veterinary students dissect the dog and receive some alternative lectures.

There is a course of general biochemistry which includes lectures on the structure, functions, and biosynthesis of the components of living tissues: proteins, nucleic acids, carbohydrates, fats, hormones, vitamins, etc. The course includes studies of enzymes, the liberation and utilisation of energy, metabolic processes and their control in animals, plants, and micro-organisms. The practical classes are designed to introduce students to biochemical methods and their application to the study of living systems. A course of lectures on chemotherapy is also included.

The physiological systems covered in the first year include nerve, neuromuscular transmission, muscle, circulation, respiration, excretion, water balance, digestion, absorption, and thermo-regulation. There are related practical classes in experimental physiology and in histology.

Lectures on Medical Genetics and on Medical Sociology are also given but are not examined in the Tripos. However, both are subjects in the Second M.B. Examination and Medical Genetics is a subject in the Second Veterinary M.B. Examination.

The Part I A examinations taken at the end of the first year are as follows:

Anatomy. The written paper consists of three sections, Sections A, B, and C, containing questions on, respectively, general anatomy, human anatomy, and veterinary anatomy. Section A will include cell and tissue anatomy, aspects of human biology, embryology, and reproductive anatomy. Section B will include questions on topographical and functional anatomy. Section C will include questions on the topographical and functional anatomy of the dog. The questions in Sections B and C will deal mainly with the general architecture of the body and will not require a detailed knowledge except of the most important regions dissected during the first year. The practical examination will include a *viva voce* examination.

Candidates may obtain exemption from Anatomy A in the Second M.B. Examination, provided that they attempt questions in Sections A and B and that they attain a satisfactory standard in the paper and in the practical examination and are otherwise qualified. Candidates may obtain exemption from Veterinary Anatomy A in the Second Veterinary M.B. Examination, provided that they attempt questions in Sections A and C and that they attain a satisfactory standard in the paper and in the practical examination and are otherwise qualified.

Biochemistry. The written paper will require a knowledge of the chemical processes associated with the life and growth of animals, plants, and micro-organisms. There will be a practical examination which will not involve laboratory work.

Candidates may obtain exemption from Biochemistry in the Second M.B. Examination and in the Second Veterinary M.B. Examination, provided that they attain a satisfactory standard and are otherwise qualified.

Physiology. The written paper will be the paper in Physiology in Part IA of the Natural Sciences Tripos; it will be of such a nature as to test the candidate's understanding of the broad principles of Physiology. There will be most emphasis on the physiology of nerve and neuromuscular transmission, muscle, autonomic nervous system, cardiovascular system, respiration, kidney, salt and water balance, digestion, absorption and temperature regulation.

In the practical examination candidates will be examined in histology and experimental physiology.

Candidates may obtain exemption from Physiology A in the Second M.B. Examination and in the Second Veterinary M.B. Examination, provided that they attain a satisfactory standard and are otherwise qualified.

Part IB

Every candidate must offer the written papers and practical examinations for the subjects of Part IB in accordance with one of the following options (*a*)–(*d*):

(*a*) Anatomy, Physiology, Psychology, one Elective Subject;
(*b*) Anatomy, Pathology, Pharmacology, Physiology, Psychology;
(*c*) Anatomy, Physiology, Veterinary Physiology;
(*d*) Anatomy, Pathology, Pharmacology, Physiology, Veterinary Physiology.

Undergraduates offering options (*a*) or (*c*) take Pathology and Pharmacology in their third year.

The course is given by members of the Departments of Anatomy, Experimental Psychology, Pathology, Pharmacology, and Physiology, together with contributions from many others in the Elective Subjects.

Teaching in Anatomy includes lectures and practical classes on embryology, morphology, and radiological anatomy. Medical students dissect the head and neck and receive lectures relating to this part. They later dissect the brain and study the structure of the central nervous system at a microscopic level. Veterinary students study the anatomy of birds and domestic ungulates and receive some alternative lectures. There are also courses in neuroanatomy and the anatomy of reproduction.

There is a course in general pathology which includes the variations which may occur in the structure and functions of living tissues and organs and discusses the causes of such changes. The course includes morbid anatomy and histology, immunology, and microbiology with particular emphasis on the biology of bacteria and viruses. Practical classes are an important feature of the course and are integrated as far as possible with the lectures.

Lectures in pharmacology deal with the general principles of drug action and on the specific effects of some drugs. They continue with a consideration of selective toxicity and the effects of drugs on the endocrine, nervous, cardiovascular, and respiratory systems.

Lectures in physiology deal with endocrinology, foetal physiology, neurophysiology, and the physiology of reproduction.

Short courses of lectures in psychology and in animal behaviour are also given.

The examinations taken at the end of the second year are as follows:

Anatomy. The written paper consists of five sections. Section A is intended for all candidates; Sections B and C are intended for candidates offering option (*a*) or (*b*) prescribed by Regulation 22 (medical students); Sections D and E are intended for candidates offering option (*c*) or (*d*) (veterinary students). Section A contains questions on reproductive biology (anatomical aspects), and cell and tissue anatomy. Section B contains questions on neuroanatomy and relevant embryology. Section C contains questions on the topographical and functional anatomy of the human head and neck and relevant embryology. Section D contains questions on neuroanatomy and relevant embryology. Section E contains questions on the comparative anatomy of the domestic animals including avian anatomy. The practical examination includes a *vive voce* examination.

Candidates may obtain exemption from Anatomy B in the Second M.B. Examination, provided that they attempt questions in Sections A, B, and C and that they attain a satisfactory standard in the paper and in the practical examination and are otherwise qualified. Candidates may obtain exemption from Veterinary Anatomy B in the

Second Veterinary M.B. Examination, provided that they attempt questions in Sections A, D, and E and that they attain a satisfactory standard in the paper and in the practical examination and are otherwise qualified.

Pathology. The examination will require an understanding of the damage caused to the structure and function of cells, tissues, and organs of higher animals and man by both living and inanimate agents. Knowledge will be required of the biology of viruses, bacteria, fungi, protozoa and metazoa as parasites, of immunological and other responses induced by these agents, and of the genetic, social, epidemiological, and preventive aspects of disease. The practical examination will include laboratory work.

Candidates may obtain exemption from Pathology in the Second M.B. Examination and in the Second Veterinary M.B. Examination, provided that they attain a satisfactory standard and are otherwise qualified.

Pharmacology. The written paper will require knowledge of the actions of drugs on whole organisms and mammalian systems, including the central nervous system, and also of the mode of drug action at the cellular, sub-cellular, and molecular levels. There will be a practical examination which will not involve laboratory work.

Candidates may obtain exemption from Pharmacology in the Second M.B. Examination and in the Second Veterinary M.B. Examination, provided that they attain a satisfactory standard and are otherwise qualified.

Physiology. The written paper contains questions of such a nature as to test the candidate's understanding of the broad principles of endocrinology, reproductive and fetal physiology, central nervous system, and sensory physiology. In the practical examination candidates will be examined in histology and in experimental physiology.

Candidates may obtain exemption from Physiology B in the Second M.B. Examination, provided that they attain a satisfactory standard in this paper and are otherwise qualified. Candidates may obtain exemption from Veterinary Physiology in the Second Veterinary M.B. Examination, provided that they attain a satisfactory standard both in this paper and in the Veterinary Physiology paper in Part IB and are otherwise qualified.

Psychology. The paper will require knowledge of experimental psychology and some of its applications to medicine. Particular topics include learning and memory; perception and information processing; intelligence and development; emotion and its physiological basis; and social psychology.

Candidates may obtain exemption from Psychology in the Second M.B. Examination, provided that they attain a satisfactory standard in this paper and are otherwise qualified.

Veterinary Physiology. The paper contains questions on certain aspects of the physiology of domestic animals, especially the ruminant.

Candidates may obtain exemption from Veterinary Physiology in the Second Veterinary M.B. Examination, provided that they attain a satisfactory standard both in this paper and in the Physiology paper in Part I B and are otherwise qualified.

Elective Subjects. The list for any year will be announced by the division of the Easter Term preceding the year in which the Examination is to be held. The following are the subjects for **1985**:

Human nutrition
History of medicine
†Human genetics and variation
†Medical statistics: measurement and experimentation
Medicine, ethics, and law
Social aspects of medicine

The examination in each will consist of one written paper.

Part II (General)

Candidates take the examination for Section I or II or III, provided that they do not offer

(*a*) any subject or Special Subject that they have previously offered in Part I B of the Natural Sciences Tripos;
(*b*) an Elective Subject which they have previously offered in Part I B of the Medical Sciences Tripos.

Section I

This is designed for undergraduates taking the three-year preclinical course. Candidates offer the papers and practical examinations in Pathology and Pharmacology; a paper in an Elective Subject; and *either* the paper in Animal Behaviour *or* the paper in Psychology.

† Candidates will be required to present to the Examiners on the first day of the written examination note-books containing a record of the practical work done by them.

Pathology. The examination will be the same as that in Pathology in Part I B and candidates may obtain exemption from Pathology in the Second M.B. Examination and in the Second Veterinary M.B. Examination provided they attain a satisfactory standard and are otherwise qualified.

Pharmacology. The examination will be the same as that in Pharmacology in Part I B and candidates may obtain exemption from Pharmacology in the Second M.B. Examination and in the Second Veterinary M.B. Examination provided they attain a satisfactory standard and are otherwise qualified.

Animal Behaviour. The paper will require knowledge of material on animal behaviour presented in the courses both for Part I B and for Part II (General).

Psychology. The subject will be concerned with the general development of human behaviour and with the study of selected issues in psychology of particular relevance to clinical medicine. These will include pain and its assessment, language and language disorders, and the effects of ageing on human performance. Consideration will be given to selected topics in social psychology, e.g. the measurement of social attitudes.

Elective Subjects. The list for any year will be announced by the division of the Easter Term preceding the year in which the Examination is to be held. The subjects in **1985** are as follows:

Medicine, ethics, and law.
History of medicine;* Biology of parasitism; Human reproduction.
Human nutrition; †Human genetics and variation; Topics in clinical physiology.
†Medical statistics: measurement and experimentation; Management of wildlife stocks; Medical aspects of neurobiology; Social aspects of medicine; Interaction and role of animals in society.

The examination in each will consist of one written paper.

SECTION II

This is designed for undergraduates taking the two-year preclinical course who want to do a third year of preclinical study but not to take a single-subject Part II from the Natural Sciences Tripos.

* Candidates will be required to submit to the Examiners, not later than the first day of Full Easter Term, an essay of not more than 4,000 words on a subject approved by the Faculty Board.

† See footnote on previous page, p. 261.

Candidates offer the papers, essay if any, and practical examination if any, prescribed for *two* of these special subjects:

Biological Resources	Physical Anthropology
History of Medicine	Social Psychology

Biological Resources. The examination is the same as that in the Special Subject in Part II (General) of the Natural Sciences Tripos.

History of Medicine. The examination consists of two written papers as follows:

1. *Medical theory and practice from antiquity to the eighteenth century*
   (Paper 7 of Section II of Part II (General) of the Natural Sciences Tripos.)
2. *Biology, medicine, and society from the eighteenth to the twentieth centuries*
   (Paper 8 of Section II of Part II (General) of the Natural Sciences Tripos.)

Physical Anthropology. A candidate shall offer written papers as follows:

either 1. *Human genetics and variation* (The paper of an Elective subject for the Tripos, or in any year in which no such subject has been announced, Paper 1 in Physical Anthropology of Part II of the Archaeological and Anthropological Tripos),

and 2. *Human ecology and adaptability* (Paper 3 in Physical Anthropology of Part II of the Archaeological and Anthropological Tripos);

or 3. *Primate biology and evolution* (Paper 2 in Physical Anthropology of Part II of the Archaeological and Anthropological Tripos),

and 4. *Primate behaviour* (A special subject in physical anthropology prescribed for Paper 4 in Physical Anthropology of Part II of the Archaeological and Anthropological Tripos).

Any practical examination shall include those parts of the practical examination in Physical Anthropology from Part II of the Archaeological and Anthropological Tripos that relate to the subjects of the written papers offered, and may include or consist wholly of a *viva voce* examination.

Social Psychology. The written papers will be as follows:

1. *Attitudes and personality* (Paper 25 of Part II B of the Social and Political Sciences Tripos).
2. *The psychology of development* (Paper 26 of Part II B of the Social and Political Sciences Tripos).

Elective Subjects. The list for any year will be announced by the division of the Easter Term preceding the year in which the Examination is to be held. It is hoped to include all those Elective subjects available in Section I (above).

SECTION III

This is for undergraduates transferring from the Natural Sciences Tripos to the Medical Sciences Tripos or from medicine to veterinary medicine (or *vice versa*). Candidates must offer

(*a*) *either* Special Subject Anatomy *or* Special Subject Veterinary Anatomy;

and

(*b*) *either* (i) one of the subjects Biochemistry, Pathology, and Pharmacology from Part I B of the Natural Sciences Tripos which has not been previously offered in Part I A of the Medical Sciences Tripos or in Part I B of either the Medical Sciences Tripos or the Natural Sciences Tripos, *or* (ii) one of the Special Subjects Biological Resources, Comparative Pathology, and Statistics from Section I of Part II (General) of the Natural Sciences Tripos.

Special Subject Anatomy. The subject includes human topographical anatomy, embryology, neuroanatomy, and tissue anatomy. The questions will deal mainly with the general architecture of the body and will require a detailed knowledge of only the more important parts. The practical examination will include or consist wholly of a *viva voce* examination.

One paper will consist of Sections A and B of the Anatomy paper in Part I A. Candidates may obtain exemption from Anatomy A in the Second M.B. Examination, provided that they attain a satisfactory standard in this paper and in the relevant part of the practical examination in Part I A and are otherwise qualified.

The other paper will consist of Sections A, B, and C of the Anatomy paper in Part I B. Candidates may obtain exemption from Anatomy B in the Second M.B. Examination, provided that they attain a satisfactory standard in this paper and in the relevant part of the practical examination in Part IB and are otherwise qualified.

Special Subject Veterinary Anatomy. The subject includes the comparative anatomy of domestic mammals, avian biology, embryology, and tissue anatomy. The practical examination will include or consist wholly of a *viva voce* examination.

One paper will consist of Sections A and C of the Anatomy paper in Part IA. Candidates may obtain exemption from Veterinary Anatomy A in the Second Veterinary M.B. Examination, provided that they attain a satisfactory standard in this paper and in the relevant part of the practical examination in Part IA and are otherwise qualified.

The other paper will consist of Sections A, D, and E of the Anatomy paper in Part IB. Candidates may obtain exemption from Veterinary Anatomy B in the Second Veterinary M.B. Examination provided that they attain a satisfactory standard in this paper and in the relevant part of the practical examination in Part IB and are otherwise qualified.

Examination in Anatomy for the Ordinary B.A. Degree

There is an Ordinary Examination in Anatomy which in each year is the examination in Anatomy in Part IB of the Medical Sciences Tripos.

A student may not be a candidate for the Ordinary Examination in Anatomy if the Examiners for Part IB of the Medical Sciences Tripos have specified that his work deserved the allowance of an Ordinary Examination in Anatomy.

M.Phil. course in History of Medicine

This is a one-year course aimed to give an insight into the historical background of the subject of medicine, to provide a suitable training for doctors and those already working in fields related to the history of medicine who intend to undertake scholarly historical work as an adjunct to their professional practice, and to act as a conversion course for further formal training in the field of History of Medicine.

The scheme of examination consists of a thesis, of not more than 15,000 words in length, including footnotes and appendices, but excluding bibliography, on a topic approved by the Degree Committee, for the Faculty of Clinical Medicine and four essays, each of about 3,000 words in length, on topics approved by the Degree Committee and related to the following areas:

(i) Life sciences and medicine up to and including the seventeenth century.

(ii) Life sciences and medicine in the eighteenth and nineteenth centuries.

(iii) A topic to be chosen by the candidate from a list announced by the Degree Committee. These topics afford the candidate the opportunity to study with various University Departments which have interests related to the History of Medicine, and they cover a wide area of study.

At least one essay must be offered from each area, but only one essay may be offered from area (iii).

The examination may include an oral examination upon the thesis and essays, and on the general field of knowledge in which they fall.

MEDICINE AND SURGERY

The two degrees, Bachelor of Medicine and Bachelor of Surgery, commonly abbreviated to M.B., B.Chir., are qualifications for provisional registration under the Medical Act, 1983. Full registration is obtained after completing one year's pre-registration service. The course of study falls into three periods: study for the First M.B. Examination (the premedical period); study for the Second M.B. Examination (the preclinical period); and study for the Final M.B. Examination (the clinical period). Cambridge Colleges do not normally admit medical students until they have passed or gained exemption from the First M.B. Examination, the commonest method of qualifying for exemption being by means of G.C.E. 'A' level passes in appropriate subjects.

Until 1976 when the Clinical School opened at Addenbrooke's Hospital, all pre-clinical students, when they had graduated with a B.A. Degree and passed or been exempted from the Second M.B. Examinations, proceeded to one of the London teaching hospitals or another university medical school for their clinical course. Now there are eighty places each year on the Cambridge Clinical Course which lasts for two years and three months. The remainder of the preclinical students continue to go to the medical school of another university for their clinical training and may in some cases opt to take the examination of that university or return to take the Cambridge Final M.B. Examination.

The course of study for the M.B., B.Chir. excluding the premedical period and pre-registration year is five years and one term for those students who pursue their clinical studies in Cambridge and six years for the remainder of the students.

Until recently there were separate regulations and examinations for students doing their clinical training in Cambridge and for those who had done clinical courses in other universities. These have now been amalgamated into a single set of regulations for the M.B., B.Chir. Degrees.

Candidates preparing for the Second M.B. Examination normally read the Medical Sciences Tripos and in their first year take the examinations in Anatomy, Biochemistry, Physiology, Medical Genetics, and Medical Sociology. In their second year students have two options: they can either take examinations in Anatomy, Neurophysiology, Physiology and Psychology, and an elective subject, or they can take examinations in all those subjects together with Pathology and Pharmacology. Students who select the first option will take the examinations in Pathology and Pharmacology together with further Psychology and a second elective in their third year. Students who take the second option will be able to choose from a wide range of Tripos examinations in the third year. The third year options open to prospective entrants to the clinical course in Cambridge include the study of a single subject leading to Part II of the Natural Sciences Tripos; a combination of subjects leading to Part II (General) of the Natural Sciences Tripos or to Part II (General) of the Medical Sciences Tripos; approved courses in Physical Anthropology leading to Part II of the Archaeological and Anthropological Tripos; or approved courses leading to examinations in the Social and Political Sciences Tripos; or courses leading to the Computer Science Tripos. At the end of the third year students will be eligible for the award of the degree of B.A.

Students are required to reach honours standard in an honours examination before proceeding to the Second M.B. Examination, the subjects of which are Anatomy A and B, Biochemistry, Physiology A and B, Pathology, Pharmacology, Medical Genetics, Medical Sociology, and Psychology. The majority of medical students will have the opportunity to obtain exemption from all these subjects (other than Medical Genetics and Medical Sociology) provided they have obtained honours in the Medical Sciences or Natural Sciences Tripos and have reached the prescribed standard in the appropriate subjects. It is not normally possible to gain exemption from Medical Sociology and medical students will rarely have the opportunity to obtain exemption in Medical Genetics. Special examinations are held twice a year for all those who have not obtained exemption from the Second M.B. Examination.

Arrangements can be made, and commonly are, for undergraduates who have begun by reading a Tripos other than the Medical Sciences Tripos to transfer to Medicine. In addition students who have taken a preclinical course in another university and have obtained a degree normally with honours in an appropriate subject may also be considered for entry to the clinical course in Cambridge. Each case raises individual problems and it is the practice of the Faculty Board of Clinical Medicine to consider individual cases on their merits and make the necessary recommendations.

The Final M.B. Examination consists of three Parts. Part I (Pathology) may be taken after fourteen months of clinical study, Part II (Obstetrics and Gynaecology) after eighteen months, and Part III (Medicine, including Clinical Pharmacology and Therapeutics, and Surgery) after two years and two months clinical study in the University or after two years and eight months of clinical study elsewhere. Each candidate must before completing the Final Examination provide evidence of five years of medical study by producing certificates of diligent attendance on certain courses of lectures and practical instructions in each year in an approved institution (either three years of pre-clinical medical study in the University or elsewhere and two years and two months clinical study in the University *or* two years of pre-clinical medical study in the University and two years and eight months of clinical study elsewhere).

The following is a brief description of each of the examinations leading to the M.B. and B.Chir. Degrees.

First M.B. Examination

The three Parts of the examination are: I (Chemistry), II (Physics), and III (Elementary Biology). The examinations are held twice a year, in March and September. The examination may be taken by any matriculated student or an unmatriculated student who is certified to be or to have been a *bona fide* candidate for admission to a College.

Exemptions from the examination may be secured as follows:

(*a*) From Part I of the First M.B. Examination by passing at Advanced level in Chemistry or in that subject in the Scottish Certificate of Sixth Year Studies;

(*b*) From Part II of the First M.B. Examination by passing
- (i) at Advanced level in Physics, or Physics-and-Mathematics, or Engineering Science; or in Physics in the Scottish Certificate of Sixth Year Studies; or
- (ii) at Ordinary level in Physics or Physical Science, or Physics with Chemistry, or Combined Science I *and* Combined Science II or in Integrated Science (double Ordinary level), and also *either* in Mathematics or Statistics at Advanced level *or* in either subject in the Scottish Certificate of Sixth Year Studies.

(*c*) From Part III of the First M.B. Examination by passing
- (i) at Advanced level in Biology, or Human Biology, or Botany, or Zoology; or
- (ii) at Ordinary level in one of those subjects and also *either* in

Mathematics or Statistics at Advanced level *or* in either subject in the Scottish Certificate of Sixth Year Studies; or

(iii) at Ordinary level in Combined Science *and* Combined Science II or in Integrated Science (double Ordinary level) and also *either* in Mathematics or Statistics at Advanced level *or* in either subject in the Scottish Certificate of Sixth Year Studies; or

(iv) at the Higher level in Biology at not less than grade B in the Scottish Certificate of Education.

(*d*) A student shall not be entitled to count an Advanced level pass in Mathematics or Statistics or a pass in either subject in the Scottish Certificate of Sixth Year Studies as contributing towards exemption from both Parts II and III of the First M.B. Examination.

(*e*) A student who has passed at Advanced level in Physical Science shall be entitled to exemption from Parts I and II of the First M.B. Examination.

(*f*) A student who has obtained honours or has reached the honours standard in the Natural Sciences Tripos in one of the subjects shown in column 2 of the table shall be entitled to exemption from the Part of the First M.B. Examination shown against it in column 1.

Column 1	*Column* 2	*Column* 2 (*continued*)
Part I	Biochemistry	
	Chemistry	
	Metallurgy and Materials Science	
Part II	Physics	
	Fluid Mechanics	
Part III	Anatomy	Botany
	Biochemistry	Genetics
	Biology of Cells	Pathology
	Biology of Organisms	Comparative Pathology
	Biological Resources	Pharmacology
	Animal Biology	Physiology
	Applied Biology	Psychology
	Environmental Biology	Experimental Psychology
	Plant Biology	Zoology

In addition the Faculty Board may exempt from the whole or from one or more Parts of the examination candidates who have passed, in this or in another university, examinations which the Board approve for the purpose.

Second M.B. Examination

The Second M.B. Examination consists of the subjects Anatomy A, Anatomy B, Biochemistry, Pathology, Pharmacology, Physiology A, Physiology B, Medical Genetics, Medical Sociology and Psychology. Candidates for the M.B., B.Chir. Degrees must pass or gain exemption from the Second M.B. Examination before they take Part I of the Final M.B. Examination. A student who has undertaken his pre-clinical studies in Cambridge will not normally be admitted to the clinical course in Cambridge until he has completed all the requirements of the Second M.B. Examination. For those entering the clinical course from another University, postponement of the examinations in Medical Genetics, Medical Sociology and Psychology may be permitted. A candidate for the Second M.B. Examination or for exemption from it, must (*a*) have completed the First M.B. Examination by having passed or been granted exemption from it, (*b*) if he is a candidate for an examination in Anatomy, produce evidence of diligent attendance on approved courses of instruction in that subject and of having satisfactorily dissected the appropriate parts of the human body, (*c*) if he is a candidate for examination in Biochemistry, Pathology, Pharmacology, Physiology, Medical Genetics, Medical Sociology or Psychology, produce evidence of diligent attendance on approved courses of instruction in the appropriate subject, (*d*) have obtained honours in an Honours Examination or, being over the standing to obtain honours in the Medical Sciences Tripos, to have attained the honours standard therein; or have obtained a degree with honours of a university other than Cambridge or other degree deemed appropriate by the Faculty Board for this purpose. The Faculty Board of Clinical Medicine may waive requirement (*a*) on condition that it is satisfied before the candidate takes either Part of the Final M.B. Examination. The Second M.B. Examination is held in June and September, except for Medical Genetics and Medical Sociology which are examined in March and September. A candidate who has gained exemption from one or more of the subjects of the examination may present himself for the remaining subject or subjects.

The Final M.B. Examination

The Final M.B. Examination is divided into three Parts, as follows:

Part I. Pathology.
Part II. Obstetrics and Gynaecology.

Part III. (*a*) Medicine including Clinical Pharmacology and Therapeutics.
(*b*) Surgery.

Parts I and II will be held in April, June and December and Part III in June and December each year. Before taking any part of the Final M.B. Examination a candidate must have completed the First and Second M.B. Examinations and produce evidence of satisfactory attendance on the approved courses of clinical instruction appropriate to that Part.

A candidate for Part III is also required to submit an essay of not more than 3,000 words on a subject related to medicine to the Clinical Dean not less than six weeks before taking Part III.

The Parts of the Final M.B. Examinations may be taken either together or separately except that a candidate will be required to have passed Part I before presenting himself as a candidate for Part III unless he has been given special permission by the Faculty Board.

MODERN AND MEDIEVAL LANGUAGES

In this subject there are courses of study followed by candidates for:

The *Modern and Medieval Languages Tripos*, which is divided into two Parts.
A *Preliminary Examination* for each Part of the Tripos.
Advanced Oral Examinations in modern languages.
Certificates of Competent Knowledge in modern languages.
Ordinary Examinations in certain modern languages for the Ordinary B.A. Degree.
The *M.Phil. in Linguistics (one-year course)*.

The Modern and Medieval Languages Tripos

The Modern Languages Tripos is in two Parts, which must be taken separately. In Part I the emphasis is on language more than on literature, philology, and linguistics. In Part II the converse is true. A very wide range of modern languages is available: Czech with Slovak, Danish, Dutch, French, German, Italian, Modern Greek, Norwegian, Polish, Portuguese, Russian, Serbo-Croat, Spanish, and Swedish. Other languages may also be approved. Details are given on pp. 274 and 278–80 of the conditions under which Classical and Oriental languages can be offered.

Part I[1]

Part I consists of a written and an oral examination. A candidate must offer two languages at the same standard and may sit his written examination at the end of his first or his second year. It is possible to offer both languages in the same year, whether first or second; it is also possible to 'split' Part I, offering one language at the end of the first year, and the other language at the end of the second. To be classed in Part I a candidate must be classed in both his languages.

Those candidates who offer two languages which they have already studied at school frequently sit both their languages at the end of their first year. Where a candidate begins the study of a new language at Cambridge, he will usually be advised to 'split' his Part I or to sit both his languages at the end of his second year. A candidate's College can often give advice concerning the possibility of taking up

[1] Further details on pp. 276 ff.

a new language and can indicate what preliminary steps, for example a summer course or a period abroad, are desirable.[1]

It is possible in Part I to offer a modern language together with either classical Greek or classical Latin. Arabic may be offered with either Spanish or Portuguese. Other combinations of a modern language and an oriental language require the consent of the Faculty Boards concerned.

Part II[2]

An extremely wide range of options is available in Part II as can be seen from the scope of Schedule II, published below. A candidate must offer from that Schedule four or five papers depending on whether he spends one or two years in preparation for Part II; the details are set out on p. 294. In addition to their Schedule II papers or papers equivalent to them, candidates must offer two language papers, an Essay paper and a Translation and Composition paper; generally these papers are offered in the same language, but a candidate who wishes to do so can sit his Essay paper in a language different from that of his Translation and Composition paper.

It is possible to specialize in the language and literature of one country or to choose papers from a variety of literatures or languages; the course can thus be virtually 'tailor-made' for the individual concerned. While the great majority of papers in Part II are concerned with the literature, history and thought of a particular period and country, there are also papers on the history of individual languages, on comparative literature and comparative philology, on phonetics, on general and historical linguistics, on specified periods of history and on the history of the visual arts, and on the history of linguistic thought. As well as the papers listed in Schedule II, a candidate has available to him papers from Part II of the Classical Tripos and also certain papers from the English Tripos and from the Anglo-Saxon, Norse, and Celtic Tripos. Details of those papers are given on pp. 296–7. Before he can offer any papers from the Oriental Studies Tripos, a candidate must have the permission of the Faculty Boards concerned.

[1] Bursaries are available to candidates firmly accepted to read a Scandinavian language to enable them to study abroad prior to coming into residence. Applications should be made to the Chairman, Scandinavian Studies Fund, Faculty of Modern and Medieval Languages, Sidgwick Avenue, Cambridge CB3 9DA.

[2] Further details on pp. 294 ff.

In Part II a candidate may offer a dissertation in addition to his papers from Schedule II or as an alternative to one of them. A candidate may offer both an 'alternative' and an 'additional' dissertation if he fulfils the specified conditions (p. 294).

[1]*Study Abroad*

A candidate for Part II of the Modern and Medieval Languages Tripos may apply through his College to the Faculty Board for permission to spend a year abroad as part of his preparation for Part II; he will thus spend four years reading for his degree. Such a candidate must satisfy the Faculty Board that he will spend the year abroad either studying at a university or in some approved teaching post. Application forms, to be obtained from the Faculty Office, are to be submitted by the Division of the Lent Term before the year to be spent abroad.

Advanced Oral Examinations

Any candidate for Part II may be a candidate for an Advanced Oral Examination in any of the modern languages available in the Tripos. The Examination is also open to candidates who have obtained honours in Part I or who have been awarded a Certificate of Competent Knowledge in a Modern Language. The examination consists of four parts: (*a*) reading aloud; (*b*) oral précis; (*c*) prepared discourse; (*d*) conversation.

Certificate of Competent Knowledge[2]

The Certificate can be taken by any member of the University in one of the languages normally available in Part I. The written examination consists of three language papers modelled on the three language papers in Part I and the candidate is expected to reach at least a second class standard in these papers. There is also an oral examination. A candidate may enter for Certificates in more than one language, and can be a candidate for a Certificate on more than one occasion.

[1] Regulations for the period of study abroad are currently under discussion and it is possible that study abroad may become a requirement of the Modern and Medieval Languages Tripos. A student in need of advice should seek it in the first instance from his College.

[2] Further details on p. 320.

Part I

A candidate may take Part I in his first or second year or, if he has obtained honours in another Tripos, one or two years after doing so but not later than his fourth year. A candidate for Part I must choose one of three options: under option A, he may offer two languages in his first year, or in his first year after obtaining honours in another Tripos; under option B, he may offer two languages in his second year, or in his second year after obtaining honours in another Tripos; under option C, he may offer one language in his first year of study for Part I and his second language in the following year. If he chooses either option B or C he will have to offer one additional paper as set out below.

Candidates for Part I are required to take papers in Composition, Translation, and Essay, and in a selected period of literary study, and to take an oral examination, in each of two languages. Candidates may combine one modern European language with either classical Latin or classical Greek, or an Oriental language, though in this last instance it is necessary for the candidate to seek, through his College, the permission of the Faculty Board of Modern and Medieval Languages; either Spanish or Portuguese with Arabic is a combination always available to candidates. The following modern European languages are available to candidates for Part I of the Modern and Medieval Languages Tripos; Czech (with Slovak), Danish, Dutch, French, German, Italian, Modern Greek, Norwegian, Polish, Portuguese, Russian, Serbo-Croat, Spanish, and Swedish. Hungarian is also currently available. Other European languages may be offered subject to the permission of the Faculty Board. Certain combinations of cognate languages are not permitted, e.g. candidates may not offer both Spanish and Portuguese, or more than one Scandinavian language. However, Latin may be combined with Italian, and classical Greek with Modern Greek.

The examination in each modern language consists of two Sections:

Section A. Three language papers and an oral examination:

A1. Passages from works in the foreign language for translation into English or for linguistic commentary.

In French, German, Italian, Portuguese, and Spanish the passages are chosen from works not earlier than 1500, in Danish and Swedish from works not earlier than 1600, in Russian from works not earlier than 1700, and in Czech (with Slovak), modern Greek, Norwegian, Polish, and Serbo-Croat from works not earlier than 1800.

A2. Passages from English to be translated into the foreign language.

A3. An essay in a foreign language chosen from a paper of subjects half of which shall bear on the literature, history, thought, and language of the country concerned, and all of which shall demand reasoned exposition.

Oral. An oral examination. Details of this examination are given below (pp. 280–1).

Section B. Papers listed in Schedule I, relating to the literature, history, thought, and language of the country the language of which may be offered, together with specified supplementary papers.

Certain papers are marked with an asterisk: a paper so marked may be offered only by a candidate who (*a*) is offering the language in his second year of study for the Tripos, and (*b*) is offering at the same examination one of the papers in Schedule I relating to the same language that is not marked with an asterisk. Any paper in the Schedule may be divided into two sections, one relating to prescribed texts to be studied in detail, the other relating to authors or topics to be studied more generally and to historical and cultural background. Candidates will be required to answer questions from each section.

A candidate who offers two modern languages in his first year of study for Part I under option A must take in each language Papers A1, A2, A3, and the oral examination, and one Section B paper chosen from among the papers listed in Schedule I that are not marked with an asterisk. A candidate who offers two modern languages in his second year of study for Part I under option B must offer

(*a*) four papers in one language, and the oral examination, as specified in option A,

(*b*) five papers consisting of

(i) four papers in the second language, as specified for a language in option A,

(ii) an additional paper chosen from among the papers listed in Schedule I, which may be *either* a paper (whether marked with an asterisk or not) in the second language, *or* one of the supplementary papers,

and the oral examination.

A candidate who offers two modern languages in successive years under option C must take four papers and the oral examination in the first year in one language as under option A, and five papers and the oral examination in the second language in the second year as in (*b*) of option B. For candidates in Arabic the regulations are slightly different (see below).

A candidate who begins his course intending to choose option A may at the end of his first year change to option C should he fail in one of the languages offered under option A. Similarly a candidate who begins having chosen option C may change to option B if he fails in the language in which he has been examined at the end of his first year. In both cases however the candidate will be prohibited from offering again the language in which he has failed. He must offer a different language in its place and, if he is changing from option A to option C, he must offer in it five papers (as in (*b*) of option B).

To obtain honours in Part I a candidate must reach the honours standard in each of his two languages either on the same occasion (under option A or option B) or in successive years (under option C).

Arabic

A candidate who offers *either* Spanish *or* Portuguese, and Arabic, must if he chooses option A offer in the modern language the papers prescribed under that option and in Arabic the following three papers from Part I of the Oriental Studies Tripos:

Ar. 1. Arabic prose composition and classical unseens.
Ar. 2. Arabic modern unseens and essay, together with the oral examination in Arabic,

and any one of the following papers:

Ar. 3. Arabic literature, 1.
Ar. 4. Arabic literature, 2.
Ar. 5. History of the Arab world.
Is. 1. Islamic history.

If he chooses option B and does not wish to offer an additional paper in his modern language, or if he has chosen option C and is offering Arabic on the second occasion, he must offer *either* a further paper chosen from among the papers Ar. 3, Ar. 4, Ar. 5 and Is. 1 of the Oriental Studies Tripos *or* one of the supplementary papers (a total of four papers).

Classical Greek

A candidate who offers one modern language and classical Greek must offer papers in the modern language prescribed under that option and in classical Greek the following papers:

(A) if he chooses option A, papers or half-papers from Part I of the Classical Tripos as follows:

either Paper 1 *or* Paper 2 (translation from Greek);
Paper 4 (four passages to be translated from Greek only*);
Paper 5 (Greek literature);

and *either* Paper 10 (translation from English into Greek).

or any one of Papers 7–9 (Greek and Roman history, philosophy and religion, art and architecture – candidates will be required to confine their answers to Greek themes only).

or one half of any two of Papers 7–9 (Greek themes only). These half papers will each consist of two questions only and will each last only one and a half hours.

(B/C) if he chooses option B and does not offer an additional paper in his modern language, or if he has chosen option C and is offering classical Greek on the second occasion, he must offer as his additional paper

either one of the supplementary papers,

or a further paper chosen from Papers 7–10 of Part I of the Classical Tripos,

or two half-papers, each consisting of two questions from one of Papers 7–9 of Part I of the Classical Tripos (as above for option A). However no candidate may offer more than two half-papers in all.

Candidates who are not already offering Paper 10 (translation from English into Greek) may offer it as an optional additional paper (see below p. 280).

* A candidate who is offering Paper 1 will be set more difficult passages than a candidate who is offering Paper 2.

Classical Latin

A candidate who offers one modern language and classical Latin must offer papers in the modern language prescribed under that option and in classical Latin the following papers:

(A) if he chooses option A:

(*a*) Translation from Latin verse from poets other than Virgil.
(*b*) Translation from Latin prose.
(*c*) Virgil, including passages for translation and commentary.
(*d*) Outlines of Latin literature, including a passage or passages for translation and commentary based on a schedule of prescribed works;

(B/C) if he chooses option B and does not offer an additional paper in his modern language, or if he has chosen option C and is offering classical Latin on the second occasion he must offer the papers prescribed for option A and in addition

either one of the supplementary papers,
or Roman history (Paper 7 of Part I of the Classical Tripos – Roman history questions only),
or Roman art and architecture (Paper 9 of Part I of the Classical Tripos–Roman art and architecture questions only).

A candidate offering classical Latin may offer additionally Paper 11 of Part I of the Classical Tripos (translation from English into Latin) and a candidate offering classical Greek may offer additionally paper 10 of Part I of the Classical Tripos (translation from English into Greek), provided he is not already offering it as a compulsory paper. In determining the place in the class-list of any candidate who has offered either Paper 10 or Paper 11 as an additional paper, the Examiners will give credit for proficiency in that paper. Distinguished and satisfactory performances in these papers will be separately indicated on the class-list of successful candidates.

Oral Examination for Part I

An oral examination is an integral component of Part I in all the scheduled languages except Classical Greek and Latin and is assessed as the equivalent of half a written paper. The examination consists of three parts: (*a*) dictation, (*b*) reading aloud, including the reading of isolated words and phrases as a phonetic test, and (*c*) conversation on one of a number of prescribed topics involving reasoned argument. The list of topics from which the examiners and candidates may choose is published in the year before that in which the examination takes place and usually incorporates the topics set in the essay paper for Part I in the year in which the list is published. The oral examinations are held at the beginning of the Easter Term, some weeks before the written papers are taken.

A list of the topics prescribed for the oral examinations in **1985** may be obtained from the Faculty Office.

The language laboratories at Sidgwick Avenue are available to undergraduates, both to improve their fluency in languages which they already know and to assist them in learning new languages.

The papers for Section B of Part I are as follows:

SCHEDULE I[1] (PAPERS FOR SECTION B OF PART I)

FRENCH

[2] *1. Introduction to French literature, thought, and history in the Middle Ages.

[2] *2. French literature, thought, and history in the sixteenth century.

3. French literature, thought, and history in the seventeenth century (with special reference to particular periods or topics to be prescribed from time to time).

4. French literature, thought, and history in the eighteenth century (with special reference to particular periods or topics to be prescribed from time to time).

5. French literature, thought, and history in the nineteenth century (with special reference to particular periods or topics to be prescribed from time to time).

GERMAN

6. Aspects of the history of the German language.

7. Introduction to German medieval literature.

8. German literature, thought, and history, from 1620 to 1700.

9. German literature, thought, and history, from 1770 to 1832.

10. German literature, thought, and history, from 1815 to 1890.

*11. German literature, thought, and history, from 1880 to 1914.

ITALIAN

*12. Introduction to the structure and varieties of the Italian language.

†13. Introduction to Dante and his age.

[1] For the asterisk, see p. 277.

[2] From 1 October 1985 this paper will be deleted.

† No candidate may offer both Papers 13 and 14.

†14. (*a*) Introduction to Dante and his age, and (*b*) the literature of the Risorgimento.
*15. Introduction to the Italian Renaissance.
16. Italian literature, thought, and history, since 1880.

Slavonic

*17. Introduction to the history and civilization of the Slavonic peoples from the sixth to the thirteenth centuries.
*18. Introduction to the study of Kievan and Muscovite Russia.
19. Russian literature and thought, from 1799 to 1900.
*20. Russian literature, thought, and history, from 1891 to 1934.
21. Czech and Slovak literature, thought, and history, from 1774 to 1939.
*22. Czech drama from 1813 to 1939.
23. Polish literature, thought, and history, from 1795 to 1914.
24. Polish literature and thought, from 1918 to 1956.
*25. Serbian literature, history, and institutions, from 1168 to 1389.
26. Serbian and Croatian literature, thought, and history, since 1800.

Scandinavian

*27. Danish literature, thought, and history, from 1800 to 1870.
28. Danish literature, thought, and history, from 1870 to the present day.
*29. Norwegian literature, thought, and history, from 1800 to 1865.
30. Norwegian literature, thought, and history, from 1865 to the present day.
*31. Swedish literature, thought, and history, from 1800 to 1870.
32. Swedish literature, thought, and history, from 1870 to the present day.

Spanish

*33. An introduction to the history of the Peninsular languages.
*34. Medieval Spain.
35. Spanish literature, thought, and history in the sixteenth century.
*36. Cervantes and the Golden Age novel, from 1500 to 1616.
*37. Benito Pérez Galdós and the nineteenth-century novel.
38. Spanish literature, thought, and history in the twentieth century.
*39. Argentina and Mexico since 1830.

Dutch

*40. The early history and literature of the Netherlands.
*41. Vondel.

† No candidate may offer both Papers 13 and 14.

*42. The literature, thought, and history of the Netherlands, from 1830 to 1918.

43. The literature, thought, and history of the Netherlands, from 1880 to 1939.

PORTUGUESE

*44. Portuguese literature, thought, and history, from 1495 to 1580.

45. Portuguese literature, thought, and history, since 1825.

MODERN GREEK

*46. Greek literature, thought, and history, from 1453 to 1700.

47. Greek literature, thought, and history, since 1800.

SUPPLEMENTARY PAPER

*48. Medieval Latin literature.

The following texts and periods have been prescribed, and authors and topics specified, for these papers in **1985** and **1986**:

SCHEDULE I

PAPERS FOR SECTION B OF PART I IN **1985**

FRENCH

**Paper 1.* *Introduction to French literature, thought, and history, in the Middle Ages*

**Paper 2.* *French literature, thought, and history, in the sixteenth century*, with special reference to the period 1515–1560, and to the following:

Rabelais, *Gargantua*, *Pantagruel*; Marot, *Œuvres poétiques*, ed. Y. Giraud (Garnier/Flammarion).

Paper 3. *French literature, thought, and history, in the seventeenth century*, with special reference to the period 1630–1700, and to the following:

Corneille; Descartes, *Discours de la méthode*; Mme de Lafayette, *La Princesse de Clèves*; La Fontaine, *Fables*; La Rochefoucauld, *Maximes*; Molière; Pascal, *Pensées* (ed. L. Lafuma, Editions du Seuil, Collection 'Points'); Racine; Church and society in France, 1630–1700.

Paper 4. *French literature, thought, and history, in the eighteenth century*, with special reference to the period 1715–1789, and to the following:

Lesage, *Gil Blas*; Montesquieu, *Lettres persanes*; Voltaire, *Zadig*, *Candide*, *Le Philosophe ignorant*; Rousseau, *Rêveries du promeneur solitaire*; Diderot, *Le Neveu de Rameau*; Marivaux, *Le Jeu de l'amour et du hasard*, *La Double Inconstance*, *Les Fausses Confidences*; Prévost, *Manon Lescaut*; Beaumarchais, *Le Barbier de Séville*, *Le Mariage de Figaro*; Laclos, *Les Liaisons dangereuses*; The rôle of the *parlements* in eighteenth-century France; Watteau.

Paper 5. *French literature, thought, and history, in the nineteenth century*, with special reference to the period 1830–1870, and to the following:

Stendhal, *Le Rouge et le noir*; Balzac, *Le Cousin Pons*; Flaubert, *Madame Bovary*; Fromentin, *Dominique*; Hugo, *Les Feuilles d'automne*; Nerval, *Les Chimères*, *Sylvie*; Gautier, *Emaux et camées*; Baudelaire, *Les Fleurs du Mal*; Romantic drama; the Revolutions of 1848; Utopian thought, 1830–51.

GERMAN

Paper 6. *Aspects of the history of the German language*

Joseph Wright, *Grammar of the Gothic Language* (Oxford, 1954), pp. 211–226; Wilhelm Braune, *Althochdeutsches Lesebuch* (Tübingen, 1969), Passage XX, sections 3–6; M. O'C. Walshe, *A Middle High German Reader* (Oxford, 1974), Section VII; Alfred Götze, *Frühneuhochdeutsches Lesebuch* (Göttingen, 1958), Sections 5, 8, 11 (235–399), 13, 14 (93–149), 22 (1–8 and 59–110), 25h, 27b, 30, 36 (1–90).

Paper 7. *Introduction to German medieval literature*

A thorough knowledge of the following works is required: *Minnesang vom Kürenberger bis Wolfram* (ed. Max Wehrli, Altdeutsche Übungstexte, Nr. 4), the poems of Der von Kürenberg, Friderich von Husen, Heinrich von Morungen, Hartman von Ouwe; Gottfried von Strassburg, *Tristan und Isold* (ed. F. Ranke, Altdeutsche Übungstexte, Nr. 3), lines 10803–12568.

A general knowledge of the following works is required: Wolfram von Eschenbach, *Parzival*, Book v (ed. E. Hartl, Altdeutsche Übungstexte, Nr. 12); Walther von der Vogelweide, *Gedichte* (ed. Max Wehrli, Altdeutsche Übungstexte, Nr. 5), sections I, II, III, IV, VIII; Wernher der Gartenære, *Meier Helmbrecht* (any available edition).

Paper 8. *German literature, thought, and history, from 1620 to 1700*

(*a*) Texts for close study: *Deutsche Barocklyrik* (ed. M. Wehrli); Gryphius, *Papinianus*; Grimmelshausen, *Die Landstörtzerin Courasche.*

(*b*) A general knowledge of the period with principal reference to Opitz, Spee, the Nuremberg School, Fleming, Gryphius, Lohenstein, Hofmannswaldau, Grimmelshausen, Beer, Reuter, Günther.

Paper 9. *German literature, thought, and history, from 1770 to 1832*, with special reference to the following:

(*a*) Texts for close study: Goethe, *Faust I*; Hölderlin, poems from the Reclam Hölderlin (RUB 6266) up to and including *Wie wenn am Feiertage*; Kleist, *Michael Kohlhaas*; *Die Marquise von O...*; *Das Erdbeben in Chili* (available in Reclam nos. 218, 7670, and 1957).

(*b*) A general knowledge of the period, with principal reference to Goethe, Schiller, Lessing, Herder, Novalis, Hölderlin, Kleist, and Grillparzer.

Paper 10. *German literature, thought, and history, from 1815 to 1890*

(*a*) Texts for close study: Büchner, *Dantons Tod*; Stifter, *Bunte Steine*; H. Heine, *Gedichte* (Reclam 8988).

(*b*) A knowledge of the literature, history, and thought of the period, with principal reference to Grillparzer, Hebbel, Heine, Büchner, Mörike, Keller, Stifter, Nietzsche, Droste, and Meyer.

**Paper 11.* *German literature, thought, and history, from 1880 to 1914*

(*a*) Texts for close study: Fontane, *Effi Briest* (Reclam 6961); Hauptmann, *Die Ratten* (Ullstein 4977); Rilke, *Neue Gedichte I.*

(*b*) A knowledge of the literature, history, and thought of the period, with principal reference to Fontane, Hauptmann, Thomas Mann, Hofmannsthal, Rilke, Schnitzler, Wedekind, Stefan George, Nietzsche, Trakl.

ITALIAN

**Paper 12.* *Introduction to the structure and varieties of the Italian language*

A general study of the present-day structure and varieties of Italian, together with a study of the general linguistic background.

†*Paper 13.* *Introduction to Dante and his age*, with special reference to the following:

Dante, *Vita nuova, Inferno, Purgatorio, Convivio* (Book I).
Prescribed topic: Dante's concept of Language.

†*Paper 14.* (*a*) *Introduction to Dante and his age, and* (*b*) *the literature of the Risorgimento*

(*a*) Dante, *Vita nuova, Inferno.*
Prescribed topic: The History of Florence, 1250–1313.
(*b*) Manzoni, *I promessi sposi*; Leopardi, *I canti.*
Prescribed topic: The Risorgimento in Italy up to and including the year 1861.

Paper 15. *Introduction to the Italian Renaissance*, with special reference to the following subjects:

(*a*) Boccaccio, *Decameron*, III, IV, V, X;
(*b*) Petrarch, *Selected poems*, eds. Griffith and Hainsworth (M.U.P.);
(*c*) Ariosto, *Orlando furioso*, selection, ed. Calvino (Einaudi);
(*d*) Giotto, The Arena Chapel; Ghiberti, The Florentine Baptistery Doors; Piero della Francesca, The Legend of the True Cross.

Students will be expected to show knowledge of at least three of the four subjects.

* See Regulations 17 and 19 (*Ordinances*, pp. 339–40).
† No candidate may offer both Papers 13 and 14.

Paper 16. ***Italian literature, thought, and history, since 1880***

(*a*) Texts for close study: Verga, *I Malavoglia*; D'Annunzio, *Alcyone*; Pirandello, *Enrico IV*; Svevo, *La coscienza di Zeno*; Moravia, *Gli Indifferenti*; Gozzano, *I colloqui*; Ungaretti, *L'Allegria*; Montale, *Ossi di seppia*; Bassani, *Il giardino dei Finzi Contini*; Pavese, *La luna e i falò*; Sciascia, *Il contesto*.

(*b*) A general knowledge of the period with special reference to Italian political history from 1918 to the present day.

Slavonic

**Paper 17.* *Introduction to the history and civilization of the Slavonic peoples from the sixth to the thirteenth centuries*, with special reference to the following:

Texts: Photius, *Homilies* III–IV (tr. and ed. C. Mango); Helmold, *Chronicle of the Slavs*, chs. 1, 11, 16, 52, 83–4 (tr. and ed. F. J. Tschan); Constantine Porphyrogenitus, *De administrando imperio*, chs. 2, 4, 5, 8, 9, 29–36 (tr. and ed. G. Moravcsik and R. Jenkins).

Topics: (*a*) The formation of the Slav states; (*b*) the conversion of the Slavs.

**Paper 18.* *Introduction to the study of Kievan and Muscovite Russia*, with special reference to the following:

Texts: Сказание... Бориса и Глеба; Моление Даниила Заточника; Повесть о разорении Рязани Батыем; Хожение Аф. Никитина, ed. V. P. Adrianova-Peretts, 1958, pp. 11–16, 18–22, 27–30; Служба кабаку (in Русская демократическая сатира XVII ь., 2 ed., 1977).

Topics: Christian culture in the Kievan period; The emergence of Muscovy (Ivan III–Ivan IV); The reign of Alexis Mikhailovich.

Paper 19. *Russian literature and thought, from 1799 to 1900*, with special reference to the following:

Texts: Pushkin, Кавказский пленник, Цыганы; Gogol, Ревизор; Lermontov, Герой нашего времени; Tolstoy, Казаки; Turgenev, Вешние воды.

Topics: Poetry 1800–1820; Chaadaev; Belinsky as literary critic; the work of Dostoevsky to 1849; the work of Tolstoy after 1878, with special reference to: Исповедь; Смерть Ивана Ильича; Хозяин и работник; Что такое искусство?

**Paper 20.* *Russian literature, thought, and history, from 1891 to 1934*, with special reference to the following:

Texts: Chekhov, Невеста, Дом с мезонином, Палата No. 6, В овраге, Дама с собачкой; Blok, *Poems* (ed. A. Pyman); Anna Akhmatova, Четки; Bunin, Жизнь Арсеньева; Fadeev, Разгром; Olesha, Зависть.

Topics: Pobedonostsev; Early Russian Marxism (1894–1905); The revolution of 1905 and the First and Second Dumas; The revolutions of 1917; The rise of Stalin (1917–1928); The collectivization of agriculture (1928–1933).

Paper 21. *Czech and Slovak literature, thought, and history, from 1774 to 1939*, with special reference to the following:

Texts: Havlíček, *Křest sv. Vladimíra*; Mácha, *Máj*; Neruda, *Malostrauské povídky*; Vrchlický, *Okna v bouři*; Karásek, *Sodoma*; Machar, *Golgatha*; Pujmanová, *Lidé na křižovatce*; Krasko, *Básnické dielo*; Jilemnický, *Zuniaci krok*.

Topics: Czech *or* Slovak Romanticism; The political thought of Palacký; The Czechoslovak Legion in Russia; Czech and Slovak Proletarian poetry; The Czech Ruralist movement; The Slovak social novel (1918–1939).

**Paper 22.* *Czech drama from 1813 to 1939*, with special reference to the following:

Tyl, *Jan Hus*; Bozděch, *Baron Gõtz*; Mrštíkové, *Maryša*; Hilbert, *Falkenštejn*; Dyk, *Posel*; Langer, *Jízdní hlídka*; Werner, *Lidé na kře*.

Paper 23. *Polish literature, thought, and history, from 1795 to 1914*, with special reference to the following:

Mickiewicz: *Sonety*; Słowacki, *Kordian*; Fredro, *Zemsta*; Sienkiewicz, *Nowele*; Żeromski, *Ludzie bezdomni*; Wyspiański, *Wesele*.

Paper 24. *Polish literature and thought, from 1918 to 1956*, with special reference to the following:

Żeromski, *Przedwiośnie*; Pollak-Matuszewski, *Poezja polska 1914–1939*; Nałkowska, *Granica*; Gombrowicz, *Ferdydurke*; Miłosz, *Wiersze* (London, 1967); Andrzejewski, *Popiół i diament*.

**Paper 25.* *Serbian literature, history, and institutions, from 1168 to 1389*, with special reference to the following:

Texts: Stojan Novaković, Примери књижевности и језика старога српско-словенскога (Beograd, 1909): pp. 209–17, 219–24, 229–38, 240–5, 247–68; N. Radojčić, Законик цара Душана (S.A.N. Beograd, 1960).

Topics: The work of St Sava; The history of Serbia from 1168 to 1355; The development of the Serbian biography; The causes leading to the Serbian defeat at Kosovo in 1389.

* See Regulations 17 and 19 (*Ordinances*, pp. 339–40).

Paper 26. *Serbian and Croatian literature, thought, and history, since 1800,* with special reference to the following:

(*a*) Ivan Mažuranić, *Smrt Smail-age Čengijića*; Branko Radičević, *Pesme*; L.K. Lazarević *Pripovetke*; Miroslav Krleža, *Povratak Filipa Latinovicza*; Ivo Andrić, *Na Drini Ćuprija*; Dobrica Ćosić, *Daleko je sunce.*

(*b*) Topics: The work of Vuk Karadžić; The history of the first and second Serbian risings 1804–1830; The Illyrian Movement; *Seoska pripovetka*; The *Moderna* and Croatian literature 1897–1914.

Scandinavian

**Paper 27.* *Danish literature, thought, and history, from 1800 to 1870,* with special reference to the following:

Adam Oehlenschläger, *Digte 1803*: Steen Steensen Blicher, *Noveller* (ed. T. Skou-Hansen); Johan Ludvig Heiberg, *Nye Digte*; H.C. Andersen, *Eventyr og Historier* (ed. V. Sørensen); Emil Aarestrup, *Digte*; Frederik Paludan-Müller, *Adam Homo*; Hans Egede Schack, *Phantasterne.*

Paper 28. *Danish literature, thought, and history, from 1870 to the present day,* with special reference to the following:

J.P. Jacobsen, *Mogens og andre Noveller*; Herman Bang, *Stuk*; Sophus Claussen, *Lyrik* (ed. F.J. Billeskov Jansen); Johannes V. Jensen, *Kongens Fald*; Martin Andersen Nexø, *Pelle Erobreren: Barndom*; Hans Kirk, *Fiskerne*; Karen Blixen, *Syndfloden over Norderney, Drømmerne.*

**Paper 29.* *Norwegian literature, thought, and history, from 1800 to 1865,* with special reference to the following:

Henrik Wergeland, *Den engelske Lods*; J.S. Welhaven, *Norges Dæmring*; Nasjonalromantikken; Bjørnstjerne Bjørnson, *Synnøve Solbakken, Arne, En glad Gut*; Henrik Ibsen, *Kongs-Emnerne*; Camilla Collett, *Amtmandens Døttre*; O. Vinje, *Ferdaminni.*

Paper 30. *Norwegian literature, thought, and history, from 1865 to the present day,* with special reference to the following:

Henrik Ibsen, *Peer Gynt*; Bjørnstjerne Bjørnson, *En Fallit, Redaktøren, Kongen*; Alexander Kielland, *Garman & Worse*; Jonas Lie, *Familjen paa Gilje*; Sigrid Undset, *Jenny*; Knut Hamsun, *Markens Grøde*; Johan Falkberget, *Den fjerde nattevakt*; Sigurd Hoel, *Møte ved milepelen.*

**Paper 31.* *Swedish literature, thought, and history, from 1800 to 1870,* with special reference to the following:

Esaias Tegnér, *Frithiofs saga*; E.J. Stagnelius, *Liljor i Saron*; C.J.L. Almqvist, *Urval* (ed. Julén); J.L. Runeberg, *Fänrik Ståls sägner* and *Kung Fjalar*; Fredrika Bremer, *Grannarne*; Viktor Rydberg, *Singoalla.*

Paper 32. *Swedish literature, thought, and history, from 1870 to the present day,* with special reference to the following:

August Strindberg, *Röda rummet, Fröken Julie, Ett drömspel*; Selma Lagerlöf, *Jerusalem*; Gustaf Fröding, *Dikter* (Stockholm, 1945); Hjalmar Söderberg, *Martin Bircks ungdom*; Hjalmar Bergman, *En döds memoarer*; Birger Sjöberg, *Kriser och kransar*; Ivar Lo-Johansson, *Godnatt, jord*; Lars Ahlin, *Min död är min.*

Spanish

**Paper 33.* *An introduction to the history of the Peninsular languages*

A general study of the present-day structures and basic external histories of Castilian and *either* Portuguese *or* Catalan. The following texts are set for special linguistic study:

Castilian: María de Maeztu, *Antología Siglo XX: Prosistas españoles*, Part two (col. Austral); Federico García Lorca, *La zapatera prodigiosa*; *Oxford Book of Spanish Verse*, 2nd ed. nos. 179–85, 189–93, 200–6, 219–27.

Portuguese: G. de Castilho (ed.), *Os melhores contos portugueses* (2. *serie*), pp. 1–97; *Contos do Brasil* (Harrap), pp. 1–57; *Oxford Book of Portuguese Verse*, 2nd ed. nos. 180–7, 200–5, 227–31, 250–4.

Catalan: J. Gili, *Introductory Catalan Grammar*, 2nd ed., pp. 122–52.

**Paper 34.* *Medieval Spain*

A general study of the literature in connexion with the historical and cultural background during the Middle Ages, with special reference to narrative poetry.

* See Regulations 17 and 19 (*Ordinances*, pp. 339–40).

Paper 35. Spanish literature, thought, and history in the sixteenth century, with special reference to the following:

(*a*) Texts for close study: Fernando de Rojas, *La Celestina*; the complete poems of Garcilaso de la Vega; San Juan de la Cruz, with special reference to his poetry; Gil Vicente, *Don Duardos*, *Auto de la Sibila Casandra*; Alfonso de Valdés, *Diálogo de las cosas ocurridas en Roma*; Lope de Vega, *Los comendadores de Córdoba*, *El remedio en la desdicha*, *El castigo del discreto*; Anon., *La vida de Lazarillo de Tormes*.

(*b*) General topics: the Spanish Inquisition; the Spanish monarchy; El Greco; the life of St Teresa.

**Paper 36. Cervantes and the Golden Age novel from 1500 to 1616*, with special reference to the following:

Amadís de Gaula (selections); *Lazarillo de Tormes*; Jorge de Montemayor, *La Diana*; Mateo Alemán, *Guzmán de Alfarache* (selections); Miguel de Cervantes, *Don Quijote*, *El celoso extremeño*, *La fuerza de la sangre*, *El coloquio de los perros*.

**Paper 37. Benito Pérez Galdós and the nineteenth-century novel*, with special reference to the following:

Benito Pérez Galdós, *Bailén*, *Prim*, *Ángel Guerra*, *La de Bringas*, *Misericordia*; Fernán Caballero, *La Gaviota*; P.A. de Alarcón, *El escándalo*; José María de Pereda, *Sotileza*; Juan Valera, *El comendador Mendoza*; Leopoldo Alas, *La Regenta*; E. Pardo Bazán, *La cuestión palpitante*.

Paper 38. Spanish literature, thought, and history in the twentieth century

(*a*) A general knowledge of the period, with principal reference to the following: the 1898 generation; *modernismo*; *poesía popular*; the Second Republic and the Civil War; Franco's Spain; the Spanish novel 1939–1960 and its setting in post Civil War Spain.

(*b*) Texts for close study: Unamuno, *Niebla*; Antonio Machado, *Soledades, galerías y otros poemas*, *Campos de Castilla*; Gabriel Miró, *either La novela de mi amigo or Las cerezas del cementerio*; Ortega y Gasset, *La deshumanización del arte*; Juan Ramón Jiménez, *Segunda antolojía poética*; García Lorca, *Bodas de sangre*, *Yerma*, *La casa de Bernarda Alba*.

**Paper 39. Argentina and Mexico since 1830*

A general study of their history and culture, with special reference to the following: Argentina: Federalism and the Capital Question, economic development, literature; Mexico: the *Reforma*, the Empire of Maximilian, Porfirio Díaz, the novel and poetry.

Prescribed texts for detailed study: José Hernández, *Martín Fierro*; D.F. Sarmiento, *Facundo, o civilización y barbarie*; Leopoldo Lugones; Julio Cortázar, *Los premios*, *Rayuela*; Mariano Azuela, *Los de abajo*; Juan Rulfo, *Pedro Páramo*; Mexican poetry in the twentieth century; Carlos Fuentes, *Cambio de piel*.

Dutch

**Paper 40. The early history and literature of the Netherlands*, with special reference to the following:

Maerlant, *Van den Lande van Oversee* and *Der Kerken Claghe* (Spectrum van de Nederlandse Letterkunde 3); *Lanceloet en het hert met de witte voet* and Segher Diengotgaf, *Tprieel van Troyen* (Spectrum... 1); Keuze uit het *Geuzenliedboek* (Spectrum... 7); *Een suverlijc boecxken* (Spectrum... 4).

**Paper 41. Vondel*, with special reference to the following:

Vondel, *Gijsbreght van Aemstel* and *Joseph in Dothan* (Spectrum van de Nederlandse Letterkunde 13); *Lucifer*; *Adam in Ballingschap*; *Kleine gedichten* (Spectrum... 9); *Verovering van Grol* and *De getemde Mars* (Spectrum... 7).

**Paper 42. The literature, thought, and history of the Netherlands, from 1830 to 1918*, with special reference to the following:

Gevoelige harten. In de ban der Romantiek (Spectrum van de Nederlandse Letterkunde 19), Multatuli, *Max Havelaar*; J.F. Willems, *Aen de Belgen*; H. Conscience, *Siska van Roosemael*; A. Vermeylen, *Kritiek der Vlaamsche Beweging* (Spectrum... 24); J. Geel, *Gesprek op den Drachenfels*, Potgieter, *Jan, Jannetje en hun jongste kind*, Busken Huet, *Over den ernst* (Spectrum... 20).

Paper 43. The literature, thought, and history of the Netherlands, from 1880 to 1939, with special reference to the following:

Een nieuw geluid. De Tachtigers in proza en poëzie (Spectrum van de Nederlandse Letterkunde 23); *Zit stil en reis. Verhalen en gedichten uit het eerste kwart van de 20e eeuw* (Spectrum... 25); Couperus, *Eline Vere*; J. Cremer, *Fabriekskinderen*, A. Bergmann, *Het Werkmansboekje*, A. Prins, *De geschiedenis van Jan Zomer*, Gorter, *Socialistische verzen*, Heijermans, *Uitkomst* (Spectrum... 22).

* See Regulations 17 and 19 (*Ordinances*, pp 339–40).

Portuguese

*Paper 44. *Portuguese literature, thought, and history, from 1495 to 1580*, with special reference to the following:
Gil Vicente, *Sátiras sociais* (ed. Saraiva); Sá de Miranda, *Cartas, Basto*; Bernardim Ribeiro, *Menina e moça*; António Ferreira, *Castro*; Camões, *Os Lusíadas*.

Paper 45. *Portuguese literature, thought, and history, since 1825*, with special reference to the following:
Almeida Garrett, *Viagens na minha terra, Frei Luís de Sousa*; Camilo Castelo Branco, *A Brasileira de Prazins*; Antero de Quental, *Sonetos*; Cesário Verde, *Poesias*; Eça de Queiroz, *O Primo Basílio*.

Modern Greek

*Paper 46. *Greek literature, thought, and history, from 1453 to 1700*, with special reference to the following:
Ανακάλημα της Κωνσταντινόπολης (ed. Kriaras); Glykos, *Πένθος Θανάτου* (ed. Zoras); Bergadis, *Απόκοπος*; *Η Βοσκοπούλα* (ed. S. Alexiou 1971); S. Alexiou, *Κρητική Ανθολογία* (2nd ed. 1969); *Ερωφίλη* (ed. Xanthoudidis 1928).

Paper 47. *Greek literature, thought, and history, since 1800*, with special reference to the following:
L. Politis, *Ποιητική Ανθολογία*, vol. IV; A. Papadiamantis, *Θαλασσινά Ειδύλλια*; A. Karkavitsas, *Ο Ζητιάνος* (ed. Mastrodimitris 1980); *Εκλογή από το Ποιητικό 'Εργο του Κωστή Παλαμά*; P. Prevelakis, *Το Χρονικό μιας Πολιτείας*; N. Kazantzakis, *Βίος και Πολιτεία του Αλέξη Ζορμπά*; O. Elytis, *'Ασμα ηρωικό και πένθιμο για το χαμένο ανθυπολοχαγό της Αλβανίας*.

Supplementary Subject

*Paper 48. *Medieval Latin literature*
This subject will include Medieval Latin literature up to A.D. 1000.
Prescribed texts: *The Oxford Book of Medieval Latin Verse* (ed. Raby), nos. 9–129; Boethius, *Consolatio Philosophiae* (ed. Rand or Büchner), Book I; Notker, *Gesta Karoli Magni* (ed. Haefele), Book II.

SCHEDULE I

Papers for Section B of Part I in 1986

French

Paper 3. *French literature, thought, and history, in the seventeenth century*, with special reference to the period 1630–1700, and to the following:
Corneille; Descartes, *Discours de la méthode*; Mme de Lafayette, *La Princesse de Clèves*; La Fontaine, *Fables*; La Rochefoucauld, *Maximes*; Molière; Pascal, *Pensées* (ed. L. Lafuma, Editions du Seuil, Collection 'Points'); Racine; Church and society in France, 1630–1700.

Paper 4. *French literature, thought, and history, in the eighteenth century*, with special reference to the period 1715–1789, and to the following:
Lesage, *Gil Blas*; Montesquieu, *Lettres persanes*; Voltaire, *Zadig, Candide, Le Philosophe ignorant*; Rousseau, *Rêveries du promeneur solitaire*; Diderot, *Le Neveu de Rameau*; Marivaux, *Le Jeu de l'amour et du hasard, La Double Inconstance, Les Fausses Confidences*; Prévost, *Manon Lescaut*; Beaumarchais, *Le Barbier de Séville, Le Mariage de Figaro*; Laclos, *Les Liaisons dangereuses*; The rôle of the *parlements* in eighteenth-century France; Watteau.

Paper 5. *French literature, thought, and history, in the nineteenth century*, with special reference to the period 1830–1870, and to the following:
Stendhal, *Le Rouge et le noir*; Balzac, *Le Cousin Pons*; Flaubert, *Madame Bovary*; Fromentin, *Dominique*; Hugo, *Les Feuilles d'automne*; Nerval, *Les Chimères, Sylvie*; Gautier, *Emaux et camées*; Baudelaire, *Les Fleurs du Mal*; Romantic drama; the Revolutions of 1848; Utopian thought, 1830–51.

German

Paper 6. *Aspects of the history of the German language*, with special reference to the following:
Joseph Wright, *Grammar of the Gothic Language* (Oxford, 1954), pp. 211–226.
Wilhelm Braune, *Althochdeutsches Lesebuch* (Tübingen, 1969), Passage XX, sections 3–6.
M. O'C. Walshe, *A Middle High German Reader* (Oxford, 1974), Section VII.
Alfred Götze, *Frühneuhochdeutsches Lesebuch* (Göttingen, 1958), Sections 5, 8, 11 (235–399), 13, 14 (93–149), 22 (1–8 and 59–110), 25h, 27b, 30, 36 (1–90).

Paper 7. Introduction to German medieval literature

A thorough knowledge of the following works is required: *Minnesang vom Kürenberger bis Wolfram* (ed. Max Wehrli, Altdeutsche Übungstexte, Nr. 4), the poems of Der von Kürenberg, Friderich von Husen, Heinrich von Morungen, Hartman von Ouwe; Gottfried von Strassburg, *Tristan und Isold* (ed. F. Ranke, Altdeutsche Übungstexte, Nr. 3), lines 10803–12568.

A general knowledge of the following works is required: Wolfram von Eschenbach, *Parzival*, Book V (ed. E. Hartl, Altdeutsche Übungstexte, Nr. 12); Walther von der Vogelweide, *Gedichte* (ed. Max Wehrli, Altdeutsche Übungstexte, Nr. 5), sections I, II, III, IV, VIII; Wernher der Gartenære, *Meier Helmbrecht* (any available edition).

Paper 8. German literature, thought, and history, from 1620 to 1700

(*a*) Texts for close study: *Deutsche Barocklyrik* (ed. M. Wehrli); Gryphius, *Papinianus*; Grimmelshausen, *Die Landstörtzerin Courasche*.

(*b*) A general knowledge of the period with principal reference to Opitz, Spee, the Nuremberg School, Fleming, Gryphius, Lohenstein, Hofmannswaldau, Grimmelshausen, Beer, Reuter, Günther.

Paper 9. German literature, thought, and history, from 1770 to 1832, with special reference to the following:

Goethe, *Faust I*; Hölderlin, poems from the Reclam Hölderlin (RUB 6266) up to and including *Wie wenn am Feiertage*; Kleist, *Michael Kohlhaas*; *Die Marquise von O...*; *Das Erdbeben in Chili* (available in Reclam nos. 218, 7670, and 1957).

A general knowledge of the period, with principal reference to Goethe, Schiller, Lessing, Herder, Novalis, Hölderlin, Kleist, and Grillparzer.

Paper 10. German literature, thought, and history, from 1815 to 1890

(*a*) Texts for close study: Büchner, *Dantons Tod*; Stifter, *Bunte Steine*; H. Heine, *Gedichte* (Reclam 8988).

(*b*) A knowledge of the literature, history, and thought of the period, with principal reference to Grillparzer, Hebbel, Heine, Büchner, Mörike, Keller, Stifter, Nietzsche, Droste, and Meyer.

**Paper 11. German literature, thought, and history, from 1880 to 1914*

(*a*) Texts for close study: Fontane, *Effi Briest* (Reclam 6961); Hauptmann, *Die Ratten* (Ullstein 4977); Rilke, *Neue Gedichte I*.

(*b*) A knowledge of the literature, history, and thought of the period, with principal reference to Fontane, Hauptmann, Thomas Mann, Hofmannsthal, Rilke, Schnitzler, Wedekind, Stefan George, Nietzsche, Trakl.

ITALIAN

**Paper 12. Introduction to the structure and varieties of the Italian language*

A general study of the present-day structure and varieties of Italian, together with a study of the general linguistic background.

†*Paper 13. Introduction to Dante and his age*, with special reference to the following:

Dante, *Vita nuova*, *Inferno*, *Purgatorio*, *Convivio* (Book I).

Prescribed topic: Dante's concept of Language.

†*Paper 14.* (*a*) *Introduction to Dante and his age, and* (*b*) *the literature of the Risorgimento*

(*a*) Dante, *Vita nuova*, *Inferno*.

Prescribed topic: The History of Florence, 1250–1313.

(*b*) Manzoni, *I promessi sposi*; Leopardi, *I canti*.

Prescribed topic: The Risorgimento in Italy up to and including the year 1861.

Paper 15. Introduction to the Italian Renaissance, with special reference to the following subjects:

(*a*) Boccaccio, *Decameron*, III, IV, V, X;

(*b*) Petrarch, *Selected poems*, eds. Griffith and Hainsworth (M.U.P.);

(*c*) Ariosto, *Orlando furioso*, selection, ed. Calvino (Einaudi);

(*d*) Giotto, The Arena Chapel; Ghiberti, The Florentine Baptistery Doors; Piero della Francesca, The Legend of the True Cross.

Students will be expected to show knowledge of at least three of the four subjects.

Paper 16. Italian literature, thought, and history, since 1880

(*a*) Texts for close study: Verga, *I Malavoglia*; D'Annunzio, *Alcyone*; Pirandello, *Enrico IV*; Svevo, *La coscienza di Zeno*; Moravia, *Gli Indifferenti*; Gozzano, *I colloqui*; Ungaretti, *L'Allegria*; Montale, *Ossi di seppia*; Bassani, *Il giardino dei Finzi Contini*; Pavese, *La luna e i falò*; Sciascia, *Il contesto*.

(*b*) A general knowledge of the period with special reference to Italian political history from 1918 to the present day.

* See Regulations 17 and 19 (*Ordinances*, pp. 339–40).

† No candidate may offer both Papers 13 and 14.

Slavonic

*Paper 17. *Introduction to the history and civilization of the Slavonic peoples from the sixth to the thirteenth centuries*, with special reference to the following:

Texts: Photius, *Homilies* III–IV (tr. and ed. C. Mango); Helmold, *Chronicle of the Slavs*, chs. 1, 11, 16, 52, 83–4 (tr. and ed. F. J. Tschan); Constantine Porphyrogenitus, *De administrando imperio*, chs. 2, 4, 5, 8, 9, 29–36 (tr. and ed. G. Moravcsik and R. Jenkins).

Topics: (*a*) The formation of the Slav states; (*b*) the conversion of the Slavs.

*Paper 18. *Introduction to the study of Kievan and Muscovite Russia*, with special reference to the following:

Texts: Сказание... Бориса и Глеба; Моление Даниила Заточника; Повесть о разорении Рязани Батыем; Хожение Аф. Никитина, ed. V. P. Adrianova-Peretts, 1958, pp. 11–16, 18–22, 27–30; Служба кабаку (in Русская демократическая сатира XVII в., 2 ed., 1977).

Topics: Christian culture in the Kievan period; The emergence of Muscovy (Ivan III–Ivan IV); The reign of Alexis Mikhailovich.

Paper 19. *Russian literature and thought, from 1799 to 1900*, with special reference to the following:

Texts: Pushkin, Кавказский пленник, Цыганы; Gogol, Ревизор; Lermontov, Герой нашего времени; Tolstoy, Казаки; Turgenev, Вешние воды.

Topics: Poetry 1800–1820; Chaadaev; Belinsky as literary critic; the work of Dostoevsky to 1849; the work of Tolstoy after 1878, with special reference to: Исповедь; Смерть Ивана Ильича; Хозяин и работник; Что такое искусство?

*Paper 20. *Russian literature, thought, and history, from 1891 to 1934*, with special reference to the following:

Texts: Chekhov, Невеста, Дом с мезонином, Палата No. 6, В овраге, Дама с собачкой; Blok, *Poems* (ed. A. Pyman); Anna Akhmatova, Четки; Bunin, Жизнь Арсеньева; Fadeev, Разгром; Olesha, Зависть.

Topics: Pobedonostsev; Early Russian Marxism (1894–1905); The revolution of 1905 and the First and Second Dumas; The revolutions of 1917; The rise of Stalin (1917–1928); The collectivization of agriculture (1928–1933).

Paper 21. *Czech and Slovak literature, thought, and history, from 1774 to 1939*, with special reference to the following:

Texts: Havlíček, *Křest sv. Vladimíra*; Mácha, *Máj*; Neruda, *Malostrauské povídky*; Vrchlický, *Okna v bouři*; Karásek, *Sodoma*; Machar, *Golgatha*; Pujmanová, *Lidé na křižovatce*; Krasko, *Básnické dielo*; Jilemnický, *Zuniaci krok*.

Topics: Czech *or* Slovak Romanticism; The political thought of Palacký; The Czechoslovak Legion in Russia; Czech and Slovak Proletarian poetry; The Czech Ruralist movement; The Slovak social novel (1918–1939).

*Paper 22. *Czech drama from 1813 to 1939*, with special reference to the following:

Tyl, *Jan Hus*; Bozděch, *Baron Gőrtz*; Mrštíkové, *Maryša*; Hilbert, *Falkenštejn*; Dyk, *Posel*; Langer, *Jízdní hlídka*; Werner, *Lidé na kře*.

Paper 23. *Polish literature, thought, and history, from 1795 to 1914*, with special reference to the following:

Mickiewicz, *Sonety*; Słowacki, *Kordian*; Fredro, *Zemsta*; Sienkiewicz, *Nowele wybrane*; Zeromski, *Ludzie bezdomni*; Wyspiański, *Wesele*.

Paper 24. *Polish literature and thought, from 1918 to 1956*, with special reference to the following:

Żeromski, *Przedwiośnie*; Pollak-Matuszewski, *Poezja polska 1914–1939*; Nałkowska, *Granica*; Gombrowicz, *Ferdydurke*; Miłosz, *Wiersze* (London, 1967); Andrzejewski, *Popiół i diament*.

*Paper 25. *Serbian literature, history, and institutions, from 1168 to 1389*, with special reference to the following:

Texts: Stojan Novaković, Примери књижевности и језика старога српско-словенскога (Beograd, 1909): pp. 209–17, 219–24, 229–38, 240–5, 247–68; N. Radojčić, Законик цара Душана (S.A.N. Beograd, 1960).

Topics: The work of St Sava; The history of Serbia from 1168 to 1355; The development of the Serbian biography; The causes leading to the Serbian defeat at Kosovo in 1389.

Paper 26. *Serbian and Croatian literature, thought, and history, since 1800*, with special reference to the following:

(*a*) Ivan Mažuranić, *Smrt Smail-age Čengijića*; Branko Radičević, *Pesme*; L. K. Lazarević *Pripovetke*; Miroslav Krleža, *Povratak Filipa Latinovicza*; Ivo Andrić, *Na Drini Ćuprija*; Dobrica Ćosić, *Daleko je sunce*.

(*b*) Topics: The work of Vuk Karadžić; The history of the first and second Serbian risings 1804–1830; The Illyrian Movement; *Seoska pripovetka*; The *Moderna* and Croatian literature 1897–1914.

* See Regulations 17 and 19 (*Ordinances*, pp. 339–40).

Scandinavian

*Paper 27. *Danish literature, thought, and history, from 1800 to 1870*, with special reference to the following:

Adam Oehlenschläger, *Digte 1803*: Steen Steensen Blicher, *Noveller* (ed. T. Skou-Hansen); Johan Ludvig Heiberg, *Nye Digte*; H. C. Andersen, *Eventyr og Historier* (ed. V. Sørensen); Emil Aarestrup, *Digte*; Frederik Paludan-Müller, *Adam Homo*; Hans Egede Schack, *Phantasterne*.

Paper 28. *Danish literature, thought, and history, from 1870 to the present day*, with special reference to the following:

J. P. Jacobsen, *Mogens og andre Noveller*; Herman Bang, *Stuk*; Sophus Claussen, *Lyrik* (ed. F. J. Billeskov Jansen); Johannes V. Jensen, *Kongens Fald*; Martin Andersen Nexø, *Pelle Erobreren: Barndom*; Hans Kirk, *Fiskerne*; Karen Blixen, *Syndfloden over Norderney*, *Drømmerne*.

*Paper 29. *Norwegian literature, thought, and history, from 1800 to 1865*, with special reference to the following:

Henrik Wergeland, *Den engelske Lods*; J. S. Welhaven, *Norges Dæmring*; Nasjonalromantikken; Bjørnstjerne Bjørnson, *Synnøve Solbakken*, *Arne*, *En glad Gut*; Henrik Ibsen, *Kongs-Emnerne*; Camilla Collett, *Amtmandens Døttre*; O. Vinje, *Ferdaminni*.

Paper 30. *Norwegian literature, thought, and history, from 1865 to the present day*, with special reference to the following:

Henrik Ibsen, *Peer Gynt*; Bjørnstjerne Bjørnson, *En Fallit*, *Redaktøren*, *Kongen*; Alexander Kielland, *Garman & Worse*; Jonas Lie, *Familjen paa Gilje*; Sigrid Undset, *Jenny*; Knut Hamsun, *Markens Grøde*; Johan Falkberget, *Den fjerde nattevakt*; Sigurd Hoel, *Møte ved milepelen*.

*Paper 31. *Swedish literature, thought, and history, from 1800 to 1870*, with special reference to the following:

Esaias Tegnér, *Frithiofs saga*; E. J. Stagnelius, *Liljor i Saron*; C. J. L. Almqvist, *Urval* (ed. Julén); J. L. Runeberg, *Fänrik Ståls sägner* and *Kung Fjalar*; Fredrika Bremer, *Grannarne*; Viktor Rydberg, *Singoalla*.

Paper 32. *Swedish literature, thought, and history, from 1870 to the present day*, with special reference to the following:

August Strindberg, *Röda rummet*, *Fröken Julie*, *Ett drömspel*; Selma Lagerlöf, *Jerusalem*; Gustaf Fröding, *Dikter* (Stockholm, 1945); Hjalmar Söderberg, *Martin Bircks ungdom*; Hjalmar Bergman, *En döds memoarer*; Birger Sjöberg, *Kriser och kransar*; Ivar Lo-Johansson, *Godnatt, jord*; Lars Ahlin, *Min död är min*.

Spanish

*Paper 33. *An introduction to the history of the Peninsular languages*

A general study of the present-day structures and basic external histories of Castilian and *either* Portuguese *or* Catalan. The following texts are set for special linguistic study:

Castilian: María de Maeztu, *Antología Siglo XX: Prosistas españoles*, Part two (col. Austral); Federico García Lorca, *La zapatera prodigiosa*; *Oxford Book of Spanish Verse*, 2nd ed. nos. 179–85, 189–93, 200–6, 219–27.

Portuguese: G. de Castilho (ed.), *Os melhores contos portugueses* (2. *serie*), pp. 1–97; *Contos do Brasil* (Harrap), pp. 1–57; *Oxford Book of Portuguese Verse*, 2nd ed. nos. 180–7, 200–5, 227–31, 250–4.

Catalan: J. Gili, *Introductory Catalan Grammar*, 2nd ed., pp. 122–52.

*Paper 34. *Medieval Spain*

A general study of the literature in connexion with the historical and cultural background during the Middle Ages, with special reference to narrative poetry.

Paper 35. *Spanish literature, thought, and history in the sixteenth century*, with special reference to the following:

(*a*) Texts for close study: Fernando de Rojas, *La Celestina*; the complete poems of Garcilaso de la Vega; San Juan de la Cruz, with special reference to his poetry; Gil Vicente, *Don Duardos*, *Auto de la Sibila Casandra*; Alfonso de Valdés, *Diálogo de las cosas ocurridas en Roma*; Lope de Vega, *Los comendadores de Córdoba*, *El remedio en la desdicha*, *El castigo del discreto*; Anon., *La vida de Lazarillo de Tormes*.

(*b*) General topics: the Spanish Inquisition; the Spanish monarchy; El Greco; the life of St Teresa.

*Paper 36. *Cervantes and the Golden Age novel from 1500 to 1616*, with special reference to the following:

Amadís de Gaula (selections); *Lazarillo de Tormes*; Jorge de Montemayor, *La Diana*; Mateo Alemán, *Guzmán de Alfarache* (selections); Miguel de Cervantes, *Don Quijote*, *El celoso extremeño*, *La fuerza de la sangre*, *El coloquio de los perros*.

* See Regulations 17 and 19 (*Ordinances*, pp. 339–40).

*Paper 37. *Benito Pérez Galdós and the nineteenth-century novel*, with special reference to the following:

Benito Pérez Galdós, *Bailén*, *Prim*, *Ángel Guerra*, *La de Bringas*, *Misericordia*; Fernán Caballero, *La Gaviota*; P.A. de Alarcón, *El escándalo*; José María de Pereda, *Sotileza*; Juan Valera, *El comendador Mendoza*; Leopoldo Alas, *La Regenta*; E. Pardo Bazán, *La cuestión palpitante*.

Paper 38. *Spanish literature, thought, and history in the twentieth century*

(*a*) A general knowledge of the period, with principal reference to the following: the 1898 generation; *modernismo*; *poesía popular*; the Second Republic and the Civil War; Franco's Spain; the Spanish novel 1939–1960 and its setting in post Civil War Spain.

(*b*) Texts for close study: Unamuno, *Tres novelas ejemplares y un prólogo*; Antonio Machado, *Soledades, galerías y otros poemas*, *Campos de Castilla*; Baroja, **either** *Aurora roja* **or** *El Mayorazgo de Labraz*; Ortega y Gasset, *Ideas sobre la novela*; Juan Ramón Jiménez, *Segunda antolojía poética*; García Lorca, *El amor de don Perlimplín con Belisa en su jardín*; Valle-Inclán, *Los cuernos de don Friolera*.

*Paper 39. *Argentina and Mexico since 1830*

A general study of their history and culture, with special reference to the following: Argentina: Federalism and the Capital Question, economic development, literature; Mexico: the *Reforma*, the Empire of Maximilian, Porfirio Díaz, the novel and poetry.

Prescribed texts for detailed study: José Hernández, *Martín Fierro*; D.F. Sarmiento, *Facundo, o civilización y barbarie*; Leopoldo Lugones; Julio Cortázar, *Los premios*, *Rayuela*; Mariano Azuela, *Los de abajo*; Juan Rulfo, *Pedro Páramo*; Mexican poetry in the twentieth century; Carlos Fuentes, *Cambio de piel*.

Dutch

*Paper 40. *The early history and literature of the Netherlands*, with special reference to the following:

Maerlant, *Van den Lande van Oversee* and *Der Kerken Claghe* (Spectrum van de Nederlandse Letterkunde 3); *Lanceloet en het hert met de witte voet* and Segher Diengotgaf, *Tprieel van Troyen* (Spectrum... 1); Keuze uit het *Geuzenliedboek* (Spectrum... 7); *Een suverlijc boecxken* (Spectrum... 4).

*Paper 41. *Vondel*, with special reference to the following:

Vondel, *Gijsbreght van Aemstel* and *Joseph in Dothan* (Spectrum van de Nederlandse Letterkunde 13); *Lucifer*; *Adam in Ballingschap*; *Kleine gedichten* (Spectrum... 9); *Verovering van Grol* and *De getemde Mars* (Spectrum... 7).

*Paper 42. *The literature, thought, and history of the Netherlands, from 1830 to 1918*, with special reference to the following:

Gevoelige harten. In de ban der Romantiek (Spectrum van de Nederlandse Letterkunde 19), Multatuli, *Max Havelaar*; J.F. Willems, *Aen de Belgen*; H. Conscience, *Siska van Roosemael*; A. Vermeylen, *Kritiek der Vlaamsche Beweging* (Spectrum... 24); J. Geel, *Gesprek op den Drachenfels*, Potgieter, *Jan, Jannetje en hun jongste kind*, Busken Huet, *Over den ernst* (Spectrum... 20).

Paper 43. *The literature, thought, and history of the Netherlands, from 1880 to 1939*, with special reference to the following:

Een nieuw geluid. De Tachtigers in proza en poëzie (Spectrum van de Nederlandse Letterkunde 23); *Zit stil en reis* (Spectrum... 25); Couperus, *Eline Vere*; L. van Deyssel, *Een liefde*; M. Emants, *Een Nagelaten Bekentenis*; Nescio, *Titaantjes*, *De Uitvreter*; A. van Schendel, *De Waterman*; Heyermans, *Uitkomst*; F. Bordewijk, *Karakter*; G. Walschap, *Houtekiet*.

Portuguese

*Paper 44. *Portuguese literature, thought, and history, from 1495 to 1580*, with special reference to the following:

Gil Vicente, *Sátiras sociais* (ed. Saraiva); Sá de Miranda, *Cartas*, *Basto*; Bernardim Ribeiro, *Menina e moça*; António Ferreira, *Castro*; Camões, *Os Lusíadas*.

Paper 45. *Portuguese literature, thought, and history, since 1825*, with special reference to the following:

Almeida Garrett, *Viagens na minha terra*, *Frei Luís de Sousa*; Camilo Castelo Branco, *A Brasileira de Prazins*; Antero de Quental, *Sonetos*; Cesário Verde, *Poesias*; Eça de Queiroz, *O Primo Basílio*.

Modern Greek

*Paper 46. *Greek literature, thought, and history, from 1453 to 1700*, with special reference to the following:

Ανακάλημα της Κωνσταντινόπολης (ed. Kriaras); Glykos, *Πένθος Θανάτου* (ed. Zoras); Bergadis, *Απόκοπος*; *Η Βοσκοπούλα* (ed. S. Alexiou 1971); S. Alexiou, *Κρητική Ανθολογία* (2nd ed. 1969); *Ερωφίλη* (ed. Xanthoudidis 1928).

* See Regulations 17 and 19 (*Ordinances*, pp. 339–40).

Paper 47. Greek literature, thought, and history, since 1800, with special reference to the following:

L. Politis, *Ποιητική Ανθολογία*, vol. IV; A. Papadiamantis, *Θαλασσινά Ειδύλλια*; A. Karkavitsas, *Ο Ζητιάνος* (ed. Mastrodimitris 1980); *Εκλογή από το Ποιητικό Έργο του Κωστή Παλαμά*; P. Prevelakis, *Το Χρονικό μιας Πολιτείας*; N. Kazantzakis, *Βίος και Πολιτεία του Αλέξη Ζορμπά*; O. Elytis, *Άσμα ηρωικό και πένθιμο για το χαμένο ανθυπολοχαγό της Αλβανίας*.

SUPPLEMENTARY SUBJECT

**Paper 48. Medieval Latin literature*

This subject will include Medieval Latin literature up to A.D. 1000, with special reference to the following:

Augustine, *Confessiones*, Book VII (Loeb or Budé); Einhard, *Vita Karoli Magni*; *The Oxford Book of Medieval Latin Verse* (ed. Raby), nos. 9–129; *Waltharius* (ed. K. Strecker or K. Langosch); Hrotsvitha (ed. H. Homeyer or P. von Winterfeld), *Gallicanus* and *Calimachus*.

The Faculty Board may allow candidates to be examined in subjects or papers other than those specified in the lists above if, in the Board's opinion, the languages of the subjects offered possess literature adequate for examination purposes and if the Board are satisfied that the requisite teaching is available. Applications must be made not later than the division of the Michaelmas Term before the examination. Permission may be refused to a candidate who wishes to offer two closely allied languages. The following language and papers have been approved for the Part I examinations in **1985** and **1986**:

Hungarian

1. Hungarian literature, thought, and history, from 1906 to 1956.
2. Hungarian literature, thought, and history, from 1849 to 1906.

The following texts have been prescribed for these papers in **1985** and **1986**:

Paper 1. Hungarian literature, thought, and history, from 1906 to 1956, with special reference to the following:

Ady, *Uj versek*; Krúdy, *A vörös postakocsi*; József Attila, *Összes versei*; Móricz, *Rokonok*; Németh László, *Iszony*; Illyés, *Kézfogások*.

*Paper 2. *Hungarian literature, thought, and history, from 1849 to 1906*, with special reference to the following:

Jókai Mór, *Az aranyember*; Arany János, *Toldi*; Madách Imre, *Az ember tragédiája*; Mikszáth Kálmán, *Az uj Zrinyiász*; Reviczky Gyula, *Összes versei*.

For general reading the relevant parts of the following works are recommended: Szerb Antal, *Magyar irodalomtörténet*; Denis Sinor, *History of Hungary*.

* See Regulations 17 and 19 (*Ordinances*, pp 379–80).

Part II

A candidate for Part II must offer:

(*a*) *either* (i) four papers, if he takes the examination in the year next after that in which he has obtained honours in another Honours Examination;

or (ii) five papers, if he takes the examination in the year next but one after that in which he obtained honours in another Honours Examination;

(*b*) an essay in a medieval or modern foreign language linked with at least one of his options;

and (*c*) a paper containing one passage of English for translation into a foreign language to which the papers of his choice appertain and one passage of that language for translation into English.

Certain papers are common to Schedules I and II; no candidate may offer from Schedule II any paper which he has previously offered in Part I.

A year spent studying abroad, with the permission of the Faculty Board (see *Study abroad*, p. 275), will be disregarded for the purpose of calculating a candidate's standing for option (i) or (ii) under (*a*) above.

*Dissertations**

With certain exceptions, which may vary from time to time, a candidate may choose to offer a dissertation on a subject approved by the Faculty Board which lies within the field of one or more of the papers listed in Schedule II (see p. 292).† A candidate may offer a dissertation

(*a*) *in substitution* for a particular paper from Schedule II which *either* he would otherwise include among the papers that he is required to offer *or* he would not be able to offer in Part II because it is identical with a paper in Part I which he has already offered. The following restrictions apply however:

* The regulations governing the submission of dissertations will be altered with effect from the examinations to be held in 1986 (see *Reporter*, 1984, p. 000).

† In **1985** candidates may not offer dissertations on the following papers,

Dutch: 73, 74.
Italian: 18.
Modern Greek: 100, 101.
Scandinavian: 64.
Slavonic: 83, 85, 86, 89, 92, 96, 122.
Spanish: 25.
Vulgar Latin and Romance Philology: 120.

Any papers from other Triposes available to Modern and Medieval Languages candidates.

(i) the candidate must already have attained at least the second class standard in the corresponding paper in the Preliminary Examination for Part II. Alternatively, in the case of a candidate who has taken more than one year to complete his Part I, the candidate must have been placed at least in the second class in Part I, and have offered there a paper from Schedule I corresponding to the paper from Schedule II for which he now wishes to substitute a dissertation.

(ii) for the purpose of proviso (i) the Board may specify certain papers from Schedule I as not corresponding to papers from Schedule II;*

(iii) if the subject lies within the field of more than one paper, the Board will decide which paper the candidate shall not be permitted to offer;

(*b*) *in addition* to the papers which he is required to take for Part II.

A candidate may offer a dissertation under either (*a*) or (*b*) above, or he may offer two dissertations, one under (*a*) and one under (*b*). If a candidate proposes to offer two dissertations the Faculty Board will not approve subjects which substantially overlap.

The procedure for dissertations for Part II is as follows: a candidate must submit his proposed subject through his Tutor to the Secretary of the Faculty Board by the end of the second week of the Full Michaelmas Term preceding the examination, stating whether the dissertation is additional to his papers, or an alternative to one of them, which he must specify. If he wishes subsequently to vary his proposal, further dates apply; details of these may be obtained from the Faculty Office. A dissertation offered under (*a*) above must be in English, but quotations from primary sources must be in the language of the original. A dissertation offered under (*b*) may be written in a modern foreign language instead of English if the Faculty Board in or after approving the subject so agree. The dissertation must be typewritten, except where a non-Roman or symbolic typeface is necessary and cannot be provided. In these cases, hand-

* The following papers have been so specified:

French: 3, 5.
German: 6, 7, 8, 9, 10, 11.
Italian: 14.
Slavonic: 18, 20, 21, 22, 23, 24, 25, 26.

written or photocopied extracts may be inserted. The dissertation must normally be not less than 8,000 words and in any case not more than 10,000 words in length (inclusive of notes and appendices but exclusive of bibliography). A dissertation within the field of comparative literature, whether offered under (*a*) or (*b*), must concern the literature of at least two languages. Two copies, accompanied by a declaration signed by the candidate that it is his own work, must be submitted through his Tutor so as to reach the Secretary of the Faculty Board by the end of the sixth week of the Full Lent Term preceding the examination. The Examiners may examine a candidate *viva voce* on his dissertation; the *viva voce* examination will be in English, or, if a candidate has offered a dissertation written in a modern foreign language, in the language in which it has been written.

Papers from other Triposes[1]

A candidate may offer not more than two of the following papers from other Triposes in place of an equivalent number of Part II subjects:

[2]Classical Tripos: any paper from Part II other than from the Schedule of Optional Papers, except that no candidate may offer both Paper E1 and Paper 111 of Part II of the Modern and Medieval Languages Tripos; both Paper E4 and Paper 120 of the Modern and Medieval Languages Tripos in any year if the Faculty Boards of Classics and of Modern and Medieval Languages in announcing the texts or subjects prescribed for those papers respectively have indicated that those papers may not in that year be offered in combination by a candidate for the Modern and Medieval Languages Tripos; a subsidiary paper in Group E and another paper from the same group; in any year from a group other than Group E a subsidiary paper and another paper from the same group if the Faculty Board of Classics in announcing the subjects prescribed for those papers have indicated that the particular combination of papers concerned may not in

[1] The Faculty Board have specified all the papers from other Triposes as papers on which candidates may not offer dissertations. Candidates who intend to spend a year abroad should not offer themselves for examination in these papers in the Preliminary Examination for Part II of the Modern and Medieval Languages Tripos without consulting with the Secretaries of the Faculty Boards concerned since these subjects may change between the Preliminary Examination and Part II of the Modern and Medieval Languages Tripos for which they will be candidates two years later.

[2] The regulations relating to papers offered from Part II of the Classical Tripos will change with effect from the examinations to be held in **1986**.

that year be offered by a candidate for the Modern and Medieval Languages Tripos.

English Tripos, Part II: Paper 2, Tragedy; Paper 3, Chaucer; Paper 4, Medieval English literature, 1066–1500; Paper 9, History and theory of literary criticism; Paper 13, History of the English language.

Anglo-Saxon, Norse, and Celtic Tripos, Paper 2, the Vikings; Paper 4, Latin literature of the British Isles, 400–1100; Paper 5, English literature before the Norman Conquest; Paper 6, Old Norse literature; Paper 7A, Medieval Welsh language and literature I; Paper 7B, Medieval Welsh language and literature II; Paper 8A, Medieval Irish language and literature I; Paper 8B, Medieval Irish language and literature II; Paper 11, Special subject II; provided that no candidate can offer both Papers 7A and 7B; or both Papers 8A and 8B; or Paper 2 if he offers Paper 50 from Schedule II.

The list of papers for the Part II examination is as follows:

SCHEDULE II* (PAPERS (OTHER THAN ESSAY AND TRANSLATION PAPERS) FOR PART II)

ROMANCE

French and Provençal

1. French literature, thought, and history, before 1300.
2. Provençal literature, thought, and history, before 1356.
3. French literature, thought, and history, from 1300 to 1510.
4. French literature, thought, and history, from 1510 to 1622.
5. French literature, thought, and history, from 1594 to 1700.
6. French literature, thought, and history, from 1690 to 1789.
7. French literature, thought, and history, from 1789 to 1898.
8. French literature, thought, and history, since 1890.
9. The history of the French language.

[1]10. (See footnote).

MEDIEVAL LATIN

12. Medieval Latin literature, from 400 to 1300.

ITALIAN

13. Italian literature, life, and history, before 1400.
14. Dante.

* An x against a paper means that it is a paper on which candidates may not offer a dissertation.

[1] There will be a new paper 10 in **1986**, 'A special subject in French culture'. The subject specified for **1986** is 'Literature and the Visual Arts in France 1527–1914'.

15. Italian literature, thought, and history, from 1400 to 1600.
16. A special subject in Italian culture.
17. Italian literature, thought, and history, since 1815.
x18. The history of the Italian language.

Spanish

20. Spanish literature, life, and history, before 1492.
21. Spanish literature, thought, and history, from 1492 to 1700.
22. Cervantes.
[1]23. Spanish literature, thought, and history, after 1700.
24. A special period or subject in Spanish literature, life, or history.
[2]25. The history of the Peninsular languages.
26. Topics in Spanish-American history.
[3]26A. Outlines of Latin-American civilization.
27. A special subject in Latin-American history or literature. (This paper has been suspended until further notice.)
28. Latin-American literature.

Portuguese

31. Portuguese literature, life, and history, before 1497.
32. Portuguese literature, thought, and history, from 1497 to 1700.
33. Portuguese literature, thought, and history, since 1700.

Germanic

German

40. German literature, thought, and history, before 1500.
41. German literature, thought, and history, from 1500 to 1700.
42. German literature, thought, and history, from 1700 to 1805.
43. Goethe.
44. German literature, thought, and history, from 1797 to 1890.
45. German literature, thought, and history, since 1890.
46. A special period or subject in German literature, thought, or history.
47. The history of the German language.

[1] This paper in **1985–86** will be titled 'Spanish literature, thought, and history, after 1820'.

[2] Every candidate will be expected to show a knowledge of the history of *either* Spanish *or* Portuguese or both, but he may be allowed to offer the history of Catalan in place of, or in addition, to these.

[3] This paper will be withdrawn in 1986.

Scandinavian

[1]50. Scandinavian literature, life, and history, before 1500.
51. Scandinavian literature, thought, and history, from 1500 to 1700.
52. Danish literature, thought, and history, from 1800 to 1870 (Paper 27 of Part I).
53. Danish literature, thought, and history, from 1870 to the present day (Paper 28 of Part I).
54. A special subject in Danish literature since 1500.
55. Norwegian literature, thought, and history, from 1800 to 1865 (Paper 29 of Part I).
56. Norwegian literature, thought, and history, from 1865 to the present day (Paper 30 of Part I).
57. Henrik Ibsen.
58. A special subject in Norwegian literature since 1800.
59. Scandinavian literature, thought, and history, from 1700 to 1800.
60. Swedish literature, thought, and history, from 1800 to 1870 (Paper 31 of Part I).
61. Swedish literature, thought, and history, from 1870 to the present day (Paper 32 of Part I).
62. August Strindberg.
63. A special subject in Swedish literature since 1500.
x64. A special subject in the literature or history of at least two of the Scandinavian countries.
[2]65. The history of *either* the Danish language *or* the Norwegian language *or* the Swedish language.

Dutch

70. The literature, life, and history of the Netherlands, before 1570.
71. The literature, life, and history of the Netherlands, from 1570 to 1730.
72. The literature, life, and history of the Netherlands, from 1730 to 1880.
x73. The literature, life, and history of the Netherlands, since 1880.
x74. The history of the Dutch language.

Slavonic

80. Russian literature, life, and history, before 1263.
81. Russian literature, life, and history, from 1263 to 1676.
82. Russian literature, life, and history, from 1676 to 1792.
x83. Russian literature and thought, from 1792 to 1883.
84. Russian literature and thought, since 1883.

[1] No candidate who offers in Part II, or has previously offered in another Honours Examination, Paper 2 of the Anglo-Saxon, Norse, and Celtic Tripos may offer this paper.

[2] In each alternative a knowledge of Old Norse will be required.

x85. Russian history, from 1801 to 1964.
x86. The history of the Russian language.
87. Czech literature, thought, and history, before 1620.
88. Czech and Slovak literature, thought, and history, since 1620.
x89. The history of the Czech and Slovak languages.
90. Polish literature, thought, and history, before 1795.
91. Polish literature, thought, and history, since 1795.
x92. The history of the Polish language.
93. Serbian and Croatian literature, thought, and history, before 1700.
94. Serbian and Croatian literature, thought, and history, since 1700.
x95. The history of the Serbo-Croat language.
x96. The history and civilization of the Slavonic Peoples from the sixth to the eleventh centuries.
97. A special period or subject in the literature, thought, or history of the Slavs.

Modern Greek

x100. Greek literature, thought, and history, from 867 to 1204.
x101. Greek literature, thought, and history, from 1204 to 1453.
102. Greek literature, thought, and history, from 1453 to 1669.
103. Greek literature, thought, and history, from 1669 to 1888.
104. Greek literature, thought, and history, since 1888.
105. The history of the modern Greek language.

Linguistics

111. General linguistics.
112. Phonetics.
113. The history of linguistic thought.
114. Historical linguistics.

Comparative Studies

[1]x120. Vulgar Latin and Romance philology, with special reference to Old French, Provençal, Spanish, and Portuguese.
121. The Teutonic languages, with special reference to Gothic, Anglo-Saxon, Early Norse, Old Saxon, and Old High German.
x122. The Slavonic languages, with special reference to Old Church Slavonic.
[2] 123. A special subject in Comparative literature (i).
[2] 124. A special subject in Comparative literature (ii).

[1] The Board may permit a candidate also to offer Catalan, Rumanian, or Rhaeto-Romance in place of one of the specified Romance languages.
[2] No candidate may offer both Papers 123 and 124.

The following texts and periods have been prescribed, and authors and topics specified, for these papers in **1985** and **1986**:

SCHEDULE II

PAPERS (OTHER THAN ESSAY AND TRANSLATION PAPERS) FOR PART II IN **1985**

ROMANCE

French and Provençal

Paper 1. French literature, thought, and history, before 1300.

Paper 2. Provençal literature, thought, and history, before 1356, with special reference to the following:

R. T. Hill and T. G. Bergin, *Anthology of the Provençal Troubadours* (second edition, Yale U.P., 1973), nos. 10–15, 22–25, 27–38, 39–43, 66–70, 73–80, 86–90, 92–94, 99–101, 105–107, 110, 111, 138–146, 180.

Paper 3. French literature, thought, and history, from 1300 to 1510.

Paper 4. French literature, thought, and history, from 1510 to 1622.

Paper 5. French literature, thought, and history, from 1594 to 1700.

Paper 6. French literature, thought, and history, from 1690 to 1789.

Paper 7. French literature, thought, and history, from 1789 to 1898.

Paper 8. French literature, thought, and history, since 1890.

Paper 9. The history of the French language, with special reference to the following:

C. W. Aspland, *A Medieval French Reader* (O.U.P., 1979), extracts nos. 1–4, 6, 7, 9, 12–15, 18, 21, 23, 26, 28–30; P. Rickard, *La Langue française au XVIe. siècle. Étude suivie de textes* (C.U.P., 1968), extracts nos. 3, 4, 9*b*, 15, 16, 18, 23, 24, 27, 28, 31, 32, 34, 36, 39, 40, 42, 43, 46, 48.

Medieval Latin

Paper 12. Medieval Latin literature, from 400 to 1300, with special reference to the following:

Notker Balbulus, *Liber Hymnorum* (ed. W. von den Steinen); *Waltharius* (ed. K. Strecker or K. Langosch); *Ruodlieb* (publ. Reclam), sections I–VII; *Carmina Burana* (publ. dtv), with particular reference to the love-songs and satires 61–77, 120–132, and the drinking-songs 193–215; *Carmina Burana* Christmas Play (227) and Passion Play (16*); Andreas Capellanus, *De amore* (ed. P. G. Walsh), Bk. II.

Italian

Paper 13. Italian literature, life, and history, before 1400, with special reference to thirteenth-century poetry, Petrarca, and Boccaccio, in connexion with the following:

Poeti del Duecento (ed. G. Contini), selections from Giacomo da Lentini, Guido delle Colonne, Stefano da Messina, Guittone d'Arezzo, Jacopone da Todi, Guido Guinizelli (I–X and XX), Guido Cavalcanti and Cino da Pistoia (I–XXIII); *Novellino*; Dino Compagni, *La Cronica* (publ. Le Monnier); Petrarca, *Rime* (ed. G. Contini, publ. Einaudi), *Secretum* (pp. 21–215 of *Prose*, publ. R. Ricciardi); Boccaccio, *Decameron*.

Paper 14. Dante, with special reference to the following:

Divina Commedia, Vita nuova, Rime.

Paper 15. Italian literature, thought, and history, from 1400 to 1600, with special reference to the following areas:

(*a*) Alberti, Poliziano, and fifteenth-century Florentine culture;
(*b*) Machiavelli, Guicciardini, and the historical background;
(*c*) Ariosto, Tasso, and the epic;
(*d*) Michelangelo, Castiglione, and High Renaissance culture.

Students will be expected to show knowledge of at least three of the four areas.

**Paper 16. A special subject in Italian culture*

The figurative arts in Tuscany, 1402–1482, with special reference to the following:

(*a*) Writings on the theory and practice of painting: Alberti, *Della pittura*, ed. Grayson; Leonardo, *Scritti scelti*, ed. A. M. Brizio, U.T.E.T., pp. 174–246; Vasari, *Vite scelte*, ed. A. M. Brizio, U.T.E.T., pp. 67–134 and 191–271;

* Candidates who intend to spend a year abroad should not offer themselves for examination in this paper in the Preliminary Examination for Part II of the Modern and Medieval Languages Tripos without consulting with the Secretary of the Faculty Board of Modern and Medieval Languages, since this variable subject may change between the Preliminary Examination and Part II of the Modern and Medieval Language Tripos for which they will be candidates two years later.

(*b*) the sculpture of Ghiberti, Donatello, and Verrocchio;
(*c*) the paintings of Masaccio, Fra Angelico, Filippo Lippi, Uccello, Domenico Veneziano, Piero della Francesca, Botticelli, and Leonardo (with particular attention to works in the galleries of Cambridge, London, and Florence).

Paper 17. Italian literature, thought, and history, since 1815, with special reference to the following:
Foscolo, *Le ultime lettere di Jacopo Ortis*, *Dei sepolcri*; Manzoni, *I promessi sposi*; Leopardi, *I canti*; Nievo, *Le confessioni di un Italiano*, Chs. I–X; Verga, *Mastro don Gesualdo*; D'Annunzio, *Il piacere*; Pirandello, *Sei personaggi in cerca d'autore*, *Il fu Mattia Pascal*; Gozzano, *I colloqui*; Fogazzaro, *Piccolo mondo antico*; Svevo, *La coscienza di Zeno*; Montale, *Ossi di seppia*, *Le occasioni*; Croce, *Breviario d'estetica*; Calvino, *Ti con zero*.

Paper 18. The history of the Italian language, with special reference to the following:
Dionisotti and Grayson, *Early Italian Texts* (2nd. ed.), passages 1–6, 9, 11–13, 15–16, 18, 19(c), (e), (f), 20(b), (c), (d), 21(a), 23, 25; Dante, *De vulgari eloquentia*; Fòffano, *Prose filologiche: La Questione della Lingua*; Bembo, *Le prose della volgar lingua*.

Spanish

Paper 20. Spanish literature, life, and history, before 1492, with special reference to the following:
(*a*) *Poema de mio Cid* (ed. C.C.Smith, Oxford); the traditional lyric of the Peninsula; Berceo, *Milagros de Nuestra Señora* (ed. Clásicos Castellanos); Alfonso X, in Solalinde's *Antología de Alfonso el Sabio* (ed. Austral or Granada); Juan Ruiz, *Libro de buen amor* (ed. Clásicos Castellanos, 2 vols.); A. Martínez de Toledo, *El Corbacho* (ed. Castalia).
(*b*) The Reconquest; the culture of Moslem Spain; the Jews in fifteenth-century Spain; the Catholic Monarchs.

Paper 21. Spanish literature, thought, and history, from 1492 to 1700, with special reference to the following:
Fray Luis de León and the Counter-Reformation in Spain; the plays of Lope de Vega; the picaresque novel; Luis de Góngora; Francisco de Quevedo; Baltasar Gracián, *El Criticón*.

Paper 22. Cervantes

Paper 23. Spanish literature, thought, and history, after 1700, with special reference to the following:
Benito Pérez Galdós; Miguel de Unamuno; the Spanish novel after 1960; *poesía pura*; surrealism.

**Paper 24. A special period or subject in Spanish literature, life, or history*
Literature in Catalan, with special reference to the following:
Ramon Llull; the chronicles; humanism; Ausiàs March; 'la decadència'; 'la renaixença'; J. Verdaguer; N. Oller; A. Guimerà; 'modernisme'; 'noucentisme'.

Paper 25. The history of the Peninsular languages, with special reference to the following:
(*a*) D.J.Gifford and F.W.Hodcroft, *Textos lingüísticos del medioevo español* (Oxford, 1966), passages 3, 6, 8–37, 38, 43, 45, 49–52, 53–4, 57, 59, 60–1, 72, 74, 81, 92, 95–6, 102, 105–6, 112, 114, 120; *Poema de Mio Cid* (ed. C.C.Smith, Madrid, 1976), *Cantar I*; Juan de Valdés, *Diálogo de la lengua* (Clásicos castellanos).
(*b*) *Oxford Book of Portuguese Verse* (pp. 1–137); Rodrigues Lapa (ed.), *Crestomatia arcaica*; *Historiadores quinhentistas* (*Textos literários*); Camões, *Os Lusiadas*, canto I.

Paper 26. Topics in Spanish-American history
Section A: Discovery and settlement of the New World, 1490–1520; the *conquistadores*; the Indian question, 1492–1544; Spanish colonial government and administration, 1550–1800.
Section B: The emancipation of Spanish America, 1780–1821.
Section C: Mexico, Argentina, and the Andean Republics, 1820–1960.

Paper 26 A. Outlines of Latin-American civilization

Paper 27. A special subject in Latin-American history or literature. This paper is suspended until further notice.

* Candidates who intend to spend a year abroad should not offer themselves for examination in this paper in the Preliminary Examination for Part II of the Modern and Medieval Languages Tripos without consulting with the Secretary of the Faculty Board of Modern and Medieval Languages, since this variable subject may change between the Preliminary Examination and Part II of the Modern and Medieval Languages Tripos for which they will be candidates two years later.

Paper 28. *Latin-American literature*, with special reference to the following:

(*a*) Hernéndez, *Martín Fierro*; Rubén Darío and *modernista* poets; López Velarde; Villaurrutia; Vallejo; Neruda; Octavio Paz.

(*b*) Sarmiento, *Facundo*; Rodó, *Ariel*; Azuela, *Los de abajo*; Güiraldes, *Don Segundo Sombra*; Gallegos, *Doña Bárbara*; Octavio Paz, *El laberinto en la soledad*; Borges; Carpentier; Rulfo; Cortázar; Fuentes; García Márquez; Vargas Llosa; Onetti.

Portuguese

Paper 31. *Portuguese literature, life, and history, before 1497,* with special reference to the following:

Crestomatia Arcaica (ed. J.J. Nunes); The Galician-Portuguese Lyric; *Cantigas de escarnho e maldizer* (ed. Rodrigues Lapa); Fernão Lopes, *Crónica de Dom João I* (Part I); Dom Duarte, *Leal Conselheiro*; Zurara and the early phase of Portuguese expansion; *Cancioneiro Geral.*

Paper 32. *Portuguese literature, thought, and history, from 1497 to 1700*, with special reference to the following:

Gil Vicente, Sá de Miranda, Bernardim Ribeiro, António Ferreira, Damião de Góis, Camões, Mendes Pinto.

Paper 33. *Portuguese literature, thought, and history, since 1700*, with special reference to the period 1820 to 1935, and to the following authors:

Almeida Garrett, Herculano, Castelo Branco, Quental, Eça de Queiroz, Oliveira Martins, Fernando Pessoa, Aquilino Ribeiro.

GERMANIC

German

Paper 40. *German literature, thought, and history, before 1500,* with special reference to the following, from which passages may be set for translation and comment:

Braune, *Althochdeutsches Lesebuch* (1969 edition*), sections XX, 5–7; XXIII, 1; XXVIII–XXXI; XXXII, 1, 4, 7, 14; XXXIV; XXXVI; XLII; XLIII; Gottfried von Strassburg, *Tristan und Isold* (ed. Ranke, Verlag Francke, Bern); Wolfram von Eschenbach, *Parzival* (ed. Hartl, Verlag Francke, Bern); Wehrli (ed. Verlag Francke, Bern), *Minnesang vom Kürenberger bis Wolfram* (the poems of Der von Kürenberg, Friderich von Husen, Heinrich von Morungen, and Wolfram von Eschenbach); Wehrli (ed.): Walther von der Vogelweide, *Gedichte* (Verlag Francke, Bern), sections II, III, IV, VII, VIII, X.

Paper 41. *German literature, thought, and history, from 1500 to 1700*

Paper 42. *German literature, thought, and history, from 1700 to 1805*†

Subjects in history for special study: Frederick the Great *and* Political, Social, and Literary Aspects of the Aufklärung.

Subject in thought for special study: Classical humanism with special reference to Herder, *Ideen...* Book 15; Kant, *Idee zu einer allgemeinen Geschichte...Beantwortung der Frage: was ist Aufklärung? Zum ewigen Frieden*; Schiller, *Über die ästhetische Erziehung des Menschen...*

Paper 43. *Goethe*†

Paper 44. *German literature, thought, and history, from 1797 to 1890*†

Subjects in history for special study: The Revolution of 1848 *and* The Foundation of the Second German Empire.

Subject in thought for special study: Theories of History with special reference to Hegel, *Philosophie der Geschichte*; Einleitung, Zweiter Teil (Die Griechische Welt), Vierter Teil, Dritter Abschnitt (Die neue Zeit) Reclam 4881–85, pp. 39–176, 320–87, 553–605); Marx, *Manifest der kommunistischen Partei*; Burckhardt, *Weltgeschichtliche Betrachtungen* chapters 5 and 6; Nietzsche, *Vom Nutzen und Nachteil der Historie für das Leben.*

Paper 45. *German literature, thought, and history, since 1890*

Subjects in history for special study: The Weimar Republic *and* National Socialism.

Subject in thought for special study: Theories of the Unconscious with special reference to S. Freud, *Abriß der Psychoanalyse*, *Das Unbehagen in der Kultur*; C. G. Jung, *Die Beziehungen zwischen dem Ich und dem Unbewußten*; A. and M. Mitscherlich, 'Die Unfähigkeit zu trauern-womit zusammenhängt: eine deutsche Art zu lieben', in *Die Unfähigkeit zu trauern. Grundlagen kollektiven Verhaltens* (Munich, 1967), pp. 13–85.

* Candidates using other editions are advised to check with the more detailed list obtainable from the Department of German.

† Questions on Goethe's *Faust*, Part I, may be set in connexion with Papers 42, 43, and 44.

*Paper 46. *A special period or subject in German literature, thought, or history*

Aspects of the German picaresque novel and *Bildungsroman.*

Paper 47. *The history of the German language*, with special reference to the following, from which passages will be set for translation and comment:

Braune, *Althochdeutsches Lesebuch* (1969 ed.†), sections VI; X; XII; XIII (*a*); XIX; XX, 5–7; XXIII, 1; XXXII, 6, 14; XXXVI; XLIV, *Heliand*, lines 1–53; Walshe, *A Middle High German Reader* (Oxford, 1974), pp. 53–5, 91–101, 119–32, 137–45; S. Singer, *Mittelhochdeutsches Lesebuch*, sections I, IV, X (lines 1–117), XII, XV; A. Götze, *Frühneuhochdeutsches Lesebuch*, sections 2*a*, *c*; 4*b*; 9*a*; 12*b*; 15*c*, 16 (lines 61–121); 20*d*; 22 (lines 1–65); 25; 27*a* (lines 1–179); 33*b*; 37 (lines 1–76).

Scandinavian

‡Paper 50. *Scandinavian literature, life, and history, before 1500*

The subject shall be divided into four sections, of which each candidate shall select two:

(*a*) Denmark before 1500, with special reference to Saxo's Danish Chronicle, the Danish medieval ballads, and the Provincial Laws of Denmark; and to the following texts, from which passages may be set for translation and comment: H. Bertelsen, *Dansk sproghistorisk Læsebog* (1905), 61–3, 111–21, 134–48, and 156–8; *Mariaklagen* (ed. J. Brøndum-Nielsen and A. Rohmann, 1929); *Danske Folkeviser i Udvalg* (ed. E. Frandsen, 1937).

(*b*) Iceland before 1500, with special reference to *Íslendingabók*, the Family Sagas, *Heimskringla*, *Sturlunga Saga*, the Icelandic scalds, Snorri's *Edda*, the Poetic *Edda*; passages may be set for translation and comment from the following texts: *Hrafnkels Saga*; *Laxdœla Saga*, chs. 40–49; *Sonatorrek*; *Vǫluspá*; Prologue to Snorri's *Edda*.

(*c*) Norway before 1500, with special reference to the Kings' Sagas, *Konungs skuggsjá*, the Norwegian scalds, the Poetic *Edda*, *Draumkvæde* (ed. Liestøl and Moe); passages may be set for translation and comment from *Hávamál*, *Vǫlundarkviða*, the fragmentary lay of Sigurðr *Ragnarsdrápa*, *Sverris saga* (ed. G. Indrebø), chs. 1–8 and 29–38, *Óláfs saga Tryggvasonar* (ed. Bjarni Aðalbjarnarson, Íslenzk Fornrit, XXVI), chs. 45–50 and 104–111; *Draumkvæde*.

(*d*) Sweden before 1500, with special reference to the songs of Eufemia, the Provincial Laws of Sweden, and the life and writings of Saint Birgitta; and to the following texts, from which passages may be set for translation and comment: E. Noreen, *Fornsvensk läsebok* (1932), II, III, VII, VIII, IX, XII, XV, XVII, XVIII, XXVII, XXX, XXXI, XXIV, XXV, Bihang II.

Paper 51. *Scandinavian literature, thought, and history, from 1500 to 1700*, with special reference to the following:

Dansk Litteratur I (Falkenstjerne/Borup Jensen); *Sveriges litteratur I–II* (Ståhle/Tigerstedt); *Norsk litteraturantologi I* (Popperwell/Støverud); *Danske Folkeviser* (E. Frandsen); *Svenska medeltidsballader* (B. R. Jonsson); *Norske Folkeviser* (R. T. Christiansen); T. Kingo, *Digte* (P. Schmidt); P. Dass, *Nordlands Trompet* (D. A. Seip); G. Stiernhielm, *Hercules* (Lindroth/Ståhle); Leonora Christina, *Jammers Minde*.

Paper 52. *Danish literature, thought, and history, from 1800 to 1870* (Paper 27 of Part I), with special reference to the following:

Adam Oehlenschläger, *Digte 1803*; Steen Steensen Blicher, *Noveller* (ed. T. Skou-Hansen); Johan Ludvig Heiberg, *Nye Digte*; H. C. Andersen, *Eventyr og Historier* (ed. V. Sørensen); Emil Aarestrup, *Digte*; Frederik Paludan-Müller, *Adam Homo*; Hans Egede Schack, *Phantasterne*; Henrich Steffens, *Indledning til philosophiske Forelæsninger*; *Fem Kierkegaard-Tekster* (ed. J. Sløk).

Paper 53. *Danish literature, thought, and history, from 1870 to the present day* (Paper 28 of Part I), with special reference to the following:

J. P. Jacobsen, *Mogens og andre Noveller*; Herman Bang, *Stuk*; Sophus Claussen, *Lyrik* (ed. F. J. Billeskov Jansen); Johannes V. Jensen, *Kongens Fald*; Martin Andersen Nexø, *Pelle Erobreren*: *Barndom*; Hans Kirk, *Fiskerne*; Karen Blixen, *Syndfloden over Norderney*, Drømmerne; Henrik Pontoppidan, *Lykke-Per*; Tom Kristensen, *Hærværk*.

*Paper 54. *A special subject in Danish literature, since 1500*

Søren Kierkegaard: Early works (1843–44).

Paper 55. *Norwegian literature, thought, and history, from 1800 to 1865* (Paper 29 of Part I), with special reference to the following:

Norway in 1814; Henrik Wergeland, *Den engelske Lods*; J. S. Welhaven, *Norges Dæmring*; Nasjonalromantikken; Ivar Aasen; Bjørnstjerne Bjørnson, *Synnøve Solbakken*, *Arne*, *En glad Gut*; Henrik Ibsen, *Kongs-Emnerne*; Camilla Collett, *Amtmandens Døttre*; O. Vinje, *Ferdaminni*.

* Candidates who intend to spend a year abroad should not offer themselves for examination in these papers in the Preliminary Examination for Part II of the Modern and Medieval Languages Tripos without consulting with the Secretary of the Faculty Board of Modern and Medieval Languages, since these variable subjects may change between the Preliminary Examination and Part II of the Modern and Medieval Languages Tripos for which they will be candidates two years later.

† Candidates using other editions are advised to check with the more detailed list obtainable from the Department of German.

‡ No candidate who offers in Part II, or has previously offered in another Honours Examination, Paper 2 of the Anglo-Saxon, Norse, and Celtic Tripos may offer this paper.

Paper 56. Norwegian literature, thought, and history, from 1865 to the present day (Paper 30 of Part I), with special reference to the following:

Henrik Ibsen, *Peer Gynt*; Bjørnstjerne Bjørnson, *En Fallit, Redaktøren, Kongen*; Alexander Kielland, *Garman & Worse*; Jonas Lie, *Familjen paa Gilje*; Sigrid Undset, *Jenny*; Knut Hamsun, *Markens Grøde*; Olav Duun, *Menneske og maktene*; Johan Falkberget, *Den fjerde nattevakt*; Sigurd Hoel, *Møte ved milepelen*; Johan Borgen, *Lillelord.*

Paper 57. Henrik Ibsen

**Paper 58. A special subject in Norwegian literature since 1800*
Knut Hamsun.

Paper 59. Scandinavian literature, thought, and history, from 1700 to 1800, with special reference to the following:

Ludvig Holberg, *Erasmus Montanus* and *Jeppe paa Bjerget*; J.H.Wessel, *Kierlighed uden Strømper*; *Rokokolyrik* (B.Julén); H.A.Brorson, *Svanesang*; J.H.Kjellgren, *Urval* (B.Julén); C.M. Bellman, *Fredmans epistlari* and *Fredmans sånger*; J.Ewald, *Levnet og Meninger*; J.Baggesen, *Labyrinthen.*

Paper 60. Swedish literature, thought, and history, from 1800 to 1870 (Paper 31 of Part I), with special reference to the following:

Esaias Tegnér, *Frithiofs saga*; E.J.Stagnelius, *Liljor i Saron*; C.J.L.Almqvist, *Urval* (ed. B. Julén) and *Drottningens juvelsmycke*; J.L.Runeberg, *Fänrik Ståls sägner* and *Kung Fjalar*; Fredrika Bremer, *Grannarne*; F.Cederborgh, *Ottar Trallings lefnadsmålning*; Clas Livjin, *Spader Dam*; Viktor Rydberg, *Singoalla.*

Paper 61. Swedish literature, thought, and history, from 1870 to the present day (Paper 32 of Part I), with special reference to the following:

August Strindberg, *Röda rummet, Fröken Julie, Ett drömspel*; Victoria Benediktsson, *Fru Marianne*; Selma Lagerlöf, *Jerusalem*; Gustaf Fröding, *Dikter* (Stockholm, 1945); Hjalmar Söderberg, *Martin Bircks ungdom*; Hjalmar Bergman, *En döds memoarer*; Birger Sjöberg, *Kriser och kransar*; Ivar Lo-Johansson, *Godnatt, jord*; Lars Ahlin, *Min död är min*; Gunnar Ekelöf, *Strountes* (Stockholm, 1955, 1966).

Paper 62. August Strindberg

**Paper 63. A special subject in Swedish literature since 1500*
Three Modern Swedish poets: Ekelöf, Lindegren, Tranströmer.

**Paper 64. A special subject in the literature or history of at least two of the Scandinavian countries*
The novel in Denmark, Norway, and Sweden after 1900.

Paper 65. The history of either *the Danish language* or *the Norwegian language* or *the Swedish language*, with special reference to the following:

For all three alternatives: E.V.Gordon, *An Introduction to Old Norse* (1957), pp. 3–20, 39–57, 87–115, and 136–41.

For Danish (65 A): P.Skautrup, *Det danske sprogs historie*, I–II; P.Didrichsen, *Dansk prosahistorie*, I; V.Falkenstjerne and E.Borup Jensen, *Håndbog i dansk litteratur* (1962), pp. 7–12, 83–8, 91–5, 96–133, 138–43, 145–80, 193–200, 207–20, 227–9.

For Norwegian (65 B): Prescribed texts: Michael Barnes, *Old Scandinavian Texts* (1968), nos. N1, N2, N4, N5, N6, N7, N9, N10, N12, N20; Eskil Hanssen, *Om norsk språkhistorie* (U-bøkene 114, no date); Ragnvald Iversen, *Norrøn grammatikk* (7th revised ed. 1972), 123–66; Vemund Skard, *Norsk språkhistorie*, I–III (1967–73); Elias Wessén, *De nordiska språken* (1957 and later editions), 3–29 (Inledning).

For Swedish (65 C): Elias Wessén, *Svensk språkhistoria* I; Elias Wessén, *Vårt svenska språk*; G.Holm, *Epoker och prosastilar*; E.Noreen, *Fornsvensk läsebok* (1932), IV, VI, VIII, X, XIII, XXVIII, Bihang I and II; E.Noreen, *Valda stycken av svenska författare 1526–1732* (1943), I, IV, VIII, IX, XIV, XXI, XXIII, XXVI, XXXII, XXXIII.

Dutch

Paper 70. The literature, life, and history of the Netherlands, before 1570, with special reference to the following:

Wie wil horen een goed nieuw lied? Liederen en gedichten uit de Middeleeuwen (Spectrum van de Nederlandse Letterkunde 4, omitting *Een suverlijc boecxken*); *Het Roelantslied* (Spectrum... 1); *De reis van Sinte Brandane* and *Beatrijs* (Spectrum... 2); *Lanseloet van Denemerken* (Spectrum... 5).

* Candidates who intend to spend a year abroad should not offer themselves for examination in these papers in the Preliminary Examination for Part II of the Modern and Medieval Languages Tripos without consulting with the Secretary of the Faculty Board of Modern and Medieval Languages, since these variable subjects may change between the Preliminary Examination and Part II of the Modern and Medieval Languages Tripos for which they will be candidates two years later.

Paper 71. The literature, life, and history of the Netherlands, from 1570 to 1730, with special reference to the following:

Hooft, *Sonnetten* (Spectrum van de Nederlandse Letterkunde 9), Uit het seste boek van *Neederlandsche Histooriën* (Spectrum... 7); Huygens, *Zede-printen* (Spectrum... 10); Bredero, *Lied-boeck* (Spectrum... 9), *Spaanschen Brabander* (Spectrum... 12); Vondel, *Jeptha.*

Paper 72. The literature, life, and history of the Netherlands, from 1730 to 1880, with special reference to the following:

'k Wou zo graag verstandig wezen. Geschriften uit de sfeer der Verlichting (Spectrum van de Nederlandse Letterkunde 16); *Verbeeldingswereld zijn geen grenzen aangewezen. Gedichten uit de Romantiek* (Spectrum... 18); Poot, *Mengeldichten* and Staring '*Mengeldichten*' (Spectrum... 17); Wolff and Deken, *De historie van Mejuffrouw Sara Burgerhart*; Multatuli, *Minnebrieven.*

Paper 73. The literature, life, and history of the Netherlands, since 1880, with special reference to the following:

Verwey, *Het blank heelal*; Heijermans, *Op Hoop van Zegen*; Vestdijk, *Terug tot Ina Damman*; Elsschot, *Het Dwaallicht*; M. Nijhoff, *Lees maar, er staat niet wat er staat* (Ooievaar 47); Hermans, *Het behouden huis*; I. Michiels, *Het boek Alfa.*

Paper 74. The history of the Dutch language, with special reference to the following:

De Oudnederlandse (*Oudnederfrankische*) *Psalmfragmenten* (ed. H. Cowan, 1957); Van Loey, *Middelnederlands Leerboek*, nos. 21–5, 28, II–VIII, XXVI, 29, 37, 38, 61*a*, 71, 74, 77, 79; A. Weijnen, *Zeventiende-eeuwse Taal*, texts 6, 7, 14, 22, 40, 42.

SLAVONIC

Paper 80. Russian literature, life, and history, before 1263, with special reference to the following:

Повесть временных лет 912–1054; Metr. Ilarion, Слово о Законе и Благодати; Чтение... Бориса и Глеба; Житие Феодосия Печерского; Поучение Вл. Мономаха; Слово о полку Игореве.

Paper 81. Russian literature, life, and history, from 1263 to 1676, with special reference to the following:

Житие Ал. Невского; Задонщина; Житие Стефана Пермского; Домострой; Житие протопопа Аввакума.

Paper 82. Russian literature, life, and history, from 1676 to 1792, with special reference to the following:

(*a*) Simeon Polotsky, Комедия о блудном сыне, Трагедия о Навуходоносоре; Повесть о матросе Василии Кориотском; Kantemir, *Satire I*; Lomonosov, Письмо о пользе стекла; Sumarokov, Синав и Трувор; Fonvizin, Бригадир; Chulkov, Пригожая повариха (in "Русская проза XVIII века", 1950); Derzhavin, На смерть князя Мещерского, Фелица, Видение Мурзы, Водопад.

(*b*) Prokopovich, Слово о власти и чести царской; Хрестоматия по истории СССР, ed. Dmitriev and Nechkina, том II, pp. 63–92 (Peter I) and pp. 235–58 (Pugachev rebellion; Жалованная грамота дворянству); the Наказ in *Documents of Catherine the Great*, ed. Reddaway; Shcherbatov, О повреждении нравов в России.

(*c*) A general knowledge of the literature, thought, and culture of the period.

Paper 83. Russian literature and thought, from 1792 to 1883, with special reference to the following:

(*a*) Texts for close study, passages from which may be set for comment: Pushkin, Евгений Онегин; Gogol, Мертвые души; Leskov, Очарованный странник; Tolstoy, Анна Каренина; Dostoevsky, Бесы.

(*b*) Topics: The early Slavophiles; Turgenev as novelist, in connexion with: Рудин, Дворянское гнездо, Накануне, Отцы и дети, Дым, Новь; the poetry of Lermontov; Herzen; radical thought in the 1860s; conservative thought, 1861–1883; the poetry of Tyutchev.

Paper 84. Russian literature and thought, since 1883, with special reference to the following:

The drama, 1890–1916, in relation to the plays of Chekhov, Andreev, Gorky, Blok; the poetry of Blok, Mayakovsky, Mandel'shtam, Akhmatova; the short stories of Andreev, Gorky, and Bunin; Bely as a novelist; literature and the State, 1917–34; the work of Zamyatin, Kaverin, Babel', and Olesha; the Soviet novel, with reference to Leonov and Sholokhov; Bulgakov; Pasternak; Soviet literature from 1956.

Paper 85. Russian history, from 1801 to 1964 with special reference to the following:

(*a*) Documents for close study in relation to their historical setting: N. M. Karamzin, Записка о Древней и Новой России; Десятилетие министерства народного просвещения 1833–43 гг. ("Эпоха Николая I" под ред. М. О. Гершензона, 1910, стр. 115–18); P. L. Lavrov, Исторические Письма; S. Yu. Witte, Воспоминания (ed. Moscow, 1960), Vol. I, chs. 10, 14, 16, 18; Vol. II, chs. 19, 27, 38, 45, 51; Vol. III, chs. 52, 56, 61, 62; V. I. Lenin, Апрельские Тезисы (Полн.

Собр. Соч., 5th ed. 1962), Vol. XXXI (March–April 1917), pp. 99–118, 123–4, 530–2; О задачах хозяйственников...I. V. Stalin, "Вопросы Ленинизма", II-е изд, 1945, стр. 322–30).

(*b*) The period 1801–1894.

(*c*) The period 1894–1964.

Paper 86. The history of the Russian language, with special reference to the following, from which passages will be set for translation and comment:

Obnorsky and Barkhudarov, Хрестоматия по истории русского языка (2nd ed., 1952), nos. 1 (pp. 13–end), 8, 11, 13, 17 (pp. 57–60), 24 (iii), 25 (pp. 82–4), 30 (pp. 102–13), 34, 42, 53 (pp. 230–1), 55 (sections 4 and 5), 59 (iii), 64, 66 (i), 67 (pp. 309–10); Lehr-Spławiński and Witkowski, *Wybór tekstów do historii języka rosyjskiego*, part I, no. 3.

Note. All the passages from the first *Chrestomathy* may be read in the second one.

Paper 87. Czech literature, thought, and history, before 1620, with special reference to the following, from which passages may be set for translation and comment:

Výbor z české literatury od počátků po dobu Husovu (ed. B. Havránek et al., Prague, 1957), pp. 108–19, 134–5, 139–43, 153–67, 171, 177–80, 200–8, 212–17, 248–60, 317–21, 335–47, 360–81, 394–405, 414–16, 426–9, 498–515, 575–8, 688–95; *Výbor z české literatury doby husitské* (ed. B. Havránek et al., Prague, 1963–64), vol. I, pp. 192–7, 281–3, 357–67, 391–5; vol. II, pp. 45–51, 118–26.

Paper 88. Czech and Slovak literature, thought, and history, since 1620, with special reference to the following:

Komenský, *Labyrint světa a ráj srdce*; Mácha, *Máj, Krkonošská pouť* and lyrical poems; Neruda *Trhani*; Hlaváček, *Básnické dílo*; Zeyer, *Jan Maria Plojhar*; K. M. Čapek, *Turbina*; Durych, *Rekviem*; Nezval, *Básně noci*; Bednár, *Hodiny a minúty*; Páral, *Mladý muž a bílá velryba.*

Paper 89. The history of the Czech and Slovak languages, with special reference to the following, from which passages will be set for translation and comment:

Chrestomatie k vyvoji českého jazyka (ed. Jaroslav Porák, Prague, 1979), pp. 35–8, 52–3, 106–7, 147–8 (lines 1–34), 257–8 (lines 23–53), 355–6 (lines 1–33), 399–401; Eugen Pauliny, *Dejiny spisovnej slovenčiny* (Bratislava, 1971), passages quoted on pp. 68–73, 84–5, 101–2.

Paper 90. Polish literature, thought, and history, before 1795, with special reference to the following:

Kochanowski, *Pieśni*; Sęp Szarzyński, *Rytmy abo wiersze polskie*; Pasek, *Pamiętniki*; Krasicki, *Satyry*; Trembecki, *Wiersze wybrane*; Zabłocki, *Fircyk w zalotach.*

Paper 91. Polish literature, thought, and history, since 1795, with special reference to the following:

Malczewski, *Maria*; Mickiewicz, *Pan Tadeusz*; Słowacki, *Balladyna*; Norwid, *Vade Mecum*; Prus, *Lalka*; Irzykowski, *Paluba.*

**Paper 92. The history of the Polish language*, with special reference to the following, from which passages will be set for translation and comment:

St. Vrtel-Wierczyński, *Wybór tekstów staropolskich* (1963 edition), pp. 3–8, 12–15 (*Kazania* IV–VI), 34–5 and 42–3 (*Kazania* 1 and 9), 44–7, 65–9, 70–4 (*Genesis*, I–III), 114–16, 120–3, 158–61, 162–7, 188–90, 210–15, 297–300, 317–20.

Paper 93. Serbian and Croatian literature, thought, and history, before 1700, with special reference to the following:

Sava, *Žitije svi Simeona* (ed. Ćorović); Konstantin Filozof, *Žitije Stefana Lazarevića* (ed. Bašić, Srp. knj. zad.); Marko Marulić, *Judita*, Djore Drzić, *Radmioi Ljubmir*; Petar Hektorović, *Ribanje i ribarsko prigovaranje*; Marin Držić, *Dundo Maroje*; Ivan Gundulić, *Dubravka*; *Osman*; Ivan Bunić, *Plandovanja.*

Paper 94. Serbian and Croatian literature, thought, and history, since 1700, with special reference to the following:

Antun Reljković, *Satir*; Dositej Obradović, *Život i priključenja*; P. P. Njegoš, *Gorski Vijenac*; Laza Kostić, lyrical poetry; Ante Kovačić, *U registraturi*; Vladimir Vidrić, *Pjesme*; Borisav Stanković, *Koštana*; Miloš Crnjanski, *Seobe*; Ivo Andrić, *Prokleta avlija*; Miodrag Bulatović, *Crveni petao leti prema nebu*; Vladan Desnica, *Proleća Ivana Galeba*; Antonije Isaković, *Paprat i vatra.*

Paper 95. The history of the Serbo-Croat language, with special reference to the following, from which passages will be set for translation and comment:

Vondrák, *Církevněslovanská chrestomatie* (Brno, 1925), pp. 148–9; M. Pavlović, Примери историског развитка српскохрватског језика, pp. 29–30, 33–8, 42–5, 50–1, 63–7, 70–3, 83–8 91–7, 101–4, 106–9, 166–73, 176–84.

* There will be no teaching in this subject until further notice.

Paper 96. The history and civilization of the Slavonic peoples from the sixth to the thirteenth centuries, with special reference to the following:

Texts for close study, passages from which will be set for comment: Повесть временных лет (to 911); Житие Константина философа (II, XIII–XVIII); Житие св. Наума; На светого Вещеслава исповедника; the *Bull* of 1136; Nemanja's Hilandar charter.

Topics: (*a*) The formation of the Slav states; (*b*) the function of the Church in the development of culture.

**Paper 97. A special period or subject in the literature, thought, or history of the Slavs*

Dostoevsky.

MODERN GREEK

Paper 100. Greek literature, thought, and history, from 867 to 1204, with special reference to the following:

Constantine Porphyrogenitus, *De Administrando Imperio* (ed. Moravcsik-Jenkins), chs. 1–22; John Mavrogordato, *Digenes Akrites* (Oxford, 1956); Hesseling-Pernot, *Poèmes Prodromiques*; Cecaumenos, *Strategicon* (ed. Wassiliewsky-Jernstedt); Nicetas Choniates (ed. van Dieten), pp. 275–354; Anna Comnena, *Alexias* (Teubner edition), Books X–XIII.

Paper 101. Greek literature, thought, and history, from 1204 to 1453, with special reference to the following:

Χρονικόν του Μορέως (ed. John Schmitt), pp. 184–506; *Καλλίμαχος και Χρυσορρόη* (ed. M. Pichard, Paris, 1956); *Διήγησις Αχιλλέως* (ed. D. C. Hesseling); *Βέλθανδρος και Χρυσάντζα* (ed. E. Kriaras); M. Phalieros, *Λόγοι Διδακτικοί* (ed. Bakker-van Gemert); Michael Ducas (ed. Grecu, Bucharest, 1958), chs. 35–42; Makhairas, *Χρονικόν της Κύπρου*(ed. R. M. Dawkins), sections 449–525.

Paper 102. Greek literature, thought, and history, from 1453 to 1669, with special reference to the following:

L. Politis, *Ποιητική Ανθολογία*, vol. II; V. Kornaros, *Ερωτόκριτος* (ed. S. Alexiou 1980); *Η Θυσία του Αβραάμ* (ed. G. Megas, 2nd ed., 1954); G. Chortatsis, *Πανώρια* (ed. E. Kriaras 1975); M. A. Foskolos, *Φορτουνάτος* (ed. A. Vincent 1980).

Paper 103. Greek literature, thought, and history, from 1669 to 1888, with special reference to the following:

N. Politis, *Εκλογαί από τα Τραγούδια του Ελληνικού Λαού*; *Χρονικό του Γαλαξειδιού* (ed. Valetas); D. Solomos, *Ποιήματα* (ed. L. Politis 1948); A. Kalvos, *Ωδαί*; L. Politis, *Ποιητική Ανθολογία*, vol. V; Makriyannis, *Απομνημονεύματα*, Book I (ed. Vlachoyannis); E. Roidis, *Η Πάπισσα Ιωάννα*.

Paper 104. Greek literature, thought, and history, since 1888, with special reference to the following:

J. Psycharis, *Το Ταξίδι μου*; K. Palamas, *Ασάλευτη Ζωή*, *Ο Δωδεκάλογος του Γύφτου*; A. Papadiamantis, *Η Φόνισσα*; S. Myrivilis, *Η Ζωή εν Τάφω*; C. P. Cavafy, *Ποιήματα* (ed. Savidis 1975); G. Seferis, *Collected Poems* (ed. Keeley and Sherrard); O. Elytis, *Προσανατολισμοί*; N. Kazantzakis, *Ο Χριστός Ξανασταυρώνεται*.

Paper 105. The history of the modern Greek language, with special reference to the following:

Malalas, Book XVIII (Bonn edition); Hesseling-Pernot, *Poèmes Prodromiques*, pp. 48–83; *Le Roman de Phlorios et de Platzia Phlore* (ed. Hesseling), lines 1–426; M. Phalieros, *Ιστορία και 'Ονειρο* (ed. van Gemert); M. A. Foskolos, *Φορτουνάτος* (ed. Vincent), pp. 108–134; Makriyannis, *Απομνημονεύματα* Book II (ed. Vlachoyannis); D. Solomos, *Dialogue on the Language*; J. Psycharis, *Το Ταξίδι μου*, chs. 1–8.

LINGUISTICS

Paper 111. General linguistics
Paper 112. Phonetics
Paper 113. The history of linguistic thought
Paper 114. Historical linguistics

} Details may be obtained from the Department of Linguistics.

COMPARATIVE STUDIES

Paper 120. Vulgar Latin and Romance philology, with special reference to Old French, Provençal, Italian, Spanish, and Portuguese

Every candidate will be expected to show a knowledge of two at least of the Romance languages. Prescribed texts:

Vulgar Latin: G. Rohlfs, *Sermo Vulgaris Latinus* (3rd ed., 1969), passages 5, 7, 8, 13, 17, 18, 25, 29, 34 (i).

Romance Languages: R. Sampson (ed.), *Early Romance Texts*, passages 50–65 (French), 31–49 (Provençal), 73–90 (Italian), 11–22 (Spanish), 1–10 (Portuguese).

* Candidates who intend to spend a year abroad should not offer themselves for examination in this paper in the Preliminary Examination for Part II of the Modern and Medieval Languages Tripos without consulting with the Secretary of the Faculty Board of Modern and Medieval Languages, since this variable subject may change between the Preliminary Examination and Part II of the Modern and Medieval Languages Tripos for which they will be candidates two years later.

Paper 121. The Teutonic languages, with special reference to Gothic, Anglo-Saxon, Early Norse, Old Saxon, and Old High German

Every candidate will be expected to show a knowledge of Gothic and of two at least of the other languages. Prescribed texts from which passages for translation and comment will be selected:

Gothic: St Mark's Gospel, as contained in Wright's *Grammar of the Gothic Language.*

Old High German: Braune, *Althochdeutsches Lesebuch* (1969 edition*), sections V, 2; VIII Cap. III; X; XX; XXIII, 14; XXXII, 7, 12; XLI.

Old Saxon: Holthausen, *Altsächsisches Elementarbuch* (1921), pp. 201–22.

Anglo-Saxon: *Sweet's Anglo-Saxon Reader*, rev. D. Whitelock (Oxford, 1967), nos. II, VIII, XVI, XXI, XXV, lines 1–76.

Old Norse: E.V.Gordon, *An Introduction to Old Norse*, rev. A.R.Taylor, nos. II, III, VIII, X.

Paper 122. The Slavonic languages, with special reference to Old Church Slavonic

Every candidate is expected to show a knowledge of Old Church Slavonic and of at least two other Slavonic languages. Passages will be set for translation and comment from the following specified texts in Old Church Slavonic:

R.Auty, *Handbook of Old Church Slavonic*, part II, *Texts and Glossary*, passages nos. 1*a* (pp. 24–7 (Matth. vii)), 2*a*, 3, 4 (pp. 52–4), 5*c*, 6*a*, 9*b*, 13*i*, 14.

†‡*Paper 123. A special subject in comparative literature* (i)

Medieval European drama

The topics that can be covered are: Secular comedy; Plays with topical reference; Miracle-plays; Biblical plays; Allegorical and moral plays.

The paper will be in two sections:

A. Passages for comment: four passages to be chosen from a larger selection in various languages. (This question will be compulsory.)

B. Essays on groups of plays and general problems of medieval drama: *two* questions to be chosen from a wide selection.

Candidates will be expected to show firsthand knowledge of a selection of plays in at least *three* languages, from among English, French, German, Dutch, Italian, and Latin.

There are no prescribed texts, but a list of reading suggestions is available from the Faculty of Modern and Medieval Languages, and from the Faculty of English.

*†‡*Paper 124. A special subject in comparative literature* (ii)

Avant-garde movements in Europe, 1910–1939

The paper will be in three sections:

A. Experiments in Form

B. Explorations of the Unconscious

C. Art and Society

Candidates will be required to answer *three* questions, not more than two from any one section.

There are no prescribed texts, but a list of reading suggestions is available from the Faculty of Modern and Medieval Languages.

SCHEDULE II

PAPERS (OTHER THAN ESSAY AND TRANSLATION PAPERS) FOR PART II IN **1986**

Note: Candidates for papers marked with an asterisk (*) who intend to spend a year abroad should not offer themselves for examination in these papers in the Preliminary Examination for Part II of the Modern and Medieval Languages Tripos without consulting with the Secretary of the Faculty Board of Modern and Medieval Languages, since these variable subjects may change between the Preliminary Examination and Part II of the Modern and Medieval Languages Tripos for which they will be candidates two years later.

ROMANCE

French and Provençal

Paper 1. French literature, thought, and history, before 1300.

Paper 2. Provençal literature, thought, and history, before 1356, with special reference to the following:

Les chansons de Guillaume IX, duc d'Aquitaine, 1071–1127, ed. A.Jeanroy (C.F.M.A. 9); *Les chansons de Jaufré Rudel*, ed. A.Jeanroy, 2. éd. revue (C.F.M.A. 15); *Bernard de Ventadour: chansons*

* Candidates using other editions are advised to check with the more detailed list obtainable from the Department of German.

† Candidates who intend to spend a year abroad should not offer themselves for examination in these papers in the Preliminary Examination for Part II of the Modern and Medieval Languages Tripos without consulting with the Secretary of the Faculty Board of Modern and Medieval Languages, since these variable subjects may change between the Preliminary Examination and Part II of the Modern and Medieval Languages Tripos for which they will be candidates two years later.

‡ No candidate may offer both Papers 123 and 124.

d'amour, ed. M. Lazar (Paris: Klincksieck, 1966); *The Poetry of Arnaut Daniel*, ed. J. J. Wilhelm (New York and London: Garland, 1981); *Les Troubadours I, Jaufre, Flamenca, Barlaam et Josaphat*, 2. éd. revue (Paris: Desclée Brouwer, 1979).

Paper 3. French literature, thought, and history, from 1300 to 1510.

Paper 4. French literature, thought, and history, from 1510 to 1622.

Paper 5. French literature, thought, and history, from 1594 to 1700.

Paper 6. French literature, thought, and history, from 1690 to 1789.

Paper 7. French literature, thought, and history, from 1789 to 1898.

Paper 8. French literature, thought, and history, since 1890.

Paper 9. The history of the French language, with special reference to the following:

C. W. Aspland, *A Medieval French Reader* (O.U.P., 1979), extracts nos. 1, 2, 3, 6, 9, 12, 15, 21, 23, 26, 30; P. Rickard, *La Langue française au XVIe. siècle. Étude suivie de textes* (C.U.P., 1968), extracts nos. 3, 4, 9*b*, 15, 18, 24, 28, 39, 46; C. F. de Vaugelas, *Remarques sur la langue française* (ed. Streicher; Slatkine, 1934, reprinted 1970) and A. Arnauld et C. Lancelot, *Grammaire générale et raisonnée* (ed. H. E. Brekle; Friedrich Frommann Verlag, 1966).

Paper 10. A special subject in French culture: Literature and the visual arts in France, 1527–1914, with special reference to the following: The First School of Fontainebleau; Poussin and classicism†; Representation in the nineteenth century (Romanticism to Impressionism); *Fins et débuts de siècle.*†

Medieval Latin

Paper 12. Medieval Latin literature, from 400 to 1300, with special reference to the following:

Boethius, *Consolatio Philosophiae* (ed. K. Büchner or E. K. Rand), Book V; *Ruodlieb* (publ. Reclam), sections VIII–XVIII; *Carmina Cantabrigiensia* (ed. K. Strecker or W. Bulst); *Carmina Burana* (publ. dtv): the love-songs nos. 75–100 and the plays nos. 227, 228, and *16; Bernardus Silvestris, *Cosmographia* (ed. P. Dronke), Book II; *Ludus de Antichristo* (publ. Reclam).

Italian

Paper 13. Italian literature, life, and history, before 1400, with special reference to thirteenth-century poetry, Petrarca, and Boccaccio, in connexion with the following:

Poeti del Duecento (ed. G. Contini), selections from Giacomo da Lentini, Guido delle Colonne, Stefano da Messina, Guittone d'Arezzo, Jacopone da Todi, Guido Guinizelli (I–X and XX), Guido Cavalcanti and Cino da Pistoia (I–XXIII); *Novellino*; Dino Compagni, *La Cronica* (publ. Le Monnier); Petrarca, *Rime* (ed. G. Contini, publ. Einaudi), *Secretum* (pp. 21–215 of *Prose*, publ. R. Ricciardi); Boccaccio, *Decameron*.

Paper 14. Dante, with special reference to the following:

Divina Commedia, *Vita nuova*, *Rime*.

Paper 15. Italian literature, thought, and history, from 1400 to 1600, with special reference to the following areas:

(*a*) Alberti, Poliziano, and fifteenth-century Florentine culture;
(*b*) Machiavelli, Guicciardini, and the historical background;
(*c*) Ariosto, Tasso, and the epic;
(*d*) Michelangelo, Castiglione, and High Renaissance culture.

Students will be expected to show knowledge of at least three of the four areas.

**Paper 16. A special subject in Italian culture*

The figurative arts in Tuscany, 1402–1482, with special reference to the following:

(*a*) writings on the theory and practice of painting: Alberti, *Della pittura*, ed. Grayson; Leonardo, *Scritti scelti*, ed. A. M. Brizio, U.T.E.T., pp. 174–246; Vasari, *Vite scelte*, ed. A. M. Brizio, U.T.E.T., pp. 67–134 and 191–271;
(*b*) the sculpture of Ghiberti, Donatello, and Verrocchio;
(*c*) the paintings of Masaccio, Fra Angelico, Filippo Lippi, Uccello, Domenico Veneziano, Piero della Francesca, Botticelli, and Leonardo (with particular attention to works in the galleries of Cambridge, London, and Florence).

Paper 17. Italian literature, thought, and history, since 1815, with special reference to the following:

Foscolo, *Le ultime lettere di Jacopo Ortis*, *Dei sepolcri*; Manzoni, *I promessi sposi*; Leopardi, *I canti*; Nievo, *Le confessioni di un Italiano*, Chs. I–X; Verga, *Mastro don Gesualdo*; D'Annunzio, *Il piacere*; Pirandello, *Sei personaggi in cerca d'autore*, *Il fu Mattia Pascal*; Gozzano, *I colloqui*; Fogazzaro, *Piccolo mondo antico*; Svevo, *La coscienza di Zeno*; Montale, *Ossi di seppia*, *Le occasioni*; Croce, *Breviario d'estetica*; Calvino, *Ti con zero*.

Paper 18. The history of the Italian language, with special reference to the following:

Dionisotti and Grayson, *Early Italian Texts* (2nd. ed.), passages 1–6, 9, 11–13, 15–16, 18, 19(c), (e), (f), 20(b), (c), (d), 21(a), 23, 25; Dante, *De vulgari eloquentia*; Fòffano, *Prose filologiche: La Questione della Lingua*; Bembo, *Le prose della volgar lingua*.

† In 1987 a further option will be available: Diderot and 'le Retour à l'antique'.

Spanish

Paper 20. Spanish literature, life, and history, before 1492, with special reference to the following:

(*a*) *Poema de mio Cid* (ed. C.C. Smith, Oxford); the traditional lyric of the Peninsula; Berceo, *Milagros de Nuestra Señora* (ed. Clásicos Castellanos); Alfonso X, in Solalinde's *Antología de Alfonso el Sabio* (ed. Austral or Granada); Juan Ruiz, *Libro de buen amor* (ed. Clásicos Castellanos, 2 vols.); A. Martínez de Toledo, *El Corbacho* (ed. Castalia).

(*b*) The Reconquest; the culture of Moslem Spain; the Jews in fifteenth-century Spain; the Catholic Monarchs.

Paper 21. Spanish literature, thought, and history, from 1492 to 1700, with special reference to the following:

Fray Luis de León and the Counter-Reformation in Spain; the plays of Lope de Vega; the picaresque novel; Luis de Góngora; Francisco de Quevedo; Baltasar Gracián, *El Criticón*.

Paper 22. Cervantes

Paper 23. Spanish literature, thought, and history, after 1820, with special reference to the following:

Benito Pérez Galdós; Miguel de Unamuno; the Spanish novel after 1960; *poesía pura*; surrealism.

**Paper 24. A special period or subject in Spanish literature, life, or history*

Literature in Catalan, with special reference to the following:

Ramon Llull; the chronicles; humanism; Ausiàs March; 'la decadència'; 'la renaixença'; J. Verdaguer; N. Oller; A. Guimerà; 'modernisme'; 'noucentisme'.

Paper 25. The history of the Peninsular languages, with special reference to the following:

(*a*) D.J. Gifford and F.W. Hodcroft, *Textos lingüísticos del medioevo español* (Oxford, 1966), passages 3, 6, 8–37, 38, 43, 45, 49–52, 53–4, 57, 59, 60–1, 72, 74, 81, 92, 95–6, 102, 105–6, 112, 114, 120; *Poema de Mio Cid* (ed. C.C. Smith, Madrid, 1976), *Cantar I*; Juan de Valdés, *Diálogo de la lengua* (Clásicos castellanos).

(*b*) *Oxford Book of Portuguese Verse* (pp. 1–137); Rodrigues Lapa (ed.), *Crestomatia arcaica*; *Historiadores quinhentistas* (*Textos literários*); Camões, *Os Lusiadas*, canto I.

Paper 26. Topics in Spanish-American history

Paper 27. A special subject in Latin-American history or literature. This paper is suspended until further notice.

Paper 28. Latin-American literature, with special reference to the following:

(*a*) Hernéndez, *Martín Fierro*; Rubén Darío and *modernista* poets; López Velarde; Villaurrutia; Vallejo; Neruda; Octavio Paz.

(*b*) Sarmiento, *Facundo*; Rodó, *Ariel*; Azuela, *Los de abajo*; Güiraldes, *Don Segundo Sombra*; Gallegos, *Doña Bárbara*; Octavio Paz, *El laberinto en la soledad*; Borges; Carpentier; Rulfo; Cortázar; Fuentes; García Márquez; Vargas Llosa; Onetti.

Portuguese

Paper 31. Portuguese literature, life, and history, before 1497, with special reference to the following:

Crestomatia Arcaica (ed. J.J. Nunes); The Galician-Portuguese Lyric; *Cantigas de escarnho e maldizer* (ed. Rodrigues Lapa); Fernão Lopes, *Crónica de Dom João I* (Part I); Dom Duarte, *Leal Conselheiro*; Zurara and the early phase of Portuguese expansion; *Cancioneiro Geral.*

Paper 32. Portuguese literature, thought, and history, from 1497 to 1700, with special reference to the following:

Gil Vicente, Sá de Miranda, Bernardim Ribeiro, António Ferreira, Damião de Góis, Camões, Mendes Pinto.

Paper 33. Portuguese literature, thought, and history, since 1700, with special reference to the period 1820 to 1935, and to the following authors:

Almeida Garrett, Herculano, Castelo Branco, Quental, Eça de Queiroz, Oliveira Martins, Fernando Pessoa, Aquilino Ribeiro.

GERMANIC

German

Paper 40. German literature, thought, and history, before 1500, with special reference to the following, from which passages may be set for translation and comment:

Braune, *Althochdeutsches Lesebuch* (1969 edition†), sections XX, 5–7; XXIII, 1; XXVIII–XXXI; XXXII, 1, 4, 7, 14; XXXIV; XXXVI; XLII; XLIII; Gottfried von Strassburg, *Tristan und Isold* (ed. Ranke, Verlag Francke, Bern); Wolfram von Eschenbach, *Parzival* (ed. Hartl, Verlag Francke, Bern);

† Candidates using other editions are advised to check with the more detailed list obtainable from the Department of German

Wehrli (ed. Verlag Francke, Bern), *Minnesang vom Kürenberger bis Wolfram* (the poems of Der von Kürenberg, Friderich von Husen, Heinrich von Morungen, and Wolfram von Eschenbach); Wehrli (ed.): Walther von der Vogelweide, *Gedichte* (Verlag Francke, Bern), sections II, III, IV, VII, VIII, X.

Paper 41. German literature, thought, and history, from 1500 to 1700

Paper 42. German literature, thought, and history, from 1700 to 1805‡

Subjects in history for special study: Frederick the Great *and* Political, Social, and Literary Aspects of the Aufklärung.

Subject in thought for special study: Classical humanism with special reference to Herder, *Ideen...* Book 15; Kant, *Idee zu einer allgemeinen Geschichte...Beantwortung der Frage: was ist Aufklärung? Zum ewigen Frieden*; Schiller, *Über die ästhetische Erziehung des Menschen...*

*Paper 43. Goethe**

Paper 44. German literature, thought, and history, from 1797 to 1890‡

Subjects in history for special study: The Revolution of 1848 *and* The Foundation of the Second German Empire.

Subject in thought for special study: Theories of History with special reference to Hegel, *Philosophie der Geschichte*; Einleitung, Zweiter Teil (Die Griechische Welt), Vierter Teil, Dritter Abschnitt (Die neue Zeit) Reclam 4881–85, pp. 39–176, 320–87, 553–605); Marx, *Manifest der kommunistischen Partei*; Burckhardt, *Weltgeschichtliche Betrachtungen* chapters 5 and 6; Nietzsche, *Vom Nutzen und Nachteil der Historie für das Leben.*

Paper 45. German literature, thought, and history, since 1890

Subjects in history for special study: The Weimar Republic *and* National Socialism.

Subject in thought for special study: Theories of the Unconscious with special reference to S. Freud, *Abriß der Psychoanalyse, Das Unbehagen in der Kultur*; C. G. Jung, *Die Beziehungen zwischen dem Ich und dem Unbewußten*; A. and M. Mitscherlich, 'Die Unfähigkeit zu trauern-womit zusammenhängt: eine deutsche Art zu lieben', in *Die Unfähigkeit zu trauern. Grundlagen kollektiven Verhaltens* (Munich, 1967), pp. 13–85.

**Paper 46. A special period or subject in German literature, thought, or history*

Aspects of the German picaresque novel and *Bildungsroman.*

Paper 47. The history of the German language, with special reference to the following, from which passages will be set for translation and comment:

Braune, *Althochdeutsches Lesebuch* (1969 ed.†), sections VI; X; XII; XIII (*a*); XIX; XX, 5–7; XXIII, 1; XXXII, 6, 14; XXXVI; XLIV, *Heliand*, lines 1–53; Walshe, *A Middle High German Reader* (Oxford, 1974), pp. 53–5, 91–101, 119–32, 137–45; S. Singer, *Mittelhochdeutsches Lesebuch*, sections I, IV, X (lines 1–117), XII, XV; A. Götze, *Frühneuhochdeutsches Lesebuch*, sections 2*a*, *c*; 4*b*; 9*a*; 12*b*; 15*c*, 16 (lines 61–121); 20*d*; 22 (lines 1–65); 25; 27*a* (lines 1–179); 33*b*; 37 (lines 1–76).

Scandinavian

‡*Paper 50. Scandinavian literature, life, and history, before 1500*

The subject shall be divided into four sections, of which each candidate shall select two:

(*a*) Denmark before 1500, with special reference to Saxo's Danish Chronicle, the Danish medieval ballads, and the Provincial Laws of Denmark; and to the following texts, from which passages may be set for translation and comment: H. Bertelsen, *Dansk sproghistorisk Læsebog* (1905), 61–3, 111–21, 134–48, and 156–8; *Mariaklagen* (ed. J. Brøndum-Nielsen and A. Rohmann, 1929); *Danske Folkeviser i Udvalg* (ed. E. Frandsen, 1937).

(*b*) Iceland before 1500, with special reference to *Íslendingabók*, the Family Sagas, *Heimskringla, Sturlunga Saga*, the Icelandic scalds, Snorri's *Edda*, the Poetic *Edda*; passages may be set for translation and comment from the following texts: *Hrafnkels Saga*; *Laxdœla Saga*, chs. 40–49; *Sonatorrek*; *Vǫluspá*; Prologue to Snorri's *Edda.*

(*c*) Norway before 1500, with special reference to the Kings' Sagas, *Konungs skuggsjá*, the Norwegian scalds, the Poetic *Edda, Draumkvæde* (ed. Liestøl and Moe); passages may be set for translation and comment from *Hávamál, Vǫlundarkviða*, the fragmentary lay of Sigurðr, *Ragnarsdrápa, Sverris saga* (ed. G. Indrebø), chs. 1–8 and 29–38, *Oláfs saga Tryggvasonar* (ed. Bjarni Aðalbjarnarson, Íslenzk Fornrit, XXVI), chs. 45–50 and 104–111; *Draumkvæde.*

(*d*) Sweden before 1500, with special reference to the songs of Eufemia, the Provincial Laws of Sweden, and the life and writings of Saint Birgitta; and to the following texts, from which passages may be set for translation and comment: E. Noreen, *Fornsvensk läsebok* (1932), II, III, VII, VIII, IX, XII, XV, XVII, XVIII, XXVII, XXX, XXXI, XXIV, XXV, Bihang II.

* Questions on Goethe's *Faust*, Part I, may be set in connexion with Papers 42, 43, and 44.

† Candidates using other editions are advised to check with the more detailed list obtainable from the Department of German.

‡ No candidate who offers in Part II, or has previously offered in another Honours Examination, Paper 2 of the Anglo-Saxon, Norse, and Celtic Tripos may offer this paper.

Paper 51. Scandinavian literature, thought, and history, from 1500 to 1700, with special reference to the following:

Dansk Litteratur I (Falkenstjerne/Borup Jensen); *Sveriges litteratur I–II* (Ståhle/Tigerstedt); *Norsk litteraturantologi I* (Popperwell/Støverud); *Danske Folkeviser* (E. Frandsen); *Svenska medeltidsballader* (B. R. Jonsson); *Norske Folkeviser* (R. T. Christiansen); T. Kingo, *Digte* (P. Schmidt); P. Dass, *Nordlands Trompet* (D. A. Seip); G. Stiernhielm, *Hercules* (Lindroth/Ståhle); Leonora Christina, *Jammers Minde*.

Paper 52. Danish literature, thought, and history, from 1800 to 1870 (Paper 27 of Part I), with special reference to the following:

Adam Oehlenschläger, *Digte 1803*; Steen Steensen Blicher, *Noveller* (ed. T. Skou-Hansen); Johan Ludvig Heiberg, *Nye Digte*; H. C. Andersen, *Eventyr og Historier* (ed. V. Sørensen); Emil Aarestrup, *Digte*; Frederik Paludan-Müller, *Adam Homo*; Hans Egede Schack, *Phantasterne*; Henrich Steffens, *Indledning til philosophiske Forelæsninger*; *Fem Kierkegaard-Tekster* (ed. J. Sløk).

Paper 53. Danish literature, thought, and history, from 1870 to the present day (Paper 28 of Part I), with special reference to the following:

J. P. Jacobsen, *Mogens og andre Noveller*; Herman Bang, *Stuk*; Sophus Claussen, *Lyrik* (ed. F. J. Billeskov Jansen); Johannes V. Jensen, *Kongens Fald*; Martin Andersen Nexø, *Pelle Erobreren: Barndom*; Hans Kirk, *Fiskerne*; Karen Blixen, *Syndfloden over Norderney*, Drømmerne; Henrik Pontoppidan, *Lykke-Per*; Tom Kristensen, *Hærværk*.

**Paper 54. A special subject in Danish literature, since 1500*

Søren Kierkegaard: Early works (1843–44).

Paper 55. Norwegian literature, thought, and history, from 1800 to 1865 (Paper 29 of Part I), with special reference to the following:

Norway in 1814; Henrik Wergeland, *Den engelske Lods*; J. S. Welhaven, *Norges Dæmring*; Nasjonalromantikken; Ivar Aasen; Bjørnstjerne Bjørnson, *Synnøve Solbakken, Arne, En glad Gut*; Henrik Ibsen, *Kongs-Emnerne*; Camilla Collett, *Amtmandens Døttre*; O. Vinje, *Ferdaminni*.

Paper 56. Norwegian literature, thought, and history, from 1865 to the present day (Paper 30 of Part I), with special reference to the following:

Henrik Ibsen, *Peer Gynt*; Bjørnstjerne Bjørnson, *En Fallit, Redaktøren, Kongen*; Alexander Kielland, *Garman & Worse*; Jonas Lie, *Familjen paa Gilje*; Sigrid Undset, *Jenny*; Knut Hamsun, *Markens Grøde*; Olav Duun, *Menneske og maktene*; Johan Falkberget, *Den fjerde nattevakt*; Sigurd Hoel, *Møte ved milepelen*; Johan Borgen, *Lillelord*.

Paper 57. Henrik Ibsen

**Paper 58. A special subject in Norwegian literature since 1800*

Knut Hamsun.

Paper 59. Scandinavian literature, thought, and history, from 1700 to 1800, with special reference to the following:

Ludvig Holberg, *Erasmus Montanus* and *Jeppe paa Bjerget*; J. H. Wessel, *Kierlighed uden Strømper*; *Rokokolyrik* (B. Julén); H. A. Brorson, *Svanesang*; J. H. Kjellgren, *Urval* (B. Julén); C. M. Bellman, *Fredmans epistlar* and *Fredmans sånger*; J. Ewald, *Levnet og Meninger*; J. Baggesen, *Labyrinthen*.

Paper 60. Swedish literature, thought, and history, from 1800 to 1870 (Paper 31 of Part I), with special reference to the following:

Esaias Tegnér, *Frithiofs saga*; E. J. Stagnelius, *Liljor i Saron*; C. J. L. Almqvist, *Urval* (ed. B. Julén) and *Drottningens juvelsmycke*; J. L. Runeberg, *Fänrik Ståls sägner* and *Kung Fjalar*; Fredrika Bremer, *Grannarne*; F. Cederborgh, *Ottar Trallings lefnadsmålning*; Clas Livijn, *Spader Dam*; Viktor Rydberg, *Singoalla*.

Paper 61. Swedish literature, thought, and history, from 1870 to the present day (Paper 32 of Part I), with special reference to the following:

August Strindberg, *Röda rummet, Fröken Julie, Ett drömspel*; Victoria Benediktsson, *Fru Marianne*; Selma Lagerlöf, *Jerusalem*; Gustaf Fröding, *Dikter* (Stockholm, 1945); Hjalmar Söderberg, *Martin Bircks ungdom*; Hjalmar Bergman, *En döds memoarer*; Birger Sjöberg, *Kriser och kransar*; Ivar Lo-Johansson, *Godnatt, jord*; Lars Ahlin, *Min död är min*; Gunnar Ekelöf, *Strountes* (Stockholm, 1955, 1966).

Paper 62. August Strindberg

**Paper 63. A special subject in Swedish literature since 1500*

Three Modern Swedish poets: Ekelöf, Lindegren, Tranströmer.

**Paper 64. A special subject in the literature or history of at least two of the Scandinavian countries*

The novel in Denmark, Norway, and Sweden after 1900.

Paper 65. *The history of* either *the Danish language* or *the Norwegian language* or *the Swedish language*, with special reference to the following:

For all three alternatives: E. V. Gordon, *An Introduction to Old Norse* (1957), pp. 3–20, 39–57, 87–115, and 136–41.

For Danish (65A): P. Skautrup, *Det danske sprogs historie*, I–II; P. Didrichsen, *Dansk prosahistorie*, I; V. Falkenstjerne and E. Borup Jensen, *Håndbog i dansk litteratur* (1962), pp. 7–12, 83–8, 91–5, 96–133, 138–43, 145–80, 193–200, 207–20, 227–9.

For Norwegian (65B): Prescribed texts: Michael Barnes, *Old Scandinavian Texts* (1968), nos. N1, N2, N4, N5, N6, N7, N9, N10, N12, N20; Eskil Hanssen, *Om norsk språkhistorie* (U-bøkene 114, no date); Ragnvald Iversen, *Norrøn grammatikk* (7th revised ed. 1972), 123–66; Vemund Skard, *Norsk språkhistorie*, I–III (1967–73); Elias Wessén, *De nordiska språken* (1957 and later editions), 3–29 (Inledning).

For Swedish (65C): Elias Wessén, *Svensk språkhistoria* I; Elias Wessén, *Vårt svenska språk*; G. Holm, *Epoker och prosastilar*; E. Noreen, *Fornsvensk läsebok* (1932), IV, VI, VIII, X, XIII, XXVIII, Bihang I and II; E. Noreen, *Valda stycken av svenska författare 1526–1732* (1943), I, IV, VIII, IX, XIV, XXI, XXIII, XXVI, XXXII, XXXIII.

Dutch

Paper 70. *The literature, life, and history of the Netherlands, before 1570*, with special reference to the following:

Wie wil horen een goed nieuw lied? Liederen en gedichten uit de Middeleeuwen (Spectrum van de Nederlandse Letterkunde 4, omitting *Een suverlijc boecxken*); *Het Roelantslied* (Spectrum... 1); *De reis van Sinte Brandane* and *Beatrijs* (Spectrum... 2); *Lanseloet van Denemerken* (Spectrum... 5).

Paper 71. *The literature, life, and history of the Netherlands, from 1570 to 1730*, with special reference to the following:

Hooft, *Sonnetten* (Spectrum van de Nederlandse Letterkunde 9), Uit het seste boek van *Neederlandsche Historiën* (Spectrum... 7); Huygens, *Zede-printen* (Spectrum... 10); Bredero, *Lied-boeck* (Spectrum... 9), *Spaanschen Brabander* (Spectrum... 12); Vondel, *Jeptha*.

Paper 72. *The literature, life, and history of the Netherlands, from 1730 to 1880*, with special reference to the following:

'k Wou zo graag verstandig wezen. Geschriften uit de sfeer der Verlichting (Spectrum van de Nederlandse Letterkunde 16); *Verbeeldingswereld zijn geen grenzen aangewezen. Gedichten uit de Romantiek* (Spectrum... 18); Poot, *Mengeldichten* and Staring '*Mengeldichten*' (Spectrum... 17); Wolff and Deken, *De historie van Mejuffrouw Sara Burgerhart*; Multatuli, *Minnebrieven*.

Paper 73. *The literature, life, and history of the Netherlands, since 1880*, with special reference to the following:

Vestdijk, *Terug tot Ina Damman*; Elsschot, *Het Dwaallicht*; M. Nijhoff, *Lees maar, er staat niet wat er staat*; Hermans, *Het behouden huis*; G. K. van het Reve, *De Avonden*; H. Claus, *Suiker*; J. Wolkers, *Terug naar Oegstgeest*; H. Mulisch, *De Aanslag*.

Paper 74. *The history of the Dutch language*, with special reference to the following:

De Oudnederlandse (*Oudnederfrankische*) *Psalmfragmenten* (ed. H. Cowan, 1957); Van Loey, *Middelnederlands Leerboek*, nos. 21–5, 28, II–VIII, XXVI, 29, 37, 38, 61*a*, 71, 74, 77, 79; A. Weijnen, *Zeventiende-eeuwse Taal*, texts 6, 7, 14, 22, 40, 42.

SLAVONIC

Paper 80. *Russian literature, life, and history, before 1263*, with special reference to the following:

Повесть временных лет 912–1054; Metr. Ilarion, Слово о Законе и Благодати; Чтение... Бориса и Глеба; Житие Феодосия Печерского; Поучение Вл. Мономаха; Слово о полку Игореве.

Paper 81. *Russian literature, life, and history, from 1263 to 1676*, with special reference to the following:

Житие Ал. Невского; Задонщина; Житие Стефана Пермского; Домострой; Житие протопопа Аввакума.

Paper 82. *Russian literature, life, and history, from 1676 to 1792*, with special reference to the following:

(*a*) Simeon Polotsky, Комедия о блудном сыне, Трагедия о Навуходоносоре; Повесть о матросе Василии Кориотском; Kantemir, *Satire I*; Lomonosov, Письмо о пользе стекла; Sumarokov, Синав и Трувор; Fonvizin, Бригадир; Chulkov, Пригожая повариха (in "Русская проза XVIII века", 1950); Derzhavin, На смерть князя Мещерского, Фелица, Видение Мурзы, Водопад.

(*b*) Prokopovich, Слово о власти и чести царской; Хрестоматия по истории СССР, ed. Dmitriev and Nechkina, том II, pp. 63–92 (Peter I) and pp. 235–58 (Pugachev rebellion; Жалованная грамота дворянству); the Наказ in *Documents of Catherine the Great*, ed. Reddaway; Shcherbatov, О повреждении нравов в России.

(*c*) A general knowledge of the literature, thought, and culture of the period.

Paper 83. *Russian literature and thought, from 1792 to 1883,* with special reference to the following:

(*a*) Texts for close study, passages from which may be set for comment: Pushkin, Евгений Онегин; Gogol, Мертвые души; Leskov, Очарованный странник; Tolstoy, Анна Каренина; Dostoevsky, Бесы.

(*b*) Topics: The early Slavophiles; Turgenev as novelist, in connexion with: Рудин, Дворянское гнездо, Накануне, Отцы и дети, Дым, Новь; the poetry of Lermontov; Herzen; radical thought in the 1860s; conservative thought, 1861–1883; the poetry of Tyutchev.

Paper 84. *Russian literature and thought, since 1883,* with special reference to the following:

The drama, 1890–1916, in relation to the plays of Chekhov, Andreev, Gorky, Blok; the poetry of Blok, Mayakovsky, Mandel'shtam, Akhmatova; the short stories of Andreev, Gorky, and Bunin; Bely as a novelist; literature and the State, 1917–34; the work of Zamyatin, Kaverin, Babel', and Olesha; the Soviet novel, with reference to Leonov and Sholokhov; Bulgakov; Pasternak; Soviet literature from 1956.

Paper 85. *Russian history, from 1801 to 1964* with special reference to the following:

(*a*) Documents for close study in relation to their historical setting: N. M. Karamzin, Записка о Древней и Новой России; Десятилетие министерства народного просвещения 1833–43 гг. ("Эпоха Николая I" под ред. М. О. Гершензона, 1910, стр. 115–18); P. L. Lavrov, Исторические Письма; S. Yu. Witte, Воспоминания (ed. Moscow, 1960), Vol. I, chs. 10, 14, 16, 18; Vol. II, chs. 19, 27, 38, 45, 51; Vol. III, chs. 52, 56, 61, 62; V. I. Lenin, Апрельские Тезисы (Полн. Собр. Соч., 5th ed. 1962), Vol. XXXI (March–April 1917), pp. 99–118, 123–4, 530–2; О задачах хозяйственников... I. V. Stalin, "Вопросы Ленинизма", II-е изд, 1945, стр. 322–30).

(*b*) The period 1801–1894.

(*c*) The period 1894–1964.

Paper 86. *The history of the Russian language,* with special reference to the following, from which passages will be set for translation and comment:

Obnorsky and Barkhudarov, Хрестоматия по истории русского языка (2nd ed., 1952), nos. 1 (pp. 13–end), 8, 11, 13, 17 (pp. 57–60), 24 (iii), 25 (pp. 82–4), 30 (pp. 102–13), 34, 42, 53 (pp. 230–1), 55 (sections 4 and 5), 59 (iii), 64, 66 (i), 67 (pp. 309–10); Lehr-Spławiński and Witkowski, *Wybór tekstów do historii języka rosyjskiego,* part I, no. 3.

Note. All the passages from the first *Chrestomathy* may be read in the second one.

Paper 87. *Czech literature, thought, and history, before 1620,* with special reference to the following, from which passages may be set for translation and comment:

Výbor z české literatury od počátků po dobu Husovu (ed. B. Havránek et al., Prague, 1957), pp. 108–19, 134–5, 139–43, 153–67, 171, 177–80, 200–8, 212–17, 248–60, 317–21, 335–47, 360–81, 394–405, 414–16, 426–9, 498–515, 575–8, 688–95; *Výbor z české literatury doby husitské* (ed. B. Havránek et al., Prague, 1963–64), vol. I, pp. 192–7, 281–3, 357–67, 391–5; vol. II, pp. 45–51, 118–26.

Paper 88. *Czech and Slovak literature, thought, and history, since 1620,* with special reference to the following:

Komenský, *Labyrint světa a ráj srdce*; Mácha, *Máj, Krkonošská pouť* and lyrical poems; Neruda *Trhani*; Hlaváček, *Básnické dílo*; Zeyer, *Jan Maria Plojhar*; K. M. Čapek, *Turbina*; Durych, *Rekviem*; Nezval, *Básně noci*; Bednár, *Hodiny a minúty*; Páral, *Mladý muž a bílá velryba.*

Paper 89. *The history of the Czech and Slovak languages,* with special reference to the following, from which passages will be set for translation and comment:

Chrestomatie k vyvoji českého jazyka (ed. Jaroslav Porák, Prague, 1979), pp. 35–8, 52–3, 106–7, 147–8 (lines 1–34), 257–8 (lines 23–53), 355–6 (lines 1–33), 399–401; Eugen Pauliny, *Dejiny spisovnej slovenčiny* (Bratislava, 1971), passages quoted on pp. 68–73, 84–5, 101–2.

Paper 90. *Polish literature, thought, and history, before 1795,* with special reference to the following:

Kochanowski, *Pieśni*; Sęp Szarzyński, *Rytmy abo wiersze polskie*; Skarga, *Kazania sejmowe*; K. Opaliński, *Satyry*; Trembecki, *Wiersze wybrane*; Staszic, *Przestrogi dla Polski.*

Paper 91. *Polish literature, thought, and history, since 1795,* with special reference to the following:

Malczewski, *Maria*; Mickiewicz, *Dziady III*; Słowacki, *Beniowski*; Norwid, *Vade Mecum*; Prus, *Lalka*; M. Dąbrowska, *Noce i dnie,* vols. I–II.

†Paper 92. *The history of the Polish language,* with special reference to the following, from which passages will be set for translation and comment:

St. Vrtel-Wierczyński, *Wybór tekstów staropolskich* (1963 edition), pp. 3–8, 12–15 (*Kazania* IV–VI), 34–5 and 42–3 (*Kazania* 1 and 9), 44–7, 65–9, 70–4 (*Genesis,* I–III), 114–16, 120–3, 158–61, 162–7, 188–90, 210–15, 297–300, 317–20.

Paper 93. *Serbian and Croatian literature, thought, and history, before 1700,* with special reference to the following:

Sava, *Žitije svi Simeona* (ed. Ćorović); Konstantin Filozof, *Žitije Stefana Lazarevića* (ed. Bašić, Srp. knj. zad.); Marko Marulić, *Judita,* Djore Drzić, *Radmioi Ljubmir*; Petar Hektorović, *Ribanje*

† There will be no teaching in this subject until further notice.

i ribarsko prigovaranje; Marin Držić, *Dundo Maroje*; Ivan Gundulić, *Dubravka*; *Osman*; Ivan Bunić, *Plandovanja*.

Paper 94. Serbian and Croatian literature, thought, and history, since 1700, with special reference to the following:

Antun Reljković, *Satir*; Dositej Obradović, *Život i priključenja*; P. P. Njegoš, *Gorski Vijenac*; Laza Kostić, lyrical poetry; Ante Kovačić, *U registraturi*; Vladimir Vidrić, *Pjesme*; Borisav Stanković, *Koštana*; Miloš Crnjanski, *Seobe*; Ivo Andrić, *Prokleta avlija*; Miodrag Bulatović, *Crveni petao leti prema nebu*; Vladan Desnica, *Proleća Ivana Galeba*; Antonije Isaković, *Paprat i vatra*.

Paper 95. The history of the Serbo-Croat language, with special reference to the following, from which passages will be set for translation and comment:

Vondrák, *Církevněslovanská chrestomatie* (Brno, 1925), pp. 148–9; M. Pavlović, Примери историског развитка српскохрватског језика, pp. 29–30, 33–8, 42–5, 50–1, 63–7, 70–3, 83–8 91–7, 101–4, 106–9, 166–73, 176–84.

Paper 96. The history and civilization of the Slavonic peoples from the sixth to the thirteenth centuries, with special reference to the following:

Texts for close study, passages from which will be set for comment: Повесть временных лет (to 911); Житие Константина философа (II, XIII–XVIII); Житие св. Наума; На светого Вещеслава исповедника; the *Bull* of 1136; Nemanja's Hilandar charter.

Topics: (*a*) The formation of the Slav states; (*b*) the function of the Church in the development of culture.

**Paper 97. A special period or subject in the literature, thought, or history of the Slavs*:

Dostoevsky.

MODERN GREEK

Paper 100. Greek literature, thought, and history, from 867 to 1204, with special reference to the following:

Constantine Porphyrogenitus, *De Administrando Imperio* (ed. Moravcsik-Jenkins), chs. 1–22; John Mavrogordato, *Digenes Akrites* (Oxford, 1956); Hesseling-Pernot, *Poèmes Prodromiques*; Cecaumenos, *Strategicon* (ed. Wassiliewsky-Jernstedt); Nicetas Choniates (ed. van Dieten), pp. 275–354; Anna Comnena, *Alexias* (Teubner edition), Books X–XIII.

Paper 101. Greek literature, thought, and history, from 1204 to 1453, with special reference to the following:

Χρονικόν του Μορέως (ed. John Schmitt), pp. 184–506; *Καλλίμαχος και Χρυσορρόη* (ed. M. Pichard, Paris, 1956); *Διήγησις Αχιλλέως* (ed. D. C. Hesseling); *Βέλθανδρος και Χρυσάντζα* (ed. E. Kriaras); M. Phalieros, *Λόγοι Διδακτικοί* (ed. Bakker-van Gemert); Michael Ducas (ed. Grecu, Bucharest, 1958), chs. 35–42; Makhairas, *Χρονικόν της Κύπρου* (ed. R. M. Dawkins), sections 449–525.

Paper 102. Greek literature, thought, and history, from 1453 to 1669, with special reference to the following:

L. Politis, *Ποιητική Ανθολογία*, vol. II; V. Kornaros, *Ερωτόκριτος* (ed. S. Alexiou 1980); *Η Θυσία του Αβραάμ* (ed. G. Megas, 2nd ed., 1954); G. Chortatsis, *Πανώρια* (ed. E. Kriaras 1975); M. A. Foskolos, *Φορτουνάτος* (ed. A. Vincent 1980).

Paper 103. Greek literature, thought, and history, from 1669 to 1888, with special reference to the following:

N. Politis, *Εκλογαί από τα Τραγούδια του Ελληνικού Λαού*; *Χρονικό του Γαλαξειδιού* (ed. Valetas); D. Solomos, *Ποιήματα* (ed. L. Politis 1948); A. Kalvos, *Ωδαί*; L. Politis, *Ποιητική Ανθολογία*, vol. V; Makriyannis, *Απομνημονεύματα*, Book I (ed. Vlachoyannis); E. Roidis, *Η Πάπισσα Ιωάννα*.

Paper 104. Greek literature, thought, and history, since 1888, with special reference to the following:

J. Psycharis, *Το Ταξίδι μου*; K. Palamas, *Ασάλευτη Ζωή*, *Ο Δωδεκάλογος του Γύφτου*; A. Papadiamantis, *Η Φόνισσα*; S. Myrivilis, *Η Ζωή εν Τάφω*; C. P. Cavafy, *Ποιήματα* (ed. Savidis 1975); G. Seferis, *Collected Poems* (ed. Keeley and Sherrard); O. Elytis, *Προσανατολισμοί*; N. Kazantzakis, *Ο Χριστός Ξανασταυρώνεται*.

Paper 105. The history of the modern Greek language, with special reference to the following:

Malalas, Book XVIII (Bonn edition); Hesseling-Pernot, *Poèmes Prodromiques*, pp. 48–83; *Le Roman de Phlorios et de Platzia Phlore* (ed. Hesseling), lines 1–426; M. Phalieros, *Ιστορία και 'Ονειρο* (ed. van Gemert); M. A. Foskolos, *Φορτουνάτος* (ed. Vincent), pp. 108–134; Makriyannis, *Απομνημονεύματα* Book II (ed. Vlachoyannis); D. Solomos, *Dialogue on the Language*; J. Psycharis, *Το Ταξίδι μου*, chs. 1–8.

LINGUISTICS

Paper 111. General linguistics

Paper 112. Phonetics

Paper 113. The history of linguistic thought

Paper 114. Historical linguistics

(Papers 111–114:) Details may be obtained from the Department of Linguistics.

COMPARATIVE STUDIES

Paper 120. Vulgar Latin and Romance philology, with special reference to Old French, Provençal, Italian, Spanish, and Portuguese

Every candidate will be expected to show a knowledge of two at least of the Romance languages. Prescribed texts:

Vulgar Latin: G. Rohlfs, *Sermo Vulgaris Latinus* (3rd ed., 1969), passages 5, 7, 8, 13, 17, 18, 25, 29, 34 (i).

Romance Languages: R. Sampson (ed.), *Early Romance Texts*, passages 50–65 (French), 31–49 (Provençal), 73–90 (Italian), 11–22 (Spanish), 1–10 (Portuguese).

Paper 121. The Teutonic languages, with special reference to Gothic, Anglo-Saxon, Early Norse, Old Saxon, and Old High German

Every candidate will be expected to show a knowledge of Gothic and of two at least of the other languages. Prescribed texts from which passages for translation and comment will be selected:

Gothic: St Mark's Gospel, as contained in Wright's *Grammar of the Gothic Language*.

Old High German: Braune, *Althochdeutsches Lesebuch* (1969 edition†), sections v, 2; VIII Cap. III; X; XX; XXIII, 14; XXXII, 7, 12; XLI.

Old Saxon: Holthausen, *Altsächsisches Elementarbuch* (1921), pp. 201–22.

Anglo-Saxon: *Sweet's Anglo-Saxon Reader*, rev. D. Whitelock (Oxford, 1967), nos. II, VIII, XVI, XXI, XXV, lines 1–76.

Old Norse: E. V. Gordon, *An Introduction to Old Norse*, rev. A. R. Taylor, nos. II, III, VIII, X.

Paper 122. The Slavonic languages, with special reference to Old Church Slavonic

Every candidate is expected to show a knowledge of Old Church Slavonic and of at least two other Slavonic languages. Passages will be set for translation and comment from the following specified texts in Old Church Slavonic:

R. Auty, *Handbook of Old Church Slavonic*, part II, *Texts and Glossary*, passages nos. 1*a* (pp. 24–7 (Matth. vii)), 2*a*, 3, 4 (pp. 52–4), 5*c*, 6*a*, 9*b*, 13*i*, 14.

*‡*Paper 123. A special subject in comparative literature* (i)

Medieval European drama

The topics that can be covered are: Secular comedy; Plays with topical reference; Miracle-plays; Biblical plays; Allegorical and moral plays.

The paper will be in two sections:

A. Passages for comment: four passages to be chosen from a larger selection in various languages. (This question will be compulsory.)

B. Essays on groups of plays and general problems of medieval drama: *two* questions to be chosen from a wide selection.

Candidates will be expected to show firsthand knowledge of a selection of plays in at least *three* languages, from among English, French, German, Dutch, Italian, and Latin.

There are no prescribed texts, but a list of reading suggestions is available from the Faculty of Modern and Medieval Languages, and from the Faculty of English.

*‡*Paper 124. A special subject in comparative literature* (ii)

Avant-garde movements in Europe, 1910–1939

The paper will be in three sections:

A. Experiments in Form
B. Explorations of the Unconscious
C. Art and Society

Candidates will be required to answer *three* questions, not more than two from any one section.

There are no prescribed texts, but a list of reading suggestions is available from the Faculty of Modern and Medieval Languages.

As in the case of Part I (see above, p. 288), the Faculty Board may allow candidates to be examined in subjects or papers other than those specified in the lists above. The following additional language and papers have been approved for the Part II examinations in **1985** and **1986**:

† Candidates using other editions are advised to check with the more detailed list obtainable from the Department of German.
‡ No candidate may offer both Papers 123 and 124.

Hungarian

1. Hungarian literature, thought, and history, before 1825.
2. Hungarian literature, thought, and history, since 1825.
3. The history of the Hungarian language.

The following texts have been prescribed for these papers in **1985** and **1986**:

Paper 1. *Hungarian literature, thought, and history, before 1825*, with special reference to the following:

Balassi Bálint, *Összes versei*; Zrinyi Miklós, *Szigeti veszedelem*; Mikes Kelemen, *Törökországi levelek*; Csokonai Vitéz Mihály, *A méla Tempefői*; Katona, *Bánk bán*.

Paper 2. *Hungarian literature, thought, and history, since 1825*, with special reference to the following:

Petőfi Sándor, *Összes versei*; Kemény Zsigmond, *Zord idő*; Mikszáth, *Különös házasság*; Kosztolányi, *Összes versei*; Ottlik, *Iskola a határon*; Pilinszky, *Harmadnapon*.

Paper 3. *The history of the Hungarian language*, with special reference to the following, from which passages may be set for translation and comment:

Bisztray-Kerecsényi, *Régi magyar próza*; Horváth János, *Magyar versek könyve*; *Hét évszázad magyar versei, Vol. 1. Magyar Költészet Bocskaytó Rákócziig.*

The Preliminary Examination for Part I

In the Preliminary Examination for Part I of the Tripos written papers are set, if there are candidates, in each of the languages that may be offered in Part I. There is also a separate preliminary oral examination similar in format to that in Part I (see above p. 280). Papers are not set on the papers marked with an asterisk in Schedule I of the Tripos. Each candidate must offer four written papers, which must include three language papers and one paper which must be chosen from among the papers listed in Schedule I for Part I of the Tripos and which must relate to one of the languages in which he is offering his language paper. Every candidate must also take an oral examination in one of the languages in which he offers a written paper. (No oral examination is set in classical Greek, classical Latin, or Arabic.) If a candidate wishes to offer less than the required number of papers, or not to offer an oral examination, he may do so; his name will not appear in the class-list, but his marks will be communicated to his Tutor.

A candidate who offers classical Greek may offer one or more papers from among Papers 1, 2, 4, and 5 of the Preliminary Examination for Part I of the Classical Tripos; a candidate who chooses to offer Paper 4 is required to answer three questions only, and if he offers Paper 4 he may not offer a paper from Schedule I.

A candidate who offers classical Latin may offer any or all of the special papers in classical Latin for Part I of the Modern and Medieval Languages Tripos, but if he offers Paper (*d*) he may not offer a paper from Schedule I.

A candidate who offers Arabic and Spanish or Portuguese must take Papers Ar. 1 and Ar. 3 of the papers prescribed for Arabic Studies in the Preliminary Examination for Part I of the Oriental Studies Tripos, together with two papers in Spanish or Portuguese, one of which must be a language paper and the other a paper chosen from among the papers listed in Schedule I for Part I of the Tripos, together with an oral examination in Spanish or Portuguese.

The prescribed texts for the Preliminary Examination for Part I in **1985** are the same as those for Part I of the Tripos in **1986** with the following exceptions:

(The papers are numbered as in Schedule I for Part I of the Tripos.)

Paper 13. Introduction to Dante and his age
Dante, *Inferno, Purgatorio.*

Paper 14. (a) Introduction to Dante and his age, and (b) the literature of the Risorgimento
(*a*) Dante, *Inferno.*
(*b*) Manzoni, *I promessi sposi*; Leopardi, *I canti.*

A list of the topics prescribed for the oral examinations in the Preliminary Examination for Part I in **1985** is available from the Faculty Office.

The Preliminary Examination for Part II

In the Preliminary Examination for Part II there are set, if there are candidates, any of the papers in Schedule II of the Tripos, and any additional paper that may have been approved by the Faculty Board. A candidate must offer three papers selected from Schedule II, together with *either* an essay in a medieval or modern foreign language *or* a paper containing a passage of English for translation into a foreign language and a passage of that language for translation into English. The essay or the translation paper must be in a language relating to at least one of the papers chosen by the candidate. A candidate may offer, in place of one or two of the Part II papers, one or two papers chosen from among

either Papers 2, 4, 5, 6, 7, and 8 of the Preliminary Examination for the Anglo-Saxon, Norse, and Celtic Tripos;

or [1]any paper from Part II of the Classical Tripos, other than from the optional papers, except that he may not offer:
(i) both E1 (Classical Tripos) and Paper 111;

[1] The regulations relating to papers offered from Part II of the Classical Tripos will change with effect from the examinations to be held in **1986**.

(ii) both E4 (Classical Tripos) and Paper 120 (subject to such announcement having been made beforehand);

(iii) any paper in Group E marked with an asterisk and another paper from the same group;

(iv) any paper marked with an asterisk from a group other than Group E and another paper from the same group (subject to such announcement having been made beforehand);

or Papers 2, 3, 4, 9, and 13 of Part II of the English Tripos.

The prescribed works, authors, and topics for **1985** are the same as those for Part II of the Tripos in **1986** with the following exceptions:

(The papers are numbered as in Schedule II for Part II of the Tripos.)

Paper 10. *A special subject in French culture: Literature and the visual arts in France, 1527–1914*, with special reference to the following: The First School of Fontainebleau; Poussin and classicism†; Representation in the nineteenth century (Romanticism to Impressionism); *Fins et débuts de siècle*.†

Paper 14. *Dante*, with special reference to the following:
Divina Commedia.

Paper 47. *The history of the German language*, with special reference to the following, from which passages will be set for translation and comment:

Braune, *Althochdeutsches Lesebuch* (1969 edition*), sections VI; X; XII; XIII(*a*); XIX; XX, 5–7; XXIII, 1; XXXII, 6, 14; XXXVI; XLIV, Heliand, lines 1–53; Walshe, *A Middle High German Reader* (Oxford, 1974), pp. 53–5, 91–101, 119–32, 137–45.

Certificates of Competent Knowledge in modern languages

A student who has satisfied the examination requirements for matriculation or the Matriculation Board and kept at least two terms may in any one year be a candidate for a Certificate of Competent Knowledge in one of the languages (other than classical Latin or classical Greek) specified for Part I of the Modern and Medieval Languages Tripos, provided that no student may be a candidate for a Certificate in a language which he is in the same term offering as a candidate for honours in the Tripos. In each language there will be an oral examination and a written examination which will consist of three papers of three hours each as follows:

1. Passages from works in the foreign language for translation into English.
2. Passages from works in English to be translated into the foreign language.
3. An essay in the foreign language.

* Candidates using other editions are advised to check with the more detailed list obtainable from the Department of German.
† These options will not be available until 1986. In 1987 a further option will be available: Diderot and 'le Retour à l'antique'.

The form, scope, and standard of Papers 1 and 2 will be the same as that of the corresponding papers in Part I of the Modern and Medieval Languages Tripos. The essay must be chosen from a paper of subjects some of which will bear on the literature, history, thought, and language of the country concerned, and all of which will demand reasoned exposition. The oral examination will be similar in format and standard to the oral examination in Part I (see above p. 280) and must be taken in the same term in which the written papers for the Certificate are taken.

A candidate who wishes to offer any language other than Czech (with Slovak), Danish, Dutch, French, German, Italian, Modern Greek, Norwegian, Polish, Portuguese, Russian, Serbo-Croat, Spanish, or Swedish, must first obtain permission from the Faculty Board in accordance with the regulations for the Tripos. Applications must be made before the division of the Michaelmas Term before the examination.

To obtain a Certificate of Competent Knowledge the candidate must attain a standard not lower than the second class in the corresponding papers in Part I of the Tripos.[1]

A list of the topics prescribed for the oral examinations for the Certificate of Competent Knowledge in **1985** is available from the Faculty Office.

Examinations in modern languages for the Ordinary B.A. Degree

There are Ordinary Examinations in Czech (with Slovak), Danish, Dutch, French, German, Italian, Modern Greek, Norwegian, Polish, Portuguese, Russian, Serbo-Croat, Spanish, and Swedish. In each language the examination consists of an oral examination and three written papers:

(1) Passages from works in the foreign language for translation.

(2) Passages of English for translation into the foreign language.

(3) An essay in the foreign language on a subject of a general character.

The written papers and the prescribed topics for the oral examinations in any year are the same as *either* (*a*) those for the Preliminary

[1] For the purposes of the Ordinary B.A. Degree, a candidate who attains this standard is deemed to have passed a Special Examination, and a candidate who does not do so may be allowed a Special Examination.

Examination for Part I of the Tripos, *or* (*b*) those for Part I of the Tripos.

A student who has been classed in, or received an allowance on, the Preliminary Examination for Part I of the Modern and Medieval Languages Tripos, or who has received an allowance on Part I of the Tripos, shall not offer option (*a*).

A student may not count towards the Ordinary B.A. Degree both the Ordinary Examination in a modern language and also anything that he has to his credit in the same language as the result of another examination.

M.Phil. in Linguistics

A one-year course leading to the degree of Master of Philosophy is offered by the Department of Linguistics. Candidates will normally be expected to possess at least a good Upper Second Class degree or its equivalent. The course will comprise: (*a*) in the Michaelmas Term lectures and classes in the following areas: theoretical linguistics, phonetics, phonology, syntax, semantics and pragmatics; (*b*) in the Lent Term seminars in the following areas: (i) phonetics and phonology; (ii) syntax, semantics and pragmatics; (iii) any two from a list of topics announced by the Degree Committee of Modern and Medieval Languages, such as: language universals, history of linguistics, sociolinguistics, applied linguistics. By the end of the Easter Vacation candidates must submit four studies of not more than 5,000 words each (excluding footnotes, tables, appendices, and bibliography), one from each of the four seminars attended. At the end of the Easter Term candidates must submit a dissertation of not more than 15,000 words (excluding footnotes, tables, appendices, and bibliography) on a topic chosen by themselves, subject to the approval of the Degree Committee.

MUSIC

The Music Tripos

The Music Tripos consists of three Parts: Part I A, Part I B, and Part II.

The normal programme for an undergraduate who intends to spend three years reading music will be as follows:

Part I A of the Tripos at the end of the first year
Part I B of the Tripos at the end of the second year
Part II of the Tripos at the end of the third year

The attainment of honours in Part I B is an essential qualification for taking Part II.

Part I A

Subjects of examination:

1. Harmony

Candidates will be required to compose a complete theme and set it as it might appear in a classical sonata, write an accompaniment for a given melody in an eighteenth- or early nineteenth-century idiom, and write simple variations on a ground or chord sequence.

2. Counterpoint

Candidates will be required to work counterpoint in sixteenth-century style in not more than four parts, including the setting of a Latin text, and a canon in two parts above a bass.

3. History of music

Questions will be set on the development of European music in the period 1550–1750 in its various manifestations: opera, sacred and secular vocal music, solo instrumental music, chamber music, and concerto.

4. Analysis and notation

Extracts from compositions of the period 1550–1750 will be provided for analysis and comment. A facsimile from the period 1550–1620 will be provided for transcription and editing, with extracts from modern editions thereof for comment.

5. Set work

An extended movement in the Viennese classical style will be prescribed not less than two weeks before the date of the written paper. Candidates will be permitted to bring unmarked copies of the score into the examination and will be required to answer questions on it.

Practical examination

Aural tests will include a memorization test (melodies), dictation exercises (four-part chorale harmonization and three-part counterpoint), a mistake-spotting test, and aural analysis (a movement from the period 1700–1830).

Keyboard tests will include the reading of a score of a string quartet, of a vocal score with C clefs, the harmonizing of a given melody, and the realizing of a figured bass at the keyboard.

A candidate must offer all five papers and take the practical examination.

Part IB

Subjects of examination:

1. Stylistic composition (also serves as Paper 7 of Part II)

Candidates will be required to demonstrate their knowledge of a composer's distinctive style by completing settings of which only one part throughout or the *incipit* alone will be provided in the examination paper. Candidates will be given a choice of settings and will be required to answer questions on one or more of the composers prescribed. The composers prescribed are:

For **1985**: Byrd, Victoria.
For **1986**: Purcell, Corelli.

2. Subjects in the history of music (also serves as Paper 2 of Part II)

This paper will be divided into at least two sections, for each of which a separate subject will be prescribed. Candidates will be required to answer questions from at least two of the sections. The subjects prescribed in **1985** are:

Music of the Western Court and Church, 1320–1420.
Cross-currents and contradictions, 1920 to the present day.
Symphony and sonata, 1760–1828.
The symphony from Berlioz to Mahler.
Art music of North Africa and the Near East.

3. Analysis

Short pieces or extracts of extended forms, including compositions of twentieth-century composers, will be provided in the examination for analysis and comment.

4. Acoustics

Nature of sound; noise and musical sound; transmission of sound, especially in relation to buildings. Sound production and the acoustics of musical instruments. Temperament. Hearing. Principles of recording and reproduction. Candidates will be expected to show an understanding of the physical principles involved, but questions demanding a specialized knowledge of mathematics or physics will not be asked.

Portfolio of tonal compositions

Candidates will be required to submit a portfolio of two tonal compositions in different forms chosen from the following: sonata, rondo, scherzo, variations, ternary slow movement, ritornello. Each composition shall be of not more than five minutes' duration and shall be for an ensemble of not more than five players.

Practical examination

Aural tests will include a memorization test (two-part counterpoint), a mistake-spotting test, aural analysis, and a test related to the perception of orchestral timbres.

Keyboard tests will include reading an orchestral score, realizing a figured bass at the keyboard, harmonizing a melody, and transposition.

A candidate must offer Papers 2–4, take the practical examination, and offer *either* Paper 1 *or* the portfolio of tonal compositions. The portfolio, if offered, must be submitted through the candidate's Tutor to the Chairman of Examiners so as to reach him not later than the fifteenth day of Full Easter Term and the compositions must have been written during the previous twelve months. Each work must be initialled by the lecturer or supervisor under whose direction the work was done, as an indication that he approves the submission.

Part II

Subjects of examination:

1. Fugal forms

Candidates will be required to compose *either* a fugue in not more than four parts from a choice of subjects, *or* a chorale prelude or chaconne with fugal elements on a given chorale or bass.

2. Subjects in the history of music (see Paper 2 of Part IB)

The subjects in **1985** will be:

Music of the Western Court and Church, 1320–1420.
Cross-currents and contradictions, 1920 to the present day.
Symphony and sonata, 1760–1828.
The symphony from Berlioz to Mahler.
Art music of North Africa and the Near East.

3. Analysis

Candidates will be required to choose one from the list of prescribed compositions and to answer questions on it. They will be permitted to bring unmarked copies into the examination.

4 and 5. Notation of early music I and II

Candidates will be required to transcribe and edit from original sources, and to evaluate editorial practices and techniques. Paper 5 will include questions on the history of notation, the relationship between notation and composition, and questions on appropriate periods of the history of music falling within the period 1350–1650.

6. History of performance practice

The study of notations, performance conventions, instrumental techniques and, where relevant, organology.

7. Stylistic composition (see Paper 1 of Part IB)

8–13. Additional papers

Additional papers may include subjects such as those shown in the following list: Ars Nova, Asian musics, Stravinsky, Elgar, Organ music of J. S. Bach.

The papers in **1985** will be:

8. Mode and melody in Asian music.

9. The music of Aaron Copland.
10. Berg's operas.
11. Byrd.
12. Theatre orchestration.

Portfolio of tonal compositions (see Part IB)

Portfolio of free compositions

Candidates will be required to submit a portfolio of four compositions which shall include a fugal composition and a setting of words in not less than three vocal parts. The compositions must be presented in normal staff notation.

Dissertation

A dissertation, of not less than 6,000 and not more than 7,000 words (exclusive of appendices), on a musical subject of the candidate's choice approved by the Faculty Board falling wholly or substantially outside the subjects chosen by the candidate for Paper 2 of Part II and for any of Papers 8–13 that he may choose to offer. The subject of the dissertation proposed by the candidate must be submitted through his Tutor to the Secretary of the Faculty Board so as to reach him not later than the end of the Full Michaelmas Term preceding the examination and approval must be obtained from the Faculty Board not later than the end of the first quarter of the Lent Term.

Test of performance

(*a*) *on an historical instrument*

Candidates will be required to demonstrate the technical and musical aspects of performance on their chosen instrument, by presenting a recital of not longer than fifteen minutes' playing time which shall include one piece set by the Examiners after consultation with the candidate during the Michaelmas Term preceding the examination. Candidates must inform the Secretary of the Faculty Board not later than the division of that term of the instrument chosen, and details of the complete programme must be sent through the candidate's Tutor to the Secretary of the Faculty Board for approval, so as to reach him not later than the division of the Lent Term preceding the examination. The candidates will be questioned by the Examiners on matters relevant to their recitals.

(*b*) *on a modern instrument*, *or in singing*

The test will consist of a recital of not more than eighteen minutes' playing time, including a piece or a song (or songs) prescribed not later than the end of the Michaelmas Term preceding the examination. Candidates must inform the Secretary of the Faculty Board not later than the division of that term of the instrument chosen or type of voice, and details of the complete programme must be sent through the candidate's Tutor to the Secretary of the Faculty Board for approval, so as to reach him not later than the division of the Lent Term preceding the examination.

Candidates for the Test of Performance should note that they must make their own arrangements to provide an accompanist or page turner or both, if required, and that they should bring to the examination two copies of the pieces to be performed.

Interview

The Examiners are empowered for the purpose of drawing up the class-list for Part II to request a candidate to present himself for interview on matters arising from the examination, but they shall take account of that interview only if it would be to the candidate's advantage.

A candidate for Part II shall offer Papers 1, 2 and 3, and

either (*a*) four other papers chosen from Papers 4–13,

or (*b*) a combination which amounts to four papers and options, chosen from Papers 4–13 and from the options numbered (i)–(iv) below:

(i) the portfolio of tonal compositions,
(ii) the portfolio of free compositions,
(iii) the dissertation,
(iv) the test of performance *either* on an historical instrument *or* on a modern instrument, *or* in singing,

provided always that

(1) no candidate shall offer for Paper 2 any subject which he has already offered for Paper 2 of Part I B,
(2) neither of Papers 4 and 5 shall be offered without the other,
(3) no candidate who offered Paper 1 in Part I B shall offer Paper 7,
(4) no candidate who offered the portfolio of tonal compositions in Part I B shall offer option (i),
(5) a candidate who offers option (iv) shall also offer Paper 6.

The portfolio of tonal compositions or free compositions, if offered, must be submitted in the same manner as the portfolio of tonal compositions in Part IB (see above).

The dissertation, if offered, must be submitted through the candidate's Tutor to the Chairman of Examiners so as to reach him not later than the eighth day of Full Easter Term. The Examiners shall have power to require the candidate to resubmit his dissertation in typescript if, in their opinion, the original work submitted is not sufficiently legible.

The degree of Bachelor of Music (new regulations)*

A student who has obtained honours in any Part of the Music Tripos may, in his third year or later, be a candidate for the Mus.B. Examination (he cannot in the same year be a candidate both for the Mus.B. and for any other University examination except that for the Certificate of Competent Knowledge in a Modern Language).

The examination consists of two Sections, as follows:

Section I

An instrumental or vocal recital. Candidates must submit a programme lasting approximately ninety minutes of instrumental or vocal music. From this the Examiners will hear a recital of at least forty minutes' music. Each candidate must be responsible for providing his own accompanist and page turner, where required, and must provide an additional copy of the works for the Examiners.

Section II

(*a*) A dissertation of between 10,000 and 15,000 words (excluding appendices) on a subject chosen from a list of subjects announced by the Faculty Board not later than 1 April of the year preceding the examination concerned.

The subjects announced for **1985** are:

1. Eighteenth-century organ music.
2. Nineteenth-century solo piano music.
3. Historical treatises and performance tutors.
4. Choral institutions and performance during the fifteenth and sixteenth centuries.
5. Methods of musical notation, 1925–1975.
6. Twentieth-century composers as their own interpreters.

* The old regulations, which are set out in the *Handbook* for 1981–82, remain in force until 1987 to enable candidates who have already passed one Section of the examination under those regulations to take another Section to complete the requirements for the degree.

(*b*) A paper of three hours' duration on the background of the subject of the candidate's dissertation. A candidate may be examined orally on questions arising from his recital or dissertation.

The two Sections of the examination must be taken together, whether at a candidate's first attempt or at any subsequent attempt, except that if a candidate has failed in not more than one Section he may be allowed to present himself for re-examination in that Section alone.

A candidate must send to the Secretary of the Faculty Board of Music, not later than the division of the Michaelmas Term preceding the examination, a list of the works that he proposes to perform, for approval by the Faculty Board, and, not later than 1 December preceding the examination, the subject of his dissertation. He must submit his dissertation to the Secretary not later than the eighth day of Full Easter Term.

M.Phil. Degree in Musical Composition

This is a one-year course of study in Musical Composition. The examination consists of:

(*a*) Two written papers, each of three hours' duration:

1. Analytical studies in the music of a composer, including appropriate consideration of the background and literature about his work.
2. *either* (i) The problems and methods of teaching composition in a period of the history of music,
   or (ii) the theories and philosophies of twentieth-century music.

The candidate's choice of composer for Paper 1 and, if he chooses Paper 2(i), of a period of the history of music, will be subject to the approval of the Degree Committee for the Faculty of Music.

(*b*) Two compositions which must be notated in a conventional manner:

(i) a composition incorporating fugal elements, requiring not less than five and not more than ten minutes to perform, for five-part chorus or for at least three melody instruments and piano;

(ii) a composition, requiring not less than twelve and not more than fifteen minutes to perform, for a large chamber ensemble or orchestra with or without soloists and/or chorus; this composition may be in any idiom of the candidate's choice.

The composition must be submitted to the Secretary of the Board of Graduate Studies not later than 31 August.

The examination will at the Examiners' discretion include an oral examination.

M.Phil. Degree in Musicology

This is a one-year course of study in Musicology. The examination consists of:

(*a*) a thesis of not more than 25,000 words in length (inclusive of tables, footnotes, and appendices, but excluding bibliography, music examples, and transcriptions) on a subject in the history of music approved by the Degree Committee for the Faculty of Music;

(*b*) an exercise consisting of:

either (i) a transcription of a piece or pieces of music, with editorial commentary and full introduction,

or (ii) a full analysis of a piece or pieces of music.

The candidate's choice of music will be subject to the approval of the Degree Committee.

The thesis and exercise must be submitted to the Secretary of the Board of Graduate Studies not later than 31 August.

The examination will at the Examiners' discretion include an oral examination on the thesis and the exercise and on the general field of knowledge within which it falls.

NATURAL SCIENCES

In the Natural Sciences there are courses of study followed by candidates for:

The *Natural Sciences Tripos*, which is divided into four Parts.

The *Preliminary Examinations for Part II and for Section II of Part II (General) of the Natural Sciences Tripos.*

Ordinary Examinations in the Natural Sciences for the Ordinary B.A. Degree.

Certificates of Post-graduate Study in Natural Science.

The *M.Phil. Degree* (one-year courses) in *Applied Biology, Biochemistry, History and Philosophy of Science, Pharmacology, Plant Breeding*, and *Quaternary Research.*

The Natural Sciences Tripos

The Natural Sciences Tripos is divided into four Parts – I A, I B, II, and II (General). It is possible for a candidate to take all four Parts, which will take him four years, but normally he spends three years on taking three Parts. Part I A has to be taken in a candidate's first year (except that a candidate transferring from another Tripos may take Part I A in his third year). Part I B has to be taken in a candidate's second year, and Part II or Part II (General) in his third or fourth year.

It is possible to transfer, after passing Part I A or Part I B, to another Tripos. The new subjects taken up will depend on the candidate's interests, but common transfers are to Law or Economics after either Part I A or Part I B, and to Part II Engineering, Electrical Sciences or Part I Chemical Engineering after Part I B. Transfer to the Mathematical Tripos after Part I A, Part I B, or Part II is also possible and may be appropriate for those interested in theoretical physics. Transfer to Medicine is a special case, on which detailed advice is required, but in general it may be said that it is possible for a candidate who has passed Part I A to complete in another two years all courses necessary to prepare him for clinical work, either (if he has not read Physiology in Part I A) by transfer to the Medical Sciences Tripos, or by reading appropriate subjects in Part I B of the Natural Sciences Tripos and then transferring to the Medical Sciences Tripos.

Transfers from other Triposes to the Natural Sciences Tripos are also possible. Some intending physicists may find it worthwhile to take Part I A of the Engineering or of the Mathematical Tripos and then transfer to Part IB Natural Sciences in Advanced Physics and Mathematics, and Part II Natural Sciences in Physics and Theoretical Physics. Transfer to Part II Genetics from other Triposes, especially the Medical Sciences Tripos, may be made. Transfer to Part II Psychology is also possible in certain circumstances, particularly from the Philosophy Tripos, and various Triposes provide a satisfactory basis for transfer to History and Philosophy of Science in Part II (General).

An affiliated student may: (*a*) take Part IB of the Tripos in his first year; (*b*) if the Faculty Board concerned permit, take Part II of the Tripos or, if the History and Philosophy of Science Syndicate permit, take Section II of Part II (General) of the Tripos, in his first or second year as if he had obtained honours in Part IB.

Part IA

Candidates are required to offer three of the following subjects for Part IA:

- Biology of Cells
- Biology of Organisms
- Chemistry
- Crystalline Materials
- Geology
- Physics
- Physiology

They may also offer Mathematics, Biological Mathematics, or Elementary Mathematics for Biologists as a fourth subject if they wish to do so.

The structure of Part IA is such as to encourage the study of at least one subject not previously studied by a candidate at school. The knowledge that candidates are assumed already to possess is indicated in the descriptions of each subject. Candidates offering Physics or Chemistry need to have studied that subject to Advanced level in the G.C.E. Examination, but the teaching of the other experimental subjects in Part IA is so designed as to provide for candidates with no previous knowledge of those subjects.

Biology of Cells. The course aims to provide a basic introduction to biology at the cellular level, and considers what cells are, what they look like, and how they work. The Biology of Cells course is complete in its own right, but it also provides a useful introduction to further studies in biology, for both biologists and non-biologists. The course is organized jointly by the Departments of Biochemistry, Botany,

Genetics, and Zoology. All Lecturers for the course issue printed lecture notes.

In the first term, the lectures deal with the basic structure of cells, with the structure and function of cell membranes, and with the essential biochemistry of cell metabolism. The second term's lectures are concerned with viruses; with genetics (including both the inheritance of genetic information and its expression in the cell) and protein synthesis; and with cell growth and multiplication. The lectures in the Easter Term are concerned with cells in multicellular organisms. An examination of mechanisms of cell differentiation and pattern formation leads to consideration of cell interaction and communication. Then various specialized cell functions are discussed. These include such topics as motility, the cellular basis of the immune response, secretion and neurobiology.

The practical side of the course is organized so that, as far as possible, the experiments are related to the subject matter of the concurrent lecture course.

Those who have 'A' level Biology find this a help, as much of the course will be familiar to them. Since Cell Biology is still an expanding field, however, recent material is included and many of the topics are treated in greater detail and often from a different viewpoint from 'A' level courses. Students without 'A' level Biology are not at a disadvantage, except that they will find that initially they have to assimilate a large amount of factual information; because of this, such students will find it useful to have done some preliminary reading before coming up. Knowledge of 'A' level Chemistry is assumed, and students would be unwise to take the course without this qualification.

Biology of Organisms. As its title implies, this course is intended to complement the Biology of Cells course: most, but not all, students studying 'Organisms' also study 'Cells'. The course is given jointly by the Departments of Botany, Genetics, and Zoology and aims at introducing students to the variety of multicellular organisms, their adaptations, and the genetical mechanisms underlying adaptation in general.

In the first term two parallel approaches will be made to a study of the range and variety of animals. One is concerned with the evolutionary relationships and functional anatomy of most of the major groups (which will be looked at also in the Practical classes) except for the Vertebrates to be studied in the second year. The second approach, which will include vertebrate examples, deals with animal engineering, and the extent to which the range of shapes and sizes, and the performance of animals, is limited by the nature of biological materials and of the physical world in which animals have evolved.

The second term deals with two major groups of organisms: the seed plants (16 lectures) and the fungi (8 lectures). The general aim is to show what has led to the wide distribution and diversity of these groups during evolution. The lectures on seed plants deal with the integration of plant structure, biochemistry, physiology and development throughout the life cycle of seed plants. A range of plant types are analysed in this way, illustrating adaptations which enable the seed plants to colonise a variety of environments. The lectures on fungi, in addition to considering their range of form and mode of growth and such comparable topics as adaptations to dry and wet environments, emphasize their role in the carbon cycle and their inter-relations with seed plants as parasites. The practical classes are closely related to the lectures and involve both observation and experiment.

In the third term there is a consideration of the processes of evolution. This course is designed to consider the mechanisms which may have influenced the development and diversification of life on earth. After a brief introduction to evolutionary theories, molecular evolution will be considered to show how similarities and differences between amino-acid sequences of particular proteins can give an indication of phylogenetic relationships between species. Changes in chromosomal arrangements will be treated in a similar way, and will lead on to a consideration of the various levels at which variation within a species can be studied and how it may be measured. The way such variation is propagated through various natural breeding systems will then be investigated (sexual versus asexual reproduction, inbreeding versus outbreeding). The enormous quantity of genetic variation within and between species provides a basis for a consideration of the evidence for natural selection, the way natural selection operates and the other factors which may affect the maintenance of genetic variations in a population. Geographical variation within species may be produced as an outcome of selection, and the conditions under which this may lead to speciation are discussed. Finally, there is a summary of the relevance to human populations and races of the principles of evolutionary change which have been developed in the course.

Although most students taking this course will have done at least one biological subject at A-level, this is not essential, but students who have not done an ‘A’ level in Biology are advised to consult their Colleges about doing some preliminary reading before coming up.

Chemistry. This is a general course containing aspects of organic, inorganic, and physical chemistry appropriate to provide an integrated background for the later study of chemistry as a whole. A previous knowledge of chemistry up to Advanced level in G.C.E. is assumed. Practical work is an essential part of the course and is particularly geared towards the illustration of modern techniques and general principles.

This foundation course is designed to emphasize the scope of modern chemistry and its central position as an enabling subject for many other disciplines.

Crystalline Materials. This course is presented jointly by the Departments of Metallurgy and Materials Science, and of Earth Sciences. It covers the study of the internal structure of crystalline solids and its relationship to important properties of materials. Specific topics treated include the crystal structure and chemical stability of simple materials, deformation and dislocations, study of materials by diffraction and by optical and electron microscopy, phase transformations, and the influence of the structural make-up of materials on selected physical and mechanical properties. The practical work is closely related to the lectures and forms an essential part of the course.

The Crystalline Materials course serves as an introduction to all aspects of the study of the solid state. It is highly desirable preparation for those intending to read Crystalline State, Mineralogy and Petrology, or Metallurgy and Materials Science in Part IB, and it is valuable for all physical scientists. No prior knowledge of crystallography is assumed.

Geology. The course is an introduction to the whole field of earth science. It covers the nature and properties of the Earth, particularly of the mantle and the crust; observed and deduced processes of change; biological, physical, and chemical methods of dating; and major economic considerations. It illustrates the principles of geology as they apply to a broadscale picture of a segment of the Earth. Emphasis is placed on practical and field work including general identifications and interpretation of rocks, interpretation of geological maps of large areas, and the use of fossils and rocks in determining the successive changes in the crustal environment. Much of the course is concerned with application of principles of physics, chemistry, and biology to rocks and their distribution, so that a school background in some or all of these subjects is a good preparation. Previous knowledge of geology is not necessary: it is recommended that any study of geology preliminary to the course should include the maximum of field experience.

Physics. The year starts with an introductory course on fundamentals, covering mechanics, gravitation, relativity, and quantum theory. Further lectures follow on thermal physics, electromagnetism, and vibrations. The course assumes familiarity with physics and mathematics at Advanced level in G.C.E. The mathematical skill required is such that a candidate who does not also offer either the A or B course in Part IA Mathematics will be at some disadvantage. Practical work (4 hours per week) is an essential part of the course.

Physiology. The biology of living organism includes consideration of structure and function. Physiology is primarily the study of function, though it inevitably involves some study of structure, particularly of the fine structure of tissues and cells.

The course does not assume any previous knowledge of biology, and in fact, for many of the topics studied, those students who have read physics and chemistry and possibly mathematics at school find that these constitute a groundwork as useful as that given by biological subjects. Physiology therefore forms an eminently suitable third subject for those Tripos candidates who are primarily interested in the physical sciences but also wish to cover a biological subject.

The first-year course can be taken simply as a one-year course or as the first part of a two-year course. It does not attempt to cover all aspects of physiology but studies selected topics in considerable detail and these topics are not dealt with again in the second year. The course concentrates on vertebrate, mammalian, and human physiology. It starts with a detailed study of the mechanisms of nerve conduction and muscle contraction, both from the physico-chemical and biological aspects. The circulatory, respiratory, and excretory mechanisms and the processes of intestinal absorption, energy balance and thermoregulation, together with their control systems, are studied in relation to the need to maintain the stability of the internal environment. A considerable proportion of the course is devoted to practical work, particularly in experimental and histological studies.

Mathematics. This subject is principally designed for physical scientists who have studied mathematics to Advanced level in G.C.E. There are two courses which differ in their level.

The A course is the easier of the two and includes lectures on calculus, vector algebra, matrices, ordinary and partial differential equations, and statistics. The B course covers all the material of the A course and also contains an introduction to vector analysis. It is more difficult than the A course, and it should only be attended by students who are well prepared in mathematics. Those who intend to continue with mathematics in Part IB of the Tripos will find it an advantage to attend the B course in Part IA but this is not a necessity.

Biological Mathematics. This subject is designed to show how biological understanding can be enhanced by the sensible use of mathematical techniques. It is intended for students who have taken one subject mathematics at Advanced level in the G.C.E. (or its equivalent). The material is presented through particular biological examples drawn from biochemistry, animal and plant physiology, ecology, genetics. Mathematical topics include simple treatments of ordinary differential equations, the diffusion equation, vector algebra, matrix algebra, probability, statistics, and computing. The lectures are supplemented by classes.

Elementary Mathematics for Biologists. This subject is designed to cover those parts of elementary mathematics that are of immediate use to biologists. No knowledge of mathematics is assumed beyond that required for mathematics at Ordinary level in G.C.E. The course consists of elementary calculus, an introduction to differential equations, statistics and computing; the lectures are supplemented by classes.

Part IB

Candidates are required to offer either two subjects or three subjects for Part IB, not more than one subject being chosen from any one of the nine groups set out below. If only two subjects are being offered one of them must be Advanced Physics or Advanced Chemistry.

(i) Chemistry; Advanced Chemistry.
(ii) Pathology; Physics; Advanced Physics.
(iii) Animal Biology; Metallurgy and Materials Science.
(iv) Crystalline State; Physiology.
(v) Biochemistry; Mineralogy and Petrology.

(vi) Plant Biology; Experimental Psychology; Fluid Mechanics.
(vii) Environmental Biology; Mathematics; Pharmacology.
(viii) Stratigraphic Geology.
(ix) History and Philosophy of Science.

Advanced Chemistry and Advanced Physics may not be offered together, nor may Stratigraphic Geology be offered together with either Advanced Chemistry or Advanced Physics. Mathematics may not be offered together with only one other subject unless the candidate has previously attained a qualifying standard in Mathematics in Part I A, or unless he has been placed in a class not lower than the second class in Part I A of the Engineering Tripos, or been classed in Part I A of the Mathematical Tripos, or is an Affiliated Student. A candidate may not offer Mathematics if he has previously obtained honours in Part I B of the Mathematical Tripos. No subject, other than Physiology, may be offered which has already been offered in the Medical Sciences Tripos.

Animal Biology. This course follows the Part I A courses in Biology of Cells, Biology of Organisms, and Physiology. Most students will have read at least two of these in Part I A; a minority come across from the 'physical' side, having read only Biology of Cells in Part I A. Centred on the Department of Zoology, the course consists of two streams one of which emphasises 'whole animal' biology and the other emphasises various cellular aspects. The streams provide options so that a series of choices is available throughout the course. Students may elect to take all 'whole animal' options, all cellular options or a mixture of both. The first term begins with an option on behavioural ecology, considering how animal species adapt to their environment, and an *alternative* option on molecular strategies (common to Animal and Plant Biology courses). The following alternative options deal with insect biology *or* with molecular biology of the cell nucleus. The first options of the Lent Term cover vertebrate biology (structure, function, evolution and development) *or* structure and function of cell cytoplasm. These are followed by options dealing with the ways in which the brains of a wide range of animals function in the control and integration of behaviour *or* parasitism and immunity, examining various aspects of the host–parasite relationship. In the third term there are again two options, one dealing with comparative physiology (including ionic and thermal regulation, respiration and metabolism) *or* one dealing with animal development (emphasising experimental studies).

Biochemistry. The aim of this course is to describe, in molecular terms, how DNA stores information and expresses it to enable cells to function as integrated and highly controlled metabolic systems, and to differentiate into the diverse organs that go to make up plants and animals. Consequently, the course initially emphasizes the theme 'The flow of information', in which lectures are presented that include discussions of DNA structure and function, the control of gene expression, the mechanisms of translation of such information into the structure of proteins, the various forms in which proteins occur and how they function, the intracellular sorting of proteins and the manner in which they span and cross cell membranes. Thereafter, the course emphasizes the theme 'Metabolism and the control of energy supply'. It shows how plants transduce solar to chemical energy and harness it in photosynthesis, and how the controlled degradation of the products of photosynthesis enables animals and micro-organisms to release that energy and use it for biosynthetic and other energy-requiring purposes. The course also describes how antibodies are made and how they function, and discusses some of the ways in which our knowledge of biochemistry can be utilized for the benefit of man, as biotechnology.

Although the course may be approached from any first-year courses in biological or physical subjects, Biology of Cells is regarded as the usual and most useful preparation.

Advanced Chemistry and Chemistry. The Advanced Chemistry course develops the subjects of physical, inorganic, and organic chemistry to a considerably greater depth and range than in Part I A and, in addition, includes aspects of theoretical chemistry. Those proposing to take chemistry in Part II are normally expected to take the Advanced Chemistry course.

The Chemistry course is less comprehensive. It comprises an initial core course covering physical, inorganic, and organic chemistry followed by a choice of two optional continuations, one designed principally for biochemists and biologists, the other mainly for chemical engineers and metallurgists.

There are no practical examinations for either Advanced Chemistry or Chemistry but the laboratory work is continually assessed.

Crystalline State. The purpose of this course is to extend the understanding of the basic theory of crystalline matter and of the techniques for its study acquired in Part I A Crystalline Materials, and to show how, with this more advanced knowledge, particular problems in the solid state can be tackled. Topics in the course include: the interaction of X-rays, electrons, and neutrons with crystals (both diffraction and image formation, including crystal structure determination); the anisotropy of physical properties; non-stoichiometry; the search for compounds with specific properties; solid-state transformations. Laboratory practicals and paper demonstrations are closely linked to the lectures.

This course, given in the Earth Sciences Department, is a valuable second subject for physicists and chemists. It is complementary to Metallurgy and Materials Science on the one hand, and to Part IB Mineralogy and Petrology on the other, and it is essential for the Mineral Sciences option in Part II Geological Sciences.

Environmental Biology. This course, run jointly by the Departments of Applied Biology, Botany, Genetics and Zoology, is concerned with the biotic and abiotic components of ecological systems and the interactions between them. Starting from general considerations of the structure and dynamics of ecosystems and populations detailed treatments are developed in four major areas; ecological genetics, the aerial environment with emphasis on energy and its utilization by plants, the nature and features of aquatic systems, and the special features of soils. A discussion of man and his environment closes the course. At all stages any necessary physical and chemical material is closely integrated with coverage of the nature and responses of organisms. Practicals, which are assessed for examination purposes, include both set material and the possibility of individual work.

The Part IA Biology of Organisms course is a valuable, though not essential, previous study. The important preliminary Long Vacation course is especially advised for students unfamiliar with the range of plants and animals or without any geological background. Environmental Biology should be attractive to students with interests in ecology and applied biology and makes a valuable introduction to Part II courses in Applied Biology, Botany, Genetics and Zoology.

Experimental Psychology. Experimental Psychology attempts to use the methods of natural science to understand the behaviour and mental processes of human beings and animals. The course is intended to provide an introduction to experimental findings and related theories on the following topics: how human beings perceive the world, process and remember information; language, thought, and intelligence and the development of these processes and abilities in childhood; motivation, learning, and memory, how these may be studied in animals, and what brain processes may underlie them; abnormal psychology and mental illness and how research in experimental psychology may help us to understand them. The course does not include any work in social psychology.

Most parts of the course are accompanied by practical work, which include individual and group experiments on human or animal behaviour, demonstrations, and films. There will be teaching on the applications of elementary psychological statistics and on basic neurobiology for non-biologists. It is useful, although not essential, to have some previous knowledge of biology such as would be gained by taking Biology of Organisms, Physiology, or both, in Part IA. Some knowledge of physical science or of mathematics is a valuable alternative preparation for the course.

Fluid Mechanics (and Transfer Processes). The course includes lectures on the fundamentals of fluid motion, dynamical similarity, flow in pipes and channels and the motion in boundary layers, rotating machinery, fluid/particle systems, drops, bubbles and foams. The section on transfer processes deals with heat transfer, the analogy between heat, mass and momentum transfer and simultaneous heat and mass transfer. There are a corresponding laboratory course and examples classes.

History and Philosophy of Science. The course is intended to introduce the student to some of the historical and philosophical problems relating to the rise of science in Western civilization and to the nature of scientific knowledge. Examples are taken from many different branches of science, and students will be able to concentrate to some extent on the history and philosophy of the sciences that interest them. Students are expected to read a substantial amount of material in the subject, including some original sources. Further details of the courses, and recommended reading for the previous Long Vacation, are available from the Department. The examination consists of two papers, one with questions of a primarily historical character, the other with questions on more philosophical topics.

Mathematics. This course is especially useful for students intending to study Physics and Theoretical Physics in Part II. It is also attended by students taking Chemistry. The following topics are included: introduction to group theory; more advanced matrix theory; Cartesian tensors; more advanced theory of differential equations (including solution in power series and expansions in characteristic functions); Fourier and Laplace transforms; calculus of variations; functions of a complex variable. An opportunity is provided for practical work in numerical analysis using a computer.

Metallurgy and Materials Science. Through a systematic study of the scientific principles involved this course aims to provide an understanding of the reasons underlying the selection and use of materials, metallic and non-metallic, in a wide range of applications from electronic through structural to electrochemical. Topics covered include: the development and optimization of microstructures; extraction and production of materials; electrochemistry, including corrosion and degradation; mechanical and physical properties and their control; fabrication of materials.

Study of the subject Crystalline Materials in Part I A is a desirable, although not essential, preparation. Whilst this course is self-contained and so can usefully be taken by those planning to proceed to Part II in another subject, it also forms an important prerequisite for Metallurgy and Materials Science in Part II.

Mineralogy and Petrology. The nature and formation of igneous and metamorphic minerals and rocks form the core of this course, together with methods of their determination such as optics, diffraction, isotope analysis and phase equilibrium studies. This traditional 'hard rock' geology course concludes by considering the build-up of a complete orogenic belt. Practical work and map analysis are emphasized, and there is a Field Course in the Easter Vacation.

The course develops one half of Geology but is complete in itself. Together with the complementary subject Stratigraphic Geology it leads on to Part II Geological Sciences.

Pathology. This is a course in general pathology, treated from the standpoint of abnormal biology. It includes the variations which may occur in disease in the structure and functions of living cells, tissues and organs and discusses the causes of such changes. The course includes morbid anatomy and histology, immunology, and microbiology with particular emphasis on the biology of bacteria and viruses. Practical classes are an important feature of the course and are integrated as far as possible with the lectures. The course is thus suitable for all biological students though primarily designed as an introduction to the systematic pathology included in the clinical curriculum for degrees in medicine and veterinary medicine.

Pharmacology. The emphasis of the course is on pharmacology considered as the action of chemical substances on biological systems and in particular the mechanisms by which drugs produce their actions considered at the molecular, sub-cellular, and cellular levels. A knowledge of the basic biochemistry and physiology of living systems is an advantage. The practical course is designed in parallel to the lecture course to illustrate the principles by which pharmacological actions can be assessed.

Physics and Advanced Physics. The *Physics* course is designed for those who intend to offer some subject other than Physics in Part II. It is also a preparation for Metallurgy and Materials Science in Part II. It includes practical work (about four hours a week) and lecture courses on waves and imaging instruments, quantum physics, and energy physics. A knowledge of Part I A *Physics* is assumed.

The *Advanced Physics* course is designed mainly for those who intend going on to *Physics and Theoretical Physics* in Part II, but it is also a useful, though not essential, preparation for Metallurgy and Materials Science in Part II, or for the Electrical Sciences Tripos. It includes six hours a week of practical work and twice as many lectures as the *Physics* course. The lectures cover electromagnetism, dynamics, wave mechanics, optics, thermodynamics, and quantum physics. A knowledge of Part I A *Physics* is assumed. There is a solid state physics course of lectures on symmetry properties of solids for those who have not taken Crystalline Materials in their first year, and who wish to proceed to *Physics* Part II, and an optional course of lectures on mathematical methods for those who are not attending the Mathematics course for Part I B.

There are further examples classes on computing and mathematical methods and optional lectures on analytical dynamics which are especially important for those who contemplate specializing in theoretical physics in *Physics* Part II.

Physiology. The course is designed as a continuation of the Physiology Part I A course but students who elect to read Physiology

I B without having attended the Part I A course will not be placed at a significant disadvantage, since most of the Part I B course does not require a previous study of Physiology. The major topics that are covered include an extensive study of endocrine organs and their control systems, the physiology of reproduction in selected species and the functioning of the eye, the ear, the brain, and the spinal cord.

Plant Biology. This subject continues the study, begun in the Part I A courses on Biology of Cells and Biology of Organisms, of higher and lower plants, their structures, physiology, biochemistry, genetics and ecology; there is no overlap with the subject *Environmental Biology*. Centred on the Department of Botany, but with contributions from the Department of Genetics, this course has a series of internal options, enabling the student to follow plant cell biology courses or whole organism plant biology courses through the year. The first term starts with alternative courses on plants, pathogens and partners or on molecular strategies of gene organization and expression; these are followed by alternative courses on aquatic microbiology, phytoplankton, and seaweeds or on plant cell manipulation. The second term offers two parallel alternative courses, one on plant metabolism, the other on land plant evolution, palaeoecology and plant distribution. The third term's course also offers two alternatives, one dealing with experimental taxonomy and ecology, the other with the regulation of development in plants. It will be noted that the options dealing with plant development complement analogous developmental options in the *Animal Biology* course. Most students selecting this subject will have read Biology of Cells and/or Biology of Organisms in their first year.

Stratigraphic Geology. The traditional 'soft rock' aspects of Geology, including evolutionary palaeontology and the nature and genesis of sedimentary rocks, together with methods of study such as well-logging and seismic profiling, are accompanied in this course by sections on rock deformation and large-scale tectonic evolution. Practical geology, including map interpretation, is emphasized, and there is a Field Course in the Easter Vacation.

The course develops one side of Geology but is complete in itself. Together with the complementary subject Mineralogy and Petrology it leads on to Part II Geological Sciences.

Part II

Candidates are required to offer one of the following subjects or combinations of subjects:

Anatomy	Pathology
Applied Biology	Pharmacology
Biochemistry	Physics and Theoretical Physics
Botany	Physiology
Chemistry	Physiology with Psychology
Genetics	Psychology
Geological Sciences	Zoology
Metallurgy and Materials Science	

Anatomy. The Anatomy Department offers an advanced course of lectures and practicals presented in modules. In the *Cell Biology* module, students study functional aspects of cell structure, the musculo-skeletal system of the cell, the organization of cell membranes, nuclear organization and division, structural aspects of gene transcription and translation, production of cell secretions and matrix. In the *Neurobiology* module, lectures are offered on the neuroanatomy of sexual behaviour, aggression, depression and mental disorder, the neurological mechanisms by which environmental influences on behaviour are mediated, neuroendocrine control systems, neurocytological studies of brain tracts and neuronal degeneration and repair. In the *Developmental Anatomy* module, lectures are offered on the control of gamete production, molecular mechanisms of sperm–egg interaction, cellular, molecular and genetic aspects of early development, cell movement and differentiation, endocrine and immunological aspects of implantation, abnormal and teratogenic development. In addition special topic lectures are offered on vascularization patterns, grafting, the functional and anatomical basis of environmental specializations, and the rule of computers in clinical and biological science.

Students have access to practical instruction in a variety of techniques including scanning and transmission electron microscopy and freeze-fracture replication, histochemistry, tissue culture, computing, radioimmunoassay, neurosurgery, and cell biology. In addition, students undertake an ambitious research project in close co-operation with members of the academic staff and research workers. The research project occupies the major part of their experimental work and results in a dissertation. A long vacation course is arranged in some years as an introduction to techniques and for initiation of the project work. Students are selected from those who have read Part IB of the Natural or Medical Sciences Tripos. No prior knowledge of human morphology is required.

Applied Biology. Students select for detailed study a group of subjects appropriate to their interests from a wide range. The subjects available include: soils, ecology, crop physiology and productivity, phytopathology, plant breeding and floral biology in plant sciences; ecology and exploitation, pests and disease carriers, domestication, breeding and nutrition of vertebrates, especially mammals; insect biology and pest management; conservation and management of wildlife in tropical and temperate areas. Students can select, for example, some of the subjects related only to animals, or to plants; alternatively they may choose an inter-disciplinary selection essential to ecology or conservation, or specialize in pests, disease control and the breeding of resistant varieties. All students receive some training in experimental design, and may specialize in quantitative methodology if they wish. Experimental and field practical work during the year takes the form of projects, and these are assessed in place of part of a practical examination. The Department's large farm is used for teaching. Inter-disciplinary seminars provide co-ordination of subject matter, and there are also general lectures on the problems of the environment, and natural resources.

Those who have taken one or more of Animal Biology, Environmental Biology and Plant Biology for Part IB, together with some who have completed their medical or veterinary preclinical studies in their first two undergraduate years, make up the majority of the Class. But those who have a background primarily in the physical sciences, or in Part IB Geography, are accepted. A short course during the Long Vacation period of residence is important for students intending to choose the entomological and some of the plant courses. Guided reading is advised for students not attending in the Long Vacation, or those taking up new subjects.

The course provides ideal training towards careers in industry, particularly those associated with food and agriculture, in conservation and pollution, and work in the developing countries: or a valuable broad background for business, administration and teaching. There are facilities for postgraduate research in all the subjects represented in the Applied Biology course.

Biochemistry. This is an advanced course in general Biochemistry, which includes topics in related physical, chemical and biological disciplines; it continues and extends the study of subjects introduced in Part I. The study of Biochemistry either in Part IB of the Natural Sciences Tripos, or in Part IA of the Medical Sciences Tripos, is the normal preparation for the Part II course.

The Part II course is divided into a 'core' of lectures and practical work, which is taken by all students, followed by a series of 'Options', from which students are expected to select a restricted number to cater for their special interests. The 'core' course occupies the Long Vacation period of residence and part of the Michaelmas Term; the 'Options' extend over the Lent Term. Two options are the interdepartmental courses on the control of Gene Expression in Eukaryotes and Developmental Biology. For details of these courses see p. 358. No formal practical classes are held during the latter part of the Michaelmas Term nor during the Lent Term; a literature survey exercise is conducted in the Michaelmas Term and a major practical research project occupies the student's time in the Lent Term.

There are opportunities for students, who satisfactorily complete the Part II course in Biochemistry, to proceed to Higher Degrees by research; the Department is well equipped for research on a wide range of biochemical topics. The Part II course is also a good preparation for careers in Industry, Teaching and the Hospital Laboratory Service.

Botany. The modern study of plants is dealt with comprehensively at an advanced level, timetabled to allow attendance at any combination of courses. There are lectures and practicals or project work in: plant ultrastructure; plant pathology, mycology and virology; plant biochemistry; plant biophysics; developmental physiology; genetic manipulation; cytology and genetics; ecology; tropical botany; palaeoecology and flora history; genecology; taxonomy and systematics; statistics. The Department participates in the interdepartmental Part II Course in Developmental Biology (see p. 358). It is not necessary to take all the courses offered; students are encouraged to specialize by taking their own choice of about half of the total.

A three-week Long Vacation course, in the Long Vacation preceding the Part II year, is an obligatory part of the course. The Long Vacation course is primarily concerned with field work in ecology, taxonomy, and plant pathology, as well as providing a substantial general background to the Part II course.

There are extensive facilities in the Department for training in research in all the above aspects of the study of plants. Many openings exist for good botanists in agriculture, horticulture, forestry, industry and other fields at home and abroad; there is a particular shortage of persons with degrees in botany who have been trained in physics, chemistry, and mathematics up to advanced level in G.C.E.

Chemistry. It is normally a necessary requirement of entry into the Part II course for students to have studied Advanced Chemistry in Part IB. The course is framed in a manner allowing maximum flexibility attuned to the individual choice of the student. It readily allows increased specialization for those who wish it, without restricting those who want a more general coverage. The initial lecture programme comprises Inorganic, Organic, Physical and Theoretical Chemistry courses which lay the basis for an informed choice from fifteen more specialized 'packages' from which the student has an unfettered choice of five.

There are four papers in the examination. The first two deal with general material based on the IB course and the initial courses of Part II. The third and fourth papers comprise material from each of the fifteen specialized 'packages' with wide freedom of choice. There are no practical examinations but the laboratory work of the year is continuously assessed; this includes a four-week practical course in Inorganic Chemistry which is held in the Long Vacation preceding the Part II year.

Openings for chemistry graduates are no longer confined to teaching or purely scientific posts in research and development and graduates with good degrees have proved very acceptable in such fields as management, administration and the patent and information retrieval aspects of industry. Many of those who attain a high class of degree continue for postgraduate study and research.

Genetics. The course is broad in scope, covering molecular and classical genetics of both procaryotes and eucaryotes, evolution and the genetics of populations, cytology and the genetics of cell differentiation and development. All Part II Genetics students attend the interdepartmental course in Developmental Biology (see p. 358). The time for practical work is divided between practical classes and individual projects. The project work is in the Lent Term and the reports prepared by students constitute part of the final assessment in the examination. It is strongly recommended that those aspiring to Part II Genetics should have read Biochemistry and at least one other biological subject in Part IB, but these are by no means absolute requirements.

Openings for geneticists who have taken the Part II course occur in plant and animal breeding, and applied microbiology as well as in the new area of 'genetic engineering' and many aspects of medical and more pure biological research. Those who contemplate teaching will find the course of value. Departmental facilities are available in a relatively wide range of topics for students wishing to do post-graduate research. Openings for those who go on to a higher degree have so far been readily obtained.

Geological Sciences. The courses cover all important aspects of the structure, composition and history of the earth: geophysics and structural geology; geochemistry, including isotope geochemistry; petrological processes and the use of experimental data in deducing thermal gradients and magma sources; topics in mineralogy, including mineral chemistry and physics; sedimentary petrology; historical geology; advanced palaeontology. A combination of courses emphasising mineralogy forms an option known as 'mineral sciences'.

There are openings for graduates with the Institute of Geological Sciences, with oil and mining companies, and in connection with refractories, ceramics, cements, etc. For the best students there are research scholarships for advanced study and research leading to academic posts and senior positions in geological surveys and museums.

Metallurgy and Materials Science. The structure of this course provides for a broadly-based study of all aspects of Metallurgy and Materials Science in the 'Core' courses followed by gradual specialisation through optional courses. Individual courses within the Core cover the mechanical, chemical, and physical properties of materials and the selection and usage of materials in a wide range of technological applications. Principal options involve further study of properties and applications in any two of the three important areas of the subject: surfaces, device materials, and ceramics, polymers and composites. Finally the special topics, of which one should be chosen, cover a wide selection of more advanced topics in the science and application of metals and materials. Members of staff in the Department will be happy to give advice on appropriate combinations best matched to a student's particular interests and future plans. In addition to the lecture courses, there will be demonstrations of specialized equipment, examples classes, metallography and laboratory work, including a small research project.

There are openings for metallurgists and materials scientists in the U.K. and abroad. The training provides a preparation for research or applied scientific work on problems over a wide field in many industries concerned with metallic and non-metallic materials, for example the steel, non-ferrous metals, electronic, ceramics, and polymer industries. The course also provides a good background for men and women looking for administrative or technical management posts in industry generally.

Study of Metallurgy and Materials Science together with one of Advanced Chemistry, Advanced Physics, Crystalline State, or ordinary Physics in Part IB is normally a necessary preparation. Attendance at a four-week course in the Long Vacation prior to the course is important.

Pathology. This course offers study in the four main constituent disciplines of Pathology. In order to facilitate study in depth each discipline is presented as an optional subject. Students take any two options.

(1) *Cellular Pathology:* This is concerned with the function and structure of cells in disease. The principles are illustrated by a close study of cell behaviour in inflammation, arterial disease, neoplasia and transplantation.

(2) *Immunology:* This aims to give a comprehensive course in Immunology, dealing with such topics as the molecular biology of antibodies, the cellular basis of the immune response and its genetic control, the effector mechanisms, immunity and hypersensitivity, and immunopathology.

(3) *Parasitism and Disease:* This concerns the principles of infection and infectious disease. It deals with parasites both large and small (from helminths to viruses) and their relationships with vertebrate and other host species.

(4) *Virology:* This deals with molecular and general virology including structure and function of the virion, the processes of replication and its control, virus genetics, pathogenesis, epidemiology and oncogenesis.

Students take practical classes in each of their chosen options and undertake a research project in one of these. The course is a suitable prelude for those wishing to make research careers in the biological sciences as well as for those going on to do clinical and veterinary medicine. There are no particular requirements for entry though Part I courses in one or more biological disciplines are essential. Similar experience is required for entry by Affiliated Students.

Pharmacology. Lectures on selected topics in pharmacology, especially those of current research interest, are presented at an advanced level. The course emphasizes molecular mechanisms of drug action. Especially detailed attention is given to (*a*) effects of drugs upon cytomembranes and subcellular components, (*b*) pharmacology of the central nervous system and peripheral synapses, especially biochemical and biophysical aspects of transmitters, (*c*) drugs affecting transport processes, (*d*) physical processes involved in drug action, and (*e*) actions on cell growth and division. A part of the course covers comparative aspects, and there are a few lectures on historical or environmental topics of interest to pharmacologists.

There is no Long Vacation course. In the Michaelmas Term the practical laboratory work occupies 3–3½ days a week and introduces the student to the application of advanced techniques and equipment to pharmacological problems. In the Lent Term each student is expected to undertake a practical research project supervised by a member of the staff. The results of these projects are presented by the student at a seminar in the Easter Term, and the work is written up as a short dissertation.

Normally students entering this course are expected to have attended the course in Pharmacology for Part IB of the Medical Sciences Tripos or the Natural Sciences Tripos.

The final examination consists of four written papers and a *viva voce* examination together with the submission of the project report. There are substantial vocational opportunities for natural scientists reading pharmacology as well as for medical students who do so before proceeding to clinical studies.

Physics and Theoretical Physics. The lectures in this course form a continuation of the course for Advanced Physics given in the second year, and offer each candidate a considerable choice of subject matter. In the Long Vacation period of residence before the start of the Part II lecture courses, candidates may carry out extended experimental work or attend mathematics lectures and examples classes, or a mixture of both; this work is assessed and the marks transmitted to the Examiners, who customarily attach considerable significance to them. Candidates who do not attend during the Long Vacation will therefore suffer substantial handicap unless, as an alternative, they spend five weeks or more in an established laboratory undertaking an approved experimental investigation.

The examination consists of five written papers, together with a general essay. The first tests the candidate's general knowledge and ability to solve problems, both qualitative and quantitative. The second and third papers are based on the lecture material common to all candidates, that is the courses up to the end of the Michaelmas Term, including material presented in previous years. In either the fourth or the fifth paper every candidate must write an essay on a prepared topic, which may be one of a number proposed by the Examiners during the Michaelmas Term or one proposed by the candidate and approved by the Examiners. The rest of these papers is taken up with questions relating to the examples classes in theoretical physics and to the special topics covered in the Lent Term lectures. A great variety of courses is available, and sufficient questions will be set to allow a candidate to confine his study to a very limited number. Candidates may elect to carry out an experimental or theoretical project or an extended exercise in computation. They may, if they so wish, substitute the assessment of this work for some part of Papers 4 and 5, according to a scheme of equivalence announced by the Head of the Department but they are permitted to offer the project work in addition to the written papers on the understanding that the extra work will carry credit only if it is of a quality comparable to the rest.

In addition to the examinable courses outlined above, a series of examples classes is available during the Michaelmas Term to encourage facility in problem-solving in the basic fields of physics; and opportunities are provided for hearing about the research fields pursued in the Cavendish Laboratory.

Physiology. The lectures in this course are given by staff members engaged in research and cover selected topics rather than the whole field of advanced physiology. The number of students is limited, and this encourages discussion between students and staff and makes it possible for advanced experimental techniques to be used in the practical laboratory work which occupies much of the time. The importance of studying original literature is emphasized. The course is divided into three broad divisions: mammalian physiology, biophysics, and neurobiology. Students are generally encouraged to study topics from the whole range of physiology but the examination is arranged such that candidates may, if they wish, avoid answering questions on any one of the above broad divisions.

For those who do well in Part II there are opportunities to take up physiological research either immediately or after the completion of clinical medical or veterinary studies.

Physiology and Psychology. The course is given in part in the Physiological Laboratory and in part in the Department of Experimental Psychology, and leads to an examination which includes two papers from the Part II Physiology examination and two papers in Psychology set specially for candidates taking this course. It is a combination suitable for those who wish to study sensory, neural and functional processes on the general border between Physiology and Psychology. Physiology and Experimental Psychology in Part IB, or the Medical Sciences Tripos Physiology and Neurobiology, are an essential preparation.

Psychology. Teaching is organized so that students may, if they so wish, concentrate upon a few areas studied in detail. The areas within which teaching is given may vary slightly from year to year but will usually include:

Sensory processes, psychophysics and perception.
Human performance (including signal detection, decision and choice, vigilance, selective attention, and reaction time).
Human learning and memory.
Language, thought and intelligence.
Comparative psychology of learning and cognition
Physiological psychology.
Developmental psychology.
Personality and abnormal psychology.

Students usually study about half the range of subjects listed above. The scheme of the examination is that four papers must be offered. Each paper is divided into five sections, four of which contain questions on a particular field of study drawn from those areas listed above. The fifth section contains questions which call for a wider treatment or which are, for instance, concerned with experimental design and treatment of results. Three questions must be answered in each paper, of which not more than two may be chosen from any single section. Alternatively, a Dissertation may be substituted for one paper. Dissertations must be on an approved topic and may not exceed eight thousand words.

Practical work is not organized in discrete classes; instead each student conducts, under supervision, a single research project throughout the year and submits a report on the result obtained.

In the selection of applicants for this course, preference is given to those who have previously taken Experimental Psychology in Part IB of the Natural Sciences Tripos or Empirical Psychology in Part IB of the Philosophy Tripos. Medical students are also considered for a one-year course in Part II. Other students, if they are in a position to devote two years to the course, are also considered. For the latter, transfer from previous study of an Arts subject may be practicable.

Students who have read Experimental Psychology in Part IB and Psychology in Part II, or those who have not read Experimental Psychology in Part IB but have devoted two years to the Part II course, are qualified to work in clinical, educational or industrial psychology; or may find their training relevant in other fields of activity, such as market research. Some of these vocational opportunities may require attendance at a postgraduate course after Part II. For students who do well in Part II there are opportunities to take up research in pure or applied branches of the subject.

Zoology. The courses are arranged in 'modules' of which students select two (or more if they wish) in each of the Michaelmas and Lent terms. The modules are as follows: Behaviour, Coastal and Marine Ecology, Vertebrate Evolutionary Studies, Physiological Control Systems, Cellular Neurobiology, Cell Biology and Molecular Biology of Eukaryote Cells, which are given in the Michaelmas Term; and Population and Behavioural Ecology, Mammalian Evolution and Faunal History, Invertebrate Biology, Neural Mechanisms of Behaviour, Physiological Integration and Locomotion, Control of Gene expression in Eukaryotes, and Developmental Biology, which are given in the Lent Term. The Easter Term is kept free for reading, seminars and excursions.

Students are expected to attend courses in the Long Vacation between Part IB and Part II unless they can satisfy the Head of Department that they will be engaged in biological studies of comparable value (e.g. expeditions involving substantial field studies). The courses may include biological statistics, insect systematics and diversity, cell structure and function, structure of nervous systems, and field ecology and behaviour.

Behaviour: will deal with the ways in which inherited and environmental factors interact in the development of behaviour; with the structure of social behaviour; with the analysis of communication; and with ways in which behaviour is controlled from moment to moment.

Coastal and Marine Ecology: investigates the ecology of salt-marshes and other intertidal systems, estuaries, and coastal and open-ocean waters from the level of the behaviour of individual species up to that of the structure and diversity of marine eco-systems. Accent is placed on whole-organism biology and on an integration of information from all relevant disciplines.

Vertebrate Evolutionary Studies: placing equal emphasis on living and fossil forms, evolutionary relationships from fishes to birds are reviewed, paying special attention to controversial issues. Alternative approaches to classification and phylogeny are compared and exquisite specimens from the Museum research collections form the basis of practical work.

Physiological Control Systems: the aim of this course is to consider the role of systems which affect the whole physiology of the animal. In particular, systems involved in the control of a wide variety of cellular processes, in ionic and osmotic regulation, and in controlling circadian and annual changes in the physiology of whole organisms will be considered.

Cellular Neurobiology: this module describes how nerve cells function and interact, dealing with neural structure, electro-physiology and neurochemistry in vertebrate and invertebrate nervous systems.

Cell Biology: deals with the structure and functions of the cyto-plasm and their analysis at the molecular level. It begins with a study of self-assembly and morphogenesis, goes on to deal with the cyto-skeleton, mitosis and motility, and concludes with lectures on membrane organisation and membraneous organelles.

Molecular Biology of Eukaryote Cells: concentrates on the inter-disciplinary nature of the subject and is illustrated by systems amenable to structural, physiological, biochemical, genetic and im-munological approaches, e.g. (1) the mammalian cell *in vitro*, its surface, proliferation, hybridization, mutagenesis and repair; (2) the eukaryote genome and chromosome, RNA processing and DNA replication.

Population and Behavioural Ecology: evolution of behaviour in relation to ecology, optimality models, competition for food, mates and territories, mating systems, co-operation and conflict in animal societies; communication; reproductive strategies, and life history variables in mammals.

Mammalian Evolution and Faunal History: starts with a consideration of structure, function, mode of life, relationships and basic systematics of mammals (and mammal-like reptiles). It then deals with modes of evolutionary change, changes in mammalian faunas during the Pleistocene, and finishes with a brief account of numerical approaches to biogeography and evolution.

Invertebrate Biology: in this module the adaptive radiation of selected groups of invertebrates will be discussed. Groups currently dealt with include: Protozoa, the Nemertines, the Pogonophora, the Protochordates, and the social insects.

Physiological Integration and Locomotion: the first half of the module deals with the metabolic changes which occur during times of intense activity, growth or reproduction, and the role of the endocrine system in relation to these changes. In the second half of the module the evolutionary implications of the mechanics and energetic costs of locomotion on land, sea and air will be discussed.

Neural Mechanisms of Behaviour: takes as its starting point the functioning of a single neurone and then attempts to explain how groups of neurones interact to produce simple patterns of behaviour. The functions of nervous systems with relatively small numbers of neurones are discussed before proceeding to more complex nervous systems and how these also function in the control and integration of behaviour.

Control of Gene Expression in Eukaryotes: Zoology students may include this interdepartmental course as one of their modules. Details are provided in a separate entry in this handbook (see p. 358).

Developmental Biology: Zoology students may include this interdepartmental course as one of their modules. Details are provided in a separate entry in this handbook (see p. 358).

Interdepartmental Courses

Control of Gene Expression in Eukaryotes. This module is shared as a joint option with students reading Part II Biochemistry. It is taught by members of both departments with additional lectures from members of the MRC Laboratory of Molecular Biology. It examines various ways in which gene expression is regulated in eukaryotic cells. The introductory lectures consider gene structure and the following lectures examine selected examples of gene regulation ranging from the early stages of animal development to immunoglobulin gene expression in differentiating lymphocytes. The power of recombinant DNA techniques (gene cloning and mutagenesis *in vitro*) for analysis of gene regulation is emphasized.

Developmental Biology. This course of 24 lectures is offered jointly by the Departments of Biochemistry, Botany, Genetics, and Zoology in the Lent Term as an optional course for students taking Part II subjects. It deals with development in both animals and plants at molecular and cellular level and brings together material previously taught for separate Part II subjects. The course includes practical work which will be arranged departmentally. Questions on the course may be set in the examination papers for individual Part II subjects.

Part II (General)

For this examination candidates choose one of two alternative sections

Section I

For this section candidates have to offer an essay paper and one of the following:

Either (*a*) Advanced Chemistry or Advanced Physics and one other subject from Part IB not previously offered;
or (*b*) One subject from Part IB not previously offered and one Special Subject;
or (*c*) Two Special Subjects.

The Special Subjects are as follows:

Biological Resources	Physics
Chemistry	Statistics

Candidates must choose their two subjects in such a way that not more than one is drawn from any one of the ten groups set out below:

(i) Chemistry; Advanced Chemistry; Special Subject Chemistry; Statistics.
(ii) Pathology; Physics; Advanced Physics; Special Subject Physics.
(iii) Animal Biology; Metallurgy and Materials Science.
(iv) Crystalline State; Physiology.
(v) Biochemistry; Mineralogy and Petrology.
(vi) Plant Biology; Experimental Psychology; Fluid Mechanics.
(vii) Environmental Biology; Mathematics; Pharmacology.
(viii) Stratigraphic Geology.
(ix) History and Philosophy of Science.
(x) Biological Resources.

In addition no candidate may offer:

(*a*) Advanced Chemistry with Advanced Physics, or Stratigraphic Geology together with either Advanced Chemistry or Advanced Physics.
(*b*) Biological Resources with Advanced Chemistry or Advanced Physics.
(*c*) Any subject previously offered in the Medical Sciences Tripos.
(*d*) Mathematics with Statistics.
(*e*) Mathematics if he has previously obtained honours in Part IB or Part II of the Mathematical Tripos.
(*f*) The subject Physics or the subject Chemistry if he has previously offered the corresponding advanced subject.
(*g*) The subjects Physics or Fluid Mechanics if he has previously obtained honours in Parts IB or II of the Engineering Tripos.
(*h*) Experimental Psychology from Part IB if he has previously offered Paper 9 in Part IB of the Philosophy Tripos.

Details of the Special Subjects are as follows:

Biological Resources. A course of lectures, seminars, practical classes, and demonstrations on the evolution of human communities and the biological resources by which they are maintained. The course is provided by the Department of Applied Biology. It is an advantage for candidates to have read a biological subject previously, but that is not essential.

Chemistry. The course consists of about half the lectures and practical work attended by a candidate offering Chemistry in Part II. Candidates are free to make any selection from the courses available, except that some courses may be excluded because the lectures take place at the same times as those for the candidate's other subject. The examination requires a knowledge of some of the subject-matter covered by the courses given in Advanced Chemistry in Part I B. Candidates who have not taken Advanced Chemistry in Part I B may take the course, but they need special advice as to which lectures they are equipped to understand.

Physics. The course consists of about half the lectures and practical work expected of a candidate offering Physics and Theoretical Physics in Part II. The lectures in the Michaelmas Term normally consist of the courses on quantum physics, nuclear physics, and solid state physics, and, in the Lent Term, of one or more optional courses, although other combinations may be possible. A prior knowledge of physics equivalent to the material covered in Advanced Physics in Part I B will be assumed.

Statistics. The course deals with the principles of statistical inference and with their applications in the design and analysis of biological experiments; the elements of probability theory are illustrated by simple biological examples. Candidates require little previous mathematical knowledge.

Section II

History and Philosophy of Science

The general aim of the course is to give insight into the historical and intellectual development of modern science (including medicine) within Western society, and into its philosophical structure and presuppositions. While a general knowledge of science is a valuable background for the course, students whose background is for example in the humanities will *not* be at a disadvantage: the insights they can bring from their previous training will compensate for any lack of knowledge of science. Advanced knowledge of present-day sciences is not required, but historical and philosophical interest is essential. Students who have not already read the subject in Part I B are advised to attend the Part I B lectures in addition to those given specifically for Part II.

The Part II courses are normally arranged under eight groups, each of which corresponds to one paper in the examination. Candidates *either* take any four of Papers 1–8 together with Paper 9 (a three-hour essay on one of a number of general topics); *or* take any four of Papers 1–8 and submit a dissertation; *or* take Paper 9 and any three of Papers 1–8 and submit a dissertation in lieu of one of the remaining papers. This freedom of choice of papers means in effect that courses can be chosen, according to individual inclinations, to emphasize either the historical or the philosophical side or to give equal weight to both. A dissertation submitted in lieu of a paper must be on a topic that falls solidly within the subject area of that paper. A dissertation must be of not more than 15,000 words, and is expected to embody a substantial piece of study on a given topic; it must be submitted by the first day of Easter Full Term; possible topics should be discussed with any of the teaching officers, preferably before the preceding Long Vacation but otherwise as early as possible in the academic year. It is generally inadvisable for students who have not previously read the subject in Part IB to attempt a dissertation.

The scope of the courses is indicated by the titles of the papers, which are as follows:

1. Scientific ideas and practice from antiquity to the Renaissance.
2. The scientific revolution 1500–1700.
3. The physical sciences since 1600: special topics.
4. Philosophy of science: general principles.
5. Philosophy of science: historical sources.
6. Philosophical problems of the human sciences.
7. Medicine from antiquity to the end of the seventeenth century.
8. Medicine, biology, and society since the seventeenth century.

No candidate may offer Paper 7 or Paper 8 having previously offered the Special Subject History of Medicine in Part II (General) of the Medical Sciences Tripos.

Further details of the courses, and recommended reading for the previous Long Vacation, are available from the Department.

The Preliminary Examinations for Part II and for Section II of Part II (General) of the Natural Sciences Tripos

The examinations are intended for the very few candidates spending two years preparing for Part II or for Section II of Part II (General) of the Natural Sciences Tripos.

The examination for Part II is in the subjects of that Part of the Tripos. The examination in Physics and Theoretical Physics consists of *either* (i) the written papers for Advanced Physics in Part IB of the Tripos, *or* (ii) the written papers for Advanced Physics and for Mathematics in Part IB of the Tripos. The examination in Chemistry consists *either* (i) of the written papers for Advanced Chemistry in Part IB of the Tripos, *or* (ii) of the first two of the four written papers for Chemistry in Part II of the Tripos. Candidates who previously offered Advanced Chemistry in Part IB offer the examination specified in (ii) and other candidates offer the examination specified in (i). The examination in Psychology consists of the papers in Experimental Psychology in Part IB of the Tripos. In subjects other than Chemistry, Physics and Theoretical Physics, and Psychology the examination consists of the written papers and, in subjects in which a practical or oral examination is set, the practical or oral examination set in Part II of the Tripos.

The examination for Section II of Part II (General) consists of Papers 1–8 set for Section II of Part II (General) of the Tripos. Each candidate is required to offer four papers.

Examinations in the Natural Sciences for the Ordinary B.A. Degree

There are Ordinary Examinations in each of the subjects included in Part IB of the Natural Sciences Tripos. The examination and Schedule for each Ordinary Examination in any year is the same as that for the corresponding subject of Part IB of the Tripos.

A student may not count towards the Ordinary B.A. Degree an Ordinary Examination in Natural Science in

(*a*) any subject for which the Examiners for Part IB of either the Natural Sciences or the Medical Sciences Tripos have specified that his work deserved the allowance of an examination for the Ordinary B.A. Degree;

(*b*) Chemistry or Physics, if he has offered the corresponding advanced subject in Part IB of the Natural Sciences Tripos;

(*c*) any subject, except Physiology, for which the Examiners for Part IA of the Medical Sciences Tripos have specified that his work deserved the allowance of an examination for the Ordinary B.A. Degree;

(*d*) any subject for which the Examiners for any examination (except the Natural Sciences or Medical Sciences Tripos) have specified that his work deserved the allowance of an examination for the Ordinary B.A. Degree;

nor if he has obtained honours in any Tripos other than the Natural Sciences Tripos may he count an Ordinary Examination in Natural Science in any subject which he has offered in that other Tripos Examination, except that a student who has obtained honours in Part IA of the Medical Sciences Tripos may count an Ordinary Examination in Physiology.

Certificate of Post-graduate Study in Natural Science

Certificates are awarded for advanced study and training in research in certain specific sciences. A candidate must have been admitted as a Graduate Student, on the recommendation of the Degree Committee concerned, by the Board of Graduate Studies, who will fix the date of commencement of his candidature. He must also *either* (*a*) have graduated, or have completed the examination and residence requirements for graduation, in the University, and have been classed in Part II of the Mathematical, Natural Sciences, or Engineering Tripos, or in the Chemical Engineering Tripos, *or* (*b*) if not a member of the University, satisfy the Appropriate Degree Committee of his fitness to study for the Certificate.

The course of instruction extends over three consecutive terms, but a candidate may be permitted in exceptional circumstances to spend up to two years in study for the Certificate.

Each candidate is required to submit a dissertation and to take an oral examination, which may include practical tests, on the subject of the dissertation and on the general field of knowledge within which it falls, and which may be supplemented by a written examination. In addition he may be required to take one or more written papers. By the end of the second term of his candidature a candidate must send to the Secretary of the Board of Graduate Studies the proposed title of his dissertation for approval by the Board. He must submit two copies of his dissertation to the Secretary of the

Board of Graduate Studies before the division of the third term of his candidature, unless he has been granted an extension; a statement of the sources from which his information is derived must be included.

A candidate for a Certificate may be allowed to count the whole or some part of the period for which he has been a candidate towards a course of research for the degree of Ph.D., M.Sc., or M.Litt., but, if such an allowance is made, he will not be entitled to receive a Certificate so long as he remains on the register of Graduate Students, nor subsequently if he should submit a dissertation for the degree of Ph.D., M.Sc., or M.Litt. A candidate is not entitled to receive a Certificate until he has kept at least three terms.

A candidate who is not awarded a Certificate may not be a candidate again either in the same field or in any other field.

Subjects of examination

Certificates are awarded in Biochemistry, Chemistry, Genetics, Metallurgy and Materials Science, and Physics.

For a Certificate in Biochemistry, the study and training include courses of lectures proposed by the Head of Department, and a research investigation.

For Certificates in Chemistry, Metallurgy and Materials Science, and Physics the study and training includes (*a*) Courses of lectures, and (*b*) Practical work carried out in one or more of the following ways: (i) organized experiments or theoretical exercises of an advanced type, (ii) assistance with a piece of research, (iii) a small research investigation, (iv) training in some technique. The examination may include one or two written papers on subjects cognate to the lectures attended by the candidate; for Certificates in Chemistry and Metallurgy and Materials Science the written papers may include passages of scientific literature in a foreign language for translation into English, for which the use of a dictionary is allowed.

For a Certificate in Genetics, the study and training include a course of lectures, and training in research by means of one or more original investigations which may be practical, theoretical, or both combined.

M.Phil. courses (one-year) in Natural Science subjects

One-year courses leading to the M.Phil. Degree provide advanced study and training in research in certain specific sciences. A candidate must have been admitted as a Graduate Student, on the recommendation of the Degree Committee concerned, by the Board of Graduate Studies, who will fix the date of commencement of his candidature.

The course of instruction extends over three consecutive terms but a candidate may, in exceptional circumstances, be permitted to continue beyond that period.

The examination may consist of written papers or the submission of a dissertation or both written papers and a dissertation. Where the examination consists of the submission of a dissertation the candidate will be expected to take an oral examination on the subject of that dissertation and on the general field of knowledge within which it falls. By the division of the second term of his candidature a candidate must send to the Secretary of the Board of Graduate Studies

(*a*) the papers in which he is to be examined, and
(*b*) the subject of the dissertation, if any, which the Degree Committee have approved for him.

He must submit two copies of this dissertation to the Secretary of the Board of Graduate Studies by a date which shall be not later than the end of the third term of his candidature, unless he has been granted an extension.

A candidate for the M.Phil. will be allowed to count the whole of that period for which he has been a candidate for that degree towards a course of research for the degree of Ph.D. or M.Sc.

Subjects of examination

One-year courses for the M.Phil. Degree are provided in Applied Biology, Biochemistry, History and Philosophy of Science, Pharmacology, Plant Breeding, and Quaternary Research.

M.Phil. course in Applied Biology

These one-year advanced courses are intended to provide a training for research or for work in a specialized field. They are usitable for students wishing to transfer from pure to applied science. A student selects *one* of seven specified subjects for study, namely one from Animal Nutrition, Applied Entomology, Biometry, Crop Physiology, Mammal Ecology, Parasitology, Plant Ecology, Plant Pathology. His course comprises lectures, seminars, practical work and an individual research project. Importance is attached to students acquiring an adequate knowledge of biometry, and teaching is provided in this subject for all students.

Requests for further information should be addressed to the Secretary, Department of Applied Biology, Pembroke Street, Cambridge, CB2 3DX.

M.Phil. course in Biochemistry

The course is designed to provide further study and training in research in biochemistry. The course includes lectures, instruction in specialized techniques and associated practical work; this part of the course occupies a period less than the equivalent of one full term. For the remainder of the academical year the candidate carries out a course of research in biochemistry under the supervision of a member of the staff of the Department. The examination consists of a thesis, of not more than 15,000 words in length, exclusive of tables, footnotes, bibliography and appendices, on a subject approved by the Degree Committee for the Faculty of Biology 'B'. The examination includes an oral examination on the subject of the thesis and the general field of knowledge in which it falls.

M.Phil. course in History and Philosophy of Science

The scheme of examination for the one-year course in History and Philosophy of Science consists of:

(*a*) a thesis, of not more then 15,000 words in length, including footnotes and appendices, but excluding bibliography, on a subject approved by the Degree Committee for the Faculty of Philosophy;

and

(*b*) four essays, each of about 3,000 words, and, except as provided below, each on a subject approved by the Degree Committee for the Faculty of Philosophy which is related to one or more of the following areas:

Ancient, medieval, and renaissance science
Physical sciences since the seventeenth century
Life sciences since the seventeenth century
The epistemology of science
Philosophy of the natural and social sciences
History of the philosophy of science

Not more than two essays may be chosen from any one area. With the permission of the Degree Committee one of the four essays may be offered in an area which is not listed above but is related to History and Philosophy of Science.

The examination will include an oral examination of the subjects of the thesis and of the four essays.

Further details regarding these areas for essays are as follows:

1. Ancient, medieval, and renaissance science

Mathematics, the natural sciences, and technology, from antiquity to the early seventeenth century, including scientific method, apparatus, institutions, and the dissemination of ideas and techniques.

2. Physical sciences since the seventeenth century

Mathematics, the physical sciences and natural philosophy, and related technology, from the early seventeenth to the twentieth century, including scientific method, apparatus, institutions, and the dissemination of ideas and techniques.

3. Life sciences since the seventeenth century

Biology, geology, physiology, and the study of disease from the early seventeenth to the twentieth century, including their philosophical and social aspects, and their relation to biological and medical theory and practice.

4. The epistemology of science

Causation, explanation, reduction, and scientific law; natural kinds and classification; change and commensurability of meaning in theoretical science.

Induction and confirmation theory; theories of probability; measures of confirmation of scientific laws and theories; analogical inference and simplicity criteria.

5. Philosophy of the natural and social sciences

Theories of space, time, and geometry; cause, chance, and determinism philosophical problems of quantum physics.

Individualism, holism, and reducibility; functional explanation and teleology.

Comparison of methods in the natural and social sciences; reasons and causes, *Verstehen* and ideal types; objectivity and values; ideology and the sociology of knowledge.

6. History of the philosophy of science.

Themes in the philosophy of science of the seventeenth and eighteenth centuries (Descartes to Kant).

Kant's philosophy of science: the regulative approach to scientific theory; the metaphysical foundations of science.

The Kantian heritage; the inductive tradition; emphasis on hypothesis; positivistic and related approaches; conventionalism; relations between nineteenth- and early twentieth-century philosophy of science.

M.Phil. course in Pharmacology

The course is designed to provide further study and training in research in pharmacology. The course includes lectures, instruction in specialized techniques and associated practical work; this part of the course occupies a period less than the equivalent of one full term. For the remainder of the academical year the candidate carries out a course of research in pharmacology under the supervision of a member of the staff of the Department. The examination consists of a thesis, of not more than 15,000 words in length, exclusive of tables, footnotes, bibliography and appendices, on a subject approved by the Degree Committee for the Faculty of Biology 'B'. The examination includes an oral examination on the subject of the thesis and the general field of knowledge in which it falls.

M.Phil. course in Plant Breeding

This is a one-year course, given by academic staff of the Departments of Applied Biology and Genetics and the Plant Breeding Institute, Trumpington. It is designed to provide a thorough grounding at advanced level in the principles of genetics and other disciplines relevant to plant breeding and is intended primarily as a training for research or for specialist employment in the field of plant breeding. The course comprises lectures, seminars, practical work, and individual research projects.

It is desirable that applications for the course should reach the Secretary, Board of Graduate Studies, by the beginning of April.

Requests for further information should be addressed to the Administration Secretary, Department of Applied Biology, Pembroke Street, *or* Professor J.R.S.Fincham, Department of Genetics, Downing Street, Cambridge, or to the Director, Plant Breeding Institute, Maris Lane, Trumpington, Cambridge.

M.Phil. course in Quaternary Research

This one-year course is intended to provide training in fundamental aspects of Quaternary research and in selected fields of the subject, including biological, geological, geographical and physical aspects. The course consists of lectures, seminars and practical work, together with a research investigation. The examination consists of a thesis, not more than 15,000 words in length, and five essays or exercises on particular topics in Quaternary research. Requests for further information should be addressed to the Director, Sub-department of Quaternary Research, Botany School. Downing Street, Cambridge, CB2 3EA.

ORIENTAL STUDIES

In this subject there are courses of study followed by candidates for:

The *Oriental Studies Tripos*, which is divided into two Parts.
The *Preliminary Examination* for Part I of the Oriental Studies Tripos.
Ordinary Examination in Oriental Studies for the Ordinary B.A. Degree.

The Oriental Studies Tripos

The Oriental Studies Tripos is an Honours Degree course dealing with the major Oriental civilizations which have flourished in Asia and adjoining areas during a period of over five thousand years. The teaching provided by the Faculty covers a number of Oriental languages (Ancient Egyptian, Coptic, Akkadian, Hebrew, Aramaic; Arabic, Turkish, Persian; Sanskrit, Prakrit, Hindi; Chinese, Japanese) and also the literature, history, philosophy, religion, art, and archaeology of these widely differing civilizations.

Each student undertakes a course which is based on either one Oriental language or two related Oriental languages, and which also introduces him to the cultural background of the civilization concerned. The balance between the amount of language study and the study of the connected literature, history, philosophy, etc., naturally varies from course to course, but the main emphasis in all courses is laid on the attainment of a satisfactory knowledge of the language or languages studied, as the key to the original source material essential to the proper understanding of each civilization. Some of the courses pertain to civilizations that have passed away, others to civilizations with both classical and modern forms. Attention is also paid to the modern spoken forms of Arabic, Persian, Turkish, Hebrew, Hindi, Chinese, and Japanese.

The Tripos is divided into two Parts. Part I, normally taken at the end of two years, is mainly concerned with providing as thorough a knowledge as possible of the one or two Oriental languages being studied together with a general introduction to the literature, history, and general cultural background of the civilization. Knowledge of the languages is fostered by an intensive and detailed study of a number of set texts, which include significant examples of the literature concerned. At the end of the first year of the two years spent on Part I there is a Preliminary Examination. Part II is taken at the end of the third or fourth year of study, depending on the particular course of study. In Part II knowledge of the language or languages is further advanced, normally by continued detailed study of set texts, while at the same time specialization is often permitted in one or more options. These options may range from philological and linguistic studies to the literature, history, art, and archaeology pertaining to the language and civilization concerned. Those studying certain languages may, with the permission of their Colleges, spend one year after Part I attending an approved course or undertaking approved study in the country of the language they are learning.

The courses which involve the study of a single civilization and the various forms of one language or language group are Arabic Studies, Chinese Studies, Hebrew Studies, Indian Studies, and Japanese Studies in both Parts of the Tripos, and also Assyriology and Egyptology in Part II. The courses which involve a combination of two languages and their related civilizations are, in both Parts of the Tripos, Hebrew and Arabic, Hebrew and Aramaic, Hebrew and Assyriology, Hindi and Persian, and Islamic and Middle Eastern Studies. Other combinations of Oriental languages or of an Oriental language with a language from the Modern and Medieval Languages Tripos may in certain circumstances be permitted if early application is made through the student's Tutor.

Since Oriental languages are not generally taught in schools, all the courses leading to Part I start from the beginner's level. Oriental studies do not demand a particular bent of mind or type of intellectual training. The courses are, however, intensive and the learning of Oriental scripts and the study of set texts may require concentrated application and regular attendance at lectures. The most successful students are usually those who have studied classical or modern languages or history at school. A complete course in both Parts I and II is the most desirable for those wishing to choose careers in the Oriental field, but Part I alone is not infrequently taken in two years by those who have taken Part I in another Tripos in their first or second year.

The languages and civilizations covered in the Tripos are as follows:

The Ancient Near East

Egyptology. Egyptology is the study of the language, literature, history, religion, institutions, art, and archaeology of ancient Egypt. The civilization of ancient Egypt began during the fourth millennium B.C. and lasted until the Arab conquest in A.D. 640. Five stages of the language can be distinguished. Down to the time of the Roman Occupation three written forms (hieroglyphic, hieratic, demotic) were in use. After the conversion of Egypt to Christianity a new script, based on a modified Greek alphabet, was adopted, and this has continued in use in the liturgy of the Coptic Church.

Assyriology. Historical records of the ancient civilizations of Mesopotamia which include documents written in the Sumerian and Akkadian (Babylonian and Assyrian) languages cover a period from about 3000 B.C. to the time of the fall of Babylon in the sixth century B.C. and beyond. A study of archaeology and of the ancient history of the Near East forms an essential part of Assyriology, and both archaeological and written evidence throw light on the history, laws, religions, and customs of early Mesopotamian culture and society.

Hebrew. Old Testament literature, which covers a period of about a thousand years (about 1100 to 165 B.C.), is written in Classical Hebrew, and Hebrew studies involve, in Part II, a knowledge of comparative Semitic philology, Semitic epigraphy, Rabbinical and modern Hebrew. There is a vast corpus of Post-Biblical literature in Hebrew (commentaries, philosophy, history, and law).

Aramaic. The Aramaic language was the Semitic dialect originally current in Mesopotamia and the adjoining areas. Its literature, including texts written in Syriac, extends from the fifth century B.C. to the thirteenth century A.D., and inscriptions, dating from the eighth century B.C. and onwards, are also important for the study of archaeology, the Old and New Testaments, Rabbinics, early Church history, law, institutions, and philosophy.

Islamic Studies

Islamic civilization is approached through a study of its three major languages, Arabic, Persian, and Turkish. Of these, Arabic may be studied by itself, but a wide range of options is available for those who wish to combine it with another language. The Tripos lays stress on the continuity of the languages and all candidates are introduced to both their classical and their modern forms. The emphasis in the Part I course is placed on linguistic competence and background knowledge, while Part II allows for a measure of specialization. Optional sections within individual papers provide considerable flexibility. Stress is laid on the comparative approach, through the interconnections between Islam and Europe in history, literature and philosophy, but the main purpose of the course is to give a framework for an appreciation of Islamic civilization itself.

Arabic. Arabic is the mother tongue of about 60 million people at present, and has acted as the classical language of the whole of the Islamic world. Apart from the Koran, there is an extensive literature covering some fourteen centuries. The subject has important associations with Greek and Latin studies (especially in regard to the transmission of Greek philosophy, science, and medicine), medieval and modern history, medieval geography, medieval and modern languages (particularly Spanish), law, ecclesiastical history, and theology.

Persian. Since the beginning of the Islamic period in Iran and Central Asia, which dates from the seventh century A.D., Persian has been of next importance to Arabic as the language of literary, spiritual, and philosophic significance in the Islamic world. The 'classical' hegemony of Persian as the language of literature, poetry, historical annals, and legal documents also comprehends the study of Indian history since the fourteenth century; Persian was the court language of the Mogul emperors. Persian is today spoken in Iran, Afghanistan, and large areas of the U.S.S.R. and is still cultivated for scholarly and literary purposes in Pakistan.

Turkish. Turkic dialects are found wherever the Turks who came from Central Asia successfully infiltrated – from the south-east of Europe to the lands near the Yenisei river and the borders of China. The subjects studied include the dialect of an eleventh-century Islamic–Turkish civilization of Central Asia; the language, literature, and history of the Islamic Ottoman Empire (*c.* 1300–1918); and the written and spoken language of the subsequent modern Turkish Republic.

India

Indian Studies: Vedic, Sanskrit, Pali, Prakrit, and Hindi. Vedic, Classical Sanskrit, Pali, and the various Prakrits extended over a period of 3,000 years of Indian history and contained three main literatures (Hindu, Buddhist, and Jain). A very large volume of literary output includes all types of composition – religious texts, epic poems, dramas, lyrics, novels, histories, and technical treatises on subjects such as phonetics, systems of grammar, astronomy, astrology, medicine, mathematics, and law. Vedic in particular is important for comparative Indo-European linguistic studies. Indian archaeology, of both the prehistoric and historic periods, includes the history of art and architecture, and may be read in conjunction with epigraphy and ancient history. Modern Indian history and politics may be read in both Parts of the Tripos with Hindi. The Hindi dialects of Northern India evolved from about A.D. 1000 with a rich literature including devotional verse. Modern standard Hindi developed from the nineteenth century and is now spoken in one form or another by nearly 300 million people.

East Asia

Chinese. China's written culture extends from the first period of writing (about 1500 B.C.) until the present day, but from a practical point of view the study of Chinese civilization may be divided into the periods before and after 1840. Several stages of development can be traced during the earlier period, which witnessed the organization of the Chinese empires, the evolution of society, and the growing application of technical skills. The modern period is characterized by more intensive contacts with western countries, and has been marked by external and internal conflicts in which other parts of the world have been increasingly concerned. China's rich and varied literature has influenced the growth of civilization in the traditional and the modern styles; and the study of art, history, literature, philosophy, and religion forms an integral part of the Tripos. Part I comprises a standard course, without options, in which undergraduates receive a basic training in the classical and modern (*Putonghua*) forms of the language and in aspects of China's cultural history; the examination includes an oral test in modern spoken Chinese. Part II includes some papers taken by all candidates which enable them to extend their knowledge of early and modern literature and, in addition, allow a choice of specializing in literature, history, linguistics, archaeology or art. Among the requirements for the Part II examination are the presentation of a dissertation, and an oral test in modern spoken Chinese.

Japanese. Japanese civilization developed very rapidly under Korean and Chinese influence from about the middle of the first millennium A.D. and soon acquired a characteristic form of its own. The essential elements of the Japanese language are not related to Chinese and were retained despite the adoption of the Chinese script. A wide literature of merit dates from the seventh century onwards.

Teaching in Japanese Studies includes history, art, literature, religion, and thought, as well as classical and modern forms of the language.

Japan during the past hundred years has become the third most important industrial nation in the world.

Part I includes an option on modern Japan intended for students who have taken a Part I in another Tripos such as History or Economics and Politics. (This option is not suitable for students who wish to proceed to Part II, since it requires no knowledge of the classical language.)

A new feature of Part II is the inclusion, along with written tests of a traditional type, of a short dissertation on an agreed topic within the field of Japanese Studies, wherein candidates may show evidence of reading, critical ability and power of expression. Both Parts of the Tripos include an oral test in modern spoken Japanese.

The subjects of examination in each Part of the Tripos are described below. The Faculty Board of Oriental Studies may however give permission to candidates to present themselves for examination in Oriental languages and subjects and combinations of languages other than those specified for each Part, provided that the Board are satisfied that such Oriental languages possess literatures adequate for the purposes of examination and that the general scope of such Oriental subjects is similar to that of the Oriental subjects (Assyriology, Chinese Studies, Egyptology, Hebrew Studies, Indian Studies, Islamic and Middle Eastern Studies, and Japanese Studies) which are regularly included in the Tripos. Applications must be submitted not later than 21 October next preceding the examination. Permission will be given only if the Board are satisfied that the requisite teaching is available.

No student may present himself as a candidate for honours in either Part I or Part II on more than one occasion, or in Part I and Part II in the same term.

Part I*

A candidate may take Part I in his first or second year or, if he has obtained honours in another Tripos, one or two years after doing so, but not later than his fifth year.

* There are also ten papers on Iranian Studies. Details are obtainable from the Faculty Board.

Subjects of examination

The following papers are set:

Aramaic

Am. 1. Aramaic specified texts, 1, and unspecified texts.

Candidates are required to use the square Hebrew script or, where appropriate, any of the Syriac scripts.

Am. 2. Aramaic specified texts, 2, and composition.

Am. 3. Aramaic literature and its historical background.

Assyriology

As. 1. Akkadian specified texts (may also serve as a special subject for Paper 5 in option (*e*) in Archaeology of Part II of the Archaeological and Anthropological Tripos).

As. 2. Akkadian unspecified texts and composition.

As. 3. Introduction to the history and archaeology of the Ancient Near East.

Chinese Studies

C. 1. Classical Chinese texts, 1.

C. 2. Classical Chinese texts, 2.

C. 3. Modern Chinese texts, 1.

C. 4. Modern Chinese translation and composition.

C. 5. Modern Chinese texts, 2.

C. 6. Chinese history: specified subject, 1.

C. 7. Chinese history: specified subject, 2.

Egyptology

E. 1. Middle Egyptian specified texts.

E. 2. Middle Egyptian unspecified texts.

E. 3. Coptic specified texts (Sa'īdic dialect).

E. 4. Coptic unspecified texts (Sa'īdic dialect).

E. 5. The development of early societies (Paper 1 of Part I of the Archaeological and Anthropological Tripos).

E. 6. The archaeology of Europe and neighbouring areas (Paper 2 of Part I of the Archaeological and Anthropological Tripos).

E. 7. Introduction to Egyptian civilization.

E. 8. The archaeology of the Nile valley: predynastic and archaic periods.

Hebrew

H. 1. Hebrew specified texts.

H. 2. Hebrew unspecified texts and composition.

In the above papers candidates will be required to use the square Hebrew script.

H. 3. Israelite and Jewish history and literature.
H. 4. Post-biblical Hebrew.
H. 5. Post-biblical Jewish history and literature.

Indian Studies

In. 1. Classical Indian specified texts.*
In. 2. Classical Indian unspecified texts.*
In. 3. Hindi specified texts.
In. 4. Hindi unspecified texts.
In. 5. Composition, and grammar or essay, in an Indian language.

This paper contains three sections: (*a*) passages in English for translation into an Indian language; (*b*) questions on Sanskrit and Prakrit (including Pali) grammar; and (*c*) subjects for an essay to be written in Hindi. Candidates are required to offer section (*a*), and either (*b*) or (*c*).

In. 6. Indian literature.
In. 7. Indian religion.
In. 8. Indian cultural history.

Islamic and Middle Eastern Studies (Arabic, Persian, and Turkish)

Ar. 1. Arabic prose composition and classical unseens.
Ar. 2. Arabic modern unseens and essay.
Ar. 3. Arabic literature, 1.
Ar. 4. Arabic literature, 2.
Ar. 5. History of the Arab world.
P. 1. Persian prose composition and unseens.
P. 2. Persian literature.
P. 3. Persian history.
Tk. 1. Turkish prose composition and unseens.
Tk. 2. Turkish literature.
Tk. 3. Turkish history.
Is. 1. Islamic history.

Japanese Studies

J. 1. Classical Japanese specified texts.
J. 2. Classical Japanese unspecified texts.
J. 3. Modern Japanese specified texts.
J. 4. Modern Japanese unspecified texts.

* Questions are set on texts in Sanskrit and Prakrit (including Pali), and questions on both languages have to be answered.

J. 5. Japanese composition and essay.
J. 6. Japanese cultural history.
J. 7. Japanese literature.
J. 8. Modern Japanese history.
J. 9. Modern Japanese literature.
J. 10. Modern Japanese economic development.
J. 11. Modern Japanese politics.
J. 12. Modern Japanese thought and religion.

The papers on specified texts may contain questions on grammar and literary history arising out of the texts, and the papers on unspecified texts may contain questions arising immediately out of the passages set for translation.

Oral examinations are held in the modern spoken forms of Arabic, Chinese, Hebrew, Hindi, Japanese, Persian, and Turkish.

In order to obtain honours in Part I a candidate must reach the standard for honours *either* in the papers specified in **one** of the following sections (*a*)–(*n*)* *or* in the papers set for another Oriental language or subject or combination of languages approved by the Faculty Board of Oriental Studies. He must reach the honours standard in *each* language offered if he wishes to be classed.

(*a*) Assyriology and Arabic
As. 1–3; Ar. 1, 3, Is. 1.

(*b*) Chinese Studies
C. 1–7, Chinese oral.

(*c*) Egyptology
Either (i) if he is a candidate in the first, second, or third term after his first term of residence or after obtaining honours in an Honours Examination in the year previous:
either (1) *philological option*:
E. 1–4, E. 6, E. 7;
or (2) *archaeological option*:
E. 1, E. 2, E. 5–8;
or (ii) if he is a candidate in the fourth, fifth, or sixth term after his first term of residence or after obtaining honours in an Honours Examination in the year next but one previous;
E. 1–8;

* Items (*k*), Iranian Studies, and (*l*), Iranian and Persian, are not included here.

provided that no candidate for this section may offer any paper which he has previously offered in any other examination.

(*d*) Hebrew Studies
H. 1–5, Hebrew oral (when Modern Hebrew is prescribed for Paper H. 4); Am. 1.

(*e*) Hebrew and Arabic
H. 1–3; Ar. 1, 3, Is. 1.

(*f*) Hebrew and Aramaic
H. 1–3; Am. 1–3.

(*g*) Hebrew and Assyriology
H. 1–3; As. 1–3.

(*h*) Hebrew and Egyptology
H. 1–3; E. 1, E. 2, E. 7.

(*i*) Hindi and Persian
In. 3–5, Hindi oral; P. 1, 2, Persian oral; *either* In. 8 *or* P. 3.

(*j*) Indian Studies
Either (i) In. 1, 2, 5 and three papers chosen from In. 3, 4, 6–8, provided that a candidate who offers In. 3 must offer In. 4 also and *vice versa*;
or (ii) In. 3–5 and three papers chosen from In. 1, 2, 6–8, provided that a candidate who offers In. 1 must offer In. 2 also and *vice versa*;

and provided that any candidate who offers In. 3 and In. 4 must offer Hindi oral.

(*m*) Islamic and Middle Eastern Studies (Arabic, Persian, Turkish)
Two papers chosen from Ar. 1, Ar. 2, P. 1, T. 1; two papers chosen from Ar. 3, Ar. 4, P. 2, T. 2; two papers chosen from Ar. 5, P. 3, T. 3, Is. 1; provided that a candidate who offers Ar. 2 must offer Arabic oral; a candidate who offers P. 1 must offer Persian oral; and a candidate who offers T. 1 must offer Turkish oral.

(*n*) Japanese Studies
Either (i) J. 1–7, Japanese oral;
or (ii) J. 3–5, 8, 9, Japanese oral; *either* J. 10, 11, *or* J. 11, 12.

Specified texts, specified subjects and periods, and special subjects for Part I of the Tripos in **1985** and **1986** have been published in the University *Reporter* and copies may be obtained from the office of the Faculty of Oriental Studies.

Part II*

A candidate who has obtained honours in Part I may take Part II one or two years after doing so, but not earlier than his third nor later than his fourth year. A candidate who has obtained honours in another Tripos may take Part II one or two years after doing so, but not earlier than his third nor later than his fifth year.

Subjects of examination

The following papers are set:

Aramaic

Am. 11. Aramaic specified texts, 1, and unspecified texts.

Candidates are required to use the square Hebrew script.

Am. 12. Aramaic specified texts, 2.

Am. 13. Aramaic unspecified texts and composition.

Am. 14. Special subject.

Assyriology

As. 11. Akkadian specified texts.

As. 12. Akkadian unspecified texts.

As. 13. History of Mesopotamia (also serves as Paper 3 for option (*e*) in Archaeology of Part II of the Archaeological and Anthropological Tripos).

As. 14. Civilization of Mesopotamia.

As. 15. Special subject in Assyriology.

As. 16. Art and archaeology of Mesopotamia (also serves as Paper 4 for options (*e*) and (*g*) in Archaeology of Part II of the Archaeological and Anthropological Tripos).

As. 17. Practical examination in Mesopotamian archaeology.

Chinese Studies

C. 11. Classical Chinese texts, 1.

C. 12. Classical Chinese texts, 2.

C. 13. Modern Chinese texts, 1.

C. 14. Modern Chinese texts, 2.

C. 15. Chinese literature (specified subject).

C. 16. Chinese literature (specified readings).

C. 17. Chinese history (specified subject).

C. 18. Chinese history (specified readings).

C. 19. Chinese linguistics (specified subject).

* There are also ten papers in Iranian Studies. Details are available from the Faculty Board.

Egyptology

E. 11. Old, Middle, and Late Egyptian specified texts (may also serve as a special subject for Paper 5 in option (*e*) in Archaeology for Part II of the Archaeological and Anthropological Tripos).

E. 12. Old, Middle, and Late Egyptian unspecified texts.

E. 13. Specified texts in hieratic book hands of the Middle and New Kingdoms.

In Paper E. 13 passages are set for transcription into hieroglyphic as well as translation into English.

E. 14. Coptic specified texts.

E. 15. Coptic unspecified texts.

E. 16. Coptic composition, Coptic grammar and literary history.

In Papers E. 14, 15, and 16 questions are set relating to the Sa'īdic, Akhmīmic, Fayyūmic, and Bohairic dialects of Coptic, but candidates other than those who offer Egyptology under (*d*) (ii) (p. 380) are required to answer questions relating to the Sa'īdic and Bohairic dialects only.

E. 17. Ancient Egyptian civilization.

E. 18. Special subject in Egyptology.

E. 19. Art and archaeology of Ancient Egypt (also serves as Paper 4 for option (*e*) in Archaeology of Part II of the Archaeological and Anthropological Tripos).

E. 20. Early history of the Coptic church, monasticism and art.

E. 21. Practical examination in Egyptian archaeology.

E. 22. History of Ancient Egypt.

General Linguistics

G. 1. General linguistics (Paper 111 of Part II of the Modern and Medieval Languages Tripos).

G. 2. Phonetics (Paper 112 of Part II of the Modern and Medieval Languages Tripos).

Hebrew

H. 11. Hebrew specified texts.

H. 12. Classical Hebrew language.

H. 13. General paper.

H. 14. Post-biblical Jewish texts.

H. 15. Modern Hebrew, 1.

H. 16. Modern Hebrew, 2.

H. 17. Semitic specified texts and philology.

H. 18. Special subject.

Indian Studies

In. 11. Sanskrit specified texts.

In. 12. Sanskrit specified and unspecified texts.

In. 13. Prakrit specified texts.

In. 14. Prakrit specified and unspecified texts.

In. 15. Classical Indian language and composition.

In. 16. Hindi specified texts, 1.

The texts in Paper In. 16 will be in medieval Hindi.

In. 17. Hindi specified texts, 2.

The texts in Paper In. 17 will be in modern Hindi.

In. 18. Hindi unspecified texts.

In. 19. Hindi essay, and history of the Hindi language.

In. 20. Indian religion.

In. 21. Prehistory and protohistory of India.

In. 22. Indian art and archaeology (500 B.C.–A.D. 400).

In. 23. Indian epigraphy.

In. 24. Medieval Indian literature.

In. 25. Specified subject in nineteenth- or twentieth-century Indian history.

In. 26. Special subject in modern South Asian history, 1.[1]

In. 27. Special subject in modern South Asian history, 2.

In. 28. Specified subject in South Asian Studies (may also serve as one of the subjects for Paper 15 of Part II of the Economics Tripos, and as Paper 41 of Part II of the Social and Political Sciences Tripos). This paper will be 'The sociology and politics of South Asia'. The paper deals with the social institutions of South Asia, broadly defined; the impact of towns, industrialization and the development of agriculture, the growth of literacy, and modern religious and cultural movements. In the study of politics some attention is given to the closing decade of imperial rule, but the main emphasis is on the development of politics in India since 1947. The political system, and the operation of parties within it, the problems of 'one party dominance' and of factionalism receive special attention. The politics of Pakistan, Bangladesh, and Sri Lanka also fall within the scope of the paper.

In. 29. Selected readings in a north Indian language.

Bengali or Urdu, as may be specified from time to time by the Faculty Board.

[1] The special subject in **1984**: Gandhi, reform, and agitation: Indian politics, 1916–1922.

Islamic and Middle Eastern Studies (Arabic, Persian, and Turkish)

- Ar. 11. Arabic prose composition and unseens.
- Ar. 12. Arabic unseens and essay.
- Ar. 13. Arabic literature, 1.
- Ar. 14. Arabic literature, 2.
- Ar. 15. History of the Arab world.
- P. 11. Persian prose composition and unseens.
- P. 12. Persian unseens and essay.
- P. 13. Persian literature, 1.
- P. 14. Persian literature, 2.
- P. 15. Persian history.
- T. 11. Turkish prose composition and unseens.
- T. 12. Turkish unseens and essay.
- T. 13. Turkish literature, 1.
- T. 14. Turkish literature, 2.
- T. 15. Turkish history.
- Is. 11. Islamic history.

Japanese Studies

- J. 21. Classical Japanese specified texts.
- J. 22. Classical Japanese unspecified texts.
- J. 23. Modern Japanese specified texts.
- J. 24. Modern Japanese unspecified texts.
- J. 25. Japanese composition and essay.
- J. 26. Japanese literature (specified subject).
- J. 27. Japanese history (specified subject).

Each paper in Part II is set for three hours. A candidate in Assyriology or Hebrew Studies, or Hebrew and Arabic, or Hebrew and Aramaic, or Hebrew and Assyriology or Hebrew and Egyptology or Indian Studies may, subject to the permission of the Faculty Board, opt to submit, and a candidate in Chinese or Islamic and Middle Eastern, or Japanese Studies must submit a dissertation of not more than twelve thousand words (inclusive of appendices and notes) on a subject approved by the Faculty Board of Oriental Studies. The dissertation should show evidence of reading, judgement, and a power of exposition, but not necessarily evidence of original research, and must give full references to the sources used. Each dissertation must be accompanied by a summary of not more than 300 words in English; candidates offering papers in Chinese Studies must furnish instead a summary in Chinese of not less than 600 characters. A candidate must submit his proposed subject through his Tutor to the Secretary of the Faculty Board so as to reach him not later than the division of the Michaelmas Term preceding the examination and a candidate who opts to submit a dissertation subject to the permission of the Faculty Board must submit his application for permission at the same time as he applies for approval of his subject. The Secretary will communicate to the candidate's Tutor the approval of his subject by the Board. Two copies of the dissertation marked with the candidate's name and College must be submitted through a candidate's Tutor so as to reach the Secretary of the Faculty Board not later than the third day of the full Easter Term. If the Examiners consider that a dissertation is not sufficiently legible, they may require that it be resubmitted in typescript.

The papers on specified texts may contain questions on the subject-matter and criticism of those texts, and the papers on unspecified texts may contain questions arising immediately out of the passages set for translation.

Oral examinations are held in the modern spoken forms of Arabic, Chinese, Hebrew, Hindi, Japanese, Persian, and Turkish.

In order to obtain honours in Part II a candidate must reach the standard for honours *either* in the papers listed in *one* of the following sections (*a*)–(*o*)* *or* in the papers set for another Oriental language or subject or combination of languages approved by the Faculty Board of Oriental Studies. He must take the oral examination in the modern spoken form of the language where specified. He must reach the honours standard in *each* language offered if he wishes to be classed; and he must submit or, subject to the permission of the Faculty Board, opt to submit a dissertation as specified below:

(*a*) Assyriology

As. 14, 16, 17; *either* As. 15 *or* a dissertation; *either* As. 1, 2, 13 *or* As. 11–13 *or* H. 11–13 *or* Am. 11–13.

(*b*) Assyriology and Arabic

As. 11, 12; Ar. 11, 13, 14; *either* As. 14 *or* Is. 11 *or* a dissertation.

(*c*) Chinese Studies

C. 11–14; *either* C. 15, 16, *or* C. 17, 18, *or* C. 19 and G. 1 *or* G. 2; a dissertation; Chinese oral.

* Items (*l*), Iranian Studies, and (*m*), Iranian and Persian, are not included. Details available from the Faculty Board.

(*d*) Egyptology

Either (i) *philological option*:
E. 11–15, 17, 22;

or (ii) *archaeological option*:
E. 11, 12, 17–19, 21, 22;

or (iii) *Coptic and Arabic*:
E. 14-16, E. 20; Ar. 1, 3; Is. 1;

or (iv) *Coptic and Syriac*:
E. 14–16, E. 20; Am. 12–14.

(*e*) Hebrew Studies
H. 11–16, Hebrew oral (when Modern Hebrew is prescribed for Paper H. 15); Am. 11; *either* H. 17 *or* H. 18 *or* a dissertation.

(*f*) Hebrew and Arabic
H. 11–14; Ar. 11, 13, 14; *either* H. 17 *or* H. 18 *or* Is. 11 *or* a dissertation.

(*g*) Hebrew and Aramaic
H. 11–14; Am. 11–13; *either* H. 17 *or* H. 18 *or* Am. 14 *or* a dissertation.

(*h*) Hebrew and Assyriology
H. 11–14; *either* As. 1–3 *or* As. 11–13; *either* H. 17 *or* H. 18 *or* As. 14 *or* As. 15 *or* a dissertation.

(*i*) Hebrew and Egyptology
H. 11–13; E. 11, 12, 22; *either* Am. 11 *or* E. 17 *or* H. 14 *or* H. 15 *or* H. 17 *or* H. 18 *or* a dissertation.

(*j*) Hindi and Persian

Either (i) In. 16–19, 24, Hindi oral; *either* P. 1, 2, Persian oral *or* P. 11, 13.

or (ii) P. 11, 13, 15; Hindi oral; *either* In. 3–5 *or* In. 16–18.

(*k*) Indian Studies

Either (i) *Classical Indian Studies*: In. 15; not less than three papers chosen from In. 11–14; additional papers chosen from In. 20–23 so as to bring the total number of papers offered by the candidate to seven, provided that one of the papers chosen from In. 20–23 may be replaced by a dissertation;

or (ii) *Modern Indian Studies*: In. 16–19; Hindi oral; and three papers chosen from In. 20; In. 24–29; provided that

(1) a dissertation may be offered in place of one paper from In. 20, 24, 25, 28, and 29,

(2) a candidate who offers In. 26 must offer In. 27 also and *vice versa*;

or (iii) *Classical and Modern Indian Studies*: two papers chosen from In. 11–14 (of which one must be *either* In. 12 *or* In. 14); *either* In. 16 *or* In. 17; In. 18; *either* In. 15 *or* In. 19; two papers chosen from In. 20–29; Hindi oral; provided that

(1) a dissertation may be offered in place of one paper from In. 20, 24, 25, 28, 29,

(2) a candidate who offers In. 26 must offer In. 27 also and *vice versa*.

(*n*) Islamic and Middle Eastern Studies (Arabic, Persian, and Turkish)

Either (i) if he is a candidate in the year next after obtaining honours in another Honours Examination, a dissertation and **five** papers as follows: two papers chosen from Ar. 11, Ar. 12, P. 11, P. 12, T. 11, T. 12; one paper or two papers chosen from Ar. 13, Ar. 14, P. 13, P. 14, T. 13, T. 14; two papers or one paper (as the case may be) chosen from Ar. 15, P. 15, T. 15, Is. 11;

or (ii) if he is a candidate in the year next but one after obtaining honours in another Honours Examination, a dissertation and five papers in accordance with (i) above, together with a **sixth** paper chosen from the papers there specified;

provided that a candidate under (i) or (ii) who offers Ar. 12 must offer Arabic oral; a candidate who offers P. 12 must offer Persian oral; and a candidate who offers T. 12 must offer Turkish oral.

(*o*) Japanese Studies

J. 21–25; *either* J. 26 *or* J. 27 *or* C. 1, 2 *or* G. 1; Japanese oral; a dissertation.

No candidate for Part II may offer, from the alternatives prescribed in (*a*), (*d*), (*j*), (*k*), (*l*), (*m*) or (*o*) above, a paper or a pair or group of papers from among the Part I papers if, as a candidate for Part I, he has previously offered that paper or a paper of that pair or group of papers.

Specified texts, specified periods and subjects, and special subjects selected for Part II of the Tripos in **1985** and **1986** have been published in the University *Reporter* and details may be obtained from the office of the Faculty of Oriental Studies.

The Preliminary Examination for Part I

In the Preliminary Examination each paper in the list given below is set if a candidate wishes to present himself for examination therein. The questions set are simpler than those set for the Tripos.

Arabic Studies

Ar. 1. Classical Arabic specified texts and grammar.
Ar. 2. Classical Arabic unspecified texts and composition.
Ar. 3. Islamic institutions.
Ar. 4. Modern Arabic specified texts.
Ar. 5. Modern Arabic unspecified texts.

Aramaic

Am. 1. Aramaic specified texts.
Am. 2. Aramaic unspecified texts and composition.

Assyriology

As. 1. Akkadian specified texts.
As. 2. Akkadian unspecified texts, grammar, and syntax.

Chinese Studies

C. 1. Classical Chinese texts.
C. 2. Modern Chinese texts.
C. 3. Modern Chinese translation and composition.
C. 4. Chinese cultural history.

Hebrew Studies

H. 1. Hebrew specified texts.
H. 2. Hebrew unspecified texts, grammar, and syntax.
H. 3. Modern Hebrew specified and unspecified texts.
H. 4. Jewish history, 1800–1918.

Indian Studies

In. 1. Classical Indian specified texts.
In. 2. Classical Indian unspecified texts and composition.
In. 3. Hindi specified texts.
In. 4. Hindi unspecified texts and composition.
In. 5. Introduction to Indian studies, 1.
In. 6. Introduction to Indian studies, 2.

Japanese Studies

J. 1. Modern Japanese specified texts.
J. 2. Modern Japanese unspecified texts.
J. 3. Modern Japanese composition and grammar.
J. 4. Japanese history and thought.

Persian

P. 1. Persian specified texts and grammar.
P. 2. Persian unspecified texts and composition.

Turkish

Tk. 1. Turkish specified texts and grammar.
Tk. 2. Turkish unspecified texts and composition.

Oral examinations are held in the modern spoken forms of Hindi, Chinese, Japanese, and Turkish.

A candidate must offer *either* the papers appropriate to one of the following sections: (*a*) Arabic Studies; (*b*) Arabic and Persian; (*c*) Arabic and Turkish; (*d*) Chinese Studies; (*e*) Hebrew Studies; (*f*) Hebrew and Arabic; (*g*) Hebrew and Aramaic; (*h*) Hebrew and Assyriology; (*i*) Hindi and Persian; (*j*) Indian Studies; (*k*) Japanese Studies; (*l*) Persian and Turkish; *or* special papers as may be approved by the Faculty Board of Oriental Studies if he proposes to offer himself for examination in the Tripos in Oriental languages and subjects which are not specified for the Tripos; provided that, if he offers the papers appropriate to sections (*b*), (*c*), (*f*), (*g*), (*h*), (*i*) or (*l*), or offers special papers in two languages approved by the Faculty Board, he must pass in both languages. Applications to take such special papers must be made to the Faculty Board not later than 21 October next preceding the examination.

In respect of each of the sections (*a*) to (*l*), a candidate must take the following papers and must take the oral examination in the modern spoken form of the language specified:

(*a*) Arabic Studies: Ar. 1–5.
(*b*) Arabic and Persian: Ar. 1–3; P. 1–2.
(*c*) Arabic and Turkish: Ar. 1–3; Tk. 1–2, Turkish oral.
(*d*) Chinese Studies: C. 1–4, Chinese oral.
(*e*) Hebrew Studies: H. 1–4.
(*f*) Hebrew and Arabic: H. 1–2; Ar. 1–3.
(*g*) Hebrew and Aramaic: H. 1–2; Am. 1–2.
(*h*) Hebrew and Assyriology: H. 1–2; As. 1–2.
(*i*) Hindi and Persian: In. 3, 4, Hindi oral; P. 1–2, Ar. 3.

(*j*) Indian Studies: *either* (i) In. 1, 2 and two papers chosen from In. 3–6, *or* (ii) In. 3, 4 and two papers chosen from In. 1, 2, 5, 6, provided that any candidate who offers In. 3 or In. 4 must offer Hindi oral. Paper In. 5 will include questions on art, archaeology, and history. Paper In. 6 will include questions on language, literature and religion.

(*k*) Japanese Studies: J. 1–4, Japanese oral.

(*l*) Persian and Turkish: P. 1–2; Tk. 1–2, Turkish oral, Ar. 3.

Specified texts for the Preliminary Examination for Part I for **1985** have been published in the *Reporter* and details may be obtained from the Faculty of Oriental Studies.

Examination in Oriental Studies for the Ordinary B.A. Degree

The papers for the Ordinary Examination in Oriental Studies, and the specified texts, are the same as those set for the Preliminary Examination for Part I. A candidate for the Ordinary Examination must offer all the papers that he would be required to offer if he were a candidate for that Preliminary Examination.

M.Phil. Degree in Oriental Studies (one-year course)

There will be a one-year course consisting of lectures, seminars, and individual supervision, leading to an examination in Oriental Studies for the M.Phil. Degree (one-year course). The scheme of examination will consist of:

(*a*) a thesis of not more than 15,000 words, inclusive of footnotes, appendices, and bibliography, on a topic approved by the Degree Committee for the Faculty of Oriental Studies, which must fall within one of the following subject areas:

(i) Assyriology;
(ii) Chinese Studies;
(iii) Indian Studies;
(iv) Islamic Studies,

and in respect of which the Degree Committee may in giving their approval specify a minimum length for the thesis;

and

(*b*) three written papers, which shall fall within the same subject area as the thesis offered by the candidate under section (*a*) above, and shall be chosen, subject to the approval of the Degree Committee for the Faculty of Oriental Studies, from prescribed papers 1–3.

Details of these papers are obtainable from the Faculty Board of Oriental Studies.

PHILOSOPHY

In this subject there are courses of study followed by candidates for:

The *Philosophy Tripos*, which is divided into three Parts, I A, I B, and II.
The *Preliminary Examination for Part I B of the Philosophy Tripos.*
The *Preliminary Examination for Part II of the Philosophy Tripos.*
The *Ordinary Examination* in Philosophy for the Ordinary B.A. Degree.

The Philosophy Tripos

Philosophy is a study of problems which are ultimate and very general, being those concerned with the nature of reality, knowledge, truth, morality, and human purpose. In university courses it is studied in a manner which lays considerable emphasis on precise and careful argument. In the earlier stages of the Cambridge course, the central elements are logic, metaphysics, ethics, and philosophy of mind; while attention is also paid to political philosophy, philosophy of religion, philosophy of science, and aesthetics. As the course proceeds the number of optional elements increases, so that in Part II there are no compulsory papers.

The Tripos consists of three separate Parts, and it is possible for students to read the subject for one, two, or three years, and also either before or after reading another subject. It is not necessary for students to have done any work in philosophy before reading the subject at Cambridge and Part I A of the Tripos is taught on the assumption that they have not. Students with both Arts and Science A-levels are acceptable.

Part I A provides an introduction to the fundamental topics of metaphysics and the philosophy of mind, ethics, and logic, together with detailed work on prescribed texts.

Part I B contains further study of metaphysics, logic, and philosophy of mind. Candidates also take two further papers from a list comprising empirical psychology, ethics, prescribed texts, philosophy of science, political philosophy, and aesthetics.

Both Parts I A and I B also contain an essay paper.

In Part II, students who have taken I B must choose any four of eleven papers, together with an essay paper or an extended essay written during the year and submitted in advance. The Examiners may call a candidate for interview in connexion with his extended essay, and may require him to resubmit it in typescript if the original work is not sufficiently legible. The subjects covered are metaphysics, ethics, two papers in the history of modern philosophy from Descartes (for which works of different authors are prescribed), history of ancient philosophy, philosophy of science, mathematical logic, philosophical logic, political philosophy, and aesthetics. There is also provision for a special subject paper to be set from time to time. It will not be set in 1985 and 1986.

Change to philosophy after one or two years in another subject:

(1) Students who change to philosophy at the end of their *first* year may attempt (i) Part IB in one year, (ii) Part IB in two years, or (iii) Part II in two years, with the following special arrangements:

Part IB in two years. The Part IA papers serve as a preliminary examination after one year.

Part II in two years. A preliminary examination is provided after one year.

(2) Students who change to philosophy at the end of their *second* year may attempt (i) Part IB in one year or (ii) Part II in one year, with the following special arrangements:

Part II in one year. Candidates who obtained honours in a Tripos examination in their previous subject the year before *may* take one fewer paper (other than the essay paper or extended essay); if they do not, their worst paper is discounted.

Part II also caters for students able to study ancient philosophy in the original texts, especially those who have obtained honours in Part I of the Classical Tripos. Such a candidate may combine the essay paper or extended essay and any two other papers in Part II (except that in ancient philosophy) with Papers B1 and B2 of Part II of the Classical Tripos (if he takes Part II in one year) or with Papers B1, B2, and B3 (if he takes Part II in two years).

Parts IA, IB, and II of the Tripos

Details of the topics prescribed for the various papers in Parts IA, IB, and II of the Tripos are given below. Although students are not expected to have studied any philosophy before embarking on the Tripos, it is certainly useful for them to have read some books on the subject first, if only to enable them to get a better idea of what their work will be like. Any of the books in the following brief list, especially Russell's *Problems of Philosophy*, can be recommended as being a significant contribution to the subject, and representative of what is to be expected in studying philosophy:

Descartes, *Meditations*; Berkeley, *Principles of Human Knowledge*; B. Russell, *The Problems of Philosophy*; A. J. Ayer, *Language, Truth and Logic*; I. Hacking, *Why Does Language Matter to Philosophy?*; K. Campbell, *Body and Mind*; C. G. Hempel, *Philosophy of Natural Science*; Hume, *Enquiry Concerning the Principles of Morals*; J. S. Mill, *Utilitarianism*; B. Williams, *Morality*.

Part IA

Part IA may be taken only at the end of a student's first year as an undergraduate. All the following papers must be taken.

In Papers 1–4 candidates are asked to answer four questions out of at least ten set.

1. Metaphysics and philosophy of mind

Things and properties. Past, present, and future. Necessity and contingency*. Meaning and* verification. Induction, evidence. Knowledge and scepticism. Deity, Identity, including personal identity. Free-will. Perception. Belief. Mind and matter.

2. Ethics

Moral and non-moral reasons for action. Amoralism. Theories of moral judgement. Virtues and moral character. Actions, consequences and motives. The 'categorical imperative'. Practical reason. Justice and happiness. Rights. Fact and Value.

3. Logic

Questions will be set on some of the following and related topics:

The province of logic. Logic and language: sentences, statements, and propositions; formal languages.

Propositional logic: truth-functions, tautologies, implication; problems of translation; formal proof, including methods of natural deduction. The concept of a many-valued logic.

Introduction to predicate logic: translation into the language of quantifiers and variables; validity and counter-examples; elements of the logic of identity, descriptions, classes, and relations. The concept of number.

Axiomatic method: theories, including consistency and completeness; proof, entailment and strict implication.

Introduction to the philosophy of logic.

* To be deleted from 1 October 1985.

4. Set text or texts

In **1985** and **1986**: Hume: *Dialogues Concerning Natural Religion*; Plato, *Meno*.

5. Essay

Part IB

A student may take Part IB in any but his first year. He must take Papers 1, 2, 3, and 10 and two other papers. No candidate who has previously offered Experimental Psychology in Part IB in the Natural Sciences Tripos may offer Paper 9.

1. Metaphysics (also serves as Paper O4 of Part II of the Classical Tripos)

Questions may be set on the topics for Part IA Metaphysics and on some of the following and related topics:

The nature of philosophy. Truth. Meaning*. Realism and idealism. Time. Primary and secondary qualities. Causality and change. Nature and grounds of religious belief. God.

2. Philosophy of mind

The general character of mind and the mental. Privacy, intentionality. Mental states, acts, dispositions. Behaviourism, functionalism. Memory, intellect, and will. The emotions. Pleasure. Sensation. Action. Motivation. Voluntariness. The unconscious. Self-deception. Mental illness.

3. Logic

Questions may be set on the topics for Part IA Logic and on some of the following and related topics:

In **1985**: Introduction to theories of meaning and theories of truth. Logical form. Necessity and analyticity. Definition. Existence. Names and descriptions. Extensionality.

Predicate logic, including the semantics of quantified sentences. Elements of modal logic. Elements of many-valued logic.

From **1986**: Introduction to the philosophy of language. Logical form. Necessity and analyticity. Definition. Existence. Names and descriptions. Extensionality.

Predicate logic, including the semantics of quantified sentences. Elements of modal logic. Elements of many-valued logic.

Selected topics or texts may be prescribed from time to time.

* To be deleted from 1 October 1985.

4. Ethics

The themes of Part IA, pursued in greater depth, with additional reference to:

Concepts of 'good' and 'bad', 'right' and 'wrong'. Naturalism. Responsibility. Punishment. Ignorance, error, and constraint. Means and ends. The individual and society. Religion and morality.

5. Set texts

Texts from the history of particular areas of philosophy are prescribed. More general questions may also be asked about some of the areas covered by the texts; such areas will be specified when the texts are prescribed.

In **1985** and **1986**: Plato: *Republic* 475–535. Aristotle: *Nicomachean Ethics*. *J. E. McTaggart: *Some Dogmas of Religion.*

6. Philosophy of science

Questions will be set on some of the following and related topics:

Scientific method in natural and social sciences. Scientific explanation. Scientific theories. Scientific laws. Natural kinds. Causation†. Probability.

7. Political philosophy

Questions will be set on some of the following and related topics:

Anarchism, authority, and power. Scope and legitimacy of government. Political obligation. Democracy. State of nature and social contract. Rights. Liberty, justice, equality, welfare. Law and morality.

8. Aesthetics (also serves as Paper 11 of Part II)

A wide range of basic questions is set, on topics such as the following:

Nature of art. Understanding and evaluation. Individuation of works of art. Representation. Expression. Intentions. Imagination, originality. Art and morality. Art and nature.

9. Empirical psychology

The aims of empirical psychology. The relation of psychological studies to those of other biological sciences. Elements of the structure and function of the nervous system and sense organs.

* More general questions will be set on the philosophy of religion, the area of philosophy with which this text is concerned.

† To be replaced in 1986 by 'Causation in natural and social sciences'.

Experimental and theoretical investigations within the general field of experimental psychology. These fall broadly into the categories of studies of instinct and maturation; sensory process and perception; learning and memory; language; reaction times and the control of human skilled behaviour; social development and studies of the behaviour of infants. In most of these areas reference is made to experiments on both animal and human behaviour.

Elements of mental testing.

10. Essay

Part II

Part II may be taken in one year after Part IB or in two years or one after another honours examination. In the first two cases a candidate must offer four out of Papers 1–11 and either Paper 12 or an extended essay, provided that no candidate may offer Aesthetics if he has taken the Aesthetics paper in Part IB.

A candidate who takes Part II one year after obtaining honours in another Tripos must offer three or four out of Papers 1–11, and either Paper 12 or an extended essay. If he offers four out of Papers 1–11 the one considered by the Examiners least good will be discounted.

If a candidate has either obtained honours in Part I of the Classical Tripos or has satisfied the Faculty Board of Classics that he has the necessary Greek and Latin to benefit by the course, he may offer two out of Papers 1–4 and 6–11 and Paper 12 or an extended essay, together with papers taken from Papers B1, B2, and B3 of Part II of the Classical Tripos as follows:

(*a*) in the year after obtaining honours in Part IB or another honours examination, Papers B1 and B2, or (*b*) in the year next but one, Papers B1, B2, and B3.

The title of a proposed extended essay must be submitted for approval by the end of November, and the essay itself by the end of the Lent Term. It must be between three and six thousand words, and include due acknowledgement of sources and supervision. A candidate may be examined orally on his extended essay. Any candidate who does not submit such an essay is automatically entered for the essay paper, which carries the same weight in the examination.

In Papers 1 and 2, and 5 to 11, candidates are asked to answer three questions out of at least ten set. In Papers 3 and 4 at least fifteen questions will be set.

1. Metaphysics

Questions may be set on the topics for Paper 1 of Part IA and Paper 1 of Part IB and on some of the following and related topics in metaphysics, theory of knowledge, the philosophy of mind, and the philosophy of religion:

Ontology. The rationality of belief. Miracles. God and human freedom. Mind and body. Consciousness. Understanding. Meaning. Images and imagination. Mental events, states, and dispositions.

2. Ethics

The paper will include, besides central questions in ethics, questions in the philosophy of mind (on such topics as decision, intention, the will, motivation, action, responsibility and self-knowledge).

3. History of modern philosophy I. The prescribed texts are:

In **1985** and **1986**: Descartes, *Meditations, Discourse on the Method*; Spinoza, *Ethics*; Locke, *An Essay Concerning Human Understanding*; Leibniz, *Discourse on Metaphysics, Philosophical Writings* (ed. G.H.R. Parkinson, Everyman); Hume, *A Treatise of Human Nature*, Book I, Parts i, iii, and iv; Berkeley, *The Principles of Human Knowledge, Three Dialogues between Hylas and Philonous.*

4. History of modern philosophy II. The prescribed texts are:

In **1985**: Kant, *The Critique of Pure Reason* to the end of the Transcendental Logic (A704, B732), Hegel, *Phenomenology of Mind*, Introduction, Consciousness, Self-consciousness (§73–230); *Encyclopaedia of the Philosophical Sciences*, Book I (*Logic* §1–111); Schopenhauer, *On the Basis of Morality, The Freedom of the Will, The World as Will and Representation*, Books 1 and 2; Nietzsche, *Genealogy of Morals, Beyond Good and Evil, Twilight of the Idols, The Gay Science, The Birth of Tragedy.*

In **1986**: Kant, *The Critique of Pure Reason* to the end of the Transcendental Logic (A704, B732); Hegel, *Phenomenology of Mind*, Introduction, Consciousness, Self-consciousness (§73–230), *Encyclopaedia of the Philosophical Sciences*, Book I (Logic, §1–111); Nietzsche, *Genealogy of Morals, The Gay Science, The Birth of Tragedy, Thus Spoke Zarathustra.* All Nietzsche texts in translations by Walter Kaufmann.

5. History of ancient philosophy

The prescribed texts for study in translation are:

In **1985**: Plato, *Sophist*; Aristotle, *De Anima*.

In **1986**: Plato, *Theaetetus*; Aristotle, *De Anima*.

6. Philosophy of science

Questions may be set on the topics for Part IB Philosophy of science and on some of the following and related topics:

Objectivity in science. The role of values in natural and social sciences. The meaning and ontology of scientific theories. The reducibility of one science or theory to another. Scientific progress. The acceptance, confirmation, testing and refutation of hypotheses. Principles of decision-making. Space and time. Problems in the philosophy of physics; of biology; of psychology.

7. Mathematical logic

Questions will be set on some of the following and related topics:

First-order and second-order logic. Formal theories, consistency, completeness, axiomatisability, decidability, models and categoricity. Gödel's theorem. Recursive functions and computability. Proof theory. Intuitionism. Set theory. Infinity. Modal logic. Many-valued logic.

8. Philosophical logic

Questions may be set on the topics for Paper 3 of Part IB and on some of the following and related topics:

In **1985**: Truth. Meaning. Reference. Modality and quantification. Iterated modalities. Speech-acts. The semantic paradoxes. Identity. Subject and predicate. Conditionals. Mathematical truth and the existence of mathematical objects. Pure and applied mathematics.

From **1986**: Semantics. Reference. Modality and quantification. Iterated modalities. Speech-acts. The semantic paradoxes. Identity. Subject and predicate. Conditionals. Mathematical truth and the existence of mathematical objects. Proof. Pure and applied mathematics.

Selected topics and texts may be prescribed from time to time.

9. Special subject specified by the Faculty Board

In **1985** and **1986**: No paper will be set.

10. Political philosophy

Questions may be set on the topics for Part IB Political Philosophy and on some of the following and related topics:

Representation, participation, social decision-making. Nature and justification of law and judicial punishment. Coercion. Paternalism. Civil disobedience. Fundamental concepts of marxist theory.

Selected texts may be specified from time to time.

In **1985** and **1986**: Marx and Engels: *The German Ideology*, Part I. Hobbes: *Leviathan*, Introduction; Part I; Part II.

11. Aesthetics (Paper 8 of Part IB)

12. Essay.

The Preliminary Examination for Part IB

The examination consists of the same papers as compose Part IA. Candidates must offer the Essay paper and three or four of the other papers. A candidate who offers the Essay paper and four other papers will be classed on the basis of the Essay paper and the three best of his other papers.

The Preliminary Examination for Part II

Eleven papers are available. Papers 1–8 and 10 are the same as the correspondingly-numbered papers of Part IB. The others are:

9. Outlines of mathematical logic and philosophy of mathematics

Questions may be set on the topics specified for Paper 7 of Part II and on the topics in philosophy of mathematics specified for Paper 8 of Part II.

11. Outlines of modern philosophy

Questions will be set on philosophers from Descartes to Kant.

Candidates must offer Paper 10 and three or four of the other papers. A candidate who offers Paper 10 and four other papers will be classed on the results of Paper 10 and the three best of his other papers.

The Examination in Philosophy for the Ordinary B.A. Degree

The examination consists of the Essay paper and any three of the other papers set for Part I B of the Philosophy Tripos.

A student who has passed or received an allowance on Part I A or Part I B of the Philosophy Tripos may not be a candidate.

M.Phil. Degree in History and Philosophy of Science

For details of this one-year course, see p. 366.

POLAR STUDIES

The M.Phil. (one-year course)

The course leading to the M.Phil. Degree in Polar Studies is intended to meet the needs of persons already working in the polar field who wish to broaden their knowledge on an interdisciplinary basis, and to enable others to gain knowledge of the polar regions in preparation for a career in which this will be relevant. Candidates need not have had any previous training in specifically polar areas of study. The possibility exists for further study towards a higher degree after completion of the M.Phil. course.

A candidate must write a thesis of up to 20,000 words on a subject proposed by him in consultation with his supervisor, and five essays or exercises on topics set by the Examiners. This work is to be done in the candidate's own time, with access to source materials, but must be submitted by specified dates. There will be an oral examination on the subject of the thesis and of the essays or exercises.

A candidate for the M.Phil. Degree must

(*a*) have been admitted to the status of Graduate Student and accepted as a candidate for the M.Phil. Degree by the Board of Graduate Studies on the recommendation of the Degree Committee of the Faculty of Geography and Geology; and

(*b*) have graduated at Cambridge or another university; *or*

(*c*) have produced other evidence to satisfy the Degree Committee and the Board of Graduate Studies of his fitness to study for the M.Phil. Degree.

An application for admission as a candidate for the M.Phil. must be sent to the Secretary of the Board of Graduate Studies and be accompanied by the names of not less than two referees and by a statement of the candidate's previous studies, attainments, and qualifications.

Subjects for essays or exercises are set by the Examiners from the following areas of study:

Environment

Climate. General geology. Oceanic circulation. Floating Ice. Ecology. Terrestrial environment – soils, permafrost, surface glaciology, flora and fauna. Marine environment – primary and secondary production, freshwater ecology.

Peoples

Ethnography of indigenous and immigrant peoples of Arctic and sub-Arctic.

History

History of exploration of northern Eurasia, northern North America, Greenland, Arctic Ocean, Antarctic.

Resources and problems of development

Renewable and non-renewable resources. Engineering problems in snow, ice, and permafrost. Transport systems and techniques. Human adaptation and health.

Administration

Government administrative structure. Relations with native peoples. International law, treaties, political and strategic factors. Territorial claims.

Research

Importance of polar regions for scientific research. International organisation of polar science and scientists.

A candidate is required to select the subject of each essay or exercise from two subjects set and to submit his essay or exercise not more than two weeks of Full Term after the announcement of the subjects. The thesis must be submitted by 30 June. In assessing a candidate's performance, the Examiners allocate half the marks to the thesis and half to the five essays or exercises.

SOCIAL AND POLITICAL SCIENCES

In this field the courses of study offered to candidates are:

The *Social and Political Sciences Tripos*, Part II.
The *Preliminary Examination* for the Social and Political Sciences Tripos, Part II.

The University of Cambridge has long had a distinguished record of postgraduate research in social anthropology, political science and sociology. The Social and Political Sciences Tripos enables undergraduates to study these subjects in a multi-disciplinary context. Part II, usually taken over two years, offers an opportunity to specialize in either sociology, or politics, or social psychology or social anthropology, and includes optional papers in related subjects such as linguistics and demography.

Within the framework of Part II it is possible to pursue many particular interests. A few compulsory papers ensure familiarity with the principal theories, findings and procedures of the social sciences, and emphasize the interdependence of theories, problems and methods in the study of society. Class work in statistics is provided and some competence in statistical and other quantitative techniques of analysis is assumed in several of the papers. Part II is distinguished from degree courses in the social sciences in many other universities by its concern with the study of pre-industrial and developing nations, the logic and philosophy of the social sciences, the social institutions of past societies, the sociology of long-term historical change and various problems and topics requiring an approach from more than one discipline. Papers are also provided in standard subjects such as kinship and the family, the sociology of economic life, political sociology, and social psychology. The papers set in Part II serve for the Preliminary examination as well. The Preliminary examination is composed of selected papers from Part II and a paper in data analysis. Part II candidates may also submit a dissertation for assessment by the Examiners for Part II.

In Part II, the student takes two papers devoted to theoretical and methodological issues in the social and political sciences and four other papers. These are chosen from a range which includes six papers in social anthropology, three in sociology, three in political science, and two in social psychology, as well as six or more papers dealing with selected topics from a multi-disciplinary standpoint, and single papers in international relations, linguistics and development. The groups of papers available in political science include special subject papers in which the student will be able to work in depth on a specified limited topic using source materials and gaining a first hand familiarity with the methods of research appropriate to the discipline. Several of the multi-disciplinary papers provide similar opportunities for concentrated study for students who wish to specialize in sociology or social psychology. One-year candidates should consult their Director of Studies and/or the relevant paper organizer when considering whether to take Social Anthropology papers.

The range of papers in Part II can thus be combined in many ways to suit varied individual interests and to give scope for different kinds of previous training. It is possible to concentrate on the study of politics, including political philosophy, and political history, or on the study of pre-industrial societies, or on the application of quantitative methods to sociological problems in contemporary economics and political life, or on the social organization of personality, values, and culture. Accordingly, the Tripos should appeal to anyone interested in the disciplined study of different types of society or in the possibility of a scientific treatment of social phenomena, whatever his previous fields of study have been. Students who have previously studied history or mathematics will perhaps feel particularly at home in the Social and Political Sciences Tripos, but those who have specialized in economics, geography, or languages will also find ample scope for their abilities.

Candidates for the Tripos Examination must be in their third or fourth year and must have been classed in another Tripos Examination either one or two years previously. Preference is not given to any particular Tripos in this respect although candidates who have read a Part I in Economics, Archaeology and Anthropology, History, Philosophy, Natural Sciences, or Mathematics will probably find themselves at an advantage. Students transferring from a Tripos with a two-year Part I such as History can take the Social and Political Sciences Tripos Part II in one year. If they take Part II, they may take either four or six papers. Candidates taking only four papers will be classed separately from those taking six papers since their qualifications as graduate social scientists are not the same as those of students who have spent two years on the course or have mastered six papers in one year. It is intended that eventually the Social and Political Sciences Tripos will become a two-part Tripos so that, instead of having to take a Part I of another Tripos before proceeding to the Social and Political Sciences Tripos, candidates who wish to devote the whole of the three years' study necessary for the B.A. Degree to the social and political sciences will be able to begin reading for the Tripos immediately on entering the University.

As with other Triposes, only a small proportion of those who read the Social and Political Sciences Tripos will be able to proceed to academic careers in the subject. More generally, the Tripos can provide a suitable training for careers in the civil service, in business, and in social and public administration. It should also qualify people for the wide variety of challenging posts which are opening up for social scientists on the staffs of local authorities and development corporations both at home and abroad. Numerous international organizations and research institutes are also now seeking qualified social scientists and, although the course does not qualify for the social work professions without further training, it does provide the best kind of academic background for such training.

Booklists may be obtained from Directors of Studies or from the Secretary of the Social and Political Sciences Committee, Free School Lane.

The Social and Political Sciences Tripos

The Tripos consists of one Part, Part II, and the scheme of the examination is as follows:

Part II

Group A: Common Core

1. Theories in the social sciences.
2. Research methods and analysis.
3. Introduction to theory and method.

Main subject groups: Groups B, C, D, and E

Group B: Social Anthropology

5. Non-industrial economics (Paper 1 of Group I(*a*) of Part II of the Archaeological and Anthropological Tripos).
6. Religion, ritual, and ideology (Paper 2 of Group I(*a*) of Part II of the Archaeological and Anthropological Tripos).
7. Kinship, marriage, and the family (Paper 3 of Group I(*a*) of Part II of the Archaeological and Anthropological Tripos).
8. Political anthropology (Paper 4 of Group I(*a*) of Part II of the Archaeological and Anthropological Tripos).
9. Change, development, and decline (Paper 6 of Group I(*a*) of Part II of the Archaeological and Anthropological Tripos).

10. Urban and ethnic studies (Paper 7 in Social Anthropology of Part II of the Archaeological and Anthropological Tripos).

Group C: Sociology

15. The sociology of politics.
16. The sociology of economic life.
17. The sociology of education.

Group D: Political Science

20. Political philosophy (Paper 5 of Part II of the Historical Tripos).
21. The politics of a specified society.

In **1985** and **1986**: The political culture of the United States since 1900.

22. A special subject.
In **1985** and **1986**: Revolution.

Group E: Social Psychology

25. Attitudes and personality.
26. The psychology of development.

Group F: Other main papers

30. The sociology and politics of development.
31. General linguistics (Paper 111 of Part II of the Modern and Medieval Languages Tripos).

Group G: Specialized papers

40. Population studies.
41. The sociology and politics of South Asia.[1]
43. The sociology and politics of Latin America.
44. The politics and sociology of the U.S.S.R. since 1917.
45. Women in society.
46. The development of the international system since the seventeenth century (the subject specified for Paper 7 of Part II of the Historical Tripos).
47. A period in the history of political thought (Paper 4 of Part II of the Historical Tripos, option (*b*)).
48. Deviance.
49. Social aspects of medicine.

[1] For so long as the subject has been specified by the Faculty Board of Oriental Studies for Paper I. 28 of the Oriental Studies Tripos.

Except in certain circumstances permitted by the Social and Political Sciences Committee (in which case the entry of papers for a particular candidate will be specified, Scheme X), a candidate who takes Part II in the year next after obtaining honours in another Honours Examination must offer

either Papers 1 and 2 from Group A, and any one of Schemes J–N (see below);

or Paper 3 from Group A, one paper from any group, and any one of the following Schemes O–S:

either	Scheme O	two papers from any one of Groups B, or C, or D, or E;
or	Scheme P	Paper 17 and one paper from Group E;
or	Scheme Q	Paper 15 and one paper from Group D;
or	Scheme R	Paper 30 and *either* Paper 15 *or* Paper 16;
or	Scheme S	Paper 26, and either Paper 7 or Paper 31.

A candidate who takes Part II in the year next but one after obtaining honours in another Honours Examination must offer Papers 1 and 2 *and*

either	Scheme J	two papers from Group B and two papers from any group or groups;
or	Scheme K	two papers from Group C, one paper from Group C or G, and one paper from any group;
or	Scheme L	*either* two papers from Group D *or* Paper 15 and one paper from Group D, *and* one paper from Group G and one paper from any group;
or	Scheme M	two papers from Group E, and two papers from any group or groups;
or	Scheme N	two papers from any one of Groups B, or C, or D, or E, and two papers from another one of these groups.

A candidate for Part II may be allowed to offer a combination of papers not specified above, provided that his Tutor makes the necessary application before the division of the Michaelmas Term before the examination. This combination would be specified in the entry of papers as Scheme X. It is also possible to submit in place of any one paper other than a paper from Group A, a dissertation of not less than 6,000 words and not more than 10,000 words, exclusive of footnotes, but inclusive of appendices, on an approved topic within the scope of the papers concerned. Each page of statistical tables is regarded as equivalent to a page of text of the same size.

A candidate wishing to offer a dissertation must submit his proposed topic for approval through his Tutor to the Secretary of the Social and Political Sciences Committee in accordance with any instructions issued by the Committee and in any case not later than the last day of Full Michaelmas Term, and must obtain the approval of the Committee for his topic not later than the division of the Lent Term, next preceding the examination. Each candidate whose topic has been approved must submit his dissertation through his Tutor to reach the Secretary not later than the end of the first week of the Full Easter Term in which the examination is to be held.

The contents of the papers are as follows:

PART II

Group A: Common Core

1. Theories in the social sciences

The object of this paper is to examine major schools of thought in the development of social theory since the early nineteenth century. The paper is explicitly interdisciplinary, and covers traditions of thought relevant to one or more of the following problem-areas: the logical status of the social sciences; the relation of the individual and society; the organization of economic and political institutions. Traditions of thought covered include: the early development of Marxism; Comtean positivism; the emergence of psychoanalytic theory; functionalism in anthropology and sociology; the hermeneutic tradition; interpretative social science; structuralism; and contemporary developments in Marxism and critical theory.

2. Research methods and analysis

The relationship between theories and methods in the social sciences. Modes of explanation, theory construction, models, and hypotheses. Special difficulties of and opportunities for explanation in social analysis. The nature, collection, and analysis of data: the logical continuity of qualitative and quantitative data. The relation of indices to concepts, problems of measurement, scaling techniques, the use of descriptive statistics, sampling. Research design and analysis; theoretical and technical determinants of design; controlled and uncontrolled experiments; multivariate analysis, statistics of relationship, significance. Continuities in social research.

Candidates will be expected to discuss the relevance of methods studied to the analysis of selected soicological problems.

3. Introduction to theory and method

Social science and its historical development. Introduction to the philosophy of social science. The distinction between description and analysis in social science. The distinctive concepts and methods of various social and political sciences. The place of experiment in social science.

Group B: Social Anthropology

5. Non-industrial economics (Paper 1 of Part II, Social Anthropology, of the Archaeological and Anthropological Tripos)

6. Religion, ritual, and ideology (Paper 2 of Part II, Social Anthropology, of the Archaeological and Anthropological Tripos)

7. Kinship, marriage, and the family (Paper 3 of Part II, Social Anthropology, of the Archaeological and Anthropological Tripos)

This paper will attempt to cover the kinship and family of non-European, peasant, and industrial societies, but there will be a sufficient choice of questions to enable students to concentrate upon two of these fields.

8. Political anthropology (Paper 4 of Part II, Social Anthropology, of the Archaeological and Anthropological Tripos)

9. Change, development, and decline (Paper 6 of Part II, Social Anthropology, of the Archaeological and Anthropological Tripos)

10. Urban and ethnic studies (Paper 7 in Social Anthropology of Part II of the Archaeological and Anthropological Tripos)

Group C: Sociology

15. The sociology of politics

The development of western liberal democracy: capitalism, liberalism, and social democracy. The formation and structure of capitalist states: the economy and the policy; ruling classes, élites, 'dominant' and 'counter' ideologies.

Capitalism and the non-liberal State: fascist movements, ideologies, and fascist states.

Meta-theories of state socialism: Marxist–Leninist, totalitarian, convergence, mobilization. Counterpoints to the Soviet Union: workers' control in Yugoslavia, the Cultural Revolution in China, the Czechoslovak Reform Movement. Social equality and inequality under state socialism.

'Nation-building', nationalism, and imperialism. Citizenship and social class. Class, party, and voting. Theories of 'stable democracy'. The political system and political culture, political leadership, and élites.

16. The sociology of economic life

Economy and society. The sociology of economic growth. Divergence and convergence in the economic systems of advanced societies. Sociological theories of industrialization, industrialism, and imperialism.

General features of peasant societies. Past and present peasant societies. The position of non-peasant elites. The political role of peasants in social change.

Industrial man and industrial institutions. The social structure of the modern business enterprise: the organization of management; the social and cultural organization of work; alienation, participation, and democracy. Industrial relations and industrial conflict; the sociology of strikes.

The analysis of social class: theories of social class and class conflict; comparative analysis of the class structure of capitalist and socialist societies. Changes in class structure; social and economic changes affecting the position of the manual working classes; the rise of the 'new middle class'; the effect of the separation of industrial ownership and control on class structure. Social mobility and career structures: the bases, rates, and avenues of social mobility; the influence of education upon social mobility and occupational recruitment.

The sociology of occupations. Occupational recruitment. The attitudes and behaviour of different occupational groups. Trade unions and other occupational associations.

The sociology of consumer behaviour. The relationship of work and non-work roles.

17. The sociology of education

Education as a social institution; education and social structure, including the relationship with other social institutions: economy, polity, religion, kinship, etc., as well as the various forms of social differentiation (class, status, sex, ethnicity, race) and social mobility; education and social change; educational 'institutions' and processes in local community context; educational 'institutions' as complex organizations; social aspects of educability; literacy and non-literacy: social causes and consequences; sociology of the curriculum; education as a profession; theoretical developments in the sociology of education; case studies and comparative analysis of selected educational systems in various types of society.

Group D: Political Science

20. Political philosophy (Paper 5 of Part II of the Historical Tripos)

21. The politics of a specified society

The politics of a particular country will be selected for detailed analysis.

For the examinations to be held in **1985** and **1986** the subject will be: The political culture of the United States since 1900.

The paper is concerned with the nature of the American political culture: the dominant (and deviant) political beliefs, values and goals, and their relationship to political institutions and actions. Among topics to be considered are:

(*a*) the nature of American democracy; limited government, pluralism and consensus; liberalism, conservatism, radicalism and socialism;
(*b*) constitutionalism and federalism; national, state and local authority institutions;
(*c*) political motivation; movements, parties and groups; voting behaviour; public opinion;
(*d*) political implications of social structure: class, immigration, race, and ethnic politics;
(*e*) aspects of the political culture: ideology, idealism and self-interest; pluralism and power; stability and change.

22. A special subject: Revolution

Approaches to the understanding of revolution: history of ideas, political theory, political sociology, comparative history.

The development of the concept of revolution: regime-transformation and historical process; the transition from sacred to secular conceptions of historical process. The English Revolution of the seventeenth century. The French Revolution. The concept of bourgeois revolution. The emergence of the role of professional revolutionary. The development of counter-revolutionary thought. Major theorists of revolutionary process: De Tocqueville, Marx, Lenin, Trotsky, Mao.

The critical assessment of revolutionary political theory: the concept of proletarian revolution; the role of the party; permanent revolution; imperialism; the transition to socialism; cultural revolution.

'Theories' of revolution and social change in sociology: conceptual and methodological problems. The relationship between sociological explanation and revolutionary consciousness: Marxism and sociology. Fascist ideologies, movements, and states.

The analysis of particular revolutions and attempted revolutions: England, France, Russia, China, Mexico, Germany, Italy, Yugoslavia, Vietnam, Cuba.

Group E: Social Psychology

25. Attitudes and personality

Problems in defining the nature and scope of social psychology. Theories of personality and personality development. The measurement of personality traits and classification of personality types.

The concept and measurement of attitudes. Theories of attitude organization, and function.

Acquisition of attitudes. The role of cognitive socialization, identification, and personality defence. Stereotypes and prejudice.

Processes of attitude change. Factors affecting changes in opinion. The role of consistency and conflict in attitude change.

Relation of attitudes to group membership, group norms, organizational roles, and reference groups. Problems of conformity and deviance. Personality predispositions to persuasibility, conformity, and prejudice.

26. The psychology of development

The development of social relations.

Theories and concepts of development. Early experience and later behaviour. The origins of social behaviour; mother–child interaction. The growth of social relationships within the family and the wider social world. Sexual differentiation and sex roles. The acquisition of social norms.

The development of cognitive abilities. Intelligence and I.Q. testing. Language acquisition. Social class differences in cognitive skills.

Social norms and abnormal behaviour. Some issues in psychopathology.

Group F: Other main papers

30. The sociology and politics of development

The history of the idea of 'development' for poorer countries since 1945. Theories of economic, social, and political change in poorer countries, including theories of development. Aspects of social and political change in selected countries, including strategies for and experiences of development.

31. General linguistics (Paper III of Part II of the Modern and Medieval Languages Tripos)

Group G: Specialized papers

40. Population studies

The elements of population analysis. General theories of the dynamics of animal and human populations. Human demography: sources of data; measurement of characteristics; some simple techniques of analysis.

The demography of pre-industrial, early industrial and contemporary non-industrial populations. The relationships between demographic variables and economic activity, social institutions, and social norms. Theories of population optima. Some case studies.

Population policy and population control.

41. The sociology and politics of South Asia (for so long as this subject has been specified by the Faculty Board of Oriental Studies for Paper In. 28 of the Oriental Studies Tripos)

43. The sociology and politics of Latin America

The emphasis of this paper is on the following topics: relations between Latin America and the world capitalist system; in particular, the effects of these on social structure of Latin-American countries; patterns of agrarian change, rural social movements. Agrarian Reform; the experience of populism and military government; urbanization and rural–urban migration; trade unions; the Mexican and Cuban Revolutions. Students will be encouraged to concentrate their efforts on a limited number of countries.

44. The politics and sociology of the USSR since 1917

Historical development of the USSR. The 1917 Revolution, the Civil War, the New Economic Policy, industrialization and collectivization, the 1941–45 war, de-Stalinization, the Brezhnev–Kosygin era, modern economic reform.

The Political System. The emergence of a one-party state, changes in the composition and role of the CPSU, the Stalin era and the cult of the personality. Elites and groups in Soviet politics; consent, dissent, deviance; the politics of market and plan.

Social change. The evolution of the Soviet social structure, the Soviet cultural revolution, changes in the structure and function of the family, developments in education and the social services; religion, nationalities, and ethnic groups, population, social stratification.

Ideology. The development of Soviet Marxism: Lenin's theories of revolution, party organization, and the State, Stalin's views on the construction of socialism, contemporary ideas about the transition to Communism. Critical theories of Soviet society: totalitarianism, state capitalism, workers' state, industrial society.

45. Women in society

The central theme of this paper is sex differences – their nature and explanation. The origins and acquisition of sex differences, and their relationship to biological, psychological, social, political, and economic factors will be considered. Specific but not exclusive attention will be given to the position of women. Particular emphasis will be given to problems of relating and integrating different approaches and different forms of explanation. The study of sex differences will be used to illustrate and explore fundamental issues in the social sciences.

The scope of the paper is as follows:

Biological factors associated with behavioural differences; the relevance of studies of animal social and sexual behaviour to human behaviour; sex differences in infancy, and parental behaviour and attitudes, and their possible explanation in terms of biological, motivational, and role considerations; the acquisition of concepts of social identity; the notions of sexual identification in psychoanalytic theory; the usefulness of concepts of 'identification' and 'role'. Cross-cultural analysis of women's role within family and kinship systems, and its connexion with their roles within the economic and political spheres, with reference to tribal, peasant, and industrialized societies. Feminist movements and theories; the structure of women's rights and activities in present-day Britain and the legal, economic, and social determinants of this; the legal status of women in modern Britain, its historic development, with reference to property and divorce; the development of social security provisions in twentieth-century Britain and its effects on the family as a social and economic unit.

46. The development of the international system since the seventeenth century (the subject specified for Paper 7 of Part II of the Historical Tripos)

47. A period in the history of political thought (Paper 4 of Part II of the Historical Tripos, option (*b*)

48. Deviance

Definitions of deviance: crime, delinquency, sexual deviance, mental illness, drug use, aggression, and dishonesty. The creation of rules, laws, and morality: conflict or consensus? The relationship between legal and social change. Functions of deviance. Formal and informal systems of social control. Explanations of deviance: scientific theories and telling stories.

Psychoanalytic and social learning theories. The personalities of deviants. Social psychological experiments on deviance: factors promoting or inhibiting deviant behaviour, the effects of observing deviance, the evaluation of deviance, reactions of others to deviance, reactions of the individual to his own deviance.

Deviance and social structure: economic theories, culture conflict, social disorganization, anomie theory, subcultural theories. The interactionist approach: social reaction and the process of identification; the creation and maintenance of deviant identities; deviant careers. Accounts by deviants of their actions. Phenomenology and the study of deviance.

49. Social aspects of medicine

Conceptual models of health, illness, and disease used by doctors, administrators, and patients, including selected cross-cultural aspects.

Medicine as social control. The definition of problems as the concern of doctors.

The organization of health care in Britain and selected other countries. The role of professionals and non-professionals. Medical and para-medical education and training. Institutional structures and individual behaviour. Decision-making and organizational theories. Economic factors.

Doctor–patient relationships viewed from psychological, sociological, and historical perspectives.

Social aspects of diagnosis and treatment, including discussion of self-medication, 'fringe' medicine, and the pharmaceutical industry.

Preliminary Examination for Part II

The Preliminary Examination may be taken only by candidates in their second or subsequent years who intend to spend two years working for Part II. The examination consists of the same papers as comprise Groups B, C, D, and E of Part II, together with Paper 3 from that part and a further paper, Paper 4, on statistics and computing for the social sciences. A candidate must offer Papers 3 and 4, and any two other papers, to be included in the list of successful candidates.

THEOLOGY AND RELIGIOUS STUDIES

In this subject there are courses of study followed by candidates for:

The *Theological and Religious Studies Tripos*, which consists of three Parts.

The *Preliminary Examination* for Parts I B and II of the Theological and Religious Studies Tripos.

The *Ordinary Examinations* for the Ordinary B.A. Degree: the Ordinary Examination in Religious Studies, and the Ordinary Examination in Biblical and Historical Theology.

The *Diploma in Theology.*

The *M.Phil. Degree.*

In all the examinations in Theology the Examiners will in general use the following texts of the Bible:

Hebrew: *Biblia Hebraica Stuttgartensia.*

Greek: Nestle/Aland text (26th edition).

English: Revised Standard Version.

The Theological and Religious Studies Tripos

Note: New regulations for the Theological and Religious Studies Tripos come into force from 1 October 1985. Details are available from the Faculty Office. Only students beginning Theology in 1985 or later will be affected by the changes to any significant degree. Directors of Studies have been informed of certain Temporary Regulations governing the choice of papers that will be available in Part II to students who come into residence in 1984.

The Faculty holds a one-day conference each year, in which senior and junior members try to give sixth-formers an idea of what reading Theology and Religious Studies involves; teachers are also welcome.

The courses in this Tripos are intended not only for prospective ordinands and teachers, but for all who are interested in asking basic questions about human existence and studying objectively the answers that have been given, especially in the Jewish–Christian tradition, to which the bulk (but not all) of the material studied in the Tripos belongs. A wide variety of intellectual disciplines, philosophical, historical, literary, and linguistic, is involved, and school subjects which provide training in these are helpful as a preparation for the course.

The Theological and Religious Studies Tripos is in three Parts, with some overlapping of papers, especially between Parts I B and II. Part I A is a one-year course, subtitled 'Religious Studies', which may be taken by freshmen, or by those who come over for one year from another Faculty. It is designed to be attractive to those who approach theology from the standpoint of some adjoining area of study – philosophy, ethics, science, the phenomenology of religion, or the history of culture. Part I B is a two-year course, with the stress on biblical studies, theological method, and the development of Christian doctrine. Part II offers a wide choice of subjects and the opportunity for a certain measure of specialization. It is taken in one year after I B; otherwise, it is normally a two-year course. A one-year version of Part II, with wide choice, is available for those who come over to theology for a single year.

The B.A. Degree can be obtained by taking honours in Parts I A and II or Parts I B and II, or in any one Part, together with a Part of another Tripos.

There are several possible combinations of courses for those who take a Part of another Tripos; full details and comments may be obtained from the Faculty office. To a freshman coming up to read theology for three years there are two possibilities: (*a*) Part I A after one year, and Part II after two further years; (*b*) Part I B after two years, and Part II after one further year.

Prospective candidates for I B with no Greek or Hebrew are advised to begin the study of one language before coming into residence. Introductory courses in Greek and Hebrew are provided in the Long Vacation Residence (July–August). Those who intend to begin the study of theology in October may care to avail themselves of these, for, although classes are provided for beginners, starting in October, the first year's work will be more profitable for those with some knowledge of at least one of the languages. In addition, they should read some books on the methods of theology and the grounds for belief, and also on the background and the main lines of biblical history. Directors of Studies will give advice on particular books.

Prospective candidates for I A should either consult their Director of Studies, or apply to the Faculty Office, Divinity School, for lists of suggested reading.

Affiliated students do not take Part I A or I B but may take Part II after two years. They have the opportunity of including certain of the I A papers.

No Greek or Hebrew is required in Part I A; some work in at least one of the two languages is normally required in Parts I B and II.

A Preliminary Examination is set at the end of the first year of the two years that may be spent preparing for Parts I B and II; it covers part of the syllabus, and affords a test of progress.

The M.Phil. Degree in Theology is an advanced course of study leading to an examination at the end of two years. A dissertation is also required. The M.Phil. in Theology is divided into six sections, corresponding to the main branches of Theology, and students may not offer more than one section. Application is made in the first instance to the Board of Graduate Studies.

For those who can spend only one year on an advanced course, a course leading to a Diploma in Theology is available. The syllabus is very similar to that for the M.Phil., but without the dissertation.

Theological and Religious Studies Tripos

The papers set for Part I A: Religious Studies are:

1. Introduction to philosophy I.
2. Introduction to philosophy II.
3. Introduction to the comparative study of religions I: problems of truth and dialogue.
4. Introduction to the comparative study of religions II: the study of religion.
5. Jewish and Christian origins: the religion and life of the biblical communities I.
6. Jewish and Christian origins: the religion and life of the biblical communities II.
7. Christian theology in the age of science I.
8. Christian theology in the age of science II.
9. Christian culture in the western world I: Church and Society, 950–1300.
10. Christian culture in the western world II: special period.

The papers for Parts I B and II are as follows:

11 A. Hebrew I. (Elementary Hebrew.)
11 B. Hebrew II.
12 A. Elementary New Testament Greek.
12 B. New Testament Greek.

13. New Testament theology and ethics.
14. Study of theology.
15. Hebrew III.
16. The religion and literature of the Old Testament.
17. Old Testament and intertestamental studies.
18. Jewish history, thought, and religion, 200 B.C.–A.D. 135.
19. New Testament introduction.
20. New Testament Epistles in Greek and English.
21. Doctrine: special paper.
22. Christian life and thought to A.D. 461.
23. A special subject or subjects in the Christian life and thought of the early or medieval periods.
24. Christian life and thought, 1500–1714.
25. A special subject or subjects in the Christian life and thought of the medieval or Reformation periods.
26. Christian life and thought from 1800 to the present day.
27. A special subject or subjects in the Christian life and thought of the Reformation or modern periods.
28. Elements of philosophical theology I.
29. Elements of philosophical theology II.
30. The comparative study of religions I.
31. The comparative study of religions II.
32. Essay.

These papers are more fully defined as follows:

Part I A[1]

1. Introduction to philosophy I

This paper will contain questions on (*a*) elementary metaphysics especially the theory of knowledge, and (*b*) the nature and grounds of religious belief. Candidates must answer questions from both sections of the paper.

2. Introduction to philosophy II

This paper will contain questions on (*a*) elementary moral philosophy, and (*b*) ethics and Divine authority. Candidates must answer questions from both sections of the paper.

[1] The examination for Part I A herein described will be held for the last time in **1985**. For details of the new Part I in 1986, see *Reporter*, 1983–84, p. 614.

3. Introduction to the comparative study of religions I: problems of truth and dialogue

This paper will contain questions on problems arising out of the encounter of Christianity and the world religions, such as the principles and approaches of inter-religious dialogue and truth-claims in religion. The Board will from time to time prescribe texts for special study. No texts for special study are prescribed for **1985.**

4. Introduction to the comparative study of religions II: the study of religion

The subject of this paper will be: an introduction to the anthropological and sociological understandings of religion.

5. Jewish and Christian origins: the religion and life of the biblical communities I, and Paper 6. Jewish and Christian origins: the religion and life of the biblical communities II

In these papers candidates will be required to show a knowledge of the biblical period from the exile onwards. The papers may contain questions on the development of religious traditions and institutions, the biblical and extra-biblical literature that came into being at this time, the formation of the Old Testament canon, the emergence of sectarian movements, and the Synoptic Gospels and their underlying traditions. Questions will not be set on Christian texts from outside the New Testament. Candidates for Paper 6 should be prepared to answer questions on at least three of the following topics, which are prescribed for special study in **1985**: Judaism and Hellenism; the rise of Jewish apocalyptic; the Qumran community; the Trial of Jesus; worship in the Early Church.

7. Christian theology in the age of science I

This paper will contain questions on the effects upon Christian thought of (*a*) the rise of classical physics from the time of Galileo to that of the deistic controversies; and (*b*) the rise of modern geology and biology from 1750 to 1900.

8. Christian theology in the age of science II

In this paper candidates are invited to compare and contrast the knowledge-systems developed by religious and scientific communities, and their interaction. This includes consideration of the role in the formation of these knowledge-systems of models; analogies; tests of truth; authority and experience. Questions are drawn from the modern debate in Christian theology concerning the following topics: (i) creation, cosmology, and aspects of modern physics; (ii) *evolutionary biology and the nature of man; and (iii) the psychological critique of religion since William James.

In some years one of these topics may not be available but in that case due notice will be given.

9. Christian culture in the western world I: Church and society, 950–1300

This paper will be concerned with Christian life, thought, art, and institutions in the central Middle Ages. The paper will contain questions on such subjects as the development of ecclesiastical institutions, especially the papacy, the religious orders, and the schools; society and its aspirations – celibacy and the pursuit of perfection; love and marriage; knightly and crusading ideas; Christian art and thought; popular religious movements; the twelfth-century renaissance and scholasticism; dissent and heresy.

The Board may also prescribe texts for special study.

10. Christian culture in the western world II: special period

For this paper the Board will from time to time prescribe periods for special study (not necessarily from within the period A.D. 950–1300) of which the candidates shall select one. When entering for this paper a candidate must state which period he has selected. After the division of the Lent Term he will not be permitted to alter the period to any period which has not already been selected by another candidate. Special periods in **1985**:

Either (*a*) Oxford and Cambridge: the Universities in the late Middle Ages;

or (*b*) English spirituality, 1500–1750.

Texts for special study may also be prescribed.

Prescribed texts for (*b*) are: Erasmus, *In Praise of Folly* and the *Colloquies* (as edited by C. R. Thompson, Chicago, 1965); Colet, *Sermon before the Convocation*, 1512 (see J. H. Lupton, *A Life of John Colet*, 1887; text printed as an appendix); More, *Correspondence* (ed. E. F. Rogers, Princeton, 1947); Nicholas Harpsfield, *The Life and Death of Sir T. More* (ed. C. V. Hitchcock and R. W. Chambers, for the E.E.T.S.); *The New Testament translated by William Tyndale*, 1534 (C.U.P. reprint, 1938); Tyndale, *Obedience of a Christian Man*, 1527–8 (ed. H. Walter, for the Parker Society, C.U.P. 1848) and *The Practice of Prelates*, 1530 (ed. H. Walter, for the Parker Society, C.U.P. 1849); Cranmer, *Preface to the Bible*, 1540, and

* Topic (ii) will not be available in **1985**.

the *Homily of Salvation* (ed. J. E. Cox, for the Parker Society, C.U.P. 1846); *The Book(s) of Common Prayer*, 1549 and 1552 (ed. J. Ketley, *Liturgies of Edward VI*, Parker Society, C.U.P. 1844); H. C. Porter (ed.), *Puritanism in Tudor England*, pp. 122–138, 182–197, and 272–300; Hooker, *Of the Laws of Ecclesiastical Polity*, Chapter VIII of the Preface (ed. H. C. Porter, *Puritanism in Tudor England*, pp. 243f.); I. Walton, *Lives* (for Hooker, in O.U.P. World's Classics, No. 303); *The Works of George Herbert* (ed. F. E. Hutchinson, Oxford, 1941), pp. 223–290; *The Autobiography of Richard Baxter* (ed. N. H. Keeble, Everyman Library), Parts 1 and 2; *The Journal of George Fox* (ed. Nickalls, Cambridge, 1952), Chapters 1–6, and 10; Bunyan, *Grace Abounding* (ed. R. Sharrock, Oxford, 1962); *Records of a Church of Christ at Bristol* (ed. R. Hayden, for the Bristol Record Society, 1974); C. A. Patrides, *The Cambridge Platonists* (C.U.P. 1980), pp. 90–144, 213–287, 326–336; Dr Josiah Woodward's *Account of the Religious Societies*, 1698 (ed. D. E. Jenkins, Liverpool, 1935); John Wesley's *Journal* (ed. Nora Ratcliff, in one volume, London, 1940); J. Chandos (ed.), *In God's Name: Examples of Preaching in England, 1534–1662* (1971); T. Ingram and D. Newton (ed.), *Hymns as Poetry* (London, 1956).

Parts I B and II[1]

11 A. Hebrew I (Elementary Hebrew)

This paper contains (*a*) questions on Hebrew grammar, and (*b*) passages for translation, linguistic comment, pointing, and retranslation from a portion or portions of the Old Testament, which the Board from time to time prescribe.

11 B. Hebrew II

This paper contains (*a*) questions on Hebrew grammar, and (*b*) passages for translation, linguistic and exegetical comment, pointing, and retranslation from portions of the Old Testament which the Board from time to time prescribe.

The portions of the Old Testament prescribed in **1985** and **1986** will be:
Paper 11 A: *Either* Genesis xxxvii and xl–xlv *or* Deuteronomy v–xv
Paper 11 B: Genesis xxxvii and xl–xlv; Deuteronomy v–xv; Judges vi–xviii.
(In **1986**: Judges will be replaced by I Kings xvi–xxii; II Kings i–xiii.)

12 A. Elementary New Testament Greek

This paper contains (i) passages for translation from one or more portions which the Board from time to time prescribe from the Gospels,

[1] The examinations herein described will be held for the last time in **1986**.

together with questions on the grammar of Hellenistic Greek, and sentences for translation from English into Greek, which will employ chiefly the vocabulary of the prescribed portions, (ii) passages for translation from these and other prescribed portions which may be from anywhere in the New Testament. Candidates may offer *either* (i) *or* (ii). Copies of a Greek lexicon will be available in the examination for those who wish to make use of them.

The passages for translation prescribed will be:

Either (i) (for candidates offering grammar):

In **1985**: Luke iii. 1–ix. 50.
In **1986**: Mark i–ix.

Or (ii) (for candidates offering translation only):

In **1985**: Matthew; Luke iii. 1–ix. 50; John; Acts; Galatians; I John.
In **1986**: Mark i. 1–ix. 1; Luke; John; Acts; Galatians; I John.

12 B. New Testament Greek

This paper contains passages for translation from portions which the Board prescribe from time to time from anywhere in the New Testament together with questions on the grammar of Hellenistic Greek, and sentences for translation from English into Greek, which will employ chiefly the vocabulary of the prescribed portions. Candidates will be examined on *all* the portions prescribed. Copies of a Greek lexicon will be available in the examination for those who wish to make use of them. The prescribed texts are:

In **1985**: Matthew; Luke iii. 1–ix. 50; John; Acts; Galatians; I John.
In **1986**: Mark i. 1–ix; Luke; John; Acts; Galatians; I John.

13. New Testament theology and ethics

This paper includes questions on a special subject, prescribed from time to time by the Board: and also passages for comment or exegesis, printed in Greek accompanied by an English translation. A candidate for Part II who has not obtained honours in Part IB and takes the examination in the year next after he has obtained honours in an Honours Examination need not attempt any question on the special subject.

In **1985** and **1986**: The Holy Spirit.

14. Study of theology

This paper contains questions on theological method as illustrated by the writings of certain Christian theologians. It is divided into three sections, Section A (patristic and medieval texts), Section B (Reformation and modern texts), and Section C (general questions). Candidates are required to answer questions from all three sections.

Candidates must show knowledge of prescribed texts which the Board prescribe from time to time.

The texts prescribed in **1985** and **1986** are:

Origen, *On First Principles*, Book I, preface and 1 (transl. by G. W. Butterworth, London, 1936, pp. 1–14); Gregory of Nazianzus, *Second Theological Oration* i–xxi (*LCC*, Vol. III, ed. E. R. Hardy [London, 1954], pp. 136–50); Augustine, *Confessions*, Book VII (*LCC*, Vol. VII, ed. A. C. Outler [London, 1955], pp. 134–56); Aquinas, *Summa Theologiae* 1a, 1 (*Summa Theologiae*, Vol. I, *Christian Theology*, transl. and ed. T. Gilby [London, 1964]); J. Calvin, *Reply to Sadolet* (*LCC*, Vol. XXII [London, 1954], pp. 219–56); F. D. E. Schleiermacher, *The Christian Faith* (Edinburgh, 1928) (introduction, paras. 11–31, pp. 52–128); K. Barth, *Church Dogmatics* (Edinburgh, 1955) (1, 2, ch. 4 [paras. 23–4], pp. 797–884); K. Rahner, 'The Experience of God Today', *Theological Investigations*, Vol. XI (London, 1974), pp. 149–65; 'Possible Courses for the Theology of the Future', *Theological Investigations*, Vol. XIII (London, 1974), pp. 32–60.

15. Hebrew III

This paper will contain passages for translation, with grammar and exegesis, from selected portions of the Old Testament, including some parts of the prophetic and poetic books; unseen translation; composition; and pointing, not necessarily from the selected portions. Candidates will be required to offer either unseen translation or composition, but not both.

In **1985** and **1986**: Isaiah i–vii; Psalms viii, xix, xxii, xxiii, li, civ; and *either* Deuteronomy v–vx, *or* II Samuel xi. 1–xix. 9.

A candidate may not offer in Paper 15 any prescribed text that he has already offered in Paper 11A or 11B.

16. The religion and literature of the Old Testament

In this paper knowledge will be required of the contents of the canonical books of the Old Testament and their background, and of the main lines of Old Testament religion and literature. Prescribed for special study:

In **1985**: Genesis i–xi; Jeremiah i–xxv.
In **1986**: Genesis i–xi; Ezekiel i–xxiv.

17. Old Testament and intertestamental studies

Candidates are required to offer *two* of the following subjects:

(*a*) Old Testament theology.
(*b*) Intertestamental literature.
(*c*) Text, Canon and Versions.
(*d*) Ancient Near Eastern texts in their relation to Old Testament studies.
(*e*) Biblical archaeology.

Candidates who offer Paper 18 may not offer (*b*).

18. Jewish history, thought, and religion, 200 B.C.–A.D. 135

Candidates are expected to make a general study of the period with particular attention to a prescribed subject. The prescribed subject is:

For **1985** and **1986**: The Jewish revolts against Rome between A.D. 66 and 135.

19. New Testament introduction

This paper contains questions on the historical background of the New Testament, on the date, authorship, and textual criticism of the books of the New Testament, and on the circumstances in which they were written. There may be questions on the historical problems raised in the study of Jesus and of Paul, and of the origin and development of the church. Special attention should be given to the Four Gospels, Acts, and Galatians. Candidates are required to make critical comment on passages from these books, and will have the opportunity of doing so on passages from elsewhere in the New Testament. The passages will be printed in English, and the references will be given. Copies of the New Testament in Greek are available in the examination for candidates who wish to make use of them.

20. New Testament Epistles in Greek and English

The Board from time to time prescribe certain Epistles or portions of Epistles for special study. The paper contains passages from the New Testament Epistles for translation, exegesis, and critical comment, with special reference to the selected Epistles. Candidates must show knowledge of the Greek text of the selected Epistles; the remaining Epistles they may offer in either Greek or English. Questions may be set on background, content, theology, and problems of criticism and interpretation and, also on language, style, and text. Copies of the New Testament in Greek are available in the examination for candidates who wish to make use of them.

The Epistles prescribed are:

In **1985**: I Corinthians vii–xv; I Thessalonians; I, II, III John.

In **1986**: II Corinthians i–ix; Ephesians; James.

21. Doctrine: special paper

In **1985** and **1986**: Twentieth-century Christology.

22. Christian life and thought to A.D. 461 (also serves as Paper O 7 of Part II of the Classical Tripos)

Paper 22 includes questions on such subjects as: the development, organization, thought, and worship of the early church, its relations with the state, its mission, and its contacts with philosophy. Candidates are expected to show knowledge of the literary and archaeological evidence for the period, and are required to answer a question requiring comment on extracts from contemporary sources which will be drawn primarily but not exclusively from books prescribed by the Board. The books prescribed in **1985** and **1986** are:

J. Stevenson, *A New Eusebius* (London, 1957).

J. Stevenson, *Creeds, Councils and Controversies* (London, 1966).

M. F. Wiles and M. Santer, *Documents in Early Christian Thought* (Cambridge/London, 1975).

23. A special subject or subjects in the Christian life and thought of the early or medieval periods

The special subject prescribed will be as follows:

In **1985** and **1986**: The life, times, and thought of St Augustine of Hippo.*

24. Christian life and thought, 1500–1714

This paper will include questions on such subjects as: the background to the Reformation; the changing political, economic, and social situation in Western Europe; intellectual history – humanism and the 'New Divinity'; the advance of the 'new religion' with special reference to the principal persons and centres of 'Protestant' activity; biblical authority, ministry

* List of primary sources, together with lists of recommended reading, may be obtained from the office of the Faculty of Divinity.

and sacraments; the 'Radical' Reformation; the Catholic Reformation, the Jesuits and the Council of Trent; post-Tridentine Catholicism: the Reformation in England and Scotland; Lollardy and Lutheranism in England; Cranmer, Ridley, Hooper, and the Edwardine Reformation; the Elizabethan religious settlement; prelates, puritans, and apologists; changing concepts and patterns of ministry; the Laudian revival; the Commonwealth and Protectorate; Anglicans, Presbyterians, and Independents; the Restoration settlement 1662–65; nonconformity and the rise of dissent; the Catholic problem and the revolution of 1688–89; the non-juring schism; religious toleration and its consequences.

Candidates are required to answer a question requiring comment on extracts from contemporary sources which will be drawn primarily but not exclusively from books prescribed by the Board.

The books prescribed in **1985** and **1986** are:

J. Chandos (ed.), *In God's Name: Examples of Preaching in England 1534–1662* (Hutchinson, 1971); A. G. Dickens and D. Carr (eds.), *The Reformation in England to the Accession of Elizabeth I* (Documents of Modern History, Arnold, 1967); H. J. Hillerbrand (ed.), *The Reformation in its own Words* (SCM, Harper & Row, 1964), J. C. Olin, *The Catholic Reformation: Savonarola to Loyola* (Harper & Row, 1971); Parker Society Edition, *Liturgies of Edward VI* (CUP, 1844); R. L. De Molen (ed.), *Erasmus* (Documents of Modern History, Arnold, 1973); E. G. Rupp and B. Drewery (eds.), *Martin Luther* (Documents of Modern History, Arnold, 1970); G. R. Potter (ed.), *H. Zwingli* (Documents of Modern History, Arnold, 1978); H. J. Schroeder (ed.), *The Canons and Decrees of the Council of Trent* (New York, 1941); T. Corbishley (ed.), *The Spiritual Exercises of St Ignatius Loyola* (Anthony Clark, 1973); Teresa of Avila, *Autobiography* (Penguin pbk); Blaise Pascal, *Provincial Letters* (Penguin pbk).

25. A special subject or subjects in the Christian life and thought of the medieval or Reformation periods

The special subject will be:
In **1985** and **1986**: Luther and Lutheranism, 1525–1534.*

26. Christian life and thought from 1800 to the present day

This paper includes questions on such subjects as: the history of the established and non-established churches in Great Britain: the relationship

* Lists of primary sources, together with lists of recommended reading, may be obtained from the office of the Faculty of Divinity.

of church and state in Europe: ultramontanism, liberalism, and modernism in the Roman Catholic Church; the churches and social questions; the missionary and ecumenical movements; the history of theological thought; the development of biblical criticism; the relationship between theology and the sciences; and the problems posed by secularization. Particular emphasis will be laid on the history of Christian life and thought in Great Britain.

Candidates are required to answer a question requiring comment on extracts from contemporary sources which are primarily but not exclusively from books prescribed by the Board.

The books prescribed by the Board in **1985** and **1986** are:

H. Bettenson, *Documents of the Christian Church* (2nd edition) xi, nos. 7–12, xiii, xiv (London, 1967); A. O. J. Cockshut, *Religious Controversies of the Nineteenth Century* (London, 1966); S. Z. Ehler and J. B. Morrall, *Church and State through the Centuries*, vii and viii (London, 1954); R. P. Flindall, *The Church of England, 1815–1948* (London, 1972); J. Macquarrie, *Contemporary Religious Thinkers* (London, 1968); B. M. G. Reardon, *Religious Thought in the Nineteenth Century* (Cambridge, 1966); D. M. Thompson, *Nonconformity in the Nineteenth Century* (London, 1972).

27. A special subject or subjects in the Christian life and thought of the Reformation or modern periods

In **1985** and **1986**: Church, State, and Society in late Stuart England, 1660–1714*.

28. Elements of philosophical theology I

This paper contains questions on the following subjects:

(i) Metaphysical argument, especially theistic argument, as illustrated by and criticized in prescribed texts.

(ii) Problems in philosophical theology, including: the question of transcendence; the existence of God; analogical knowledge of God; the relation of God to the world; the concept of divine action; the problem of evil; the soul and immortality. Special attention should be paid to the problem of analogical discourse about God.

The prescribed texts in **1985** and **1986** are:

* Lists of primary sources, together with lists of recommended reading, may be obtained from the office of the Faculty of Divinity.

Plato's *Republic*, Book v, 475e4 to the end of Book vii, in F. M. Cornford's translation, from p. 178: 'And whom do you mean by the genuine philosophers?'; D. Hume's *Dialogues Concerning Natural Religion*, ed. N. Kemp Smith (Oxford, 1935); I. Kant, *Critique of Pure Reason*, translated by M. Kemp Smith (London, 1934), *Dialectic*, Book ii, ch. iii, sections 4–7 and *Appendix* (pp. 500–49).

29. Elements of philosophical theology II

The subject of this paper is 'The relations of religion and morality'. The paper contains questions on such topics as 'the autonomy of ethics', the relation of morality to nature and to the will of God, the form and content of Christian ethics, both personal and social, and the adequacy of Christian ethics.

30. The comparative study of religions I

This paper contains questions on topics, prescribed by the Board, as they occur in one or more non-Christian religions. Reference to Christianity may be included.

The papers prescribed in **1985** and **1986** are:

Either (*a*) Religious traditions of India: Hinduism and Buddhism.

Or (*b*) The concept of the legal system (Halakhah) in medieval and modern Judaism.

31. The comparative study of religions II

This paper contains questions on topics, prescribed by the Board, as they occur in Christianity, and one or more other religions.

The papers prescribed in **1985** and **1986** are:

Either (*a*) The self and salvation in Indian and Western thought.

Or (*b*) Worship in Judaism and Christianity.

Rules for offering papers – General

A candidate may not offer in any Part any paper, other than Paper 32, which he has already offered in a previous Part, or in a Part of another Tripos except that a candidate who has offered Paper 11A in Part IB may offer Paper 11B in Part II, but not *vice versa*, and that a candidate who has offered Paper 12A in Part IB may offer Paper 12B in Part II, but not *vice versa*. No candidate may offer in the same examination more than one paper from among Papers 11 A, 11 B, and 15 nor more than one paper from among Papers 12 A, 12 B, and 20.

Part I A: Religious Studies

The following may present themselves as candidates for honours in Part I A:

(*a*) a student who has not obtained honours in an Honours Examination, provided that he has kept one term and that three complete terms have not passed after his first term of residence;
(*b*) a student who has obtained honours in an Honours Examination of another Tripos in the year next after he has so obtained honours, provided that he has kept four terms and that twelve complete terms have not passed after his first term of residence.

A candidate for Part I A must offer the following papers:

(*a*) if he has not obtained honours in an Honours Examination, two pairs of papers chosen from among Papers 1 and 2, 3 and 4, 5 and 6, 7 and 8, and 9 and 10;
(*b*) if he has already obtained honours in an Honours Examination, two pairs of papers chosen from among Papers 1 and 2, 3 and 4, 5 and 6, 7 and 8, 9 and 10, and one other paper chosen from among Papers 1–10.

Part I B: Biblical and Historical Theology

A student who has not obtained honours in an Honours Examination may present himself as a candidate for honours in Part I B, provided that he has kept four terms and that six complete terms have not passed after his first term of residence.

A candidate for Part I B must offer Papers 14, 16, 19, 22, and 32; and *either* Paper 11 B *or* Paper 12 B. He may, if he so wishes, offer one additional paper, chosen from among Papers 11 A, 11 B, 12 A and 12 B.

Part II

The following may present themselves as candidates for honours in Part II:

(*a*) a student who has obtained honours in Part I B or in any

Honours Examination other than Part IA of the Theological and Religious Studies Tripos in the year next after he has so obtained honours, provided that he has kept seven terms and that fifteen complete terms have not passed after his first term of residence;

(*b*) a student who has not obtained honours in Part IB but has obtained honours in Part IA or any other Tripos, in the year next but one after he has so obtained honours, provided that he has kept seven terms and that fifteen terms have not passed after his first term of residence;

A candidate for Part II must offer papers as follows (subject to Rules for offering papers – General, p. 429):

(*a*) if he has obtained honours in Part IB, he must offer:

(i) Papers 13 and 32;

and (ii) *either* (1) three other papers chosen from among Papers 11B, 12B, and 14–31; and, if he so wishes, one additional paper chosen from among Papers 3, 4, 7–12B, and 14–31;

or (2) two other papers chosen from among Papers 11B, 12B, and 14–31, *and* a dissertation on a topic approved by the Faculty Board; and, if he so wishes, one additional paper chosen from among Papers 3, 4, 7–12B, and 14–31;

(*b*) if he has not obtained honours in Part IB and takes the examination in the year next after he has obtained honours in an Honours Examination, he must offer:

(i) Papers 13 and 32;

and (ii) three other papers chosen from among Papers 11A, 11B, 12A, 12B, and 14–31;

(*c*) if he has not obtained honours in Part IB and takes the examination in the year next but one after he has obtained honours in an Honours Examination or if he is an Affiliated Student he must offer:

(i) Papers 13 and 32;

and (ii) *either* (1) four other papers chosen from among Papers 11B, 12B, and 14–31; and, if he so wishes, one additional paper chosen from among Papers 3, 4, 7–12B, and 14–31;

or (2) three other papers chosen from among Papers 11B, 12B, and 14–31, *and* a dissertation on a topic approved by the Faculty Board; and, if he so wishes, one additional paper chosen from among Papers 3, 4, 7–12 B, and 14–31;

and (iii) Paper 11 A or 12 A, unless he offers Papers 11 B, 12 B, 15, or 20 among the papers offered under (ii).

Whether he offers papers under (*a*) or (*b*) or (*c*) above he may be required by the Examiners to present himself for a *viva voce* examination.

The Faculty Board has power to exempt from the requirement to offer Paper 11 A or Paper 12 A any candidate for Part II under (*c*) above who produces evidence that he has done work of a satisfactory standard in Greek or in Hebrew, whether in Cambridge or elsewhere. Such a candidate cannot offer in Part II the paper from which he has been exempted. Before the beginning of the Michaelmas Term preceding each examination the Board will draw up a list of those to whom they have granted exemption, indicating for each candidate whether the exemption is granted with reference to Paper 11 A or to Paper 12 A, and they will communicate the information to the Registrary and to the Tutor of each candidate. Any application for exemption on behalf of any other candidate will be made through the candidate's Tutor to the Registrary so as to reach him before the division of the Michaelmas Term preceding the examination, and will include details of the applicant's qualifications.

Dissertations

A candidate for Part II who intends to submit a dissertation must give notice of his intention and proposed topic to the Secretary of the Faculty Board not earlier than the beginning of the Easter Term and not later than the division of the Michaelmas Term next preceding the examination. The Secretary will inform him as soon as possible, and in any case before the end of Full Michaelmas Term, whether his topic has been approved by the Faculty Board. The dissertation must be of not more than ten thousand words (inclusive of notes), and must be clearly marked with the author's name, College, and the Part of the Tripos for which he is a candidate. The candidate must send his dissertation to the Registrary so as to reach him not later than the eighth day of the Full Term in which the examination is to be held, together with a written declaration that it is his own original work. The dissertation should show evidence of reading, judgement, and criticism, and of a power of exposition but not necessarily of original research, and should give full references to sources used. It may be on any topic relating to the subject of any paper in any Part of the Tripos, but the Board may, when giving approval to a particular topic, impose the condition that a candidate who offers a dissertation on that topic may not offer a particular paper or a particular prescribed subject in a paper. It must be written in English unless the candidate has received permission from the Board to use some other specified language. A request for such permission must be made when the original notice of intention is given. The Examiners may require a candidate to re-submit his dissertation in typescript if in their opinion it is not reasonably legible.

Preliminary Examination for Parts IB and II of the Theological and Religious Studies Tripos

The papers in this examination are as follows:

1. The religion and literature of the Old Testament (Paper 16 of the Tripos)

A candidate must offer:

either the full syllabus as prescribed for Tripos candidates, but with a special study of Ezekiel i–xxiv in place of the passages prescribed for special study by candidates for the Tripos in **1985**;

or a more restricted syllabus as follows: the religion and literature of the Old Testament with special reference to the prophets and in particular to Ezekiel i–xxiv.

2. Elementary Hebrew (Paper 11 A, *Hebrew I*, of the Tripos)

The paper contains questions on (*a*) Hebrew grammar and (*b*) passages for translation, linguistic comment, pointing, and retranslation from prescribed texts. The texts prescribed in **1985** are:

either Genesis xxxvii and xl–xlv;

or Deuteronomy v–xv.

3. The Synoptic Gospels

Candidates are required to make critical comments on *four* passages, *including at least one from each Gospel.* Nine passages are set, three from each Gospel, which will be printed in both Greek and English. References will be given. The paper contains questions on literary, critical and historical problems, and also on problems of theology and ethics.

4. Introduction to the New Testament

Candidates are required to show a knowledge of the New Testament writings in their historical setting with special reference to Acts and Galatians, but excluding Hebrews, II Peter, I, II, and III John, Jude, and Revelation. Passages are set for critical comment, printed in English. Detailed questions are not set on the Synoptic Gospels, but their place within the development of the New Testament should be understood. Copies of the New Testament in Greek are provided in the examination room.

5. The Gospel according to St John and the Epistle to the Romans

Passages are set for critical comment, printed in English. Optional passages for translation are set from Romans v–viii. Copies of the New Testament in Greek are provided in the examination room.

6. Elementary New Testament Greek (Paper 12A, *New Testament Greek*, of the Tripos)

This paper contains (i) passages for translation from one or more portions which the Board prescribe from the Gospels, together with questions on the grammar of Hellenistic Greek, and sentences for translation from English into Greek, which will employ chiefly the vocabulary of the prescribed portions, (ii) passages for translation from these and other prescribed portions which may be from anywhere in the New Testament. Candidates may offer *either* (i) *or* (ii). Copies of a Greek lexicon will be available in the examination for those who wish to make use of them.

The texts prescribed for this paper in **1985** are:

either (i) (for candidates offering grammar):
Luke iii. 1–ix. 50;

or (ii) (for candidates offering translation only):
Luke iii. 1–ix. 50; Matthew; John; Acts; Galatians; I John.

7. Introduction to theology (Paper 14 of the Tripos)

A candidate must show knowledge of prescribed texts (in English) as follows:

Origen, *On First Principles*, Book I, preface and 1 (translated by G. W. Butterworth, London, 1936, pp. 1–14).

Gregory of Nazianzus, *Second Theological Oration*, i–xxi (*LCC*, Vol. III, ed. E. R. Hardy [London, 1954], pp. 136–50).

Augustine, *Confessions*, Book VII (*LCC*, Vol. VII, ed. A. C. Outler [London, 1955], pp. 134–56).

Aquinas, *Summa Theologiae* Ia, 1 (*Summa Theologiae, Vol. I, Christian Theology*, translated and edited by T. Gilby [London, 1964]).

A candidate must also answer at least one general question on theological method.

8. Christian life and thought to A.D. 461 (Paper 22 of the Tripos)

A candidate must offer *either* the full syllabus of the paper as prescribed for Tripos candidates, *or* a more restricted syllabus as follows:

Christian life and thought to A.D. 337.

9. Christian life and thought, A.D.1500–1714 (Paper 24 of the Tripos)

A candidate must offer *either* the full syllabus of the paper as prescribed for Tripos candidates, *or* a more restricted syllabus as follows:

Christian life and thought, 1500–1565.

10. Christian life and thought, from 1800 to the present day (Paper 26 of the Tripos)

A candidate must offer *either* the full syllabus of the paper as prescribed for Tripos candidates, or a more restricted syllabus as follows:

Christian life and thought *either* (*a*) from 1800 to 1889 *or* (*b*) from 1889 to the present day.

11. Introduction to philosophical theology

This paper contains questions on:

(i) Plato, *Republic*, Book V 475e4 to the end of Book VII, in F. M. Cornford's translation (Oxford, 1941), pp. 178 ff. (Paperback 1975, reprint of 1945, pp. 183 ff.) from 'And whom do you mean by the genuine philosophers?...'; and Hume, *Dialogues Concerning Natural Religion*, ed. N. Kemp Smith, second ed. (Oxford, 1947).

(ii) The problem of evil.

12. Introduction to the study of particular religions*

Either (*a*) Introduction to the study of Indian religions, with special reference to Hinduism and Buddhism; particular attention will be paid to the basic themes and ideas underlying the life, thought, and worship of these religions.

* A candidate must indicate on his entry which option he is offering.

Or (*b*) Introduction to the life, thought, and worship of Modern Judaism.

13. Essay

Papers to be offered

A candidate must offer papers as follows:

(*a*) if three complete terms have not passed after his first term of residence, at least four papers chosen from among Papers 1–8;
(*b*) if he is an Affiliated Student, or if three or more complete terms have passed after his first term of residence, Papers 3 and 13, and at least three other papers.

No candidate may offer both Paper 4 and Paper 5.

Diploma in Theology *

To qualify for the award of a Diploma in Theology, a candidate must pursue the prescribed course of study and must pass the examination for the Diploma. He must also reside for three terms. A candidate for the Diploma must normally be a graduate and must have been admitted as a Graduate Student by the Board of Graduate Studies.

A candidate may not present himself for examination more than once and he may not be a candidate in the same term for any other University examination.

A candidate for admission to the course must apply to the Secretary of the Board of Graduate Studies normally not later than 31 July in the year before that in which he wishes his candidature to begin.

A candidate must pursue his studies in Cambridge under the direction of a Supervisor appointed by the Degree Committee of the Faculty of Divinity.

A candidate may be allowed by the Board of Graduate Studies to count all or part of the period during which he has been a candidate for the Diploma towards a course of research but, if he does so, he may not also be awarded the Diploma.

The scheme of examination consists of six sections, and an Essay

* Lists of primary sources set for study in Section III may be obtained from the Faculty Library, and lists of recommended reading may be obtained from the office of the Faculty of Divinity.

paper common to all the sections (see p. 443). No candidate may present himself for examination in more than one section.

The sections are as follows:

SECTION I. *Old Testament and Hebrew*

1. Old Testament theology

This paper will include the theological ideas of the Old Testament Apocrypha. In preparing for this paper, the attention of students should be directed towards such subjects as the nature and methods of Old Testament theology, ideas of God, and Israelite monotheism; the formation of the Old Testament canon; the relationship between the Old and New Testaments; the relationship between the religion of Israel and the religions of other peoples of the ancient Near East; revelation, election, covenant, and universalism; holiness, righteousness, sin, and redemption; priestly and sacrificial institutions; the nature of prophecy; the kingdom of God, and the messianic hope; the Law; wisdom; the problem of suffering; life after death.

2. Old Testament general paper

This paper will be divided into two parts. The first will contain at least four essay questions on the texts prescribed for Paper 3. The second will contain at least ten questions on such subjects as the Hebrew language, and its relation to other Semitic languages; textual criticism, and the versions; archaeology and Old Testament study; Ugaritic and other ancient Near Eastern texts in their relation to Old Testament studies; inter-Testamental literature, including the Qumran scrolls. Candidates are required to attempt four questions, and to draw at least one from each part and at least two from the second.

3. A selected portion or portions of the Old Testament, including always some poetical texts.

This paper will contain questions on a selected portion or portions of the Old Testament in Hebrew concerning (*a*) translation; (*b*) grammar; (*c*) pointing; (*d*) textual criticism (questions involving a knowledge of the Septuagint translation of the prescribed texts may be included); (*e*) subject-matter. As an alternative to questions on some chapters of the selected portions of the Old Testament in Hebrew, candidates will be allowed to answer questions on either (i) a selected portion or portions of the Aramaic parts of the Old Testament, or (ii) a selected portion or portions of the Septuagint. The part of the paper concerned with (i) will contain questions on (*a*) translation; (*b*) grammar; (*c*) pointing; (*d*) textual criticism; (*e*) subject-matter. The part of the paper concerned with (ii) will contain questions on (*a*) translation; (*b*) grammar; (*c*) comparison of the Hebrew and Greek texts.

The selected portions of the Old Testament in **1985** will be: Psalms i–xx; Proverbs x–xii; Song of Songs; *either* Amos; *or* The Aramaic portions of Daniel; *or* The LXX of Isaiah xl–xliv, xlix–lv.

4. Passages for translation from the Old Testament (Hebrew) generally, Hebrew composition, and pointing.

Candidates must offer all four papers and the Essay paper.

SECTION II. *New Testament*

1. General paper on the New Testament

This paper will contain questions on the background of the New Testament, on the authorship and date of the books of the New Testament, and on the circumstances in which they were written: on the general principles of the textual criticism of the New Testament; and on the outlines of the history of the formation of the canon. Some questions of a more advanced character will also be set on textual criticism and on the history of the canon, but candidates will not be expected to show detailed knowledge of more than one of those subjects.

2. The Gospels in Greek, with special reference to a selected Gospel

For **1985**: Mark.

3. The Acts, Epistles, and Apocalypse in Greek, with special reference to a selected portion

For **1985**: Acts.

4. New Testament theology, with special reference to a selected subject

For **1985**: The Church in the New Testament.

Candidates must offer all four papers and the Essay paper.

SECTION III. *Church History*

1. History of the church, including doctrine, to A.D. 461
2. General church history, A.D. 461–1500
3. General church history, A.D. 1500–1800
4. General church history from 1800 to the present day.
5. A subject in the early and patristic period
   For **1985**: The rise and development of Monasticism up to A.D. 461.
6. A subject in the medieval period
   For **1985**: St Anselm of Canterbury.
7. A subject in the Reformation and Counter-reformation period
   For **1985**: John Calvin's Second Geneva Ministry, 1541–64.
8. A subject in the modern period
   For **1985**: The life and thought of William Temple, 1881–1944.

A candidate must offer the Essay paper and three papers as follows:

either (*a*) two papers chosen from Papers 1–4, and one paper chosen from Papers 5–8;

or (*b*) if the Degree Committee decide on the evidence supplied that he is already qualified in general knowledge of church history, one paper chosen from Papers 1–4 and two papers chosen from Papers 5–8. Application for such permission must be made not later than the end of the Michaelmas Term preceding the examination.

A candidate who in the judgement of the Degree Committee is not already qualified in general knowledge of the period covered in Paper 1 must offer Paper 1; a candidate whom they decide to be so qualified must not offer Paper 1. A candidate for this section must be informed by the Degree Committee as soon as his application is approved whether he must, or must not, offer Paper 1.

SECTION IV. *Dogmatics*

1. History of Christian doctrine to the close of the Council of Chalcedon

2. A subject from the patristic period in connexion with original documents

   For **1985**: The doctrine of the Trinity from Tertullian to Augustine.

3. A subject from the medieval period, i.e. A.D. 800–1500, in connexion with original documents

   For **1985**: Eucharistic doctrine from A.D. 800 to 1400.

4. History of Christian doctrine from Luther to the close of the Council of Trent

5. A subject from modern theology in connexion with original documents

   For **1985**: The doctrine of the saving work of Christ in writings from 1870 to the present day (the ways in which theologians have represented the significance and continuing efficacy of the work of Christ in and for the individual, the community, and the world).

6. Selected portions of liturgies and service-books in their relation to the history of Christian doctrine

   For **1985**: The action of the worshipping community as reflected in eucharistic and baptismal rites of the patristic, Reformation, and contemporary periods.

A candidate must offer the essay paper and three papers as follows:

either (*a*) Paper 1 and two other papers, provided that he offers at least one chosen from Papers 2, 3, and 5;

or (*b*) if the Degree Committee decide on the evidence supplied that he is already qualified in general knowledge of the subject covered in Paper 1, either or both Papers 4 and 6, and at least one paper chosen from Papers 2, 3, and 5.

A candidate for this section must be informed by the Degree Committee as soon as his application is approved whether he must, or must not, offer Paper 1.

SECTION V. *Philosophy of Religion and Christian Ethics*

1. The history of the philosophy of religion

2. Fundamental problems in the philosophy of religion

The subjects of Papers 1 and 2 are defined below. These subjects are to be studied historically and critically. Students are expected to have a general knowledge of the history of the subject, but alternatives to questions on the history before Descartes are set from the modern period.

The nature and grounds of religious belief: the functions of reason, feeling, and volition in producing faith; the theory of the relativity of knowledge as applied to man's knowledge of God; the different conceptions of divine revelation; the possibilities of revelation; reason and revelation.

The idea of God: the arguments for the existence of God; the value-judgement in religion; pluralism; pantheism; theism; divine personality and the absolute.

Theories of the universe: dualism; materialism; naturalism; idealism, law in relation to providence; prayer and miracle; the problem of evil.

Human nature: personality, freedom, immortality.

3. Christian ethics

Types of moral theory, ancient and modern.
Faith and morals.
Christian ideals and motives.

4. *Either* (*a*) Some major philosopher or school of philosophers or philosophical problem in its theological aspects

For **1985**: Time and eternity.

or (*b*) A special subject in ethics

For **1985**: Law, love, and freedom.

A candidate must offer Papers 1–3, and the Essay paper. But the Degree Committee may permit a candidate who is already well qualified in general knowledge of the philosophy of religion to offer Paper 4(*a*) or Paper 4(*b*) in place of one of Papers 1–3. Application for such permission must be made not later than the end of the Michaelmas Term preceding the examination.

SECTION VI. *Christian Theology in the Modern World*

1. Church and society in England since 1800

The relation between the Churches and civil society. History of the established and non-established Churches; the effects upon them of, and their reactions to, social change, including the conditions of life and labour, the development of political and economic democracy and the welfare state.

2. Ecumenical movements since 1800

The history and theology of developments in inter-Church relations since 1800. This paper will also include some questions on the contribution of liturgical movements to closer relations between the Churches.

3. The Church's mission in the modern world

Developments since 1750 of Christian missionary thought and action in relation to non-Christian faiths and world-views. The paper will include two sections: (*a*) Missions and Society; (*b*) The Christian Faith and Other Faiths – A Study of Their Encounter. Candidates will be required to answer questions from both sections.

4. Religious thought since 1781

The impact of science, philosophy, and historical studies upon the understanding of the nature of religion and of theology.

5. Christian doctrine

The study in its setting in the twentieth century of *either* the thought of a selected theologian *or* the interpretation of a particular doctrine.

The subject of the examination in **1985** is: Eschatological hope in the twentieth century (Christian thought concerning the goal and outcome of human and cosmic history, in relation to other representations).

6. Christian ethics

The moral implications of Christian belief. The relation between Christian and other contemporary ethical attitudes with special reference to a select group of problems, such as crime and punishment, war and peace, sex and the family.

For **1985**: Law, love, and freedom.

Candidates must offer any three papers and the Essay paper.

An Essay paper common to all the Sections

This paper contains subjects for an English essay, which are so chosen that each Section, for which there are candidates, is represented by at least three subjects. Candidates are directed to choose a subject cognate to their own section. No candidate may write on more than one subject.

The Examination in Theology for the M.Phil. Degree

To qualify for the award of the Degree of Master of Philosophy in Theology a candidate must pursue the prescribed course of study and must pass the examination for the Master of Philosophy. He must also reside for six terms. He must normally be a graduate and must have been admitted as a Graduate Student by the Board of Graduate Studies.

A candidate may not present himself for examination more than once and he may not be a candidate in the same term for any other University examination.

A candidate for admission to the course must apply to the Secretary of the Board of Graduate Studies normally not later than 31 July in the year before that in which he wishes his candidature to begin.

A candidate must pursue his studies in Cambridge under the direction of a Supervisor appointed by the Degree Committee of the Faculty of Divinity.

A candidate may be allowed by the Board of Graduate Studies to count all or part of the period during which he has been a candidate for the M.Phil. towards a course of research, but if he does so, he may not also be awarded the M.Phil. Degree.

The scheme of examination consists of six sections. No candidate may present himself for examination in more than one section. Every candidate is also required to submit a short thesis not exceeding 20,000 words, including footnotes, references, and appendices, but excluding bibliography. The six sections are as follows:

Section I. Old Testament and Hebrew

1. Old Testament theology

This paper includes the theological ideas of the Old Testament Apocrypha. In preparing for this paper, the attention of students is directed towards such subjects as the nature and methods of Old Testament theology, ideas of God, and Israelite monotheism; the formation of the Old Testament canon: the relationship between the Old and New Testaments; the relationship between the religion of Israel and the religions of other peoples of the ancient Near East; revelation, election, covenant, and universalism; holiness, righteousness, sin, and redemption; priestly and sacrificial institutions; the nature of prophecy; the kingdom of God, and the messianic hope; the Law; wisdom; the problem of suffering; life after death.

2. Old Testament general paper

This paper is divided into two parts. The first contains essay questions on the texts prescribed for Papers 3 and 5. The second contains questions on such subjects as the Hebrew language, and its relation to other Semitic languages; textual criticism, and the versions; archaeology and Old Testament study; Ugaritic and other ancient Near Eastern texts in their relation to Old Testament studies; inter-Testamental literature, including the Qumran scrolls.

3. A selected portion or portions of the Old Testament in Hebrew, including always some poetical texts.

This paper contains questions on a selected portion or portions of the Old Testament in Hebrew concerning (*a*) translation; (*b*) grammar; (*c*) pointing; (*d*) textual criticism (questions involving a knowledge of the Septuagint translation of the prescribed texts may be included); (*e*) subject-matter.

The portions prescribed in **1985** are: Exodus i–xii; Amos, Psalms i–xx; Proverbs x–xii; Song of Songs. In **1986**: Exodus i–xii; Amos, Psalms i–x, cxx–cxxxii; Proverbs xxix–xxxi, Song of Songs.

4. Passages for translation from the Old Testament (Hebrew) generally, Hebrew composition, and pointing.

5. *Either* (*a*) Isaiah xl–lxvi in Hebrew,
or (*b*) Aramaic,

or (*c*) A selected portion or portions of the Septuagint, including both prose and poetical books of the canonical Old Testament.

5(*a*) contains questions on (i) translation; (ii) grammar; (iii) pointing; (iv) textual criticism (questions involving a knowledge of the Septuagint translation of Isaiah xl–lxvi may be included); (v) subject-matter.

5(*b*) contains questions on (i) translation; (ii) grammar; (iii) pointing; (iv) textual criticism (questions involving a knowledge of the Greek versions of the Aramaic portions of the Old Testament may be included); (v) subject-matter, and may contain a passage from an unspecified text for translation from Aramaic into English.

5(*c*) contains questions on (i) translation; (ii) grammar; (iii) comparison of the Hebrew and Greek texts; (iv) the history and criticism of the Septuagint Version.

The following Aramaic texts are prescribed for study in **1985** and **1986**: The Aramaic portions of the Old Testament; Targum Neofiti on Genesis xii–xiv, in A. Diez Macho, *Neophyti I*, i (1968); the Targum of Jonathan on I Samuel i–vi, in A. Sperber, *The Bible in Aramaic*, ii (1959).

The selected portions of the Septuagint prescribed in **1985** and **1986** are: Exodus xiii–xxiv; Isaiah xl–xliv, xlix–lv.

A candidate must offer all five papers in Section I.

Section II. New Testament

1. General paper on the New Testament

This paper contains questions on the background of the New Testament, on the authorship and date of the books of the New Testament, and on the circumstances in which they were written; on the general principles of the textual criticism of the New Testament; and on the outlines of the history of the formation of the canon. Some questions of a more advanced character are also set on textual criticism and on the history of the canon, but candidates are not expected to show detailed knowledge of more than *one* of those subjects.

2. The gospels in Greek, with special reference to a selected gospel

The selected gospel in **1985**: Mark. In **1986**: John.

3. The Acts, Epistles, and Apocalypse in Greek, with special reference to a selected portion

In **1985**: Acts. In **1986**: II Corinthians.

4. New Testament theology, with special reference to a selected subject

This paper will include passages for translation, explanation, or paraphrase.

The selected subject in **1985**: The Church in the New Testament. In **1986**: Ethics.

5. A selected portion or portions from (*a*) Philo, (*b*) Josephus

This paper contains passages for translation from the prescribed portion or portions, with questions on relevant matters of language, history, or thought.

The selected portion in **1985** and **1986** is from Philo, *de Opificio Mundi.*

6. A selected portion or portions of writings in Aramaic

This paper will be set on a portion or portions of one or more books in Aramaic. It will contain:

(i) passages for translation from the prescribed portion or portions, with questions (mainly linguistic) on the passages set;

(ii) general questions on the history of the language and of the Targums. Passages for retranslation may be set, but these will be optional.

The selected portion in **1985** is: Isaiah xl–xlv in *The Targum of Isaiah*, ed. J. F. Stenning (Oxford, 1949). In **1986**: Isaiah xlix–liii in *The Targum of Isaiah*, ed. J. F. Stenning (Oxford, 1949) and columns xx–xxi in *The Genesis Apocryphon of Qumran Cave 1*, ed. J. A. Fitzmyer (Rome, 2nd edn, 1971).

A candidate must offer Papers 1–4 and *either* 5 *or* 6 in Section II.

Section III. Church History

1. History of the church, including doctrine, to A.D. 461

2. General church history, A.D. 461–1500

3. General church history, A.D. 1500–1800

4. General church history, from 1800 to the present day

A candidate must offer all four papers in Section III.

Section IV. Dogmatics

1. History of Christian doctrine to the close of the Council of Chalcedon

2. A subject from the patristic period in connexion with original documents

The subject in **1985** is: The doctrine of the Trinity from Tertullian to Augustine. In **1986**: Doctrines of Grace, Necessity, and Free Will from Augustine to Godescalc.

3. A subject from the medieval period, i.e. A.D. 800–1500, in connexion with original documents

The subject in **1985** is: Eucharistic doctrine from A.D. 800 to 1400. In **1986**: The doctrine of the Trinity from Boethius to Aquinas.

4. History of Christian doctrine from Luther to the close of the Council of Trent

5. A subject from modern theology in connexion with original documents

The subject in **1985** and **1986** is: The doctrine of the saving work of Christ in writings from 1870 to the present day (the ways in which theologians have represented the significance and continuing efficacy of the work of Christ in and for the individual, the community, and the world).

6. Selected portions of liturgies and service-books in their relation to the history of Christian doctrine

The prescribed subject in **1985** and **1986** is: The action of the worshipping community as reflected in eucharistic and baptismal rites of the patristic, Reformation, and contemporary periods.

In Section IV a candidate must offer one paper from Papers 1, 4, and 6, one from Papers 2, 3, and 5, and two others chosen from Papers 1–6.

Section V. Philosophy of Religion and Christian Ethics

1. The history of the philosophy of religion

2. Fundamental problems in the philosophy of religion

The subjects in these papers are to be studied historically and critically. Students will be expected to have a general knowledge of the history of the subject, but alternatives to questions on the history before Descartes will be set from the modern period.

(*a*) *The nature and grounds of religious belief:* the functions of reason, feeling, and volition in producing faith; the theory of the relativity of knowledge as applied to man's knowledge of God; the different conceptions of divine revelation; the possibilities of revelation; reason and revelation.

(*b*) *The idea of God:* the arguments for the existence of God; the value–judgement in religion; pluralism; pantheism; theism; divine personality and the absolute.

(*c*) *Theories of the universe:* dualism; materialism; naturalism; idealism; law in relation to providence; prayer and miracle; the problem of evil.

(*d*) *Human nature:* personality; freedom; immortality.

3. Christian ethics

(*a*) Types of moral theory, ancient and modern.
(*b*) Faith and morals.
(*c*) Christian ideals and motives.

4. *Either* (*a*) Some major philosopher or school of philosophers or philosophical problem in its theological aspects,

In **1985** and **1986**: Time and eternity.

or (*b*) A special subject in ethics.

In **1985** and **1986**: Law, love, and freedom.

A candidate must offer all four papers in Section V.

Section VI. Christian Theology in the Modern World

1. Church and society in England since 1800

The relation between the Churches and civil society. History of the established and non-established Churches; the effects upon them of, and their reactions to, social change, including the conditions of life and labour, the development of political and economic democracy and of the welfare state.

2. Ecumenical movements since 1800

The history and theology of developments in inter-Church relations since 1800. This paper will also include some questions on the contribution of liturgical movements to closer relations between the Churches.

3. The Church's mission in the modern world

Developments since 1750 of Christian missionary thought and action in relation to non-Christian faiths and world-views. The paper will include two sections: (*a*) Missions and Society; (*b*) The Christian Faith and Other Faiths – A Study of Their Encounter. Candidates will be required to answer questions from both sections.

4. Religious thought since 1781

The impact of science, philosophy, and historical studies upon the understanding of the nature of religion and of theology.

5. Christian doctrine

The study in its setting in the twentieth century of either the thought of a selected theologian or the interpretation of a particular doctrine. The Faculty Board will determine and announce which of the alternative subjects shall be the subject of the examination in a particular year.

The subject in **1985** and **1986** is: Eschatological hope in the twentieth century (Christian thought concerning the goal and outcome of human and cosmic history, in relation to other representations).

6. Christian ethics

The moral implications of Christian belief. The relation between Christian and other contemporary ethical attitudes with special reference to a select group of problems, such as crime and punishment, war and peace, sex and the family.

In **1985** and **1986**: Law, love, and freedom.

A candidate must offer four papers from Papers 1–6 in Section VI.

Ordinary Examinations for the B.A. Degree

(i) **Religious Studies**

The examination consists of any two pairs of papers chosen by the candidate from among Papers 1 and 2, 3 and 4, 5 and 6, 7 and 8, 9 and 10, of the papers specified for the Theological and Religious Studies Tripos.

A candidate who has obtained honours, or been allowed an Ordinary Examination, on Part I A of the Theological and Religious Studies Tripos may not offer any paper that he offered in that examination.

(ii) **Biblical and Historical Theology**

The examination consists of certain of the papers specified for the Theological and Religious Studies Tripos as defined below.

No student may be a candidate for this examination who has obtained honours, or been allowed an Ordinary Examination, in Part IB or Part II of the Theological and Religious Studies Tripos.

A candidate who has been classed, or obtained an allowance, on the Preliminary Examination for Part IB and for Part II of the Theological and Religious Studies Tripos must offer Paper 13 and four other papers chosen by himself from among Papers 14, 16, 19, 22, 24, and 26.

Every other candidate must offer Paper 13 and two other papers chosen by himself from among Papers 16, 19, 22, 24, and 26.

VETERINARY MEDICINE

The veterinary courses at Cambridge are divided into preclinical and clinical parts. The first three years[1] are concerned with the basic preclinical sciences and lead to the B.A. Degree. This part of the course is taught in the laboratories in Downing Street and lies mainly within the framework of the Medical Sciences Tripos (see p. 255 of the Handbook). The final examination for the degree of Bachelor of Veterinary Medicine (Vet.M.B.) is taken after clinical courses which extend over a further three years.

The Medical Sciences Tripos

Part IA

First-year veterinary students attend courses in Anatomy, Biochemistry, Medical Genetics, and Physiology, and with the exception of Medical Genetics take a written paper and a practical examination in all of these subjects in Part IA of the Medical Sciences Tripos at the end of the year. The examination in Medical Genetics forms part of the Second Veterinary M.B. Examination and may be taken at the end of the Lent Term or in September: see Second Veterinary M.B. Examination below.

Part IB

The courses available to second-year veterinary students offer an element of choice. Those students who, with the approval of their Directors of Studies, wish to study a single subject in depth during their third (Part II) year, will attend courses in Anatomy and Veterinary Anatomy, Pathology, Pharmacology, and Physiology and Veterinary Physiology. They will be examined in all of these subjects in Part IB of the Medical Sciences Tripos at the end of their second year. The examinations will consist of a practical and oral and the relevant sections of the written paper in Anatomy, the practical examination and written paper in each of Pathology, Pharmacology, and Physiology, and the written paper in Veterinary Physiology. Alternatively, some students may prefer to spread the range of basic medical subjects over three years instead of two: these

[1] Two years for affiliated students, who must take the two-year course for Parts IA and IB of the Medical Sciences Tripos.

candidates postpone the courses in Pathology, and Pharmacology until their third year of residence but take a course of lectures in Animal Behaviour. For these students the subjects Pathology, Pharmacology, and Animal Behaviour are not examined in Part IB of the Tripos. Unlike medical students, veterinary students taking the three-year option will not be required to offer a second-year Elective Subject in Part IB.

Part II (General)

The choice of a Part II course in the third preclinical year will largely follow from the subjects taken in Part IB of the Medical Sciences Tripos. Those students who have postponed Pathology and Pharmacology from the second year will be required to offer both these subjects in Section I of Part II (General) of the Medical Sciences Tripos. They will also be required to attend a further course in Animal Behaviour and a course in an Elective Subject, and, with Pathology and Pharmacology, will be examined in these subjects at the end of the year. The list of Elective Subjects may show slight changes from one year to the next, but students will be informed of the choices available by the division of the Easter Term of their second year of residence. Section I of Part II (General) of the Medical Sciences Tripos will consist for veterinary students of one written paper and a practical examination in each of the subjects Pathology and Pharmacology, a short written paper in Animal Behaviour, and a written paper in an Elective Subject.

Students who have read Anatomy, Pathology, Pharmacology, and Physiology in Part IB of the Medical Sciences Tripos are free to take any of the courses leading to Section II of Part II (General) of the Medical Sciences Tripos or to Part II of the Natural Sciences Tripos: the Clinical Veterinary Medicine Syndicate imposes no restrictions on candidates' freedom of choice. The courses for Part II of the Natural Sciences Tripos include Anatomy, Applied Biology, Biochemistry, Genetics, Pathology, Pharmacology, Physiology, Psychology, and Zoology: full details of these courses may be found on pp. 346–57 of the Handbook. Students who wish to read subjects from other Tripos examinations may in certain circumstances be allowed to do so, but they are strongly recommended to seek early advice from Tutors and Directors of Studies.

It should be noted that the choice between the two- and three-year courses for the Medical Sciences Tripos will normally be made at the end of the first year of residence, and that candidates who opt for the three-year course will be unable to read for any Part II other than Section I of Part II (General) of the Medical Sciences Tripos. On the other hand a student who chooses the two-year course and who subsequently regrets his decision should immediately consult his Tutor and Director of Studies. He may then be allowed to transfer to the three-year course, *provided he makes arrangements to do so before the middle of the Michaelmas Term.* Such a student would defer continuation of his courses in Pathology, and Pharmacology until his third preclinical year, and at the end of that year would be examined in Pathology, Pharmacology, Animal Behaviour, and one Elective Subject in Section I of Part II (General) of the Medical Sciences Tripos.

Transfers

In certain circumstances it is possible for students to transfer to Veterinary Medicine from other Triposes, but as places are in short supply it is essential for candidates considering the possibility of transfer to obtain early and detailed advice from their Colleges. A student who has *not* read Physiology in Part I A of the Natural Sciences Tripos may in exceptional circumstances be permitted to transfer in his second year to the two-year Medical Sciences Tripos course. Such a student should read Anatomy, Biochemistry, and Physiology in his second year, and Anatomy, Physiology, Pathology, and Pharmacology in his third year. A student who *has* read Physiology in Part I A of the Natural Sciences Tripos should normally read Biochemistry, Pharmacology, and Physiology for Part I B of that Tripos, thus enabling him in his third year to read Pathology, and Special Subject Veterinary Anatomy in Section III of Part II (General) of the Medical Sciences Tripos (for details see p. 000 of the Handbook). Students who transfer to Veterinary Medicine should arrange to attend the course and take the examination in Medical Genetics in the Second Veterinary M.B. Examination, unless they have already gained exemption from Medical Genetics by attaining the prescribed standard in Biology of Cells in Part I A of the Natural Sciences Tripos. They must also attend the course in Veterinary Physiology and take the relevant section or sections of the examination in Veterinary Physiology in the Second Veterinary M.B. Examination.

Professional Training

The three years which follow the preclinical courses are based on the Department of Clinical Veterinary Medicine at Madingley Road. During this time all students take the various parts of the Final Veterinary Examination which leads to the Vet.M.B. Degree.

Veterinary students, like medical students, must comply with certain standards laid down by the University in order to qualify for membership of the appropriate professional body. For veterinary students at Cambridge these standards are embodied in the First M.B. Examination, the Second Veterinary M.B. Examination and the Final Veterinary Examination, Parts I, II, and III.

The First M.B. Examination

Veterinary students normally gain exemption from the First M.B. Examination before they come up to Cambridge by obtaining appropriate passes in G.C.E. at 'O' and 'A' levels. Details of the examination and the exemption requirements may be found on p. 269 of the Handbook.

The Second Veterinary M.B. Examination

Candidates may obtain exemption from all subjects of the Second Veterinary M.B. Examinations except Medical Genetics by attaining the prescribed standards in Anatomy, Biochemistry, and Physiology in Part I A of the Medical Sciences Tripos; in Anatomy, Physiology, and Veterinary Physiology, in Part I B, and in Pathology, and Pharmacology either in Part I B or in Section I of Part II (General) of that Tripos. Most candidates who transfer to Veterinary Medicine from the Natural Sciences Tripos will, with the possible exception of Medical Genetics and Veterinary Physiology, be able to complete their exemption requirements by reading Pathology and Special Subject Veterinary Anatomy in Section III of Part II (General) of the Medical Sciences Tripos in their third year (see Transfers above).

For all candidates who have not obtained exemption, the Second Veterinary M.B. Examination is held in June and September of each year. The examination in Medical Genetics is held at the end of the Lent Term and in September of each year.

The Final Veterinary Examination, Parts I, II, and III

No candidates are exempted from these examinations, nor may students take Parts II or III of the Final Veterinary Examination until they have successfully completed the previous Part or Parts. The examinations take place at the end of the Easter Term, and are held again at the beginning of the Michaelmas Term for candidates who may not have passed on previous occasions. The Vet.M.B. Degree is conferred on students who have passed Parts I, II, and III. It qualifies them for membership of the Royal College of Veterinary Surgeons and so to practise.

Part I

Part I of the Final Veterinary Examination is held at the end of the fourth academic year. A candidate for this examination must have satisfied the following requirements:

(*a*)* that he or she has passed all parts of the Second Veterinary M.B. Examination or has obtained exemption from the relevant parts by achieving the prescribed standards in Parts IA, IB, or Sections I or III of Part II (General) of the Medical Sciences Tripos;

(*b*) that he or she, since attaining the age of sixteen years, has spent a total of at least twelve weeks on a farm or farms working with the larger animals, and can produce the necessary certificates from the farmers concerned;

(*c*) that he or she has satisfied the requirements for the necessary certificates of attendance for the first three terms of clinical instruction.

The courses are divided into three sections as follows:

(i) *Animal Pathology and Microbiology*

This section includes morphological, histological, and clinical aspects of pathology, and the epidemiology, pathogenesis, laboratory diagnosis, and principles of control of viral, bacterial, and mycotic diseases.

(ii) *Animal parasitology*

This section includes helminths, arthropods, and protozoal infections of domestic animals.

* Requirement (*a*) must in practice be satisfied before the student starts the clinical courses.

(iii) *Animal health and production*

This section includes the husbandry and management of healthy animals, including nutrition, livestock improvement, and housing.

The examination for each section consists of two three-hour written papers, a practical examination, and a *viva voce* examination.

Part II

Part II of the Final Veterinary Examination is held at the end of the fifth academic year. A candidate for this examination must have passed all sections of Part I of the Final Veterinary Examination and must have satisfied the requirements for the necessary certificates of attendance. The courses which lead to the examination cover public health (including meat and milk inspection), poultry diseases, and the principles of diagnosis and therapeutics. The latter presents a common approach to medicine and surgery, with particular emphasis on the clinical examination of animals. The examination, now retitled *Veterinary Medicine* (preliminary clinical subjects), consists of two three-hour written papers, a practical examination, and a *viva voce* examination.

During this year students also complete the first three terms of a six-term course of instruction in the Principles and Practice of Animal Surgery. This part of the course is examined in Section (ii) of Part III of the Final Veterinary Examination at the end of the sixth academic year.

Part III

Part III of the Final Veterinary Examination is held at the end of the sixth academic year. A candidate for this examination

(*a*) must have passed Parts I and II;

(*b*) must have satisfied the requirements for the necessary certificates of attendance;

(*c*) must produce written evidence of 26 weeks of practical veterinary experience as approved for this purpose by the Clinical Veterinary Medicine Syndicate.

The examination has two sections as follows:

(i) *Veterinary Medicine.* This section deals with the prevention and medical treatment of diseases in the domestic animals; it includes questions on jurisprudence.

(ii) *Animal Surgery.* This section deals with the principles and practice of animal surgery; it includes questions on anaesthesia, infertility, and obstetrics.

The examination for each section consists of two three-hour written papers, a clinical examination, and a *viva voce* examination.

5

RESEARCH AND COURSES OF ADVANCED OR FURTHER STUDY

The University offers the research degrees of Doctor of Philosophy (Ph.D.), Master of Science (M.Sc.) and Master of Letters (M.Litt.) to graduates, and in exceptional cases to non-graduates, who can show the ability to profit from a course of supervised research; and the degree of Master of Philosophy (M.Phil.) to similar candidates who can demonstrate their ability to profit from either a two-year course of advanced study or a one-year course of further study and training in research. In all cases the student works under the general direction of a Supervisor appointed by the Degree Committee for the Faculty concerned, and the resources of the University Library, the Departmental and College libraries and, in appropriate cases, the scientific laboratories, are open to him. For the Ph.D., M.Sc. and M.Litt. Degrees the student presents for examination a dissertation in English embodying the results of his research, and undergoes an oral, or in exceptional cases a written, examination on the dissertation and the general field of knowledge in which it falls. The M.Phil. Degree (two-year course) is examined by written papers and a thesis; and the M.Phil. Degree (one-year course) is examined by written papers, or by a thesis, or by written papers and a thesis, according to the subject.

General conditions of admission

Enquiries about admission as a Graduate Student and requests for forms of application should be made to the Secretary of the Board of Graduate Studies, at 4 Mill Lane, Cambridge, CB2 1RZ. The forms of application should be completed in accordance with the instructions, and returned to the Secretary of the Board of Graduate Studies, who will also handle the applicant's admission to a College, under the provisions of the Cambridge Intercollegiate Graduate Application Scheme.

In exceptional cases persons who are not graduates of a university may be admitted as Graduate Students, provided that they give such evidence of general educational qualification as may be approved by the Board of Graduate Studies.

Applications for admission in any one academical year should, if possible, reach the Secretary of the Board of Graduate Studies, together with all the necessary documents, not later than the end of March in the preceding academical year. The Degree Committees for the Faculties, which consider applications in the first instance, do not normally meet during the Long Vacation.

No application will be favourably considered unless (i) it appears at the time that the course proposed can conveniently be pursued within the University; and (ii) it appears that the applicant is well qualified for the particular course which he has proposed.

Candidates for the M.Phil. Degree are so registered on their admission, but the Board of Graduate Studies and the Degree Committee concerned almost invariably require a person who proposes to work for the Ph.D. Degree, or the M.Sc. Degree or the M.Litt. Degree to spend a probationary period before registration as a candidate for a degree, and may require him to take a progress examination, either a special examination, or, if more convenient, papers or questions set in a Tripos or other University examination, provided that this examination is not held later than the vacation following the second term after the term of admission. The Board determine how many, if any, of the terms previous to examination shall be counted towards the requirements for a degree.

Before anyone can be admitted as a Graduate Student and allowed to count residence or claim other privileges, he must have been admitted to one of the Colleges.

A Graduate Student is not admissible as a candidate for any University Prize, Scholarship, or Studentship which is open only to undergraduates.

Courses of research for the Ph.D., M.Sc., and M.Litt. Degrees

A person who has been admitted as a Graduate Student is required to pursue a course under direction and supervision prescribed by the Degree Committee which has recommended approval of his application, and under such other conditions, if any, as may be laid down by that Degree Committee or by the Board of Graduate Studies.

He must pursue in the University under supervision a course of research, if he seeks the degree of Master of Science or of Master of Letters, for not less than six terms; if he seeks the degree of

Doctor of Philosophy, for not less than nine terms, with the following exceptions:[1]

(i) A Graduate Student who is a candidate for the degree of Doctor of Philosophy or M.Sc. or M.Litt. may be exempted from three terms of research if, before he was admitted as a Graduate Student, he had been engaged to an extent satisfactory to the Degree Committee and the Board of Graduate Studies either in full-time or part-time research or in other work done after graduation, which is deemed by the Degree Committee and the Board to have provided training for the course of research that he has undertaken.

(ii) The Board may allow a Graduate Student who is a candidate for the Ph.D. Degree, or the M.Sc. Degree, or the M.Litt. Degree, or for certain other qualifications, to spend all but three terms of his course of research, or any less numbers of terms, working under supervision outside the University under conditions approved by the Degree Committee and the Board.

(iii) The Board may allow a Graduate Student to intermit his course of research for one or more terms on account of illness or other sufficient cause.

(iv) The Board may allow a Graduate Student who is qualified to receive, but who has not received the Certificate of Post-graduate Study in Natural Science, or in Engineering, or in Chemical Engineering; the Diploma in Economics, or in Historical Studies, or in International Law, or in Legal Studies, or in Theology to count towards his course of research not more than three terms of the period during which he was a candidate for one of these Certificates or Diplomas.

(v) The Board may grant a Graduate Student, to whom an allowance of terms of residence has been made in respect of work done by him in the University before matriculation, a similar allowance towards the period during which he is required to pursue his course of research in the University.

Specific application must be made to the Secretary of the Board whenever exemption or other allowance is applied for, and must be accompanied by a written opinion from the student's Supervisor on the proposal made.

At least three terms must have been kept by residence by any

[1] All these exemptions and special privileges are exceptional and will not be granted unless the applicant satisfies the Board that he deserves them.

Graduate Student who is admitted to a degree, except any term which the Council of the Senate may allow on account of illness or other grave cause. Graduate Students who are graduates of the University may count for this purpose previous residence *in statu pupillari*, but they must in addition comply with the separate requirements about terms of research.

The Board of Graduate Studies may deprive any person of the status of Graduate Student

(i) if he is no longer a member of a College;

(ii) if he has failed to pay the fees due from him as a Graduate Student;

(iii) if, in the opinion of the Degree Committee, the report made on the examination taken in his probationary period is such as to show that he is not qualified to continue in his course;

(iv) if, after completing three terms as a Graduate Student, he has not been registered as a candidate for a degree, diploma, or certificate;

(v) if the Degree Committee under whose control he has been placed have satisfied the Board that he has not been working to their satisfaction, or that in their opinion he is not likely to reach the standard of the M.Sc. or M.Litt. Degree, or M.Phil. Degree (two-year course), or M.Phil. Degree (one-year course) or of any other qualification for which he might be registered as a candidate, or that he has not complied with the conditions laid down for him.

Submission of dissertations for the Ph.D., M.Sc., and M.Litt. Degrees

A Graduate Student registered for a degree who has kept all but one of the terms required to be kept by him may submit a dissertation embodying the results of his research not earlier than the beginning of the term during which he expects to complete the period of research required under the regulations and not later than the end of the vacation following the eleventh term after the term in which his registration became effective; by special permission of the Board of Graduate Studies a dissertation may be submitted later than this. An allowance of terms counts in calculating his standing.

Courses of advanced study for the M.Phil. Degree (two-year course), and of further study and training in research for the M.Phil. Degree (one-year course)

Candidates for the M.Phil. Degree are admitted as Graduate Students by the Board of Graduate Studies on the recommendation of the Degree Committee concerned.

A two-year course of advanced study is offered in Theology, and one-year courses of further study and training in research are offered in a number of subjects, details of which may be obtained from the Secretary of the Board of Graduate Studies.

Candidates for both the two-year course and the one-year course follow a course of study and research under the general responsibility of the Degree Committee concerned and are examined, in the case of candidates for the two-year course, by written papers and a thesis and, in the case of candidates for the one-year course, by written papers, or a thesis, or written papers and a thesis, according to the subject.

A candidate who has been approved for the M.Phil. Degree (two-year course) may be registered for the Ph.D. Degree, but he will be required to complete five further terms of research, of which three terms must be spent in Cambridge. If the candidate has proceeded to the M.Phil. Degree, the Ph.D. Degree Examiners will take no account of any work which was included in the M.Phil. Degree thesis. A candidate for the M.Phil. Degree (two-year course) who has not presented himself for examination for that degree may be allowed to count not more than three terms of research towards the required terms for the Ph.D., M.Sc., and M.Litt. Degrees.

A candidate who has been approved for the M.Phil. Degree (one-year course) may, with the approval of the Board of Graduate Studies, be allowed to count not more than three terms of his candidature for that degree towards the requirements of the Ph.D., M.Sc., and M.Litt. Degrees. If this allowance is made, the candidate is not prevented from proceeding to the M.Phil. Degree.

Fees and Expenses

The cost of a period of graduate study at Cambridge includes payment of the University Composition fee, College fees, and the expense incurred in the student's maintenance. Before an applicant's admission can finally be confirmed the Board of Graduate Studies must have evidence that the applicant will have sufficient financial support. The sum concerned will be specified as a condition of admission in formal offers of admission issued by the Board's office and will represent the estimated total of the following elements:

(1) University Composition Fees: for graduate students starting their course in October 1984 these will be as follows:

U.K. and EEC students:	£1,569 a year	(£523 a term)
Overseas students:		
Arts	£3,300 a year	(£1,100 a term)
Science	£4,200 a year	(£1,400 a term)
Clinical Medicine	£7,400 a year	(£2,466.67 a term)

There could well be substantial increases above these sums from October 1985.

(2) College Fees: students should allow a further £1,100, **in addition to the sums mentioned above.** However, College fees vary from College to College; further information may be sought from the College concerned.

(3) Maintenance and living expenses

In addition to the costs of University and College fees, it is estimated that students admitted from October 1985 will need financial support in accordance with **at least** the following rates to cover their own maintenance and living expenses:

	£
A United Kingdom student staying for 12 months or more	2,625 a year
A United Kingdom student staying for 9 months	2,100
An EEC or Overseas student staying for 12 months or more	3,325 a year
An EEC or Overseas student staying for 9 months	2,660

In addition a married student accompanied by a wife or husband and other dependants, will need a further £1,350 a year for the wife or husband and £650 a year for each dependant. Students accompanied by children should make additional provision, where necessary, for the cost of child-minding and should not expect the University or their College to bear this cost for them. It is suggested that at least £40 per week per child should be allowed for this purpose, in addition to the sum for which the Board of Graduate Studies require a guarantee.

It cannot be emphasized too strongly that, because of inflation, expenses including fees are likely to rise substantially over a three-year period of research, and applicants and their sponsors should take this into account. Students from overseas should also allow for possible fluctuations in currency exchange rates.

Students pursuing research which requires the provision of abnormally expensive laboratory materials may sometimes be required to contribute towards the cost of their research, in addition to their paying the usual University and College fees. The Board of Graduate Studies will inform successful applicants for admission of any additional fees that they will be called on to pay for this purpose, and the Board will increase accordingly the amount of the financial support for which those students will be required to provide a guarantee.

6

UNIVERSITY SCHOLARSHIPS AND OTHER AWARDS

UNIVERSITY SCHOLARSHIPS

TABLE OF AWARDS

KEY: † Award published in the Awards number of the *Reporter*. Please consult this for further details, especially where indicated.
B.G.S.: Board of Graduate Studies, 4 Mill Lane, Cambridge, CB2 1RZ.
G.B.: General Board of the Faculties, The Old Schools, Cambridge, CB2 1TT.
U.R.: University Registry, The Old Schools, Cambridge, CB2 1TN.
* Awards also open to prospective members of the University. Other awards are open only to people who are already members of the University.

N.B. Due to the limited space available, certain details (e.g. closing dates) have been omitted from the Table of Awards. Prospective candidates are strongly advised to make further enquiries before applying to funds or competing for a prize.

GENERAL AWARDS, RELATED TO MORE THAN ONE SUBJECT

Award	Subject/Purpose	Eligibility	When offered	Details (and forms when applicable) from:
†Allen Scholarships	**Research in 'arts' subjects**	Graduates of the University, under 29 on 1 October following application	Annually	B.G.S.
†Bell, Abbott, and Barnes Funds/Exhibitions	Subject unrestricted. General financial assistance	Undergraduates needing assistance	Each Term	College Tutors
*Cambridge Commonwealth Trust Awards	Subject unrestricted	Graduates or undergraduates from the Commonwealth, Burma, Pakistan, or Sudan	Annually	B.G.S. (Graduates); College Tutors (Undergraduates)
*Cambridge Livingstone Trust Awards	Subject unrestricted. For Bachelor level degrees, or postgraduate courses	Graduates who are domiciled, resident, or normally resident in Botswana, Lesotho, Malawi, Namibia, South Africa, Swaziland, Zambia, or Zimbabwe	Annually	U.R.
*†H. M. Chadwick Studentship	For advanced study or research in the history, religion, and culture	Open to graduates or research students of universities in U.K.	Annually	G.B.

[1] **Full details of the regulations governing awards are given in the *Statutes and Ordinances of the University of Cambridge*. Most University Scholarships, Studentships, and Prizes are advertised in the Awards number of the *Reporter* which appears annually in November. Notices also appear in the official and unofficial parts of the *Reporter* throughout the year.**

Award	Subject/Purpose	Eligibility	When offered	Details (and forms when applicable) from:
H. M. Chadwick Studentship (*cont.*)	(all aspects) of any of the peoples of the British Isles or Scandinavian peoples before A.D. 1050, of the Teutonic/Celtic peoples before A.D. 600, of the peoples of the Near East before 1000 B.C., or of any modern primitive peoples, or the general history or comparative study of culture (*excluding* subjects wholly or mainly relating to Western Europe since A.D. 1050, the classical periods of Greece, Rome, or India, or other periods of advanced culture)	or Eire (preference to Cambridge candidates)		
†Bartle Frere Exhibitions	For study or research in any branch of knowledge requiring travel to any part of the Commonwealth except U.K., India, and Bangladesh	Preference given to Graduate Students intending to undertake research, but undergraduates may also apply	Annually	B.G.S.
*†Robert Gardiner Memorial Scholarships	Unrestricted	Undergraduates or graduates of Irish universities	Annually	U.R.
*†Le Bas Research Studentships	Research in Literature	Applicants must gain admission as Graduate Students	Annually	B.G.S.
†Lundgren Research awards	Research in scientific subjects, including Mathematics	Candidates for the Ph.D. Degree, who are not ordinarily resident in the U.K., and who have completed four terms of research as registered Graduate Students	Twice a year	B.G.S.
†W. A. Meek Scholarships	Research in 'science' subjects	Graduates of the University under 29 on 1 October following application	Annually	B.G.S.
†Mary Euphrasia Mosley Fund Grants	Travel to British Commonwealth countries for study or research	Members of the University below the standing of M.A.	Annually	U.R.

Award	Subject/Purpose	Eligibility	When offered	Details (and forms when applicable) from:
†A. M. P. Read Scholarships	Research in 'arts' and 'science' subjects	Graduates of the University under 29 on 1 October following application	Annually	B.G.S.
†Research Maintenance Fund Grants	Research for the Ph.D. Degree	Those who have graduated (or about to graduate) with a B.A. Degree of the University. Applicants must gain admission as a Graduate Student and must apply within two academical years of graduating	Annually	B.G.S.
Sims Fund and Scholarship	Study or research in Physics, Chemistry, Mathematics, or Medicine	Graduates of the University born in Great Britain or N. Ireland, or whose parents were British subjects at the time of the candidate's birth. Registered Graduate Students, who are not graduates of the University, but are qualified in every other respect, may apply for a grant when the Scholarship is offered	When vacant	U.R.
†Smuts Memorial Fund Grants	Study or research in Commonwealth studies	Members of the University	Each Term	G.B.
†Worts Travelling Scholars Fund Grants	Travel outside Great Britain investigating various subjects	Members of the University. Preference given to below standing of M.A.	Annually	B.G.S.
		AWARDS IN PARTICULAR SUBJECTS		
		Agriculture		
†A. J. Keith Studentships	Graduate studies in Agriculture	Members of the University	When vacant	Department of Applied Biology
		Anglo-Saxon		
†Dame Bertha Phillpotts Memorial Scholarships and Grants	Advanced study or research in Old Norse or Icelandic	Members of the University	Annually	Faculty of Modern and Medieval Languages

Award	Subject/Purpose	Eligibility	When offered	Details (and forms when applicable) from:
		Archaeology and Anthropology		
*†Evans Fellowship	Research in Anthropology and Archaeology in relation to South East Asia	A graduate of any university	Annually	The Secretary of the Fund, Museum of Archaeology and Anthropology, Downing Street
†Fortes Fund Grants	Towards the expenses of publications in Social Anthropology	Members of the University. Preference given to those under 40 and those with children under 10	Annually	Department of Social Anthropology
†Mark Gregson Prize	For an essay on an archaeological subject	Undergraduates may compete in the year they are candidates for Part II of the Archaeological and Anthropological Tripos. See † for more details	Annually	U.R.
†Richards Fund	Fieldwork in Social Anthropology	Graduate Students registered for field research in the Department of Social Anthropology	Annually	Department of Social Anthropology
†Ridgeway-Venn Travel Studentship	Archaeology and Anthropology	Members of the University *in statu pupillari*. See † for more details	Annually	U.R.
Henry Ling Roth Scholarships	Research in Ethnology	Members of the University, who are working, or have worked, in the Faculty of Archaeology and Anthropology	When funds permit	Faculty of Archaeology and Anthropology
†Anthony Wilkin Studentship and Grants	Research in Ethnology and Archaeology	Members of the University who are not of standing to become M.A. Certain preferences apply. See †	When funds permit	U.R.
		Architecture and History of Art		
†Kettle's Yard Travel Fund	Travel abroad to study Art or Architecture	Members of the University who have graduated in Architecture	Annually	Faculty of Architecture and History of Art

Award	Subject/Purpose	Eligibility	When offered	Details (and forms when applicable) from:
Kettle's Yard Travel Fund (*cont.*)		or in History of Art. Preference given to those below standing of M.A.		
†Edward S. Prior Prize	For a portfolio of drawings which show the best understanding of building construction and use of materials	Students of Architecture who have completed the studio-work for Parts I B and II of the Architecture Tripos	Annually	Faculty of Architecture and History of Art
		Bibliography		
Gordon Duff Prize	Essay on any of the following subjects: Bibliography, Palaeography, Typography, Book-binding, Book-illustration, or the Science of Books and Manuscripts and the Arts relating thereto. Subject must be approved	Members of the University, under 30	Triennially (next 1985)	U.R.
		Classics		
†Craven, Prendergast Sandys, H. A. Thomas Studentships, and G. C. Winter Warr and Charles Oldham Scholarships	Various branches of Classical research in Cambridge and abroad	Graduates of the University. See † for more details	Annually	Faculty of Classics
†Henry Carrington and Bentham Dumont Koe Studentship	Travel in lands where Greek is spoken, preferably in connexion with the study of Greek literature	Graduates of the University, whose age on the first day of the term of the election is not more than 28	Annually	Faculty of Classics
†Walston Studentship	Travel to Greek lands for the furtherance of research in Classical Archaeology	Cambridge students of Archaeology or Architecture. See † for more details	Annually	Faculty of Classics
†Sir William Browne's Medals	For composition of a Greek ode or elegy, or epigram, or Latin ode or elegy, or epigram, on a prescribed theme	Resident undergraduates may compete not later than their third year	Annually	U.R.

Award	Subject/Purpose	Eligibility	When offered	Details (and forms when applicable) from:
†Montagu Butler Prize	For an original exercise in Latin Hexameter Verse on a prescribed theme	Resident undergraduates may compete not later than their third year	Annually	U.R.
†Porson Prize	For a translation of a set passage from an English poet into Greek verse	Resident undergraduates may compete not later than their third year	Annually	U.R.
†Hare Prize	A dissertation on an approved subject pertaining to the history, literature, philosophy, law, or archaeology of ancient Greece or Rome	Members of the University, under 30, who have either been admitted to a degree in the University or have been elected Fellows of a College or have been appointed University Officers	Triennially (next 1987)	U.R.
*†Jebb Scholarship	Approved course of Literary study either in Greek and Latin or in one of these languages, together with English, or some other European language and literature. Normally required to become an Affiliated Student, and a candidate for an appropriate Tripos Examination. In special cases a Scholar may be allowed to be a Graduate Student	British subjects who have completed a course in Classics (or Latin or Greek, together with English or some other European language or literature), who are graduates of a university in the Commonwealth (excluding Great Britain and N. Ireland) and who have received an approved degree	Annually	U.R.
†Members' Classical Essay Prizes	Two Prizes for essays on approved subjects, primarily concerned with the study of Ancient Greece or Rome. See † for more details	One Prize is open to members of the University *in statu pupillari* of not more than seven years' standing, other than Graduate Students or candidates for the Diploma in Classical Archaeology, who are eligible for the other Prize	Annually	U.R.

Award	Subject/Purpose	Eligibility	When offered	Details (and forms when applicable) from:
†Members' Classical Reading Prizes	For the reading out loud of Greek or Latin	Any member of the University *in statu pupillari*, other than a Graduate Student, who has not kept more than seven terms at the beginning of the academical year in which he competes	Annually	U.R.
†Members' Classical Translation Prizes	For translation of Greek or Latin verse	Any member of the University *in statupupillari*, other than a Graduate Student, who has not kept more than seven terms at the beginning of the academical year in which he competes	Annually	U.R.
†F. S. Salisbury Fund	Grants for those engaged in excavations on Roman sites in Britain	Any member of the University *in statu pupillari*	Annually	Faculty of Classics
		Computing		
*ICL Research Studentship	Computing	Graduates of any university	When vacant	The Computer Laboratory, Corn Exchange Street
		Economics		
†Price Waterhouse Prize	For an essay on some subject that is within the scope of any paper in Part II of the Economics Tripos, or on an approved subject	Any second year undergraduate. See † for more details	Annually	U.R.
†Adam Smith Prize	For an essay on some subject that is within the scope of the syllabus of any paper in Part II of the Economics Tripos	Any candidate for Part II of the Economics Tripos or any undergraduate who has obtained honours in Part I of the Economics Tripos and has kept by residence not less than six terms. See † for more details	Annually	U.R.
†Stevenson Prize	For an essay on some question in Economics, Economic History, or Statistics since 1800	Open to (*a*) any registered Graduate Student, provided that the minimum number of terms of	Annually	U.R.

Award	Subject/Purpose	Eligibility	When offered	Details (and forms when applicable) from:
Stevenson Prize (*cont.*)		research or study required for the degree or qualification registered for have not been completed; (*b*) B.A.s not of standing to become M.A.s		
†Wrenbury Scholarships	Study and research in Economics, Political Economy, or Economic History subsequent to 1800	Candidates for Part II of the Economics Tripos in the year of application	Annually	U.R.
		Elocution		
†Winchester Reading Prizes	Reading out loud passages in Classical English Prose and Poetry; in the Old and New Testament and English Liturgy. See † for more details	Students in their third and fourth years	Annually	U.R.
		Engineering		
†William George Collins Fund	Research in Engineering, but preference given to Electrical and Mechanical	Members of the University in the Department of Engineering	Any time	The Secretary of the Degree Committee for the Faculty of Engineering
†Ford of Britain Trust Fund	General financial support	Graduate Students in the Department of Engineering	Any time	The Secretary of the Degree Committee for the Faculty of Engineering
†Charles Hesterman Merz Fund	Grants for research	Members of the University in the Faculty of Engineering, who are citizens of the Commonwealth of Nations	Any time	The Secretary of the Degree Committee for the Faculty of Engineering
†Rex Moir Fund	General financial support	Postgraduate or Graduate Students in the Department of Engineering	Any time	The Secretary of the Degree Committee for the Faculty of Engineering
*†Taylor Woodrow Fund	Grants for Postgraduate Studies in Civil Engineering	Applicants must have obtained an honours degree in a U.K. university, or some other approved qualification, and must become members of the University	Any time	The Secretary of the Degree Committee for the Faculty of Engineering

Award	Subject/Purpose	Eligibility	When offered	Details (and forms when applicable) from:
†Hamilton Prize	(See Natural Sciences)			
†John Winbolt Prize	For a paper, already accepted for publication in an established professional or learned journal, on some subject related to the profession of a civil engineer. All subjects studied for Parts IB and II of the Engineering Tripos are deemed acceptable	B.A.s not of standing to become M.A.s, or registered Graduate Students holding the status of B.A. working under the supervision of the Degree Committee for the Faculty of Engineering	Annually	U.R.
		English		
†Chancellor's Medal for an English Poem	For an original English poem	Resident undergraduates may compete not later than their third year	Annually	U.R.
†Harness Prize	For an English essay upon some subject connected with Shakespearean Literature	Undergraduates, or graduates of not more than 3 years' standing from their first degree	Triennially (next 1986)	U.R.
†Jebb Scholarship	(See Classics)			
†Jebb Studentships	(See Modern and Medieval Languages)			
†Le Bas Prize	For an essay on an approved literary subject	Any member of the University, who is a graduate of this or another university, under 30	Annually	U.R.
†Members' English Prize	For an essay on a literary subject chosen by the candidate	Graduate Students working under the supervision of the Degree Committee for the Faculty of English, who were admitted not earlier than 1 August next but one preceding the academical year they compete	Annually	U.R.
†Charles Oldham Shakespeare Scholarship	For an examination and essay on the works of Shakespeare	Undergraduates, B.A.s, LL.B.s, or LL.M.s under the New Regulations, provided that not more than nine complete terms have	Annually	U.R.

Award	Subject/Purpose	Eligibility	When offered	Details (and forms when applicable) from:
Charles Oldham Shakespeare Scholarship (*cont.*)		passed after their first term, and they are under 25		
		Geography		
Philip Lake Fund II Grants	Research or field-work in any approved branch of Geography	Graduate Students in the Department of Geography below the standing of M.A. Candidates for Part II of the Geographical Tripos may also apply at the beginning of the term they propose to present themselves	Annually	Department of Geography, Downing Place
†David Richards Travel Scholarships	Geography	British-born students who in the previous academical year have been classed in Part I A of the Geographical Tripos and are now reading for Part I B	Annually	U.R.
		History		
*†Stanley Baldwin Studentships and Grants	Study or research in British Political History in the years 1919 to 1939	Any person who is, or is about to become registered as, a Graduate Student in the University	Annually	Faculty of History, West Road
†Archbishop Cranmer Prize	For an essay on changes in doctrine, organization, and ritual within the Church of England between A.D. 1500 and A.D. 1700	Graduates of the University of not less than three years' standing from their first degree	Annually	U.R.
*†Archbishop Cranmer Studentships and Grants	For the furtherance of original research in English Ecclesiastical History between 1500 and 1700	Any person who is, or is about to become, registered as a Graduate Student in the University. Grants are also open to senior members of the University	When funds permit	Faculty of History, West Road

Award	Subject/Purpose	Eligibility	When offered	Details (and forms when applicable) from:
†Dr Lightfoot's Scholarship	For an examination in Ecclesiastical History. See † for more details	Members of the University who, having resided at least one year and being still in residence, or having taken their first degree, are under 25 when the examination begins	Annually	U.R.
†Ellen McArthur Prizes	Any work in Economic History	Any graduate of the University	Annually	Faculty of History, West Road
*Ellen McArthur Studentships	Original research in Economic History	Any person who is, or is about to become registered as, a Graduate Student in the University, with the intention of becoming a candidate for the Ph.D. Degree	Annually	Faculty of History, West Road
*Mellon Research Fellowships	Original research in American History	It is expected that candidates will either have completed a Ph.D. dissertation or be able to submit substantial written work if requested	Annually	Faculty of History, West Road
†Members' History Prize	For an essay on an historical subject chosen by the candidate	Graduate Students working under the supervision of the Degree Committee for the Faculty of History, who were admitted not earlier than 1 August preceding the academical year they compete	Annually	U.R.
†Sara Norton Prize	For an essay on an approved subject, on some aspect of the political history of the U.S.A.	Graduate Students and graduates of the University, under 25, who have kept not less than three terms	Annually	U.R.
†Prince Consort and Thirlwall Prizes	For a dissertation on an approved subject involving original historical research	Graduates of the University under 28	Annually (Prince Consort even years, Thirlwall odd years)	U.R.
*†Holland Rose Studentship	Study of some subject connected with the general history or development of the British	Any British subject, who is a graduate of the University or some other university in the	Annually	U.R.

Award	Subject/Purpose	Eligibility	When offered	Details (and forms when applicable) from:
Holland Rose Studentship (*cont.*)	Empire since 1815, or of Commonwealth, or with present problems thereof	U.K or Commonwealth, with high honours in History or in another relevant subject. Candidates may apply if not more than three complete academical years have elapsed since they took their first degree, or if they have been registered Graduate Students for not more than nine terms		
		Land Economy		
*†Harold Samuel Studentships	Research in economic, legal, or social matters relating to the use, tenure, or development of the land	Open, but tenure conditional upon the student being a registered Graduate Student of the University	Annually	Department of Land Economy, Silver Street
		Law		
*†Humanitarian Trust Senior Studentship	Advanced study in International Law	Open to candidates not more than 30 years, who hold or are about to obtain a degree or diploma of an approved university or college	Biennially (next 1985)	U.R.
†Arnold McNair Scholarships	Study or research in International Law	Members of the University, who have kept at least eight terms, who are candidates for, or have been classed in either Part IB or Part II of, the Law Tripos	Annually	U.R.
*F. W. Maitland Fund	Grants for research in the History of Law and of Legal Language and Institutions	Open to those appropriately qualified for research proposed	Any time	Faculty of Law, The Syndics Building, Old Press Site
†Rebecca Flower Squire Fund	Grants for the study of law to those who declare their	Resident members of the University, under 25, who are	Any time	Faculty of Law, The Syndics Building, Old Press Site

Award	Subject/Purpose	Eligibility	When offered	Details (and forms when applicable) from:
Rebecca Flower Squire Fund (*cont.*)	intention of practising the legal profession	British subjects and who are children of British subjects domiciled in England or Wales at the time of the candidate's birth		
*†Squire Scholarships	For those who declare their intention of practising the legal profession and are reading for an examination in Law	Undergraduates, or candidates for admission, under 25, who are British subjects and who are children of British subjects domiciled in England or Wales at the time of the candidate's birth	Annually	Faculty of Law, The Syndics Building, Old Press Site
†Ver Heyden de Lancey Prizes	For an essay on any aspect of Medico-Legal Studies, approved by the Managers	Graduates of the University (in any subject), who are also professionally qualified in Medicine (including Dentistry, but not Veterinary Medicine) or in Law	Annually	U.R.
*†Whewell Scholarships	Awarded on examination in International Law, certain papers being identical with that for Section D of the LL.M. examination, plus a paper on Problems and Disputed Points in this subject	Open to persons who have not attained the age of 25 on the 1 January following the election in the Easter Term	Annually	U.R.
*†Wright Rogers Law Scholarships	Study or research relating to the Laws of England	Any person who has a degree of any university or polytechnic in the U.K., and has spent at least one year studying law	Annually	Faculty of Law, The Syndics Building, Old Press Site
†Yorke Prizes	For an essay on a legal subject (including the history, analysis, administration, and reform of law), approved by the Faculty Board of Law	Graduates of the University, or those who have been admitted or have been registered as a Graduate Student, who are under 32	Annually	Faculty of Law, The Syndics Building, Old Press Site

Award	Subject/Purpose	Eligibility	When offered	Details (and forms when applicable) from:
		Mathematics		
†Adams Prize	For an essay on a set subject in Pure Mathematics, Astronomy, or other branch of Natural Philosophy	Graduates of the University, and those who, on or before the closing date for entries, are Fellows of a College or University Officers. See † for more details	Biennially (next 1985–86)	U.R.
†J. T. Knight Prizes	For essays on any subject in Mathematics and its applications	Any member of the University who is not a graduate of the University. See † for more details	Annually	U.R.
†Smith's and Rayleigh Prizes	For essays on any subject in Mathematics and its applications	B.A.s of the University. See † for more details	Annually	U.R.
		Medicine		
†Henry Roy Dean Prize	Awarded on the results of a special examination in Clinical Pathology	Any member of the University who is pursuing clinical studies in Cambridge and has been entered as a candidate for Part I of the Final M.B.	Annually	U.R.
†Denis Dooley Prize	For an essay on a subject in the field of Clinical Anatomy	Any member of the University pursuing a course of clinical study for the degrees of M.B. and B.Chir.	Annually	The Department of Anatomy
*Elmore Medical Research Studentships	For research in Medicine	Certain restrictions apply	When funds permit	The Secretary of the Fund, The Clinical School, Addenbrooke's Hospital, Hills Road
E. G. Fearnsides Research Scholarship	Original Clinical research on the organic diseases of the nervous system	Graduates of the University; preference given to graduates in Medicine	When funds permit	The Secretary of the Fund, The Clinical School, Addenbrooke's Hospital, Hills Road

Award	Subject/Purpose	Eligibility	When offered	Details (and forms when applicable) from:
†Glennie Prizes	For the best and next best annotated case history of a child with psychosomatic illness seen during the clinical course leading to the Final M.B. Examination	Any member of the University who is pursuing clinical studies in Cambridge and is a candidate for the Final M.B.	Annually	U.R.
*Grimshaw-Parkinson Studentships	Research in the diseases of the heart and circulation	Registered medical practitioners and holders of medical degrees approved by the Managers	When funds permit	The Secretary of the Fund, The Clinical School, Addenbrooke's Hospital, Hills Road
*†William Harvey Studentships and Grants	Clinical Medicine	Any student intending to pursue a course of clinical instruction in the University leading to the degrees of M.B. and B.Chir.	Annually	The Secretary of the Fund, The Clinical School, Addenbrooke's Hospital, Hills Road
†John and Margaret Henderson Memorial Prize	For an essay on a subject chosen by the candidate, in the field of either Gerontology or Geriatrics	Members of the University who are pursuing clinical studies in Cambridge for the degrees of M.B. and B.Chir., and have not yet presented themselves as candidates for Part III of the Final M.B.	Annually	U.R.
†Paediatric Prizes				
(*a*) Cow and Gate Prize	For best annotated case history or study in the field of Clinical Nutrition	Any member of the University pursuing clinical studies in Cambridge and who is a candidate for the Final M.B.	Annually	U.R.
(*b*) Fisons Prize	For best annotated case history or study concerning a child with allergic disease	Any member of the University pursuing clinical studies in Cambridge and who is a candidate for the Final M.B.	Annually	U.R.
*Pinsent-Darwin Studentship	Original research in Mental Pathology	Candidates must be qualified in medicine, psychology, or an allied subject	When funds permit	The Secretary of the Fund, The Clinical School, Addenbrooke's Hospital, Hills Road
*Gwynaeth Pretty Research Studentship	Research in Aetiology, Pathology, or treatment of diseases, with	A recent first degree is required	When funds permit	The Department of Pathology,

Award	Subject/Purpose	Eligibility	When offered	Details (and forms when applicable) from:
Gwynaeth Pretty Research Studentship (*cont.*)	particular reference to those which disable in early life			Tennis Court Road
†Marmaduke Sheild Scholarship	Human Anatomy	Undergraduates of not more than three years' standing and B.A.s of not more than one year's standing, who have passed the First M.B. See † for more details	Annually	U.R.
Sims Scholarship	(See General Awards)			
†Eliot Slater Prize	Awarded on a special examination in Psychiatry	Any member of the University pursuing clinical studies in Cambridge and who was a candidate for Part I of the Final M.B. Examination at the last occasion it was held	Annually	U.R.
†Department of Surgery Prize	For a dissertation on a subject of the candidate's choice related to Surgery	Any person who has pursued clinical studies in the University for the degrees of M.B. and B.Chir., provided that no entry shall be eligible if it is submitted more than two years after the candidate has passed the Final M.B.	Annually	U.R.
†Ver Heyden de Lancey Prizes	(See Law)			
*John Lucas Walker Studentship	Research, or for study and training for research in Pathology	Candidates must be of post-doctoral status	When funds permit	Department of Pathology, Tennis Court Road
		Modern and Medieval Languages		
*†Dorothea Coke Fund Grants	To aid publications contributing to the knowledge of the history and culture of Denmark, Iceland, Norway, and Sweden before A.D. 1500	British authors, who are not necessarily members of the University	When funds permit	The Faculty of Modern and Medieval Languages, Sidgwick Avenue

Award	Subject/Purpose	Eligibility	When offered	Details (and forms when applicable) from:
†Gibson Spanish Scholarship	Advanced study or research in Spanish Literature. See † for more details	Graduates of the University, provided that not more than 17 complete terms have elapsed after their first term of residence	Biennially (next 1986)	U.R.
†Jebb Studentships	Advanced study of some subject in the field of European Literature from the foundation of Constantinople onwards	Graduates of the University, under 26	Annually	U.R.
†Brita Mortensen Fund Grants	To visit Scandinavia to study culture, literature, and the arts	Undergraduates	Annually	The Faculty of Modern and Medieval Languages, Sidgwick Avenue
†Scandinavian Studies Studentship	Advanced study or research in Sweden, Denmark, Norway, or Iceland	Members of the University, who have passed some final examination for the B.A. Degree, provided that not more than 24 terms have elapsed since the end of their first term of residence	Annually	The Faculty of Modern and Medieval Languages, Sidgwick Avenue
†Tennant Studentship	Advanced study or research in Norway	Members of the University, who have passed some final examination for the B.A. Degree, provided that not more than 24 terms have elapsed since the end of their first term of residence	Annually	The Faculty of Modern and Medieval Languages, Sidgwick Avenue
*†Scandinavian Studies Fund Grants	For study connected with Scandinavian countries	Any member, or prospective member of the University	Annually	The Faculty of Modern and Medieval Languages, Sidgwick Avenue
†Tennant Fund Grants	For furtherance of study in Norway	Members of the University	Annually	The Faculty of Modern and Medieval Languages, Sidgwick Avenue
†Tiarks German Scholarship	Advanced study or research in German Language or Literature. See † for more details	Any graduate of the University, provided that not more than 17 complete terms have elapsed after the first term of residence	Annually	U.R.

Award	Subject/Purpose	Eligibility	When offered	Details (and forms when applicable) from:
†J. B. Trend Fund Grants	To visit Spanish- and Portuguese-speaking countries to study the language, literature, history, or music	Undergraduates or registered Graduate Students. See † for more details	Annually	U.R.
†Wallenberg Prize	For an essay on an approved subject connected with the language, literature, history, or civilization of one or more of the Scandinavian peoples	Members of the University who have kept seven terms, and if graduates, not more than nine complete terms have passed since they were admitted to their first degree at this, or any other university	Annually	U.R.
		Music		
†Ord Travel Fund Grants	For travel in Europe and in the Mediterranean countries of Africa or Asia, or exceptionally elsewhere to increase interest and understanding of the art and practice of music	Members of the University, who have spent at least two terms studying for a Part of the Music Tripos. See † for more details	Annually	U.R.
†William Barclay Squire Essay Prize	For an essay on an approved subject relating to the history of music	Members of the University, *in statu pupillari*, other than Graduate Students, who have kept at least six terms	Annually	U.R.
†John Stewart of Rannoch Scholarship in Sacred Music	For a dissertation on a set topic. A *viva voce* examination on the entry will also be held. See the Awards Number	Students of not more than three years' standing	Annually	U.R.
		NATURAL SCIENCES		
		Astronomy		
*†Isaac Newton Studentship	Study and research in Astronomy (especially Gravitational Astronomy, but also other	Graduates of any university, under 26 on 1 January in the year of the election	Annually	U.R.

Award	Subject/Purpose	Eligibility	When offered	Details (and forms when applicable) from:
Isaac Newton Studentship (*cont.*)	branches of Astronomy and Astronomical Physics). See † for more details			
		Biochemistry and Biophysics		
*†Broodbank Fellowships	Research in Biochemistry and Biophysics with special reference to the Principles and Practice of Food Preservation	Open, but preference given to postdoctoral applicants	Annually	U.R.
Benn W. Levy Studentship	Original research in Biochemistry	Graduates of the University	When vacant	The Secretary of the Fund, The School of Biological Sciences, 19 Trumpington Street
		Biology		
		Botany		
†Sir Albert Howard Travel Exhibition	For Botanical research	Students offering Botany in Part II of the Natural Sciences Tripos in the year of the award	Annually	U.R.
†Frank Smart Studentships	Research in Botany	Graduates of the University, not more than six years' standing from matriculation, or Graduate Students of not more than three years' standing from matriculation	When vacant	U.R.
		Colloid Science		
*†Oliver Gatty Studentship	Whole-time study and training for research in Biophysical and Colloid Science	Graduates of all universities. Preference given to graduates of universities outside Great Britain	When vacant	U.R.

Award	Subject/Purpose	Eligibility	When offered	Details (and forms when applicable) from:
		Communications		
†Hamilton Prize	For a dissertation embodying research on the theory or practice of electrical physics associated with any aspect of communications using electro-magnetic radiation, or with communication systems in general	Members of the University, who are, or have been, Graduate Students, provided that not more than nine terms of their course of research have been completed since admission as a Graduate Student. See † for more details	Annually	U.R.
		Entomology		
†Balfour-Browne Fund	For the advancement of study of entomology. Preference to studies in the field, especially in the U.K.	Any person working in the University, who need not be a member. Preference is given to persons *in statu pupillari*. Registered Graduate Students are not eligible for support with their courses of study or research	Any time	The Secretary of the Faculty Board of Biology 'A', The Department of Zoology
		Geology		
Cowper Reed Travelling Grants	Research in Palaeontology	Members of the University	Any time	Department of Earth Sciences, Downing Street
†Harkness Scholarship	Research in Geology, including Palaeontology	Members of the University, who have, within the previous $3\frac{1}{2}$ years, passed a final examination for the B.A. Degree	Annually	U.R.
Philip Lake Fund I Grants	For travelling expenses incurred when on Geological studies	Students and University Officers in the Department of Earth Sciences	Any time	Department of Earth Sciences, Downing Street
†Marr Memorial Fund Grants	For study of Geology in the field	Members of the University. Preference given to those who have obtained honours in Part IB of the Natural Sciences Tripos	Annually	U.R.

Award	Subject/Purpose	Eligibility	When offered	Details (and forms when applicable) from:
†Sedgwick Prize	For an essay on a set subject in Geology or kindred sciences	Graduates of the University, who have resided 60 days during the 12 months preceding the date entries are sent in	Triennially (next 1985)	U.R.
		Metallurgy		
*Ulick Richardson Evans Fund Studentship and Grants	Research in the study and the prevention of corrosion and oxidation of metals and related fields	Any person who is, or is about to become, a registered Graduate Student	When funds permit	The Goldsmiths' Professor of Metallurgy, The Department of Metallurgy and Materials Science, Pembroke Street
		Organic Chemistry		
*Herchel Smith Fellowship	Research work in Organic Chemistry. To be undertaken in the University Chemical Laboratory	Junior Faculty or senior post-doctoral organic chemists who are U.S. citizens	When funds permit	G.B.
		Physics		
Clerk Maxwell Scholarship	Original research in Experimental Physics, especially Electricity, Magnetism, and Heat	Members of the University, who have been for one term or more in the Cavendish Laboratory	When vacant	The Department of Physics, Madingley Road
		Physiology (see also Medicine)		
†Michael Foster Studentship	Research in Physiology	B.A.s of the University, not of standing to become M.A.s	Annually	U.R.
†Gedge Prize	For an essay on original observations in Physiology or in any branch thereof. The subject must be approved	Members of the University, of five to seven years' standing, or, in the case of Graduate Students, of three to five years' standing from matriculation. See † for more details	Biennially (next 1986)	U.R.

Award	Subject/Purpose	Eligibility	When offered	Details (and forms when applicable) from:
		Zoology		
Hanne and Torkel Weis-Fogh Fund Grants	*a*) Research in Zoology and Zoophysiology at the Department of Zoology, Cambridge University, and the Departments of Zoology and Zoophysiology in the Universities of Copenhagen and Aarhus (*b*) To support exchange visits by those engaged in the above research in these departments	Those carrying out research in the specified fields in the Department of Zoology	When funds permit	Department of Zoology, Downing Street
J. Arthur Ramsay Funds Grants	For research in Experimental Zoology	Graduate Students in the Department of Zoology. Candidates for Part II of the Natural Sciences Tripos intending to offer Zoology, to pursue a course of experimental research in the vacation	When funds permit	Department of Zoology, Downing Street
		Oriental Studies		
†Professor A. J. Arberry Travelling Scholarship	For visiting Arabic or Persian speaking countries	Students whose mother-tongue is English, and are citizens of the Commonwealth. Must have acquitted themselves with distinction in Arabic or Persian or both languages in either Part of the Oriental Studies Tripos	Triennially (next 1987)	U.R.
†Bendall Sanskrit Exhibition	Awarded on an examination in Sanskrit	Any member of the University, not being a Graduate Student, of not more than four years' standing, or if still qualified to be a candidate for the Oriental Studies Tripos in the term of the award. More details may be obtained from the U.R.	Annually	U.R.

Award	Subject/Purpose	Eligibility	When offered	Details (and forms when applicable) from:
*†E. G. Browne Memorial Research Studentship Fund Grants	Research in Persian Studies	Graduates of universities who have obtained honours in Persian or in Iranian	Annually	U.R.
*†C. H. W. Johns Studentship	Whole-time and training for research in Assyriology	Graduates of any university	When vacant	U.R.
*†Thomas Mulvey Egyptology Fund Grants	For field-work in Egyptology	Open	Annually	Herbert Thompson Reader in Egyptology, Sidgwick Avenue
†Rapson Scholarship	Study or research in Sanskrit, Pali, or Avestan	Any member of the University who has obtained honours in a Part of the Classical or Oriental Studies Tripos, but not of standing to become M.A. See † for more details	Annually	U.R.
†John Stewart of Rannoch Scholarship in Hebrew	Awarded on a special examination in Hebrew, including a test paper in Greek and Latin	Students of not more than hree years' standing	Annually	U.R.
†Tyrwhitt's Hebrew Scholarships and Mason Hebrew Prize	Awarded on a special examination in Hebrew	B.A.s, LL.B.s, or LL.M.s under the New Regulations, if not more than seven years have elapsed since matriculation	Annually	U.R.
†Wright Studentship	Study of the Arabic language and literature and of subjects closely connected	Graduates of the University under 28	Annually	U.R.
†Ghulam Yazdani Essay Prize	For an essay on an approved topic in the field of Ancient Deccan History and Archaeology	Any member of the University *in statu pupillari*	Annually	U.R.
		Philosophy		
†Arnold Gerstenberg Studentship	Philosophical study	Members of the University, up to their sixth year, who have attained honours in Part IA, or Part IB or Section I of Part II (General) or Part II of the Natural Sciences Tripos., or Part IB of the Medical Sciences Tripos	When vacant	U.R.

Award	Subject/Purpose	Eligibility	When offered	Details (and forms when applicable) from:
		Theology		
*†Bethune-Baker Fund Grants	Theological Studies	Open	Each Term	The Divinity School, St John's Street
†Gregg Bury Prize	For an essay on a set subject connected with the Philosophy of Religion	Members of the University in their second to sixth years	Annually	U.R.
†Burney Prize	For an essay on a set subject connected with the Philosophy of Religion	Members of the University in their third to sixth years	Annually	U.R.
†Burney Studentship and Fund	Study or research in the Philosophy of Religion	Members of the University in their third to sixth years N.B. Research Students ineligible for the Studentship may apply for grants	Annually	U.R.
†Carus Greek Testament Prizes	Awarded on a special examination to encourage the accurate study of the New Testament in Greek	Members of the University in their third to seventh years	Annually	U.R.
†Crosse Studentship	Advanced study or research for the furtherance of the knowledge of the Holy Sciptures in Hebrew and Greek, Ecclesiastical History, and Christian Theology	B.A.s of the University and Registered Graduate Students of not more then three years standing	Annually	U.R.
†Divinity (German Language Fund) Grants	For acquiring or developing knowledge of the German language	Members of the University pursuing or intending to pursue a course of study or research in Divinity in the University	Annually	The Divinity School, St John's Street
†Evans Prizes	Awarded on a special examination on selected Greek and Ecclesiastical writings earlier than A.D. 461	Members of the University in their third to seventh years	Annually	U.R.
*†Hort Memorial Fund Grants	For Biblical, Hellenistic, and Patristic research	Open	Each Term	The Divinity School, St John's Street
†Hulsean Prize	For an essay on an approved subject connected with the history of the Christian Religion	Members of the University, who are in their fourth year onwards, and who are under 27	Annually	U.R.

Award	Subject/Purpose	Eligibility	When offered	Details (and forms when applicable) from:
†Jeremie Prizes	Awarded on a special examination in either Septuagint or Hellenistic writings	Members of the University in their third to seventh years	Annually	U.R.
†Kaye Prize	For a dissertation upon some approved subject relating to Ancient Ecclesiastical History, Biblical Studies which aid enquiry relating to the Scriptural authority for Christian doctrines, or advance the knowledge of Biblical History or Biblical Hebrew and Greek	Graduates of not more than 10 years' standing from their first degree	Every fourth year (next 1987)	U.R.
†Alasdair Charles Macpherson Fund Grants	Research expenses incurred by students in the Faculty of Divinity	Students of not more than ten years' standing from their first degree	Annually	The Divinity School, St John's Street
†Peregrine Maitland Studentship	Comparative Religion	Graduates of the University, with preference to those preparing for missionary work	Triennially (next 1987)	U.R.
†Norrisian Prize	For an essay on a set subject in Christian Doctrine. See † for more details	Graduates of not more than 13 years' standing from their first degree	From time to time (next 1985)	U.R.
†Seatonian Prize	For a poem on a set sacred subject	Members of the Senate, and all persons who are possessors of the status of M.A. See † for more details	Annually	U.R.
†Steel Studentships	For further study in preparation for taking Holy Orders in the Church of England	Resident members of the University, who have completed the examination requirements for the B.A. Degree	Annually	U.R.
†Theological Studies Fund Grants	Pecuniary assistance to those engaged in the study of theology in the University or elsewhere	Students who have kept one term, but no grants are paid until four terms have passed after the first term of residence	Annually	U.R.

Award	Subject/Purpose	Eligibility	When offered	Details (and forms when applicable) from:
†George Williams Prize	For an essay on an approved subject connected with liturgical study	Members of the University in their third to seventh years	Annually	U.R.
†Wordsworth Studentships	Divinity	Members of the University, intending to take Holy Orders in the Church of England. See † for more details	Annually	U.R.
		Veterinary Medicine		
†Jowett Fund Grants	Research into diseases of animals, especially those transmissible to man and tropical diseases of domestic animals	Members of the University	Annually	The Secretary, Department of Clinical Veterinary Medicine, Madingley Road

AWARDS OFFERED BY OTHER BODIES

With no restriction of subject, or for a wide field

Under the *Commonwealth Scholarship and Fellowship Plan* Scholarships are offered to Commonwealth students to enable them to study in countries other than their own in the Commonwealth. The Scholarships are normally for two years to be spent in advanced study or research, but some awards may be made to those who wish to follow undergraduate courses. Particulars of the Scholarships may be obtained from the Joint Secretaries, Commonwealth Scholarship Commission in the United Kingdom, 36 Gordon Square, London, WC1H 0PF.

Harkness Fellowships are awarded annually to men and women between twenty-one and thirty years of age for study and travel in the U.S.A. Candidates should have completed both their schooling and university education within the United Kingdom. Information and application papers may be obtained from The Harkness Fellowships (U.K.), 38 Upper Brook Street, London, W1Y 1PE, and completed forms must be submitted by the beginning of October of each year.

One *Henry Fellowship* tenable at Harvard or Yale University (tenable for one year) is offered annually. Candidates must be unmarried British subjects, men or women, under twenty-six on 1 January of the year of the award, who are *either* graduates of a recognized university in their first year of postgraduate work (under review *or* undergraduates of a British university who have completed at least six terms' residence in that university. Notice is given in the *Cambridge University Reporter*. Applications close in November.

The *Goldsmiths' Company* offer each year Studentships to students preparing for a higher degree at a United Kingdom university and wishing to work for at least one academic year in any part of the world other than the United Kingdom, Europe, or North America. Particulars of these awards are published from time to time in the *Cambridge University Reporter*.

Gladstone Memorial Trust Travelling Scholarships are offered annually to enable undergraduates and postgraduate students to travel who would not otherwise be able to do so without some financial help. Candidature is limited to members of the Universities of Oxford or Cambridge who are in full-time residence and have not proceeded to the M.A. Degree. Applications from Cambridge applicants must be sent to Mr J. S. Morrison, Wolfson College, Cambridge, by mid-March.

Jane Eliza Procter Visiting Fellowships at Princeton University, New Jersey (tenable for one year, with a possibility of re-election) are offered annually by Princeton University. Notices appear in the *Reporter*. Applications close in November.

A Visiting Fellow must be a citizen of the British Commonwealth, under thirty years of age on 1 January of the year of election. Candidates must hold a degree in distinctively liberal studies, and must be of high character, excellent education, and exceptional scholarly power. The purpose of the Fellowship is to provide for resident independent advanced study and investigation in the purely liberal arts and sciences, exclusive of professional, technical, or commercial subjects. Applications are invited each year by notice in the *Cambridge University Reporter*, and close in November.

The *Joseph Hodges Choate Memorial Fellow* at Harvard University (tenable for one year) is nominated by the Vice-Chancellor and is open to graduates of the University who are of British nationality. Applications are invited each year by notice in the *Cambridge University Reporter*, and close in November.

Frank Knox Memorial Fellowships (tenable for one year, but renewable for degree programmes of more than one year's duration), at Harvard University, are offered annually to graduate students from the U.K. who wish to pursue postgraduate study in one of the Faculties of Harvard University. Details of the Fellowships and the method of application may be obtained from the Secretary, The Association of Commonwealth Universities, 36 Gordon Square, London, WC1H 0PF.

The Council of the *Royal Institution of Chartered Surveyors* offer awards for postgraduate study or research in the theory and practice of surveying, in any of its branches, subject to the candidates being accepted by the Board of Graduate Studies of the University. Applications should be submitted to the Honorary Secretary, R.I.C.S. Education Trust, 12 Great George Street, Westminster, London, SW1P 3AD. Full particulars may be obtained from the Head of the Department of Land Economy, Cambridge.

Certain awards tenable at Cambridge are made from time to time by the Worshipful Companies of Carpenters, of Cutlers, of Drapers, of Fishmongers, of Grocers, of Haberdashers, of Leathersellers, and of Mercers.

Classics

A Studentship, tenable at the British School of Archaeology in Athens, is offered to a student following a definite course of graduate study in some branch of Classics or Archaeology. The value of the Studentship may be supplemented in accordance with the needs of the student. Further information may be obtained from the Secretary, British School at Athens, 31–34 Gordon Square, London, WC1H 0PY.

History

The *Royal Historical Society* offers annually the *Alexander Prize* for Historical Research. Particulars may be obtained from the Society at University College, Gower Street, London, WC1E 6BT.

Law

Harmsworth, Astbury, and Benefactors Law Scholarships (tenable for two years) may be awarded every October. Candidates must be members of the Middle Temple who intend to practise at the English Bar. The Harmsworth Scholarships are open to graduates or undergraduates of universities in England, Scotland, Wales, or Northern Ireland, whilst the Astbury Scholarships are limited to men who are members of Oxford or Cambridge Universities and who are or have been undergraduates in either of those Universities. Candidates must be nominated by the Vice-Chancellor of their university; the names of candidates should be sent to the Vice-Chancellor through Heads of Colleges before 30 June. Nomination forms for Scholarships can be obtained from the Under-Treasurer, Middle Temple, London, EC4Y 9AT.

Science

The *Smithson Research Fellowship* in Natural Sciences (tenable for four years, possibly renewable for a further period of one year) is administered by a Committee appointed by the Royal Society and the University of Cambridge. Copies of the regulations and forms of application for the Fellowship when this is being advertised (usually not more than once every five years) may be had from the Executive Secretary of the Royal Society, 6 Carlton House Terrace, London, SW1Y 5AG.

Fellowships of the Royal Commission of 1851. The Royal Commissioners for the Exhibition of 1851 award every year about four Research Fellowships, intended to give to a few young research workers, of proved capacity for original work, the opportunity of devoting their whole time for not less than two years to the prosecution of scientific research. These Fellowships are subject to some special provisions, and nominations can be made by a number of universities, including the University of Cambridge. A candidate must submit particulars of his or her academic record, and must present a published paper or thesis embodying the results of his or her work, together with a recommendation from the Professor or Head of a Laboratory under whom he or she has worked. In considering the claims of a candidate, special importance will be attached to skill in original research.

The Secretary General sends annually to the Heads of all scientific Departments in the University circulars inviting recommendations for nomination. A candidate must be a citizen of the British Commonwealth or of the Republic of Ireland or of the Republic of South Africa and should generally be under thirty years of age.

British Gas Research Scholarships are granted annually, through Heads of Departments or research schools, to graduates for research in the physical sciences or engineering at universities in the U.K. The Scholarships are tenable for three years. The closing date for applications is early December. Particulars and application forms may be obtained from the Director of Research, British Gas Corporation, 326 High Holborn, London, WC1V 7PT.

Royal Society and Nuffield Foundation Commonwealth Bursaries are offered twice yearly for study in natural and applied sciences in Commonwealth countries. The Bursaries provide travel and maintenance at a rate depending on the applicant's circumstances and the living costs in the country concerned, and are normally tenable for periods of six to twelve months. Application forms and full particulars may be obtained from the Executive Secretary of the Royal Society, 6 Carlton House Terrace, London, SW1Y 5AG.

A *Shell Scholarship in Geophysics* (tenable for two years, with possible renewal for a third year) is offered from time to time by the Royal Dutch/Shell Group of Oil Companies. The Student pursues a course of training in research in Geophysics in the University of Cambridge and must be or must become registered as a Graduate Student. Inquiries should be addressed to the Secretary of the Department of Geophysics, Madingley Rise, Madingley Road, Cambridge, CB3 0EZ.

The *George Henry Lewes Studentship* for research in Physiology (tenable for one, two, or three years: stipend at a rate determined by the Trustees) is awarded from time to time and is at present tenable in the Physiological Laboratory, Cambridge. Inquiries should be addressed to the Professor of Physiology, Physiological Laboratory, Cambridge.

The *Rolleston Memorial Prize* is offered in alternate years (1984, 1986, etc.) for original research in Animal and Vegetable Morphology, Physiology and Pathology, and Anthropology, to certain members of the University of Oxford or to B.A.s, M.B.s, or Graduate Students of the University of Cambridge, of not more than six years' standing. Inquiries should be addressed to the Registrar, University Offices, Wellington Square, Oxford, OX1 2JD.

The *Nuffield Foundation* offer annually five Research Scholarships for science graduates and up to three Research Scholarships for medically qualified students to provide experience and knowledge for subsequent research in food safety.

Social Anthropology

Postgraduate Studentships in Social Anthropology are offered by the Social Science Research Council. Information can be obtained from the Secretary, Department of Social Anthropology, Downing Street, Cambridge.

Theology

Exhibitions are awarded from the *Cambridge Graduates Ordination Candidates' Fund* to graduates of the University who are preparing to take Holy Orders in the Church of England, and who undertake to study for such Part or section of a Part of the Theological Tripos, or for such other Theological Examination, as the awarders shall approve. Candidates should send their applications to the Regius Professor of Divinity at the Divinity School not later than 31 May.

Candidates may obtain advice about other possible sources of financial assistance from the Secretary, Advisory Council for the Church's Ministry, Church House, Dean's Yard, London, SW1P 3NZ.

The Awards Information Service of the Association of Commonwealth Universities

The Service produces four publications which are listed below. They are revised every two years and are available for reference in many university and public libraries, and can be purchased from the A.C.U. office in London (John Foster House, 36 Gordon Square, London, WC1H 0PF).

1. *Awards for Commonwealth University Academic Staff.* Sixth edition (for 1984–86): price £8.40; 212 pages.

2. *Grants for Study Visits by University Administrators and Librarians.* Second edition (for 1983–85): price £2.00; 20 pages.

3. *Scholarships Guide for Commonwealth Postgraduate Students.* Fifth edition (for 1983–85): price £7.90; 328 pages.

4. *Financial Aid for First Degree Study at Commonwealth Universities.* Fifth edition (for 1984–86); price £2.25; 39 pages.

7

UNIVERSITY CAREERS SERVICE

Secretary: W. P. KIRKMAN, M.A.

Senior Assistant Secretary: J. N. COOPE, M.A.

Assistant Secretaries: G. A. CURRY, M.A. (part-time); Mrs A. C. M. DINHAM, B.A.; A. J. FAWCITT, B.SC., M.A.; M. S. GAVIN, B.SC., M.A., Mrs M. G. LLOYD, B.SC., M.A.; A. J. RABAN, M.A.; Mrs R. E. SMITH, M.A. (part-time); D. F. T. WINTER, M.A.

Assistant to the Secretaries (Information Officer): MISS A. W. SYME, M.A.

The Cambridge Appointments Association was founded in 1899 and in 1902 was superseded by the University Appointments Board (for men, as women were not then full members of the University).

The functions of the Service are:

(i) To provide a service of information and advice about careers in general, and individual employers in particular.

(ii) To help people to decide on their future plans.

(iii) To act as a link between employers seeking recruits and graduates and undergraduates seeking appointments.

The Service is open to past as well as present members of the University.

Men and women are welcome to consult the Service at any time during their period at Cambridge. Ideally they should first make contact well before their final year. Because the pressure of work with final year people is greatest in the first half of the academic year, it is helpful if first and second year people come from February onwards.

Those registering in their final year are put on mailing lists to receive details of specific appointments if they wish. Anyone who has had preliminary discussions before his or her final year should resume contact in the final year. The Careers Advisers do not usually put on to their active lists automatically those who have made preliminary contact in their first or second years.

The Service is in regular contact with about 3,000 employees, covering an immense range of occupations, in the educational, professional, and non-commercial fields as well as in industry and commerce, and including small organizations as well as 'household names'.

There is an Information Room containing a selection of literature about particular occupations and individual employers, and about postgraduate courses and training. It includes material produced by the staff, material provided by employers and material from other sources such as newspapers and is widely used by people at all stages in their University career. No appointment is necessary to use the Information Room, which may be consulted at any time during office hours.

Many people approaching the Service have little or no idea of what they want to do on graduating. The task of the Careers Advisers, therefore, is to help determine the possible range of choice, to suggest how more information can be obtained and to provide a frame of reference for judging the pros and cons of various fields of work. To this end, the Service arranges various courses and workshops, careers evenings, talks etc., as well as individual discussions.

In 1969 a joint committee was set up, consisting of the staff of the Service and a number of undergraduate and graduate representatives, to participate in the day to day work of the Service. It meets regularly.

The offices are at Stuart House, Mill Lane, Cambridge, CB2 1XE (tel. 64851). They are open from 9 a.m. to 5.30 p.m. Mondays to Fridays in Full Terms, except during the Easter Term when they are closed between 1 and 2 p.m. On Saturdays they are open from 10 a.m. to 12.30 p.m., from October to March only. During vacations the offices are closed between 1 and 2 p.m., and in the Long Vacation from 5 p.m.

8

TRAINING FOR THE MINISTRY

Candidates for Holy Orders in the Church of England are advised to obtain from the Advisory Council for the Church's Ministry, Church House, Dean's Yard, London, SW1P 3NZ, a leaflet of general information entitled *Ordination in the Church of England.* Men and women who are in residence should consult the Dean or Chaplain of their College.

The normal course of training for the priesthood in the case of men, the diaconate in the case of women, is for those who have read a degree, or a substantial part of their first degree, in Theology, to take a two years' course of theological, pastoral, and spiritual training at a recognized Theological College. Graduates in other subjects are expected to undertake three years of training, of which, in the case of suitable persons, two years may be spent in reading for Part II of the Theological and Religious Studies Tripos. Candidates must satisfy the requirements of the General Ordination Examination insofar as they are not covered by university courses which have been taken. Members* of the Cambridge Federation of Theological Colleges take the Cambridge Federation Examination in Theology, which is a recognized equivalent of the General Ordination Examination.

Ridley Hall

Ridley Hall is a Theological College, founded in 1877 mainly for the preparation of graduate candidates for Ordination in the Church of England.

Applications for admission should be made to the Principal.

Further information may be obtained from the Principal: The Rev. H. F. de Waal, M.A.

Wesley House

Wesley House is a Theological College for the training of accepted candidates for the ministry of the Methodist Church. Students of the College, who are usually graduates, become members of the University and read for a degree or take the Examination in Theology of the Cambridge Federation of Theological Colleges.

Applications for admission should be made to the Principal, Rev. Dr Ivor H. Jones, M.A.

* The members are Ridley Hall, Wesley House, Westcott House, and Westminster College.

Westcott House

Westcott House was founded as 'The Cambridge Clergy Training School' in 1881 by Dr B. F. Westcott, then Regius Professor of Divinity and subsequently Bishop of Durham. It received its present name after Dr Westcott's death. In 1972 it entered a Federation with the other theological colleges in Cambridge.

Most, but not all, members are graduates of a university and all must have been accepted for training by their diocesan bishop. Members of the University who are prospective ordinands may be accepted as Associates.

Applications from those desiring to become Members or Associates should be made to the Principal.

Westminster College and the Cheshunt Foundation

Westminster College, Cambridge, is a Theological College of the United Reformed Church, and it houses the Cheshunt Foundation which continues the work of Cheshunt College, founded by Selina, Countess of Huntingdon.

The College is open to receive candidates, men and women, for the ministry, not only of the United Reformed Church, but of any Church. It also welcomes qualified students who desire to undertake advanced or research studies in theology.

Detailed information about the conditions of admission may be obtained from the Principal of Westminster College, Rev. M. H. Cressey, M.A.

INDEX

Abbott Fund, 466
Academical dress, 34
Adams Prize, 479
Administrative officers, 2
Admission, undergraduates, 24: graduates, 458, overseas candidates, 24
Advanced Course in Production Methods and Management (Engineering), 171
Aeronautics: *see* Engineering
Affiliation, 13
Agriculture awards, 468
Alexander Prize (offered by the Royal Historical Society), 494
Allen Scholarship, 466
A. M. P. Read Scholarships, 468
Anatomy: *see* Medical Sciences *and* Natural Sciences
Anglo-Saxon, Norse, and Celtic, Courses of Study and Examinations in, 42: Scholarships and other awards, 468
Anthropology: *see* Archaeology and Anthropology
Applied biology, M.Phil. Degree in, 365
Arberry Travelling Scholarships, 487
Archaeology and Anthropology, Courses of Study and Examinations in, 49 Studentships and other awards, 469
Archaeology, M.Phil. Degree in, 63
Architecture, Courses of Study and Examinations in, 69: Scholarships and other awards, 468
Architecture, M.Phil. Degree in, 77
Astbury Scholarships, 494
Astronomy: *see* Mathematics
Awards Information Service, Association of Commonwealth Universities, 497

B.A. Degree, examinations leading to, 34: for courses of study, *see under the various subjects, e.g.* Architecture, etc.
Baldwin, Stanley, studentships and grants, 475
Balfour Studentship, 484
Balfour-Browne Fund, 485
Barnes Fund, 466
Bartle Frere Exhibitions, 467
Bell, Abbott, and Barnes funds/exhibitions, 466
Bendall Sanskrit Exhibition, 487
Benefactors Law Scholarships, 494
Bethune Baker Fund, 489
Biochemistry, M.Phil. Degree in, 366
Biological Anthropology, M.Phil. Degree in, 65
Biology: *see* Natural Sciences
Biophysics: *see* Natural Sciences

Boards and Syndicates, 1
Botany: *see* Natural Sciences
British Gas Research Scholarships, 495
British Institute of Management, exemption from examinations of, 168
British School of Archaeology at Athens, Studentship, 494
Broodbank Fellowships, 484
Browne, E. G., Memorial Research Studentship (Persian), 488
Browne, Sir William, Medals (Classics), 470
Burney Fund, 489: Prize, 489: Studentship, 489
Bury, Gregg, Fund, 489: Prize, 489
Butler, Montagu, Prize, 471

Cambridge Admissions Prospectus, 23, 24
Cambridge Commonwealth Trust Awards, 466
Cambridge Inter-collegiate Applications Scheme, 23, 451
Cambridge Livingstone Trust Awards, 466
Cambridge University Reporter, 1, 2
Careers Service, 498
Carrington, Henry, and Bentham Dumont Koe Studentship, 470
Carus Greek Testament Prizes, 489
Celtic: *see* Anglo-Saxon, Norse, and Celtic
Certificate in Education, 134
Certificate of Diligent Study, 35
Certificate of Advanced Study in Chemical Engineering, 84
Certificates of Competent Knowledge in modern languages, 275, 320
Certificates of degrees, 35
Certificates of Post-graduate Study in Chemical Engineering, 84: in Natural Science, 363
Chadwick, H. M., Studentship, 466
Chancellor, 1, 2
Chancellor's Medals: for an English poem, 473
Chemical Engineering, Courses of Study and Examinations in, 79
Chemistry: *see* Natural Sciences
Cheshunt Foundation, 501
Choate, Joseph Hodges Memorial Fellowship, 493
Classics, Courses of Study and Examinations in, 86: Scholarships, Studentships, etc., 470
Coke, Dorothea, Fund, 481
Colleges, general, 23
Collins, William George, Fund, 473
Colloid Sciences, awards in, 477; *see also* Natural Sciences, 484
Commonwealth Scholarship and Fellowship Plan, 492
Comparative Pathology: *see* Natural Sciences
Computer Science Tripos, Courses of Study and Examination in, 105
Computer speech and language processing, M.Phil. Degree in, 170
Congregation, 1: general admission, 34; procedure for taking degrees at, 35
Control Engineering and Operational Research, M.Phil. Degree in, 169
Council of Engineering Institutions (C.E.I.), exemption from examinations of, 168

Council of the Senate, 1
Cow and Gate Prize, 480
Cranmer, Archbishop, studentships, 475
Craven Studentship, 470
Criminology, M.Phil. Degree in, 245
Crosse Studentship, 489
Czech (with Slovak) Language and Literature: *see* Modern and Medieval Languages

Danish Language and Literature: *see* Modern and Medieval Languages
Dean, Henry Roy, Prize, 479
Degrade, permission to, 28
Degrees, 34: entry of candidates for, 34: presentation and admission to, 35: degrees by incorporation, 17: in virtue of office, under Statute B, III, 6:18; B.A., 35; B.D., B.Ed., LL.B., M.B., 37; Mus.B., B.Chir., Vet.M.B., 38; M.A., LL.M., M.Litt., 38; Mus.M., M.Phil., M.Sc., M.Chir., 39; D.D., LL.D., Litt.D., M.D., 40; Mus.D., Ph.D., Sc.D., 41
Department of Surgery Prize, 481
Development Studies, 109
Diplomas, in Architecture, 75: in Classical Archaeology, 102: in Development Studies, 109: in Legal Studies, 244: in Computer Science, 107: in Economics, 131: in Education, 151: in Historical Studies, 212: in International Law, 244: in Mathematical Statistics, 253: in Theology, 436
Divinity, Bachelor of, 35: Doctor of, 40: *see also* Theology
Divinity (German Language Fund) grants, 489
Dooley, Denis, Prize, 479
Duff, Gordon, Prize, 470
Dutch Language and Literature: *see* Modern and Medieval Languages

Economics and Politics, Courses of Study and Examinations in, 110: Scholarships and Prizes, 472: Economics Qualifying Examination in Elementary Mathematics, 155
Education, Courses of Study and Examinations in, 134: Diplomas in, 151
Education, Bachelor of, 35
Egyptology: *see* Oriental Studies
Electrical Sciences Tripos, 165
Elmore, F. E., Medical Research Studentships, 479
Elocution, prizes for, 473
Engineering, Courses of Study and Examinations in, 152: Scholarships, Studentships, etc., 473: exemptions from the examinations of Professional Institutions, 168
English, Courses of Study and Examinations in, 172: Scholarships, Studentships, etc. 474
Entomology grants, 485
Environmental Biology: *see* Natural Sciences
Ethics: *see* Philosophy
Ethnology: *see* Archaeology and Anthropology
Evans Fellowship, 469

Evans, Prizes, 489
Evans, Ulick Richardson, Research Fund, 486
Examination entry, 27: Allowances, 28
Examination requirements for matriculation, 9

Fearnsides, E.G., Research Scholarship, 479
Financial Board, 1
Fine Arts: *see* History of Art
Fisons Prize, 480
Fitzwilliam Museum, 20
Ford of Britain Trust Fund, 473
Fortes Fund grants, 469
Foster, Michael, Studentship, 486
French Language and Literature: *see* Modern and Medieval Languages

Gardiner, Robert, Memorial Scholarships, 462
Gas, British, Research Scholarships, 495
Gatty, Oliver, Studentship, 484
Gedge Prize, 486
General Admission to Degrees, 37
General Board of the Faculties, 1
Genetics: *see* Natural Sciences
Geography, Courses of Study and Examinations in, 188: Scholarships, etc., 475
Geology: *see* Natural Sciences
German Language and Literature: *see* Modern and Medieval Languages
Gerstenberg, Arnold, Studentship, 488
Gibson Spanish Scholarship, 482
Gladstone Memorial Prize, 492
Gladstone Memorial Trust Travelling Scholarships, 492
Glennie Prizes, 480
Goldsmiths' Company Studentships, 492
Graduates Ordination Candidates' Fund, 496
Greek: *see* Classics *and* Modern and Medieval Languages
Gregson, Mark, Prize, 469
Grimshaw-Parkinson Studentships, 480

Hamilton Prize, 474, 485
Hare Prize, 471
Harkness Fellowships, 492
Harkness Scholarship, 485
Harmsworth Law Scholarships, 494
Harness Prize, 474
Harvey, William, Studentships, 480
Hebrew Scholarships and Prizes, 488
Henderson, John and Margaret, Memorial Prize, 480
Henry Fellowships, 492
Herchel Smith Fellowship, 486
History, Courses of Study and Examinations in, 194: Awards for study and research, 475

History and Philosophy of Science, 360: M.Phil. Degree in, 366
History of Art, Courses of Study and Examinations in, 214
History of Medicine, M.Phil. Degree in, 265
Holy Orders, Training of Candidates for, 500: Ridley Hall, 500: Westcott House, 501: Westminster College and Cheshunt Foundation, 501: Wesley House, 500: Exhibitions and grants for candidates for ordination, 496
Honours examinations: tables of standing, 30
Hort Memorial Fund, 489
Howard, Sir Albert, Travel Exhibition, 484
Hulsean Prize, 489
Humanitaran Trust Senior Studentship, 477
Hungarian Language and Literature: *see* Modern and Medieval Languages
Hydraulics: *see* Engineering

I.C.L. Research Studentship, 472
Incorporation, 17
Institution of Electrical Engineers, exemption from examinations of, 168
Institution of Mechanical Engineers, exemption from examinations of, 168
International Relations, M.Phil. Degree in, 212
Irish Language and Literature, Early: *see* English *and* Anglo-Saxon, Norse, and Celtic
Italian Language and Literature: *see* Modern and Medieval Languages

Jebb Scholarship, 471, 474: Studentships, 482
Jeremie Prizes, 490
Johns, C.H.W., Studentship, 488
Jowett Fund, 491

Kaye Prize, 490
Kettle's Yard Travel Fund, 469
Knight, J.T., Prizes, 479
Knox, Frank, Memorial Fellowships, 493

Lake, Philip, Funds, 475, 485
Land Economy, Courses of Study and Examinations in, 221: Studentships, 477
Latin: *see* Classics *and* Modern and Medieval Languages
Latin-American Studies, M.Phil. Degree in, 231
Law, Doctor of, 40: Master of, 38
Law, Courses of Study and Examinations in, 235: Scholarships, Studentships, etc., 477: exemption from professional examinations, 240
Le Bas Prize, 474
Le Bas Research Studentship, 467
Letters, Doctor of, 45: Master of, 43; *see also Chapter 5*
Levy, Benn W., Studentship, 484
Lewes, George Henry, Studentship, 495
Lightfoot Scholarships, 476
Linguistics, M.Phil. Degree in, 322
Livingstone Trust Scholarships, 466
Logic: *see* Philosophy

McArthur, Ellen, Prizes, 476
McNair, Arnold, Scholarships, 477
Macpherson, Alasdair Charles, Fund, 490
Madingley Hall, 22
Maitland, Frederic William, Memorial Fund, 490
Maitland, Peregrine, Studentship, 490
Marr Memorial Fund, 485
Mason Hebrew Prize, 488
Mathematics, Courses of Study and Examinations in, 248: Studentships, Prizes, etc., 479: *see also under* Natural Sciences
Matriculation, 9
Maxwell, Clerk, Scholarship, 486
Medical Sciences Tripos, 255
Medicine and Surgery, Courses of Study and Examinations in, 267: First M.B. Examination, 269; Second M.B. Examination, 271: Final M.B. Examination, 271: Studentships and Second Scholarships, etc., 479
Medicine, Doctor of, 40: Bachelor of Medicine, 37, or Surgery, 38: Master of Surgery, 39
Medieval Languages and Literature: *see* Modern and Medieval Languages
Meek, W. A., Scholarship, 467
Mellon Research Fellowships, 476
Members' Classical Essay Prizes, 471; Members' Classical Translation Prizes, 472; Classical Reading Prizes, 472; Members' English Prize, 474; Members' History Prize, 476
Merz, Charles Hesterman, Fund, 473
Metallurgy: *see* Natural Sciences
Meteorology: *see* Natural Sciences
Mineralogy and Petrology: *see* Natural Sciences
Modern and Medieval Languages, Courses of Study and Examinations in, 273: Scholarships, Studentships, etc., 481
Moir, Rex, Fund, 473
Mortensen, Brita, Fund, 482
Mosley, Mary Euphrasia, Fund grants, 467
Mulvey, Thomas, Prize, 488
Music, Courses of Study and Examinations in, 323: Scholarships and Prizes, 483
Music, Bachelor of, 38: Master of, 39: Doctor of, 41
Musical Composition, M.Phil. Degree in, 330
Musicology, M.Phil. Degree in, 331

Natural Sciences, Courses of Study and Examinations in, 332: Fellowships Studentships, etc., 483
Newton, Isaac, Studentships, 483
Norrisian Prize, 490
Norton, Sara, Prize, 476
Norwegian Language and Literature: *see* Modern and Medieval Languages
Nuffield Foundation Research Scholarships, 496

Oldham, Charles, Shakespeare Scholarship, 474

Ord Travel Fund, 483
Ordinances, 1
Ordinary B.A. Degree, 36: *for particulars of special Examinations, see under the several subjects*
Ordination Candidates Fund, 496
Organic Chemistry: *see* Natural Sciences
Oriental Studies, Courses and Examinations in, 370: Studentships, Scholarships, etc., 487
Oriental Studies, M.Phil. Degree in, 389
Overseas Candidates for Admission, 24

Paediatric Prizes, 480
Pharmacology, M.Phil. Degree in, 368
Phillpotts, Dame Bertha, Memorial Fund and Scholarship, 468
Philosophy, Courses of study and Examinations in, 391; Studentship, 488
Philosophy, Doctor of, 41, Master of, 39: *see also Chapter 5*
Physics and Theoretical Physics, *see* Natural Sciences
Physiology: *see* Medical Sciences *and* Natural Sciences
Physiology and Psychology: *see* Natural Sciences
Pinsent-Darwin Studentship, 480
Plant Breeding, M.Phil. Degree in, 368
Polar Studies, M.Phil. Degree in, 401
Polish Language and Literature: *see* Modern and Medieval Languages
Porson Prize, 464, 471
Portuguese Language and Literature: *see* Modern and Medieval Languages
Praelectors, 35
Preliminary Examinations, 29: *see also under the various subjects*
Prendergast Studentship, 470
Pretty, Gwynaeth Research Studentship, 480
Price Waterhouse Prize, 472
Prince Consort Prize, 476
Prior, Edward S., Prize, 470
Proctor, Jane Eliza, Visiting Fellowships, 493
Production Methods and Management, Advanced Course in, 171
Production Engineering Tripos, 165
Proctors, 2
Professors, 3
Psychology: *see* Medical Sciences, Natural Sciences, *and* Philosophy

Quaternary Research, M.Phil. Degree in, 369

Ramsay, J. Arthur, Fund, 487
Rapson Scholarship, 488
Rayleigh Prizes, 479
Read, Amy Mary Preston, Scholarship, 468
Readers, 7
Reed, F. R. Cowper, Fund, 485
Regent House, 1
Registrary, 2

Research and courses of advanced or further study, 458
Research Maintenance Grants Fund, 468
R.I.B.A.: exemption from Intermediate Examination of, 69: Anderson and Webb Scholarship for Architecture, 69
Richards Fund, 469
Ridgeway-Venn Travel Studentship, 469
Ridley Hall, 500
Rolleston Memorial Prize, 496
Rose, Holland, Studentship, 476
Roth, Henry Ling, Scholarship, 469
Royal Commission for the Exhibition of 1851, Fellowships, 494
Royal Historical Society: Prize for historical research, 494
Royal Institution of Chartered Surveyors: postgraduate awards offered by the Council of, 493
Royal Society and Nuffield Foundation Commonwealth Bursaries, 495
Russian Language and Literature: *see* Modern and Medieval Languages

Salisbury, F.S., Fund, 472
Samuel, Harold, Studentships, 477
Scandinavian Languages and Literature: *see* Modern and Medieval Languages
Scandinavian Studies Fund, 482
Science, Doctor of, 41: Master of, 39
Science, History and Philosophy of: *see* Natural Sciences
Seatonian Prize, 490
Secretary General of the Faculties, 2
Sedgwick Prize, 485
Senate, 1
Serbo-Croat Language and Literature: *see* Modern and Medieval Languages
Shell Fund for Chemical Engineering, 462: Scholarship in Geophysics, 495
Sims Fund and Scholarship, 468, 481
Slater, Eliot, Prize, 481
Slavonic Languages and Literature: *see* Modern and Medieval Languages
Smart, Frank, Studentships, 484
Smith, Adam, Prize, 472
Smith's Prizes, 479
Smithson Research Fellowship, 494
Smuts Memorial Fund, 468
Social and Political Sciences Courses of Study and Examinations in, 403
Social Anthropology, M.Phil. Degree in, 65
Social Anthropology, Studentships offered by the Social Science Research Council, 496
Sociology: *see* Archaeology and Anthropology *and* Economics and Politics
Soil Mechanics, M.Phil. Degree in, 170
Spanish Language and Literature: *see* Modern and Medieval Languages
Squire Fund, Rebecca Flower, 477
Squire Law Scholarships, 478
Squire, William Barclay, Essay Prize, 483
Standing of candidates for examinations and degrees, 33
Statistics: *see* Natural Sciences

Status: of B.A., 19: of M.A., 18
Statutes, 1
Steel Studentships, 490
Stevenson Prizes, 472
Stewart of Rannoch, John, Scholarships for: Music, 483: Hebrew, 488
Surgery, Bachelor of, 38: Master of, 39
Surgery, Dept of, Prize, 481
Swedish Language and Literature: *see* Modern and Medieval Languages

Teachers, Training of, *see* Education, 134
Tennant Fund, 482
Theological Studies Fund, 490
Theology and Religious Studies, Courses of Study and Examinations in, 416: Studentships, Prizes etc., 489: *see also under* Holy Orders
Theology, M.Phil. Degree, 443
Thirlwall Prize, 476
Thomas, Henry Arthur, Studentships, Prizes, and Travel Exhibition, 470
Tiarks German Scholarships, 482: Fund, 482
Training for the Ministry, 500
Treasurer, 2
Trend, J.B., Fund, 483
Triposes, *see Chapter 4*: privileges accorded to Affiliated Students, 13
Tyrwhitt's Hebrew Scholarships, 488

University Careers Service, 498
University Examinations and Degrees, 27
University Library, 19
University Classical Scholarships, 470
University scholarships and other awards, 465

Ver Heyden de Lancey Prizes, 478, 481
Veterinary Medicine, Bachelor of, 38
Veterinary Medicine, Courses of Study and Examinations in, 451
Vice-Chancellor, 1, 2

Walker, John Lucas, Studentships, 481
Wallenberg Prize, 483
Walston Studentship, 470
Warr, George Charles Winter, Scholarship, 470
Waterhouse, Price, Prize, 472
Weis-Fogh, Hanne and Torkel, Fund grants, 487
Welsh Language and Literature: *see* English *and* Anglo-Saxon, Norse, and Celtic
Wesley House, 500
Westcott House, 501
Westminster College, 501
Whewell Scholarships, 478
Wilkin, Anthony, Studentship, 469

Williams, George, Prize, 491
Winbolt, John, Prize, 474
Winchester Reading Prizes, 473
Wishart, John, Prizes, 472
Woodrow, Taylor, Fund, 473
Wordsworth Studentships, 491
Worts Travelling Scholars Fund, 468
Wrenbury Scholarship, 473
Wright Studentship, 488
Wright Rogers Law Scholarships, 478

Yazdani, Ghulam, Essay Prize, 488
Yorke Prizes, 478

Zoology: *see* Natural Sciences